UNITY FROM ZERO TO PROFICIENCY (INTERMEDIATE)

Third Edition

A step-by-step guide to programming your first FPS in C#.

Patrick Felicia

UNITY FROM ZERO TO PROFICIENCY

(INTERMEDIATE)

THIRD EDITION

Copyright © 2022 Patrick Felicia

All rights reserved. No part of this book may be reproduced, stored in retrieval systems, or transmitted in any form or by any means, without the prior written permission of the publisher (Patrick Felicia), except in the case of brief quotations embedded in critical articles or reviews.

Every effort has been made in the preparation of this book to ensure the accuracy of the information presented. However, the information contained in this book is sold without warranty, either expressed or implied. Neither the author and its dealers and distributors will be held liable for any damages caused or alleged to be caused directly or indirectly by this book.

- First published: April 2016
- Second Edition published: February 2018
- Third Edition published: October 2019
- Third Edition updated: December 2022
- Published by Patrick Felicia

CREDITS

Author: Patrick Felicia

ABOUT THE AUTHOR

Patrick Felicia is a **lecturer and researcher** at Waterford Institute of Technology, where he teaches and supervises undergraduate and postgraduate students. He obtained his MSc in Multimedia Technology in 2003 and PhD in Computer Science in 2009 from University College Cork, Ireland. He has published several books and articles on the use of video games for educational purposes, including the Handbook of Research on Improving Learning and Motivation through Educational Games: Multidisciplinary Approaches (published by IGI), and Digital Games in Schools: a Handbook for Teachers, published by European Schoolnet. Patrick is also the Editor-in-chief of the **International Journal of Game-Based Learning (IJGBL)**, and the Conference Director of the **Irish Conference on Game-Based Learning**, a popular conference on games and learning organized throughout Ireland.

Support and Resources for this Book + Free Book

To complete the activities presented in this book you need to download the startup pack on the companion website; it consists of free resources that you will need to complete your projects, including bonus material that will help you along the way (e.g., cheat sheets, introductory videos, code samples, and much more).

These resources also include the final completed project so that you can see how your project should look like in the end.

Amongst other things, the resources for this book include:

- Cheat sheets with tips on how to use Unity.
- 3D characters and animation that you can use in Unity.
- A library of over 40 tutorials (video or text).

To download these resources, please do the following:

- Open the following link: **http://learntocreategames.com/books/**
- Select this book ("**Unity from Zero to Proficiency - Intermediate**").
- On the new page, click on the link labelled "**Book Files**", or scroll down to the bottom of the page.
- In the section called "**Download your Free Resource Pack**", enter your email address and your first name, and click on the button labeled "**Yes, I want to receive my bonus pack**".
- After a few seconds, you should receive a link to your free start-up pack.
- When you receive the link, you can download all the resources to your computer.

This book is dedicated to Mathis

TABLE OF CONTENTS

Contents

Credits iv
About the Author v
Support and Resources for this Book + Free Book... vi
Table of Contents 1
Preface.. 6
Content Covered by this Book... 7
    Part 1: 3D Games Creation (First-Person Shooter) 8
    Part 2: Mastering Artificial Intelligence for NPCs 9
    Part 3: 2D Games Creation (Space Shooter) 10
What you Need to Use this Book 11
Who this Book is for 12
Who this Book is not for.. 13
How you will Learn from this Book... 14
Format of each Chapter and Writing Conventions 15
    Special Notes 16
How Can You Learn Best from this Book... 17
Feedback.. 18
Downloading the Solutions for the Book 19
Improving the Book... 20
Supporting the Author.. 21
1 Adding Simple AI.. 22
    Resources necessary for this chapter 23
    Instantiating projectiles 24
    Managing collision 43
    Finishing our first game 49
    Detecting when the player has reached the end of the game 61
    Level Roundup.. 64
        Checklist.. 64
        Quiz... 65
        Solutions to the Quiz 67
        Challenge 1... 68
        Challenge 2... 68
2 Creating and Managing Weapons... 69

Setting-up the environment 71
Detecting objects ahead using raycasting 74
Creating a weapon 79
Managing Damage 84
Collecting and managing ammunitions 86
Building a weapon management system with arrays 90
Managing the collection of ammunitions 101
Creating a grenade launcher 106
Level Roundup 115
   Checklist 115
   Quiz 116
   Answers to the Quiz 117
   Challenge 1 118
   Challenge 2 118

3 Using Finite State Machines 119
Introduction to finite state machines 120
Getting started with finite-state machines in Unity 121
Controlling an Animator Controller from a C# script 128
Linking transitions to the movement of objects 133
Using Animated Characters with Mecanim 139
Making the NPC smarter 149
Adding weapons to the player 154
Adding animations for more realism 159
Applying damage to the player 164
Using Dot products for more accuracy 177
Adding a screen flash when the player is hit 184
Creating new prefabs 189
Level Roundup 190
   Checklist 190
   Quiz 191
   Answers to the Quiz 192
   Challenge 1 193
   Challenge 2 193

4 Putting it all together 194
Setting-up the environment manually 195
Setting-up the environment through scripting 202
Level Roundup 209

5 Using Off-mesh links, Areas and Costs 210
Setting up the environment 211
Simple AI (drag and drop) using Unity's built-in AI characters 212
Adding more obstacles 216
Grouping intelligent NPCs 221
Collision detection 222
Off-mesh links 225
Using areas and costs 229
Making it possible for NPCs to jump 234

Level Roundup	**236**
Checklist	236
Quiz	236
Quiz Solutions	238
Challenge 1	239
6 Using Fixed and Random Paths for NPCs	**240**
Importing our 3D character	241
Specifying a target for the npc	252
Waypoints	255
Moving randomly within a path	259
Wandering navigation	262
Level Roundup	**269**
Checklist	269
Quiz	270
Quiz Solutions	271
Challenge 1	272
7 Adding Vision and Hearing to NPCs	**273**
Setting-up the level	274
Building a new Animator Controller	276
Triggering the npc to change state from idle to patrol	283
Associating a movement to a state from the script	288
Adding Hearing	295
Adding Sight	300
Losing track of the player	305
Adding the sense of smell	307
Level Roundup	**316**
Summary	316
Checklist	316
Quiz	316
Quiz Solution	318
Challenge 1	318
8 Creating Smarter NPCs Who Can Flee or Ambush	**319**
Decisions based on internal values (health, ammos, etc.)	320
Providing weapons to the NPC	328
Ambushing	334
Adding a gun to the npc	349
Using dot products for a more accurate vision	353
Spawning NPCs	360
Fleeing	363
Level Roundup	**373**
Summary	373
Checklist	373
Quiz	373
Challenge 1	374
Quiz Solutions	374
Challenge 1	374

9 Adding and Controlling An Army of NPCs 376
Walking behind the leader 377
Attacking several targets as a group 383
Withdrawing from a battle 392
Managing damage and attacks 394
Setting-up an intelligent team 400
Applying attacks to the NPCs 410
Level Roundup 415
Summary 415
Checklist 415
Quiz 415
Quiz Answers 416
Challenge 1 416

10 Creating a 2D Shooter (Part 1): Introduction 417
Adding the spaceship 418
Shooting missiles 423
Destroying the target 427
Spawning moving targets randomly 434
Managing Damage 440
Level Roundup 443
Checklist 443
Quiz 444
Answers to the Quiz 445
Challenge 1 446
Challenge 2 446

11 Creating a 2D Shooter (Part2): Adding Special Effects 447
Introduction 448
Adding special effects to the targets 449
Adding an explosion 452
Creating a scrolling background 465
Level Roundup 471
Checklist 471
Quiz 472
Answers to the Quiz 473
Challenge 1 474

12 Creating a 2D Shooter (Part 3): Adding AI and Weapons 475
Introduction 476
Keeping the player in the field of view 477
Applying Damage to the player 481
Adding artificial intelligence 483
Level Roundup 503
Summary 503
Checklist 503
Quiz 503
Challenge 1 506

13 Creating a 2D Shooter (Part 4): Adding AI and Sound 507

  Improving AI 508
  Adding a temporary shield to the player 511
  Adding a score 520
  Adding Audio 524

14 Frequently Asked Questions 530
  Rigid Bodies 531
  Using prefabs 532
  Finite State Machines 533
  Navmesh Navigation 534
  User Interaction 535
  Firing Objects 536

15 Thank you 537

PREFACE

After teaching Unity for over 4 years, I always thought it could be great to find a book that could get my students started with Unity in a few hours and that showed them how to master the core functionalities offered by this fantastic software.

Many of the books that I found were too short and did not provide enough details on the why behind the actions recommended and taken; other books were highly theoretical, and I found that they lacked practicality and that they would not get my students' full attention. In addition, I often found that game development may be preferred by those with a programming background but that those with an Arts background, even if they wanted to get to know how to create games, often had to face the issue of learning to code for the first time.

As a result, I started to consider a format that would cover both: be approachable (even to the students with no programming background), keep students highly motivated and involved using an interesting project, cover the core functionalities available in Unity to get started with game programming, provide answers to common questions, and also provide, if need be, a considerable amount of details for some topics.

This book series entitled **From Zero to Proficiency** does just this. In this book series, you have the opportunity to play around with Unity's core features, and essentially those that will make it possible to create an interesting 3D game rapidly. After reading this book series, you should find it easier to use Unity and its core functionalities.

This book series assumes no prior knowledge on the part of the reader, and it will get you started on Unity so that you quickly master all the wonderful features that this software provides by going through an easy learning curve. By completing each chapter, and by following step-by-step instructions, you will progressively improve your skills, become more proficient in Unity, and create a survival game using Unity's core features in terms of programming (C#), game design, and drag and drop features.

In addition to understanding and being able to master Unity's core features, you will also create a game that includes many of the common techniques found in video games, including: level design, object creation, textures, collision detection, lights, weapon creation, character animations, particles, artificial intelligence, and a user interface.

Throughout this book series, you will create a game that includes both indoor and outdoor environments, where the player needs to finds its way out of the former through tunnels, escalators, traps, and other challenges, avoid or eliminate enemies using weapons (i.e., gun or grenades), drive a car or pilot an aircraft.

In this book you will learn how to create a 3D First-Person Shooter with intelligent NPCs, a 2D space shooter, a card guessing game, as well as a 2D puzzle.

Content Covered by this Book

Content Covered by this Book

PART 1: 3D GAMES CREATION (FIRST-PERSON SHOOTER)

Chapter 1, Adding Simple AI, gets you to use C# for the creation of a simple launcher. You will learn to instantiate, use and control Rigidbody objects from your script as well as creating explosions.

Chapter 2, Creating and Managing Weapons, explains how you can create and manage weapons using a simple inventory system. You will create an automatic gun and a grenade launcher, manage the collection of ammunitions, and also implement a user interface to keep track of ammunitions. In addition, you will also learn how to include these as prefabs, so that they can be reused in other levels, and to save you some coding too.

Chapter 3, Using Finite State Machines, provides an in-depth explanation of how to create and use Finite State Machines (FSM) in Unity. You will create your FSM and use it to control the behavior and movement of an animated Non-Player Character. You will also learn how to employ NavMesh navigation so that your animated NPCs can navigate easily within the scene to either follow the player or go to a specific location. Finally, you will learn how to optimize your assets so that they can be reused seamlessly in other scenes with no or little changes.

Chapter 4, Putting it All Together, makes it possible to combine the skills you have acquired in the previous chapters, and to reuse and combine all the objects that you have created so far (e.g., NPCs, weapons, inventory systems, ammunitions, etc.), and the concepts (e.g., FSM, NavMesh, RigidBody components, User Interface, etc.) that you have mastered, to create a fully functional level. You will also get to learn how to generate a maze (or a game level) dynamically from your code.

Content Covered by this Book

PART 2: MASTERING ARTIFICIAL INTELLIGENCE FOR NPCS

Chapter 5, *Using Off-mesh links, Areas and* , shows you how to create a simple AI for your 3D games with no coding involved; this includes NPCs that can detect and follow a particular target (including the player) individually or as a group, avoid obstacles, and jump over obstacles to reach their target. You will also learn how to apply the concept of navigation costs so that the NPCs can optimize their navigation.

Chapter 6, *Using Fixed and Random Paths for NPCs,* shows you how to create different types of navigation for your NPCs, including set paths, random paths, and wandering aimlessly. Along the way, you will also learn how to configure an animated 3D character, and how to combine it with a Finite State Machine and a C# script to customize the navigation and animations.

Chapter 7, *Adding Vision and Hearing to NPCs*, shows you how to add senses to the NPCs so that they can detect targets and take decisions accordingly. This will include adding the ability to hear, smell, or see the player and to start following the player accordingly. Along the way, you will also learn to configure a Finite State Machine in more details with parameters, transitions, multiple conditions for conditions, and different types of parameters (e.g., triggers, Boolean, integers, etc.)

Chapter 8, *Creating Smarter NPCs Who Can Flee or Ambush,* shows how to make the NPCs smarter by making it possible for the NPCs to take more sensible decisions based on the environment and their own state; this will include: accounting for their health or weapons, and look for ammos or health packs accordingly when these are running low; you will also learn to create other interesting behaviours, often found in 3D games, such as fleeing from, or ambushing the player as well as sub-state machines, which are very useful when dealing with a group of actions for NPCs. Finally, you will learn how to make the sight of the NPCs more accurate using what is called **dot products**, and to also spawn NPCs at run time.

Chapter 9, *Adding and Controlling An Army of NPCs,* shows how to implement group behaviours for NPCs. You will learn how to create a group of NPCs that follow the orders of the player (e.g., follow the leader, attack targets or withdraw from the battle). You will also create a team of opponents that will be led by an intelligent NPC leader. Finally, you will be able to engage these two teams (i.e., your team and the opposing team) in a battle.

Content Covered by this Book

PART 3: 2D GAMES CREATION (SPACE SHOOTER)

Chapter 10, Creating a 2D Shooter, explains how to create a simple 2D shooter where the player will pilot a spaceship, avoid asteroids, and destroy enemies, using an arcade-style vertical scrolling shooter.

Chapter 11, Creating a 2D Shooter (Part2): Adding Special Effects, explains how to add explosions and a scrolling background to make the game more realistic.

Chapter 12, Creating a 2D Shooter (Part 3): Adding AI and Weapons, explains how you can include intelligent enemies that shoot at the player based on their field of view.

Chapter 13, Creating a 2D Shooter (Part 4): Adding AI and Sound, explains how you can include a shield to the player, along with audio, a better AI, and a scoring system.

WHAT YOU NEED TO USE THIS BOOK

To complete the project presented in this book, you only need Unity 2019, or a more recent version, and to also ensure that your computer and its operating system comply with Unity's requirements. Unity can be downloaded from the official website (**http://www.unity3d.com/download**), and before downloading, you can check that your computer is up to scratch on the following page: **http://www.unity3d.com/unity/system-requirements**. At the time of writing this book, the following operating systems are supported by Unity for development: Windows XP (i.e., SP2+, 7 SP1+), Windows 8, and Mac OS X 10.6+. In terms of graphics card, most cards produced after 2004 should be suitable.

In terms of computer skills, all knowledge introduced in this book will assume no prior programming experience from the reader. So for now, you only need to be able to perform common computer tasks, such as downloading items, opening and saving files, be comfortable with dragging and dropping items and typing, and relatively comfortable with Unity's interface. This being said, because the focus of this book is on scripting, and while all steps are explained step-by-step, you may need to be relatively comfortable with Unity's interface, as well as creating and transforming objects.

So, if you would prefer to become more comfortable with Unity prior to starting scripting, you can download the first book in the series called **Unity From Zero to Proficiency (Foundations)** or its sequel called **Unity from Zero to Proficiency (Beginner)**. These books cover most of the shortcuts and views available in Unity, as well as how to perform common tasks in Unity such as creating objects, transforming objects, importing assets, using navigation controllers, creating scripts or exporting the game to the web. They also explain some of the key features available in Unity along with good coding practices.

WHO THIS BOOK IS FOR

If you can answer **yes** to all these questions, then this book is for you:

1. Are you a total beginner in Unity or programming?

2. Would you like to become proficient in the core functionalities offered by Unity?

3. Would you like to teach students or help your child to understand how to create games, using coding in C#?

4. Would you like to start creating great 3D and 2D games?

5. Although you may have had some prior exposure to Unity, would you like to delve more into Unity and understand its core functionalities in more detail?

WHO THIS BOOK IS NOT FOR

If you can answer yes to all these questions, then this book is **not** for you:

1. Can you already code in C# and implement Artificial Intelligence or manage animated characters through coding in Unity?

2. Can you already easily code a 3D game with Unity, using C#, with built-in objects, controllers, cameras, lights, terrains, AI-driven non-player characters, and weapons?

3. Are you looking for a reference book on Unity programming?

4. Are you an experienced (or at least advanced) Unity user?

If you can answer yes to all four questions, you may instead look for the next book in the series called Unity from Zero to Proficiency (Advanced). To see the content and the topics covered in this book, you can check the official website (http://www.learntocreategames.com/books/).

How you will Learn from this Book

Because all students learn differently and have different expectations of a course, this book is designed to ensure that all readers find a learning mode that suits them. Therefore, it includes the following:

- A list of the learning objectives at the start of each chapter so that readers have a snapshot of the skills that will be covered.

- Each section includes an overview of the activities covered.

- Many of the activities are step-by-step, and learners are also given the opportunity to engage in deeper learning and problem-solving skills through the challenges offered at the end of each chapter.

- Each chapter ends-up with a quiz and challenges through which you can put your skills (and knowledge acquired) into practice and see how much you know. Challenges consist in coding, debugging, or creating new features based on the knowledge that you have acquired in the chapter.

- The book focuses on the core skills that you need; some sections also go into more detail; however, once concepts have been explained, links are provided to additional resources, where necessary.

- The code is introduced progressively and is explained in detail.

- You also gain access to several videos that help you along the way, especially for the most challenging topics.

Format of each Chapter and Writing Conventions

Throughout this book, and to make reading and learning easier, text formatting and icons will be used to highlight parts of the information provided and to make it more readable.

The full solution for the project presented in this book is available for download on the official website (**http://learntocreategames.com/books/**). So if you need to skip a section, you can do so; you can also download the solution for the previous chapter that you have skipped.

SPECIAL NOTES

Each chapter includes resource sections, so that you can further your understanding and mastery of Unity; these include:

- A quiz for each chapter: these quizzes usually include 10 questions that test your knowledge of the topics covered throughout the chapter. The solutions are provided on the companion website.

- A checklist: it consists of between 5 and 10 key concepts and skills that you need to be comfortable with before progressing to the next chapter.

- Challenges: each chapter includes a challenge section where you are asked to combine your skills to solve a particular problem.

Author's notes appear as described below:

> Author's suggestions appear in this box.

Code appears as described below:

```
public int score;
public string playersName = "Sam";
```

Checklists that include the important points covered in the chapter appear as described below:

- Item1 for check list
- Item2 for check list
- Item3 for check list

How Can You Learn Best from this Book

- **Talk to your friends about what you are doing.**

    We often think that we understand a topic until we have to explain it to friends and answer their questions. By explaining your different projects, what you just learned will become clearer to you.

- **Do the exercises.**

    All chapters include exercises that will help you to learn by doing. In other words, by completing these exercises, you will be able to better understand the topic and gain practical skills (i.e., rather than just reading).

- **Don't be afraid of making mistakes.**

    I usually tell my students that making mistakes is part of the learning process; the more mistakes you make and the more opportunities you have for learning. At the start, you may find the errors disconcerting, or that the engine does not work as expected until you understand what went wrong.

- **Export your games early.**

    It is always great to build and export your first game. Even if it is rather simple, it is always good to see it in a browser and to be able to share it with you friends.

- **Learn in chunks.**

    It may be disconcerting to go through five or six chapters straight, as it may lower your motivation. Instead, give yourself enough time to learn, go at your own pace, and learn in small units (e.g., between 15 and 20 minutes per day). This will do at least two things for you: it will give your brain the time to "digest" the information that you have just learned, so that you can start fresh the following day. It will also make sure that you don't "burn-out" and that you keep your motivation levels high.

FEEDBACK

While I have done everything possible to produce a book of high quality and value, I always appreciate feedback from readers so that the book can be improved accordingly. If you would like to give feedback, you can email me at **learntocreategames@gmail.com**.

DOWNLOADING THE SOLUTIONS FOR THE BOOK

To complete the activities presented in this book you need to download the startup pack on the companion website; it consists of free resources that you will need to complete your projects, including bonus material that will help you along the way (e.g., cheat sheets, introductory videos, code samples, and much more).

These resources also include the final completed project so that you can see how your project should look like in the end.

Amongst other things, the resources for this book include:

- Cheat sheets with tips on how to use Unity.
- 3D characters and animation that you can use in Unity.
- A library of over 40 tutorials (video or text).

To download these resources, please do the following:

- Open the following link: **http://learntocreategames.com/books/**
- Select this book ("**Unity from Zero to Proficiency - Intermediate**").
- On the new page, click on the link labelled "**Book Files**", or scroll down to the bottom of the page.
- In the section called "**Download your Free Resource Pack**", enter your email address and your first name, and click on the button labeled "**Yes, I want to receive my bonus pack**".
- After a few seconds, you should receive a link to your free start-up pack.

When you receive the link, you can download all the resources to your computer.

IMPROVING THE BOOK

Although great care was taken in checking the content of this book, I am human, and some errors could remain in the book. As a result, it would be great if you could let me know of any issue or error you may have come across in this book, so that it can be solved and the book updated accordingly. To report an error, you can email me (**learntocreategames@gmail.com**) with the following information:

- Name of the book.

- The page or section where the error was detected.

- Describe the error and also what you think the correction should be.

Once your email is received, the error will be checked, and, in the case of a valid error, it will be corrected, and the book page will be updated to reflect the changes accordingly.

SUPPORTING THE AUTHOR

A lot of work has gone into this book and it is the fruit of long hours of preparation, brainstorming, and finally writing. As a result, I would ask that you do not distribute any illegal copies of this book.

This means that if a friend wants a copy of this book, s/he will have to buy it through the official channels (i.e., through Amazon, lulu.com, or the book's official website: **http://www.learntocreategames.com/books/**).

If some of your friends are interested in the book, you can refer them to the book's official website (**http://www.learntocreategames.com/books/**) where they can either buy the book, enter a monthly draw to be in for a chance of receiving a free copy of the book, or to be notified of future promotional offers.

1
ADDING SIMPLE AI

In this section we will discover how you can create very simple Artificial Intelligence (AI) to implement a canon that points in the direction of your character and fires projectiles.

After completing this chapter, you will be able to:

- Instantiate objects.
- Instantiate explosions.
- Make it possible for a canon to follow a particular object.
- Modify the firing rate of the canon.
- Detect collision between the cannon balls and the player and instantiate an explosion on impact.

RESOURCES NECESSARY FOR THIS CHAPTER

To get started with this chapter, you will be using resources that you have downloaded from the companion website. If you have not done so yet, please do the following:

- Open the following link: **http://learntocreategames.com/books/**

- Select this book ("**Unity from Zero to Proficiency - Intermediate**").

- On the new page, click on the link labelled "**Book Files**", or scroll down to the bottom of the page.

- In the section called "**Download your Free Resource Pack**", enter your email address and your first name, and click on the button labeled "**Yes, I want to receive my bonus pack**".

- After a few seconds, you should receive a link to your free start-up pack.

- When you receive the link, you can download all the resources to your computer.

Adding Simple AI

INSTANTIATING PROJECTILES

At this stage, we are getting familiar with Unity and creating C# scripts; we will now get to create a very simple AI object that will target our user and shoot cannon balls in its direction. The workflow will be as follows; we will:

- Create a simple environment.
- Add a third-person controller.
- Add a canon.
- Instantiate cannon balls frequently.
- Ensure that the canon is always facing the target and shoot in its direction.
- Detect when the cannon balls have hit the player and instantiate an explosion at the location of the impact.
- Modify the firing rate of the canon.

So, let's get started:

- Open Unity.
- Create a new project (e.g., **File | New Project**).

Once the project is open, we will add a ground and a Third-Person Controller as follows:

- Create a new box (**GameObject | 3D Object | Cube**).
- Using the **Move** tool or the **Inspector** window, change the position of this object to **(0,0,0)**.
- Using the **Scale** tool or the **Inspector** window, change the **scale** of this object to **(100,1,100)**, this will rescale it on the **x-**, and **z–axes**.
- Rename this box **ground**.

We will then add a **Third-Person Controller**:

- Import the **Characters** assets by selecting **Asset | Import Package | Characters**.

Adding Simple AI

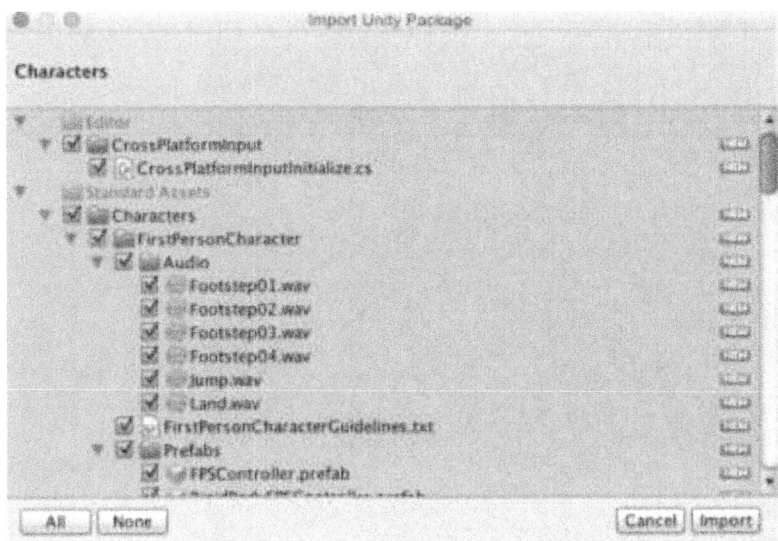

Figure 1-1: Importing the Characters Asset package

- Click **Import** to import all assets in the package.

If this option is not available, and/or if you don't already have a folder called **Standard Assets** in your **Project** folder (this is the case for Unity 2019+), you will need to import the **Standard Assets** from the **Asset Store**. For this purpose, please open the **Asset Store** window (i.e., select: **Window | Asset Store**) and search for the key words "**Standard Asset Unity**". Once you have found this asset, you can then import it into your project, this should create a folder called **Standard Assets** in your **Assets** folder.

Note that you will need to reproduce these steps (importing the Standard Assets) if you create a new project.

For more information on downloading the Standard Assets with Unity 2029+, please follow the instructions described on that blog post:

http://learntocreategames.com/importing-and-using-standard-assets-with-unity-2020/

- Once the import is complete, this will have created a folder called **Characters** in the folder **Assets | Standard Assets**.

- In the **Project** window, navigate to the folder **Assets | Standard Assets | Characters | ThirdPersonCharacter | Prefabs**.

- From this folder, drag and drop the prefab called **ThirdPersonController** to the scene, just above the box we have created.

[25]

Adding Simple AI

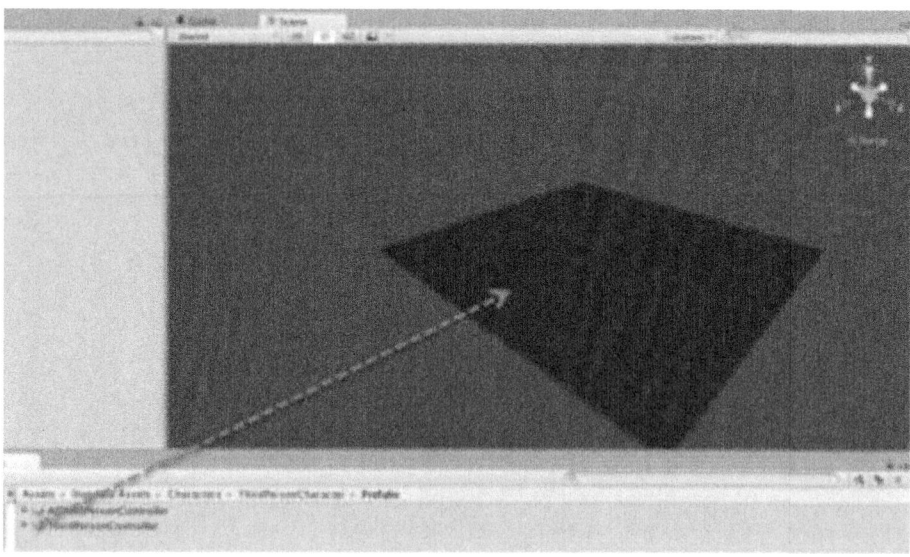

Figure 1-2: Adding a third-person controller

This will add an object called **ThirdPersonController** in the **Hierarchy** window.

And last but not least, we will add a camera that will follow the player:

> If you have already imported the **Standard Assets** from the **Asset Store**, the next steps won't be necessary as Unity will already have created a folder called **Cameras** in your **Project** window (i.e., in the folder **Assets**).

- Import the **Cameras** assets by selecting **Asset | Import Package | Cameras**.
- Leave all default options (i.e., import all assets in the package) and click **Import**.

Adding Simple AI

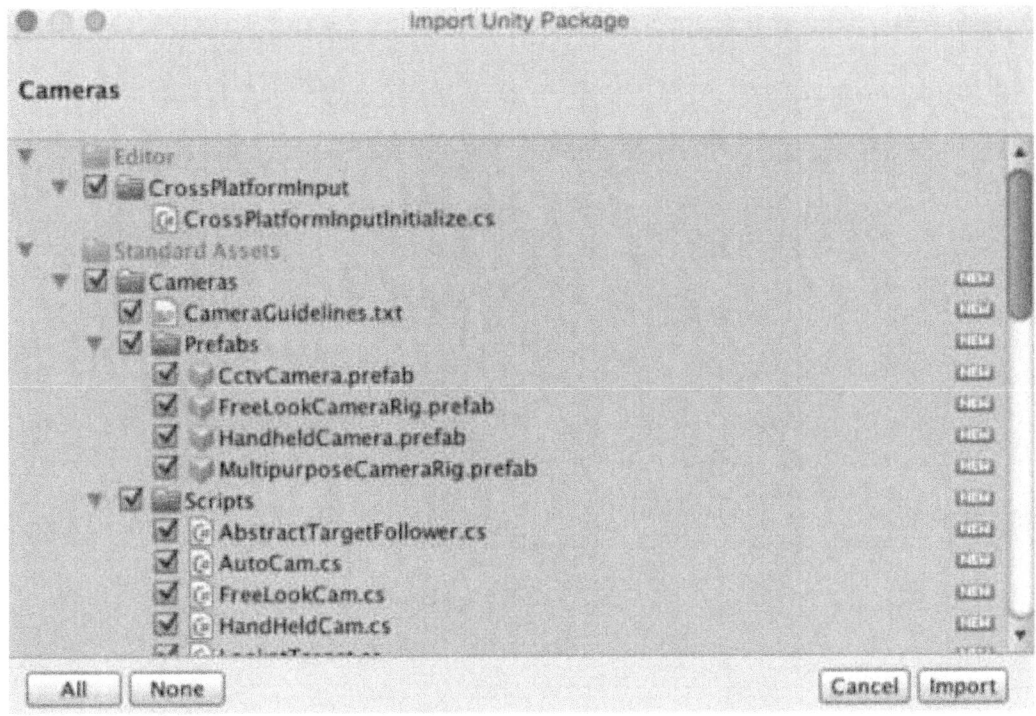

Figure 1-3: Importing the Camera asset package

- Once the import is complete, this will have created a folder called **Cameras** in the folder **Assets | Standard Assets**.

- In the **Project** window, navigate to the folder **Assets | Standard Assets | Cameras | Prefabs**.

- From this folder, drag and drop the prefab called **MultipurposeCameraRig** to the scene.

[27]

Adding Simple AI

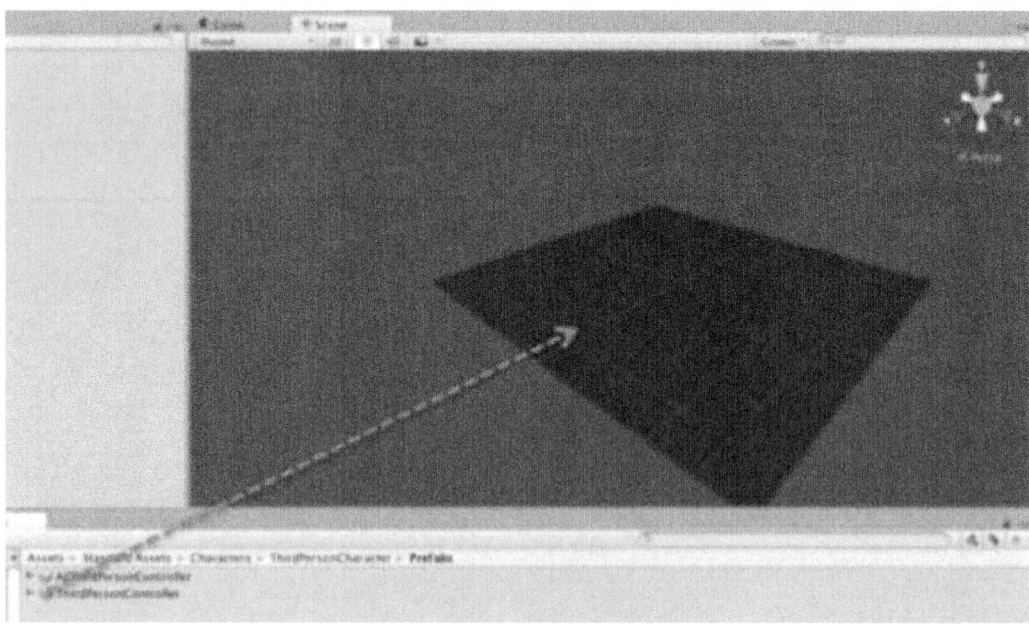

Figure 1-4: Adding a new camera

- This will add an object called **MultipurposeCameraRig** in the **Hierarchy** window.
- Select this object.
- Then drag and drop the object **ThirdPersonController** from the **Hierarchy** window to the field called **target** as described on the next figures.

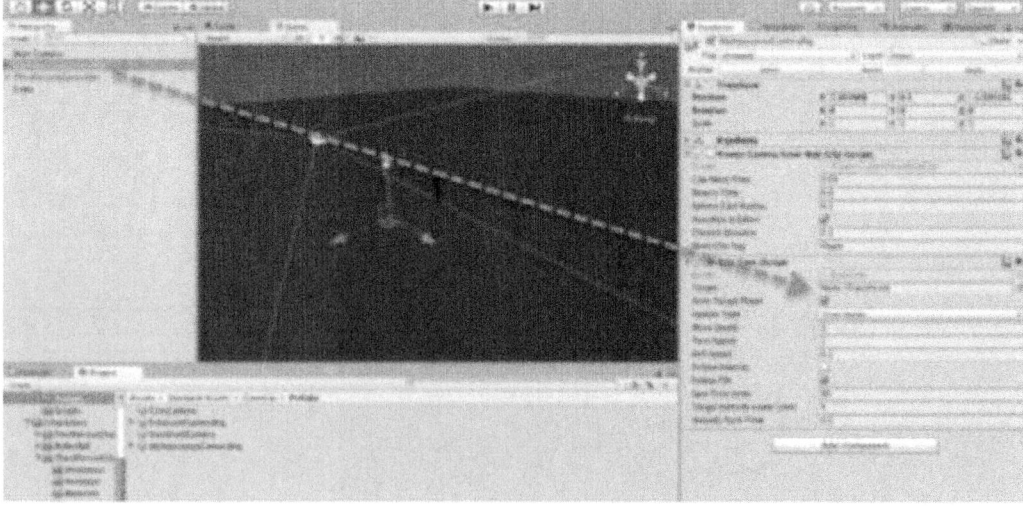

Figure 1-5: Setting-up the camera (part 1)

[28]

Adding Simple AI

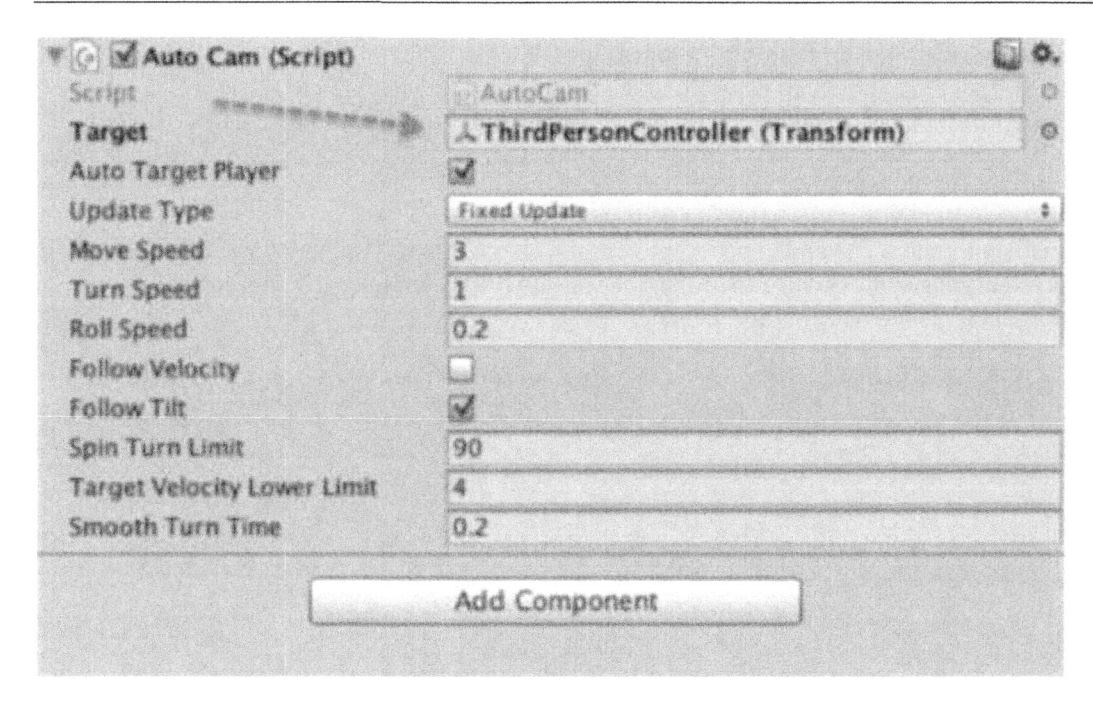

Figure 1-6: Setting-up the camera (part 2)

Finally, we will deactivate the main camera that was present in the scene at the start, since we already have a camera that follows the player, and we will also add some light.

- Select the object called **Main Camera** in the **Hierarchy** window, and, using the **Inspector** window, deactivate this object by unchecking the box located to the left of the name of the object (top-left corner)

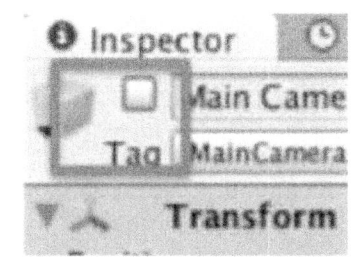

Figure 1-7: Deactivating the main camera

- Select: **Game Object | Light | Directional Light**. This will create a new directional light.
- Change the position of this light to **(0,10,0)** and its rotation to **(0,0,0)**.

So at this stage you should see that the following in the **Hierarchy** window:

- A third-person controller.

[29]

Adding Simple AI

- A **Camera** object that is set to follow this character.
- A **ground** object on which the character will be able to walk or run.
- A light for the scene.

So first, let's play the scene and experiment with the character. As you play the scene, and use the arrow keys on your keyboard, you will be able to move the character in different directions and see that the camera is following this character.

Figure 1-8: Playing the initial scene

You can now stop the scene; we will now create a launcher that will be used to fire projectiles at the character.

- Please create a new cube.
- Rename this cube **launcher**.
- Move it away from the player and make sure that it is at least 1 meter above the ground, for example at the position **(15, 2, 0)**.
- Deactivate the collider component from this object: select the **launcher** and deactivate its collider component in the **Inspector** window. This is so that any object launched through the **launcher** does not collide with it.

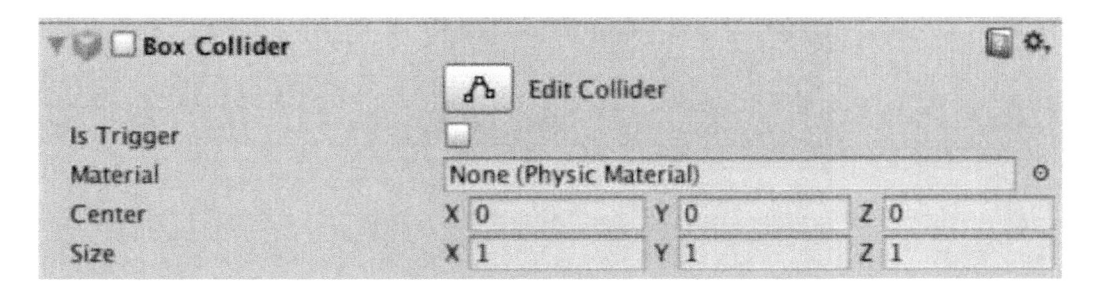

Box Collider			
	Edit Collider		
Is Trigger	☐		
Material	None (Physic Material)		
Center	X 0	Y 0	Z 0
Size	X 1	Y 1	Z 1

Figure 1-9: Deactivating the collider for the launcher

Next, we will create the actual projectile that will consist of a simple sphere. This sphere will be used as a template for any projectile fired from the launcher.

- Create a new sphere (**Game Object | 3D Object | Sphere**).

- Rename it **ball**.

- Change its scale settings to **(0.2, 0.2, 0.2)** so that its radius is **.2**.

Because this ball will be used as an airborne projectile, it will need to behave as if it was subject to gravity and emulate other physics-based behaviors. For this, we can add what is called a **rigid body** to this object; this is a component that effectively gives physics properties to an object:

- Select the object labeled **ball**.

- From the main menu, select: **Component | Physics | Rigidbody**.

- You should now see in the **Inspector** that a component called **Rigidbody** has been added to the object called **ball**, as described on the next figures.

Adding Simple AI

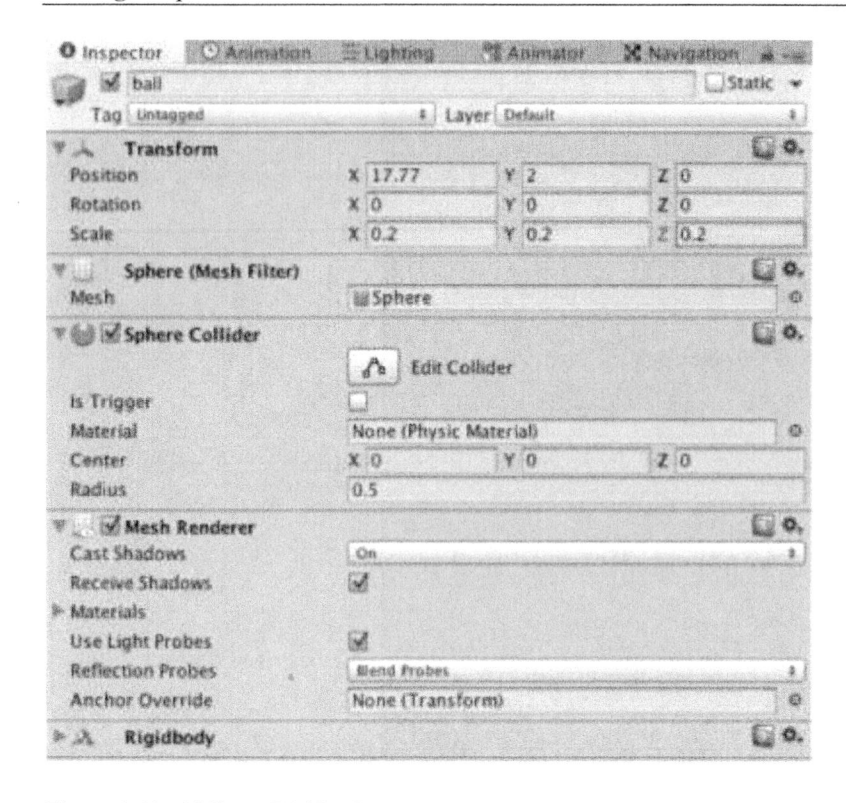

Figure 1-10: Adding a Rigidbody component

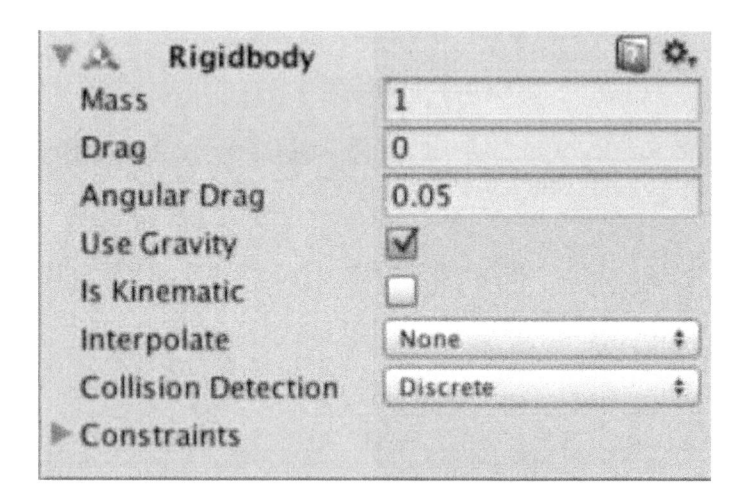

Figure 1-11: Checking the ball's physics properties

From the previous figure, we can see that this object will have a mass of 1 kilogram and that it will be subject to gravity.

Once this is done (i.e., once you have added the **Rigidbody** component), we can now create a prefab with this particular object.

Adding Simple AI

> The idea of a prefab is that sometimes you would like to instantiate or create objects based on a template. So, a prefab can be used as a template and then instantiated when needed.

In our case, we want to create several projectiles, so we will create a prefab that can be used for every projectile.

- In the **Project** window, select the folder called **Assets**.

- Then select the option **Create | Folder** as described on the next figure.

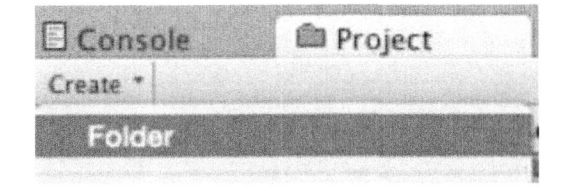

Figure 1-12: Creating a new folder

- This will create a new folder. Rename this folder **launcher** and double-click on it, so that the next asset (i.e., the new prefab) that we create is saved in this folder.

- In the **Project** window, select **Create | Prefab**, this will create a prefab symbolized by a grey cube in the **Project** window (or the folder that was selected before your created your prefab).

> If asked by Unity (i.e., Unity 2019+) whether you want to create an **Original Prefab** or a **Prefab Variant**, please use the option "**Original Prefab**".

- Rename this prefab **projectile**.

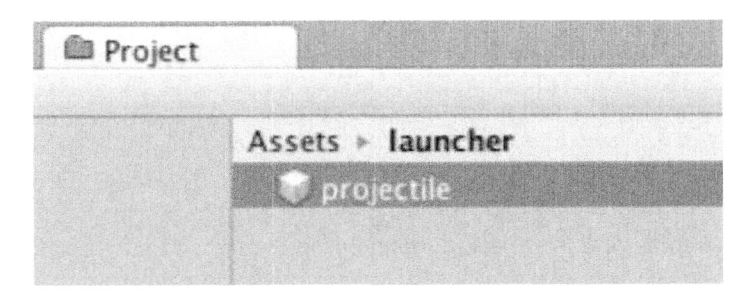

Figure 1-13: Adding a prefab

- Drag and drop the object called **ball** (from the **Hierarchy** window) on this prefab; you may notice that the prefab has turned to blue; which means that it now contains an object that can be instantiated (as illustrated on the next figure).

Adding Simple AI

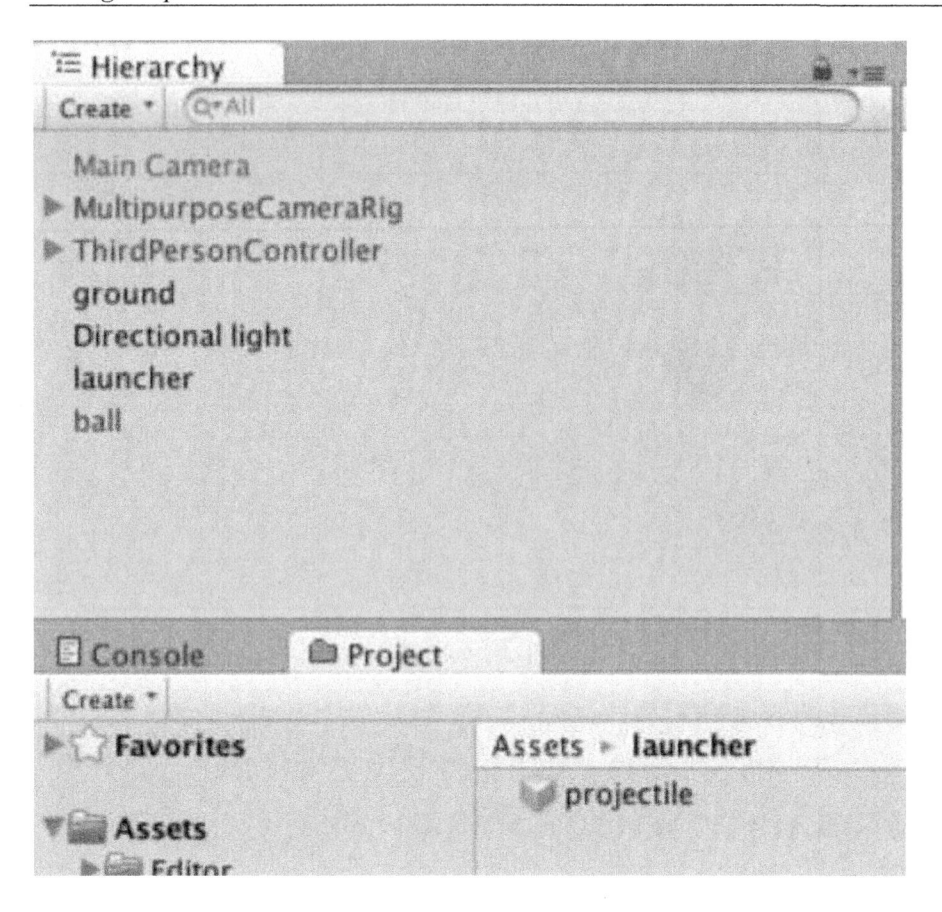

Figure 1-14: Creating a new prefab

Once the prefab has been created, it is time to create a script that will control the launcher and instantiate projectiles.

- From the **Project** window, create a new C# script (**Create | C# Script**) named **LaunchProjectile**.

- Once it has been created, please open this script in your code editor.

The first thing we will do in this script, is to create a member variable that will act as a placeholder for the projectile. So we will create a **public** variable for the projectile's prefab, so that, when the script has been attached to an object, we can drag and drop the prefab to this empty field.

- Please add the following code to the script, within the class definition (new code in bold).

Adding Simple AI

```
using UnityEngine;
using System.Collections;

public class LaunchProjectile : MonoBehaviour
{
    public GameObject projectile;
    // Use this for initialization
    void Start () {

    }

    // Update is called once per frame
    void Update () {

    }
}
```

Then, we can try to detect when the player has pressed a key on the keyboard so that an object (i.e., a projectile) can be instantiated in this case. Please enter the following code within the **Update** function.

```
void Update ()
{
    if (Input.GetKeyDown (KeyCode.P))
    {
        GameObject t = (GameObject) Instantiate (projectile, transform.position, Quaternion.identity);
    }
}
```

In the previous code:

- We check whether the key **P** has been pressed.

- We then create a new **GameObject** using the keyword **Instantiate**. This **GameObject** is created (or instantiated) from the **projectile** prefab; its position will be the same as the object linked to this script (i.e., in our case, this will be the launcher, using **transform.position**), and no rotation will be applied to this new object.

- We also add the keyword **GameObject** before the keyword **Instantiate**; this is to ensure that the object created is of type **GameObject**. In programming terms, it is called **casting**.

Adding Simple AI

> **About casting**: as you will be coding in C#, the compiler will require that every time you create or initialize a variable, that the type of the left side of the **equal** sign is the same as the type on the right side of the equal sign. Using casting can help to ensure that this condition is fulfilled. If you omit to perform this casting, Unity may throw an error that may look like "**Cannot implicitly convert type**". So if you ever get this error message, you may check the types of the variables on either sides of an equal sign and use casting, if need be.

- We can now save our script.
- After checking that it includes no errors, we can then drag and drop it on the object called **launcher** in the **Hierarchy** window.

There is now one last thing we need to do; that is, dragging and dropping the prefab we have created initially on to the field called **projectile** in the script that is attached to the launcher.

- Please select the object **launcher** in the **Hierarchy** window.
- In the **Inspector** window, you should see that there is an empty field, in the component **LaunchProjectile**, called **projectile**.

Figure 1-15: Checking the script LaunchProjectile

- Please drag and drop the **projectile** prefab from the **Project** window to this field; this will effectively set the value of the variable **projectile** in the script to the prefab, as described on the next figure.

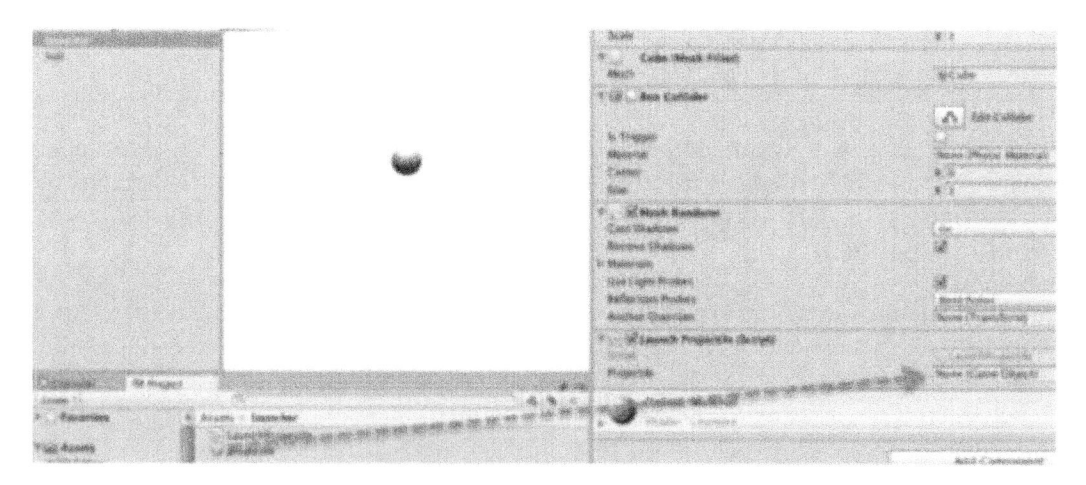

Figure 1-16: Setting a public variable with a prefab

[36]

Adding Simple AI

> Note that we can access this variable because it was previously set as **public** in our script.

Once this is done, let's play the scene and test our script.

- Please play the scene.
- Move the character near the launcher.
- Press the **P** key, and you should notice that balls are dropped from the launcher, as described on the next figure.

Figure 1-17: Testing the launcher

So at this stage, the instantiation is working properly; however, we would like now to add a force to these spheres, so that they are effectively propelled in the air (rather than being dropped on the ground). Before that, there is also another aspect that we need to look at: as we create these projectiles, they may start to overcrowd the scene and we could decide to destroy them after a few seconds, to keep performances high. For this purpose, we will use the method **Destroy**.

- Please add the following code, within the code that tests for the user input (just after the instantiation; the new code is highlighted in bold).

Adding Simple AI

```
void Update ()
{
    if (Input.GetKeyDown (KeyCode.P))
    {
        GameObject t = (GameObject) Instantiate (projectile, transform.position, Quaternion.identity);
        Destroy (t,3);
    }
}
```

In the previous code, we destroy the ball that has been instantiated after three seconds.

- Please save your code.
- Play the scene.
- Move the character near the launcher.
- Press the **P** key several times.
- Check that the balls that have been created disappear after a few seconds.

We can now start to think about adding a force to the projectiles. To do so, we will be using a method that exists for all rigid bodies, called **AddForce**. This method will add a force to a specific rigid body, based on a direction and a magnitude (i.e., intensity).

- Please add the following code just after the **Destroy** statement that we have added earlier.

```
t.GetComponent<Rigidbody>().AddForce(transform.forward * 500);
```

In the previous code:

- We access the **Rigidbody** component of our object.
- We then add a force forward with an intensity of **500**.

Now, the last modification we will make will be to ensure that the launcher is always facing the player, so that the projectile is launched towards the player. Thankfully, Unity provides a method that makes it possible to look at (or rotate to face) a particular object; this method usually needs a target to look at; in our case this will be the player. So let's create this feature.

- Please add the following code at the beginning of the class.

```
public GameObject target;
```

- This variable will be used as a placeholder so that the player becomes the target for this launcher.
- Then, we can add the following line within the code that tests for the user input.

Adding Simple AI

```
transform.LookAt(target.transform);
```

In this code, we specify that we would like our launcher to look in the direction of the target. This code should be executed before we start to instantiate the projectile, so it needs to be added just at the start of the conditional statement; so the full code should look as follows:

```
using UnityEngine;
using System.Collections;

public class LaunchProjectile : MonoBehaviour
{
    public GameObject projectile;
    public GameObject target;
    // Use this for initialization
    void Start () {

    }

    // Update is called once per frame
    void Update ()
    {
        if (Input.GetKeyDown (KeyCode.P))
        {
            transform.LookAt(target.transform);
            GameObject t = (GameObject) Instantiate (projectile, transform.position, Quaternion.identity);
            t.GetComponent<Rigidbody>().AddForce(transform.forward * 500);
            Destroy (t,3);
        }
    }
}
```

As you save your script, please switch back to Unity and check that the placeholder **target** appears in the **Inspector** window.

We can now set its value:

- Select the launcher in the **Hierarchy** window.

- Drag and drop the object **ThirdPersonController** from the **Hierarchy** window to the variable **target**, in the script attached to the launcher, as described on the next figure.

[39]

Adding Simple AI

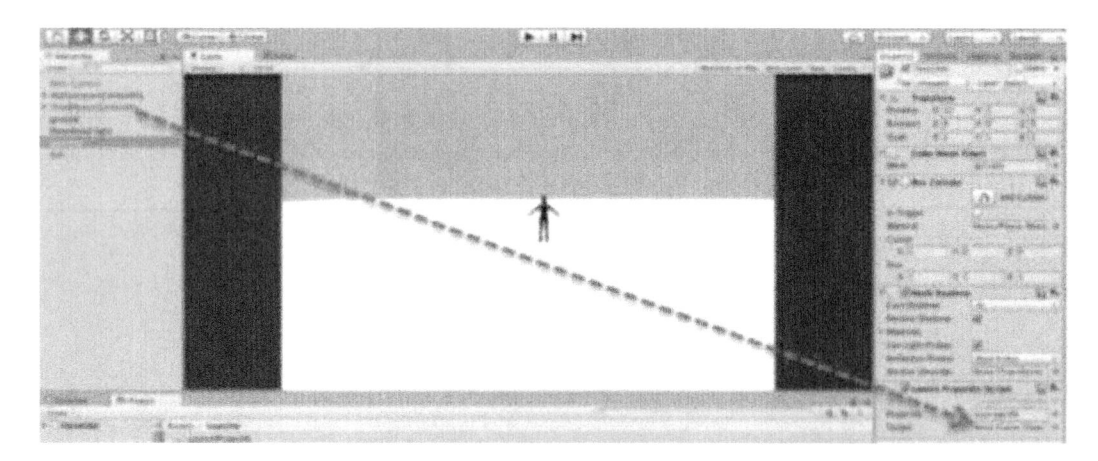

Figure 1-18: Setting the target for the launcher

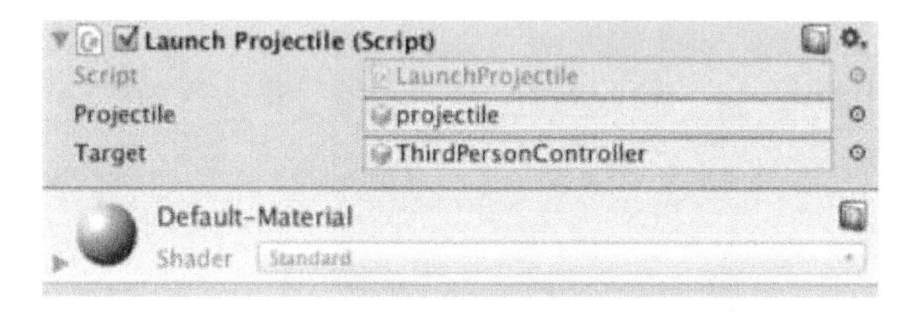

Figure 1-19: Setting the target for the launcher (close-up)

Once this is done we can test the scene, and as you play it, you will see that when you move the character around and press the *P* key, the projectiles will be fired in the direction of the player.

As you do so you may also notice that more force may need to be applied to the projectile if the player is at a medium distance from the launcher. So we could do the following:

- Open the script.
- Modify the following line so that the force applied is 1000 (instead of 500).

```
t.GetComponent<Rigidbody>().AddForce(transform.forward * 1000);
```

Now that we have managed to test whether the launcher could fire projectiles, we can now make it possible for this launcher to automatically fire projectiles (without the need to press a key). For this purpose, we just need to remove the condition (i.e., key pressed). So we can modify the code and remove this conditional statement by either deleting it or commenting it as follows.

[40]

```
//if (Input.GetKeyDown (KeyCode.P))
```

After you save your code and as you play the scene, you will notice that the firing range of the launcher has increased significantly.

Figure 1-20: Avoiding the projectiles

This being said, there is one aspect of the launcher that we could change; that is, its reload time. At present, the launcher fires projectiles indefinitely, making it relatively difficult for the player not to get hit. What we could do is to add more time between each shot. This time could be set in stone or, to increase challenge, this time could decrease over time (i.e., increasing firing rate). To implement this feature, let's modify the code with the **Update** method as follows:

- First, we can add a member variable **time** that will be used as a timer; please add this code to the start of the class.

```
float time;
```

- Then we can modify the **Update** method as follows (new code highlighted in bold).

```
void Update ()
{
        time +=Time.deltaTime;
        if (time >=2.0)
        {
                time = 0;
                transform.LookAt(target.transform);
                GameObject t = (GameObject) Instantiate (projectile, transform.position, Quaternion.identity);
                t.GetComponent<Rigidbody>().AddForce(transform.forward * 1000);
                Destroy (t,3);
        }
}
```

In the previous code:

- The value of the variable **time** is increased by one every second.

- When it reaches the value **two** it is then initialized back to 0 and a projectile is instantiated.

- As a result, a projectile will be instantiated every two seconds.

- Please save your code, and switch back to Unity.

- Check that there are no errors.

- Play the scene and see how the shooting frequency is now every two seconds.

Adding Simple AI

MANAGING COLLISION

So at this stage, we have managed to implement a relatively simple, yet effective, AI that follows the player and shoots projectiles in his/her direction. We could now modify the code that we have to date to implement the following:

- Collision detection for the projectile.
- An explosion is created at the point of impact.
- If the collision is with the player, then the player is destroyed.

So let's get started:

- Please create a new C# script and name it **CollisionWithProjectile**. You can create this new file in the folder called **launcher** or any other folder of your choice.
- Please open the script and add the following code at the beginning of the class.

```
public GameObject explosion;
```

In the previous code, we create a placeholder (i.e., a **public** variable) that we will initialize later using drag and drop from the **Inspector** window. This **explosion** object will be used to instantiate an explosion at the point of impact of the projectile.

Now, we just need to create a method that will handle the collision.

- Please add the following code just after the method **Update** (but within the class **CollisionWithProjectile**).

```
void OnCollisionEnter (Collision collision)
{
        if (collision.gameObject.tag == "Player") Destroy (collision.gameObject, 1);

        Instantiate (explosion, transform.position, Quaternion.identity);
}
```

- In the previous code, we use a built-in method called **OnCollisionEnter**. This method is usually called when an object (such as a sphere, a box, or a cylinder) collides with another object. So when this happens, Unity looks for a method spelt exactly this way, and returns information about the collision in the variable **collision.**

[43]

Adding Simple AI

> The information about the collision is returned in a variable of type **Collision**, for which we can set the name. In this case, we have called it **collision**, but using a different name (as long as its type is correct) would work just as fine.

- When this collision happens, we just check the tag of the object that we are colliding with; in this case, we look for a tag called **Player** (i.e., we will need to set our third-person controller with this tag so that it is detected accordingly also).

- If this is the case, then we will destroy the object with this tag, and also instantiate an explosion at the position of the projectile (i.e., point of impact).

- Your script should now look like the following:

```
using UnityEngine;
using System.Collections;

public class CollisionWithProjectile : MonoBehaviour
{
        public GameObject explosion;
        // Use this for initialization
        void Start () {

        }

        // Update is called once per frame
        void Update () {

        }

        void OnCollisionEnter (Collision collision)
        {
                if (collision.gameObject.tag == "Player") Destroy (collision.gameObject, 1);
                Instantiate (explosion, transform.position, Quaternion.identity);
        }
}
```

- Please save your code.

- Look at the **Console** window and check for any error.

So at this stage, we just need to add this script to the projectile prefab:

- Select the prefab called **projectile**.

- Drag and drop the script that we have just created (i.e., **CollisionWithProjectile**) on this prefab.

- Check that the script is now a component of this prefab by selecting the prefab and looking at its properties in the **Inspector** window, as described on the next figure.

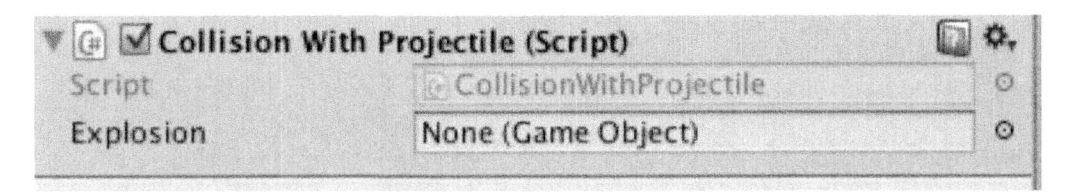

Figure 1-21: Checking that the script is added as a component

Once this done, we just need to specify a type of explosion to be used by this script when a collision occurs between the projectile and another object. For this, we can import and use built-in explosions, which are part of Unity's **Particle** built-in assets.

> If you have already imported the **Standard Assets** from the **Asset Store**, the next steps won't be necessary as it will already have created a folder called **Particle Systems** in your **Project** window.

- Please select: **Assets | Import Package | ParticleSystems**.

- The following window should appear.

Adding Simple AI

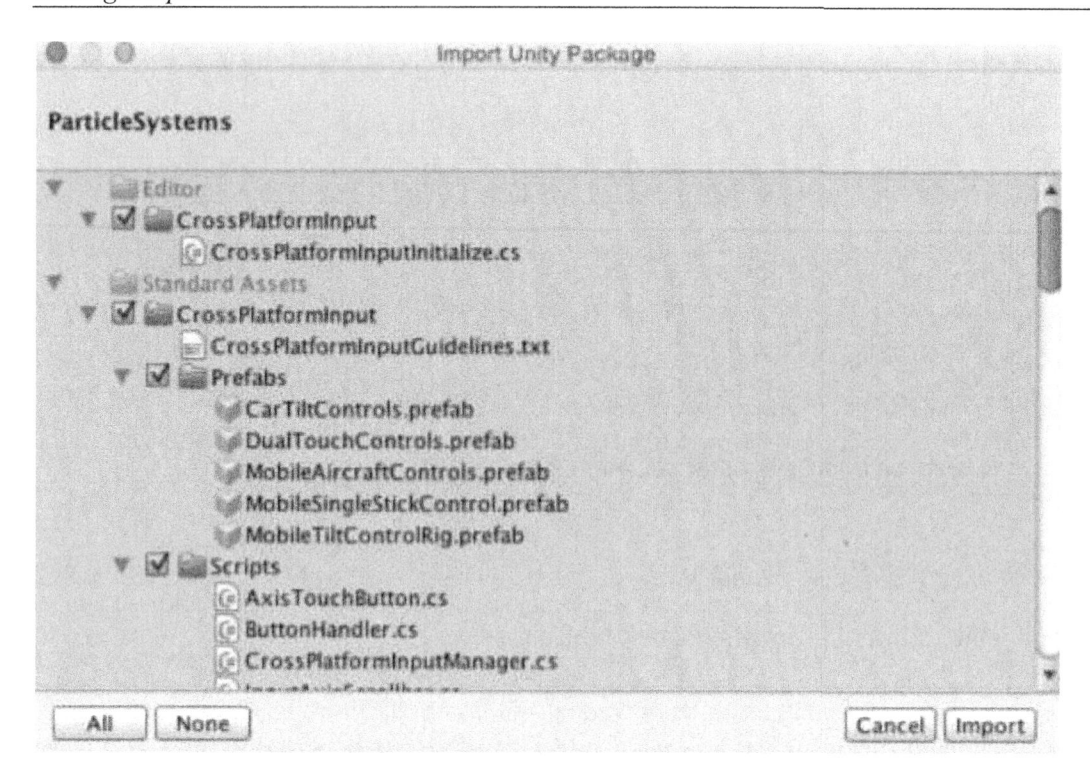

Figure 1-22: Importing the ParticleSystems package (part 1)

- Click the button labeled **Import**, to import all assets included in this package.

- Once the import is complete, a new folder called **ParticleSystems** will be created for these assets in the folder **Standard Assets**, as described in the next figure.

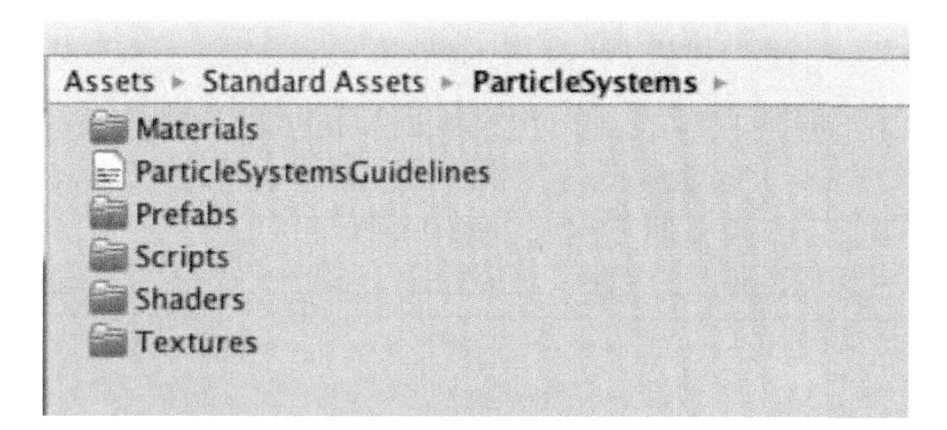

Figure 1-23: Importing the ParticleSystems package (part 2)

At this stage, we can use these new assets so that an explosion can be instantiated at the point of impact.

Adding Simple AI

- Select the object called **ball** in the **Hierarchy** window.

- Check in the **Inspector** that the script **CollisionWithProjectile** is listed as a component for this object.

- Using the **Project** window, navigate to the folder **Assets | Standard Assets | ParticleSystems | Prefabs** and drag and drop the prefab called **explosion** to the field called **explosion** from the script attached to the object called **ball**.

Figure 1-24: Adding a prefab for the explosion (part 1)

Figure 1-25: Adding a prefab for the explosion (part 2)

- Finally, update the corresponding prefab (i.e., projectile) by clicking on the button labeled Apply located in the top-right corner of the Inspector window. Since this object is used to create the prefab projectile, clicking on Apply will update the prefab also.

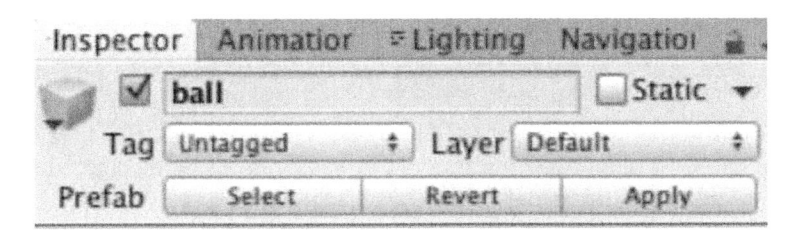

Figure 1-26: Updating the prefab using the Inspector window

[47]

Adding Simple AI

Last but not least, so that we can detect collisions with the player, we need to set a tag for the **Third-Person Controller**.

- Select the **Third-Person Controller** from the **Hierarchy** window.
- In the **Inspector** window, you will notice a section called **Tag** just below the name of the object.

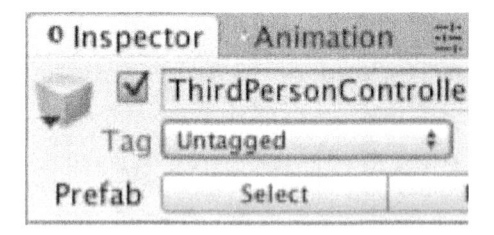

Figure 1-27: Creating a tag

- Click on the text **Untagged** and select the option **Player** from the drop-down list, as described on the next figure.

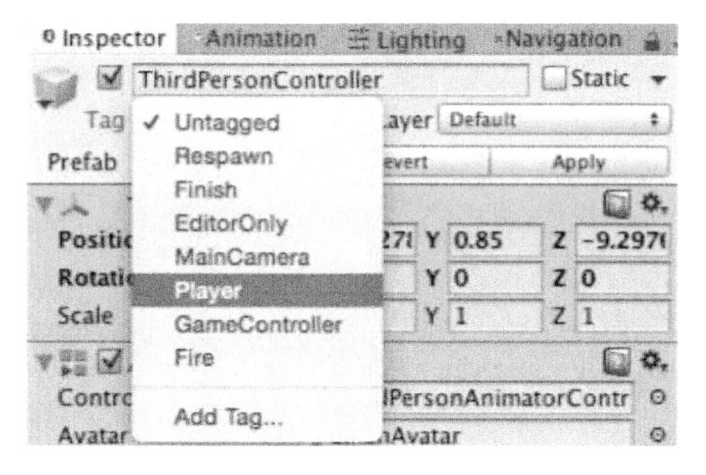

Figure 1-28: Adding a tag for the player

- Play the scene and check that your player disappears once it has been hit by a projectile, and that explosions are instantiated on impact.

[48]

FINISHING OUR FIRST GAME

So the game is working fairly well at this stage, the launcher manages to track (and shoot at) the player, and explosions are instantiated upon collision.

There are a few last things that we could do to both improve the game and to be able to reuse the code:

- To be able to reuse the objects that we have created, especially the launcher, it would be great to create a template from them (i.e., a prefab).

- Since the user will lose a life when hit by a projectile, it would be good to keep track of his/her number of lives.

- Finally, it would be nice to create a game with a goal, a scoring system, and the ability to display information onscreen about the status of the game.

So let's make these modifications. First, we will modify the game so that it uses the following gameplay:

- The player needs to collect five objects and reach a platform that symbolizes the end of the level.

- Intelligent launchers will track and shoot at the player.

- There will be four launchers in total.

- The player will avail of safe areas where he/she will be able to hide (away from the projectiles).

- The player, if hit by a projectile, has to restart the level from the starting point.

Please do the following:

- Create four spheres that will be representing the items to be collected by the player. You can rename them **sphere1**, **sphere2**, **sphere3**, and **sphere4**.

- You can then change their position so that their y-coordinate is **1.5**.

- Move them a few meters apart.

Once you have created the spheres, we need to make sure that the player can collect them; we will perform this action by (1) allocating tags to these spheres, (2) then, upon collision, a script linked to the player will detect if the player is colliding with these spheres (i.e., by checking their label), and (3) if this is the case, these spheres will be destroyed.

Adding Simple AI

First, let's create tags for the spheres.

- Select the object **sphere1** in the **Hierarchy** window.

- In the **Inspector** window, you will notice a section called **Tag** just below the name of the object.

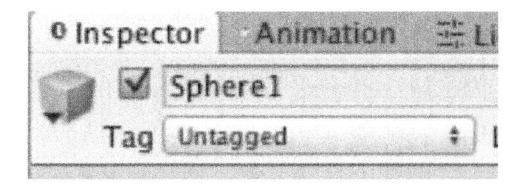

Figure 1-29: Creating a tag

At present, because no tag has been defined or selected for this object, the **Tag** section is set to **Untagged**. So we will create a new tag and allocate it to our object:

- Click on **Untagged**, this will display a list of predefined tags, as well as the option **Add tag...**

- Click on **Add Tag...**, this should display the following window.

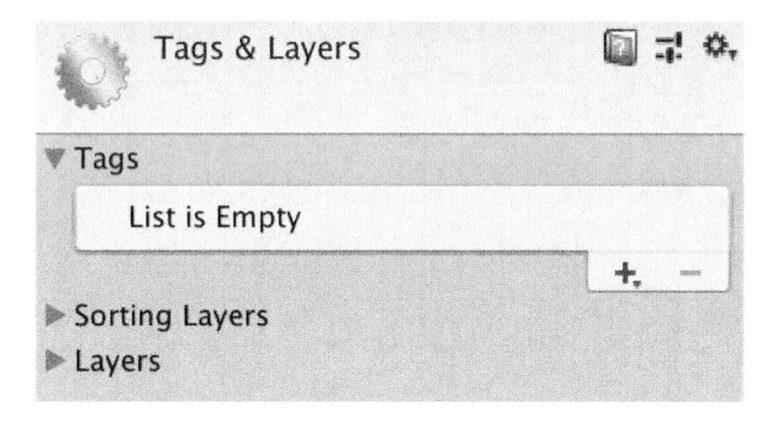

Figure 1-30: Creating a new tag

- You may notice that the section **Tags** displays the message **List is Empty**, as we have not defined any new tag yet.

- Click on the + sign to the right of the text **List Empty**, as highlighted on the previous figure.

- Then, enter the name of the new tag, **pick_me**, and press return.

Adding Simple AI

```
New Tag Name    pick_me
                Save
```

Figure 1-31: Entering the value of the new tag

Now that we have created a new tag, we just need to allocate it to an object:

- In the **Hierarchy** window, select the object **sphere1**.

- In the **Inspector**, go to the **Tag** section; you should now see the tag that you have just created in the drop-down list.

- Select this tag (i.e., click on it once), as described on the next figure.

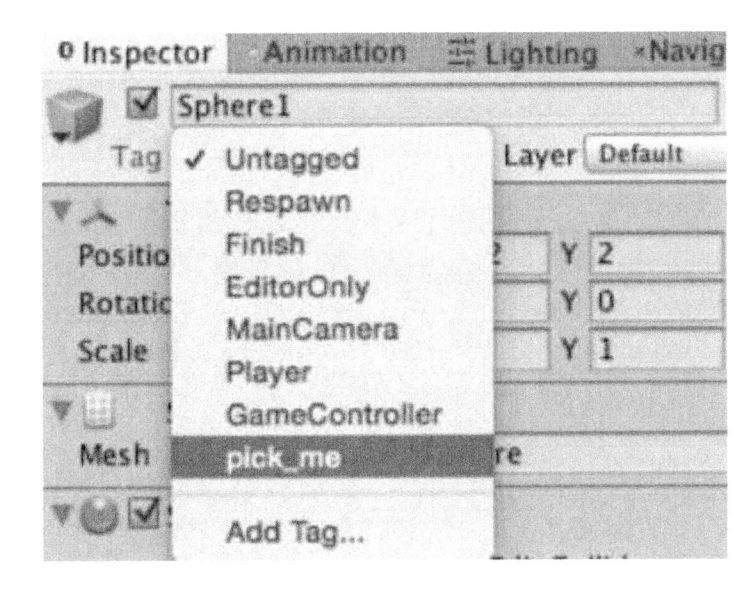

Figure 1-32: Applying a new tag

- You can now apply this tag to the three other spheres, either individually (i.e., by selecting and applying the tag to each sphere one by one, or by selecting all the spheres and applying the tag to all of them in one go).

- At this stage, the tag has been created for each sphere; we could also create a color (e.g., red) and apply it to the spheres so that they are more visible. To do so, you can create a new **red** material and apply it to the spheres (i.e., select **Create | Material** from the **Project** window and drag and drop this new material to the spheres).

Once this done, we will create a script to detect when the player collides with the objects to be picked-up.

[51]

Adding Simple AI

- Please create a new C# script named **CollisionWithPlayer**.
- Open this script and add the following code (new code highlighted in bold) to it.

```
int score;
void Start ()
{
        score = 0;
}
```

- In the previous code, we create a new member variable **score** that will be used to keep track of the score.
- We then initialize the **score** to 0.

We can then add the following code after the **Update** method.

```
void OnCollisionEnter (Collision collision)
{
        if (collision.collider.gameObject.tag == "pick_me")
        {
                Destroy (collision.collider.gameObject);
                score++;
                print ("Score" +score);
        }
}
```

In the previous code:

- We create a new method **OnCollisionEnter**.
- This is a built-in method that is called by Unity every time a collision is detected between the object linked to this script and another object (with a collider).
- Whenever the collision occurs, Unity returns information about the collision using an object of type **Collision**. In our case, this object will be called **collision**.
- If the collision occurs with an object for which the tag is **pick_me**, we then destroy this object and also increase and display the score.

So the full code should look as follows by now:

Adding Simple AI

```
using UnityEngine;
using System.Collections;

public class CollisionWithPlayer : MonoBehaviour {
    // Use this for initialization
    int score;
    void Start ()
    {
        score = 0;
    }
    // Update is called once per frame
    void Update () {
    }
    void OnCollisionEnter (Collision collision)
    {
        print ("Collided with " + collision.collider.gameObject.tag);
        if (collision.collider.gameObject.tag == "pick_me")
        {
            Destroy (collision.collider.gameObject);
            score++;
            print ("Score" +score);
        }
    }
}
```

- Please save your code and ensure that there are no errors.

- Drag and drop this script (i.e., **CollisionWithPlayer**) on the object **ThirdPersonController**.

- Please play the scene and make sure that you can collect the different spheres.

Once this is done, we can then create two platforms: a platform that symbolizes the start of the level, and a platform that symbolizes the end of the level.

Please do the following:

- Create a new cylinder (**GameObject | 3D Object | Cylinder**).

- Set its scale attribute to **(2.0, 0.2, 2.0)** and its **y** position coordinate to **.6**. This is the initial point from where the player will start.

- Rename this object **start**.

- Please repeat the last three steps to create a similar cylinder, but with the name **end** (to speed-up the process, you can duplicate the previous object).

Adding Simple AI

- Place these two cylinders at least 50 meters apart.

For now, we just need to add three more launchers; for this purpose, we will create a prefab for the launcher and reuse this prefab to create the three additional launchers.

- In the **Project** window, select the folder **launcher**, or any other folder that you have created for the items created in this scene.

- Select the object **launcher** in the **Hierarchy** window.

- Drag and drop this object to the **launcher** folder (or the **Assets** folder).

- This will automatically create a prefab, as illustrated on the next figure (if prompted to choose the type of prefab that you want to create, please chose the option "**Original Prefab**").

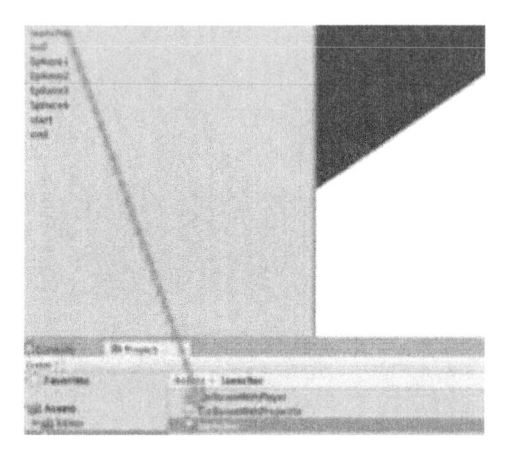

Figure 1-33: Creating a launcher prefab

- Now we can deactivate the **launcher** object that is in the scene.

- Drag and drop the **launcher** prefab on the scene four times to create four launchers.

- This should create four launchers named **launcher (1)**, **launcher (2)**, **launcher (3)**, and **launcher (4)**.

- Include the four launchers between the start and the end of the level.

If you look at the properties of one of these launchers, you may notice that the target is not set, so we will need to do this for all launchers.

- Select all four launchers in the **Hierarchy** window (*using CTRL + click or CTRL + Shift + click*).

- Drag the **ThirdPersonController** from the **Hierarchy** window to the **target** variable for the script **LaunchProjectile** present in the **Inspector** window. Because we have selected the four launchers, the target will be set for these four objects simultaneously.

- So that it is easier to locate the different objects that make up this scene from the y-axis (i.e., from above), you can create two new **Materials** (e.g., blue) and apply these to the launchers (e.g., blue) for the start and end of the level (e.g., green), as illustrated on the next figure.

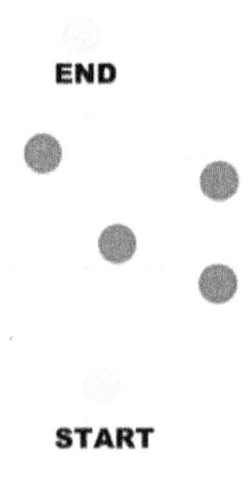

END

START

Figure 1-34: Viewing the scene from above

At this stage, all the elements are ready for our game, and we just need to add the following features:

- Make it possible to detect when the player has reached the end of the game.

- Place the player on the starting platform at the beginning of the game or after it has been hit.

Let's do the following:

- Please move the **Third-Person Controller** just 1 meter above the **start** object.

Adding Simple AI

Figure 1-35: Moving the character above the start cylinder

- Open the script **CollisionWithProjectile** and modify it so that, after it has been hit by a projectile, s/he is moved back to the start, as follows (new code highlighted in bold).

```
void OnCollisionEnter (Collision collision)
{
        //if (collision.gameObject.tag == "Player") Destroy (collision.gameObject, 1);
        if (collision.gameObject.tag == "Player")
        {
                collision.gameObject.transform.position = GameObject.Find ("start").transform.position;
        }
        Instantiate (explosion, transform.position, Quaternion.identity);
}
```

In the previous code, we move the player back to the start of the game.

As you play the game you may notice that the explosions may make the game very difficult at the start because every time the projectile explodes, the player is propelled in the air, even if s/he is far from the projectile; you may also notice that the player seems to start way above the starting platform.

To solve the first issue (i.e., the explosions), we can change the type of explosion that is instantiated when a projectile hits an object; we will replace the explosion with smoke instead:

- In the **Project** folder, locate the **projectile** prefab.

- Click on this prefab and look at the **Inspector** window: you should see a component called **CollisionWithProjectile**.

Adding Simple AI

- Click to the right of the variable called **explosion** in the script **CollisionWithProjectile**, as illustrated in the next figure.

Figure 1-36: Replacing the explosion

This will open a new window where you can specify the prefab to be used for the explosion on impact.

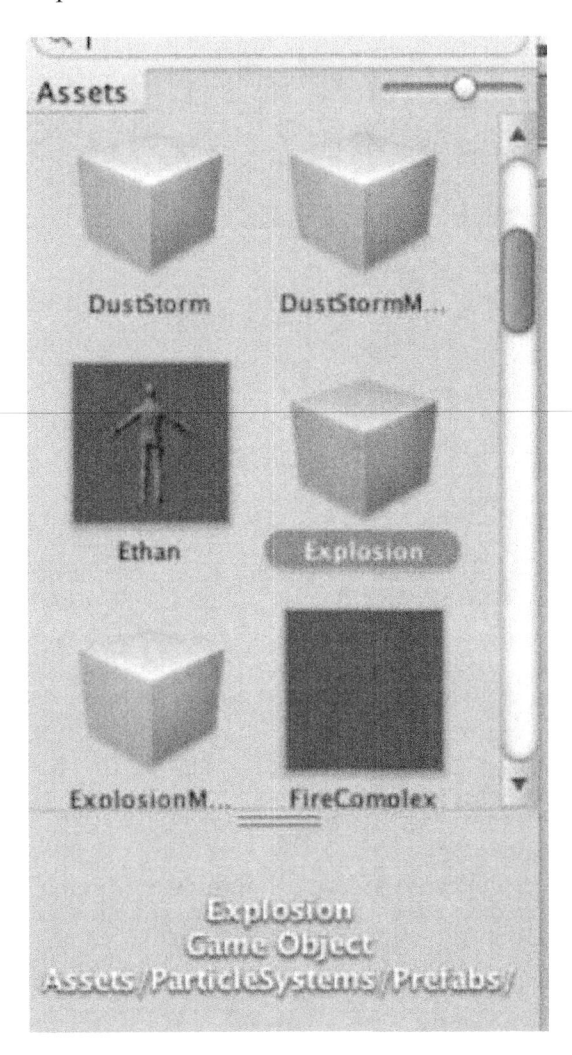

Figure 1-37: Choosing another prefab for the explosion

[57]

Adding Simple AI

- In the search window located at the top of this window, please type the word **smoke**; this should narrow down the search to two prefabs.

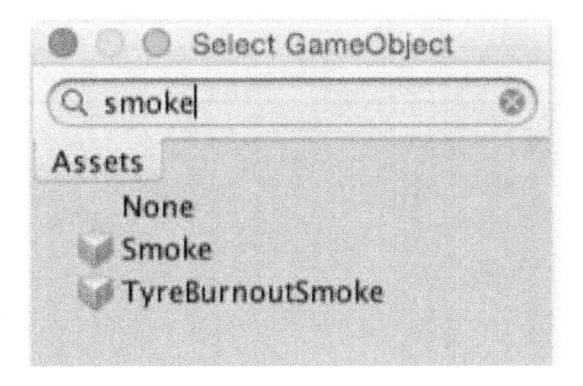

Figure 1-38: Narrowing down the search

- Select the prefab called **Smoke** (double-click on this prefab).
- This should set the explosion with the prefab **Smoke**.

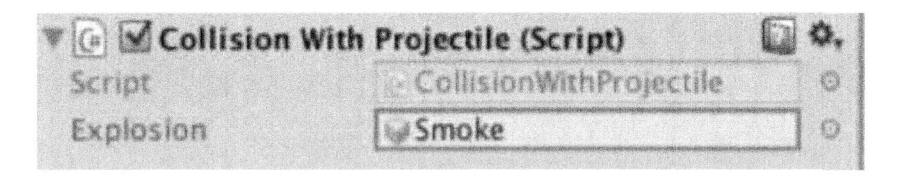

Figure 1-39: Completing the change of prefab for the explosion

Next, we will make sure that the projectile is also destroyed upon collision by modifying the method **OnCollisionEnter** in the script **CollisionWithProjectile** as follows (new code highlighted in bold):

```
Instantiate (explosion, transform.position, Quaternion.identity);
Destroy (gameObject);
```

And last but not least, we will make sure that the smoke lasts only for a few seconds:

- Select the **Smoke** prefab in the project folder (**Assets | Standard Assets | ParticleSystems | Prefabs**).
- In the **Inspector** window, change its **looping** property to **false**.

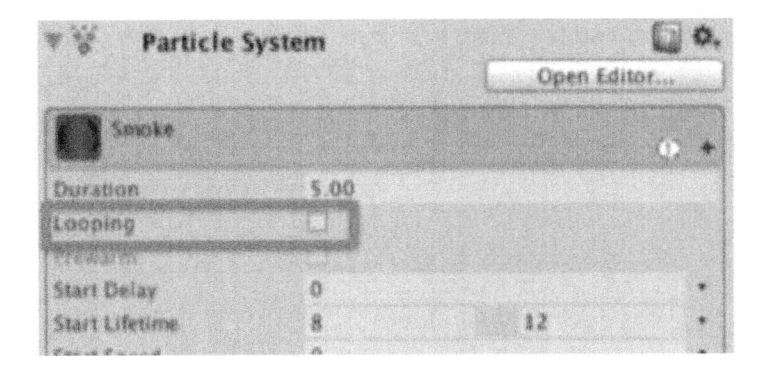

Figure 1-40: Modifying the looping property of the smoke

- Play the scene, and check that the projectiles are destroyed upon impact and also that the smoke disappears after a few seconds.

Finally, we will make sure that the colliders used for each platform (i.e., the start and the end of the game) are correct. At present, as we noticed previously, the player when placed above these, seem to be staying about one meter above its surface, whereas it should be connecting with the top part of the platform.

If we select the start platform and look at its collider, you will notice that a capsule collider is used, which means that the top part of the collider will not follow a flat surface. So we need to change to a more accurate collider that really follows the shape of our cylinder.

- Please right-click on the **start** object in the **Hierarchy** window.

- In the **Inspector**, deactivate the **Capsule Collider** component for this object by unchecking the box to the left of the label **Capsule Collider**.

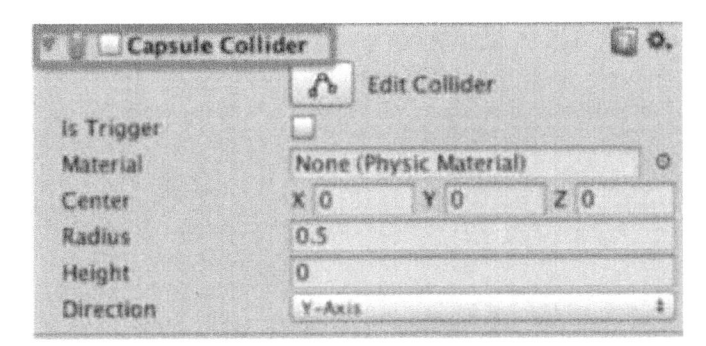

Figure 1-41: Deactivating the capsule collider.

We can now add a new collider, in our case, for increased precision, this will be a mesh collider:

- Click on the button labeled **Add Component** located at the bottom of the **Inspector** window.

[59]

Adding Simple AI

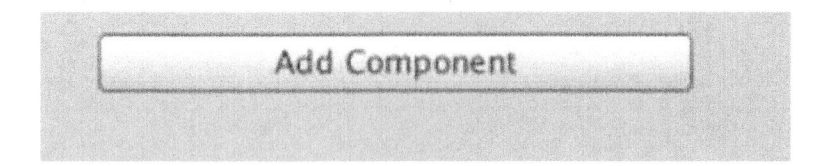

Figure 1-42: Adding a new Collider component

- From the contextual menu, select: **Physics | MeshCollider**.
- Once this is complete, a new mesh collider should be listed as a component of this object.

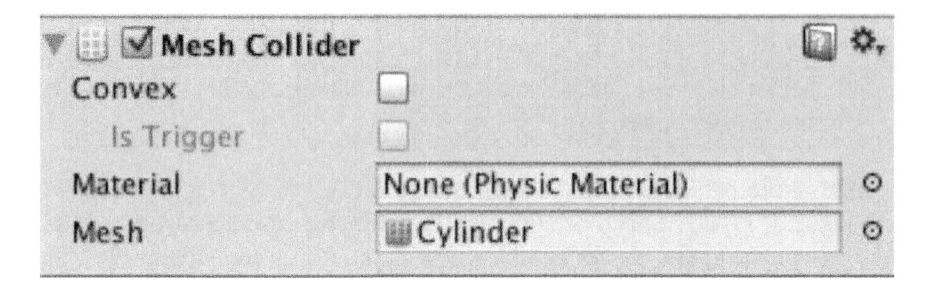

Figure 1-43: The mesh collider listed as a component

- Please repeat the last steps to modify the collider for the object called **end**.
- Play the scene and check that you can jump on both platforms easily.

DETECTING WHEN THE PLAYER HAS REACHED THE END OF THE GAME

At this stage, we need to detect whether the player has reached the end of the level (i.e., the **end** platform) after collecting four objects. So we will need to check for both conditions and then display a message (e.g., "congratulations") when both conditions have been fulfilled. Since we are already counting the number of objects collected, all we need is to access (i.e., read) the score when we have reached the **end** platform.

First, let's detect wen we have reached this platform.

- Open the script **CollisionWithPlayer** and modify it as illustrated in the next code snippet (new code highlighted in bold).

```
void OnCollisionEnter (Collision collision)
{
        if (collision.collider.gameObject.tag == "pick_me")
        {
                Destroy (collision.collider.gameObject);
                score++;
                print ("Score" +score );
        }
        if (collision.collider.gameObject.name == "end" && score == 4)
        {
                print("Congratulations!");
        }
}
```

- In the previous script, we check the name of the object we are colliding with.

- If this is the **end** platform and if the score is **4**, then we print the message **"Congratulations!"**, in the **Console** window.

- Please save your code, play the scene, collect four objects, and reach the **end** platform. A message saying **"Congratulations!"** should be displayed in the **Console** window.

Last we will display this message onscreen using **UI** objects. If you are new to **UI** objects, these make it possible to display information (e.g., text, images, menus, buttons, or sliders) onscreen as part of the user interface. So for now, we will be using a **UI Text** object.

- Create a new **UI Text** object (**GameObject | UI | Text**).

- Rename this object **message**.

- Select this object.

Adding Simple AI

Modify its properties in the **Inspector** as follows:

- PosX:0
- PosY:0
- PosZ:0
- Width: 500
- Height: 200
- Font Size: 40
- Vertical alignment: middle
- Horizontal alignment: middle
- Color: green (or any color of your choice)

We can then modify the script **CollisionWithPlayer** so that it displays a message when all spheres have been collected.

- Modify the script **CollisionWithPlayer** as follows:

```
using UnityEngine;
using System.Collections;
using UnityEngine.UI;

public class CollisionWithPlayer : MonoBehaviour {

    // Use this for initialization
    int score;
    void Start ()
    {
        score = 0;
        GameObject.Find("message").GetComponent<Text>().text ="";
    }
```

In the previous code:

- The third line introduces the name space **UnityEngine.UI**. This may be new to you, so let me explain. The **Text UI** elements are part of a sub-library called **UI**, which is part of the library **UnityEngine**. So, if we want to refer to the **Text UI** element, we can use **GetComponent** <Text> instead, and Unity will look into the library **UnityEngine.UI** to find the **UI Text** component.

Adding Simple AI

- Then we specify that the text for the object called message is set to a blank string; in other words, we initialize the text field so that no message is displayed until we reach the end platform.

We can then display the message when the player has reached the **end** platform by modifying the code in the **Update** method, in the script **CollisionWithPlayer**, as follows (new code highlighted in bold).

```
if (collision.collider.gameObject.name == "end" && score >= 2)
{
    print("Congratulations!!!");
    GameObject.Find("message").GetComponent<Text>().text = "Congratulations!";
}
```

In the previous code, we change the message, as we have done before, but this time with the string "**Congratulations**".

[63]

Adding Simple AI

LEVEL ROUNDUP

Well this is it!

In this chapter, we have learned about instantiating objects in C#. We have created a very simply AI-driven launcher that follows the player and shoots projectile in his/her direction, and at a controlled rate. We also managed to create explosions upon collision. Finally, we created a scoring system and a mini-game whereby the player has to collect four objects, and also avoid the projectiles, before reaching the end of the level. So yes, we have made some considerable progress, and we have by now looked at some simple ways to implement artificial intelligence in our games.

Checklist

You can consider moving to the next chapter if you can do the following:

- Create prefabs.
- Instantiate prefabs.
- Add **Rigidbody** components.
- Shoot projectiles (i.e., apply a force to an object with a Rigidbody component from a script).
- Understand why and how to cast variables.
- Display messages onscreen.

Adding Simple AI

Quiz

It's now time to check your knowledge with a quiz. So please try to answer the following questions. The solutions are included in your resource pack. Good luck!

1. The method **onControllerColliderHit** is called whenever a collision occurs between the **ThirdPersonController** and anther object that includes a collider.

2. To be able to access a variable from a script through the **Inspector**, this variable has to be declared as **public** in the script.

3. Write the missing line in this code to be able to destroy the object we have collided with.

```
function OnCollisionEnter (Collision collision)
{
<MISSING LINE>
}
```

4. There is only one way to create a prefab in Unity, that is through the menu **Create | Prefab**.

5. A mesh collider will detect collision more precisely than a capsule collider when applied to a spherical object.

6. Find one error in the following code.

```
void Start ()
{
    score = 0;
    GameObject.Find("message").GetComponent<UIText>().text        ="";
}
```

7. Any object selected in the **Hierarchy** window can be duplicated using the shortcut *CTRL + D*.

8. If the object attached to the next script has a **Rigidbody** component, the following code will access this component and apply a forward force to it.

```
gameObject.GetComponent<Rigidbody>().AddForce(transform.forward * 1000);
```

9. Explosions prefabs need to be imported using the **ParticleSystems** asset, in order to be used in Unity.

10. If the following error message appears "**Cannot implicitly convert type**", what do you need to do with the following code:

```
GameObject t = Instantiate (projectile, transform.position, Quaternion.identity);
```

   a) Make sure that the type of the variable to the left of the = sign is the same as the type of the variable on right of the = sign.
   b) Cast the variable to the right of the = sign using **(GameObject)**.

[65]

c) All of the above.

Solutions to the Quiz

1. FALSE (it should be **On**ControllerColliderHit).

2. TRUE.

3.
```
function OnCollisionEnter (Collision collision)
{
    Destroy (collision.collider.gameObject;
}
```

4. FALSE.

5. TRUE.

6.
```
void Start ()
{
    score = 0;
    //GameObject.Find("message").GetComponent<UIText>().text    ="";
    //should be
    GameObject.Find("message").GetComponent<UI.Text>().text    ="";
    OR
    GameObject.Find("message").GetComponent< Text>().text="";
}
```

7. TRUE.

8. TRUE.

```
gameObject.GetComponent<Rigidbody>().AddForce(transform.forward * 1000);
```

9. TRUE.

10. c (all the above)

[67]

Adding Simple AI

Challenge 1

Now that you have managed to complete this chapter and that you have improved your skills, let's modify the game to add more interaction.

- Change the onscreen message to "**You have collected an object**" every time the user has collected an object.

- Display the score onscreen (i.e., create a new **UI Text** object and access it whenever the score is updated).

- Create a timer so that this message is displayed only for 5 seconds.

Challenge 2

It is now time to try to use different prefabs:

- Look into the **ParticleSystems** assets folder and look at the different types of prefabs available.

- Successively use two different prefabs from this folder for when the ball hits an object.

- Experiment with the other prefabs and add them to the scene (e.g., steam or dust storm).

2
CREATING AND MANAGING WEAPONS

In this section we will discover how to create and manage weapons using a simple inventory system.

After completing this chapter, you will be able to:

- Create different weapons including a gun, an automatic gun, and a grenade launcher.
- Collect and manage ammunitions.
- Switch between weapons.
- Aim at targets using ray casting and a crosshair.
- Detect objects in the distance based on the crosshair.
- Simulate the impact of a bullet using particles.

Creating and Managing Weapons

In this section, we will be creating a training camp with the following features:

- The player will avail of three different weapons.
- The player will need to hit specific targets.
- The player will be able to collect ammunitions when needed.

SETTING-UP THE ENVIRONMENT

In this section we will create a very simple environment for this training camp.

So let's get started:

- Save the previous scene (**File | Save Scene**).

- Create a new scene (**File | New Scene**).

- Rename this scene **training-camp** or any other name of your choice using **File | Save Scene**.

- You may also create a new folder to store assets created in this scene (i.e., select **Create | Folder** from the **Project** window).

- Change the light settings so that the ambient light is brighter (**Window | Rendering | Light Settings**).

We will now create a simple ground and three targets.

- Create a new cube and rename it **ground**.

- Change its position to **(0, 0, 0)** and its scale properties to **(100, 1, 100)**.

- You can apply a texture to the ground by choosing one of the textures present in the resource pack (e.g., ground).

Creating and Managing Weapons

> If you import a texture to be used in Unity, please make sure that its **Texture Type** property (available from the **Inspector** window, as illustrated in the next figure) is set to **Texture**. To do so you can select the texture imported, set its type to **Texture** in the **Inspector** window, and then click on the button Apply located in the bottom-right corner of the **Inspector** window. If this texture is to be repeated several times (i.e., tiled) over the surface of an object, you may also set the option **Wrap Mode** to **Repeat**.
>
> Figure 2-1: Setting the Texture Type attribute of an imported texture

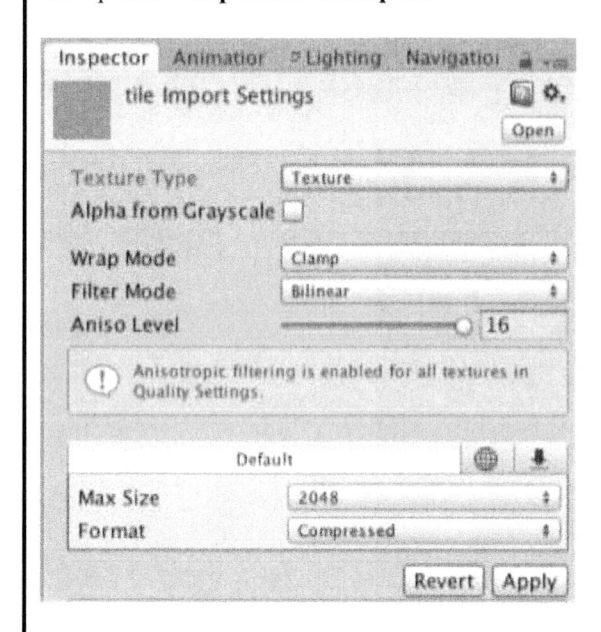

We will now create three targets that will be used for the training:

- Create a new **Cube**.

- Rename this cube **target1**.

- Using the **Rect** tool and/or the **Move** tool, rescale the cube on the y-axis so that its **position** is **(0,4,0)** and its **scale** property **(1, 6.5, 1)**. At this stage, what really matters is that this target can be seen (and targeted) easily.

- You can also paint this target in red by either applying an existing material that you have created in the previous scene, or by creating a new color material for this scene (i.e., select **Create | Material** from the **Project** window, change the color of the material and drag and drop it on the target).

- We can now duplicate this target three times, to add three identical targets. You can rename these targets **target2**, **target3**, and **target4**.

- Move these targets apart, so that they are aligned and about three meters apart; for example, they could be at the positions **(3, 4, 0)**, **(6, 4, 0)** and **(9, 4, 0)**.

So at this stage we have four targets that are aligned; we will now just add a First-Person Controller to the scene:

- Navigate to the folder **Assets | Standard Assets | Characters | FirstPersonCharacter | Prefabs**.

- Drag and drop the prefab **FPSController** to the scene, and make sure that it is just above the ground.

- This controller will be used to navigate through the scene.

- We can deactivate the object **MainCamera** so that only the camera embedded on the First-Person Controller is used.

- Play the scene (*CTRL + P*) and check that you can walk around the scene.

Creating and Managing Weapons

DETECTING OBJECTS AHEAD USING RAYCASTING

At this stage, we would like to detect what is in front of the player so that when we use our weapon (e.g., gun), we know whether an object is in the line of fire before shooting. To do so, we will use ray casting. So we will create some code to be able to detect what is in front of the player using a ray.

A ray is a bit like a laser beam; it is casted over a distance and usually employed to detect if an object is in the line of fire. In our case, we will cast a ray from the player (forward) and detect if it "collides" with another object. Before we do this, we can also use a ray in debug mode (i.e., only visible in the scene view), just to check its direction and length.

Rays can be used for many applications, from weapons to controlling objects (e.g., opening a door only if you are facing it rather than using collision).

The first ray that we will create will be used for testing purposes; it will only be visible in the scene view for the time being and will help us to gauge whether the ray casting technique used for collision detection will be successful.

- Please create a new script called **ManageWeapons**.
- Open this script and modify it as illustrated below.

```
public class ManageWeapons : MonoBehaviour
{
        Camera playersCamera;
        Ray rayFromPlayer;
        // Use this for initialization
        void Start ()
        {
                playersCamera = GetComponent<Camera>();
        }

        // Update is called once per frame
        void Update ()
        {

        }
}
```

In the previous code:

- We declare a new **GameObject** called **playersCamera**. This camera will be used for ray casting.

- We also declare a new ray called **rayFromPlayer** that will also be used for our ray casting.

- In the method **Start**, this camera is then initialized with the camera that is linked to the First-Person Controller.

Since the game, in this scene, will be using a First-Person view, the scene will be viewed through the eyes of the player; so we will cast a ray as if it was originating from the eyes of the player; since the scene is rendered through the camera attached to the First-Person controller, we will cast a ray from the middle of this lens (or the screen) and forward.

- You may just check that there is a camera attached to the **First-Person Controller** using the **Inspector** window: if you click on the object **FPSController**, you will see an object within called **FirstPersonCharacter**. If you click on this object (i.e., **FirstPersonCharacter**), and look at the **Inspector** window, you will see that, amongst other things, it includes a camera component.

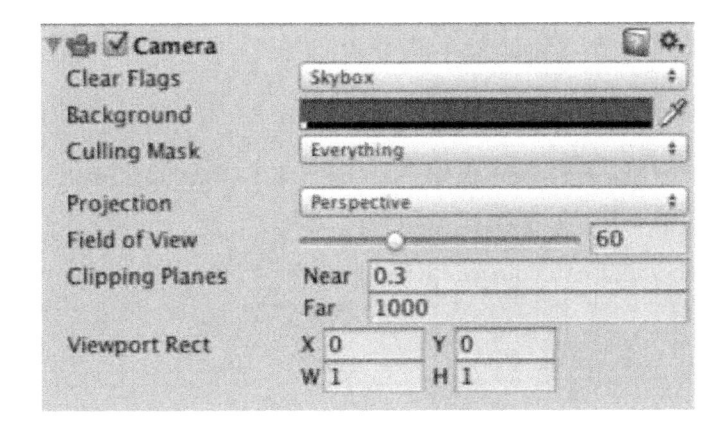

Figure 2-2: Checking the camera for the FPC

So again, this camera is linked to the object **FirstPersonCharacter** (and not the **FPSController**); this is really important because the script will be linked to the latter. If you were to add this script to the object **FPSController** instead, an error would occur because this object does not have a camera component.

- Let's further modify this script as follows.

[75]

Creating and Managing Weapons

```
void Update ()
{
        rayFromPlayer = playersCamera.ScreenPointToRay (new Vector3 (Screen.width/2, Screen.height/2, 0));
        Debug.DrawRay(rayFromPlayer.origin, rayFromPlayer.direction * 100, Color.red);

}
```

In the previous code, we do the following:

- We initialize our ray defined earlier; this ray will be originating from the camera used for the **First-Person Controller**, from the centre of the screen, which is defined by the x and y coordinates **Screen.width/2** (i.e., half the screen's width) and **Screen.height/2** (i.e., half the screen's height); the z coordinate is ignored. So at this stage, we know where the ray will start. By default, the ray will point outward.

- On the next line, we use the static method **DrawRay** and specify three parameters: the origin of the ray, its direction, and its color. By using **ray.origin** we will start the ray from the middle of the screen. By using **rayFromPlayer.direction*100**, we specify that the ray's length is 100 meters.

We are now ready to use this script:

- Please save your code and check that there are no errors left.

- Drag and drop the script form the **Project** window to the object **FirstPersonCharater** (the one within the object **FPSController**).

- Change the layout of your scene so that you can see both the **Scene** and the **Game** view simultaneously (e.g., drag the **Scene** view to the right of the **Console** tab).

- Play the scene.

- Check that you can see a ray casted from the camera of the FPS Controller, as described on the next figure.

Creating and Managing Weapons

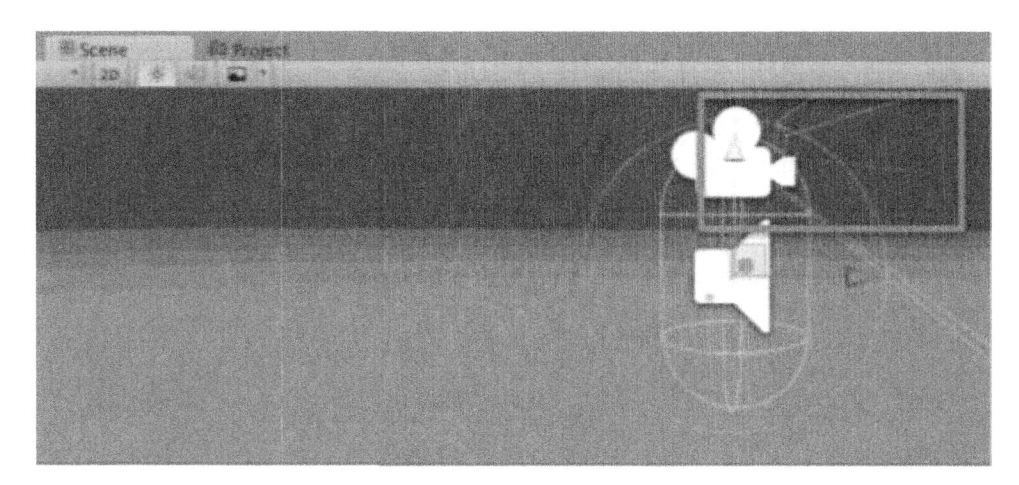

Figure 2-3: Casting a ray using the debug mode

Once this done, we can now apply a real ray casting method, by using a ray that will point in the exact same direction, but that will, in addition, detect any objects ahead of the player. To be more accurate the new ray will detect any collider attached to an object in front of the player.

- Please open the script **ManageWeapons**, and modify it as follows (new code highlighted in bold).

```
public class ManageWeapons : MonoBehaviour
{
    Camera playersCamera;
    Ray rayFromPlayer;
    RaycastHit hit;
```

In the previous code, we declare an object of type **RaycastHit**; this object will be used to store information about the collision between the ray casted from the player (i.e., from its camera), and the object in front of the player.

- We will then modify the **Update** method to cast the ray and detect any object in sight (the new code highlighted in bold):

Creating and Managing Weapons

```
void Update ()
{
        rayFromPlayer = playersCamera.ScreenPointToRay (new Vector3 (Screen.width/2, Screen.height/2, 1000));
        Debug.DrawRay(rayFromPlayer.origin, rayFromPlayer.direction * 100 , Color.red);
        if (Physics.Raycast(rayFromPlayer, out hit, 100))
        {
                print (" The object " + hit.collider.gameObject.name +" is in front of the player");
        }
}
```

In the previous code:

- We cast a ray using the keyword **Physics.RayCast**; the method **RayCast** takes three parameters: the ray (**rayFromPlayer**), an object where the information linked to the collision between the ray and another collider is stored (**hit**), and the length of the ray (**100**). The keyword **out** is used so that the information returned about the collision is easily accessible (as a reference rather than a structure; this is comparable to a type conversion or casting).

- If this ray hits an object (i.e., its collider), we print a message that displays the name of this object. To obtain this name, we access the collider involved in the collision, then the corresponding **GameObject** using **hit.collider.gameObject.name**.

- Please play the scene, and as you walk towards one of the targets, for example **target1**, the message **"target1 is in front of the player "** should be displayed in the **Console** window.

The method **Debug.DrawRay** will create a ray that we can see in the scene view and that can be used for debugging purposes to check that a ray effectively points in the right direction; however, **Debug.DrawRay** does not detect collisions with objects. So while it is useful to check the direction of a particular ray in the **Scene** view, this ray needs to be combined to a different method to be able to detect collisions; one of these methods is called **Physics.Raycast**.

CREATING A WEAPON

So, well done: at this stage we can cast rays and detect the object in front of the player. So the next step for us is to create and fire a weapon, and detect, using the ray cast, whether and where the bullet has hit a target. In this case, we will instantiate particles at the exact point of impact. So let's open the script **ManageWeapons**.

First, we will define a placeholder (i.e., a **public** variable accessible from the **Inspector**) that holds the particles to be used at the point of impact (i.e., at the intersection between the ray and the object in front of the player).

- Please modify the code to declare a new **GameObject** as follows (new code in bold).

```
public class ManageWeapons : MonoBehaviour
{
    Camera playersCamera;
    Ray rayFromPlayer;
    RaycastHit hit;
    public GameObject sparksAtImpact;
```

- We will then make sure that the ray is casted only when a specific key has been pressed, by adding the following code to the **Update** method (new code highlighted in bold).

```
Debug.DrawRay(rayFromPlayer.origin, rayFromPlayer.direction * 100, Color.red);
if (Input.GetKeyDown(KeyCode.F))
{
    if (Physics.Raycast(rayFromPlayer, out hit, 100))
    {
        print (" The object " + hit.collider.gameObject.name +" is in front of the player");
        Vector3 positionOfImpact;
        positionOfImpact = hit.point;
        Instantiate (sparksAtImpact, positionOfImpact, Quaternion.identity);
    }
}
```

In the previous code,

- We check that the key **F** has been pressed (you could have chosen any other key also) before ray casting.

- We then create a new **Vector3** variable called **positionOfImpact** that is used to store the position of the impact (i.e., this is the intersection between the ray and the object in front of the player).

Creating and Managing Weapons

- We initialize this variable with the position of impact; this position is found using the variable **hit.point**.

- We then instantiate a new **GameObject** (i.e., **sparkAtImpact**) at this exact position.

The last thing we need to do is to set the variable for the particles to be emitted on impact (**sparkAtImpact**). We can do this, as we have done before, using the **Inspector**.

- Please select the object **FirstPersonCharacter** (i.e., the object within the object **FPSController**).

- In the **Inspector** window, in the section called **ManageWeapons** for this object, click on the small circle to the right of the variable **SparksAtImpact**, as described on the next figure.

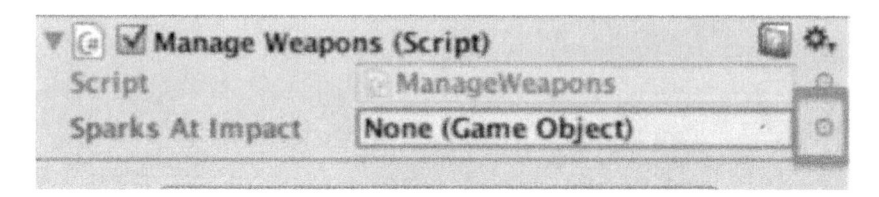

Figure 2-4: Adding a new particle effect on impact (part 1)

- Once this is done, a new window will appear where you can perform a search.

- Search for the term **smoke**, using the search field: this should return, amongst other prefabs, the prefab called **Smoke**.

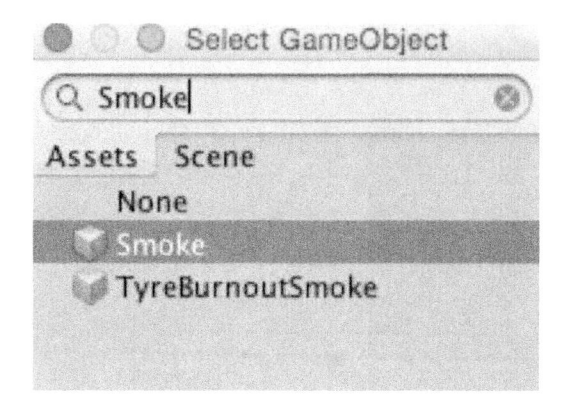

Figure 2-5: Adding a new particle effect on impact (part 2)

- Double click on the prefab called **Smoke** to select it.

- Once this is done, the **Inspector** should now list this prefab for the variable **SparksAtImpact**.

Creating and Managing Weapons

Figure 2-6: Adding a new particle effect on impact (part 3)

Once this is done, there is a last thing we can do to make shooting more accurate: adding a crosshair.

- Import the **crosshair** image from the resource pack to your project.

- Create a new **RawImage** Object (**Game Object | UI | RawImage**).

- Using the **Inspector** window, change its position to **(0, 0, 0)** so that it is displayed in the center of the screen.

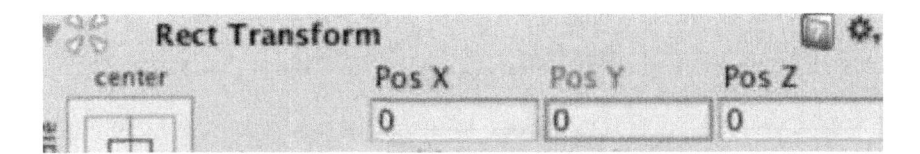

Figure 2-7: Positioning the crosshair

And finally, set its texture in the section **RawImage**, by dragging and dropping the **crosshair** texture from your **Project** window (i.e., where you have imported this texture) to the variable **Texture**.

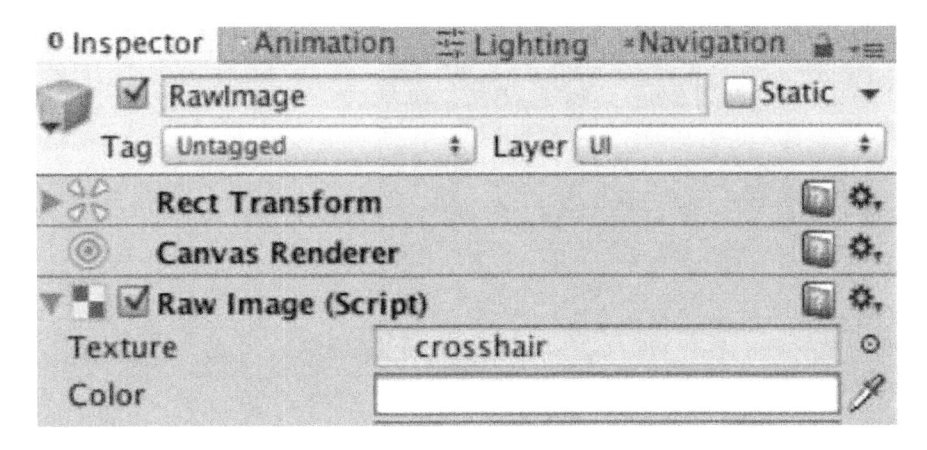

Figure 2-8: Adding the crosshair texture

[81]

Creating and Managing Weapons

- We could also rename this object **crosshair**, using the **Hierarchy** or the **Inspector** window.

- Once this is done, the **Game** view should look as follows:

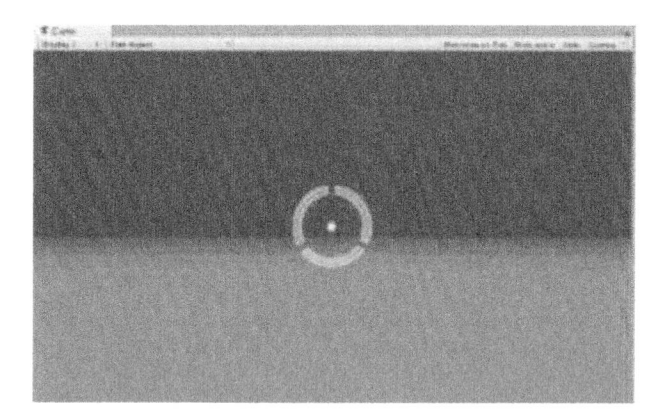

Figure 2-9: Displaying the crosshair

- Now, we can play the scene, and use the crosshair to aim at the different targets.

- As you press the **F** key, you should see that smoke is created at the point of impact.

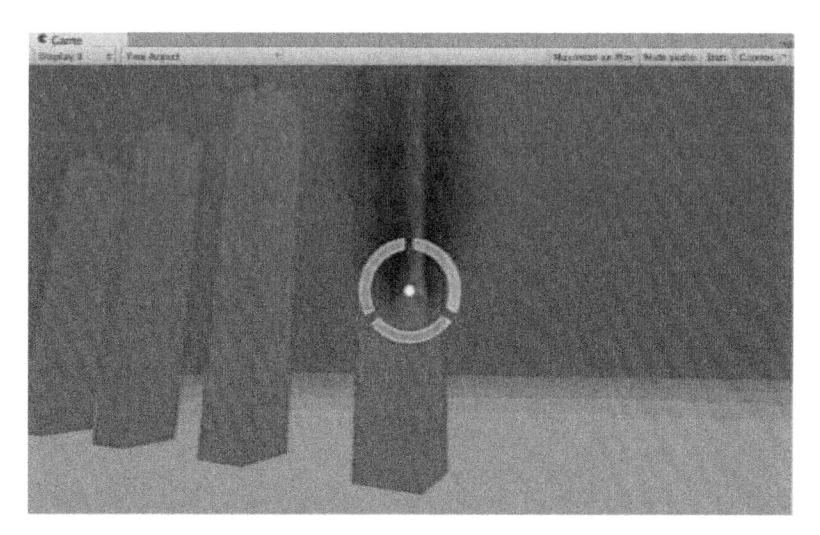

Figure 2-10: Shooting at a target.

Last but not list, we will try to manage ammunitions for this particular gun. You see, at present, the player can shoot indefinitely; so we could just give the player an initial amount of bullets, and make it possible to fire the gun only if there are bullets left.

- Please modify the start of the script as follows (new code in bold).

Creating and Managing Weapons

```
public class ManageWeapons : MonoBehaviour
{
        Camera playersCamera;
        Ray rayFromPlayer;
        RaycastHit hit;
        public GameObject sparksAtImpact;
        private int gunAmmo = 3;
```

In the previous code, we declare a new variable that will be used to store the number of ammunitions left.

- Then, we can modify the code to manage these ammunitions, as follows (new code in bold):

```
if (Input.GetKeyDown(KeyCode.F) && gunAmmo > 0)
{
        if (Physics.Raycast(rayFromPlayer, out hit, 100))
        {
                print (" The object " + hit.collider.gameObject.name +" is in front of the player");
                Vector3 positionOfImpact;
                positionOfImpact = hit.point;
                Instantiate (sparksAtImpact, positionOfImpact, Quaternion.identity);

        }
        gunAmmo --;
        print ("You have "+gunAmmo + " bullets left");
```

In the previous code:

- We check that we have enough ammunition before firing the gun.
- If this is the case, we decrease the number of bullets left.
- We then display the number of bullets left.

Please play the scene, and check that after shooting three times, you can no longer fire the gun.

[83]

MANAGING DAMAGE

So at this stage, we have managed to create a weapon and fire bullets precisely using ray casting and a crosshair. This being said, it would be great to be able to manage the targets (that we will refer to as NPCs in this section) by knowing how many times they have been hit and when they should be destroyed (e.g., after being hit three times). So for this purpose, we will create a script that will store the NPC's health, count how many times it was hit, decrease its health whenever it has been hit, and destroy it after its health has reached 0.

So let's create our script.

- Please create a new C# script and rename it **ManageNPC**.

- Add the following code (new code in bold).

```
public class ManageNPC : MonoBehaviour
{
    private int health;
    public GameObject smoke;
    void Start ()
    {
        health = 100;
    }
    public void gotHit()
    {
        health -=50;
    }
```

In the previous code:

- We declare two variables: **health** and **smoke**; the former is used to track the NPCs' health, and the latter is used so that we can instantiate particles (e.g., explosions) when and where the NPC has been destroyed.

- We then initialize the health to 100 in the **Start** function.

We also create a method **gotHit** that is declared as **public**. This means that it will be accessible from outside this script. This method will be called whenever the object has been hit; when this happens, the health is decreased by **50**.

- Please add the next code to the script (i.e., within the class **ManageNPC**; new code in bold).

Creating and Managing Weapons

```
public void Destroy()
{

    GameObject lastSmoke = (GameObject) (Instantiate (smoke, transform.position, Quaternion.identity));
    Destroy (lastSmoke,3);
    Destroy(gameObject);

}
void Update ()
{
    if (health <=0) Destroy();
}
```

In the previous code:

- In the method **Update**, we check the status of the health. If the health is **0** or less, then we call the method **Destroy**.

- In the method **Destroy**, we instantiate a **GameObject** (e.g., smoke) at the position of the NPC.

- We then destroy the smoke after 3 seconds and we also destroy the NPC.

Once these changes have been made, we can:

- Save the script.

- Drag and drop this script on all targets.

- Set the variable **smoke** for the script embedded on these targets with a particle effect of your choice (e.g., smoke) by dragging and dropping a prefab of your choice on the variable called **smoke,** for the script **ManageNPC** linked to each target, using the **Inspector**.

Once this is done, we just need to modify the script **ManageWeapons** so that we can modify the health of each NPC when it has been hit:

- Please open the script **ManageWeapons**.

- Modify the code as follows (new code in bold).

Creating and Managing Weapons

```
if (Physics.Raycast(rayFromPlayer, out hit, 100))
{
        print (" The object " + hit.collider.gameObject.name +" is in front of the player");
        Vector3 positionOfImpact;
        positionOfImpact = hit.point;
        Instantiate (sparksAtImpact, positionOfImpact, Quaternion.identity);
```
GameObject objectTargeted;
if (hit.collider.gameObject.tag == "target")
{
    objectTargeted = hit.collider.gameObject;
    objectTargeted.GetComponent<ManageNPC>().gotHit();
}
```
}
}
```

In the previous code:

- We create a new **GameObject** called **objectTargeted**.

- We then set this object with the object that is in the line of sight.

- If the tag of this object is **target** we will access its script called **ManageNPC** and call (or evoke) the method **gotHit**.

The last things we need to do is to create a tag called **target** (using the **Inspector**, as we have done before) and apply it to all the targets. We can also set the initial number of bullets, **gunAmmo**, to **10** (instead of three, in the script **ManageWeapons**) so that we can test the game properly.

- Please make these changes (i.e., add the tag target to all targets and set the initial number of ammos to 10).

- Please play the scene.

- Shoot at each target twice and check that they disappear, and that smoke has been created at their previous location.

COLLECTING AND MANAGING AMMUNITIONS

At this stage, the game level is working well, however our player may run out of ammunitions. So it would be good to create ammunitions that can be collected by the player. To do so, we will create and texture boxes that will be used as ammunitions; we will also give them a label, and detect whenever the player collides with them. We will also get to create prefabs with these so that they can be reused later (i.e., in different levels).

Creating and Managing Weapons

So let's create these ammunition boxes:

- Please create a new cube.

- Move it slightly away from the targets and above the ground, for example at the position (1.0, 1.5, 10.0).

- Use a texture of your choice or import a texture from the resource pack and apply it to the box.

- Create a new tag called **ammo_gun** and apply it to this cube.

Once this is done, we just need to detect collisions between this cube and the player, and increase the player's ammunitions accordingly. This being said, collision detection would usually be handled by the **FPSController** object rather than the **FirstPersonCharacter** object; this is because the **FPSController** object already has a collider whereas the **FirstPersonController** object doesn't have any; as a result, we could proceed in at list two ways:

(1) We could create a new script, attach it to the **FPSController**, and also copy (or transfer) all the code that we have created to date to this script; this would involve some minor to medium changes, but it would have the benefit of having all our code for the weapon and collision management associated to the player in only one script

OR

(2) We could just create a new script, to be attached to the **FirstPersonCharacter**, that detects collision and that notifies our already existing script (**ManageWeapons**) of the collision. This would only involve one line of code, and very minor changes.

So, with all of this considered, we could apply the second solution. However, bear in mind that we could have solved this challenge in many other ways.

So we will create a mechanism whereby:

- A script attached to the **FPSController** will detect collisions.

- It will then notify the script **ManageWeapons** of a collision and pass information related to this collision.

So let's get started:

- Please create a new script called **ManageCollisionWithPlayer**.

- Add the following code to this script, within the class **ManageCollisionWithPlayer**.

Creating and Managing Weapons

```
void OnControllerColliderHit (ControllerColliderHit hit)
{
transform.GetChild(0).GetComponent<ManageWeapons>().manageCollisions(hit);
}
```

In the previous code:

- We use the built-in method **OnControllerColliderHit**; this method is called whenever a collision is detected between the **FPSController** and another object.

- The information about the collision is returned in an object of type **ControllerColliderHit**.

- We name this object **hit**, and then pass it to the script **ManageWeapons** through a member method (that we yet have to create) called **manageCollisions**.

- This method is accessed using the syntax **transform.getChild**; this means that we access the first child of the object **FPSController** (i.e., the first and only child here). Again, this is due to the hierarchy of our game whereby the object **FirstPersonCharacter** is a child of the object **FPSController**.

- Please save your code, check for any error in the **Console** window.

Once this done, we can save this script and modify the script **ManageWeapons**, to add a new method within the class, as follows:

```
public void manageCollisions (ControllerColliderHit hit)
{
        print ("Collided with " + hit.collider.gameObject.name);
        if (hit.collider.gameObject.tag =="ammo_gun")
        {
                gunAmmo +=5;
                if (gunAmmo > 10) gunAmmo = 10;
                Destroy (hit.collider.gameObject);
        }
}
```

In the previous code:

- We declare a new method called **manageCollisions**. This method takes one parameter of type **ControllerColliderHit**.

- We then print the name of the object we have collided with.

- We check if we have collided with gun ammunitions.

- If this is the case, we increase the ammunitions for the player by **5**.

- We then check if we have reached the maximum number of ammos that we can carry.
- If this is the case, we cap the number of ammunitions to this maximum.
- We then destroy the ammo pack.

Please save your code, check for any errors in the **Console** window; then drag and drop the script **ManageCollisionWithPlayer** from the **Project** window on the object called **FPSController** located in the **Inspector** window (or the **Scene** view).

You can now play the scene. As you play the scene, please check that you can shoot at the targets several times, that you can collect some ammos, and also that your ammunition levels have been updated accordingly.

BUILDING A WEAPON MANAGEMENT SYSTEM WITH ARRAYS

At present, we have a relatively simple weapon management system that works with one weapon. We can collect ammos and also shoot at targets. However, in the next sections, we will be adding more types of weapons (i.e., automatic gun and grenade), so we need to find a way to manage these simply, using structures that make it easy to track the ammunitions for each of them or the time it takes to reload a weapon. So, before even creating new weapons, we will make sure that we have a structure in place that will make it possible to track the following information, for each of them:

- Whether the player has this weapon.

- The reload time for this weapon.

- The name of the weapon.

- The ammunitions that the player is carrying (or currently has) for this weapon.

- The maximum number of ammunitions that the player can carry for this weapon.

To do so, we will be using a combination of arrays and constant variables. The process will be as follows.

- We will create an array for each of the variables that are common across the weapons: an array for the weapons' name, an array for their reload time, an array to check whether the player has this weapon, an array for the corresponding ammunitions, and an array for the maximum number of ammunitions that can be carried for this weapon.

- We will then create an index for each of these weapons; for example, a gun could be referred as index 0, the automatic gun could be referred as index 1, and the grenade launcher could be referred as index 2. These indexes will be used to access information in the arrays for a particular weapon.

- Whenever the player presses the tab key, we will switch between the active weapons (i.e., the one that the player is carrying).

- When the player presses the **F** key, we check that there is enough ammunition for the current weapons, and then, if this is the case, we fire this particular weapon.

- As the player tries to shoot another time, we check the reload time for this particular weapon (e.g., 2 for a normal gun, .5 for an automatic gun, etc.).

- When we collect an ammo pack, we check its type, and also update the ammunition levels for the weapon that we currently carry.

So, this is the general principle; now that it is clearer, let's implement the corresponding code.

Creating and Managing Weapons

Please open the script **ManageWeapons**, and add the following code at the beginning of the class (new code in bold).

```
public class ManageWeapons : MonoBehaviour
{
    private const int WEAPON_GUN = 0;
    private const int WEAPON_AUTO_GUN = 1;
    private const int WEAPON_GRENADE = 2;

    private int activeWeapon = WEAPON_GUN;
    private float timer;
    private bool timerStarted;
    private bool canShoot = true;
    private int currentWeapon;

    private bool [] hasWeapon;
    private int [] ammos;
    private int [] maxAmmos;
    private float [] reloadTime;
    private string [] weaponName;
```

In the previous code:

- We first declare a set of three constant variables, **WEAPON_GUN**, **WEAPON_AUTO_GUN**, and **WEAPON_GRENADE**. These variables are constant, so their value will always be the same.

- We then declare four other variables: **activeWeapon**, **timer** (this will be used to simulate the reload time), **timerStarted** (this will be used to check whether the reload has started), **canShoot** (this will be used to check if the player can shoot or whether the reload time has elapsed).

- Finally we also declare five arrays that will share common properties across weapons including: whether the player has this weapon (**hasWeapon**), the number of ammos for a particular weapon (**ammos**), the maximum number of ammos for this weapon (**maxAmmos**), the reload time (**reloadTime**), and the name of this weapon (**weaponName**).

Now, we just need to initialize these variables; so let's add the following code to the **Start** function:

[91]

Creating and Managing Weapons

```
void Start ()
{
        ammos = new int [3];
        hasWeapon = new bool [3];
        maxAmmos = new int [3];
        reloadTime = new float [3];
        weaponName = new string [3];
```

In the previous code, we initialize all the arrays that we have declared previously; they are initialized using the syntax **new dataType [size]**. Because we only plan on having three different weapons for now, we set a size of 3 for all these arrays.

Note that each element of the arrays will be accessible using the syntax **arrayName [index]**; for example the first element of the array **ammos** will be accessible using **ammos [0]**; for each array, the first element starts at **0**, so the last element will be, in our case, at the index **2** (i.e., the size of the array minus 1). Although you can also initialize an array without specifying its size, it is good practice to set its size at the beginning if we know that it will not change overtime.

Also note that many of the errors related to the use of arrays are often linked to their size. For example, you may try to access an array element at the index 7, whereas the size of the array is 5; in this case Unity may display a message telling your that you are "**out of bounds**" which means that you are trying to access an element that is outside the bounds of this array. We will look into these types of errors later but this is something to keep in mind.

After initializing the arrays we can initialize some of values in these arrays; please add the following code to the **Start** method (after the previous code):

```
hasWeapon [WEAPON_GUN] = true;
hasWeapon [WEAPON_AUTO_GUN] = false;
hasWeapon [WEAPON_GRENADE] = false;

weaponName[WEAPON_GUN] = "GUN";
weaponName[WEAPON_AUTO_GUN] = "AUTOMATIC GUN";
weaponName[WEAPON_GRENADE] = "GRENADE";

ammos [WEAPON_GUN] = 10;
ammos [WEAPON_AUTO_GUN] = 0;
ammos [WEAPON_GRENADE] = 0;


maxAmmos [WEAPON_GUN] = 20;
maxAmmos [WEAPON_AUTO_GUN] = 20;
maxAmmos [WEAPON_GRENADE] = 5;

currentWeapon = WEAPON_GUN;
```

In the previous code:

- We first set the content of the array **hasWeapon**. For each element of the array, we use the constant variables defined earlier. So the first element of the array (index 0), is referred to using the constant variable **WEAPON_GUN**, the second element (1) is referred to using the constant variable **WEAPON_GUN_AUTO_GUN**, and so on. Using these notations, we set the elements of the array **hasweapon** to specify that we initially only have a gun.

- Then, using the same principle, we initialize the values for the array **ammos** (i.e., 10 ammos for the gun, and no ammos for the other weapons), **maxAmmos** (i.e., 20 ammos for the gun and the automatic gun, and 5 grenades).

- Finally we specify that the current weapon is the gun.

Once this is done, we need to find a system that switches between the weapons that we have whenever we press the *Tab* key on the keyboard; so the following method will be used:

- Pressing the tab key will change the index of the current weapon (0 for gun, 1 for the automatic gun, or 2 for grenades).

- If we have only one weapon, then pressing the Tab key will not cause any change.

- If we have the three weapons, pressing the tab key will select the gun, the automatic gun, or the grenades.

- If we have two weapons, pressing the tab key will toggle between these two weapons.

Creating and Managing Weapons

Let's type the corresponding code; please add the following code to the **Update** method (just before the end of this method) in the script **ManageWeapons**:

```
if (Input.GetKeyDown(KeyCode.Tab))
{
        if (hasWeapon[WEAPON_GUN] && hasWeapon[WEAPON_AUTO_GUN] && hasWeapon[WEAPON_GRENADE])
        {
                currentWeapon++;
                if (currentWeapon>2) currentWeapon = 0;
        }
        else if (hasWeapon[WEAPON_GUN] && hasWeapon[WEAPON_AUTO_GUN])
        {
                if (currentWeapon == WEAPON_GUN) currentWeapon = WEAPON_AUTO_GUN;
                else currentWeapon = WEAPON_GUN;
        }
        else if (hasWeapon[WEAPON_GUN] && hasWeapon[WEAPON_GRENADE])
        {
                if (currentWeapon == WEAPON_GUN) currentWeapon = WEAPON_GRENADE;
                else currentWeapon = WEAPON_GUN;
        }
        else if (hasWeapon[WEAPON_AUTO_GUN] && hasWeapon[WEAPON_GRENADE])
        {
                if (currentWeapon == WEAPON_AUTO_GUN) currentWeapon = WEAPON_GRENADE;
                else currentWeapon = WEAPON_AUTO_GUN;
        }
        else
        {
        }
        print ("Current Weapon: "+ weaponName[currentWeapon] + "("+ammos[currentWeapon]+")");
}
```

In the previous code:

- We first check whether the **Tab** key has been pressed.

- If this is the case, we check how many and what types of weapons the player currently has.

- In the case of three weapons, we increase the index of the current weapon; if this count is more that 2 (remember that the index starts at 0 so the third item would be at the index 2) then it is set to 1; this way we can loop through the three weapons (i.e., index goes from 0, to 1, 2, and back to 0).

- In the case where the player has two weapons (gun and automatic gun, gun and grenade, or grenade and automatic gun), we switch between the current and the second weapon.

Creating and Managing Weapons

- Finally if the player has only one weapon, nothing happens.
- We also print a message, in the **Console** window, that indicates the current weapon and the corresponding ammunitions.

Last but not least, you can modify the code in the **Start** method as follows.

```
hasWeapon [WEAPON_AUTO_GUN] = true;
```

Please save your code, and test the scene. As you press the *Tab* key, you should see the message "**Current Weapon: AUTOMATIC GUN (10)**" and "**Current Weapon: GUN (10)**" in the **Console** window.

Well, our system is working properly; now we just need to link it to the firing system, so that we can shoot depending on the current weapon and ammunitions available for this weapon.

Please modify the **Update** method as follows (new code in bold).

[95]

Creating and Managing Weapons

```
if (Input.GetKeyDown(KeyCode.F))
{
        if (currentWeapon == WEAPON_GUN && ammos [WEAPON_GUN] >=1 && canShoot)
        {
                ammos [currentWeapon]--;
                if (Physics.Raycast(rayFromPlayer, out hit, 100))
                {
                        print (" The object " + hit.collider.gameObject.name +" is in front of the player");
                        Vector3 positionOfImpact;
                        positionOfImpact = hit.point;
                        Instantiate (sparksAtImpact, positionOfImpact, Quaternion.identity);
                        GameObject objectTargeted;
                        if (hit.collider.gameObject.tag == "target")
                        {
                                print ("hit a target");
                                objectTargeted = hit.collider.gameObject;
                                objectTargeted.GetComponent<ManageNPC>().gotHit();
                        }
                }
                canShoot = false;
                timer = 0.0f;
                timerStarted = true;
                //gunAmmo --;
        }
}
```

In the previous code:

- We check that the key F has been pressed.

- We then check whether the current weapon is a gun and that we have enough ammunitions left.

- If this is the case, we decrease the number of ammunitions and proceed as we did before.

- After we have managed to fire the gun, we set the variable **canShoot** to false; this is so that the gun can't be fired while it is reloading.

- We then set-up the timer that calculates how much time it will take for the gun to reload; when this timer is up, the player will be able to use the weapon again, provided that there are enough ammunitions. So here, the time (for the timer) is set to 0 and it will then start. These variables **timer** and **timerStarted** will be used in the code that we yet need to add in the script.

Creating and Managing Weapons

Before we can add this timer, we need to set the reload time for each weapon; please add the following code at the end of the the **Start** method, for the script **ManageWeapons**:

```
reloadTime [WEAPON_GUN] = 2.0f;
reloadTime [WEAPON_AUTO_GUN] = 0.5f;
reloadTime [WEAPON_GRENADE] = 3.0f;
```

In the previous code, we indicate that it will take 2 seconds for the gun to reload, .5 seconds for the automatic gun to reload, and 3 seconds to be able to throw another grenade.

- Please add the following code at the beginning of the **Update** method:

```
if (timerStarted)
{
        timer += Time.deltaTime;
        if (timer >= reloadTime [currentWeapon])
        {
                timerStarted = false;
                canShoot = true;
        }
}
```

- In this code, if the timer is started (this will happen just after a weapon has been used), we increase the time.

- Once the time reaches the reload time for the current weapon, we can then stop the timer, and make it possible for the player to shoot again.

So let's test this system; before we do so, let's modify the code slightly so that we have enough ammunition for the automatic gun. Please modify the following code in the **Update** method:

```
if (Input.GetKeyDown(KeyCode.F))
{
        if ((currentWeapon   ==   WEAPON_GUN   ||   currentWeapon   ==
WEAPON_AUTO_GUN) && ammos [currentWeapon] >=1 && canShoot)
        {
```

In the previous code, we check whether the gun or the automatic gun are selected, that we have enough ammunitions and that the current weapon can be used (i.e., when the reload time has elapsed).

We can also modify the number of initial ammunitions for the automatic gun, by modifying the code in the **Start** method as follows (new code in bold):

Creating and Managing Weapons

```
ammos [WEAPON_GUN] = 10;
```
ammos [WEAPON_AUTO_GUN] = 10;
```
ammos [WEAPON_GRENADE] = 0;
```

To make sure that we hear when the gun is shot, and to tell the difference between the two guns, we will also add a sound when one of these is fired.

- Import the **gun_shot** sound for the resource pack into Unity.

- Select the object **FirstPersonCharacter** (which is within the object **FPSController**).

- Then add an **Audio Source** component to it by selecting: **Component | Audio | AudioSource** from the top menu.

- Once this is done, a new **Audio Source** component should be added to this object.

- You can look at its properties in the **Inspector** window.

- As you look at the **Inspector** window, in the section called **Audio Source**, please uncheck the option **Play on Awake** and drag and drop the **gun_shot** sound from the **Project** window to the variable called **Audio Clip**, as illustrated on the next figure.

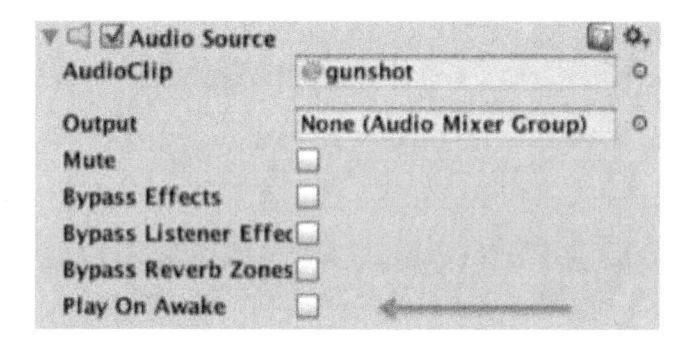

Figure 2-11: Adding an Audio Clip

Once this is done, we can trigger this sound through our script.

- Please open the script **ManageWeapons**.

- Modify the code in the **Update** method as follows (new code highlighted in bold).

```
if ((currentWeapon == WEAPON_GUN || currentWeapon == WEAPON_AUTO_GUN) && ammos [currentWeapon]
>=1 && canShoot)
{
    ammos [currentWeapon]--;
```
GetComponent<AudioSource>().Play();

In the previous code, we access the **AudioSource** component on the object **FirstPersonCharacter**, and play the default **AudioClip** associated with this **Audio Source**.

[98]

The last change that we will make will be to display the current weapon onscreen.

- Please create a new **Text UI** object (**Game Object | UI | Text**).

- Rename this object **userInfo**.

- Please move this object to the bottom-left corner of the window (if it is not already there). You may switch to the 2D mode temporarily for this.

> To move the **Text UI** component you can temporarily switch to the 2D mode, this will display the screen boundaries (i.e., white rectangle) and make it easier to position the **Text UI** component. To activate or deactivate the 2D mode, you can click on the 2D icon located below the tab labeled scene, as described on the next figure.

- You may change the color of the font for this text if you wish.

Next, we will modify the text for this object from the script to display the name of the current weapon:

- Please add the following code at the start of the script:

```
using UnityEngine.UI;
```

- The previous line makes it possible to refer to the **UI Text** component using the syntax **GetComponent<Text>**.

- Then add the following code at the end of the method **Update**.

```
GameObject.Find("userInfo").GetComponent<Text>().text = weaponName[currentWeapon]+ "("+ammos[currentWeapon]+")";
```

In the previous code, we access the **Text UI** object named **userInfo**, then its **Text** component; we then change the value of the text to the name of the current weapon.

We are now ready to go, so:

- Please save your code.

- Check for any error in the **Console** window.

- Play the scene.

- As you play the scene, try to switch between the two guns and see how the reload delay varies as you try to press the **F** key several times consecutively.

Creating and Managing Weapons

Now, at this stage, all works well; this being said we could just make a small change; that is, making it possible for the player to shoot repeatedly but without having to press the F key again; in other words, the weapon should fire, as long as the F key is kept pressed (or is down) and that we have sufficient ammos. For this, we just need to change the type of event detected. Instead of using the event **GetKeyDown**, we will use the event **GetKey**.

> While the first event (GetKeyDown) is triggered only when the key has been pressed, the second one (GetKey) is triggered as long as the key is being pressed.

Please modify the **Update** method in your code, for the conditional statement that checks whether the player has pressed the F key as follows:

```
if (Input.GetKey(KeyCode.F))
```

Play the scene and check that you can now fire consecutive shots by just keeping the F key pressed.

Creating and Managing Weapons

MANAGING THE COLLECTION OF AMMUNITIONS

Well, so far we have managed to define two different weapons and to fire them based on the corresponding ammunitions. What we need to do now is to make it possible, as we have done before, for the player to collect ammunitions, and to then update the game information accordingly. For this, we will need to do the following:

- Detect collision with ammo packs.

- Increase the number of ammunitions for a particular weapon.

- Destroy the ammo pack.

So let's modify the script **ManageWeapons** by editing the code for the method **manageCollisions** as follows.

```
public void manageCollisions (ControllerColliderHit hit)
{
        string tagOfTheOtherObject = hit.collider.gameObject.tag;
        if (tagOfTheOtherObject == "ammo_gun" || tagOfTheOtherObject == "ammo_automatic_gun" || tagOfTheOtherObject == "ammo_grenade")
        {
                int indexOfAmmoBeingUpdated = 0;
                if (tagOfTheOtherObject =="ammo_gun") indexOfAmmoBeingUpdated = WEAPON_GUN;
                if (tagOfTheOtherObject =="ammo_automatic_gun") indexOfAmmoBeingUpdated = WEAPON_AUTO_GUN;
                if (tagOfTheOtherObject =="ammo_grenade") indexOfAmmoBeingUpdated = WEAPON_GRENADE;
                ammos [indexOfAmmoBeingUpdated] +=5;
                if (ammos [indexOfAmmoBeingUpdated] > maxAmmos[indexOfAmmoBeingUpdated]) ammos[indexOfAmmoBeingUpdated] = maxAmmos[indexOfAmmoBeingUpdated];
                Destroy (hit.collider.gameObject);
        }
}
```

In the previous code:

- We create a new string called **tagOfTheOtherObject**, to store the tag of the object that we are colliding with.

- We then check whether this object is an ammo pack (e.g., for a gun, an automatic gun or grenades).

- If this is the case, we check what type of ammos we have collided with and we keep track of its type using the variable **indexOfAmmoBeingUpdated**.

Creating and Managing Weapons

- Once this is done, we increase the number of ammos for the corresponding weapon (i.e., using the variable **indexOfAmmoBeingUpdated**).

- We then check that we have not reached the maximum number of ammos that we can carry for this particular weapon.

At this stage, you should have an ammo pack with a label called **ammo_gun** in your scene. So, with this in mind, please play the scene, collect this ammo pack and check that the number of ammos for your gun has increased.

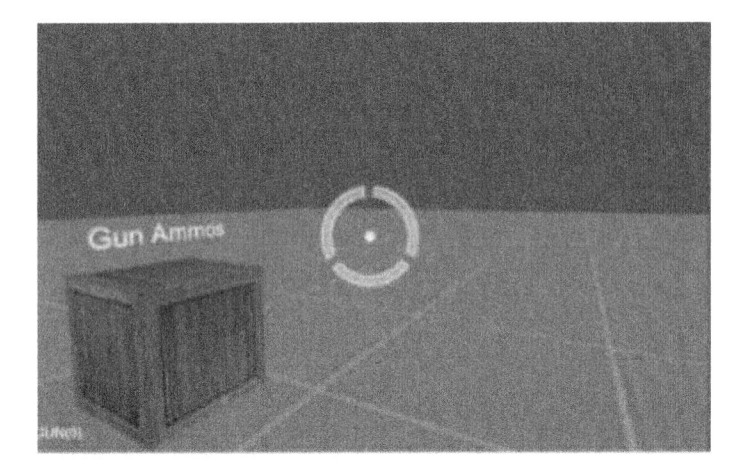

Figure 2-12: The gun ammos

We could now duplicate the object used for the ammunitions object, and change the duplicate's tag to **ammo_automatic_gun**.

- Please rename the object **Cube** (that is currently used for the ammunition) **ammo_gun**.

- Select this object.

- Duplicate this object (*CTRL + D*).

- Rename the duplicate **ammo_auto**.

- Create a new tag called **ammo_automatic_gun**.

- Apply the tag **ammo_automatic_gun** to the object **ammo_auto**.

- Using the **Scene** view, move the object **ammo_auto** apart from the other ammo pack.

- Play the scene and check that after collecting this pack (**ammo_auto**), your ammos for the automatic gun increase accordingly.

Once this is done, we will just add a 3D text to these boxes, so that it is easy to recognize them during gameplay.

Creating and Managing Weapons

- Please create a new 3D text object (**Game Object | 3D Object | 3D Text**).

- Rename this object **ammo_label**.

- Drag and drop this object on the object **ammo_gun**, so that it becomes a child of this object.

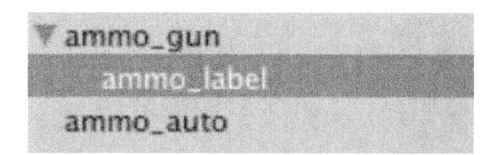

Figure 2-13: Setting the 3D text as a child of the ammo object

Then, select this object (**ammo_label**) and change its properties in the **Inspector** window as follows:

- Position: **(0, .8, 0)**.

- Scale: **(0.15, 0.15, 0.15)**.

- In the section called **Text Mesh**, change the **Text** attribute to **Gun Ammos**.

- In the section called **Text Mesh**, change the **Anchor** attribute to **Middle-centre**.

- In the section called **Text Mesh**, change the **Alignment** attribute to **Centre**.

- Once you have made these modifications, it should look as follows:

Figure 2-14: Adding 3D text to an object

Creating and Managing Weapons

- You can then repeat the previous steps to create a new 3D text label for the object **ammo_auto**, that displays the text "**Auto Gun Ammos**". You could, for example, duplicate the previous label, add the duplicate to the object **ammo_auto**, and change its position.

Figure 2-15: Two ammo packs with 3D labels

The last interesting detail we could add here, is to create prefabs from these packs, so that they can be instantiated or modified later.

> If you are prompted to choose the type of prefab that you want to create, please chose the option "**Original Prefab**".

- Drag and drop the object called **ammo_gun** to the **Project** window.
- This will create a prefab called **ammo_gun**.
- Repeat these steps for the object **ammo_auto**.

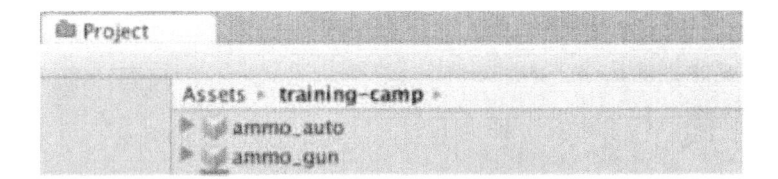

We can now:

- Deactivate the two ammos present in the scene.

[104]

- Drag and drop one of each of the ammo prefabs we have created (or more) to the scene. You may need to adjust their position so that they are above the ground, for example **y=1.2**.

- Play the scene to test whether we can still collect these ammos.

By creating prefabs for these ammo packs, we have created templates that can be reused (or instantiated) either from the scene view (i.e., by dragging and dropping these prefabs to the scene), or from the code, by instantiating these prefabs while the game is playing. This is interesting, for example when you would like to balance the game difficulty and spawn some ammos when the player is in trouble and needs them.

CREATING A GRENADE LAUNCHER

At this stage our weapon management system works well; however, we just need to add the ability to throw grenades (and to also pick-up corresponding ammos). For this purpose, we will use rigid body physics, as we have in the last chapter, to propel the grenade and also apply damage, where applicable. For this purpose we will:

- Create a launcher attached to the player.

- When the **F** key is pressed and the grenade launcher is selected, we will propel a grenade in the direction where the player is looking, provided that we have enough ammunition.

- The grenade will explode after a few seconds.

- Upon explosion, all objects within a specific radius of the grenade will be destroyed.

So let's get started.

- Create a new empty object (**Game Object | Empty Object**) and rename it **launcher**.

- Drag and drop this object on top of the object **FirstPersonCharacter** (and NOT the **FPSCOntroller**), so that the launcher becomes a child of the object **FirstPersonCharacter**.

- Modify its position to **(0, 0, 0)**.

- Create a new **Sphere** object (**Game Object | 3D Object | Sphere**).

- Rename this object **grenade**.

- Modify its scale properties to **(0.2, 0.3, 0.2)**.

- You can also add a color to it if you wish.

- Add a **Rigidbody** component to this object (i.e., the grenade) by selecting: **Component | Physics | Rigidbody**.

Once this is done, we can start to modify our script **ManageWeapons** so that we can propel this grenade:

- Open the script **ManageWeapons**.

- Add the following code at the beginning of the class, to declare a placeholder that will be accessed from the **Inspector** to set the grenade that will be launched:

Creating and Managing Weapons

```
public GameObject grenade;
```

- Also modify the code in the **Start** method, to specify that we will start the game with a grenade launcher, as follows:

```
hasWeapon [WEAPON_GRENADE] = true;
```

- You can also add the following line within the **Start** method, so that we start with 10 grenades.

```
ammos [WEAPON_GRENADE] = 10;
```

Then we just need to add code to manage the grenades. The code that we are about to add will simply check whether we have a grenade, and the corresponding ammunitions for it. It will also instantiate and propel a grenade in the air.

- Please add the following code in the **Update** function, just after the code that deals with the guns (but within the conditional statements that deals with the key **F**; if ensure, you can always check the solution code included in the resource pack).

```
if (currentWeapon == WEAPON_GRENADE && ammos [WEAPON_GRENADE] >=1 && canShoot)
{
        ammos [currentWeapon]--;
        GameObject launcher = GameObject.Find("launcher");
        GameObject grenadeF = (GameObject) (Instantiate (grenade, launcher.transform.position, Quaternion.identity));
        grenadeF.GetComponent<Rigidbody>().AddForce(launcher.transform.forward*200);
        canShoot = false;
        timer = 0.0f;
        timerStarted = true;
}
```

In the previous code:

- We check if the grenade launcher is selected and that we have enough ammunition.

- We then decrease the corresponding level of ammunition.

- We identify the **launcher** object.

- We create a new instance of the object **grenade** (i.e., a public variable that will be set later by dragging and dropping the **grenade** object on it in the **Inspector**).

- The new projectile is then propelled using the method **AddForce**.

Once this is done, you can:

- Save your code.

- Create a new grenade prefab by dragging the **grenade** object to the **Project** window.

Creating and Managing Weapons

> If you are prompted to choose the type of prefab that you want to create, please chose the option "**Original Prefab**".

- Once this is done, we can deactivate the **grenade** object already present in the scene.

- We can also select the object **FirstPersonCharacter** and drag and drop the prefab **grenade** (from the **Project** window) to the field called **grenade** for the script **ManageWeapons** attached to the object **FirstPersonCharacter**. Once this is done, you can now test the scene, switch between weapons, and check that you can throw a grenade.

After this, we just need to create an explosion and also check if other objects are close to the grenade. For this purpose, we will create a new script that will be attached to the grenade that has been instantiated.

- Please create a new C# script called **Grenade**.

- Open the script and add the following code to it (new code in bold).

```
public class Grenade : MonoBehaviour {
public float grenadeTimer;
public bool grenadeTimerStatrted;
public float grenadeTimerLimit;
public bool grenadeExplode;
public GameObject explosion;
private float radius = 5.0f;
private float power = 500.0f;
private float timer;
private float explosionTime;
private bool hasExploded;
```

In the previous script, we declare several variables that will be necessary to control and launch the grenade: variables that will determine when the grenade should explode (e.g., **grenadeTimer**, **grenadeTimerStarted**, and **grenadeTimerLimit**), a variable that checks whether the grenade has exploded (**grenadeExplode**), the radius within which objects will be affected by the explosion, and the power of the explosion.

- Then we can modify the method **Start** as follows:

```
private void Start ()
{
        timer = 0.0f; explosionTime = 2.0f;
        hasExploded = false;
}
```

In the previous code:

Creating and Managing Weapons

- We set the explosion time to 2 seconds, so that the grenade explodes two seconds after it has been propelled.

- We also specify that it has not exploded yet.

- Finally, we will modify the method **Update** as follows:

```
void Update()
{
        timer+=Time.deltaTime;
        if (timer >= explosionTime)
        {
                if (hasExploded == false)
                {
                        Vector3 explosionPos = gameObject.transform.position;
                        Collider [] colliders = Physics.OverlapSphere (explosionPos, radius);
                        for (int i = 0; i < colliders.Length; i++)
                        {
                                if (colliders [i].gameObject.GetComponent<Rigidbody>() != null && colliders [i].gameObject.tag != "Player")
                                {
                                        GameObject objectTargeted = colliders [i].gameObject;
                                        if (objectTargeted.tag == "target") objectTargeted.GetComponent<ManageNPC>().gotHitByGrenade();
                                }
                        }

                        hasExploded = true;
                        Destroy (gameObject);
                }
        }
}
```

In the previous code:

- We update the time.

- We also check whether the grenade should detonate (based on **explosionTime**).

- In this case, we look for all objects around the grenade with a **Rigidbody** component (i.e., these objects should be affected by the force exerted by the grenade); for this purpose we use the method **Physics.OverlapSphere**.

Creating and Managing Weapons

> The method **Physics.OverlapSphere** checks for the presence of rigid bodies within a specific radius; in our case, once they have been found, the colliders of these objects are saved in the variable called **colliders**.

As you can see in the previous code, we are referring to a method called **goHitByGrenade**, from the script **ManageNPC**; however, this method does not exist yet, and you may have an error in the **Console** window for this reason.

So let's modify the script **ManageNPC** accordingly:

- Please open the script **ManageNPC**.
- Add the following code to it:

```
public void gotHitByGrenade()
{
        print ("Hit by grenade");
        health = 0;
}
```

In the previous code, we set the health of the NPC to 0 if it has been hot by a grenade.

Now that the code is compiled correctly, we can update the prefab grenade:

- Please drag and drop the script **Grenade** on the object **grenade** in the **Scene** view (this object is deactivated at present).
- Select this object (i.e., grenade).
- Activate this object.
- Using the **Inspector** window, check that the script **Grenade** is now a component of the object **grenade**.
- Using the **Inspector** window, click on the button **Apply** located in the top-right corner of the **Inspector** window to be able to update the corresponding prefab.

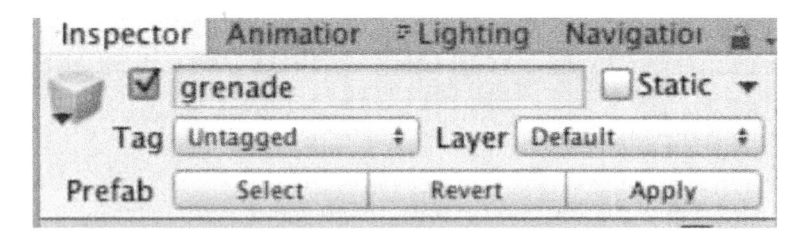

Figure 2-16: Updating the grenade prefab

Creating and Managing Weapons

- You can now deactivate this object again. It is important to apply the changes to an activated object; otherwise, if changes were applied while the object is deactivated, the object within the prefab would, in turn, also be deactivated.

> To update a prefab, you can either update the object that was used to create the prefab, and then **Apply** the changes to the prefab, or select the prefab and amend it directly.

Before we can test the scene, we just need to make sure that all the targets include a rigid body, so that the explosion affects them:

- Please select all the targets in the scene.

- Add a rigid body component to these targets using **Component | Physics | Rigidbody**.

- You can now save your code, and test the scene. As you test the scene, switch to your grenade launcher and throw some grenades. You should see that the targets within range disappear with smoke left at their previous location.

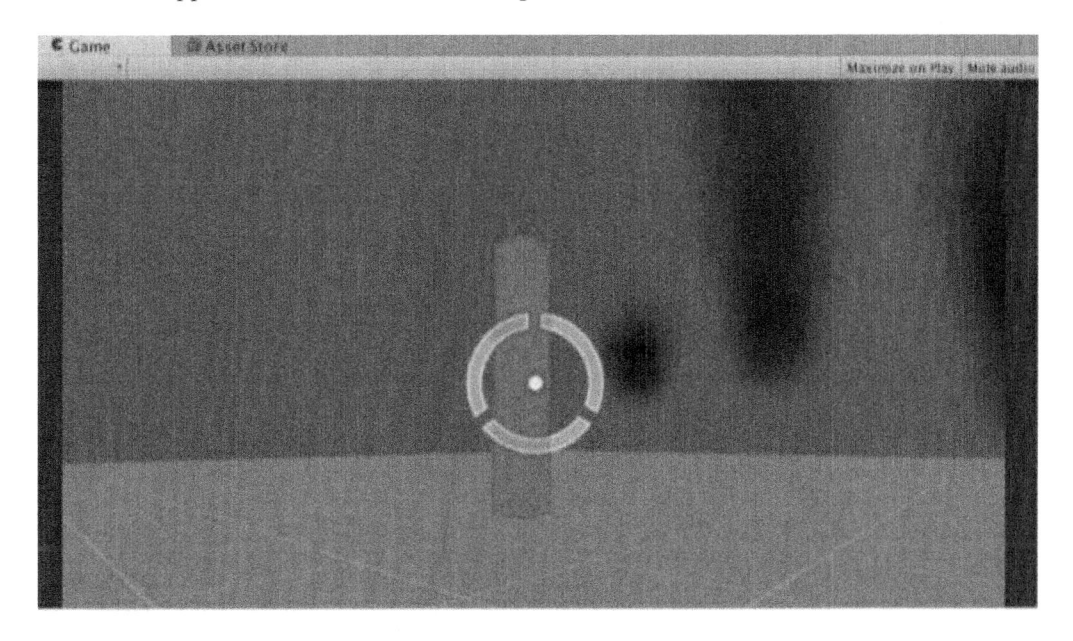

Figure 2-17: The targets disappear after being hit several times.

So, the grenades work quite well; however, it would be great to add a more visual effect, for example, using an explosion at the point of impact. For this purpose, we will instantiate an explosion (just as we have done in the previous chapter), where the grenade has exploded.

- Please select the prefab **grenade** in the **Project** window.

[111]

Creating and Managing Weapons

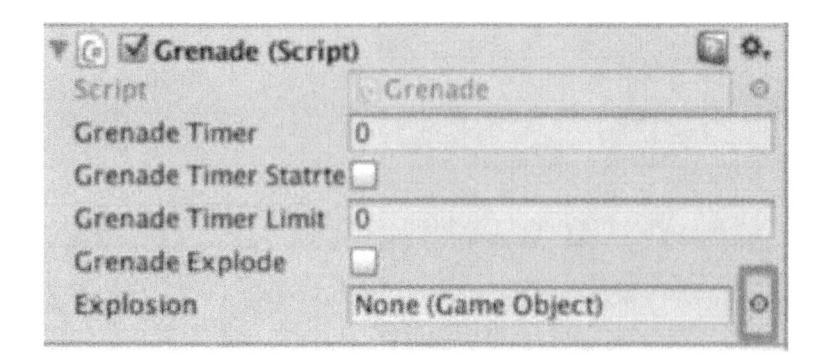

Figure 2-18: Adding an explosion to the grenade

- Using the **Inspector**, click on the circle to the right of the variable **explosion** to select a prefab for this explosion, as illustrated on the previous figure.

- In the next window, search for the word **explosion**, and choose the **explosion** prefab from the results returned.

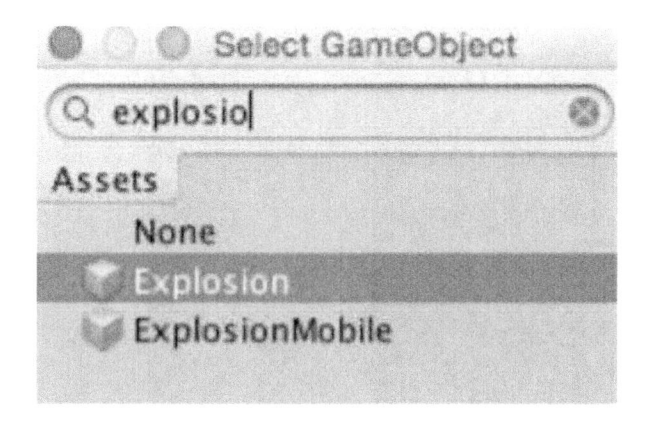

Figure 2-19: Selecting a new explosion for the grenade

Once this is done, we just need to change the code in the script called **Grenade** to instantiate a new explosion when it detonates.

- Please open the script **Grenade** and add the following code in the **Update** method (new code in bold).

GameObject.Instantiate (explosion, transform.position, Quaternion.identity);
hasExploded = true;
Destroy (gameObject);

- In the previous code we instantiate a new explosion at the point where the grenade has detonated.

- Please save your code and test the scene.

[112]

Creating and Managing Weapons

As you try to launch a grenade, it will explode; however, some of the targets that are not within range may be propelled in the air.

So, what we could do, is to give a very high weight to the targets, so that they are not propelled in the air by the explosion:

- Please select all the targets available in the scene.
- Using the **Inspector**, change their mass from 1 to 10000 (using the **Rigidbody** component).
- Play the scene again, and you should see that the targets that are not within range are not blown away by the explosion.

Last but not least, we need to create ammos for the grenades.

- Using the **Project** window, duplicate the **ammo_gun** prefab.
- Rename it **ammo_grenade**.
- Select this new prefab (i.e., **ammo_grenade**).
- Create a new tag **ammo_grenade**, and apply it to this prefab.
- Drag and drop this new prefab (i.e., **ammo_grenade**) to the scene, and adjust its position, if need be, so that it is above the ground.
- As you add it to the scene, it will create a new instance of the prefab in the scene named **ammo_grenade**; within this object, there should also be a **GUI Text** object named **ammo_label**, as described on the next figure.

Figure 2-20: Selecting the label for the grenade ammos

- Please select this object, and modify the text for its label to **Grenade Ammos**, as described on the next figure.

Creating and Managing Weapons

Text Mesh	
Text	Grenade Ammos

Figure 2-21: Modifying the text for the label of the grenade ammos

Once this is done, we can update the **grenade_ammo** prefab so that all objects instantiated from this prefab have the correct label, by clicking on the button **Apply** located in the top-right corner of the **Inspector** window, or by dragging and dropping the object **ammo_grenade** on the prefab **ammo_grenade**. This is another simple way to update the prefab.

Once this is done, you can test the scene. You may notice that the initial number of grenades is 10 and that it then drops to 5 after collecting the grenade ammos; this is because we have initialized the number of grenades to 10 in our code and set the maximum to 5; so we could change our code in the **Start** method for the script **ManageWeapons** as follows:

```
maxAmmos [WEAPON_GRENADE] = 10;
```

You can also create a new prefab for the First-Person Controller by dragging and dropping the object **FPSController** to the **Project** window, so that we can reuse it in other levels, at a later stage. You can use any name of your choice, for example, **player_with_launcher**.

LEVEL ROUNDUP

In this chapter, we have further improved our skills to learn about how to create a complete weapon management system. We became more comfortable with rays, arrays, and particles. We managed to create scripts to detect objects in the distance, fire a weapon, propel a projectile in the air, or instantiate explosions. We also optimized our game and code by creating prefabs, methods, constant variables, and arrays. So, again, we have made considerable progress since the last chapter. Well done!

Checklist

You can consider moving to the next stage if you can do the following:

- Create a **ray**.
- Create and instantiate prefabs.
- Detect objects ahead with a ray.
- Detect key strokes.
- Instantiate explosions.
- Manage and account for ammunitions.

Creating and Managing Weapons

Quiz

It's time to check your knowledge. Please answer the following questions.

1. A new prefab can be created by dragging and dropping an object to the **Project** window.

2. The following code will empty the text for the component named **userMessageUI**.

```
GameObject.Find("userMessageUI").GetComponent.<UI.Text>.text ="";
```

3. To be able to instantiate a prefab, the following code could be used:

```
Instantiate (prefab, transform.position, Quaternion.identity);
```

4. Find one error in the following code.

```
void OnControllerColliderHit (ControllerColliderHit hit)
{
        if (hit.collider.tag = "pick_me") print ("Collided with a box");
}
```

5. Any prefab can be duplicated using the shortcut *CTRL + F*.

6. If the object **myObject** does not have a Rigidbody component, and the following code is used, an error message will be displayed in the **Console** window.

```
myObject.GetComponent<Rigidbody>().AddForce (transform.forward*100);
```

7. What does this error message most likely mean "**; missing**".

    a) You have forgotten to declare a variable.
    b) One of the statements in your code is missing a semi-colon.
    c) The method that you have called does not exist.

8. There is only one way to add an **Audio Source** component to an object, and this is using the button **Add Component** button in the **Inspector** window for this object.

9. If the method **manageCollision** is defined as follows…

```
public void manageCollision()
{
        print ("Collision detected");

}
```

… it can be called from outside its containing class.

10. The following code will create an array and then access its first element.

```
int [] myArray = new int [4];
int newVar = myArray [1];
```

[116]

Answers to the Quiz

1. TRUE.
2. TRUE.
3. TRUE.
4.
```
void OnControllerColliderHit (ControllerColliderHit hit)
{
        if (hit.collider.gameObject.tag = "pick_me") print ("Collided with a box");
}
```
5. FALSE.
6. TRUE.
7. c (missing semi-colon)
8. FALSE.
9. TRUE.
10. FALSE (the second element is accessed in the code).

Challenge 1

Now that you have managed to complete this chapter and that you have improved your skills, let's put these to the test.

- Add more ammos to the scene, based on the prefabs that you have created earlier (i.e., drag and drop the prefabs to the scene).

- Test the scene and check that you can collect them and increase your ammunitions.

Challenge 2

- Create a new **UI Text** object

- Update the text for this object with the message "**You have just collected ammos**" every time you pick up an ammo pack.

- Using one of the sounds located in the resource pack, play a sound whenever an ammo pack has been collected.

3
USING FINITE STATE MACHINES

In this section, we start to work with Finite State Machines (FSM) to be able to manage NPCs and how they behave depending on the environment. We will also get to design some basic, intermediate and advanced artificial intelligence along with animated characters.

After completing this chapter, you will be able to:

- Create and manage a Finite State Machine.
- Associate character animations to different states.
- Use the FSM to implement basic and intermediate types of artificial intelligence.
- Simulate vision detection for the NPCs.
- Get the NPCs to behave realistically.

INTRODUCTION TO FINITE STATE MACHINES

So, you have probably heard about state machines in the past, but may not know exactly what it means. In a nutshell, when you create a game, you will most probably use Non-Player Characters (NPCs). These characters will probably have some levels of artificial intelligence.

When applying these different levels of intelligence, we usually want to mimic how people would behave in real life. This means that based on specific factors (e.g., low ammos or enemy in sight), the NPC will follow a specific behavior.

This behavior is often broken down into states. That is, we consider that at any time during the game, the NPC is in only one state. So the NPC will be either idle, following the player, shooting at the player, or looking for health packs.

Now, when we consider states, we also need to consider how (and why) the NPC will enter or exit a state. For example, at the start of the game, our NPC could be idle (state = **IDLE**), and then, if the NPC sees the player, it will transition to the **Follow Player** state. While following the player, the NPC may lose sight of the player, and then decide to go back to its initial position (state = **Go Back To Initial Position**), and once it has reached its initial position, it will be **IDLE** again.

So what we can see here, is that we have different states, and there are triggers and/or conditions to enter or exit a state.

Now, this is of course just one possible behavior, and we could create several different behaviors to implement different types of NPCs; but in all cases, this behavior will be determined by states, transitions, and conditions that will need to be fulfilled to transition between states.

In Unity, you can define states and transition very easily using a visual tool that makes it possible to define states, to define variables that will be assessed for transitions, and to define and check for conditions that need to be fulfilled so that transitions between states can occur. These tools are available in the **Animator** window, and we will learn to use these in the next section.

Using Finite State Machines

GETTING STARTED WITH FINITE-STATE MACHINES IN UNITY

In this section, we will become familiar with creating a simple FSM and applying it to an NPC.

- Please save your current scene.

- Create a new scene (**File | New Scene**).

- Create a new **Animator Controller** by selecting **Create | Animator Controller** from the **Project** window.

- Rename this controller **guard**. This should create an **Animator Controller**. An **Animator Controller** is effectively a way to create and manage different states. This animator controller will then be attached to an NPC to control its behavior.

> **Animator Controllers** are used to define states and also rules for transitioning between these states. They control how an object (e.g., NPC) may behave under certain conditions.

- Please display the **Animator** window by selecting: **Window | Animator**. You may change the layout of Unity as illustrated in the next figure.

- The following window will appear.

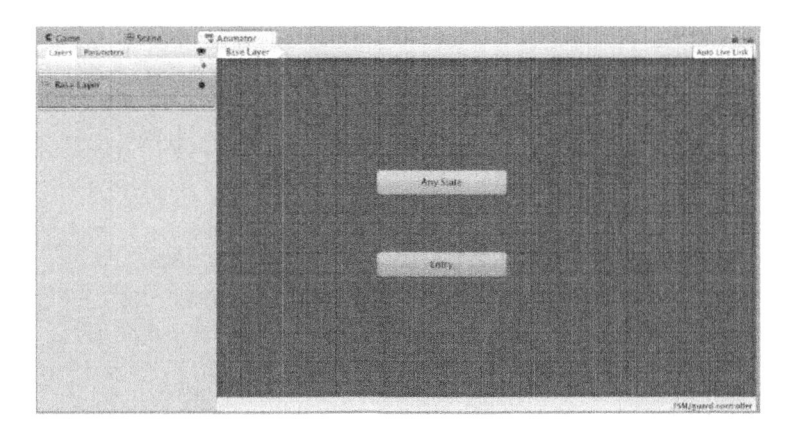

Figure 3-1: Creating a new Animator Controller

You will see that, by default, the **Animator Controller** will have two states symbolized by rectangles: a state called **Any State** and an **Entry** State. The first state (i.e., **Any State**) will be covered later in this book, and it used to define general behaviors that apply to any state (hence the name **Any State**). The **Entry** state is the point of entry for our behavior. In other words, when the FSM is started, it will be in that state. So what we will do now is to create a new state called **IDLE** in which our player will be at the start of the game (so the FSM will transition to this state at the start of the game).

Using Finite State Machines

- Please right-click on the grid (or canvas) in the **Animator** window, and select **Create State | Empty** from the contextual menu. This will create a new state called **New State** symbolized by an orange rectangle.

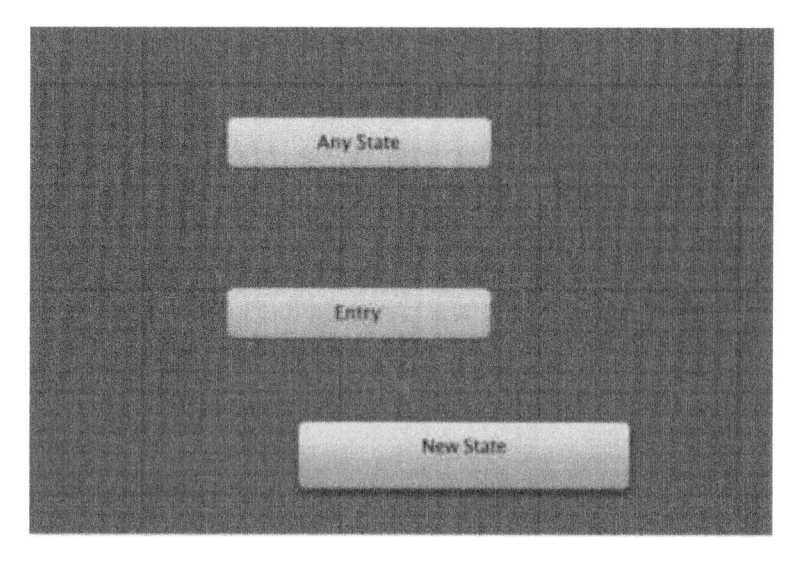

Figure 3-2: Creating a new state

- You may notice an arrow from the state **Entry** to the state **New State**. So by default, when we start the game, the new state **New Sate** will be entered.
- Let's rename this new state: select this state (i.e., **New State**) by clicking once on it, and change its name to **IDLE**, using the **Inspector** window.

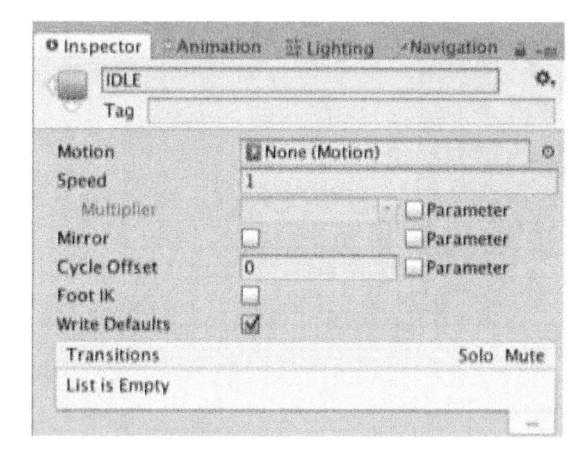

Figure 3-3: Changing the name of the state

- As you make this change, you may look at the other fields in the **Inspector** window, you will notice fields called **motion** (this will be used later in this book to add an animation), **speed** (the speed of the animation), or **transitions**.

[122]

- Once this is done, we can create a new state called **FOLLOW_PLAYER**, using the same method as previously (*CTRL + Click*, and then select **Create State | Empty**).

- Once this is done, we will create a transition between the states **IDLE** and **FOLLOW_PLAYER**, so that the FSM transitions to the later based on a condition; however, before we can specify the transition, we need to define variables. This is because the conditions used for the transitions are based on variables that we need to declare. As we will see, these variables can be of different types including **Boolean**, **string**, or **integer**. So let's create one of these parameters.

- Within the **Animator** window, click on the tab called **Parameters**.

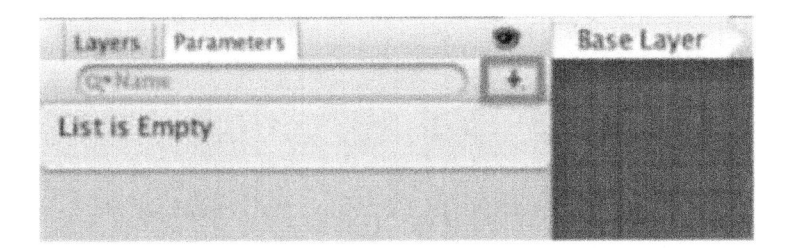

Figure 3-4: Adding a parameter (part 1)

- At present the list is empty, as we haven't defined any parameter yet.

- Please click on the + button, as highlighted on the previous figure, and select **Bool** from the contextual menu, so that you can create a **Boolean** variable.

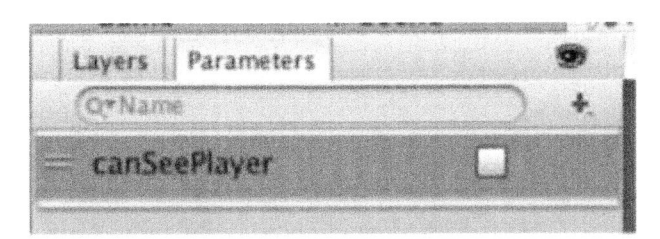

Figure 3-5: Adding a parameter (part 2)

- This should create a new **Boolean** parameter. The box to its left is unchecked, which means that its value is **false** by default. Please rename this variable **canSeePlayer** (e.g., you can double-click on the default name and then change it).

Once this is done, we can create a transition between the states **IDLE** and **FOLLOW_PLAYER**.

- Please right-click on the state **IDLE**, select **Make Transition** from the contextual menu, and click on the state **FOLLOW_PLAYER**. This should create a transition between these two states, symbolized by an arrow.

Using Finite State Machines

> If need be, you can always delete a transition by right-clicking on it and then select the option to **Delete**.

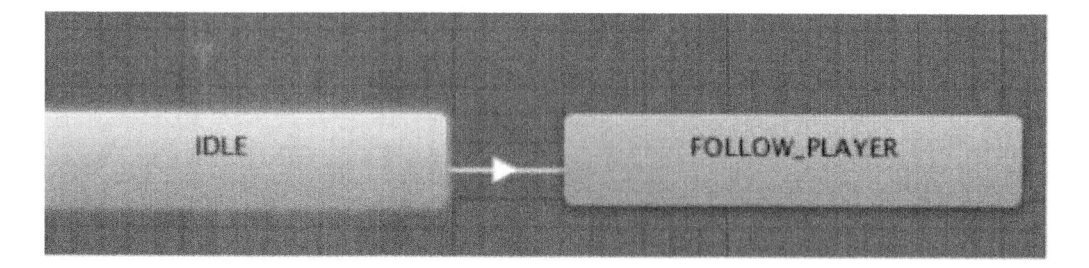

Figure 3-6: Creating a transition

Once this is done, we just need to specify when this transition should occur:

- Please select the transition by clicking on it once (i.e., the white arrow between the two states).

- This should display information about this transition in the **Inspector** window.

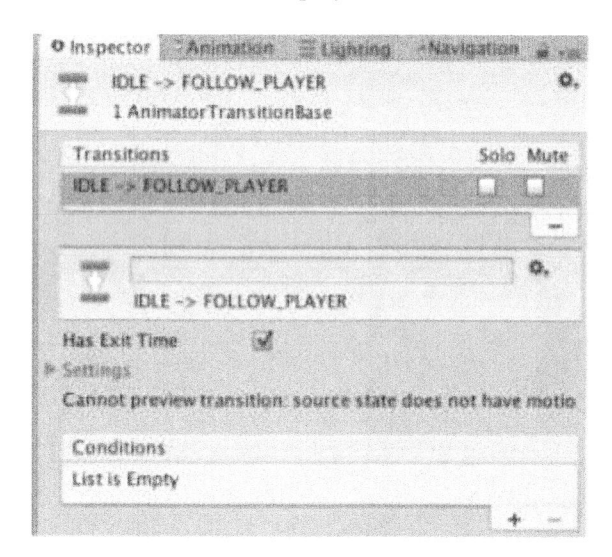

Figure 3-7: Displaying information about the transition

- You may also notice a section called **Conditions** at the bottom of the **Inspector** window, and we will use it to specify when the transition will occur (or what conditions should be fulfilled for this transition to occur).

- Please click on the + sign, as illustrated on the next figure.

[124]

Figure 3-8: Setting the condition for the transition (part 1)

Because we only have one parameter declared (i.e., **canSeePlayer**), Unity will automatically set the transition condition to **canSeePlayer = true**.

Figure 3-9: Setting the condition for the transition

- This means that the transition will occur only if this parameter is equal to true.

So at this stage, we have defined states and a basic rule that defines when the FSM should transition from the **IDLE** to the **FOLLOW_PLAYER** state. So, we now need to apply this FSM to an object and see how it works. For this purpose, we will create a simple object and attach the FSM to it. Note that nothing really happens in these states right now, but in the next section we will see how we can define what the NPC does in these states and what animations can be used for this purpose (e.g., idle, walking, etc.).

- Please create an empty object (**GameObject | Create Empty**) and rename it **testFSM**.

- Drag and drop the **Animator Controller** called **guard** that we have just created earlier, from the **Project** window to the object **testFSM** (e.g., using the **Inspector** or the **Scene** view). This will create a new component called **Animator** for the object **testFSM**. You will notice, as illustrated on the next figure, that this animator has several parameters, including a parameter called **Controller**. This controller is, in our case, the **Animator Controller** that we have created (i.e., guard). In other words, the object **testFSM** may be animated (or have a specific behavior) and this behavior will be **controlled** by the **Animator Controller** called **guard**.

Using Finite State Machines

Figure 3-10: Adding an Animator component

It is now time to test our **Animator Controller**.

- Please select the object **testFSM**.

- Play the scene.

- Click on the tab **Animator**, so that you can see the **Animator Controller**.

- You should see a blue line under the state **IDLE**; it means that this is the active state.

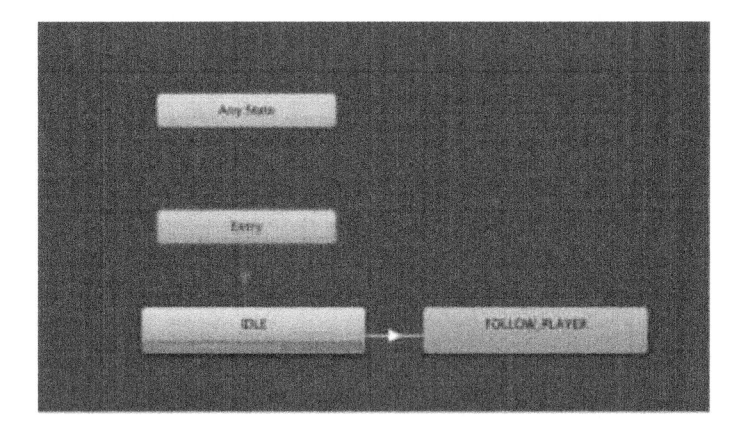

Figure 3-11: Observing our Animator Controller

> Note that you can pan the view within the **Animator** window by pressing the **ALT** key and dragging and dropping your mouse.

- Now, let's try to see if the transition is working: in the **parameter** tab within the **Animator** window, check the box for the parameter **canSeePlayer**. This will set this variable to true, and the transition to the next state (**FOLLOW_PLAYER**) should occur, as illustrated on the next figure.

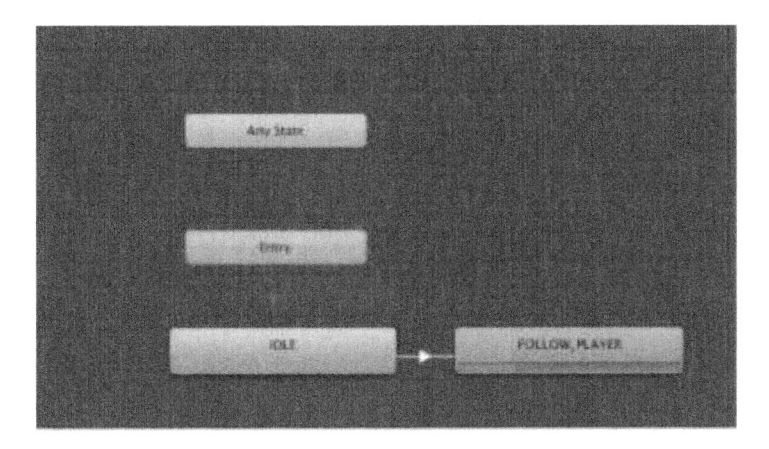

Figure 3-12: Transitioning from IDLE to FOLLOW_PLAYER

Eh Voila!

You can now stop playing the scene.

Now, you may be wondering, "Ok, this is great, but how can I link this behavior to an NPC or an object in the scene".

Well, so far we have been able to test the FSM from the **Animator** window, but there is, of course, a way to control this animator (and trigger transitions) through scripting, and we will discover how this can be done in the next section.

CONTROLLING AN ANIMATOR CONTROLLER FROM A C# SCRIPT

So at this stage, you might be comfortable with the idea of states, transitions, and **Animator Controller**; what we will do here is to control the **Animator Controller**, that we have created earlier, from our script; so we will be able to:

- Access this **Animator Controller**.
- Check what state we are in (i.e., the active state).
- Perform actions depending on the active state.
- Set values for parameters so that transitions can occur between states.

So let's get started:

- Create a new C# script called **ControlNPCFSM**.

- Drag and drop this script on the object **testFSM**.

- Once this is done, we can open our script and start editing it, bearing in mind that, because it is attached to the object **testFSM**, we will be able to access its components directly, including the **Animator Controller**.

- Please modify the code as follows (new code in bold).

Using Finite State Machines

```
using UnityEngine;
using System.Collections;

public class ControlNPCFSM : MonoBehaviour
{
    private Animator anim;
    // Use this for initialization
    void Start ()
    {
        anim = GetComponent<Animator>();
    }
    // Update is called once per frame
    void Update ()
    {
        if (Input.GetKeyDown (KeyCode.I))
        {
            anim.SetBool("canSeePlayer", true);
        }
    }
}
```

In the previous code:

- We declare a new variable of type Animator, called **anim**.

- This variable is initialized in the **Start** method, so that it points to the **Animator** component of the object **testFSM**.

- We then, using the **Update** function, detect whether the key **I** has been pressed; if this is the case, we set the value of the parameter **canSeePlayer** to true. For this purpose we use the method **anim.SetBool**; for this method, we pass two parameters: the name of the parameter to be altered (using quotes), and its new value.

> It is possible to set the values of parameters defined in a particular **Animator Controller** from a script using the methods **SetBool**, **SetString**, or **SetInt**.

Once this is done, we can save our script and test it:

- Please play the scene.

- You may move the **Game** window beside the **Console** window, so that you can see both the **Game** and the **Animator** window simultaneously. This will be helpful because we will need to click on the **Game** window before pressing the I key, so that the **Game** window is active, and so that pressing the **I** key can be detected (and processed).

Using Finite State Machines

- Click once on the **Game** view.
- Press the **I** key.
- Look at the **Animator** window and check that the **Animator Controller** has transitioned to the **FOLLOW_PLAYER** state.

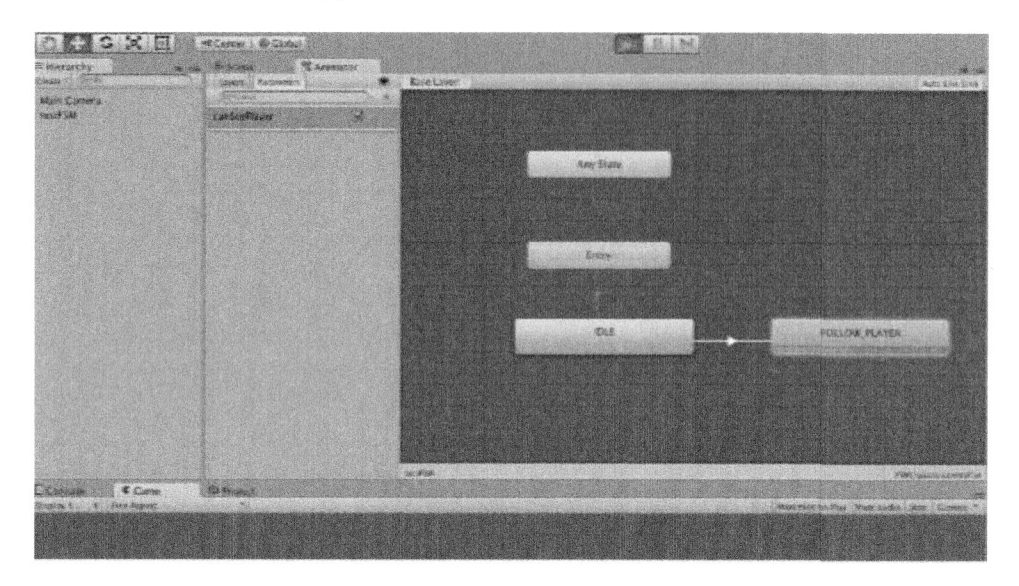

Figure 3-13: Triggering the transition from a script

Once you have checked that this is working, we will add another transition to this **Animator Controller**, so that the NPC goes back to the **IDLE** state when he can't see the player anymore.

> Whenever you make a modification to your game, please ensure that it is not playing, as any change made as the game is playing will not be kept.

- You can stop playing the scene.
- Please select the object **testFSM**.
- Open the **Animator** window.
- Create a new transition from the state **FOLOW_PLAYER** to the state **IDLE** (i.e., right-click on the **FOLLOW_PLAYER** state and select **Make Transition**).

[130]

Using Finite State Machines

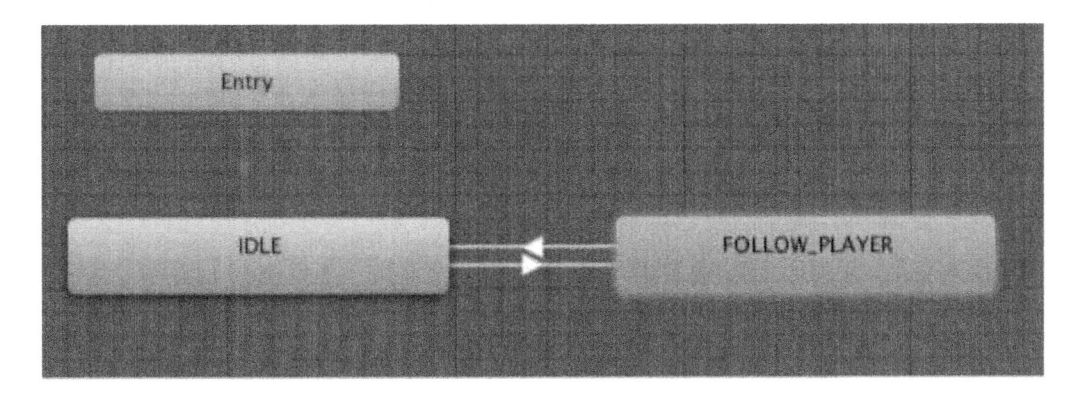

Figure 3-14: Creating a new transition to the IDLE state

- We can then select the transition and apply the condition **canSeePlayer = false** for this transition to occur (using the **Inspector**).

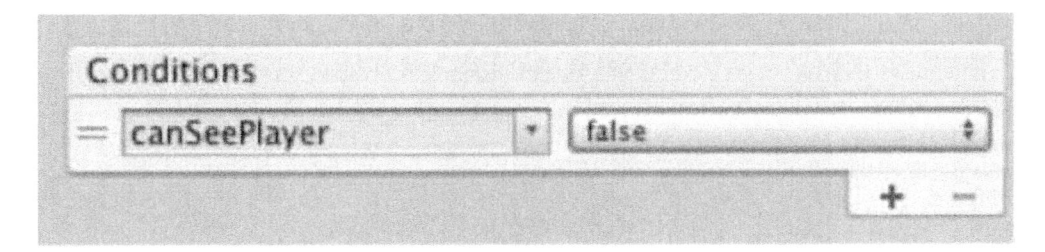

Figure 3-15: Setting the condition for the transition

> Note that transitions can be based on a combination of conditions (i.e., by checking the value of several parameters).

- We can now modify our C# script (**ControlNPCFSM**) as follows (new code in bold).

Using Finite State Machines

```
void Update ()
{
        if (Input.GetKeyDown (KeyCode.I))
        {
                anim.SetBool("canSeePlayer", true);
        }
        if (Input.GetKeyDown (KeyCode.J))
        {
                anim.SetBool("canSeePlayer", false);
        }
}
```

In the previous code, we check whether the key **J** was pressed. If this is the case, we then change the value of the parameter **canSeePlayer** to **false**, so that the transition back to the state **IDLE** can occur.

Please save your code, and play the scene. Click once in the **Game** window (so that this window is active and that the key strokes are detected). As you successively press the **I** and **J** keys, you should see that the **Animator Controller** transitions to the state **FOLLOW_PLAYER**, and then back to the state **IDLE**.

LINKING TRANSITIONS TO THE MOVEMENT OF OBJECTS

At this stage, I assume that you find it easy to understand how to control parameters from a script. However, what we could do now is to literally control the movement of an object based on the **Animator Controller**. So, we will use the controller that we have already created, and modify the associated script so that:

- The NPC will be, for the time being, symbolized by a cube.

- The NPC will be idle at the start of the scene.

- A ray is created (or casted) from the NPC and pointing forward.

- If this ray detects the player, then the NPC will start to look in the direction of the player and then move in its direction.

- Whenever the NPC loses sight of the player, it will stop on its track.

So this is a very simple behavior, to start with, and we will then customize it to add more states. So let's get started!

- Please create a ground for the scene: create a new box, at the position **(0,0,0)**, scaled on the x- and z-axis by **100** and with a texture of your choice.

- Modify the ambient light for this scene so that it is a light color (**Window | Lighting**).

- Create a new **Cube**, apply a color to it (e.g., green), rename it **NPC**, and place it just above the ground.

- Add an **FPSController** prefab to the scene from the folder **Standard Assets | Characters | FirstPersonCharacter | Prefab**.

- Assign the tag **Player** to this object.

- Deactivate the object **Main Camera** as well as the object **testFSM**.

- Select the **NPC** object, add an **Animator** component to it (**Component | Miscellaneous | Animator**), and drag and drop the **guard Animation Controller** from the **Project** window to the field called **Controller** for the **Animator** component of the object **NPC**, as described on the next figure.

Using Finite State Machines

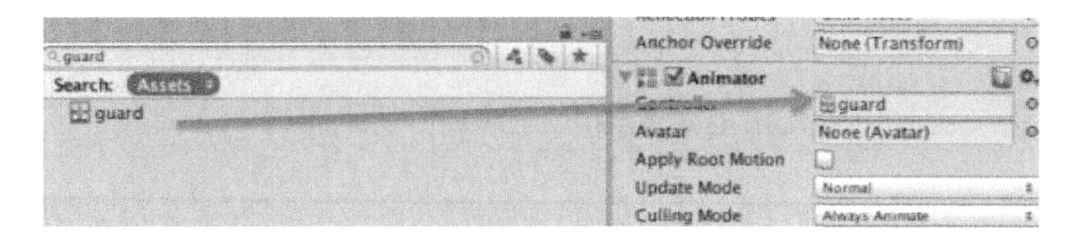

Figure 3-16: Adding the Animator Controller called guard (part 1)

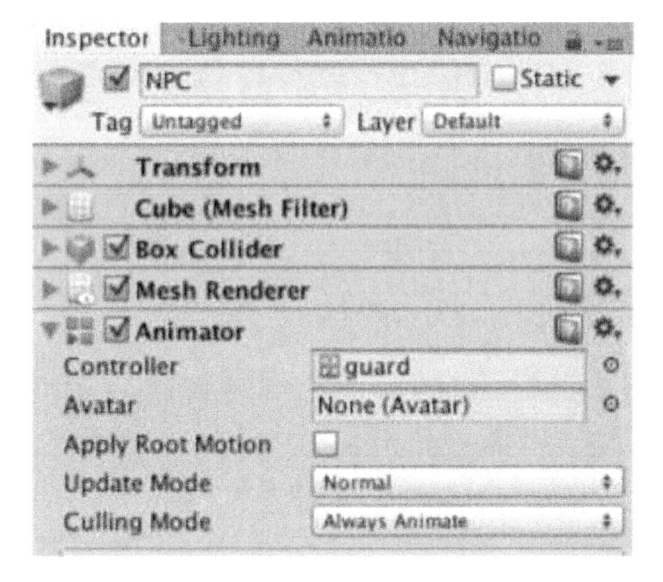

Figure 3-17: Adding the Animator Controller called guard (part 2)

- Add the script **ControlNPCFSM** to the object **NPC** (i.e., drag and drop this script on the object NPC).

So our NPC is now linked to the **Animator Controller**; it includes an **Animator** component, that is controlled by the **guard Animator Controller**, and its also includes the script **ControlNPCFSM** that we will use to access the **Animator Controller**.

We will now modify this script to create the ray casting and also change the **Animator Controller**'s parameters based on whether the player is in sight.

- Please open the script **ControlNPCFSM**.
- Add the following code at the start of the class (new code in bold).

```
public class ControlNPCFSM : MonoBehaviour {
private Animator anim;
private Ray ray;
private RaycastHit hit;
private AnimatorStateInfo info;
private string objectInSight;
```

In the previous code, we declare five variables:

- The variable **anim** will be used to link-up to the **Animator Controller** component of the object **NPC**.

- The variable **ray** will be used to cast a ray and detect objects ahead.

- The variable **hit** will be used to collect information about the collision between the ray casted and objects ahead.

- The variable **info** will be used to determine the current state for our **Animator Controller**.

- The variable **objectInSight** is used to store the tag of the object currently in sight (if any).

Next, let's modify the **Update** method by adding the following code to it (at the end of the method).

```
ray.origin = transform.position;
ray.direction = transform.forward;
info = anim.GetCurrentAnimatorStateInfo(0);
objectInSight = "";
```

In the previous code:

- We set the origin of the ray. In this case it will originate from the position of the NPC (i.e., linked to this script).

- We then set the direction of the ray (i.e., forward).

- We then initialize the variable **info**. By accessing the current state of the **Animator Controller** using the method **GetCurrentAnimatorStateInfo(0)**. Note that the parameter **0** refers to the first layer of the **Animator Controller**.

Using Finite State Machines

> There can be several layers for a particular **Animator Controller**, and in our case, only one (i.e., the first one) has been used. The number of layers can be checked using the **Animator** window, through the **Layer** tab, as illustrated on the next figure.

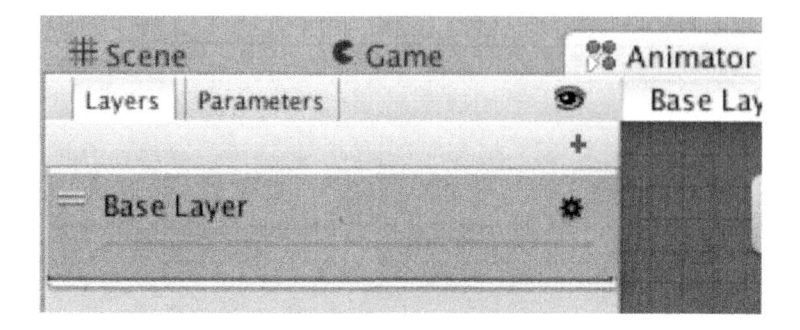

Figure 3-18: Checking the number of layers

- In the previous figure, there is only one layer for this **Animator Controller**, and it is called **Base Layer**.

Please add the following code, just after the code we have added in the **Update** method:

```
Debug.DrawRay (ray.origin, ray.direction * 100, Color.red);
if (Physics.Raycast(ray.origin, ray.direction * 100, out hit))
{
        objectInSight = hit.collider.gameObject.tag;
        print ("Object in Sight" + objectInSight);
        if (objectInSight == "Player")
        {
                anim.SetBool ("canSeePlayer",true);
                print ("Just saw the Player");
        }
}
```

In the previous code:

- We use the ray defined earlier, and cast it for debugging purposes (i.e., only seen in the **Scene** view), using the method **Debug.DrawLine**. Again, this is just for debugging purposes to visually check that the ray is pointing in the right direction.

- After this, we cast a ray using the syntax **Physics.Raycast**; this casts a ray from the NPC and forward.

- If the ray hits a collider, we save the tag of the object in front of the NPC and also print it.

- We then check for the name of the object in sight (if any).

- If this is the player, then we change the parameter **canSeePlayer** to true and also print a message in the **Console** window.

Please add the following code after the last code (i.e., at the end of the method **Update**).

```
if (info.IsName("IDLE"))
{
        print("We are in the IDLE state");
}
```

In the previous code:

- Using the variable **info**, which points to the state of the **Animator Controller**, we check if the current state is **IDLE**; if this is the case, we just print the text **"We are in the IDLE state"**.

We are almost there, we just need to include the following code after the code that you have just added:

```
else if (info.IsName("FOLLOW_PLAYER"))
{
        transform.LookAt(GameObject.Find("FPSController").transform);
        if (objectInSight != "Player")
        {
                anim.SetBool ("canSeePlayer",false);
                print ("Just lost sight of the Player");
        }
        else
        {
                transform.Translate(Vector3.forward* Time.deltaTime);
        }
        print("We are in the FOLLOW_PLAYER state");
}
```

In the previous code:

- We follow the same method used in the previous **if** statement by testing if the player is in sight.

- We look in the direction of the player using the method **LookAt**.

- If the player is not in sight then the parameter **canSeePlayer** is set to **false**.

- Otherwise, the NPC will start to move towards the player at the speed of **1** meter per second.

You can comment or delete the code that detects whether the player has pressed the keys **I** or **J**, as we will trigger events based on sight for now.

One of the last things we need to do is to add a wall to the scene, so that we can create a situation whereby the NPC loses sight of the player as it is following the player.

- Please create a cube, and add it to the scene, making sure that it is slightly above the ground, high enough (e.g., y scale of 4), and wide enough (e.g., x scale of 14).

- You can also create a new material (e.g., blue) and apply it to the wall.

Once this is done, we can now save our code and play the scene to check that:

- The NPC follows the player and transitions from the **IDLE** state to the **FOLLOW_PLAYER** state, once it "sees" the player.

- The NPC stops after losing sight of the player.

Once this is done we will, instead of using a box to represent our NPC, use an actual animated character.

Using Finite State Machines

USING ANIMATED CHARACTERS WITH MECANIM

In this section, we will replace our cubic NPC with an animated character and make some modifications to our script also.

First, let's import the animated character:

- In Unity, create a new folder (if you wish, so that it easier to find your animations) in the **Project** window (for example **military**).

- In your file system, please locate the folder called **animations** in the resource pack. Then locate the folder called **military** within the folder **animations**.

- Drag and drop the content of this folder (i.e., all files within the folder **military**) into your **Project** window (e.g., to the new folder that you have just created).

- Unity will then import these assets.

- If a window labeled **NormalMap Settings** appears, you can press the option to **Fix Now**, as illustrated on the next figure.

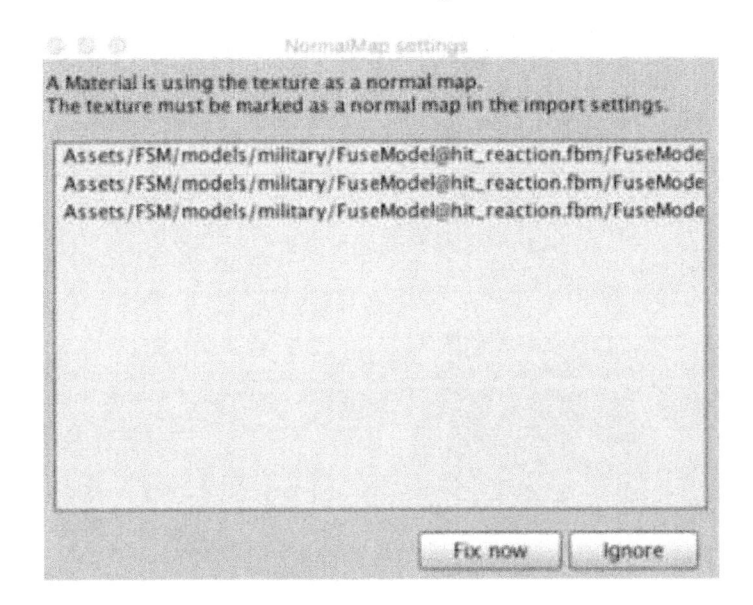

Figure 3-19: Fixing normals for imported models

- This should add several prefabs and folders that we will be able to use for the character animation.

Using Finite State Machines

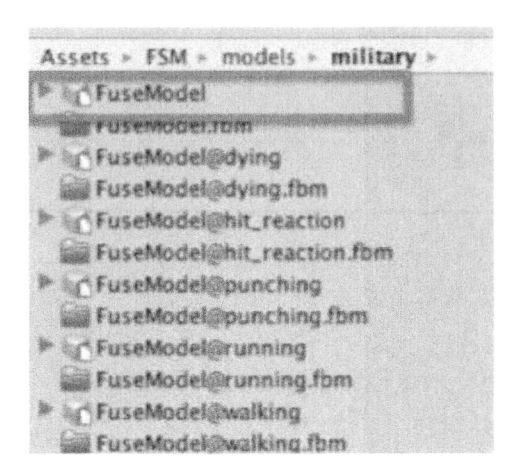

Figure 3-20: Completing the import

- Please deactivate the object called **NPC** already present in the scene.
- Drag the prefab **FuseModel** (as illustrated in the previous figure) to the **Scene** view.

Figure 3-21: Importing the model without animations

- You will notice that, for now, it is in what is called a **T pose**. However, this will change once we add animations for the different states.
- Rename this object **NPC1**.
- Attach the script **ControlNPCFSM** to it.
- Drag and drop the **Animator Controller** called **guard** from the **Project** window to this object (i.e., **NPC1**).

Using Finite State Machines

- By dragging and dropping the two previous assets to the object **NPC1**, we make sure that we can control the different states associated with our new NPC.

It is now time to configure the different states so that the object is animated depending on its state:

- Please select the object **NPC1**.
- Open the **Animator** window.
- Click on the state called **IDLE**.
- In the **Inspector** window, you will notice that the attribute **Motion** is empty.
- Please click on the circle to the right of the label **None (Motion)**, as illustrated on the next figure.

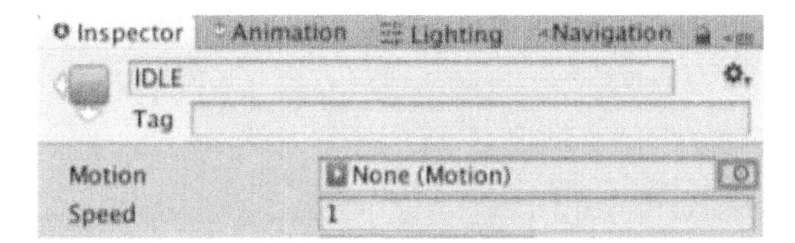

Figure 3-22: Setting the animation for the IDLE state

- In the new window, search for the animation **idle** and select it (e.g., type the text **idle** in the search field and then click on the animation **idle**).

Once this is done, we can perform a quick check by playing the scene. Since the **NPC** is in the **IDLE** mode, you will see it in an **IDLE** posture; however, it seems static (immobile); this is because we need to specify that its animation should loop.

[141]

Using Finite State Machines

Figure 3-23: The NPC in IDLE mode

So let's modify this clip to add a looping feature:

- Please stop playing the scene.

- Open the **Project** window and/or rearrange the layout of Unity so that you can see both the **Project** and the **Animation** window simultaneously.

- After making sure that the object **NPC1** is selected, use the **Animator** window to double-click on the clip **idle** that you have now added to the **IDLE** state.

- Its location should now be highlighted in yellow in the **Project** window.

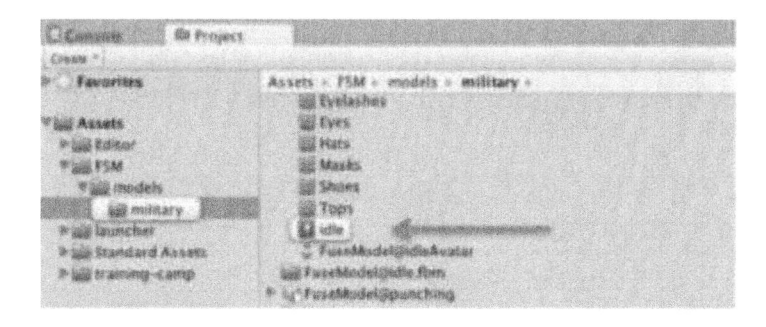

Figure 3-24: Finding the idle animation clip

- Once this is done, click on the animation clip **idle** (i.e., the one highlighted in yellow in the previous figure, in the **Project** view), this will display its properties.

- Using the **Inspector** window, click on the button **Edit** located in its top-right corner.

Using Finite State Machines

Figure 3-25: Editing an animation clip

- Once this is done, you can scroll down within the **Inspector** window, check (i.e., click on) the box **LoopTime**, so that the animation can loop indefinitely, and then press the button labeled **Apply** that is located in the bottom-right corner of the **Inspector** window, so that your changes can be applied and saved.

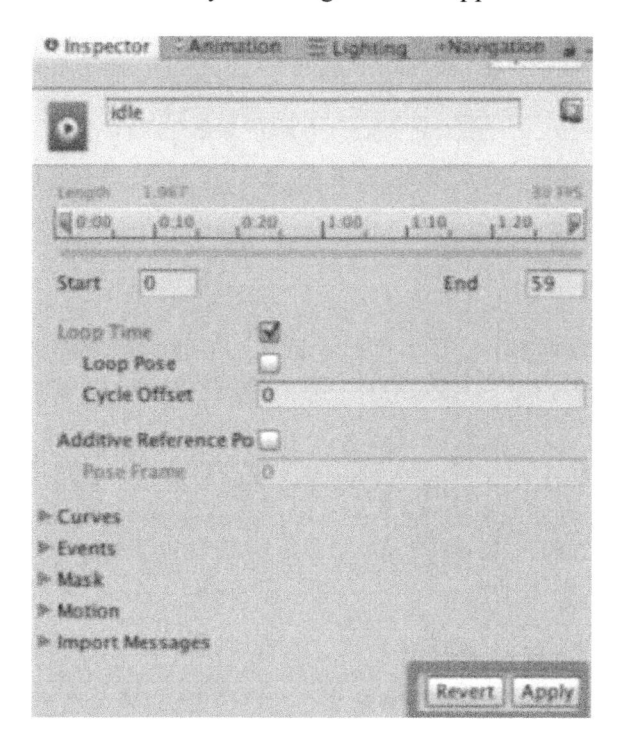

Figure 3-26: Adjusting the parameters of the animation clip

- After applying this change, you can play the scene, zoom-in on the object **NPC1** and check that it is animated and that the animation is looping.

> Whenever you apply modifications to your scene, please stop playing the scene, so that these modifications can be saved.

Next, we need to add an animation for the **FOLLOW_PLAYER** state:

- Select the object **NPC1**.

[143]

Using Finite State Machines

- Display the **Animator** window.

- In the **Animator** window, click on the state **FOLLOW_PLAYER**.

- Using the search field that is within the **Project** window, look for all animations in the **Project** by typing **t:animation**.

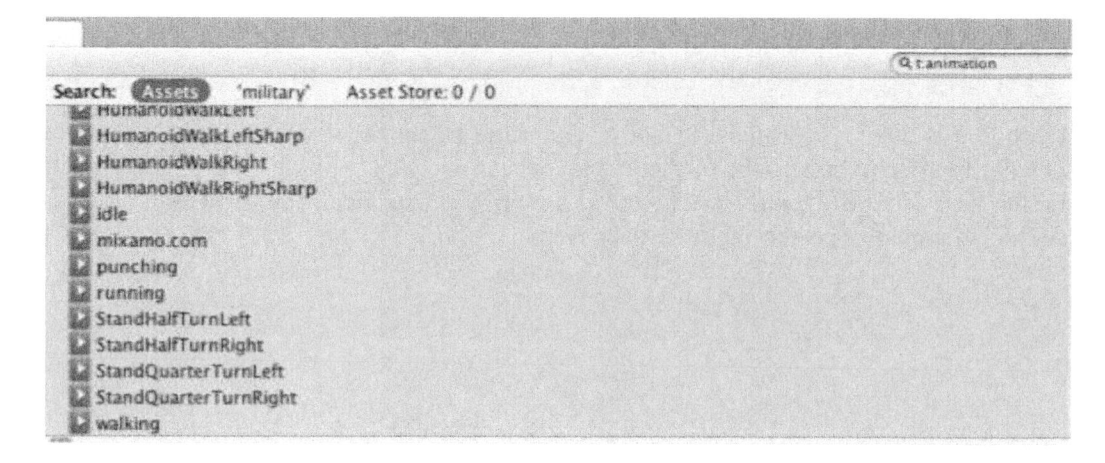

Figure 3-27: Searching for all the animations included in the project

- You can then drag and drop the animation **walking** from the results to the empty field for the attribute **Motion** of the state **FOLLOW_PLAYER**. This is another simple way of selecting an animation for a particular state.

Last but not list, we will add a mechanism that makes the ray casting from the NPC a bit more efficient; this will consist in creating an empty object, adding this object as a child of the **FPSController**, and using it as a target for the **NPC** when it casts rays to detect and follow the player.

- Please create an empty object and rename it **playerMiddle**.

- Add this object as a child of the object **FPSController**.

- Change its position to **(0, -0.67, 0)**.

Once this is done, we just need to modify our script:

- Please open the script **ControlNPCFSM**.

- Replace the line...

```
transform.LookAt(GameObject.Find("FPSController").transform);
```

...with the following code (we just specify that we now look at the centre of the FPSController, where the object **playerMiddle** has been added).

[144]

Using Finite State Machines

```
transform.LookAt(GameObject.Find("playerMiddle").transform);
```

… and replace the line…

```
ray.origin = transform.position;
```

… with the following code (this will make sure that the ray is starting 1 meter above the ground so that it can be used to detect objects ahead):

```
ray.origin = transform.position + Vector3.up;
```

Finally, we will, as for the previous clip, need to ensure that the clip for the state **FOLLOW_PLAYER** is looping:

- Please locate the animation **walking** in your project (e.g., perform a search for the word **walking** in the **Project** window).

- Click on it to see its properties in the **Inspector** window.

- Set its attribute **Loop Time** to **true**, as you have done for the previous clip (i.e., by editing the clip). Also set its attribute **Loop Pose** to **true**; this is so that the animation is executed on the same spot. If you would like to see the impact of the attribute **Loop Pause**, you can change this attribute and then preview the animation clip using the window located in the bottom corner of the **Inspector**.

- Apply these changes (i.e., click on the button **Apply** located in the bottom-right corner of the **Inspector** window).

- Play your scene and check that the game works as expected; by moving in front of the NPC and then moving away from him, you should see that the NPC is following you.

> Please note that currently, if the player changes direction too fast, the NPC may lose sight of the player very easily. So, to be more realistic, we could have implemented a vision detection based on a field of view (e.g., 110 degrees). This could be achieved by calculating the dot product between the forward vectors of the player and the NPC and we will cover this concept later in the book.

Next, we will modify the behavior of the NPC to make it more realistic.

- The NPC will not remain idle after losing site of the player.

- The NPC will keep following the player even if it loses sight of the player.

- The NPC will attack the player when it is close (e.g., close combat technique).

First, let's look at the attacking state.

Using Finite State Machines

Please select the object **NPC1**, open the **Animator** window, and modify the **Animator Controller** by creating a Boolean parameter called **withinArmsReach**.

Please modify the **Animator Controller** by creating the following state and transitions (note that you will also need to drag and drop an animation from the **Project** window to the corresponding state):

- State name: **ATTACK_CLOSE_RANGE**; animation = **punching**.

- Transition: from **FOLLOW_PLAYER** to **ATTACK_CLOSE_RANGE**, condition=" **withinArmsReach =true**".

- Transition: from **ATTACK_CLOSE_RANGE** to **FOLLOW_PLAYER**, condition=" **withinArmsReach =false**".

By creating the previous states and transitions, you modified the behavior of the NPC so that it starts attacking the player when it is within arms' reach, and then resumes following the player when it is not within arms' reach.

> Note that you will need to modify the new animation **punching** so that it loops and set its attribute **Loop Time** to true. You will also need to make sure that the attribute **Loop Pause** is set to true for this animation. To do so, you can select the animation in the project window, and **Edit** its properties using the **Inspector** window.

After creating this state and transitions, the **Animator** window should look as follows:

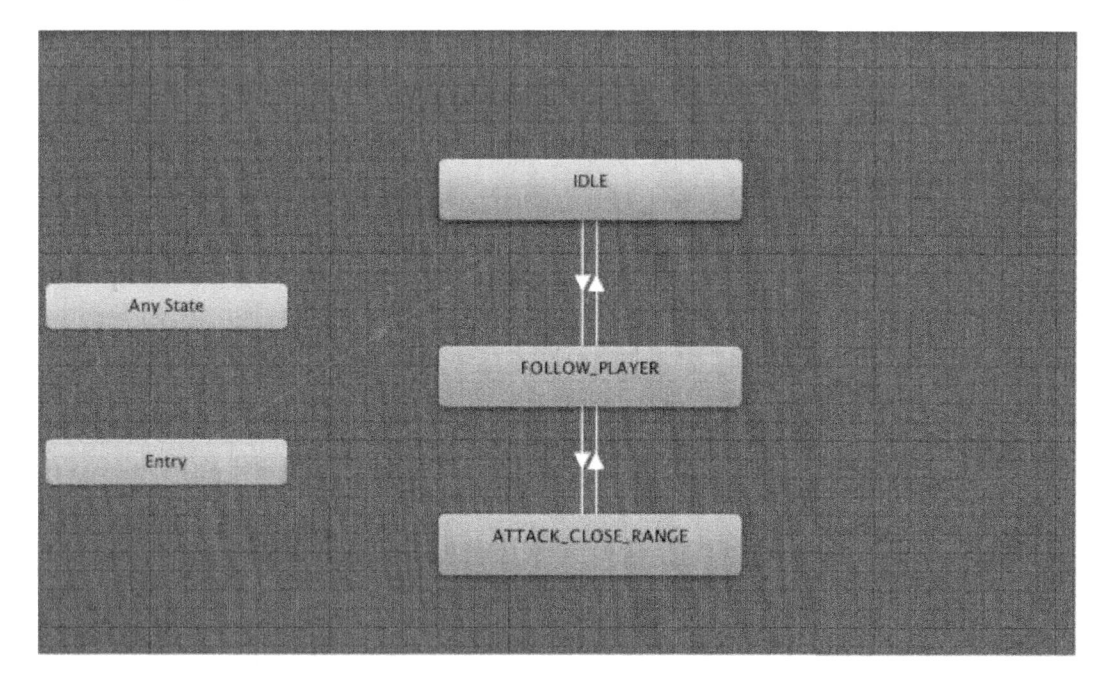

Figure 3-28: The states and transitions for our Animator Controller

Using Finite State Machines

- And the parameters should be listed as follows:

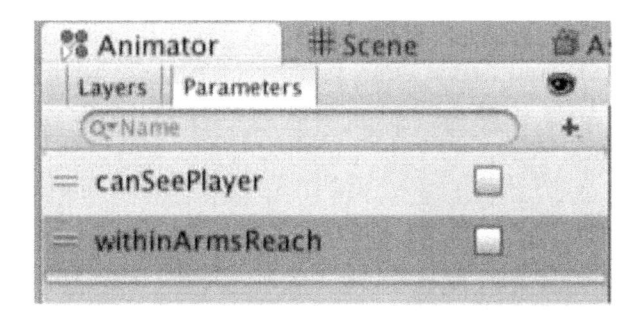

Figure 3-29: Parameters for the Animator Controller

Once this is done, we just need to make sure that the parameter we have just defined (i.e., **withinArmsReach**) is triggered from our script.

- Please open the script **ControlNPCFSM**.

- Add the following code at the beginning of the script (i.e., where other variables are declared and within the class).

```
private float distance;
```

In the previous code, we declare the variable **distance**; it will be employed to detect if the NPC is close to the player.

Add the following code at the beginning of the method **Update** (new code in bold).

```
void Update ()
{
    distance = Vector3.Distance(gameObject.transform.position, GameObject.Find("FPSController").transform.position);
    bool withinReach, closeToPlayer;
    withinReach = (distance < 1.5f);
    anim.SetBool("withinArmsReach", withinReach);
```

In the previous code:

- We calculate the distance between the player and the **NPC**.

- We declare a Boolean variable (**withinReach**) and we then set its value.

- The variable **withinReach** will be true if the distance between the NPC and the player is less than 1.5 meters.

- We then set the parameter for the **Animator Controller** using this Boolean variable.

[147]

Using Finite State Machines

That's about it!

You can now play the scene and check that if you walk in front of the NPC, it will first walk towards you; then, when close enough, the NPC should start to throw punches.

Figure 3-30: Close-range attack from the NPC

MAKING THE NPC SMARTER

At present, when the NPC follows the player and loses sight of the player, it will stop. To make this behavior more realistic, we could modify our game so that the NPC follows the player, and keeps going in his/her direction, even if it has lost sight of the player. So, we will be using the concept of Navmesh. Using a Navmesh, you can ask Unity to compute a path between an object (i.e., usually referred as a Navmesh agent), and a target.

First we will delete the transition from the state **FOLLOW_PLAYER** to the state IDLE, as the NPC will keep following the player.

- Please click on the object **NPC1**.
- Open the **Animator** window.
- Click on the transition from the state **FOLLOW_PLAYER** to the state **IDLE**.
- Press **DELETE** on your keyboard (or *CTRL + DELETE* for Mac users).
- A new window will appear asking you to confirm your choice.

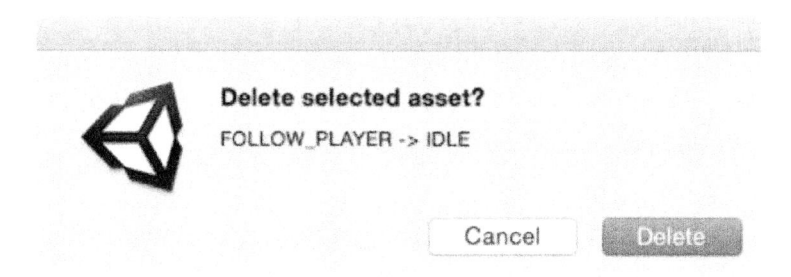

Figure 3-31: Deleting the transition from FOLLOW_PLAYER to IDLE

- Click on **Delete** to confirm that you want to delete this state.

Once this is done, the **Animator** window should look as follows.

Using Finite State Machines

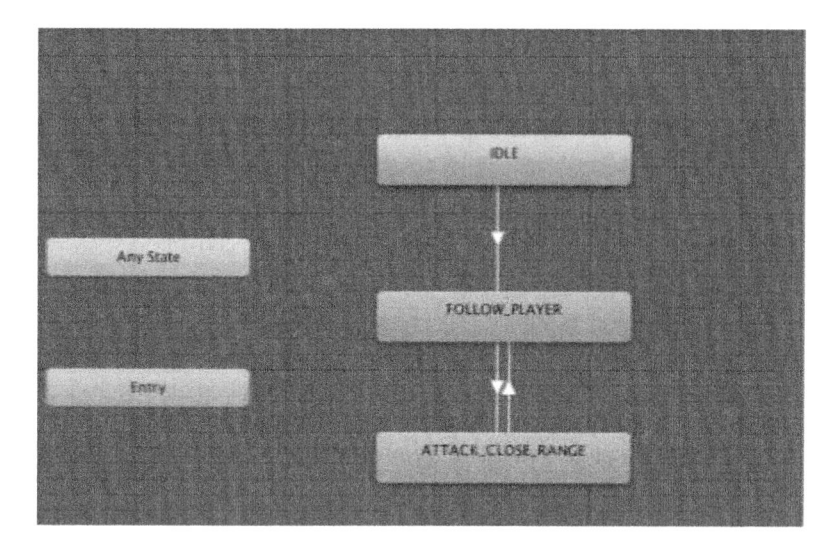

Figure 3-32: The Animator window after deleting the transition

Now that the transition has been deleted, it is time to add "smart" navigation features to our NPC. So, let's add some navigation features to the NPC.

- Please select the NPC (i.e., the object **NPC1**).

- Add a **NavMeshAgent** component to this object (using **Component | Navigation | NavMeshAgent**).

- Using the **Inspector** window, modify the **speed** attribute of this component to **1.0** (i.e., walking speed).

We can now specify the objects that the player can walk on or avoid while pursuing its target; for this purpose, we will use the **Navigation** window.

- Please open the **Navigation** window (**Window | Navigation**).

- Then, using the **Hierarchy** window, select the ground and the wall that you have created.

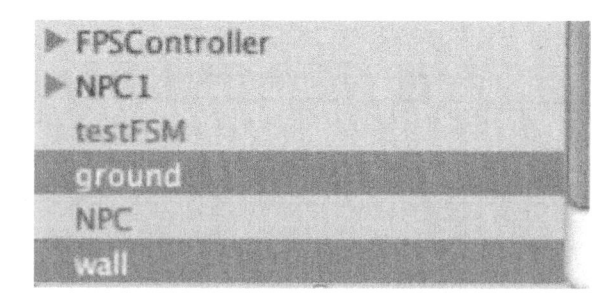

Figure 3-33: Selecting the objects to avoid

Using Finite State Machines

- Once this is done, using the **Navigation** window, in the tab labeled **Object**, click on the option **Navigation Static**.

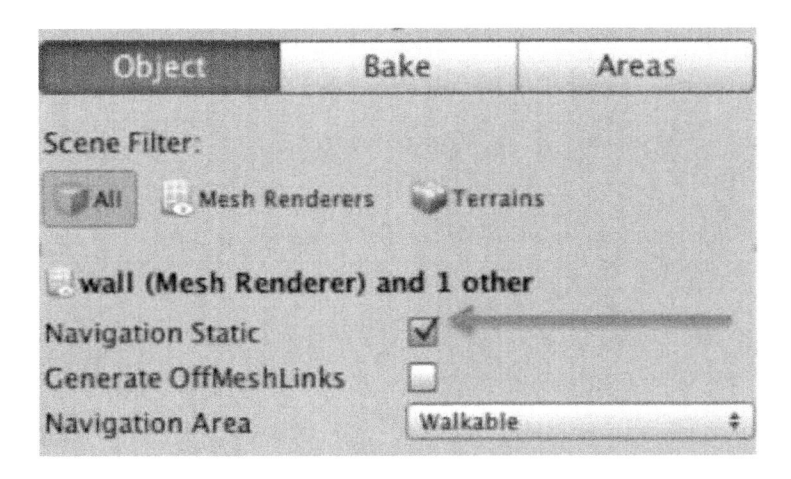

Figure 3-34: Choosing the type of navigation

- If a window labeled **Change Static Flags** appears, select the option **Yes Change Children**.

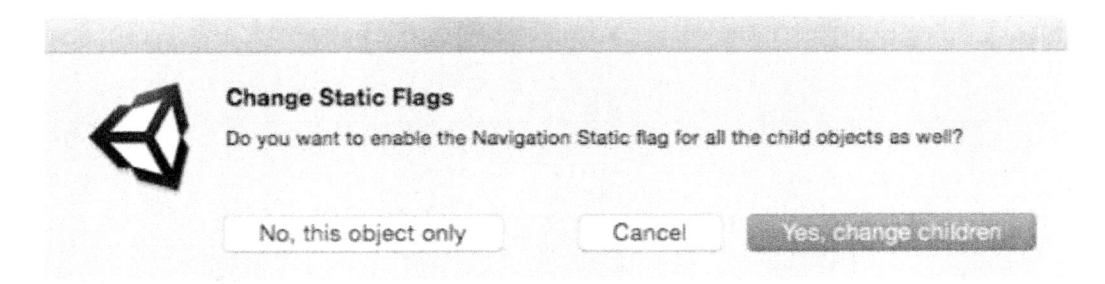

Figure 3-35: Applying navigation settings to the children

- Once this is done, just click on the **Bake** button located in the bottom-right corner of the **Navigation** window.

Figure 3-36: Baking the scene

- As the baking process is complete, your scene will look different as it includes some of the meshes calculated by Unity to define possible paths for our **NPC**.

Using Finite State Machines

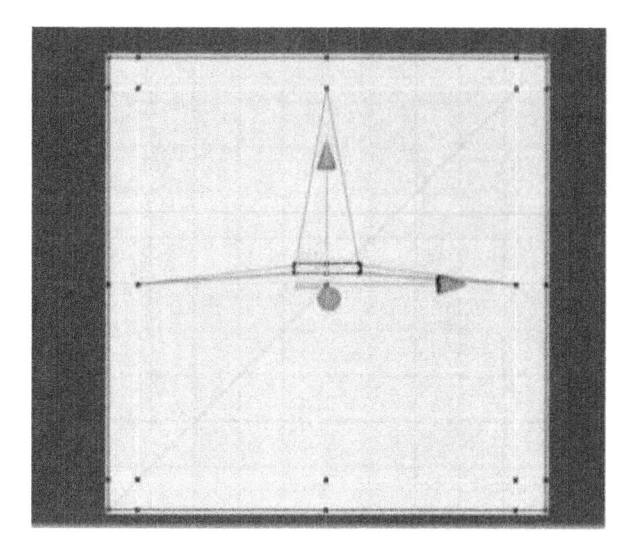

Figure 3-37: Looking at the scene after the baking process is complete

Once this is done, we just need to modify the script **ControlNPCFSM**.

- Please open the script **ControlNPCFSM**.
- Modify the code in the Update method as follows (new code in bold).

```
if (info.IsName("IDLE"))
{
        GetComponent<NavMeshAgent>().Stop();
        print("We are in the IDLE state");
}
else if (info.IsName("ATTACK_CLOSE_RANGE"))
{
        GetComponent<NavMeshAgent>().Stop();
}
else if (info.IsName("FOLLOW_PLAYER"))
{
        GetComponent<NavMeshAgent>().destination = GameObject.Find("playerMiddle").transform.position;
        GetComponent<NavMeshAgent>().Resume();
        //You can delete the code that was in this section previously
}
```

In the previous code:

[152]

- We use the code **GetComponent<NavMeshAgent>().Stop()** so that the NPC stops navigating towards the player whenever it is in the states **IDLE** or **ATTACK_CLOSE_RANGE**.

- If the NPC is in the state **FOLLOW_PLAYER**, we then set the destination (the target) to the player, and then resume the navigation.

Please play the scene, check that after losing sight of the player (e.g., after hiding behind a wall), the NPC still manages to keep track of the player and follow him/her.

ADDING WEAPONS TO THE PLAYER

At this stage, the NPC has a simple behavior whereby it will follow the player once the player is in sight and eventually throw punches when close enough. So we could, at this stage, start to equip our player so that it can use and manage weapons, using the code and prefabs we have created in the previous chapters. For this purpose, and to also keep a backup of the script that we have created in the previous chapter we will perform a series of script duplication.

- Please duplicate the script **ManageWeapons** and call it **ManageWeapons2**.

- Open this script (i.e., **ManageWeapon2**) and change the name of the class within as follows.

- Replace the following code....

```
public class ManageWeapons : MonoBehaviour
```

- ...with this code (changes in bold)...

```
public class ManageWeapons2 : MonoBehaviour
```

- We need to change the name of the class within to avoid conflict with the class **ManageWeapons** that we have already defined in the file **ManageWeapons.cs**.

> If you omit to change the name of the class within after changing the name of the file, Unity may display a message saying "**The namespace global already contains a definition for...**". This message means that this class has already been defined earlier and that there is a potential conflict.

- Please do the same with the scripts **ManageNPC**, **ManageCollisionWithPlayer**, and **Grenade**: duplicate these scripts, add a **2** to the name of the duplicate, and also modify the name of the class within.

- After making these modifications, you should have three additional scripts: **ManageNPC2**, **ManageCollisionWithPlayer2**, and **Grenade2**.

- For clarity, you can add these scripts to a new folder, for example **FSM**, as illustrated on the next figure.

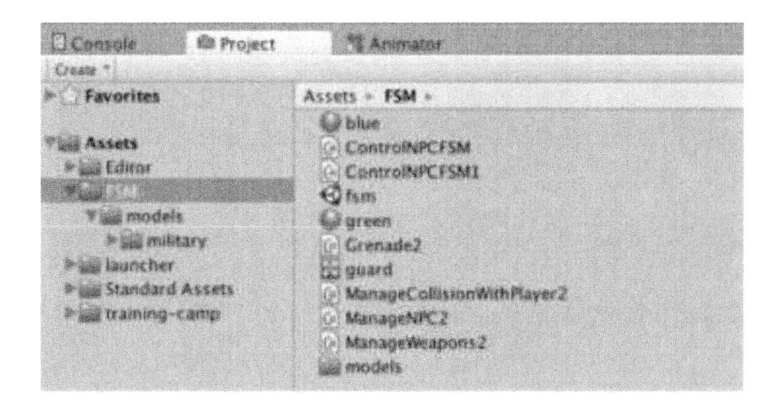

Figure 3-38: Duplicating C# files

- Create a new **RawImage** object (**Game Object | UI | Raw Image**).

- Use the **crosshair** texture that you employed in the last chapter, as a texture for this object.

- Make sure that the crosshair is centered (i.e., displayed in the middle of the screen); for example, you could set its parameters **PosX** and **PosY** to 0.

Once this is done, it is time to add weapons to the player:

- Drag and drop the script **ManageWeapons2** to the object **FirstPersonCharacter**.

- Open this script (**ManageWeapons2**) and replace this code (in the **Update** method):

```
objectTargeted.GetComponent<ManageNPC>().gotHit();
```

...with this code...

```
objectTargeted.GetComponent<ManageNPC2>().gotHit();
```

- Once this is done, select the object **FirstPersonCharacter**, and, using the **Inspector** window, focusing on the component **ManageWeapons2**, set the prefabs for the fields **grenade** and **sparksAtImpact** with the prefabs **grenade** and **smoke**, respectively. You can set these by clicking on the circle to the right of the variable that you need to change, then search for and select the corresponding prefab, as you have done in the previous sections.

Using Finite State Machines

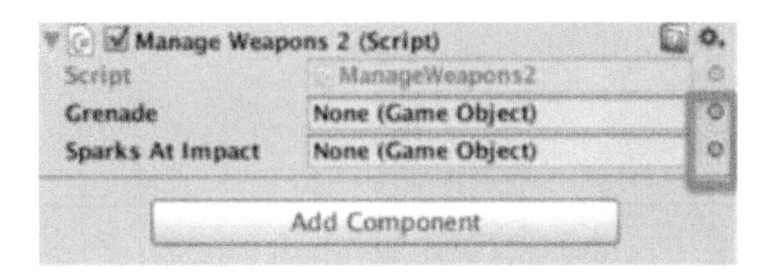

Figure 3-39: Setting the variables grenade and sparksAtImpact from the Inspector

- Finally, create a new **UI | Text** object, rename it **userInfo**, change its **width** to **400**, and set its position to the bottom-left corner of the screen; for example **(-74.5, 150.5, 0)**.

> To move the **Text UI** component you can temporarily switch to the 2D mode, this will display the screen boundaries (i.e., white rectangle) and make it easier to position the **Text UI** component. To activate or deactivate the 2D mode, you can click on the 2D icon located below the tab labeled scene, as described on the next figure.

- Drag the audio clip **gunshot** to the object **FirstPersonCharacter**. Also ensure that its option **Play on Awake** is set to false (i.e., after selecting the object **FirstPersonCharacter** and displaying its properties in the **Inspector**).

- Create a new empty object, rename it **launcher**, add it as a child of the object **FirstPersonCharacter**, and set its position to **(0, 0.2, 0)**.

- Play the scene; you should be able to use the different weapons, including the grenades, and to also see the number of ammunitions available.

Next, we will make it possible for the player to collect ammunitions:

- Drag and drop the script **ManageCollisionWithPlayer2** from the project window to the object named **FPSController**.

- Open this script and change its code as follows (new code in bold):

```
void OnControllerColliderHit (ControllerColliderHit hit)
{
            transform.GetChild(0).GetComponent<ManageWeapons2>().manageCollisions(hit);
}
```

- The modification is necessary at this stage, as the other script that manages the weapons has changed name (from **ManageWeapons** to **ManageWeapons2**).

[156]

Using Finite State Machines

- Locate the prefabs **ammo_auto**, **ammo_grenade**, and **ammo_gun** in your project (i.e., by searching for the word **ammo** in your **Project** window), and drag and drop them several times from your project to the scene, so that it creates new ammos in the scene.

- Please play the scene and check that you can pick-up different types of ammos and that the ammunition levels are updated accordingly.

At this stage, we have successfully recycled the code created in the previous chapter to add weapons to our character. The next phase will now involve applying damage to the NPCs when they are hit.

- Please drag and drop the script **ManageNPC2** on the object **NPC1**.

- Remove the component **ManageNPC** from the object **NPC1** (i.e., right-click on the component and select **Remove Component**).

- Select the object **NPC1** and, using the **Inspector**, set the **smoke** variable for the attached script **ManageNPC2** to the prefab **smoke** (i.e., click on the circle to the right of the variable smoke and search/select the prefab **smoke**).

Last but not list, we need to add colliders to the NPC. At present, the ray casting generated from the player will not detect the NPC because this NPC has no colliders yet. So we will create a collider for the NPC accordingly:

- Please select the object **NPC1**.

- Change its tag to **target**.

- Then select **Component | Physics | Capsule Collider**. This will add a capsule collider to the NPC.

- Modify the attributes of this capsule collider using the **Inspector** window as follows: **Centre (0, 0.82,0)**, **Height (1.75)**, and leave the other options as default.

After making these changes, play the scene, and check that after firing twice or more at the NPC, it disappears.

You may notice, however, that the grenade does not impact on the **NPC**; this is because the grenade object is linked to the script **Grenade.cs**, which needs to be updated.

- Please select the prefab **grenade** from the **Project** window.

- Deactivate or remove its script component **Grenade.cs**.

- Drag and drop the script **Grenade2.cs** to this object, so that it becomes a component of the **grenade** prefab.

- Set the variable **explosion** for this component (**Grenade2.cs**) to the prefab **explosion**.

Using Finite State Machines

Finally, open the script **Grenade2.cs**, and change its code as follows (new code in bold). You can replace the code that was previously within the for loop with the next code.

```
for (int i = 0; i < colliders.Length; i++)
{
        if (colliders [i].gameObject.tag == "target")
        {
          GameObject objectTargeted = colliders [i].gameObject;
          objectTargeted.GetComponent<ManageNPC2>().gotHitByGrenade();
        }
}
```

In the previous script, we check whether the objects within range have a tag called **target**; if this is the case, we then access its script and apply damage.

After making this change, please save your script and test the scene. Using the guns or grenades, you should be able to neutralize the NPC now.

ADDING ANIMATIONS FOR MORE REALISM

Ok. So we can now use our weapons to neutralize the NPC, and it works well; however, we could add more realism to the animations. For example, every time the **NPC** is hit, we could play an animation; when its health is low, we could also play an animation that shows this NPC falling to the ground. All it takes is to create states (e.g., **HIT** or **DIE**), then detect whether the player is hit, and switch to the corresponding states.

So let's get started; first we will create the two additional states:

- Please select the **NPC** (**NPC1**).
- Open the **Animator** window.
- Create two states called **HIT** and **DIE**.
- Create two new parameters: **gotHit** (type = **Trigger**) and **lowHealth** (type = **Boolean**).

> You will notice that we use a **Trigger** variable here (**gotHit**); this is because this parameter will switch back to false after it has been set to true. In other words, this state **HIT** will last for a short period of time and this variable (**gotHit**), because it is true just for a moment, will switch back to its original value right after that. So it makes more sense to use a **Trigger** parameter rather than a Boolean, as the NPC will get hit (this will last for a short moment) but will not remain in this state for a long time.

Please apply the following animations to the states created:

- State = **HIT**; animation = **hit_reaction**.
- State = **DIE**; animation = **dying**.
- You don't need to loop these animations, so no modification of the corresponding clips is necessary for now.

We just need to create the transitions now; please create the following transitions:

- From **HIT** to **DIE**: **lowHealth = true**.
- From **HIT** to **ATTACK_CLOSE_RANGE**: **withinArmsReach=true && lowHealth = false**.

Using Finite State Machines

> To include several conditions for a transition, additional transitions can be provided using the + sign in the bottom-right corner of the section **Transition**, in the **Inspector** window.
>
> | Conditions | | |
> |---|---|---|
> | = withinArmsReach | ▾ | true ⇕ |
> | = lowHealth | ▾ | false ⇕ |
> | | | + − |
>
> Figure 3-40: Adding conditions for transitions
>
> To delete a condition, you can simply click once on the = sign to the right of the variable and then press the − sign located in the bottom-right corner of the window.

- From **Any Sate** to **HIT**: **gotHit**. The state **Any State** is already present in the **Animator** by default, and you can move it by dragging and dropping it to the location of your choice.

- After you have created these states, parameters and transitions, the **Animator** window may look as follows:

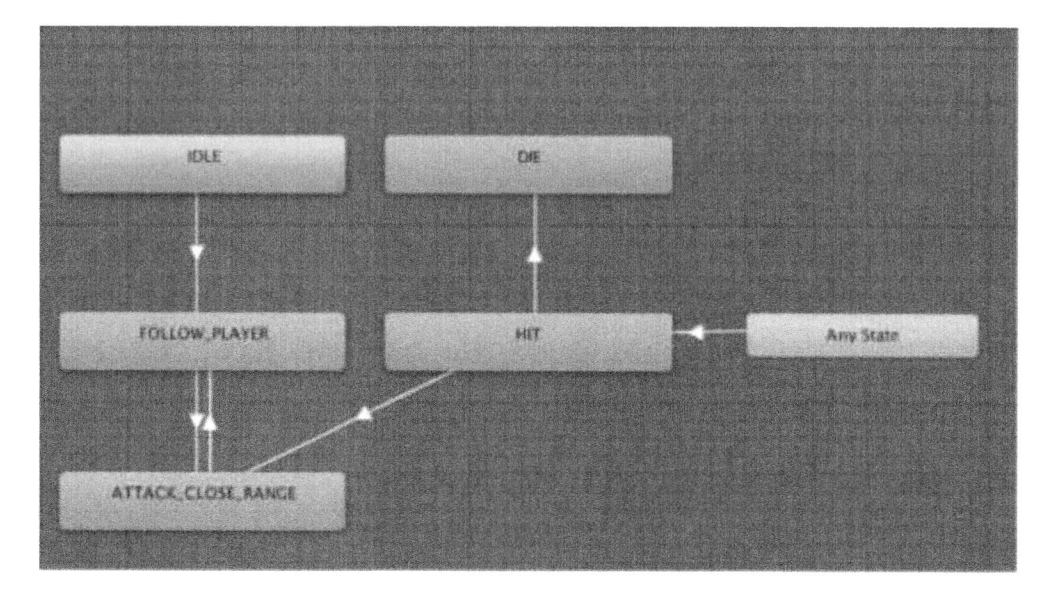

Figure 3-41: New states and transitions

- Once this done, you can check that these transitions work by just playing the scene, displaying both the **Animator** and the **Scene** views simultaneously, and clicking on the parameters and **lowHealth** and then **gotHit** in the **Animator** window.

[160]

Using Finite State Machines

- First you can change the **gotHit** variable, the **NPC** should be ducking slightly (as per the next figure); then set the variable **lowHealth** to true, set the variable **gotHit** again and the NPC should start to fall down.

Figure 3-42: The NPC is hit	Figure 3-43: The NPC falls down (part 1)	Figure 3-44: The NPC falls down (part 2)

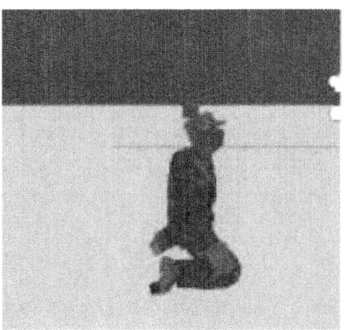

So after checking that these transitions work well, we need to link them to the game. So the process will be to detect when the **NPC** is hit, and set the parameter **gotHit** or **lowHealth** based on its **health**.

- Please open the script **ControlNPCFSM**.

- Add the following lines of code within the class (e.g., at the end of the class, just before the last closing curly bracket).

```
public void setGotHitParameter()
{
        anim.SetTrigger("gotHit");
}

public void setLowHealthParameter()
{
        anim.SetBool("lowHealth",true);
}
```

In the previous code:

- We create two member methods.

- In the first method, we set the **Trigger** variable **gotHit**.

- In the second method, we set the **Boolean** variable **lowHealth** to true.

[161]

Using Finite State Machines

> You may notice that these methods are public, which means that they will be accessible from outside this class, including from other classes.

Next, we will modify the script **manageNPC2.cs**:

- Please open the script **manageNPC2.cs**.

- Modify the methods **gotHit** and **gotHitByGrenade** as follows (new code in bold).

```
public void gotHit()
{
    print ("Got hit by bullet");
    GetComponent<ControlNPCFSM>().setGotHitParameter();
    health -=50;
}
public void gotHitByGrenade()
{
    print ("Got hit by Grenade");
    GetComponent<ControlNPCFSM>().setGotHitParameter();
    health = 0;
}
```

In the previous code:

- We create a method **gotHit**.

- In this method, we access the method **setGotHitParameter** from the script **ControlNPCFSM** that is linked to the same object. This method (i.e., **setGotHitParameter**) will set an animation parameter so that the NPC briefly transitions to the state **HIT**.

- We then decrease the health of the NPC by 50.

- We also update the method **gotHitByGrenade** and proceed as for the previous method except that **health** is set to 0 instead.

Modify the method **Destroy** as follows (new code in bold):

[162]

```
public void Destroy()
{
        /*print ("Destroying "+ gameObject.name);
        GameObject lastSmoke = (GameObject) (Instantiate (smoke, transform.position, Quaternion.identity));
        Destroy (lastSmoke,3);
        Destroy(gameObject);*/
        GetComponent<ControlNPCFSM>().setLowHealthParameter();
        Destroy(gameObject, 5);
}
```

In the previous code:

- We comment some of the code (the first 5 lines of the method).

- We access the method **setLowHealthParameter** from the script **ControlNPCFSM**. This is because the script **ControlNPCFSM** is also attached to the NPC (i.e., the object **NPC1**)

- We then destroy the **NPC** after **5** seconds (this should give enough time for the falling animation to be completed).

As you play the scene and use your gun or grenades to neutralize the NPC, you should be able to see the NPC either ducking or falling after being hit by a bullet or a grenade.

Using Finite State Machines

APPLYING DAMAGE TO THE PLAYER

In this section, we will give the opportunity for the NPC to also apply damage to the player. If you remember, we have a state called **ATTACK_CLOSE_RANGE**; in this state the NPC throws punches at the player at close range. However, no health points are withdrawn from the player yet. So we will implement this functionality. It will consist in:

- Detecting when the NPC is throwing punches.

- Decreasing a finished amount of health from the player when it's being hit.

- Provide the ability for the player to increase its health by collecting med packs.

So let's get started!

- Please create a new C# script and rename it **ManagePlayerHealth**.

- Add the following code at the beginning of the class (new code in bold).

```
public class ManagePlayerHealth : MonoBehaviour {
int health = 100;
```

Then add the following method (e.g., before the last closing curly bracket):

```
public void decreaseHealth(int healthIncrement)
{
        health -= healthIncrement;
}
```

- Save your script and drag and drop it to the object **FPSController**.

- Open the script **ControlNPCFSM**.

- Add the following code within the **Update** method after the code that deals with the **IDLE** state.

[164]

Using Finite State Machines

```
else if (info.IsName("ATTACK_CLOSE_RANGE"))
{
        GetComponent<NavMeshAgent>().Stop();
        if (info.normalizedTime%1.0 >= .98)
        {
                GameObject.Find
("FPSController").GetComponent<ManagePlayerHealth>().decreaseHealth(5);
        }
}
```

In the previous code:

- We check that we are in the state **ATACK_CLOSE_RANGE**.

- We then stop the navigation (i.e., following the player)check if the animation associated to this state is almost complete; and we then call the method **decreaseHealth**. The reason for using the following code…

`info.normalizedTime%1.0 >= .98`

… is that, if we don't check that the animation is almost completed, we would decrease the player's health continuously while the animation is played; however, we just want to decrease the player's health after each round of attack (or punch); so we wait until we have reached 98% completion of the animation before we decrease health.

> The variable **info.normalizedTime** returns a number that includes two types of information: the integer part tells us how many times the animation has looped, and the decimal part indicates the percentage of completion of the current loop. So since we are interested in the later (i.e., percentage of completion of the current loop), we use the operator modulo (%) to obtain this value.

We will add a UI component to our scene later, to display the player's health and to check that all works properly.

While this is working, we could also add some challenge in the game by allowing the NPC to shoot at the player. So let's create this behavior.

- Please select the NPC (i.e., the object **NPC1**).

- Open the **Animator** window.

- Create a new state called **SHOOT**.

- Associate this state with the animation **shooting** (i.e., by dragging and dropping the animation on the state or clicking on the circle to the right of the field called **Motion**).

Create the following transitions:

Using Finite State Machines

- From **HIT** to **SHOOT**: **withinArmsReach=false && lowHealth = false**.

- From **SHOOT** to **FOLLOW_PLAYER**: **no conditions.** This means that the state **FOLLOW_PLAYER** will be reached after the animation for the state **SHOOT** is complete.

After performing these changes, the **Animator** window should look as follows.

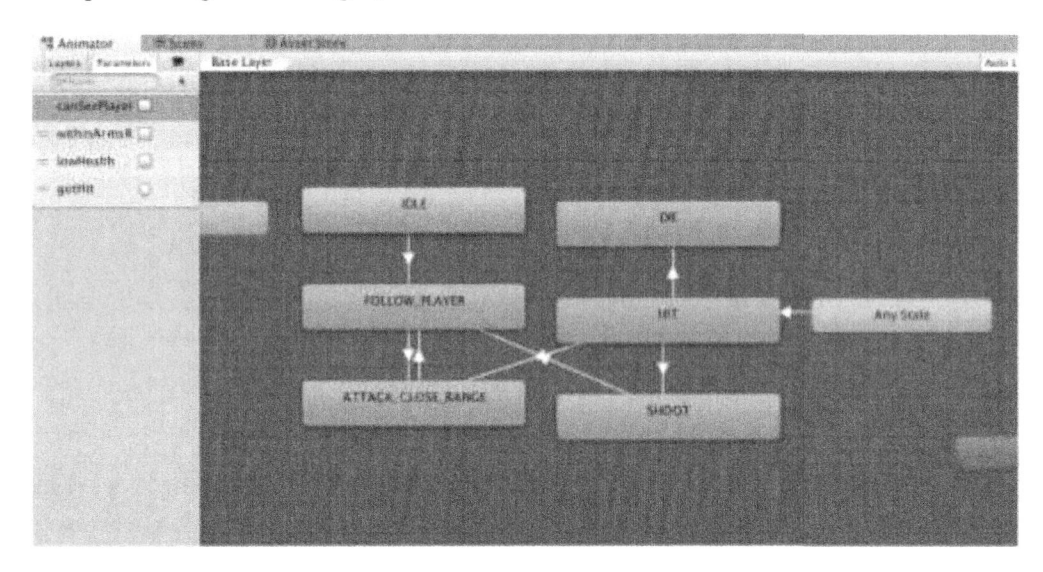

Figure 3-45: The Animator controller with an additional state

After creating these states and transitions, we just need to modify the code for the script **ControlNPCFSM**:

- Please open this script **ControlNPCFSM**.

- Add the following code within the **Update** method just after the code that deals with the state **ATTACK_CLOSE_RANGE**.

```
else if (info.IsName("HIT"))
{
        GetComponent<NavMeshAgent>().Stop();
}
else if (info.IsName("SHOOT"))
{
        GetComponent<NavMeshAgent>().Stop();
        transform.LookAt(GameObject.Find("playerMiddle").transform);
        if (info.normalizedTime%1.0 >= .98)
        {
                GameObject.Find ("FPSController").GetComponent<ManagePlayerHealth>().decreaseHealth(5);
        }
}
```

In the previous code:

- We check that we are in the state **HIT**; in this case, we make sure that the NPC is not navigating (i.e., that it is stopped).

- We then check for the state **SHOOT**; in this case, we also make sure that the NPC is not navigating (i.e., that it is stopped).

- We then make sure that the NPC is looking in the direction of the player before starting to shoot.

- We finally decrease the health of the player, following the same principle as the one we have used for the state **ATTACK_CLOSE_RANGE**.

Please play and test the scene and make sure that the NPC reacts as predicted (e.g., following the player, or shooting after being hit).

As you check the scene, you may notice that when the NPC is shooting, it has no gun yet in its hand; this is because the animation created did not include the weapon, so we need to add a gun object to this NPC when it is shooting.

So let's add this object:

- You can download a gun object form the following site and link (this model was created by Dennis Haupt):

http://tf3dm.com/3d-model/45-acp-smith-and-wesson-13999.html

- In case this link is not available anymore, it is also included in the resource pack, in the folder **3D models | handgun** (with the permission of the author of this object).

Using Finite State Machines

- Once this done, you can import the folder called **fbx** in Unity. This will include a folder with a prefab for the gun, as well as textures.

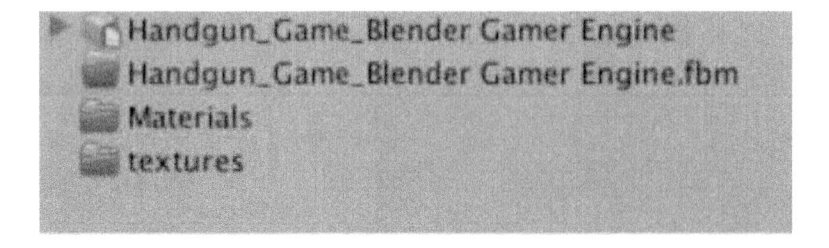

Figure 3-46: Importing a gun object

Once this is done, you can drag and drop the prefab (i.e., the blue box named **Handgun_Game_Blender Gamer Engine**) on the object **NPC1**, so that it becomes a child of the NPC.

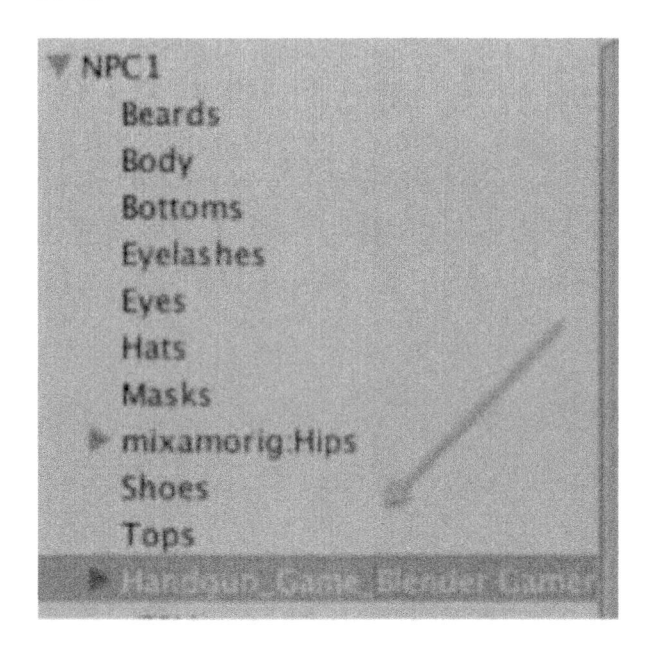

Figure 3-47: Adding the gun as a child of the NPC

We can then adjust its **Transform** settings as follows:

- Position **(0.115, 1.211, 0.759)**.
- Rotation **(0, 90, 0)**.
- Scale **(0.2, 0.2, 0.2)**.

Using Finite State Machines

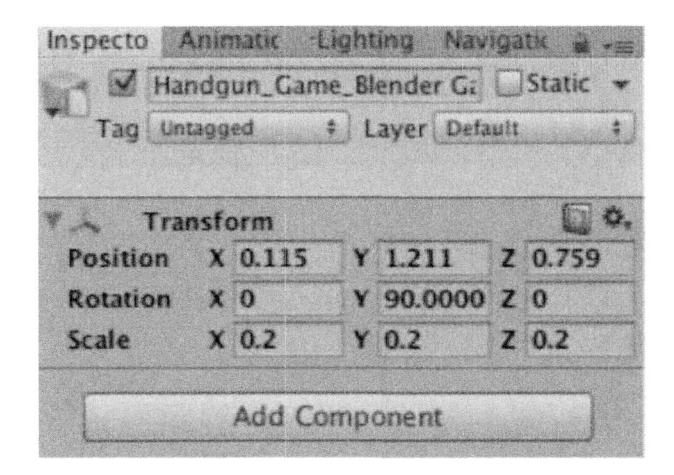

Figure 3-48: Adjusting the transform properties of the gun

- In the **Hierarchy** window, rename this object **hand_gun**.

Figure 3-49: Adding a gun to the NPC

Once this is done, you should see that the gun appears in front of the NPC in the **Scene** view. You can check that the gun is in the right position when the NPC is shooting by doing the following:

- Select the object **NPC1**.

- Focus on this object (*SHIFT + S*).

- Play the scene.

- Open the **Animator** window (you can first press **CTRL + 1** to switch to the **Scene** view and then use your mouse to select the **Animator** window).

[169]

Using Finite State Machines

- Set the variables **lowHealth** and **withinArmsReach** to **false**, and then set the variable **gotHit**.

- Observe the object **NPC1** in the scene view; it should look like the following picture.

Figure 3-50: Positioning the gun

Next, we need to enable this object only when the NPC is shooting:

- Open the script **ControlNPCFSM**.

- Add the following code at the beginning of the class.

```
private GameObject gun;
```

- Then add the following code to the method **Start**.

```
gun = GameObject.Find("hand_gun");
gun.active = false;
```

Finally, add the following code to the **Update** method (new code in bold).

[170]

Using Finite State Machines

```
else if (info.IsName("SHOOT"))
{
        GetComponent<NavMeshAgent>().Stop();
        if(anim.IsInTransition(0)&&
anim.GetNextAnimatorStateInfo(0).IsName("FOLLOW_PLAYER")) gun.active = false;
        else gun.active = true;
        transform.LookAt(GameObject.Find("playerMiddle").transform);
        if (info.normalizedTime%1.0 >= .98)
        {
                GameObject.Find ("FPSController").GetComponent<ManagePlayerHealth>().decreaseHealth(5);
        }
}
```

In the previous code that is highlighted in bold:

- We check that the **Animator Controller** is transitioning and that it is transitioning to the state called **FOLLOW_PLAYER** from the state **SHOOT**.

- When this is verified, we just deactivate the gun so that it can't be seen.

- The method **GetNextAnimatorStateInfo()** provides the next state to be reached in the first layer (hence the parameter 0). We then use the method **IsName** to obtain its name.

The last things we need to do are to:

- Display the player's health and number of lives.

- Reload the level when health levels are low.

- Increase the health levels when the player collects ammunitions.

- Decrease the number of lives by one.

So we will modify the script **ManagePlayerHealth** accordingly.

- Open the script **ManagePlayerHealth**.

- Add this code at the beginning of the class (i.e., where other variables are declared).

```
int nbLives = 3;
```

- Modify the method **decreaseHealth** as follows:

[171]

Using Finite State Machines

```
public void decreaseHealth(int healthIncrement)
{
        print ("Decreasing health by "+ healthIncrement);
        health -= healthIncrement;
        if (health <=0) restartLevel();
}
```

- Then add the following methods to the script (at the end of the class):

```
public void increaseHealth(int healthIncrement)
{
        health += healthIncrement;
}
public void restartLevel()
{
        nbLives--;
        health = 100;
        Application.LoadLevel(Application.loadedLevel);
}
public void Awake()
{
  DontDestroyOnLoad(transform.gameObject);
}
```

In the previous code:

- We create a method that increases the health of the player.

- We create a method that restarts the current level after the player has lost a life.

- We create a method that ensures that the object linked to this script (the player) is persistent. In other word, even if the scene is reloaded, this object will not be destroyed. This means that the information on health levels and the number of lives is also kept whenever the scene is reloaded.

Finally, add the following code in the **Start** function (new code in bold):

```
void Start ()
{
        GameObject [] clones = new GameObject [2];
        clones = GameObject.FindGameObjectsWithTag("Player");
        if (clones.Length > 1) Destroy (clones[1]) ;
}
```

In the previous code:

Using Finite State Machines

- As we will restart, the level will already include an object called **FPSController**.

- As a result there will be two of these objects (i.e., since the previous one will be kept using the method **DontDestroyOnLoad**).

- So we detect whether there is a duplicate and remove one of them.

- Finally we set the health to **100**.

After this, we just need to create and add health packs:

- Please duplicate the prefab **ammo_gun**.

- Rename the duplicate prefab **health_pack**.

- Create a tag **health_pack** and apply it to this prefab.

- Drag and drop this prefab to the scene.

- This should create a new object called **health_pack** and an object within called **ammo_label**, as described on the next figure.

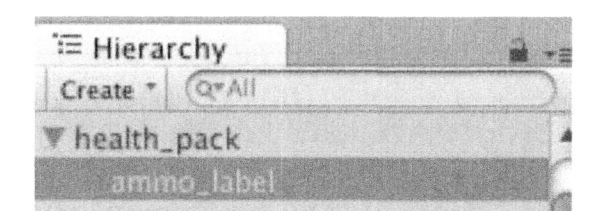

Figure 3-51: Identifying the label for the health pack

- Click on the **ammo_label** object.

- Using the **Inspector** window, change its text to **Health Pack**.

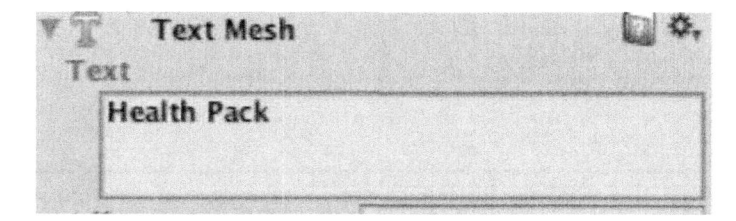

Figure 3-52: Changing the label of the health pack

- Then, so that these changes are applied to the prefab, you can select this object and, using the **Inspector** window, click on the **Apply** button located in the top right corner of the screen, as illustrated on the next figure.

[173]

Using Finite State Machines

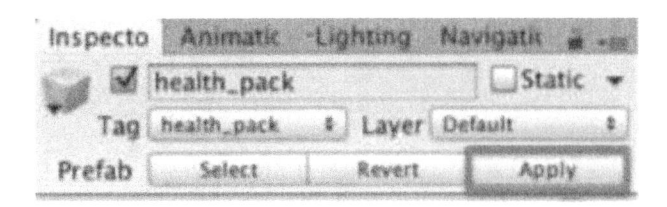

Figure 3-53: Applying changes to the prefab

We will now modify the scripts so that, upon collision with health packs, health levels are increased:

- Please open the script **ManageWeapons2.cs**.
- Add the following code at the end of the method **manageCollisions**.

```
if (tagOfTheOtherObject =="health_pack")
{
        GameObject.Find ("FPSController").GetComponent<ManagePlayerHealth>().increaseHealth(50);
        Destroy (hit.collider.gameObject);

}
```

- Modify the method **increaseHealth** in the script **ManagePlayerHealth** as follows (new code in bold).

```
public void increaseHealth(int healthIncrement)
{
        health += healthIncrement;
        if (health > 100) health = 100;
}
```

- You can also check your health levels by adding the following code to the **Update** method in the same script (i.e., **ManagePlayerHealth**).

```
print ("Health is: " + health);
```

- Please test your scene, and check that, after being hit by a bullet and having collected a health pack, your health is increased (i.e., you can check the **Console** window).

> Before testing the game, make sure that the variable **gotHit** is set to false in the **Animator** window.

Last but not list, we will display the health and life information onscreen:

- Create two new **UI | Text** objects by duplicating the object **userInfo** twice.
- Rename the duplicates **healthInfo** and **livesInfo**.

[174]

Using Finite State Machines

- Place them just above the **userInfo GameObject** (you can temporarily switch to the 2D view to see and move these objects accordingly, select one of them, and focus on it by pressing *CTRL + F*).

> To switch between the 2D/3D modes while the **Scene** view is active, you can just press the key **2** on your keyboard.

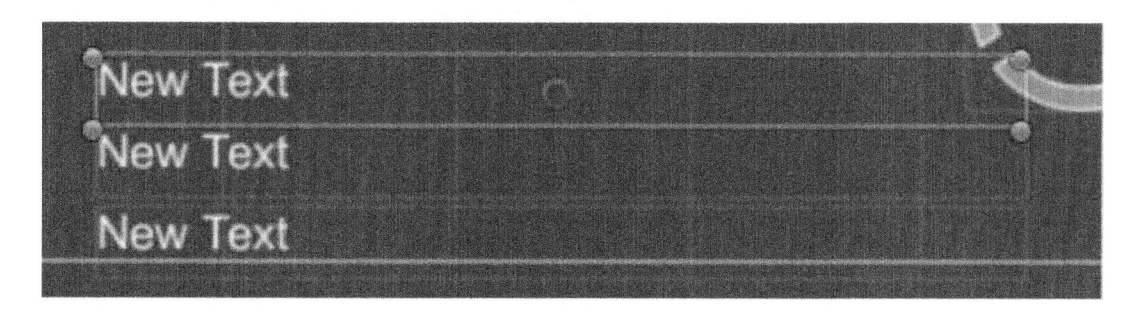

Figure 3-54: Adjusting the position of the UI Text objects

Then, we just need to modify the script **ManagePlayerHealth**.

- Please open the script **ManagePlayerHealth**.
- Add the following code at the beginning of the script.

```
using UnityEngine.UI;
```

- Modify the method **Update** as follows:

```
void Update ()
{
    print ("Health" + health);
    GameObject.Find ("healthInfo").GetComponent<Text>().text = "Health: " + health;
    GameObject.Find ("livesInfo").GetComponent<Text>().text = "Lives: " + nbLives;
}
```

> It is usually good practice not to use **GameObject.Find** or any time-consuming statements in the **Update** method. So you could, but this is only optional here, modify this code by creating a global variable that points to the object **livesInfo**. Then, you could initialize this **object** using the method **GameObject.Find** in the **Start** function; finally, you could use this object (with no use of the method **GameObject.Find**) in the **Update** function.

- You can now play the scene and check that the number of lives and health levels are displayed onscreen.

[175]

Using Finite State Machines

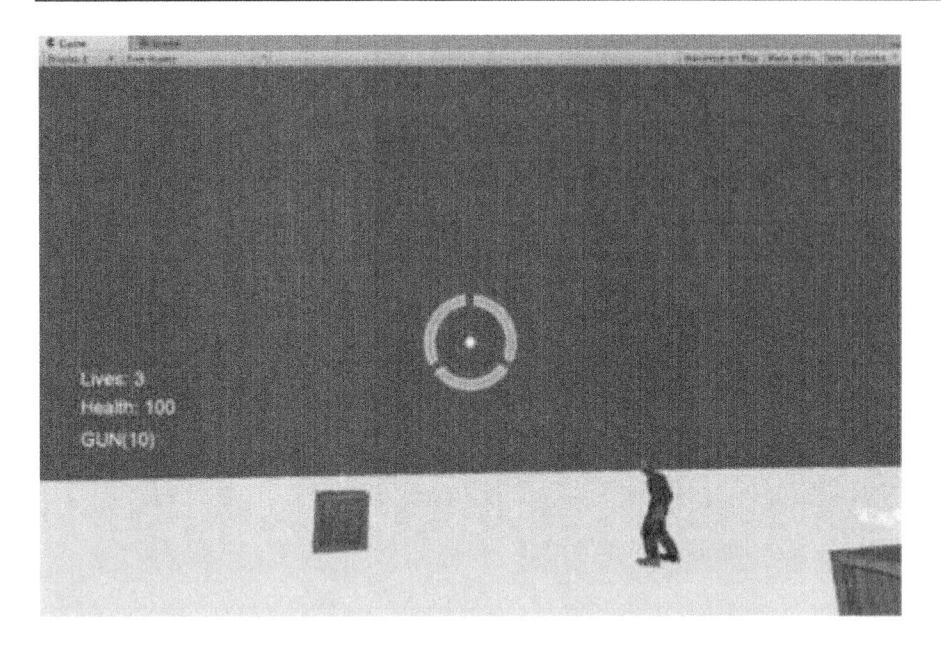

Figure 3-55: Displaying health levels and number of lives.

USING DOT PRODUCTS FOR MORE ACCURACY

Now, as you play and test the scene, you should see that the NPC will follow you whenever you walk pass him. However, the sight detection, as it is, may not be as accurate as it could be. This is because, at present, the field of view of this NPC is extremely narrow, as we expect to detect only objects at a 0 degree angle from him; not only is this not accurate, but it can cause some undesirable effects and behaviors. However, we can correct this easily using a more realistic field of view. For this we will use a bit of algebra, that is, using the dot product. The **dot product** is a mathematical concept that basically tells us about the angle between two vectors; so to mimic the field of view of the NPC, we would like to know whether the player is in front of the NPC +/- several degrees, as illustrated on the next figure.

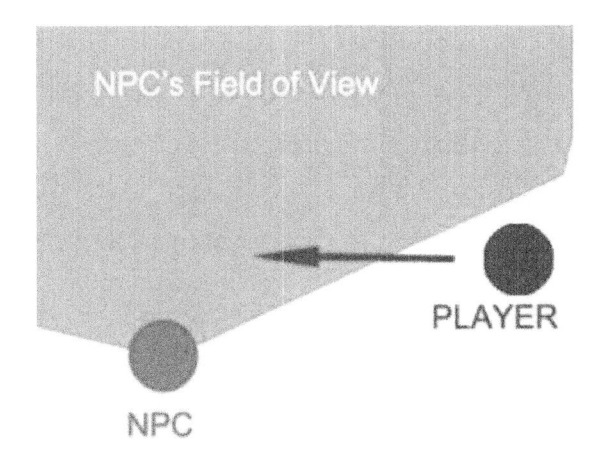

Figure 3-56: Illustrating the player's field of view

The definition of a dot product between two vectors is the product of their magnitude multiplied by the cosine of the angle between these vectors. In practical terms, we multiply the two vectors; however, to do so, we need to consider whether they are in the same direction. So the cosine will provide us with the projection of one of the vectors on the other one and multiply this projection then by the magnitude of the other vector.

> The dot product effectively tells us about the angle between these vectors and to what extent they are aligned; for example, a positive dot product indicates that the angle between the two vectors is between -90 and 90 degrees, a null dot product indicates that they are perpendicular to each other.

The formula is as follows:

D = |v1| x |v2| x Cos (alpha).

Where:

- D is the dot product between the two vectors.
- Alpha is the angle between the two vectors.

In Unity, the built-in classes make it easier to use the dot product, as demonstrated below:

```
Vector3 v1 = new Vector3 (1.0f,1.0f,1.0f);
Vector3 v2 = new Vector3 (-2.0f,-2.0f,-2.0f);
float productOfV1AndV2 = Vector3.Dot(v1,v2);
```

- Line 1: the vector v1 is created.
- Line 2: the vector v2 is created.
- Line 3: the dot product of these vectors is calculated.
- In this case, the dot product is -2; so we know that the angle between the vectors is between -90 and 90 degrees.

It would be great, however, to know more about the direction of these vectors, and more importantly if they are aligned or pointing in the same direction. For this purpose, we can normalize these vectors first (i.e., reduce their magnitude to 1). This way, if they are in the exact same direction, the dot product will be 1; and if they are in the opposite direction, the dot product will be -1. This is because when we calculate the dot product, if the magnitudes of both vectors are 1, the dot product will be equal to the cosine of the angle between these two. Because the cosine is equal to one if the angle is 0 and -1 if the angle is 180, it is now easier to check if these vectors are aligned. In Unity, we could do this as follows:

```
Vector3 v1 = new Vector3 (1.0f,1.0f,1.0f);
Vector3 v2 = new Vector3 (-2.0f,-2.0f,-2.0f);
float productOfV1AndV2 = Vector3.Dot(v1.normalized,v2. normalized);
```

- The first two lines are similar to the previous code.
- Line3: we calculate the dot product of these vectors, after they have been normalized; in this case, we will find that the dot product equals -1 (i.e., vectors are pointing to opposite directions).

If we call the field of view **alpha**, knowing whether the NPC is in the field of view is equivalent to know whether the angle determined by the direction of the NPC (V1 on the next diagram) and the vector that points at the player from the NPC (V2 in the next diagram) is comprised between -alpha/2 and alpha/2. So for a field of view of 90 degrees, the angle defined by V1 and V2 should be comprised between -45 degrees and +45 degrees. This is explained on the next diagram. As the player enters the NPCs' field of view, the vector V2 will rotate counterclockwise.

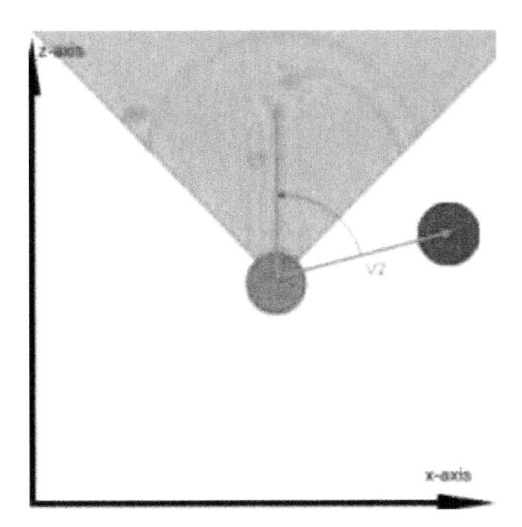

Figure 3-57: Illustrating the player entering the NPC's field of view

So, as described on the previous diagram, and knowing that cosine (45) is approximately 0.7 and that cosine (-45) is approximately also 0.7, we know that the player is in the field of view of the NPC if the angle between V1 and V2 is between -45 degrees and +45 degrees, or, in a similar way, if the cosine of the angle between the vectors V1 and V2 is comprised between 0.7 and 1. This is because when the player is on the right border of the field of view, the angle between V1 and V2 is -45° (i.e., cosine = 0.7).

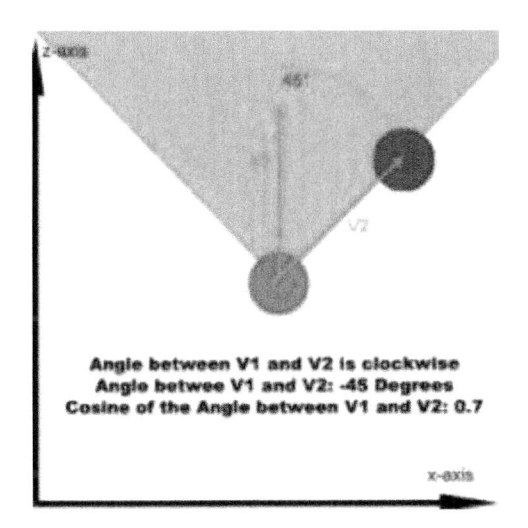

Figure 3-58: the player enters the right boundary of the field of view

- When the player is in front of the NPC, the angle between V1 and V2 is 0 (Cosine = 1).

- When the player is on the left border of the field of view, the angle between V1 and V2 is 45° (Cosine = 0.7). So effectively, when the NPC is in the field of view, the Cosine of the angle will vary between 0.7 and 1.

Using Finite State Machines

**Angle between V1 and V2 is counterclockwise
Angle betwee V1 and V2: +45 Degrees
Cosine of the Angle between V1 and V2: 0.7**

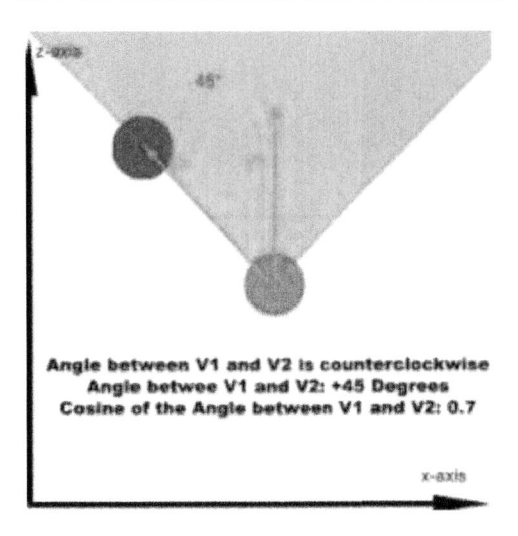

Figure 3-59: Exiting the NPC's field of view

- The field of view could be any number of your choice. We have arbitrarily chosen 90 degrees to simulate the horizontal field of view for some humans, but you could, if you wished, increase it to 100 degrees or more.

- Now that we have clarified the calculation of the **Cosine**, let's see how we can find the vectors V1 and V2.

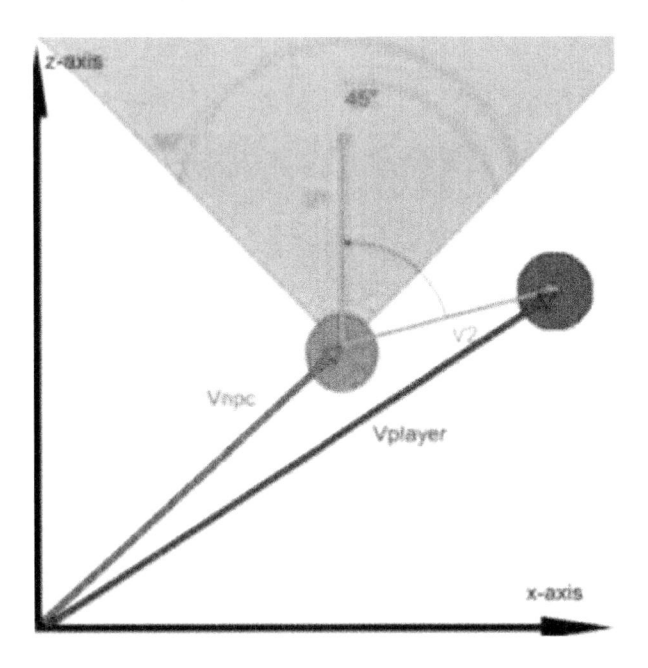

Figure 3-60: Calculating V2

- V1 is the direction of the NPC. This vector originates (on the previous diagram) from the NPC and is going in the direction of the positive z-axis. V2 is determined by the position

[180]

of both the NPC and the Player. Let's see how. As you can see on the next diagram, V2, Vnpc and Vplayer form a triangle. Vnpc is the vector for the position of the NPC. It starts at the origin of the coordinate system. Vplayer is the vector for the position of the NPC and, as for the previous vector, it starts at the origin of the coordinate system. If we operate a loop from the origin of the coordinate system, we can go from the origin of the coordinate system to the NPC by following the vector Vnpc, we follow the vector V2 (in reverse: from the head to the tail), and then following the vector Vplayer (in reverse: from the head to the tail). So we could say that: **Vnpc + V2-Vplayer = 0**; in other words, by following Vnpc, then V2 in reverse and Vplayer in reverse, we end up at the same point. Following this, we can then say that: V2 = -Vnpc + Vplayer (we add -V2 to both sides of the previous equation). This is how we can calculate V2.

- Normalizing the vectors: so at this stage, we know V1 and V2 and we just need to calculate the dot product between these to have an idea of the cosine of the angle. However, if you remember the definition of a dot product, the cosine of this angle equals the dot product only if the magnitude of the vectors is 1, or in other words, if these vectors have been normalized. Normalizing can be done easily in Unity as each vector can access the function/method **normalized** which returns a normalized version accordingly.

- At this stage, we have two normalized vectors (magnitude equals 1) and we need to calculate the cosine of the angle defined by them. You will notice that so far, we have been using degrees for angles (FOV=90°). However, the function that calculates the Cosine in Unity only takes Radians (and not Degrees) as parameters. So we will need to convert our angle in radians first before the cosine can be calculated. This can be done using the function **Mathf.Deg2Rad** in Unity.

- Now we have an angle expressed in radians and we can calculate the dot product of the normalized versions of V1 and V2. That's great! Bearing in mind that when the player is on the right boundary of the field of view, the angle between V1 and V2 is -45° (Cosine = 0.7), when the player is in front of the NPC, the angle between V1 and V2 is 0 (Cosine = 1), and that when the player is on the left border of the field of view, the angle between V1 and V2 is 45° (Cosine = 0.7), we effectively know that for the NPC to detect the player (or the player to enter the Field of View of the NPC), the cosine of the angle between V1 and V2 should be comprised between 0.7 and 1.

Now that the principle of dot products is clear, we could apply it to our own code, as follows:

- Please open the script **ControlNPCFSM**.

- Please add the following code at the beginning of the script.

```
public Vector3 direction;
public bool isInTheFieldOfView;
public bool noObjectBetweenNPCAndPlayer = false;
```

- Add the following code at the beginning of the **Update** method.

Using Finite State Machines

```
direction = (GameObject. Find("FPSController").transform.position - transform.position).normalized;
isInTheFieldOfView = (Vector3.Dot(transform.forward.normalized, direction) > .7);
Debug.DrawRay(transform.position, direction * 100, Color.green);
Debug.DrawRay(transform.position, transform.forward * 100, Color.blue);
if (Physics.Raycast(transform.position, direction * 100, out hit))
{
        if (hit.collider.gameObject.tag == "Player") noObjectBetweenNPCAndPlayer = true;
        else noObjectBetweenNPCAndPlayer = false;
}
if (noObjectBetweenNPCAndPlayer && isInTheFieldOfView)
{
        anim.SetBool ("canSeePlayer", true);
        transform.LookAt(GameObject.Find("playerMiddle").transform);

}
else anim.SetBool ("canSeePlayer", false);
```

In the previous code:

- We set the variable **direction** to be the direction between the player and the NPC.

- We then set the variable **isInTheFieldOfView** to true if the dot product between the direction of the NPC and the vector direction (i.e., direction if the NPC had to look at the player) is between .7 and 1. Note that we use normalized vectors, so the dot product can only be between -1 and 1.

- We also cast two rays that you will be able to see in the scene view: one in the NPC's direction (i.e., forward), and the other one from the NPC and toward the player.

- Once this is done, we cast a ray between the NPC and the player.

- So if this ray collides with the NPC object, we know that there is nothing between the NPC and the player.

- Finally, if there are no objects between the NPC and the player and the player is in the field of view, we set the animation parameter to true, otherwise it is set to false.

Finally, we can also comment the previous code that was used to detect if the player was in the line of sight, as follows, within the **Update** method.

Using Finite State Machines

```
/*
objectInSight = "";
Debug.DrawRay (ray.origin, ray.direction * 100, Color.red);
if (Physics.Raycast(ray.origin, ray.direction * 100, out hit))
{
        objectInSight = hit.collider.gameObject.tag;
        print ("Object in Sight" + objectInSight);
        if (objectInSight == "Player")
        {
                anim.SetBool ("canSeePlayer",true);
                print ("Just saw the Player");
        }
}
*/
```

You can now play the scene; you can look at the **Scene** view and the **Game** view simultaneously if you wish; as you move the player around, look at the two rays originating from the NPC and the angle between them, as illustrated on the next figure.

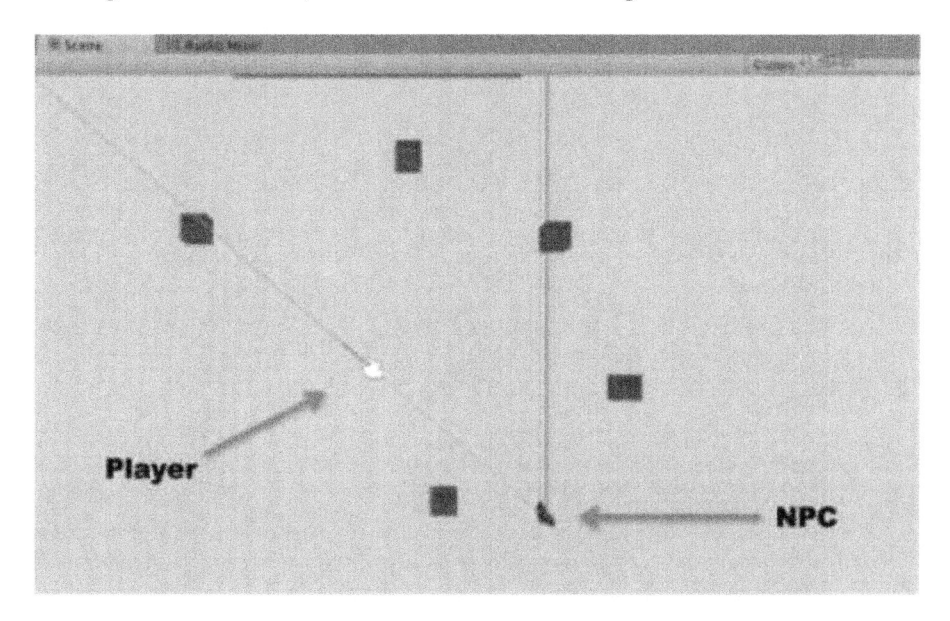

- Once you reach the 45-degree angle within the NPC's field of view, the NPC will start to follow you.

So, as you can see, simple algebra can be very handy to solve some challenges paused by game design, and dot products are extremely useful in the case of fields of view.

[183]

Using Finite State Machines

ADDING A SCREEN FLASH WHEN THE PLAYER IS HIT

As the NPC can target us, it would be great to add feedback as to when we have been hit by the NPC. One common ways to do this is to add a screen flash; that is, a brief moment when the screen flashes to red. There are many ways to achieve this effect, and one of them is to create a texture or color material and quickly fade its alpha (i.e., transparency) value from opaque to fully transparent.

So here, we will achieve this effect using a **UI Image** component.

- Please create a new **UI | Image** object.
- Rename it **screenFlash**.

Please change its **Rect Transform** properties as follows:

- Type: **Stretch/Stretch**.
- Left: **0**.
- Top: **0**.
- Pos Z: **0**.
- Right: **1**.
- Bottom: **1**.

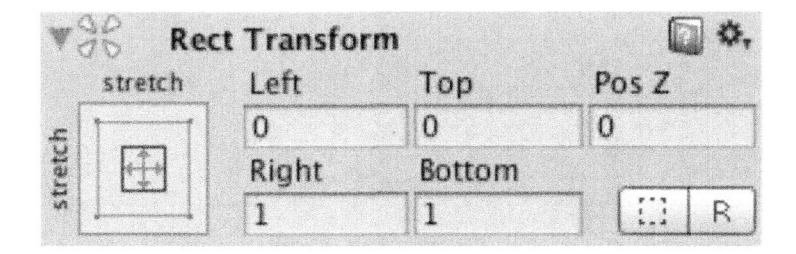

Figure 3-61: Modifying the properties of the UI Image

- This will ensure that the image fills the screen.
- Please change its **color** to **red** and its **transparency to 100%** (Alpha = 0). The transparency attribute is marked as **A** on the second figure.

Using Finite State Machines

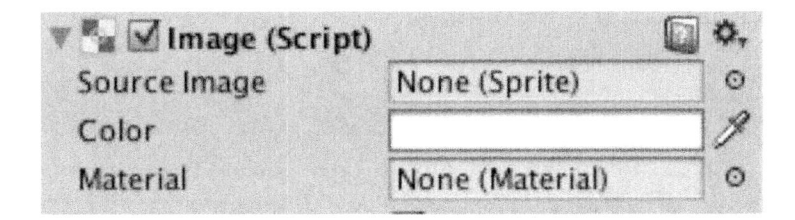

Figure 3-62: Changing the color and transparency of the UI Image (part 1)

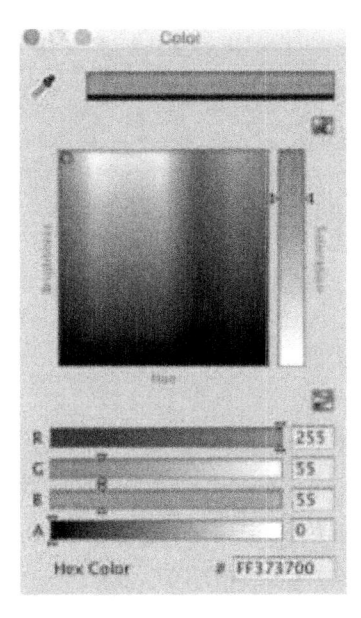

Figure 3-63: Changing the color and transparency of the UI Image (part 2)

We will now modify the script **ManagePlayerHealth** so that this red screen appears briefly whenever the player is hit.

- Please open the script **ManagePlayerHealth** and add the following code at the beginning.

```
public float alpha;
public bool screenFlashBool;
```

- Then add the following code at the end of the method **decreaseHealth**.

```
screenFlash();
```

- Add the following to the **Start** method.

[185]

Using Finite State Machines

```
alpha = 0;
GameObject.Find("screenFlash").GetComponent<Image>().color = new Color (1,0,0,alpha);
screenFlashBool = false;
```

- In the previous code, we set the color of the **screenFlash** object, using the RGB code (i.e., Red = 1, Green = 0, Blue = 0) to red and its alpha value to 0 (i.e., transparent). The RGB values are normalized here; this means that the values will range between 0 and 1;

- Add the following method at the end of the class:

```
private void screenFlash ()
{
    screenFlashBool = true;
    alpha = 1.0f;
    print ("Screen Flash");
}
```

- In the previous code, we specify that the screen flash effect should start, and we then set the **alpha** value of the **screenFlash** object to **1** (i.e., it will initially be opaque and progressively become transparent).

- Finally, add the following code to the **Update** method.

```
if (screenFlashBool)
{
    alpha -= Time.deltaTime;
    GameObject.Find("screenFlash").GetComponent<Image>().color = new Color (1,0,0,alpha);
    if (alpha <=0)
    {
        screenFlashBool = false;
        alpha = 0;
    }
}
```

In the previous code:

- We decrease the alpha value of the **screenFlash** object.

- When this value has reached **0** (i.e., totally transparent) the screen flash effect can be stopped.

- Please save your code and check that the screen flash appears whenever the player has been hit.

Using Finite State Machines

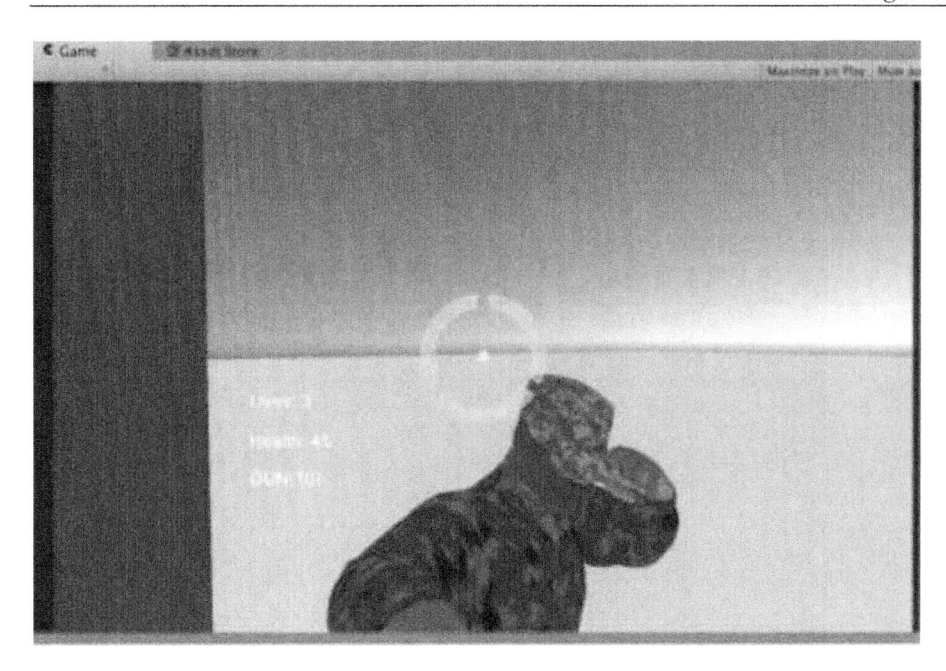

Figure 3-64: The player is about to get hit by the NPC

Figure 3-65: The screen flash is displayed when the player is hit

So all seems to work well, we can now save our NPC and create a prefab with it, so that it can be reused at a later stage.

- Please drag and drop the object **NPC1** to the project window.

- Rename the prefab **npc_guard**.
- In the **Hierarchy** window, the object **NPC1** should turn into an object called **npc_guard**.
- Drag and drop the prefab **npc_guard** several times in the scene, and test the game.

CREATING NEW PREFABS

Now that all works well, we could create prefabs with some of the objects that we may reuse later on.

We can then create groups of objects:

- Please rename the **Canvas** object **UI** (assuming that you have created all the UI objects within this canvas); Unity usually includes all UI elements within the same canvas object by default.

- Create a prefab with the object **UI** (by dragging and dropping this object to the **Project** window) so that its elements can be reused in a different scene.

- You can also create a new prefab based on the object **FPSController** (its default name will be **FPSController**; please keep this name for the prefab for now). When you do so, make sure that you create this prefab in the folder called Assets or another folder of your choice, so that you can identify and use this particular prefab easily later on.

> If you have made any modifications to the objects **npc_guard**, you can update its corresponding prefab also.

After playing the scene you may notice that the gun may always be active for some of the NPCs; this may be, in part, due to the fact that, when we created our scene initially, there was only one NPC and also only one gun; so the following code made perfect sense:

```
gun = GameObject.Find("hand_gun");
```

However, as we add more NPCs, there will inevitably be more characters, hence more objects with the name **hand_gun**. So we need to make sure that when we activate or deactivate a gun, the object that we manipulate is in this case a child of the NPC to which the script **ControlNPCFSM** is attached. To do so, we just need to replace the previous code, in the script ControlNPCFSM, with the following code:

```
gun = transform.Find("hand_gun").gameObject;
```

In the previous code, we specifically target the object named **hand_gun**, which is a child of the NPC to which the script is attached.

Please modify the script, save it, and test the scene.

Using Finite State Machines

LEVEL ROUNDUP

In this chapter, we have learned how to create and manage a finite state machine. We became more comfortable with creating states, transitions, and parameters. We managed to create NPCs that behave relatively realistically and to control their behaviors through our scripts. So, again, we have covered considerable ground to produce a relatively interesting scenario. In the next section, we will create a last level where we put all these skills together.

Checklist

> You can consider moving to the next stage if you can do the following:
>
> - Create an **Animator Controller**.
> - Create states, parameters, and transitions.
> - Add animations to a state and configure this animation.
> - Manage a state from a script.
> - Detect, from a script, if a state is transitioning.

Using Finite State Machines

Quiz

Now, let's check your knowledge! Please answer the following questions (the answers are included one the next page).

1. It is possible to duplicate an Animator Controller using the keys *CTRL + D*.

2. The following code will change the value of a Boolean parameter for an animation.

```
SetParameter("canSeePlayer", true).
```

3. The variable type **AnimatorInfo** can be used to provide information about a specific animation.

4. By default, within an Animation Controller, a Boolean parameter is set to false.

5. If the **Animator** linked to this script is in the state **FOLLOW_PLAYER**, the following code will display the message **We are in the FOLLOW_PLAYER Mode**.

```
private Animator anim;
private AnimatorStateInfo info;
anim = GetComponent<Animator>();
info = anim.GetCurrentAnimatorStateInfo(0);
if (info.IsName("FOLLOW_PLAYER")) print ("We are in the FOLLOW_PLAYER Mode");
```

6. When using finite state machines, it is possible to have two states active at the same time.

7. In Mecanim, for a transition to occur between two states, a condition always needs to be defined.

8. The following code will stop the movement of a **NavMeshAgent**.

```
GetComponent<NavMeshAgent>().Stop();
```

9. The following code, provided that the script is linked to an object that includes a **NavMeshAgent**, will display the distance between the NPC and its destination.

```
print (GetComponent<NavMeshAgent>().remainingDistance);
```

10. Complete the following code so that we can test if the **Animator** is transitioning and that the next state is **GoBacktoStart**.

```
if(anim.IsInTransition(0)&& MISSING CODE)
```

[191]

Answers to the Quiz

1. TRUE.
2. FALSE.
3. TRUE.
4. TRUE.
5. TRUE.
6. FALSE.
7. FALSE.
8. TRUE.
9. TRUE.
10.

```
if(anim.IsInTransition(0)&&
anim.GetNextAnimatorStateInfo(0).IsName("GoBacktoStart")))
```

Challenge 1

Now that you have managed to complete this chapter and that you have improved your skills, you could use these to improve the flow of your game. So for this challenge, you will be creating a new type of NPC that will behave as follows:

- It will be similar to the first NPC (guard).
- It will not move from its spot.
- It will shoot at the player when it sees him/her.

Challenge 2

In this challenge, you can create another type of NPC; this NPC will do the following:

- Always look for the player using a **NavMeshAgent**.
- Shoot at the player when the player is in sight and the distance between them is less than 10 meters.
- All other aspects of its behavior are the same as the **guard**.

4
PUTTING IT ALL TOGETHER

In this section we will put all the skills that we have learned to create a fully functional level with the following features:

- The player has three lives.

- The player will then need to collect 10 objects in the scene to win.

- The player will need to avoid or neutralize NPCs.

- The level will include a combination of safe and dangerous areas.

- Ammos will be present in places and possibly re-spawn when the player runs low on ammunitions.

- NPCs will be present at the start of the game.

- The player wins if he/she has collected all 10 objects.

- The player will lose if s/he has no lives left.

Putting it all together

SETTING-UP THE ENVIRONMENT MANUALLY

To setup the environment, we will generate an indoor scene using the duplication techniques that were covered in the very first book in the series. We will create a box, texture it, and duplicate it to generate the outline of a simple maze.

- Please save the previous scene with a name of your choice.

- Create a new scene and rename it (i.e., save it as) **gameLevel**, or any other name of your choice.

- Create a new box, rename it **ground**, set its scale property to **(100, 1, 100)** and its position to **(0, 0, 0)**.

- You can also create a material for the ground if you wish or create and apply a blue **Material** to this object.

- You can also change the **Light** settings for the scene (**Window | Lighting**) or add a new light of your choice.

Next, we will create an object that will be used to instantiate the walls.

- Please create a new cube.

- Rename it **wall**.

- Set its **scale** property to **(10, 3, 10)**.

- Set its **y** position to **2**, so that it appears just above the ground.

- You can also create and apply a red **Material** to this object.

Once this is done, you can duplicate this shape several times and move the duplicates to achieve a layout similar to the following one (viewed from above).

Putting it all together

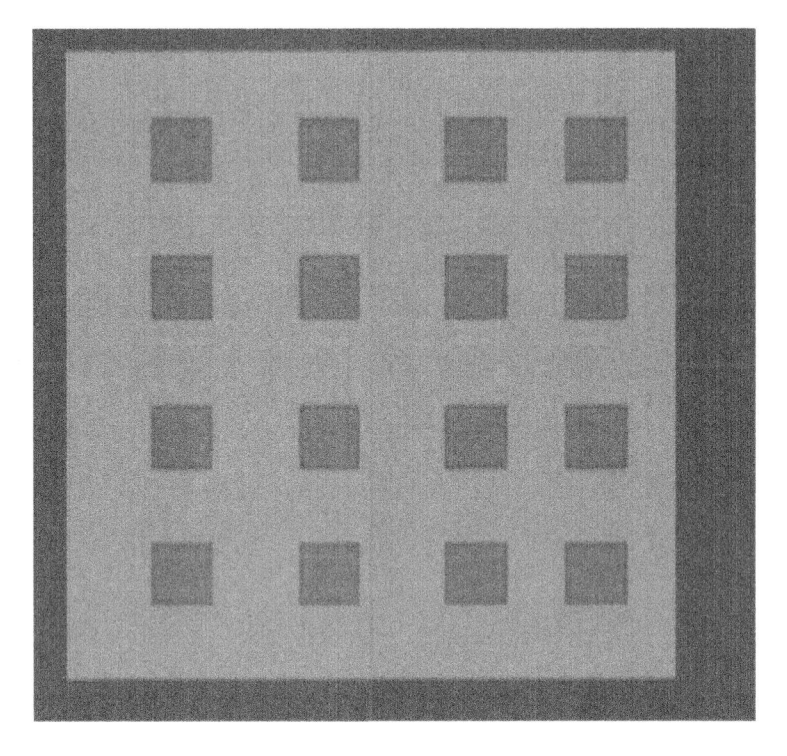

Figure 4-1: Above view of the maze

- You can deactivate the main camera.

- Drag and drop the prefab **UI** to the scene. This prefab includes UI elements that display health and ammo information too.

- Drag and drop the prefab **FPSController** (the one you have just created in the previous scene and stored in the **Assets** folder) to this scene. As you look for this prefab, you will find two prefabs with the same name (the original built-in prefab and the one you have modified in the previous chapters). So, to make sure you have the right one, select it and check in the **Inspector** window that it includes two scripts **ManagePlayerHealth** and **ManageCollisionWithPlayer2**.

- Play the scene and check that you can see your ammunitions and also use your weapons.

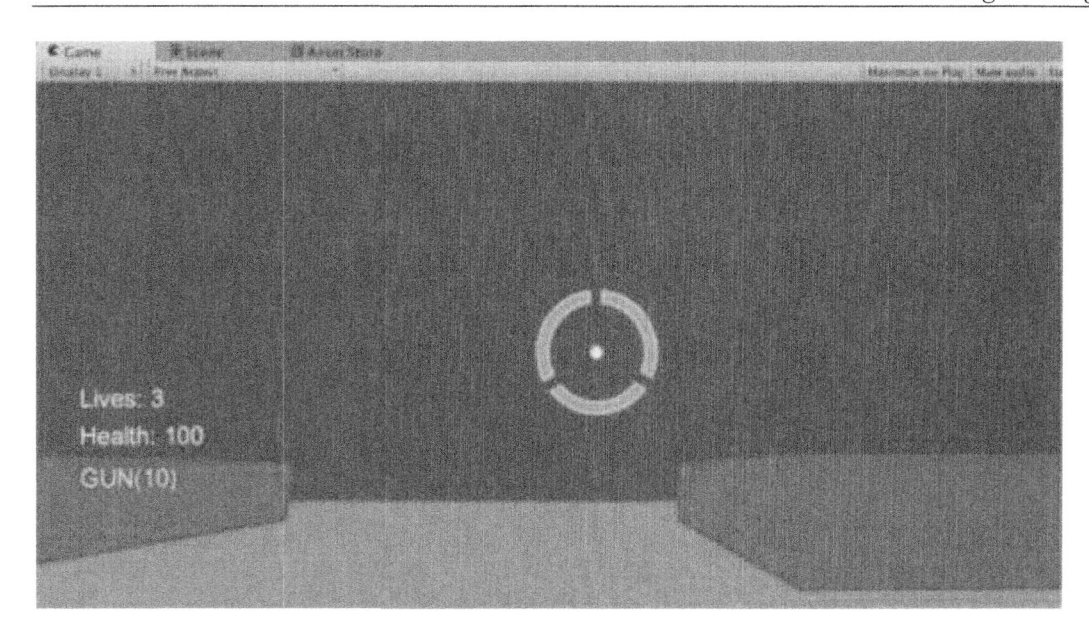

Figure 4-2: Testing the new scene made from prefabs

- Then drag and drop some ammunitions and health packs prefabs in the scene.

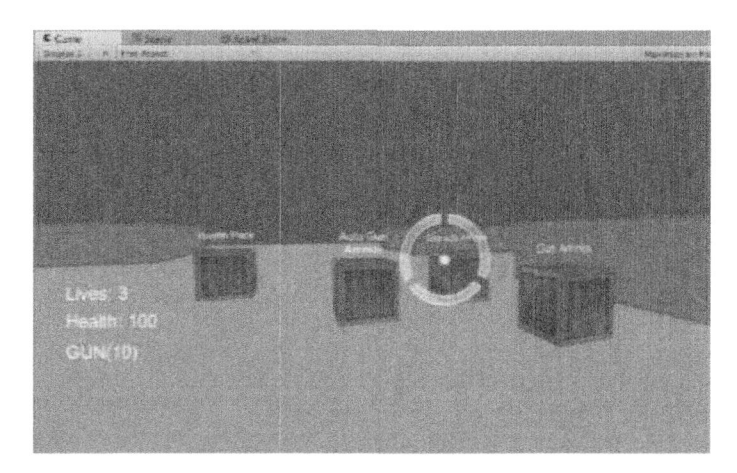

Figure 4-3: Adding med packs to the scene

Next, we can start to add NPCs by dragging one or several **npc_guard** prefabs in the scene. You can also rotate them so that they face a particular direction. To increase the difficulty of this level, you can place these guards near the ammunitions, for example.

Putting it all together

Next, we will compute the Navmesh information so that our NPC can navigate properly:

- Select all the ammos, med packs, the walls and the ground in the scene.
- Switch to the **Navigation** window.
- Check the box **Navigation Static**.

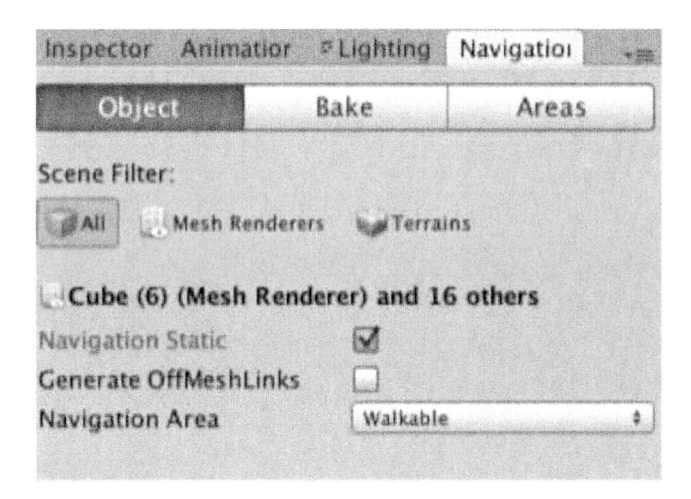

Figure 4-4: Setting navigation attributes

- And click on the button **Bake** located in the bottom-right corner of the **Navigation** window. If a window asks whether you would like to "modify the children", please click on **Yes**.
- Once the baking process is complete, the scene view should look as follows:

Putting it all together

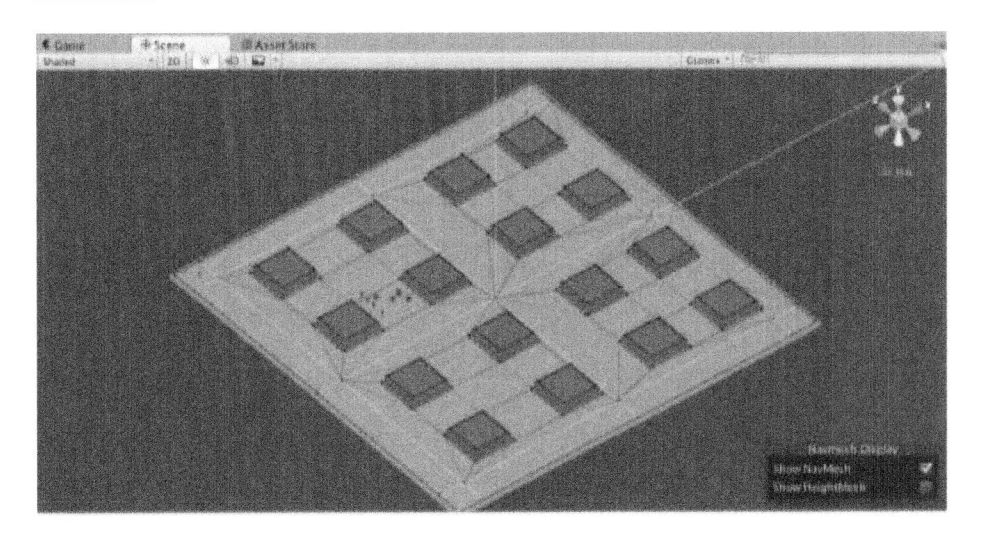

So now, we just need to:

- Add objects to collect.

- Count them as we collect them.

- Load the **Win** scene when the player has collected all of them.

- Load the **Lose** scene when the player has been killed (i.e., nbLives = 0).

First let's create two scenes: one for when the player wins and the other one for when the player loses.

- Please save the current scene.

- Create a new scene and rename it **loseScene** (e.g., using **File | Save Scene As…**).

- Add a simple **UI Text** element that says "**Too Bad, you've just lost**".

- Adjust the size and position of this object so that it is displayed onscreen.

- Save the scene.

- Copy this scene (using the **Inspector** window), rename the duplicate **winScene**, and change the **UI Text** object so that it displays **"Congratulations"**. To look for all the scenes in the project, you can use the key words **t:scene** in the **Project**'s search window. Then you can duplicate the scene by selecting it and then pressing *CTRL + D*. You can rename and open the duplicate scene to modify it.

- Once this is done, save the scene and go back to the **gameLevel** scene.

- Add this scene, as well as the **win** and **lose** scenes to the build settings (**File | Build Settings**).

Putting it all together

Once this is done, we just need to gain access to these scenes from our scripts.

- Please open the script **ManagePlayerHealth**.
- Modify the script as follows (new code in bold).

```
public void restartLevel()
{
        nbLives --;
        health = 100;
        if (nbLives >=0) Application.LoadLevel(Application.loadedLevel);
        else Application.LoadLevel("lostScene");
}
```

Next, we will work on adding objects to collect and count them.

- Create a sphere that will need to be collected by the player.
- Create a tag called **pick_me** (if not done yet), and apply it to this sphere.
- Add a color to this sphere if you wish.
- Duplicate this sphere nine times and move the duplicates in different locations (i.e., far apart from each other)

Then we will modify the scripts **ManageWeapons2**.

- Open this script.
- Create a private integer variable called **score**.
- Initialize it to 0 in the **Start** method.
- Modify the method **manageCollision** as follows (i.e., add the following code at the end of the method).

```
if (tagOfTheOtherObject =="pick_me")
{
        Destroy (hit.collider.gameObject);
        score++;
        if (score >=9) Application.LoadLevel("winScene");
}
```

Last but not least, please make sure that you have added the new scenes **gameLevel**, **winScene** and **lostScene** to the build settings (if it has no been done yet), so that they can be loaded accordingly.

Putting it all together

Please save this script (i.e., **ManageWeapons2**) and test the game; you should see that after collecting all the spheres, the scene **winScene** will be displayed.

This being said, you may also notice that there is an error message in the Console window ("**Object reference not set to an object**"). This error may occur in the scripts **ManageWeapons2** and **ManagePlayerHealth**. This is due to the fact that the player is not destroyed before the win scene is loaded.

So we will modify these scripts as follows.

- Please open the script **ManageWeapons2**.
- Replace the following line in the **Update** method....

```
GameObject.Find("userInfo").GetComponent<Text>().text = weaponName[currentWeapon]+ "("+ammos[currentWeapon]+")";
```

... with this code...

```
if(GameObject.Find("userInfo")!=null) GameObject.Find("userInfo").GetComponent<Text>().text = weaponName[currentWeapon]+ "("+ammos[currentWeapon]+")";
```

- Then open the script **ManagePlayerHealth**.
- Replace the following code...

```
GameObject.Find ("healthInfo").GetComponent<Text>().text = "Health: " + health;
GameObject.Find ("livesInfo").GetComponent<Text>().text = "Lives: " + nbLives;
```

...with this code...

```
if (GameObject.Find ("healthInfo") !=null) GameObject.Find ("healthInfo").GetComponent<Text>().text = "Health: " + health;
if (GameObject.Find ("livesInfo") != null) GameObject.Find ("livesInfo").GetComponent<Text>().text = "Lives: " + nbLives;
```

You can now test your game again and ensure that no errors appear in the **Console** window after you win the game.

SETTING-UP THE ENVIRONMENT THROUGH SCRIPTING

This section is optional; however, it may be useful if you would like to generate environments from your script; as we have seen in the previous section, you can set-up your environment manually by creating walls and moving them in particular locations; however, there are times when you would like to generate the maze from the script; this approach has several advantages including: the possibility to create random levels, less time spent moving objects to create your maze, and the possibility to use algorithms that generate the maze automatically; so the next instructions will give you a heads-up on how this can be done.

To setup the environment, we will generate an indoor level using scripting.

We will proceed as follows:

- Create an array that represents the environment.
- Read the array.
- Instantiate objects based on the numbers read in the array.

So let's get started:

- Please create a new scene and rename it **gameLevelAuto** (or any other name of your choice).
- Create a new cube and rename it **ground**.
- Make sure that the ground **scale** property is **(100, 1, 100)** and its position **(0,0,0)**.
- You can also create a material for the ground if you wish.

Next, we will create an object that will be used to instantiate the walls.

- Create a new cube.
- Rename it **wall**.
- Set its **scale** property to **(10,2,10)**.
- You can also create and apply a blue **Material** to this object or use any other texture of your choice.
- Once this is done, you can create a prefab from this object, rename this prefab **wall**, and deactivate the object **wall** in the **Hierarchy** window.

Next, we will create a script that will generate our maze.

Putting it all together

- Create a new C# script and rename it **GenerateMaze**.
- Open this script and add the following code at the beginning of the class (just before the **Start** method).

```
public GameObject wall, player, npc_guard;
private int [,] worldMap = new int [,]
{
{1,1,1,1,1,1,1,1,1,1},
{1,2,1,0,0,0,0,0,0,1},
{1,0,1,0,1,0,1,0,0,1},
{1,0,1,0,0,0,0,0,0,1},
{1,0,1,1,1,1,0,0,0,1},
{1,0,0,0,0,0,0,0,0,1},
{1,0,1,0,1,0,1,1,1,1},
{1,0,0,1,0,0,0,0,0,1},
{1,0,1,0,0,0,0,0,0,1},
{1,1,1,1,1,1,1,1,1,1},
};
```

In the previous code:

- We declare three public **GameObject** variables that will be used as placeholders in the **Inspector** window to set the objects to instantiate with the corresponding prefabs.

- We then declare an array (two-dimensional array) of integers. The structure of this array mirrors the structure of the maze that we would like to create; for example the top row could be the north wall, the bottom row could represent the south wall, etc. So each value of **1** represents a wall, and each **0** represents an empty space.

- In its entirety, the array will represent the outline of our maze; the 1s represent walls, and the 0s represent empty spaces for now. Each row of the array is defined using opening and closing brackets with values within separated by commas.

Please add the following code to the **Start** method:

Putting it all together

```
int i,j;
for (i = 0; i < 10; i++)
{
        for (j = 0; j < 10; j++)
        {
                GameObject t;
                if (worldMap [i,j] == 1) t = (GameObject)(Instantiate (wall, new Vector3 (50-i*10, 1.5f, 50-j*10), Quaternion.identity));
                if (worldMap [i,j] == 2)
                {
                        t = (GameObject)(Instantiate (player, new Vector3 (50-i*10, 1.5f, 50-j*10), Quaternion.identity));
                        t.name = "FPSController";
                }
        }
}
```

In the previous code:

- We declare two integers **i** and **j**; these will refer to specific rows and columns in our array. For example if **i equals 1 and j = 1**, we will be looking at the row **1** and the column **1**. Because each array starts at 0, these will effectively be the second row and the second column in our array.

- We then create two loops; these loops will go through each row of our array.

- We then check the value of each element read in the array.

- If the value is **1**, we instantiate a **wall** prefab accordingly.

- If the value is **2**, we instantiate a **player** prefab (i.e., First-Person Controller).

Now, we just need to finish our setup as follows:

- Save your script.

- Check that it is error-free.

- Create an empty object and rename it **generateMaze**.

- Then drag and drop the script **GenerateMaze** to the object **generateMaze**.

- Once this is done, select the object **generateMaze**.

- Make sure that the **Inspector** window is active.

- Look at the parameter called **wall** for the script **GenerateMaze** attached to this object, and drag and drop the prefab **wall** to this variable.

Putting it all together

- Drag and drop the prefab **FPSController** (ensuring it is the one that you have created in the previous chapters; this prefab should be located in your **Assets** folder and include the scripts **ManageCollisionWithPlayer2** and **ManagePlayerHealth**) to the variable **player**.

- Drag and drop the prefab **npc_guard** from the **Project** window to the variable **guard**.

- You can deactivate the object **FPSController** that is already in the **Hierarchy** (if any).

- You can deactivate the object **Main Camera** that is already in the **Hierarchy**.

- Finally, you can also drag and drop the prefab **UI** to the scene, so that you can see information on your number of lives and ammunitions.

- Once this is done, you can play the scene, and check the layout either from the **Scene** view or the **Game** view.

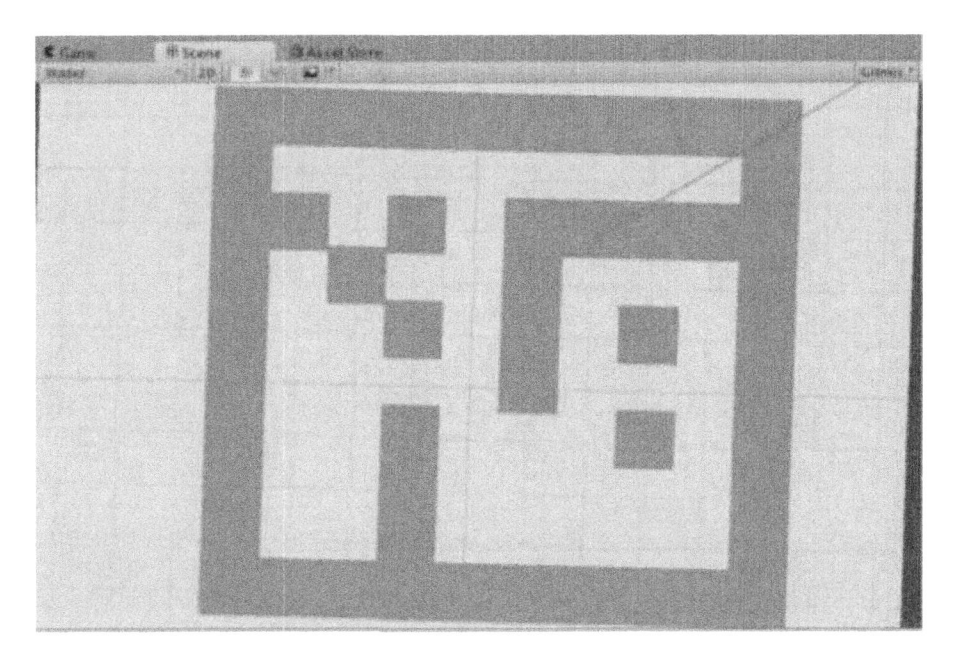

Figure 4-5: The maze viewed from above

Putting it all together

[Figure: Unity Game view showing maze from player's perspective with HUD displaying Lives: 3, Health: 100, GUN(10)]

Figure 4-6: The maze viewed from the player's perspective

Next, we could try to add a few guards by modifying the script **GenerateMaze** as follows:

- Please modify the array as follows by adding 3s in places (you can add them where you wish).

{1,1,1,1,1,1,1,1,1,1},
{1,2,1,0,0,0,0,**3**,0,1},
{1,0,1,0,1,0,1,0,0,1},
{1,0,1,0,0,0,0,0,0,1},
{1,0,1,1,1,1,0,0,0,1},
{1,**3**,0,0,0,**3**,0,0,0,1},
{1,0,1,0,1,0,1,1,1,1},
{1,0,0,1,0,0,0,0,0,1},
{1,**3**,1,0,0,0,0,0,**3**,1},
{1,1,1,1,1,1,1,1,1,1},

- Also add the following code within the **Start** method, within the conditional statement (new code in bold).

[206]

Putting it all together

```
for (i = 0; i < 10; i++)
{
    for (j = 0; j < 10; j++)
    {
        GameObject t;
        if (worldMap [i,j] == 1) t = (GameObject)(Instantiate (wall, new Vector3 (50-i*10, 1.5f, 50-j*10), Quaternion.identity));
        if (worldMap [i,j] == 2)
        {
            t = (GameObject)(Instantiate (player, new Vector3 (50-i*10, 1.5f, 50-j*10), Quaternion.identity));
            t.name = "FPSController";
        }
        if (worldMap [i,j] == 3) t = (GameObject)(Instantiate (npc_guard, new Vector3 (50-i*10, 0.5f, 50-j*10), Quaternion.identity));
    }
}
```

- Save your code.

- Check that it is error-free using the **Console** window.

- Select the object **ground**, then, using the **Navigation** window, select the option **Navigation Static**, and click on **Bake**.

- You can now test the scene.

- As a guard sees you, and possibly loses sight of the player, you may notice that it goes through the walls to reach its final destination. This is because, contrary to what we have done in previous chapters, we have not baked the scene (i.e., the walls), so Unity has not computed any of the necessary paths for the NPC.

- Unfortunately, at present there is no way to bake the scene at run time; however, there is a trick that we can use, that is, to add a **NavMeshObstacle** component to the wall component. By doing this, we ensure that the NPC will avoid the walls on its way back to the player.

So now you can do the following:

- Select the **wall** object in the scene and activate it.

- Open the **Navigation** window.

- Select the option **Navigation Static** and then click on the button **Bake**.

- The baking process is still necessary here so that the **NavMeshAgent** for our NPC finds its destination.

[207]

- Once this is done, add a **NavMeshObstacle** component to the wall (**Component | Navigation | NavMeshObstacle**).

- Update the corresponding prefab by clicking on the button **Apply** located in the top-right corner of the **Inspector** window or by dragging and dropping the **wall** object to the **wall** prefab.

- You can now deactivate the **wall** object in the scene (since the prefab has been updated).

- Once this is done, please check the scene.

Once you have checked that everything works fine, you can start to add other objects, including med packs, ammunitions, or the objects to collect using the same array (or a different array if you wish).

LEVEL ROUNDUP

In this chapter, we have learned how to combine the skills that you have acquired to date in order to design a challenging level. We looked at reusing prefabs, and also generating a level automatically, and all of that using C#. So let's take a look back from the start of the book and appreciate your progress; you have learned to:

- Create C# code.
- Create classes.
- Apply C# in your scenes.
- Use rigid bodies.
- Create simple and more complex weapons.
- Create prefabs so that you can reuse relatively complex behaviors, objects and scripts.
- Create Finite State Machines (FSMs).
- Apply these FSMs to animated characters.
- Create realistic behaviors for NPCs whereby NPCs can detect the player using sight and field of view, and then walk towards and attack the player.
- Use relatively interesting algebra concepts such as **dot product** to simulate a field of view.
- Generate a level procedurally.

So, well, you have covered a lot and congratulations for reaching this stage of the book.

5
USING OFF-MESH LINKS, AREAS AND COSTS

In this section, we will start by creating simple AI using Unity's built-in library, including:

- Simple AI (drag and drop) from Unity's built in AI characters.
- Group AI.
- Collision detection.
- Off-mesh links.
- Costs.

So, after completing this chapter, you will be able to:

- Create an NPC that follows the player.
- Create several NPCs with the same behavior.
- Detect collision between the NPC and the player.
- Use off-mesh links and costs for the NPCs' navigation.

SETTING UP THE ENVIRONMENT

In this section, we will set-up the environment; it will consist of:

- A scene with a ground (i.e., a scaled box).
- A first person-controller for the player.
- Non Player Characters (NPCs).

So, let's get started:

- Please open Unity and create a new scene.
- Locate the folder called **Characters** within the folder called **Standard Assets**, as illustrated in the next figure.

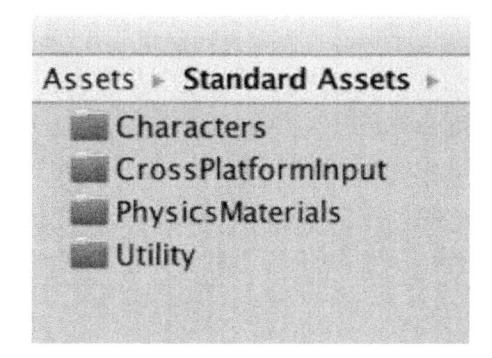

Figure 7: The Characters folder

This package includes the prefabs (or templates) that we will be able to use to implement our first-person character and the NPCs.

Once this is done, we can start to build our environment and add Non-Player Characters (NPCs) to it:

- Please create a new cube (**GameObject | 3D Object | Cube**); this will create a new object called **Cube** in the **Hierarchy** window.
- Using the **Hierarchy** window, rename this object **ground**.
- Using the **Inspector**, modify its **scale** to **(100, 1, 100)**.

SIMPLE AI (DRAG AND DROP) USING UNITY'S BUILT-IN AI CHARACTERS

Once the basic set-up is complete, we can now start to add our player and the NPCs.

- Please drag and drop the prefab called **FPSController** from the **Project** folder (within the folder called **Standard Assets | Characters | FirstPersonCharacter | Prefabs**) to the **Scene** view.

- It will create an object called **FPSController**.

- Change the position of this object to **(8, 0, -4)**.

- Please drag and drop the prefab called **AIThirdPersonController** from the **Project** folder (i.e., from within the folder **Standard Assets | Characters | ThirdPersonCharacter | Prefabs**) to the **Scene** view.

- Change its position to **(16, 0, -11)**.

Once you have added these two characters, you can test the scene (i.e., press **CTRL + P**) and walk toward the third-person controller; you should see that it is immobile, as per the next figure.

Figure 8: The NPC

What we'd like to do now, is to add the ability for the NPC to follow the player. This will involve setting a target for this NPC.

- Please select the **AIThirdPersonController** object in the **Hierarchy**.

- In the **Inspector** window, scroll down to the section (i.e., the component) called **AICharacterControl**.

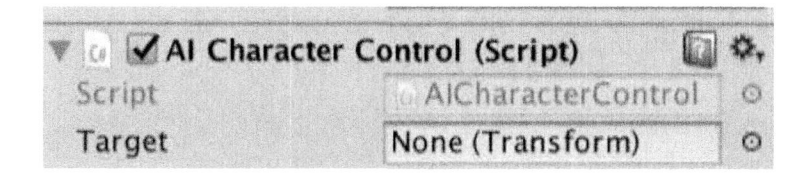

Figure 9: Setting the target (part 1)

- Drag and drop the object **FPSController** to the variable **target** from the **Hierarchy** window, as illustrated in the next figure.

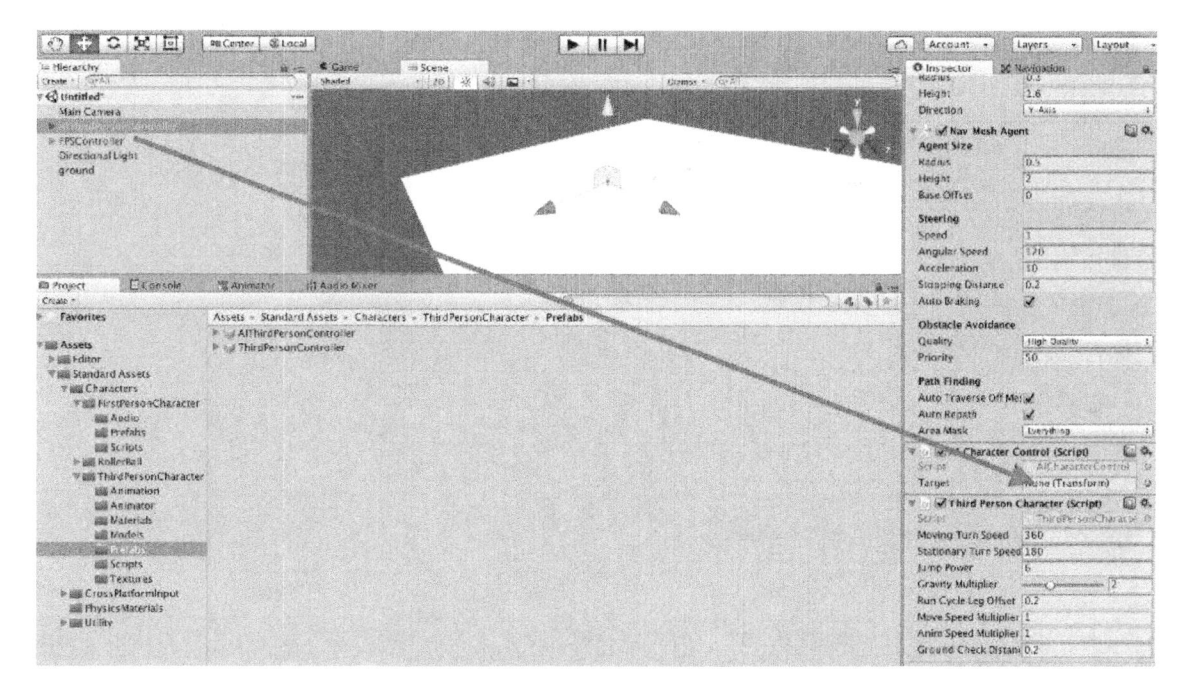

Figure 10: Setting the target (part 2)

- The **AI Character Control** component should then look like the next figure.

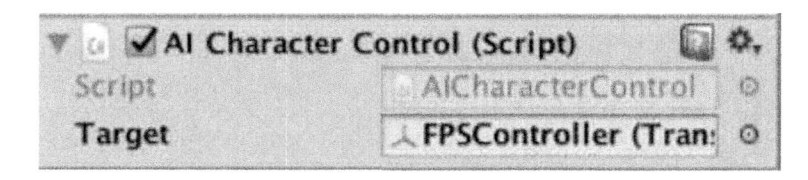

Figure 11: Setting the target (part 3)

[213]

- So, by performing this action, we have effectively specified that the target of this AI Agent (i.e., the NPC) is the player (i.e., the object **FPSController**).

Next, we need to specify how the agent (i.e., the NPC) can navigate to its target; this will be done using the **Navigation** window.

- Please select the object called **ground**.
- Open the window called **Navigation** (i.e., **Window | Navigation**).
- Click on the tab called **Object**.
- Check the box called **Navigation Static** and leave the **Navigation Area** option to **Walkable**.

Figure 12: Specifying the navigation type

- You can then click on the tab called **Bake**, and click on the button labelled **Bake**, within this tab (you may also be asked to save your scene).

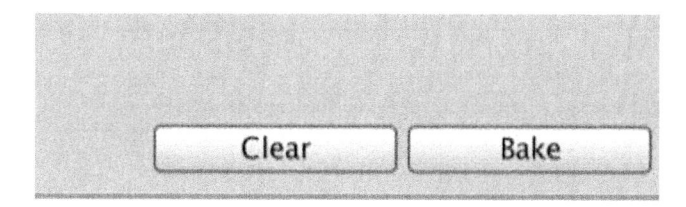

Figure 13: Baking the scene

Using Off-mesh links, Areas and Costs

> By baking the scene, you make it possible for Unity to define and calculate walkable (and static) areas in the scene that the NPC can take to reach its target; without baking the scene, the NPC will not be able to find its way to its target; so this step is very important.

Once the baking process is complete, please check that the **Inspector** window is active and also that the options called **Show NavMesh** is selected in the **Scene** view (i.e., in the bottom-right corner), as illustrated in the next figure:

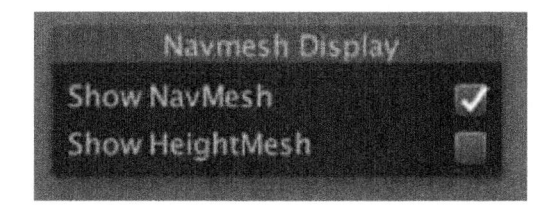

Figure 14: Checking that we can see the NavMesh

If you look at the **Scene** view from above (e.g., along the y-axis), you should see that the ground has turned to blue; indicating that walkable areas have been calculated for this scene.

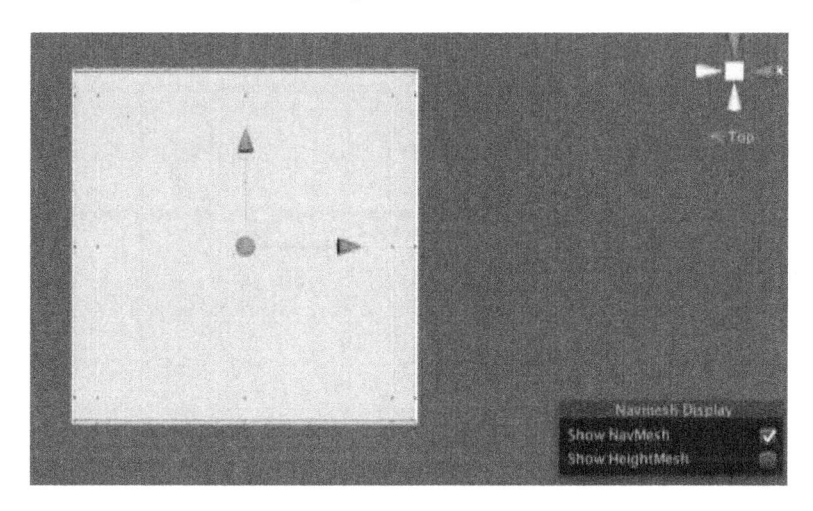

Figure 15: Displaying the NavMesh after baking the scene

You can now play the scene, and you should see that the NPC is now following you.

ADDING MORE OBSTACLES

Now that the NPC can walk towards its target, we will start to add a few obstacles to our scene so that the NPC needs to avoid them to reach the player. These will consist of boxes that we will rescale.

- Please create a new cube (i.e., **GameObject | 3D Object | Cube**) and rename it **wall**.

- Change its scale to **(10, 1, 10)** and its position to **(0, 1, 0)**.

Next we will create a new material for this wall, so that it can be seen easily.

- From the **Project** window, select: **Create | Material**.

- Rename the new material **red**.

- Select this material (i.e., **red**).

- Using the **Inspector** window, change its colour to red.

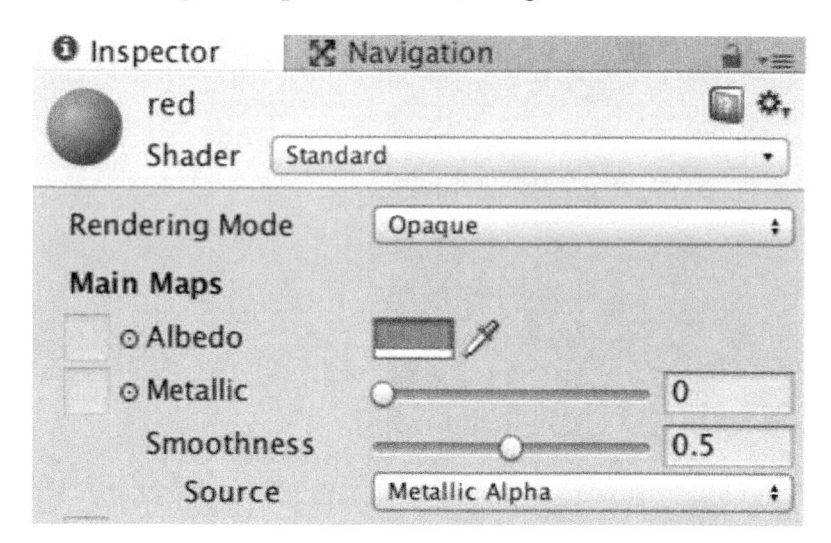

Figure 16: Creating a new material

- Once this is done, you can drag and drop this material (i.e., **red**) on the object called **wall**.

- You can then duplicate this **wall** object four times (i.e., **CTRL + D**) to create a layout similar to the next figure.

Using Off-mesh links, Areas and Costs

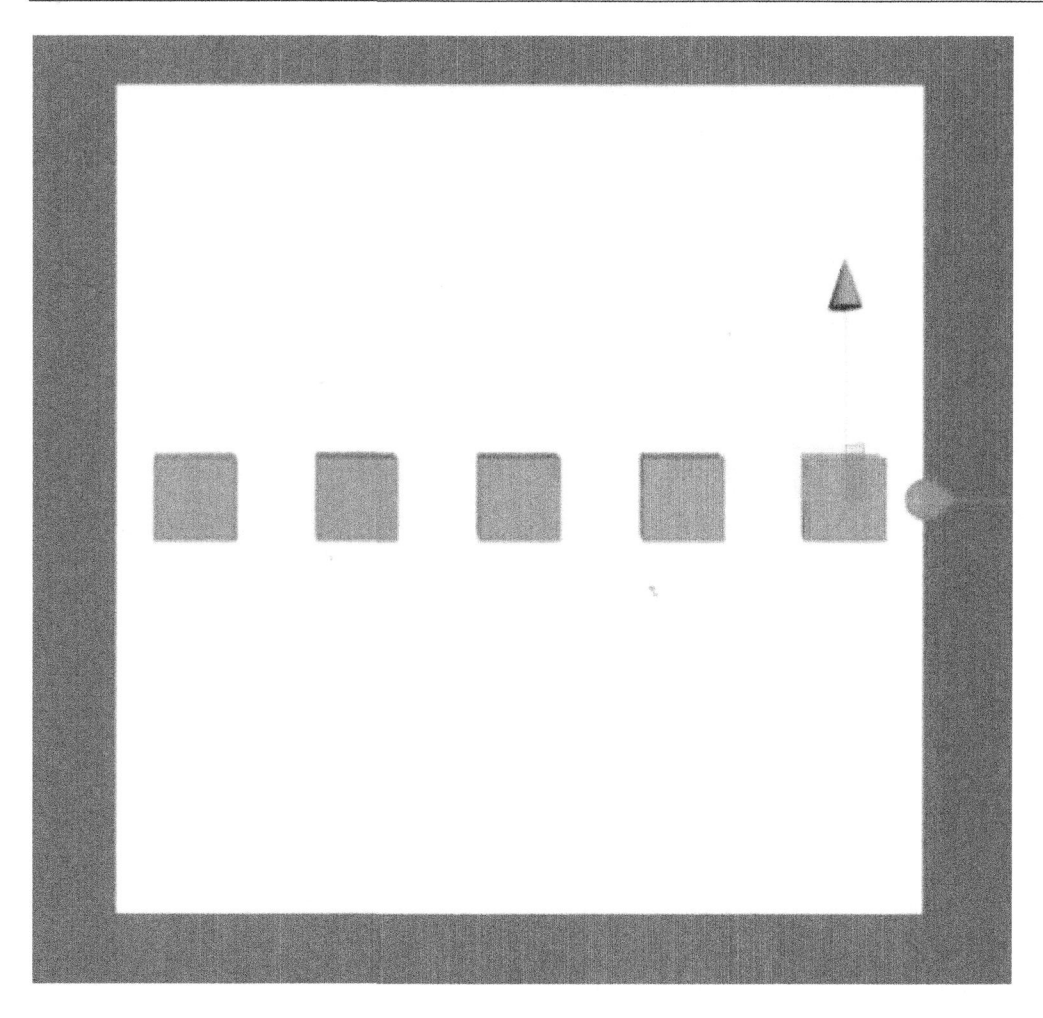

Figure 17: Creating a new layout for the scene

- In the previous example, the walls have the same **y** and **z** coordinates, but their **x** coordinate are respectively **-40**, **-20**, **0**, **20**, and **40**.

You can now duplicate this row **four times** as follows:

- Select the five walls in the **Hierarchy**.

- Duplicate them (**CTRL + D**).

- Using the **Move** tool, move the duplicates so that their **z** coordinate is **20**.

- Repeat the previous steps three times so as to obtain the following layout (i.e., a grid of 5 by 5 boxes), using rows with a z coordinate of **40, 20, 0, -20** and **-40**.

[217]

Using Off-mesh links, Areas and Costs

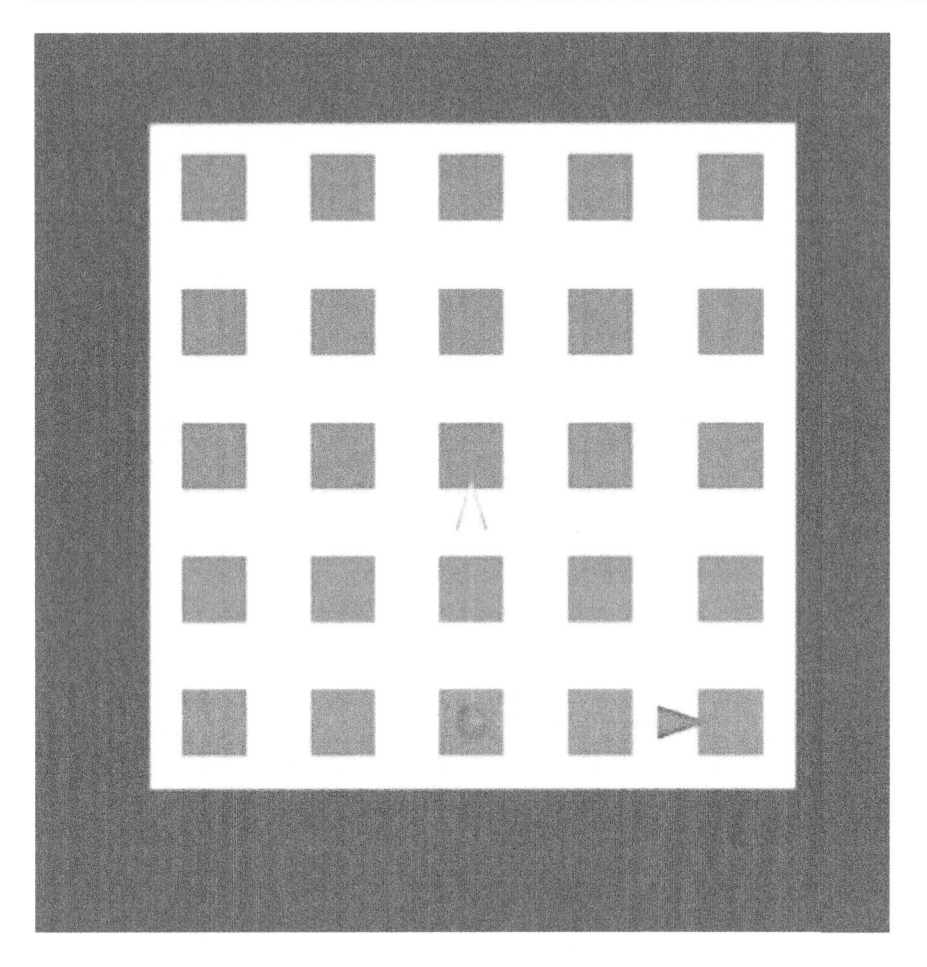

Figure 18: Layout for the scene

Once this is done, we just need to ensure that these walls will be avoided by the NPC when walking towards the player. This will be done by baking the scene again and by including the new walls in the baking process.

- Please select all the walls in the **Hierarchy** window (**Click + Shift** key or **CTRL + Click**) as well as the **ground** object.

- Open the **Navigation** window and then the tab called **Object**.

[218]

Using Off-mesh links, Areas and Costs

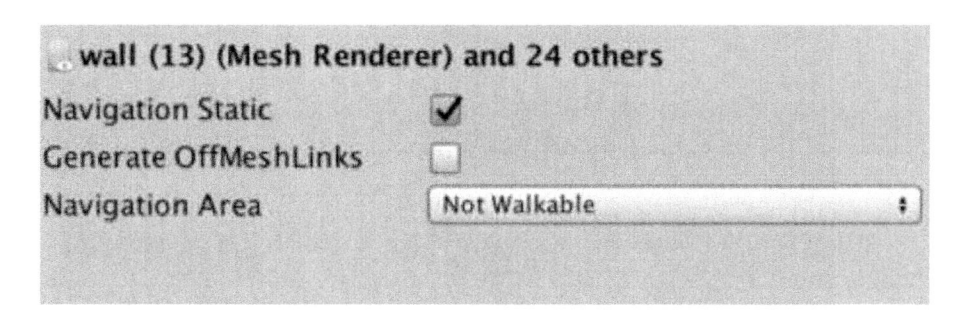

```
wall (13) (Mesh Renderer) and 24 others
Navigation Static          ✓
Generate OffMeshLinks      ☐
Navigation Area            [ Not Walkable        ▼ ]
```

Figure 19: Baking the walls

- Whereas as we have previously chosen the option **Walkable** for the ground, this time, we will choose the option "**Not Walkable**", because these are obstacles, as illustrated in the previous figure; please also click on the options **Navigation Static**, and then click on the button labelled **Bake**, that is within the tab called **Bake**.

- After baking the scene, it should look like the following figure:

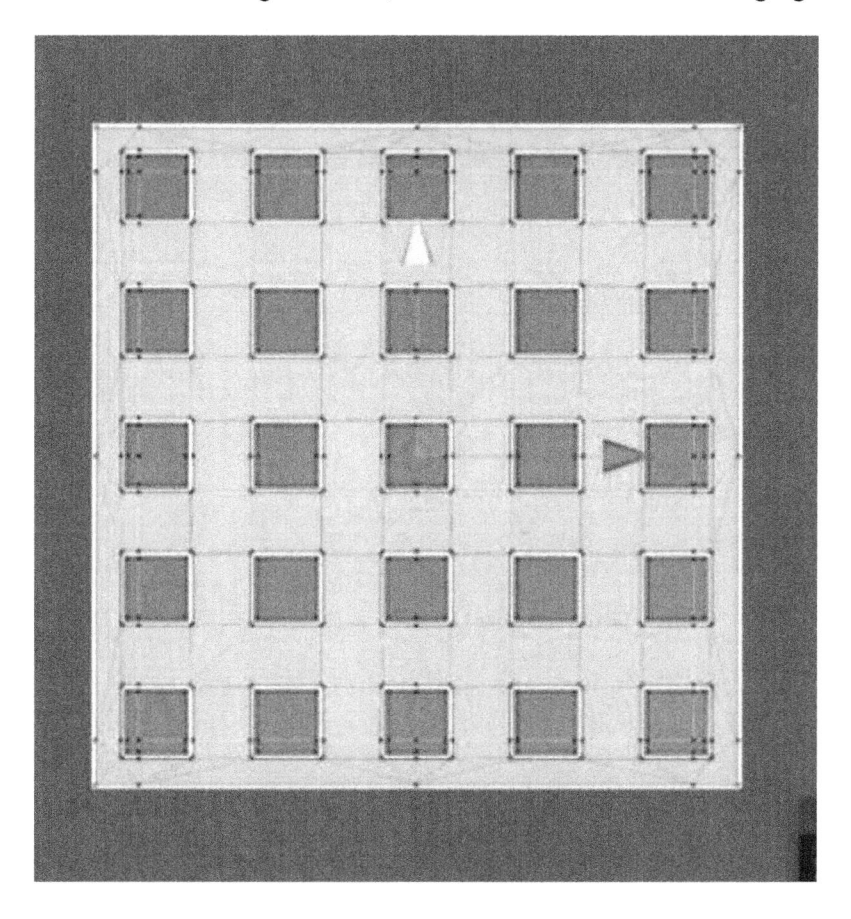

Figure 20: The scene baked

[219]

Using Off-mesh links, Areas and Costs

- For a more dramatic effect, and to really see the NPC moving towards the player, you can change the position of the player to (**-40, 0, -10**) so that the NPC has to travel a longer distance to reach the player.

- As you play the scene, you should see that the NPC follows you by avoiding the walls, as in the next figure.

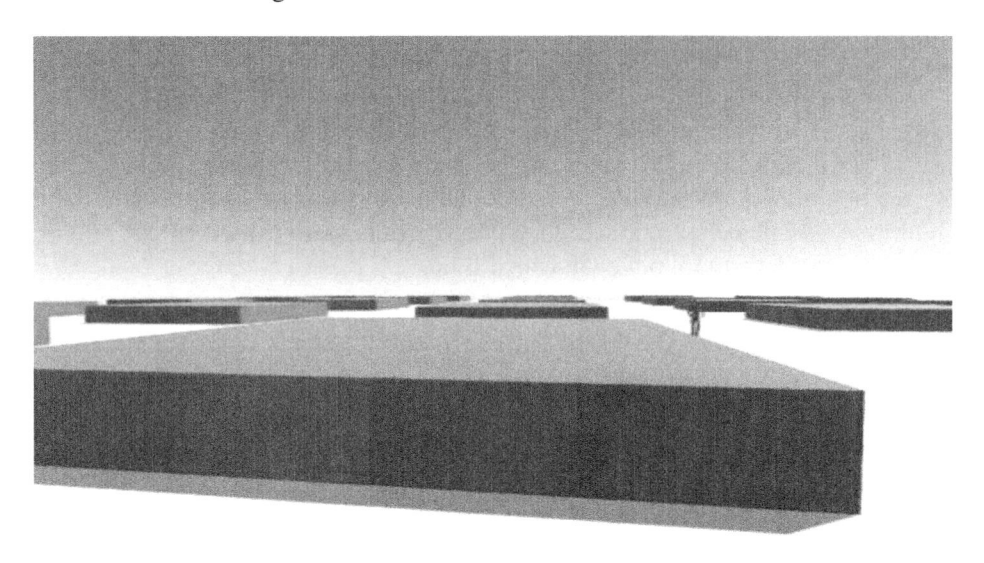

Figure 21: The NPC avoiding the walls to reach the player

GROUPING INTELLIGENT NPCS

Now, to add more challenge to the game, we could add several NPCs, in different locations, that will all be looking for and following the player. To do so, we just need to duplicate the current NPC and proceed as follows:

- Please change the name of the object **AIThirdPersonController** to **NPC**.
- Drag and drop it (i.e., the object called **NPC**) to the **Project** window.
- This will create a prefab called **NPC** (i.e., a reusable template).
- Drag the prefab **NPC** twice to the **Scene** view.
- This will create two new objects called **NPC(1)** and **NPC(2)**.
- Change the positions of the duplicates to **(28, 0, 40)** and **(28, 0, - 40)**.
- Select all three NPCs, as we will change their attributes simultaneously.
- In the **Inspector** window, scroll down to the component **AICharacterControl**.
- Drag and drop the **FPSController** from the **Scene** view to the variable called **target** for the script **AICharacterControl**. This will define the player as the target for all the NPCs.
- As you play the scene, you should see that all three NPCs are now following the player.

Figure 22: The Three NPCs following the player

COLLISION DETECTION

At this stage, we could create a simple rule, whereby the level restarts once one of these NPCs has managed to catch-up with the player; for this we need to detect collision between the player and the NPCs and to reload the current scene in this case. We may also need to decrease the speed of the NPCs, to make the game slightly easier to play.

So let's proceed:

- Please create a new script called **ManageNPC** (from the **Project** window, select **Create | C# Script**).

- Add the following code to it (new code in bold).

```
using UnityEngine;
using System.Collections;
using UnityEngine.SceneManagement;
public class ManageNPC : MonoBehaviour {

    // Use this for initialization
    void Start () {

    }

    // Update is called once per frame
    void Update () {
        GameObject player = GameObject.FindWithTag ("Player");
        float distance = Vector3.Distance (transform.position, player.transform.position);
        if (distance < 1.5)
            SceneManager.LoadScene (SceneManager.GetActiveScene ().name);

    }
}
```

In the previous script we check whether the NPC is very close to the player (i.e., the object with the tag called **Player**); if this is the case, we reload the active scene.

- Please save your script and drag and drop it to the **NPC** prefab.

- Add the tag "**Player**" to the **player**: select the **FPSController** object, and using the **Inspector** window, select the tag called **Player** from the drop-down list in the section called **Tag**, as a new tag for this object, as illustrated in the next figure.

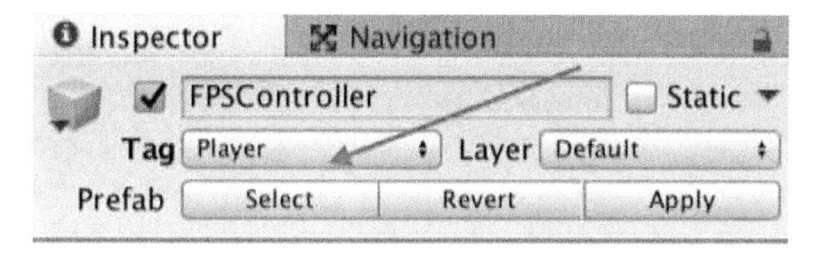

Figure 23: Applying a tag to the player

Now that we have configured the NPC and the player, we just need to ensure that it is possible to reload the current scene, if need be.

- Please save your scene as **chapter1** (i.e., **File | Save Scene As...**).

- Open the **Build Settings** (i.e., **File | Build Settings**).

- Click on the button labelled **Add Open Scenes**, as illustrated in the next figure. This will ensure that the current scene is part of the build, and that, therefore, it can be (re)loaded.

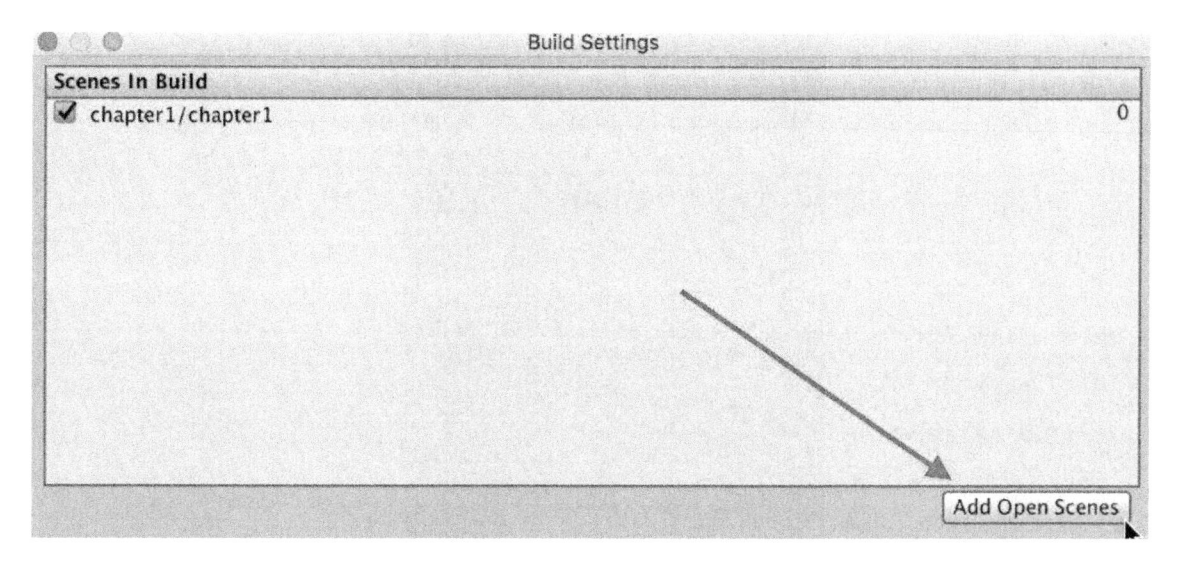

Figure 24: Adding the scene to the Build Settings

Once this is done, you can close the **Build Settings** window, and play the scene. You will notice that, if one of the NPCs is very close to the player, the scene will automatically restart.

Note that if the light in the game, after reloading the scene, seems different, you can do the following:

Using Off-mesh links, Areas and Costs

- Add a directional light to the scene (**GameObject | Light | Directional Light**).
- Change its rotation to **(90, 0, 0)**.
- Open the **Lighting** settings (**Window | Lighting | Settings**).
- Open the tab called **Scene**.
- Uncheck the box called **Auto Generate**.

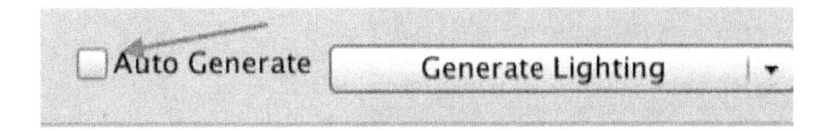

Figure 25: Modifying the light settings

Last but not least, we will decrease the speed of the NPCs, to give the player a chance to escape:

- Please select the prefab called **NPC** from the **Project** window.
- Open the **Inspector** window.
- Scroll down to the component called **ThirdPersonCharacter**.
- Change the attribute **Move Speed Multiplier** to **0.7**, as illustrated in the next figure.

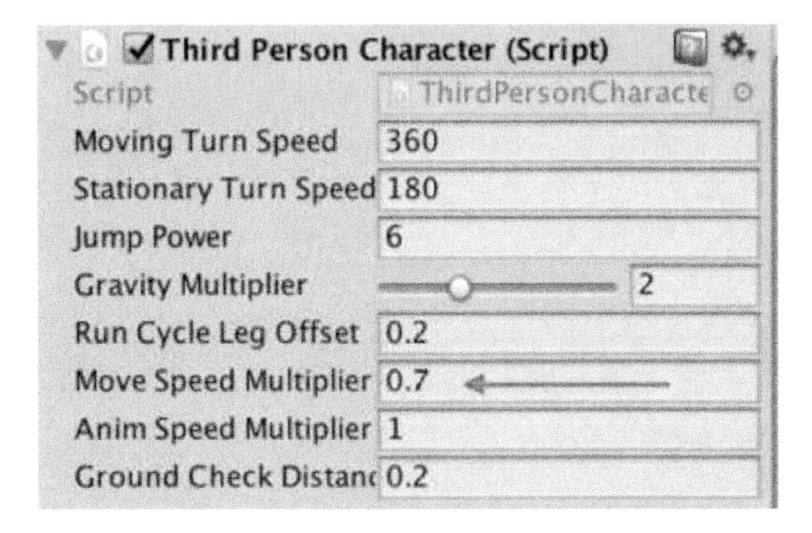

Figure 26: Modifying the speed of the NPCs

You can now test the scene and check that the NPCs are walking/running slower.

OFF-MESH LINKS

So far, we have managed to create **(NavMesh)** navigation for a continuous flat surface; however, it would be interesting to introduce a few gaps, and force the NPCs to jump, if need be, to be able to follow the player; for this purpose, we will be using off-mesh links; the idea behind off-mesh links is to provide the NPCs with a way to navigate between two walkable surfaces that may not be connected (e.g., two platforms), by specifying the maximum distance that they can jump to go from the first one to the second one.

So let's proceed:

- Please duplicate the object called **ground**.

- Rename the duplicate **ground2**.

- Change its position to **(-75, -3, 0)** and its scale to **(50, 1, 100)**.

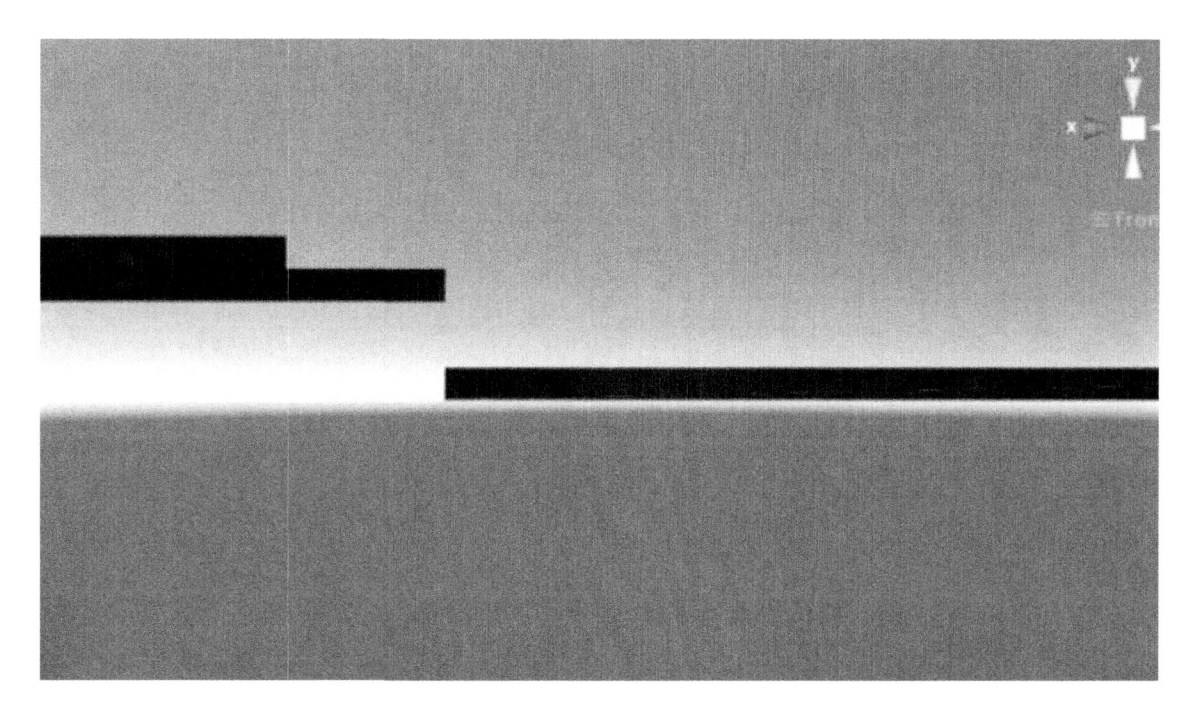

Figure 27: Creating the lower level

Once this is done, we will make sure that we allow the NPC to jump from the upper platform to the lower platform if need be:

Using Off-mesh links, Areas and Costs

- Please select both the objects **ground** and **ground2** in the **Scene** view.
- In the **Navigation** window, open the tab called **Object**, and select the option to **Generate OffMesh Links**.

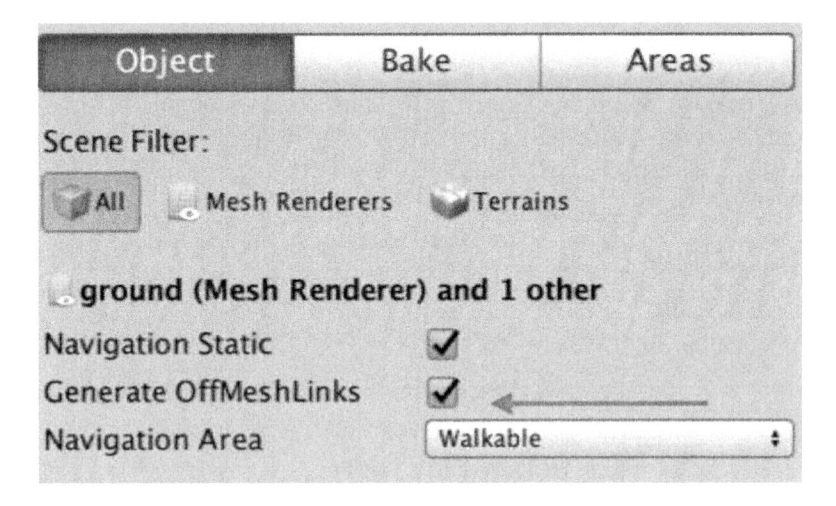

Figure 28: Setting-up navigation for both levels

- Then click on the **Bake** tab.
- Specify a **Drop Height** of **4**.

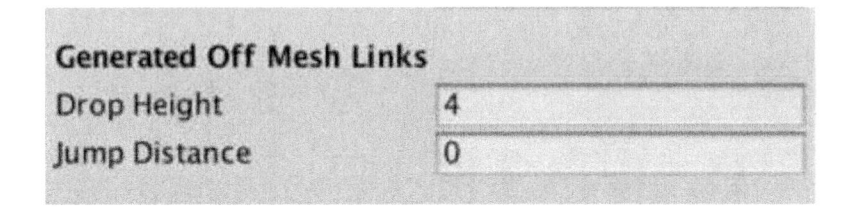

Figure 29: Modifying the jumping height

- You can then click on the **Bake** button.
- If you open the **Navigation** window, and then look closely at the **Scene** view, you should now see that Unity has generated links between the two levels, as illustrated in the next figure.

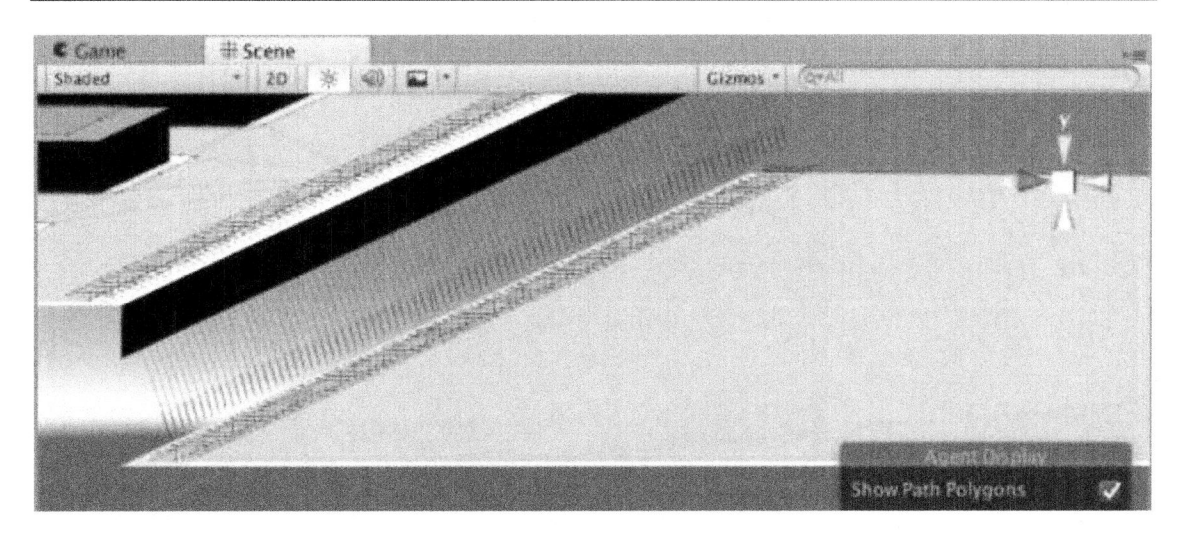

Figure 30: Off-mesh links

In order to test these changes (i.e., the ability to jump from platforms for the NPCs), we will modify the color of the lower level to blue:

- Please create a new **blue** material as we have done previously. You can also duplicate and modify the material called **red** that we have created previously.

- Apply it to the object called **ground2**.

If you play the scene, and if you then jump on the blue area and look back, you should see that the **NPCs** will also jump on your current platform to navigate towards you.

Using Off-mesh links, Areas and Costs

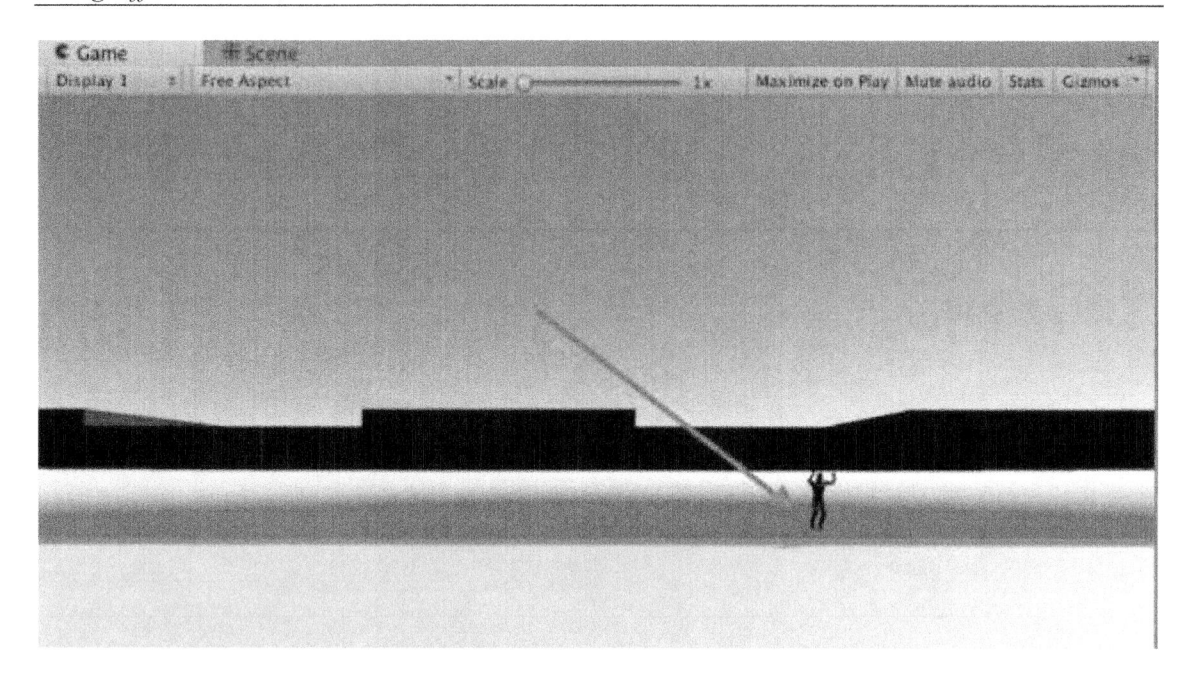

Figure 31: NPCs following NavMesh links

USING AREAS AND COSTS

In this section, we will simulate the presence of water. Although our NPCs may be able to walk through water, this environment may slow-down their progression; so the idea here is to assign costs to different environments so that the NPCs can plan their navigation accordingly and avoid areas with high costs (i.e., areas that might slow them down too much) in order to reach their destination faster.

First, let's add a few more elements to our environment:

- Please create a new cube and rename it **bridge**.

- Change its position to **(-65, 0, 12)** and its scale to **(30, 1, 3)**.

- Create another cube and rename it **platform**.

- Change its position to **(-95, 0, 12)** and its scale to **(30, 1, 30)**.

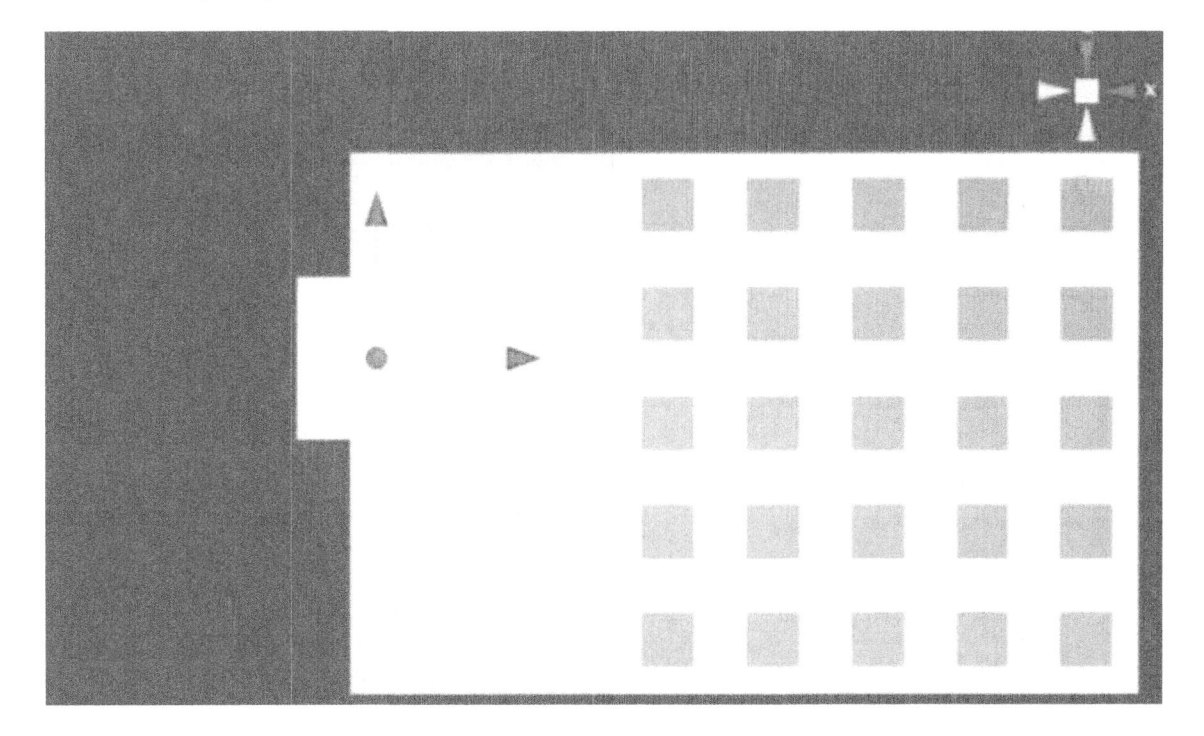

Figure 32: The scene layout

We can then define an area and its associated (navigation) cost:

- Please select the **Navigation** window, and then the tab called **Area**.

- Create a new area called **Water** with a cost of **10**, as illustrated in the next figure.

Using Off-mesh links, Areas and Costs

	Name	Cost
Built-in 0	Walkable	1
Built-in 1	Not Walkable	1
Built-in 2	Jump	2
User 3	Water	10

Figure 33: Creating a new area

As you can see, this type of area will have a higher cost than the walkable areas that were created by default; so if the NPC has to choose between these two, it should opt for the walkable area, as its cost is lower, and the NPC would therefore arrive to its destination faster.

- Please select the object called **ground2**.

- Using the **Navigation** window, and the tab called **Object**, set its **Navigation Area** attribute to **Water**.

```
Scene Filter:
   All    Mesh Renderers    Terrains

ground2 (Mesh Renderer)
Navigation Static        ✓
Generate OffMeshLinks    ✓
Navigation Area    →   [ Water    ⁞ ]
```

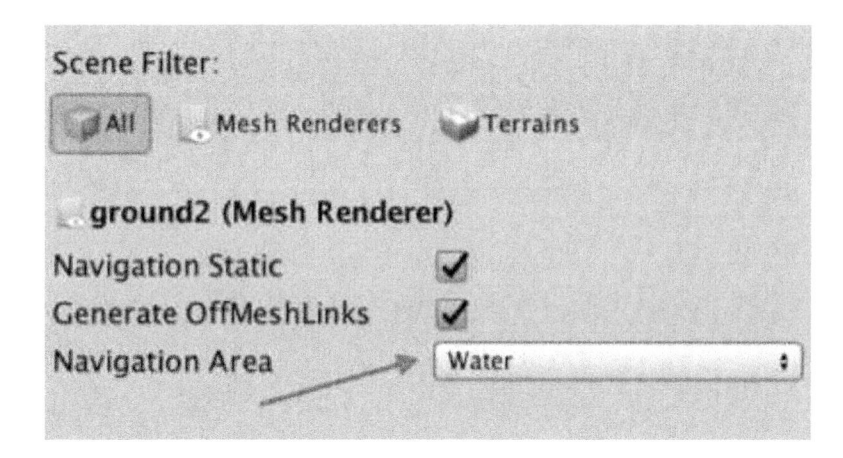

Figure 34: Setting Navigation settings

- Select the objects **bridge**, **platform**, and **ground**.

- Using the **Navigation** window set their attributes as in the next figure (Navigation Static=true, Generate OffMeshLinks=true, and Navigation Area = Walkable):

Using Off-mesh links, Areas and Costs

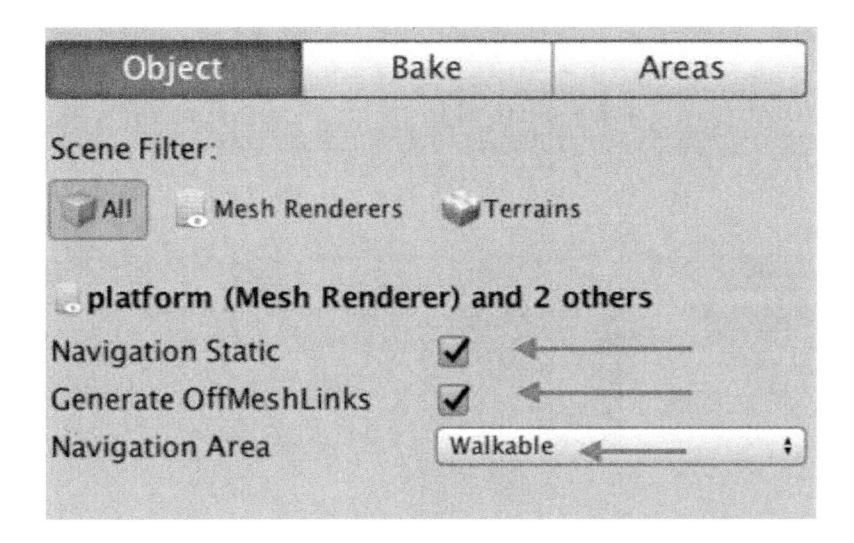

Figure 35: Setting the navigation (part 2)

In the previous steps, we have defined that the objects **bridge**, **platform**, and **ground** can be used for the NPCs navigation, that they are static, and that the NPCs can jump between them if need be, thanks to off-mesh links.

- You can now bake your scene, by selecting the tab called **Bake**, and by then clicking on the button called **Bake**.

As you play the scene, you should see that, if you walk on the bridge and look back, the NPCs will also follow you, and walk on the bridge, and they will not jump into the water (as they would have done before we made the last changes).

[231]

Using Off-mesh links, Areas and Costs

Figure 36: NPC navigation based on costs

Note that we could have achieved a similar effect by specifying that the NPCs should not walk on the water area; this can be achieved as follows:

- Select all the NPCs.

- Using the **Inspector** window, scroll down to the section called **NavMeshAgent**.

- Modify the area mask so that **Water** is <u>not</u> selected in the list, as per the next figure.

Using Off-mesh links, Areas and Costs

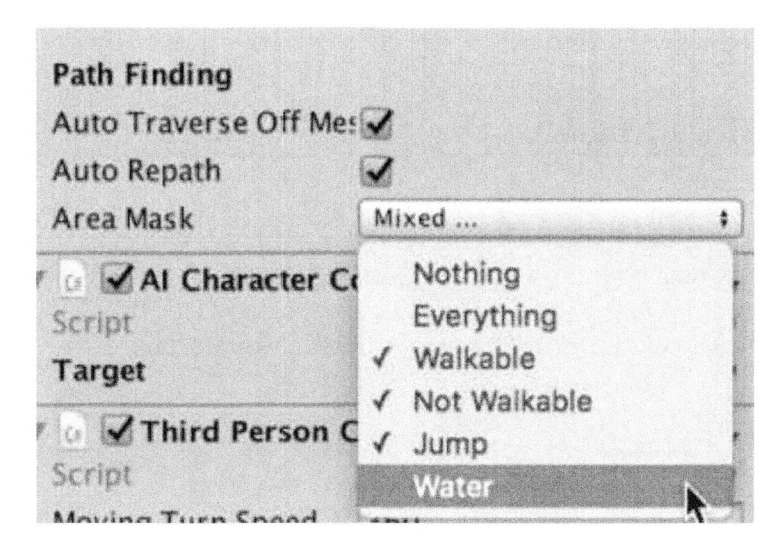

Figure 37: Setting-up the area mask

- For testing purposes, you can set the cost for the water to **1** (using the tab called **Areas** in the **Navigation** window), and play the scene, so that the changes in the NPC navigation are only linked to the area mask and not the cost.

Figure 38: NPCs using area masks

If you jump in the water and walk, you will see that the NPCs will not follow you. This is because the area called **water** is not part of the area mask for the NPCs.

[233]

MAKING IT POSSIBLE FOR NPCS TO JUMP

In this last section, we will add a feature whereby the NPCs are able to jump between two platforms. Whereas the NPCs could previously jump vertically to reach a lower level, we will now make it possible for the NPCs to jump horizontally instead.

- Please duplicate the object called **platform** and rename the duplicate **platform2**.

- Change its **x** coordinate to **-128**.

- Select the two objects **platform** and **platform2**.

- In the **Inspector** window, using the **Object** tab, make sure that the settings are as follows (i.e., Navigation Static=true, Generate OffMeshLinks=true, and Navigation Area = Walkable):

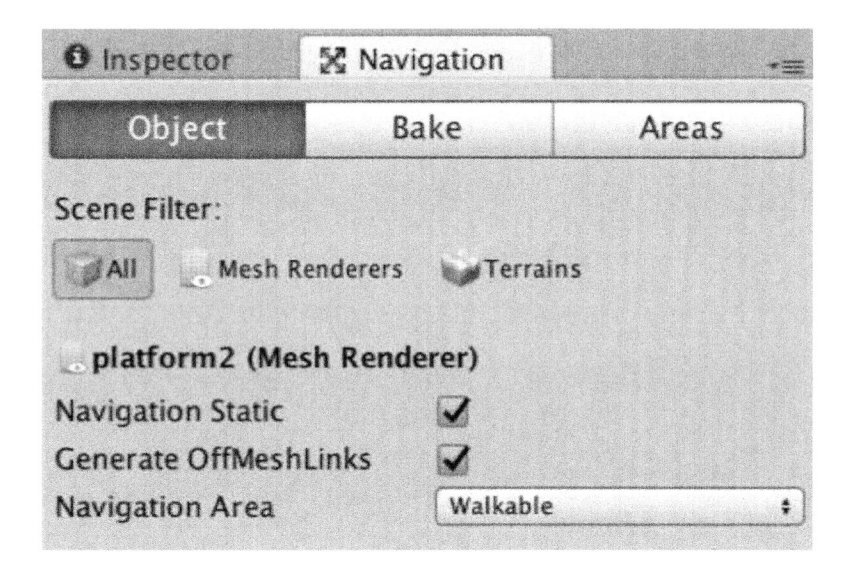

Figure 39: Modifying the Navigation settings

- Click on the **Bake** Tab.

- Change the **Jump Distance** to **4**.

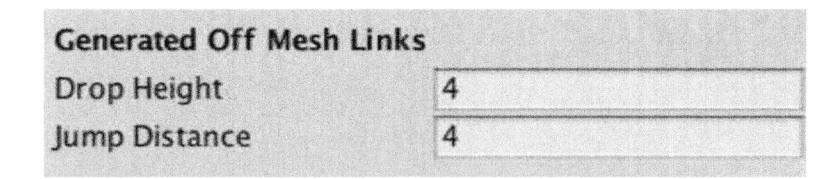

Figure 40: Setting the jump distance

[234]

- Bake the scene.

After making sure that the **Navigation** window is active, you should see that off-mesh links, symbolized as arrows, have been created between the two platforms.

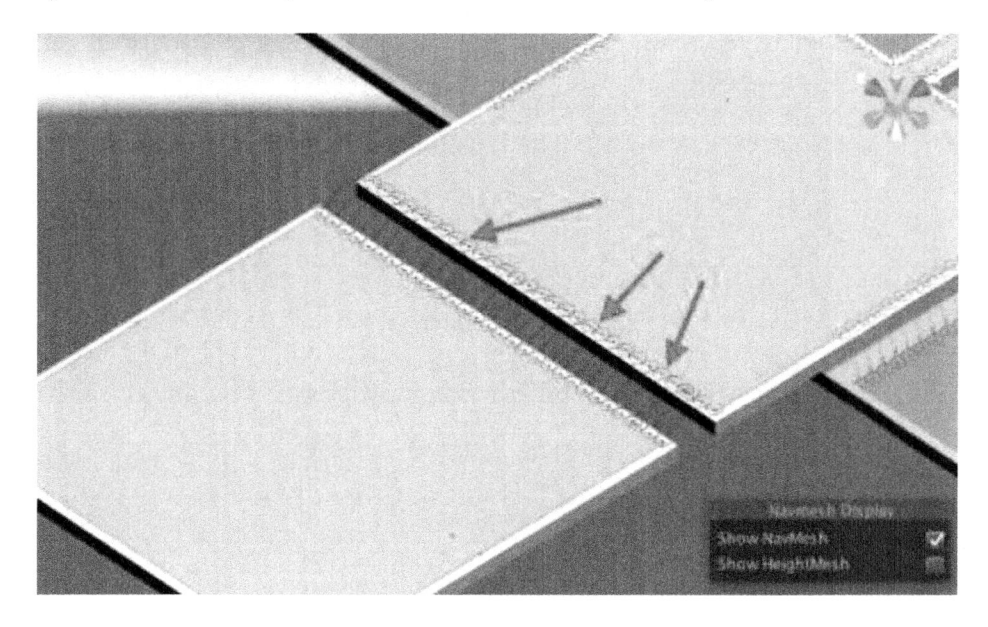

Figure 41: Off-mesh links between the two platforms

If you play the scene, and reach the second platform, you should see that not only do the NPCs use the bridge to reach the player, but they also jump between the two platforms, as per the next figure.

Figure 42: An NPC jumping between platforms

Using Off-mesh links, Areas and Costs

LEVEL ROUNDUP

In this chapter, we have learned to create simple artificial intelligence allowing the NPCs to follow the player, after avoiding obstacles. We also learnt how to define and set areas and associated costs, so that NPCs can prioritize areas to maximize their path (and speed); we also looked at area masks to specify the area where NPCs should or should not go to. So, we have covered considerable ground to get you started with your first AI features!

Checklist

You can consider moving to the next stage if you can do the following:

- Create NPCs using Unity's built-in library.
- Set-up NPCs so that they follow the player.
- Bake a scene for Navigation.
- Create areas and associated costs.
- Detect the keys pressed by the player.

Quiz

Now, let's check your knowledge! Please answer the following questions or specify if these statements are either correct or incorrect (the solutions are on the next page).

11. By default, a Unity project includes a folder called Characters.

12. The **Characters** folder needs to be imported as a package.

13. For an NPC to follow the player, it needs to have a target that is set.

14. For an NPC to follow the player, walkable areas need to be set, and the scene needs to be baked.

15. By default, the area called **Walkable** is created in Unity.

16. By default, the area called **Water** is created in Unity.

17. Off-mesh links need to be created when navigation needs to be facilitated between two platforms that are atop each other and separated by a few meters.

18. Off-mesh links need to be created when navigation needs to be facilitated between two platforms that are beside each other and separated by a few meters.

19. The attribute **Drop Height** can be used to allow vertical jumps.

20. The attribute **Jump Distance** can be used to allow horizontal jumps.

Using Off-mesh links, Areas and Costs

Quiz Solutions

Now, let's check if you have answered the questions correctly.

1. False (you need to import a pack).
2. True.
3. True.
4. True.
5. True.
6. False.
7. True.
8. True.
9. True.
10. True.

Using Off-mesh links, Areas and Costs

Challenge 1

Now that you have managed to complete this chapter and that you have created your first level, you could improve it by doing the following:

- Create a third platform where the player can go to, but that should not be accessible to the NPCs, using area masks.

- Create a second bridge leading to the first platform but with a cost of 10 (you will need to set-up a new area and the associated cost for this bridge).

6
USING FIXED AND RANDOM PATHS FOR NPCS

In this section, we will learn how to create custom navigation using a 3D character of our choice; these navigation modes will be very close to techniques found in many 3D games.

After completing this chapter, you will be able to create the following navigation systems for your NPCs:

- Walking on a set path.
- Walking on a random path.
- Wandering with no set destination.

> The code solutions for this chapter are in the **resource pack** that you can download by following the instructions included in the section entitled "Support and Resources for this Book".

IMPORTING OUR 3D CHARACTER

For this chapter, we will be using a 3D character that is not part of Unity's packages; this will make it easier to customize the movement of the character and to implement the associated navigation modes. So first, let's import this character.

- Please locate the resource pack that you have downloaded from the companion website.

- Locate the folder called **military**.

- Import it to Unity (i.e., drag and drop it to the **Project** window).

- As you import the package in Unity, the following window may appear.

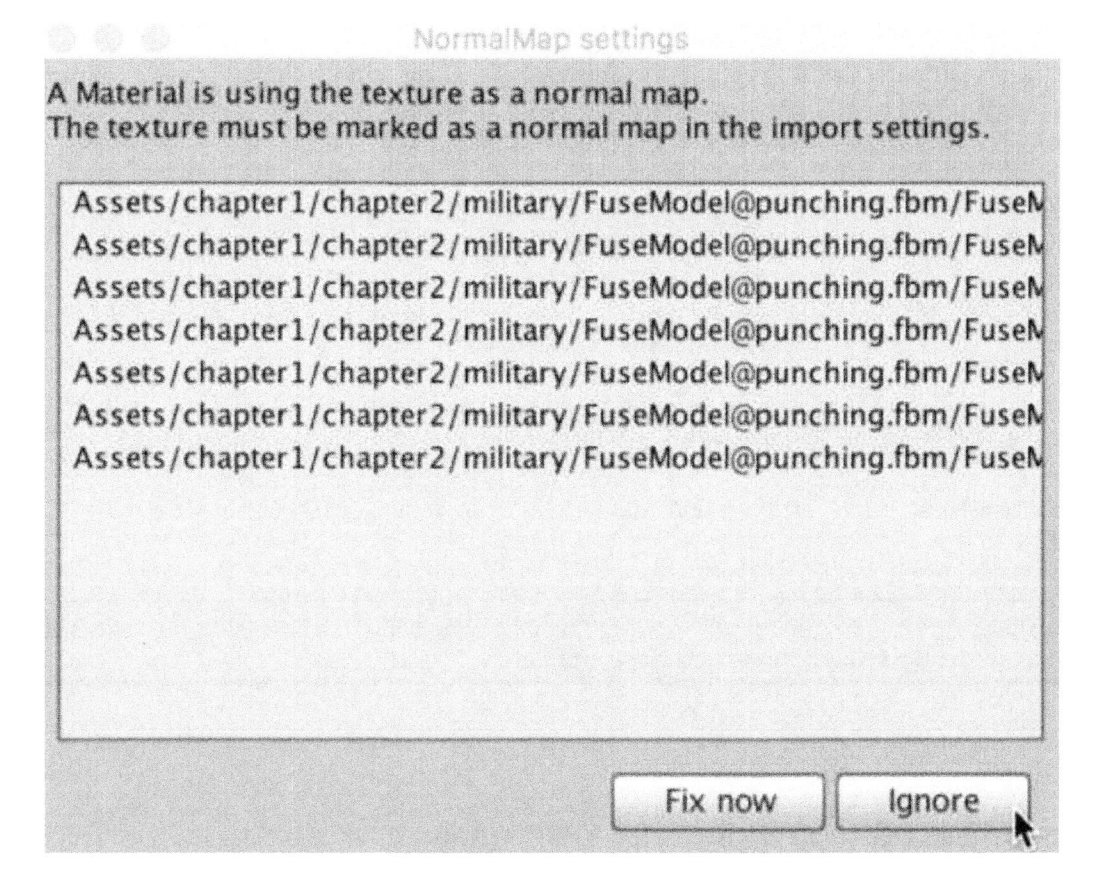

Figure 43: Importing the 3D characters (part 1)

- You can then click on the button labelled **Fix Now**.

Using Fixed and Random Paths for NPCs

- The **Project** window should then include the folder called **military**, as illustrated in the next figure.

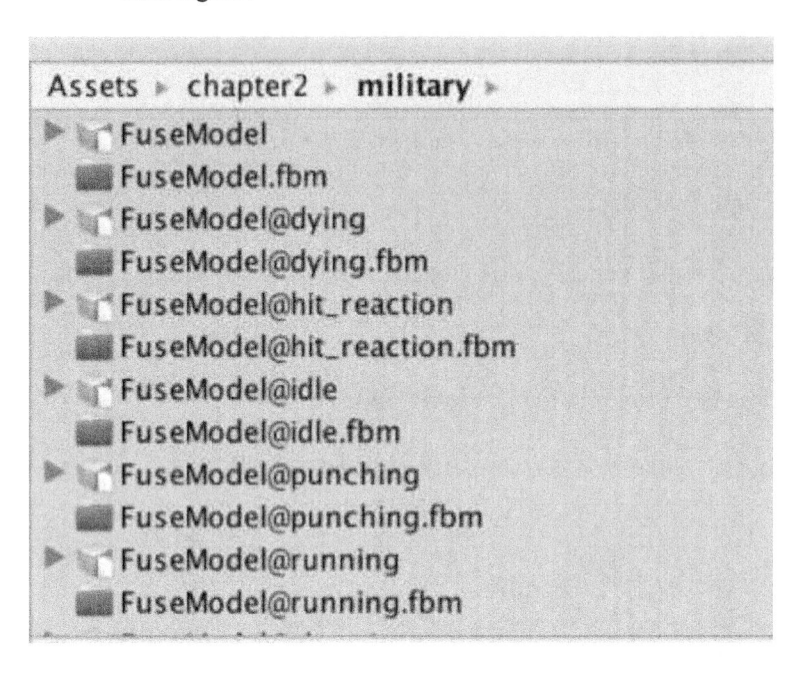

```
Assets ▶ chapter2 ▶ military ▶
▶ FuseModel
  FuseModel.fbm
▶ FuseModel@dying
  FuseModel@dying.fbm
▶ FuseModel@hit_reaction
  FuseModel@hit_reaction.fbm
▶ FuseModel@idle
  FuseModel@idle.fbm
▶ FuseModel@punching
  FuseModel@punching.fbm
▶ FuseModel@running
  FuseModel@running.fbm
```

Figure 44: Importing the 3D characters (part 2)

- Once the import is complete, you can save the previous scene (**CTRL + S**), create a new scene (**CTRL + N**), rename it **chapter2**, and open it.

- In the new scene, create a new ground by adding and rescaling a cube with a position of **(0, 0, 0)** and a scale factor of **(100, 1, 100)**, and by renaming the object **ground**.

Once the ground has been created, we will add our player, as well as a 3D character for the NPC, to the scene.

> The following step assumes that you have completed the first chapter; if this is not the case, you will need to import the **Characters** package accordingly.

- In the **Project** folder, navigate to the folder called: **Standard Assets | Characters | FirstPersonCharacter | Prefabs**.

- Please drag and drop the asset called **FPSController** from this folder to the **Scene** view. This will create a new object called **FPSController** in the **Hierarchy**.

- From the **Project** window, open the folder called **military** that you have just imported, and drag and drop the prefab called **FuseModel** to the **Scene** view.

[242]

Using Fixed and Random Paths for NPCs

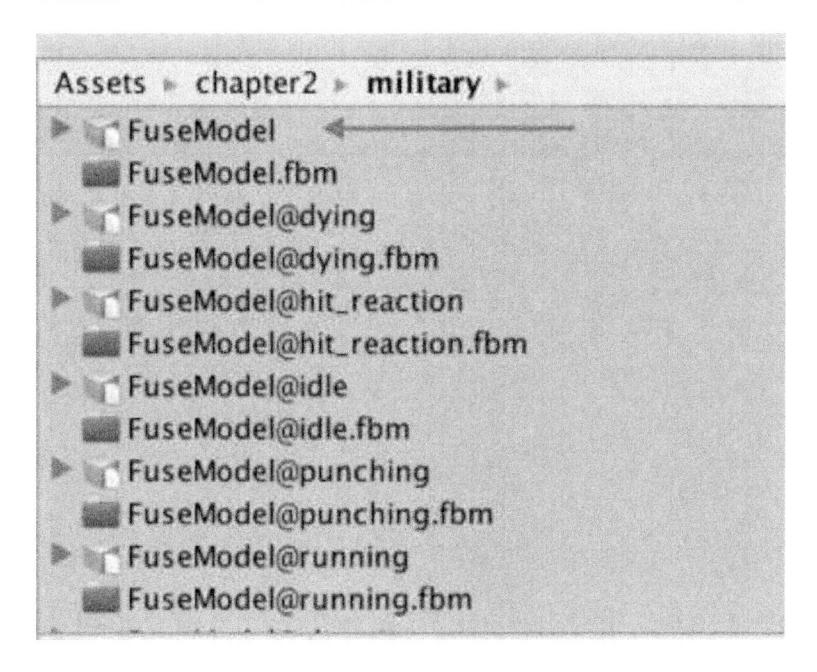

Figure 45: Creating a 3D character

- This will create an object called **FuseModel** in the **Hierarchy**, as illustrated in the next figure.

Figure 46: Adding the 3D Character for the NPC.

Using Fixed and Random Paths for NPCs

As you play the scene, you should see that the 3D character is in the **T pose**, as illustrated in the next figure.

Figure 47: The 3D character in the T pose

As you navigate the scene, you will see that the NPC is immobile. This is because we have only added a 3D model, but no animations have been linked to it. In the next section, we will animate this model so that it starts to walk.

- Using the **Hierarchy**, please change the name of the object called **FuseModel** to **NPC**.

- Change its position to **(-12, 0.5, 0)**, so that it is slightly above the ground.

- As you look at the **Inspector**, you will see, for the object **NPC**, a component called **Animator**; within this component, you will also see a field called **Controller**.

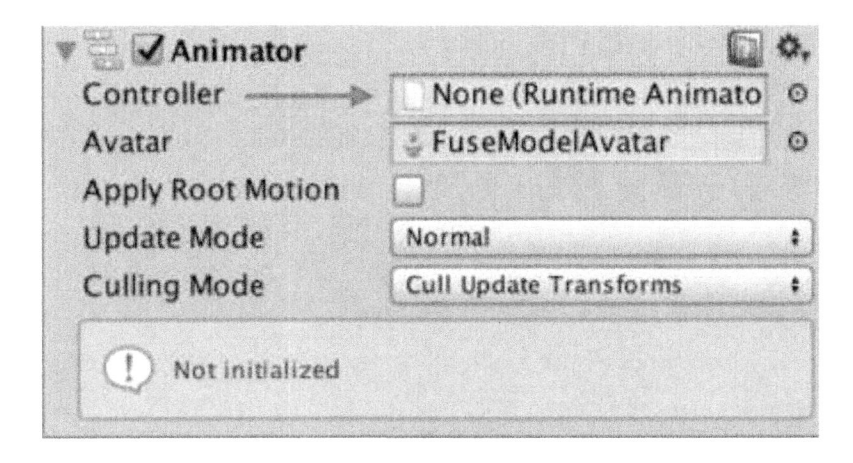

Figure 48: The Animator Controller for the NPC

- The field called **Controller** should be empty, as per the previous figure; this means that there is no animation linked to the character yet.

So to be able to animate the NPC, we will need to create a corresponding **Animator Controller**, and then drag and drop it to this field.

> An **Animator Controller** is a component that defines different states for an object (often animated), along with corresponding animations (e.g., walking, running, etc.), and transitions between these states.

So let's create our **Animator Controller**:

- In the **Project** window, select **Create | Animator Controller**.
- This will create a new **Animator Controller** asset.
- Please rename it **walkingAnimation**, as illustrated in the next figure.

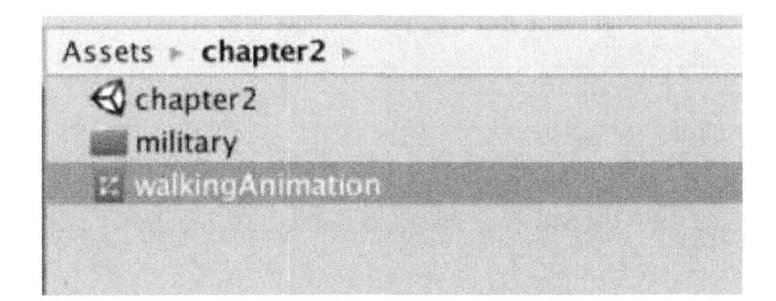

Figure 49: Creating a new Animator Controller

- You can now double click on it.

Using Fixed and Random Paths for NPCs

- This will open the **Animator** window. This window will make it possible to create and manage different states for our NPC.

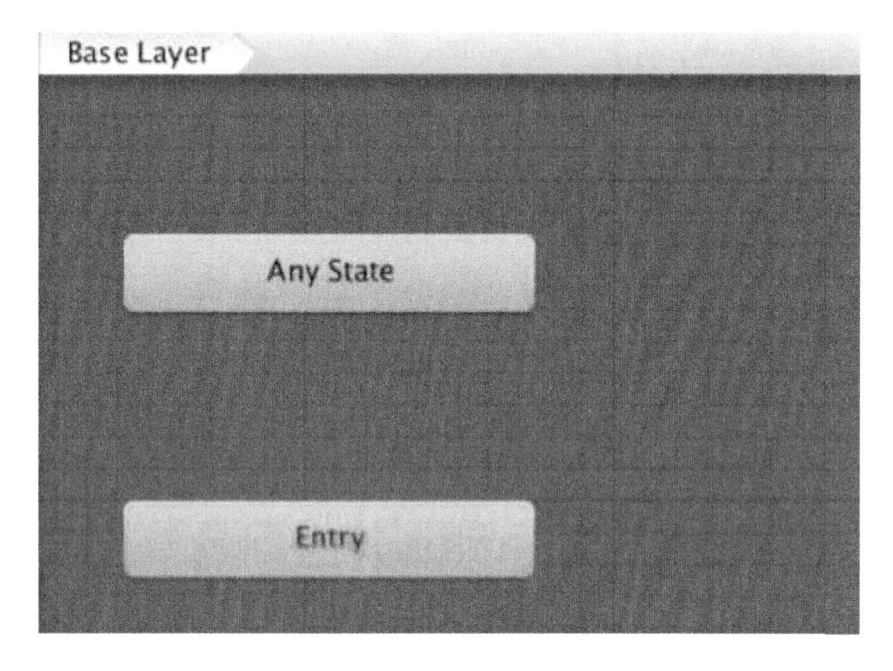

Figure 50: Opening the Animator window

- Once the **Animator** window is open, please right-click within the window and select the option **Create State | Empty** from the contextual menu.

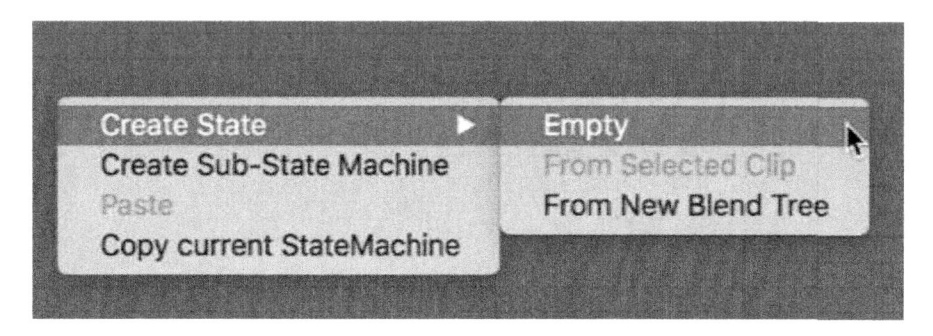

Figure 51: Creating a new state

- This will create a new state labelled **New State**, as illustrated in the next figure.

[246]

Using Fixed and Random Paths for NPCs

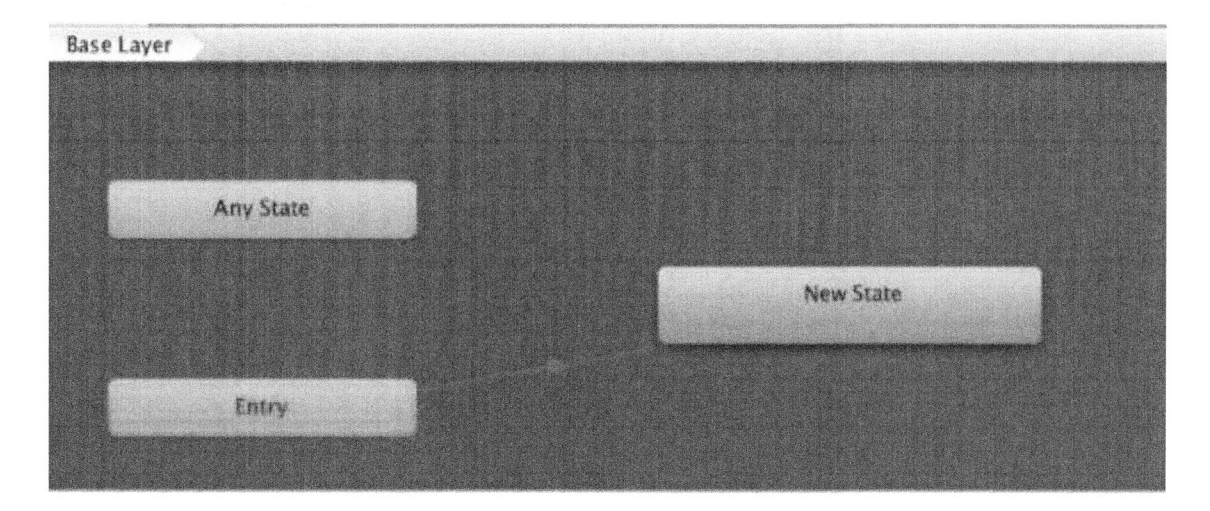

Figure 52: Adding a new state

> You may notice that an **Entry** state has been created, with an arrow pointing towards the state called **New State**; this means that from the very beginning, when this **Animator Controller** is "entered" or "initialized", the **Animator Controller** will transition to the state called **New State**.

- Please click once on the state called **New State**.
- Using the **Inspector** window, change its name to **walking**.

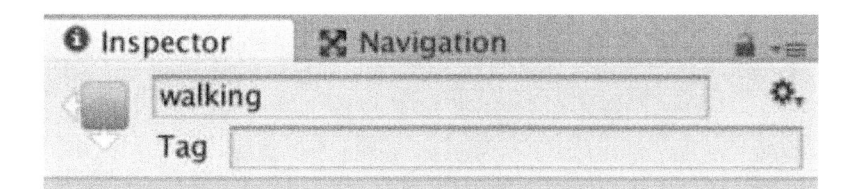

Figure 53: Changing the name of the new state

So by default, when the **Animator Controller** is linked to an object, this object will directly be in the state called **walking**.

We will now associate an animation with this state.

- Please click to the right of the label called **motion**.

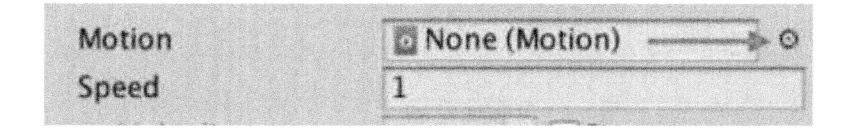

[247]

Using Fixed and Random Paths for NPCs

- This should open a new window.

- In the new window, please type the text **walking** in the search field, as illustrated in the next figure.

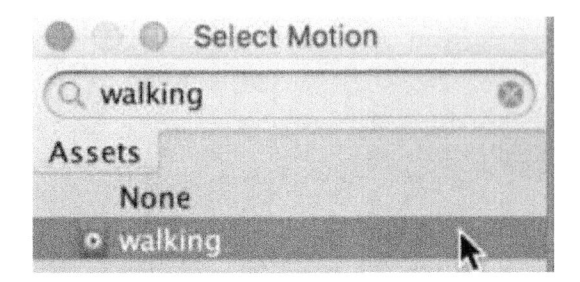

Figure 54: Looking for an animation

- Double click on the item labelled **walking** in the search results.

- This will link the state called **walking** to this particular animation, as illustrated in the next figure. In other words, whenever the state **walking** is active, the animation called **walking** will be played; as we will see later, in this animation, the 3D character is walking.

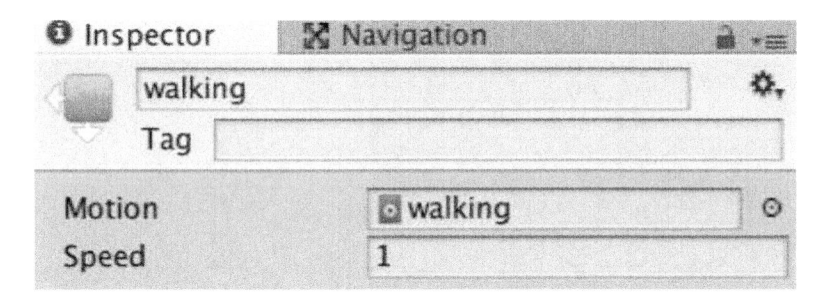

Figure 55: The animation selected for the state

Next, we will just link our newly-created **Animator Controller** to the **NPC**, so that this **NPC** can be animated accordingly.

- Using the **Hierarchy**, select the object called **NPC**.

- Drag and drop the **Animator Controller** called **walkingAnimation** from the **Project** window to the field called **Controller**, as illustrated in the next window.

[248]

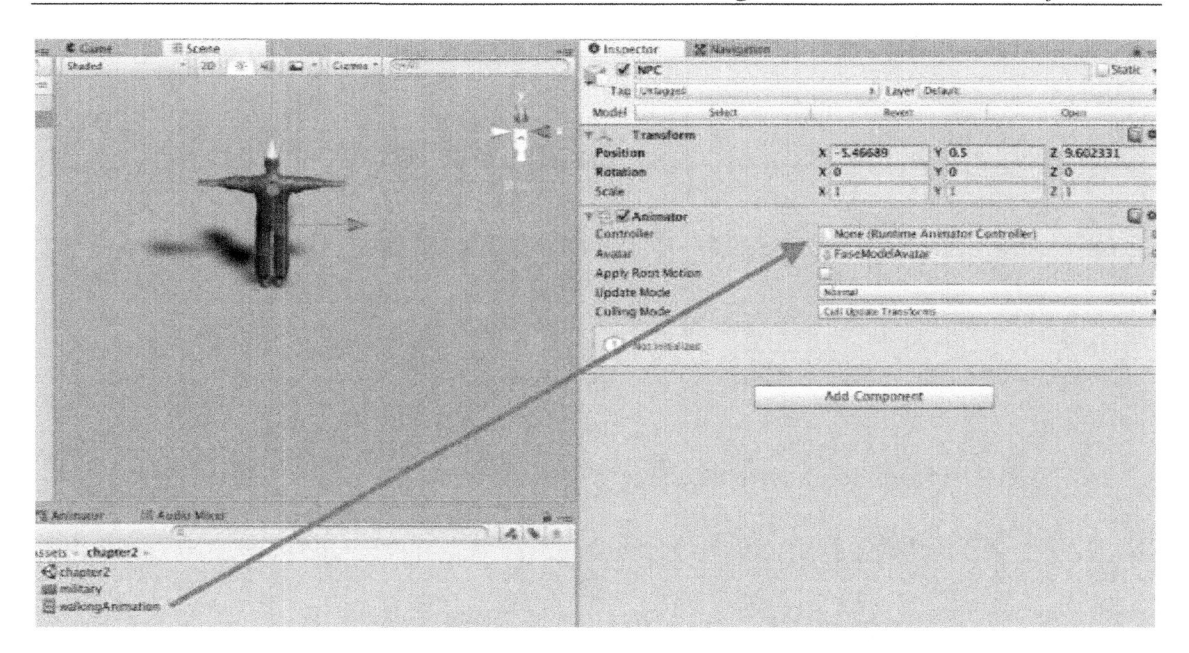

Figure 56: Adding the Animator Controller to the NPC

- After this, the **Controller** field should look as follows.

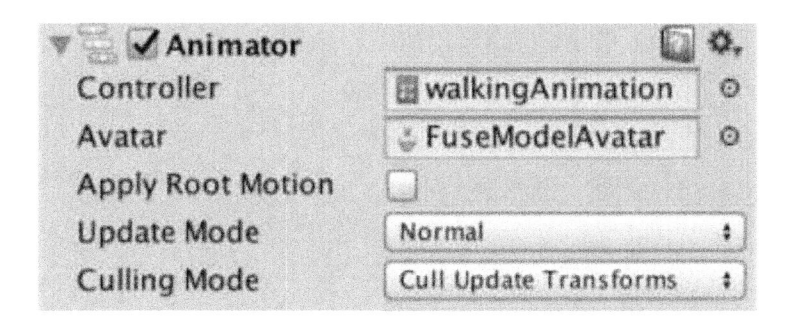

Figure 57: Setting the Controller attribute

You can now play the scene and check that the NPC is walking; you might also notice that the animation for the NPC stops after a few seconds. This is because the animation clip for the NPC animation needs to be modified slightly in order to specify that it should loop overtime.

So, in the next section, we will locate and modify the **walking** animation clip accordingly.

- In the **Project** window, use the *search* field to look for the word **walking**, as illustrated in the next window.

Using Fixed and Random Paths for NPCs

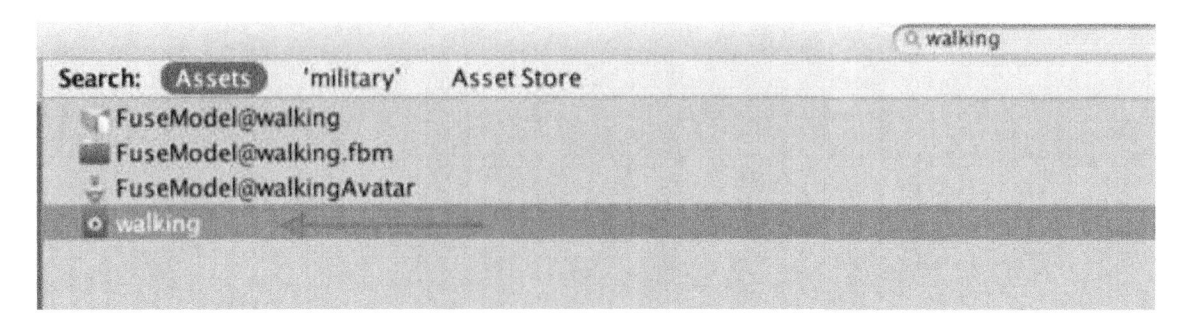

Figure 58: Locating the walking animation

- Select the fourth result (symbolized by a dark square with a triangle within).
- Using the **Inspector**, click on the button labelled **Edit** to edit this clip.

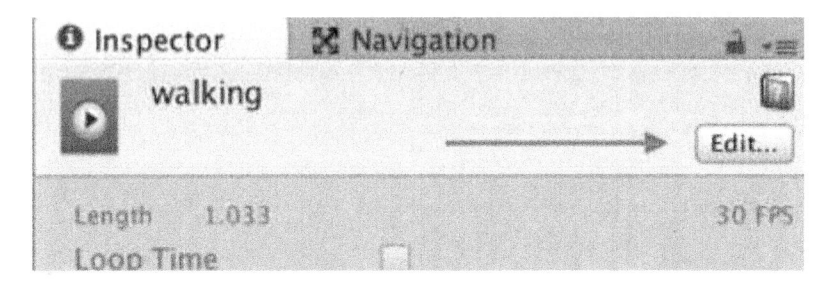

Figure 59 : Editing the animation

- Check/tick both the options **Loop Pose** and **Loop Time**.

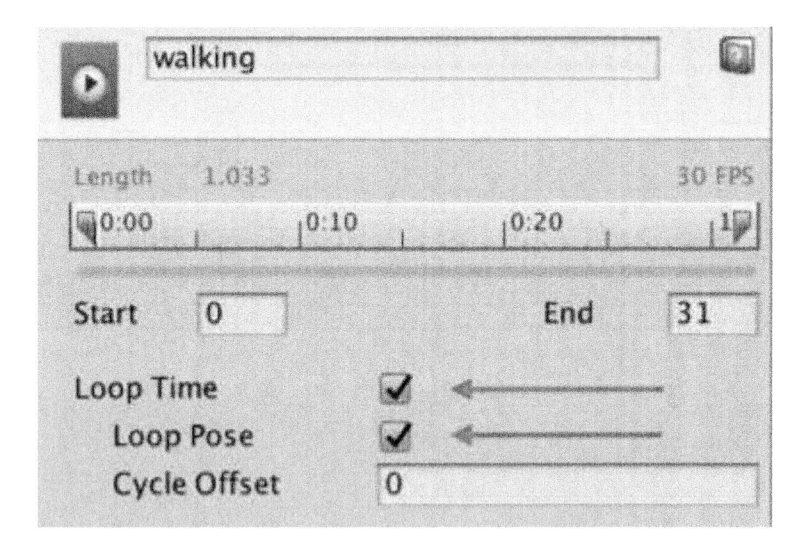

Figure 60: Modifying the animation

Using Fixed and Random Paths for NPCs

> By ticking the box called **Loop Time**, we specify that the animation should loop.
>
> By ticking the box called **Loop Pose**, we specify that the animation should be performed on the same spot.

- Once these changes have been made, you can click on the button called **Apply**, so that these changes can be applied accordingly.

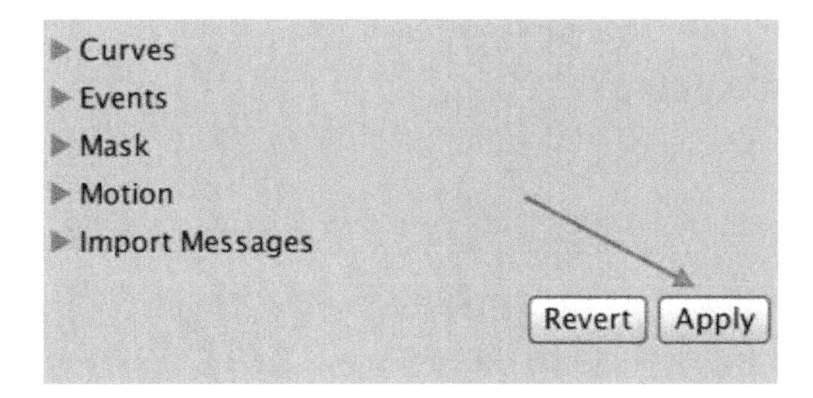

Figure 61: Applying the changes

- Please play the scene, and you should see that the NPC is now animated properly, and that the animation is looping indefinitely overtime.

Figure 62: The looping walking animation applied to the NPC

[251]

SPECIFYING A TARGET FOR THE NPC

Now that the NPC animation works well, we will start to get the NPC to move to a specific location; for this purpose, we will do the following:

- Add a **NavMesh Agent** component to the NPC.
- Create a new script that will define the next destination for the NPC.
- Set the target of the **NavMesh Agent** from this script.

So let's proceed:

- Please select the object called **NPC** in the **Hierarchy** window.
- Add a component called **NavMesh Agent** to this object (i.e., select **Component | Navigation | NavMesh Agent**).

> Adding a **NavMesh Agent** component will help to ensure that the NPC has the ability to move towards its target and to avoid obstacles; note that before this can be made possible, we will also need to select obstacles and bake the scene, using the **Navigation** window, as we have done in the first chapter.

- Please create a new script called **ControlNPC** (from the **Project** window, select **Create | C# Script**)
- Add the following code to this script (new code in bold).

```
using UnityEngine.AI;
public class ControlNPC : MonoBehaviour
{
    public GameObject target;
    void Start () {}
    void Update ()
    {
        GetComponent<NavMeshAgent> ().SetDestination (target.transform.position);
    }
}
```

In the previous code:

[252]

- We declare an object called **target**. This object will be initialized (or set) later-on through the **Inspector**, as this variable is public (and therefore accessible from outside the class).

- We then, in the **Update** function, set the target (or destination) for this NPC to be the target that we have just defined.

- This is done by accessing the component called **NavMeshAgent** from the NPC (i.e., the component that we have just added), and then by using the built-in function **SetDestination**.

Once this has been done, we can save our script.

- Please save the script, check that it is error-free and drag and drop it to the object called **NPC** in the **Hierarchy** window.

- Select the object called **NPC**.

- In the **Inspector**, scroll down to the component called **ControlNPC**.

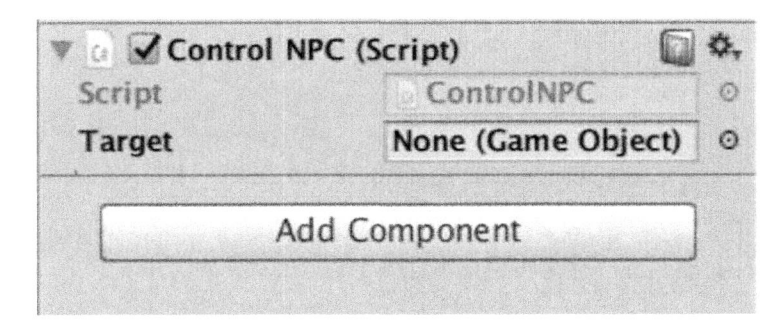

Figure 63: Identifying the component ControlNPC

- Drag and drop the object called **FPSController** from the **Scene** view to the attribute called **target**. This effectively tells Unity that we want the **NPC** to go towards the player.

Once this is done, we need to indicate how the NPC should navigate towards its destination by baking the scene through the **Navigation** window.

So let's proceed:

- Please select the **ground** object.

- Open the **Navigation** window.

- Once this is done, click on the boxes labelled **Navigation Static** and **OffMeshLinks**, as illustrated in the next figure. By doing so, we indicate that the ground can be used for navigation and that it is static.

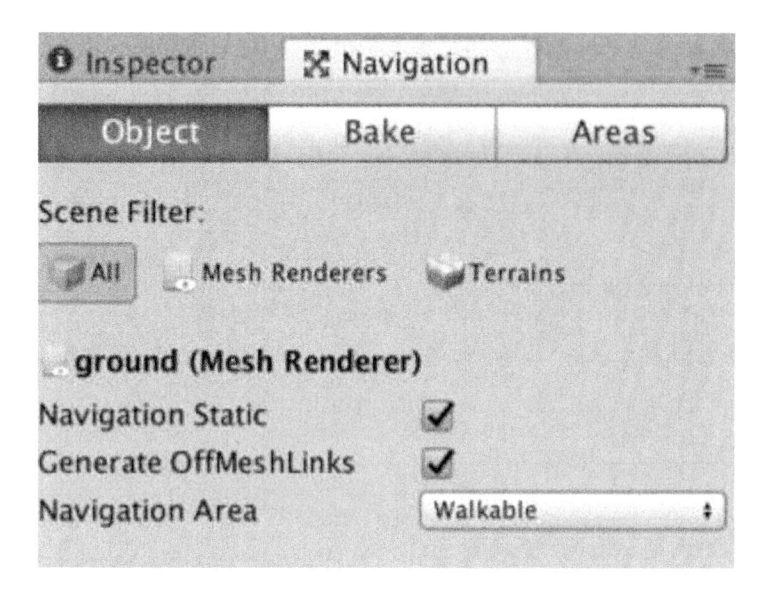

Figure 64: Setting-up navigation

- Once this is done, please click on the button labelled **Bake** that is within the tab called **Bake**.

- Play the scene, and you should see that the **NPC** is following the player at all times.

WAYPOINTS

At this stage, we will create a path for the NPC; this path will be made of waypoints which are basically successive targets that, put together, define the path. So the idea will be to:

- Create waypoints or empty objects that will be used for the navigation.
- The NPC will navigate towards a particular waypoint.
- When close to this waypoint (e.g., less than 1 meter), it will start to move towards the next waypoint.
- After reaching the last waypoint, the NPC will follow the first waypoint again.

So let's get started:

- Please create a new cube (**GameObject | 3D Object | Cube**).
- Rename it **WP1** (as in **W**ay**P**oint**1**).
- Change its position to **(10, 1, 10)**.
- Using the **Inspector** window, deactivate its collider, as illustrated in the next figure.

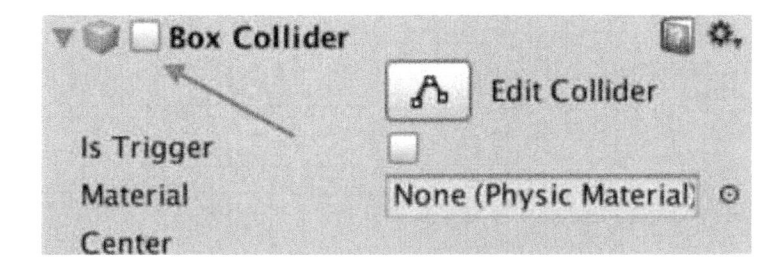

Figure 65: Deactivating the collider of the waypoint

- Select the object **WP1** in the **Hierarchy**.
- Duplicate this object three times (i.e., **CTRL + D**) and call the duplicates **WP2**, **WP3**, and **WP4**.
- Change their position respectively to **(-10, 1, 10)**, **(-10, 1, 0)**, and **(10, 1, 0)**.

Once the waypoints have been created, we can modify the script **ControlNPC** so that the NPC follows these waypoints successively.

Using Fixed and Random Paths for NPCs

- Please open the script **ControlNPC** and modify it as follows (new code in bold).

```
public class ControlNPC : MonoBehaviour
{
    public GameObject target;
    public GameObject WP1, WP2, WP3, WP4;
    int WPCount;
    GameObject[] WayPoints;

    // Use this for initialization
    void Start () {
        WP1 = GameObject.Find ("WP1");
        WP2 = GameObject.Find ("WP2");
        WP3 = GameObject.Find ("WP3");
        WP4 = GameObject.Find ("WP4");
        WayPoints = new GameObject[]{ WP1, WP2, WP3, WP4 };
        WPCount = 0;
```

In the previous code:

- We declare four objects that will correspond to the waypoints that we have just created.

- The variable **WPCount** is used to indicate the active waypoint (i.e., the waypoint that the NPC is currently following).

We can now modify the **Update** function so that the NPC navigates to each of these waypoints successively.

- Please modify the **Update** function as follows:

[256]

```
void Update ()
{
        target = WayPoints [WPCount];
        if (Vector3.Distance(transform.position,target.transform.position) < 1.0)
        {
                WPCount++;
                if (WPCount > WayPoints.Length-1) WPCount = 0;
        }
        GetComponent<NavMeshAgent> ().SetDestination (target.transform.position);

}
}
```

In the previous code:

- The new target is set to the first waypoint in the array.

- We then calculate the distance between the NPC and the current waypoint using the built-in function **Vector3.Distance**.

- If this distance is less than one meter, we increase the index of the current waypoint so that the NPC navigates towards the next waypoint; we also ensure that, if the NPC has reached the last waypoint, it follows the first waypoint instead.

- Finally, we set the destination of the NPC to be the position of the current waypoint.

Once you have saved these changes, please check that your code is error-free. You can then play the scene. You should see that the NPC navigates through the different waypoints that define the path, as illustrated in the next figure.

Using Fixed and Random Paths for NPCs

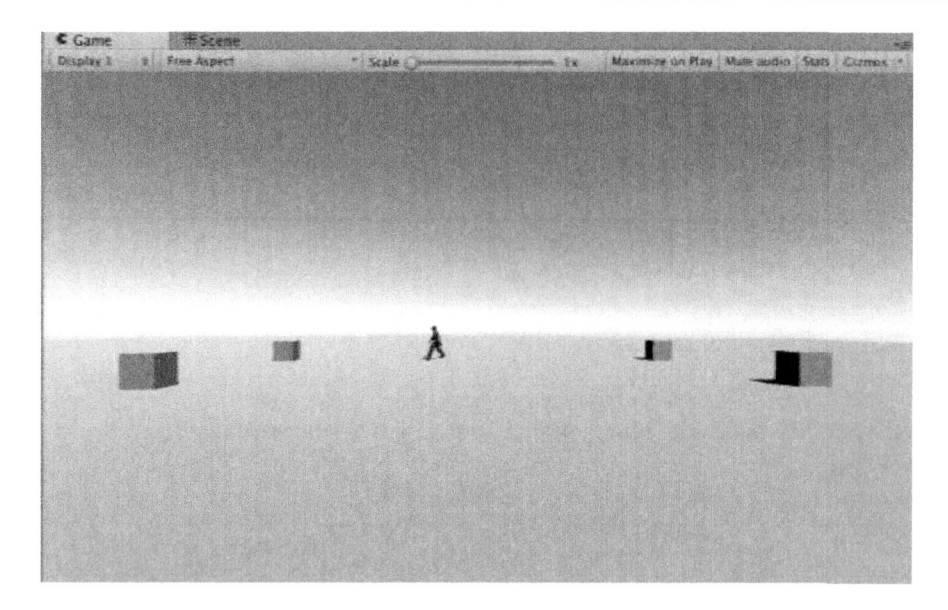

Figure 66: The NPC navigating towards each waypoint

The last thing we could do is to hide the boxes as the game starts, for more clarity.

This can be done by adding the following code to the **Start** function (at the end of the function) in the script **ControlNPC**.

```
for (int i = 0; i < WayPoints.Length; i++)
{
        WayPoints [i].GetComponent<Renderer> ().enabled = false;
}
```

In the previous code:

- We go through each waypoint available in the array called **WayPoints**.
- We access the **Renderer** component for each waypoint.
- We then disable the Renderer; this will make these objects invisible.

That's it.

As you can guess, using this principle you can define any path, by moving waypoints around using the **Scene** view or by using additional waypoints if need be. This is a very simple and flexible technique to create customized paths.

MOVING RANDOMLY WITHIN A PATH

While NPCs can be on a fixed path, it is always good to add some unpredictability to their movement. This could be used to simulate the movement of NPCs in a crowd, for example. To do so, we could set-up the NPC so that it navigates to a random waypoint that belongs to an existing path. So for example, instead of navigating the path following successively WP1, WP2, WP3, and WP4; it will start at WP1, but then it might go to any of the other waypoints.

So let's implement this feature.

Before we add any new code, we will save the previous code as follows:

- Create the following function in the script **ControlNPC**.

```
void moveToNextWP()
{
        WPCount++;
        if (WPCount > WayPoints.Length-1) WPCount = 0;
}
```

- Modify the **Update** function as follows (new code in bold):

```
if
(Vector3.Distance(transform.position, target.transform.position) < 1.0)
{
        moveToNextWP ();
//previous code deleted as added to the function moveTonextWP
}
```

Next, we will create a new function that will be used to move the NPC to a random waypoint.

- Please create the following function in the script **ControlNPC**:

Using Fixed and Random Paths for NPCs

```
void moveToRandomWP()
{
        int previous = WPCount;
        int random = 0;
        do {
                random = Random.Range (0, WayPoints.Length);
        } while (random == previous);
                WPCount = random;
}
```

In the previous code:

- We declare a function called **moveToRandomWP**.

- We create a loop using the syntax **do …while**.

- In this loop, we create a **random** number using the built-in function **Random.Range**.

- Because the variable **random** is an integer, the range will include the lower boundary (i.e., 0) but it will exclude the upper boundary (i.e., **WayPoints.Length**); so effectively, the variable **random** will range between **0** and **3** (i.e., **WayPoints.Length-1**).

- We generate a random number as long as it is the same as the current index; in other words, we only pick this number if it is not the same as the current index for the waypoints, so that the new destination is different to the current location for the NPC.

- Once this is done (i.e., once we have found a proper number), we exit the loop and set the index for the current waypoint to be the value of the variable **random**.

Now that we have made this modification, we can also modify the **Update** function as follows (new code in bold):

```
if
(Vector3.Distance(transform.position, target.transform.position) < 1.0)
{
        //moveToNextWP ();
        moveToRandomWP ();
}
```

In the previous code, we just make sure that we call the new function **moveToRandomWP** instead.

Please save your script and check that the NPC is effectively going towards waypoints randomly.

[260]

This random behavior, when applied to several NPCs, can be used to simulate a crowd for example.

WANDERING NAVIGATION

So, in the last section, we have created a way to randomize the NPC's navigation, and this works well. This being said, there are other ways, to make the NPC navigate randomly, and one of them is the idea of wandering, whereby the NPC walks aimlessly while also avoiding walls and other obstacles.

The concept that we will implement in this section will consist in the following steps:

- Set an initial goal or a target for the NPC.
- After 4 seconds choose a new direction.
- To choose the new direction, we will cast a ray in a random direction (i.e., in front of or behind the character).
- If there is an object (e.g., a wall) in this direction, then the NPC will aim to go towards this object.

> Note that we could also apply another similar principle whereby the NPC move forwards only if there are no objects in sight.

Before we do so, we will tidy-up our code slightly so that it is easier to change the behavior of our NPC in the future.

- Please add this code at the beginning of the class **ControlNPC**.

```
bool isWandering = true;
bool isFollowingWayPoints;
float timer;
GameObject wanderingTarget;
```

In the previous code:

- We create two Boolean variables **isWandering** and **isFollowingWayPoints** that will be used to specify whether the **NPC** is following waypoints or wandering.
- The variable **timer** will be used to implement a timer that will be used to decide when the NPC should change direction.
- The variable **wanderingTarget** will be used to set temporary targets for the NPC while it is in a wandering state.

Next, we will modify the **Start** function to set an initial target for the NPC.

- Please modify the **Start** function by adding the following code at the **Start** function:

```
if (isWandering)
{
        wanderingTarget = new GameObject ();
        wanderingTarget.transform.position = new Vector3 (20,0,20);
        target = wanderingTarget;
        GetComponent<NavMeshAgent> ().SetDestination (target.transform.position);
}
```

In the previous code:

- We check whether the NPC is in the **wandering** state.
- If this is the case, we create a new **GameObject** that will be used as a new target.
- We then set the position of this object to **(20, 0, 20)**.
- Once this is done, the target is set, and the new destination for the NPC is defined.

Once this is done, we can then modify the **Update** function

- Please modify the **Update** function as follows (new code in bold).

```
timer += Time.deltaTime;
if (timer > 4) {
        timer = 0;
        wander ();
}
if (isFollowingWayPoints)
{
        target = WayPoints [WPCount];
        if (Vector3.Distance(transform.position, target.transform.position) < 1.0)
        {
                //moveToNextWP ();
                moveToRandomWP ();
        }
}
GetComponent<NavMeshAgent> ().SetDestination (target.transform.position);
```

In the previous code:

- The value of the timer will increase by one every seconds.

Using Fixed and Random Paths for NPCs

- After 4 seconds, the timer is reset to zero.

- In this case, the function wander (that we will create in the next section) is called; this means that we will define a new direction (and target) for our NPC.

- The rest of the code is similar to what we have coded earlier-on, in that: if we are in the state **isFollowingWayPoints**, and if the NPC is close to its current target, then the function **moveToRandomWP** will be called.

You can now save your code, and check that it is error-free.

So at this stage we just need to declare the function called **wander** and add the code within that will determine the new direction for the NPC.

- Please create the function called **wander** by adding this code.

```
void wander()
{

}
```

- Add the following code within the function:

```
Ray ray = new Ray();
RaycastHit hit;
ray.origin = transform.position + Vector3.up * 0.7f;
float distanceToObstacle = 0;
float castingDistance = 20;
```

In the previous code:

- We create a new ray

- We define a **RaycastHit** variable that will be used to obtain information about the object that has been detected in front of the player (i.e., the object that collided with the ray).

- We then specify its origin; it will start at same the position as the player, at a height of **0.7**.

- Two additional variables are then declared: **distanceToObstacle** will be used to determine how far the object is from the NPC, and **castingDistance** will be used to specify that we will cast a ray at a maximum of 20 meters away from the NPC.

Now that the ray has been defined, we can start to define a direction for this ray,

- Please add the following code before the end of the function wander:

Using Fixed and Random Paths for NPCs

```
do
{
        float randomDirectionX = Random.Range (-1.0f, 1.0f);
        float randomDirectionZ = Random.Range (-1.0f, 1.0f);
        ray.direction = transform.forward*randomDirectionZ + transform.right * randomDirectionX;
        Debug.DrawRay (ray.origin, ray.direction, Color.red);
} while (distanceToObstacle < 1.0f);
```

In the previous code:

- We create a **while** loop.

- We will stay in this loop as long as we are very near an obstacle (i.e., if **distanceToObstacle** is less than **1.0**).

- We declare two variables; **randomDirectionX** and **randomDirectionZ**; these variables will range between **-1** and **+1** and will be employed to define a random vector.

- These values are then employed to define the direction of our ray; by default, the ray points forward; however, we add a random direction to it. So our NPC may be going left or right (depending on the variable **randomDirectionX**), and forward or back (depending on the variable **randomDirectionZ**).

- Once the origin and the direction of the ray have been set, we then use the built-in function called **Debug.DrawRay** to draw a ray that will only be visible in the **Scene** view; it is so that we can check whether the ray is pointing in a correct direction. To use this function, we specify the origin and the direction of the ray, along with a color of our choice (i.e., red).

Now that the ray has a starting point and a direction, we can start to cast this ray and to detect potential objects in front of the player.

- Please add the following code within the loop, just after the statements that starts with **Debug.DrawRay**.

```
if (Physics.Raycast (ray.origin, ray.direction, out hit, castingDistance))
        {
                distanceToObstacle = hit.distance;
        }
        else distanceToObstacle = castingDistance;

wanderingTarget.transform.position = ray.origin + ray.direction * (distanceToObstacle - 1);
target = wanderingTarget;
```

In the previous code:

- We detect objects ahead of the NPC by using the built-in function **Physics.Raycast**.

Using Fixed and Random Paths for NPCs

> Note that **Physics.RayCast** casts a ray and will detect objects ahead of the NPC, while **Debug.DrawRay** will only draw a ray that will be visible in the **Scene** view.

- In case an object has been detected ahead of the player, we save the distance between the NPC and this object in the variable called **distanceToObstacle**.

- Otherwise, we set the variable **distanceToObstacle** to the value saved in **castingDistance** (i.e., 20); this way, if there is no obstacle detected, the NPC will walk forward for 20 meters.

- Once this is done, we set the position of the **wanderingTarget** accordingly, so that it is about one meter just before our destination.

- We then set the target for the NPC accordingly.

You can now save your code and check that it is error-free.

Last but not least: in order to test our code, we will need to create walls that the NPC has to avoid. So let's go ahead and create these walls.

- Please create a new cube, and rename it **wall**.

- Set its position to **(20, 2.5, 18)** and its scale to **(10, 4, 10)**.

- Apply the **red** material to this wall.

- Duplicate the object **wall** 8 times, and move the duplicates along the x and z-axes to obtain a layout similar to the next figure.

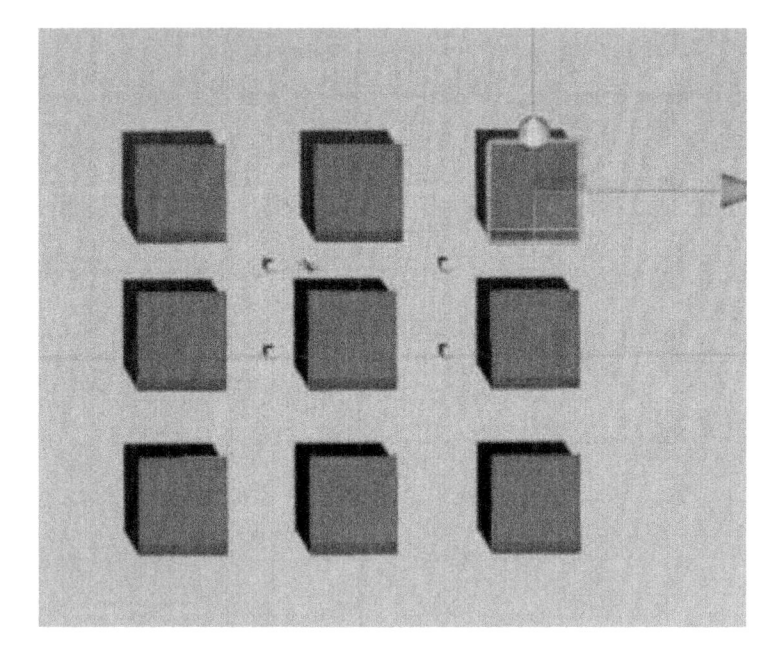

Figure 67: Creating the walls

- Once this is done, you can select the 9 walls, and bake them using the **Navigation** window, as we have done earlier-on.

Figure 68: Baking the walls

Lastly, you can change the position of the **NPC** from **(-12, 0.5, 0)** to **(-12. .5, -7),** so that it is not within any of the walls, and test your scene. You should see that the NPC is wandering around the level aimlessly.

Figure 69: The Wandering NPC

After testing the game, you may notice that the NPC may occasionally find itself stuck in a wall (i.e., walking towards the wall although very close to the wall); this is because, according to our code, the change of direction is done only every 4 seconds; this means that we will look for the presence of the wall only every 4 seconds; so, we will modify our code so that the NPC checks every frame whether a wall is 1 meter ahead; if it is the case, then the function wander will be called, and the direction will be recalculated automatically.

- Please add the following function to the script **ControlNPC**:

```
void checkAhead()
{
        Ray ray = new Ray();
        RaycastHit hit;
        float castingDistance = 2;
        ray.origin = transform.position + Vector3.up * 0.7f;
        ray.direction = transform.forward * castingDistance;
                Debug.DrawRay (ray.origin, ray.direction, Color.red);
        if (Physics.Raycast (ray.origin, ray.direction, out hit, castingDistance))
        {
                print ("object in sight at"+hit.distance);
                wander ();
        }
}
```

In the previous code:

- We detect objects that are two meters ahead of the NPC
- If an object is detected, then the function wander is called.
- We also print the distance to the object, for testing purposes.

Now that this is done, you can add the following code at the beginning of the function **Update** (new code in bold):

```
void Update ()
{
        checkAhead ();
```

LEVEL ROUNDUP

Well, this is it!

In this chapter, we have learned about creating and managing our NPC using different types of navigation from a simple target, to paths; along the way, we also managed to make this navigation less predictable by adding random destinations or by creating wandering navigation. So, we have, again, covered some significant ground compared to the last chapter.

Checklist

You can consider moving to the next chapter if you can do the following:

- Create a simple Animator Controller.
- Associate an animation to a state in an Animator Controller.
- Create a path for an NPC.

Quiz

Now, let's check your knowledge! Please answer the following questions or specify if these statements are either correct or incorrect (the solutions are on the next page).

1. An **Animator Controller** can be used to apply animations to a character.

2. An **Animator Controller** can be modified using the **Animation** window.

3. It is not possible to modify an animation imported in Unity.

4. Waypoints can be used to define a path.

5. Waypoints need to include a collider.

6. The function **Vector3.Distance** can be used to calculate the distance between two objects.

7. The function **Random.Range** can be used to generate random numbers.

8. The functions **Debug.DrawRay** can be used to detect objects ahead of the NPC.

9. The functions **Physics.Raycast** can be used to detect objects ahead of the NPC.

10. When casting a ray, its origin and direction need to be specified.

Quiz Solutions

Now, let's check if you have answered the questions correctly.

1. True.

2. False (it's the **Animator** window).

3. False.

4. True

5. False (only their position is used, so collision detection is not necessary).

6. True.

7. True.

8. False: it is only used to see how the ray is cast. But it does not detect any object.

9. True.

10. True.

Challenge 1

Now that you have managed to complete this chapter and that you have improved your skills, let's do the following.

- Create two additional paths and their corresponding waypoints, and apply these to the NPC. When an NPC has completed its current path, it will randomly be assigned to one of the other two paths.

7
ADDING VISION AND HEARING TO NPCS

In this section, we will start to add more sensing features to our NPC so that it can gather information about its environment and make decisions accordingly.

After completing this chapter, you will be able to:

- Use Finite State Machines.

- Simulate senses for the NPC (i.e., hearing, vision, or smell).

- Make it possible for the NPC to make decisions based on its senses.

- Make it possible for the NPC to make decisions based on internal values (e.g., health, ammos, hearing, etc.)

- Make it possible for the NPC to make decisions based on known information (i.e., omniscient behaviour).

The code solutions for this chapter are in the **resource pack** that you can download by following the instructions included in the section entitled "Support and Resources for this Book".

SETTING-UP THE LEVEL

If you remember well, in the second chapter, we have already created an NPC as well as a corresponding environment with a ground and walls; so, to save us extra (and unnecessary) work, but to also make it possible for you to go back to the settings in the second chapter (if need be), we will duplicate the second level, and also create a new class based on the one created in the second level.

First, let's duplicate the second level and the NPC.

- Please drag and drop the object called **NPC** to the project window (this will create a prefab called **NPC**), and rename the prefab **NPC1**. This will also rename the corresponding object in the **Hierarchy** window to **NPC1**.

- Please save the current scene (**CTRL + S**).

- In the **Project** window, select the folder called **Assets**, and create a new folder called **chapter3** within by selecting **Create | Folder**.

- Then locate the scene called **chapter2**, that you have created in the second chapter, duplicate it (i.e., **CTRL + D**), rename the duplicate **chapter3**, and move this duplicate to the folder called **chapter3**.

Figure 70: Creating a new scene

- Once this is done, we can open the scene called **chapter3** by double clicking on it.

- Locate the script called **ControlNPC**.

- Duplicate it (i.e., **CTRL + D**), this will create a file called **ControlNPC1**.

- Rename this class **ControlNPC2**;

At this stage, Unity will display an error because the name of the class **ControlNPC2** is not identical to the name of the class within the file; so we will need to modify the file accordingly.

- Please open the file **ControlNPC2** (i.e., double click on it).

- Change this line...

```
public class ControlNPC : MonoBehaviour {
```

to this code...

```
public class ControlNPC2 : MonoBehaviour {
```

- Please save your code.

- In the **Hierarchy** window, rename the object **NPC1** to **NPC2**.

- Drag and drop the object **NPC2** to the **Project** window; this will create a new prefab called **NPC2**. So any change made to this object can be applied to the corresponding prefab and vice versa.

At this stage, if you play the scene, the NPC will behave in the exact same way as in chapter2, by wandering aimlessly in the level.

In the next section, we will learn to modify its behavior so that it takes decisions based on its senses.

BUILDING A NEW ANIMATOR CONTROLLER

Because this NPC will behave differently to the one created in the second chapter, we will create a corresponding **Animator Controller**.

- In the **Project** window, please select the option: **Create | Animator Controller**.

- This will create a new **Animator Controller**.

- Rename it **ControlNPC2** and then double click on this **Animator Controller** to open it in the **Animator** window.

- Once the **Animator** window is open, create a new state by right-clicking within the **Animator** window and by selecting the option **Create State | Empty** in the contextual menu.

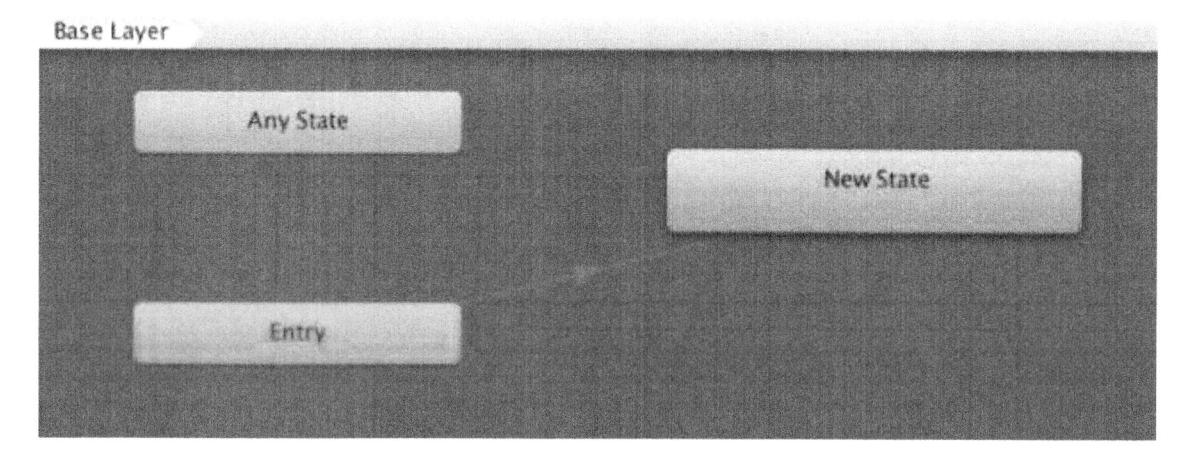

Figure 71: Creating a new state

- Select the new state that you have just created, and using the **Inspector**, change its name to **idle**. So by default, once we have linked this **Animator Controller** to the NPC, the NPC will be in the state called **idle**.

- In the **Inspector**, please click to the right of the label called **motion**.

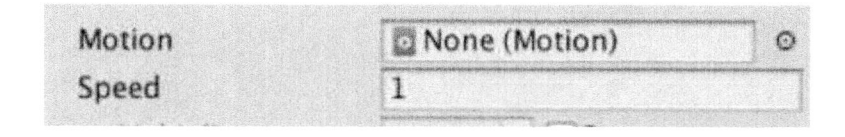

- This should open a new window.

Adding Vision and Hearing to NPCs

- In the new window, please type the text **idle** in the search field, as illustrated in the next figure.

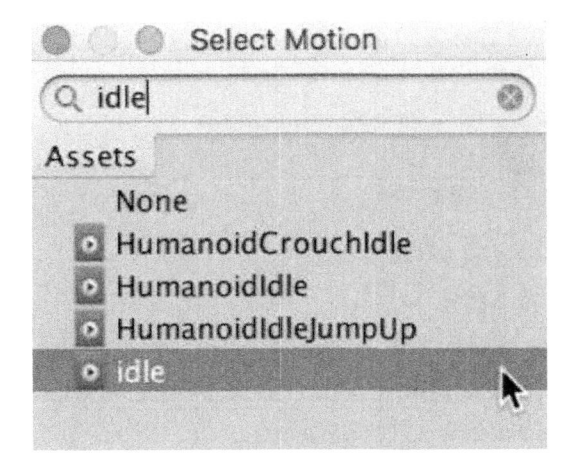

Figure 72: Selecting the idle clip (part 1)

- You can then double click on the clip **idle** listed in the results.

- Looking at the **Inspector**, you should now see that the clip called **idle** has now been selected for this state, as illustrated in the next figure.

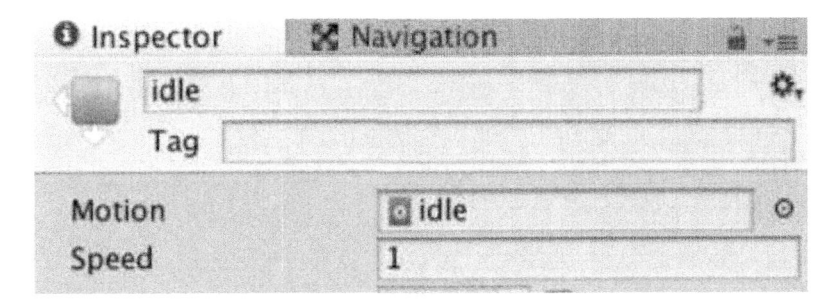

Figure 73: Selecting the idle clip (part 2)

Now that we have specified a new state and a corresponding animation, we can allocate this **Animator Controller** to the NPC.

- Using the **Hierarchy**, select the object **NPC2**.

- Using the **Inspector**, scroll down to the component called **Animator**, you should see that the active animator is the one we have created in the last chapter (i.e., **walkingAnimation**).

Adding Vision and Hearing to NPCs

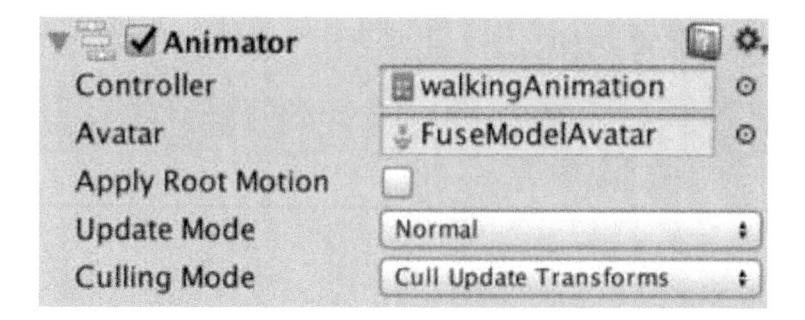

Figure 74: The Animator attribute

- So now, we can replace this animation with the one that we have just created, by dragging and dropping the **Animator Controller** called **ControlNPC2** from the **Project** window to this field, as illustrated in the next figure.

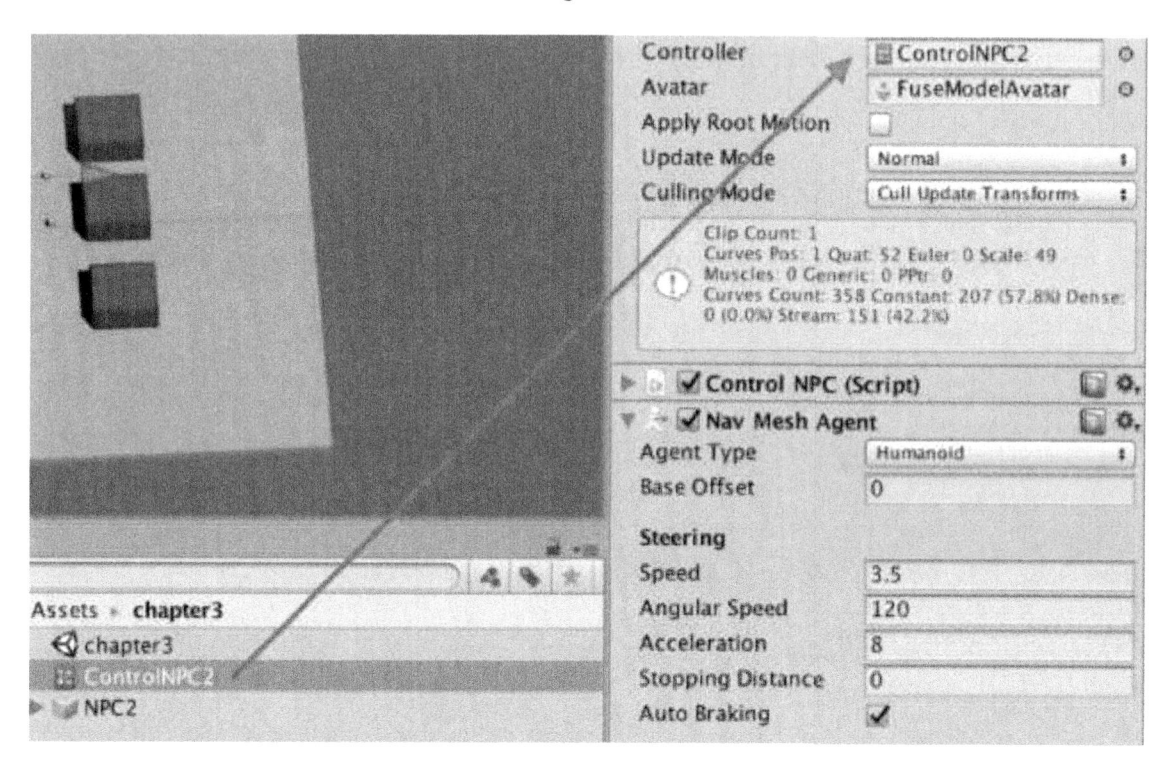

Figure 75: Applying the new Animator Controller to the NPC

Before we can play the scene, we just need to modify the script attached to the NPC, because, as it is, the NPC would be wandering indefinitely otherwise.

- Please select the object **NPC2**.

- Using the **Inspector**, delete the component called **ControlNPC**; we no longer need this script, as we will be using the new script **ControlNPC2** instead for this NPC. To delete this component, you can right-click on it in the **Inspector** window, and then select the option **Remove Component** from the contextual menu, as illustrated in the next figure.

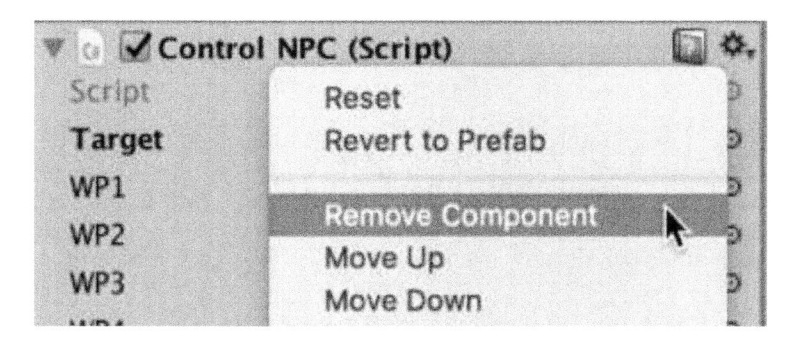

Figure 76: Removing the component ControlNPC

- Once this is done, drag and drop the script called **ControlNPC2** from the **Project** window to the object **NPC2** (or to the **Inspector** window), so that the object **NPC2** now includes a new component called **ControlNPC2**, as illustrated in the next figure.

Figure 77: Adding the new Animator Controller

Now that the script is linked to the NPC, we just need to temporarily deactivate the wandering and patrolling movements.

Please open the script **ControlNPC2**.

- Modify the function **Start** as follows (new code in bold)

```
void Start () {
isWandering = false;
isFollowingWayPoints = false;
```

In the previous code, we just specify that the NPC will neither be wandering nor following waypoints.

- Please comment the following line in the **Update** function also:

Adding Vision and Hearing to NPCs

```
//GetComponent<UnityEngine.AI.NavMeshAgent>().SetDestination (target.transform.position);
```

- Comment this lines in the **Update** function.

```
//wander ();
```

... and this line also.

```
//checkAhead();
```

- Save your code and check that it is error-free.

You can now play the scene and check that the NPC is idle; if you walk closer to the NPC, you might also notice that the animation for the NPC stops after a few seconds. This is because the animation clip for the NPC animation needs to be modified slightly in order to specify that it should loop overtime, as we have done earlier for the walking clip.

- In the **Project** window, please use the *search* field to look for the word **idle**, as illustrated in the next window.

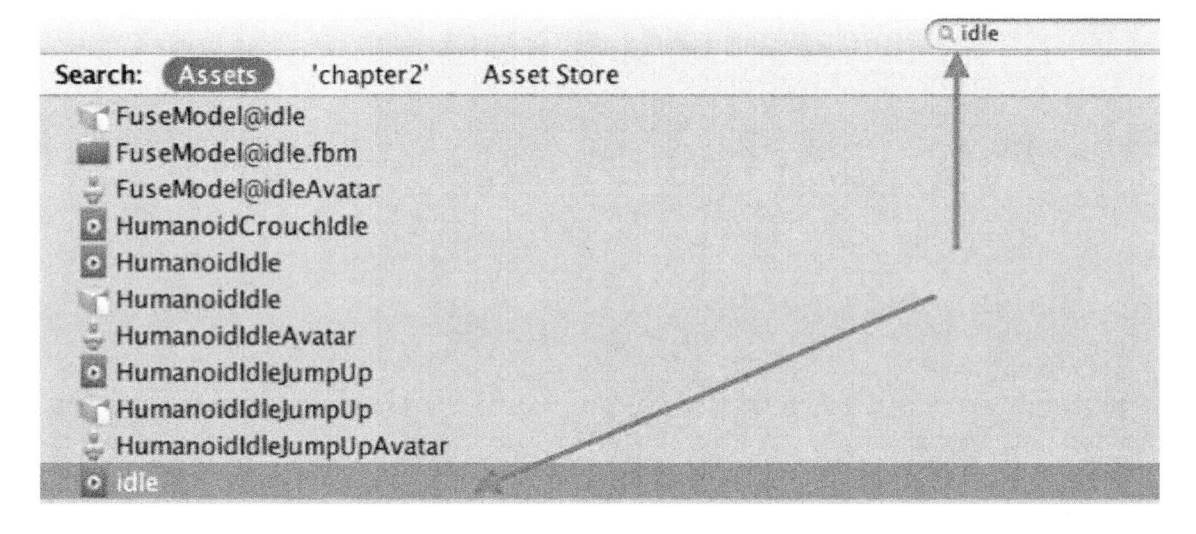

Figure 78: Locating the idle animation

- Select the **idle** clip (symbolized by a dark square with a triangle within), as illustrated in the previous figure.
- Using the **Inspector**, click on the button labelled **Edit** to edit this clip.

[280]

Adding Vision and Hearing to NPCs

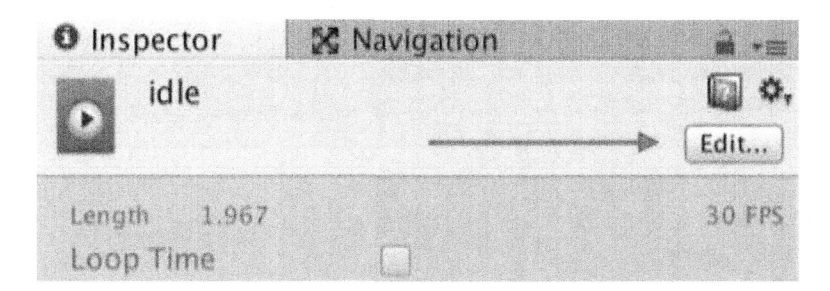

Figure 79 :Editing the animation

- Check (i.e., select) both the options **Loop Pose** and **Loop Time**.

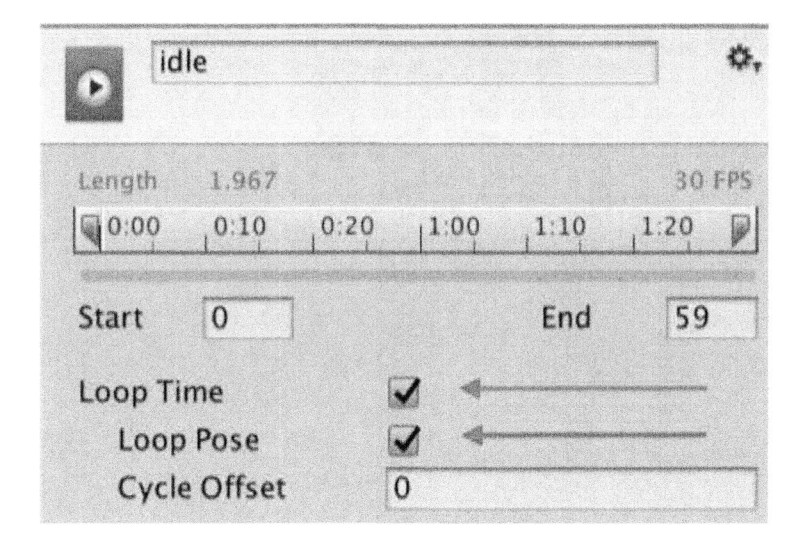

Figure 80: Modifying the animation

- Once these changes have been made, you can click on the button called **Apply**, so that these changes can be applied accordingly to the **idle** animation.

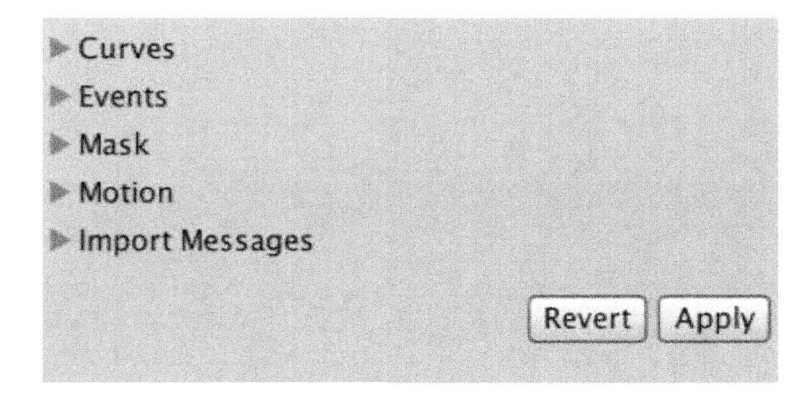

Figure 81: Applying the changes

[281]

Adding Vision and Hearing to NPCs

- Please play the scene, and you should see that the NPC is now animated properly, and that the animation is looping overtime.

Figure 82: The looping idle animation applied to the NPC

TRIGGERING THE NPC TO CHANGE STATE FROM IDLE TO PATROL

At this stage, the NPC is idle with a corresponding state and animation; the idea that we will apply in this section is as follows:

- At frequent intervals (e.g., every couple of seconds), the NPC will start to patrol the scene and follow the waypoints that we have defined earlier.

- Once it has completed its "round", the NPC will go back to its initial position and become idle for another while.

To create such a behavior, we will proceed as follows:

- Create a new state called **patrol**.

- Create a transition between the two states **idle** and **patrol**.

- Triger this transition based on parameters defined in the **Animator Controller**.

- Control the value of this "trigger" from the script, so that the trigger is set accordingly after a specific number of seconds.

So first, let's create the state called **patrol**, as you have done for the previous state.

- Open the Animator Controller **ControlNPC2** in the **Animator** window.

- Create a new state and rename it **patrol**.

- Add (i.e., link) the animation called **walking** to this state.

- After ensuring that the **Parameter** tab is active in the **Animator** window, click on the + button to the right of the search field and select the option **Trigger** from the contextual menu, as in the next figure.

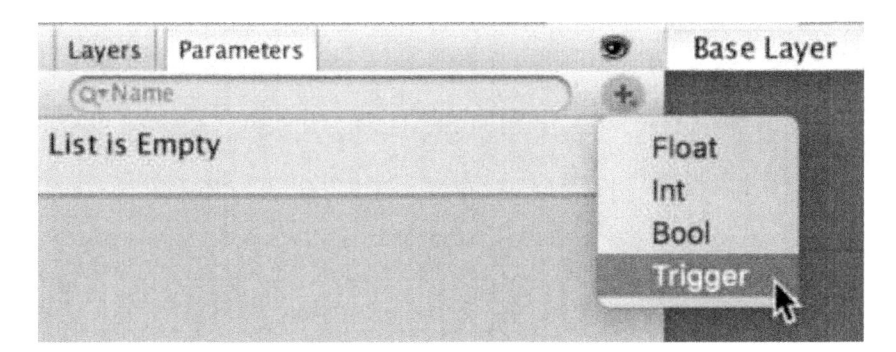

Figure 83: Creating a new trigger

Adding Vision and Hearing to NPCs

> Note that other types of variables can be created and used in **Animator Controllers** including **Booleans**, **Integer**, and **Float**. Triggers are comparable to Booleans in the sense that they are either true or false; the key difference is that if they are used in a transition (as it will be the case in the next section) their value will be reset after the transition has occurred; for example, if a trigger is initially false, and then set to true to trigger a transition, its value will be reset to false after the transition has occurred between two states.

- This will create a new trigger that you can rename **startPatrol**.

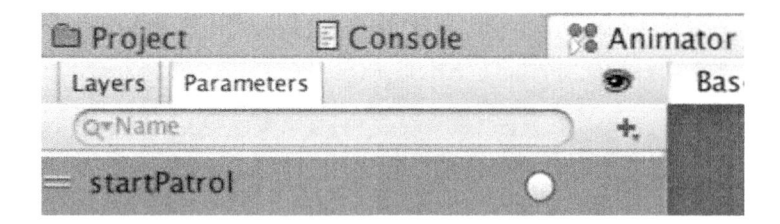

Figure 84: Creating a trigger

This trigger will be used in the next section to manage the transition between the states idle and patrol.

Next, we will create a transition between the two states and specify that it should occur only when the variable **startPatrol** is true.

- Please right-click on the state **idle**.

- From the contextual menu, select **Make Transition**.

- Then click on the state **patrol**.

- This should create a transition, symbolized by a white arrow, between the two states, as illustrated in the next figure.

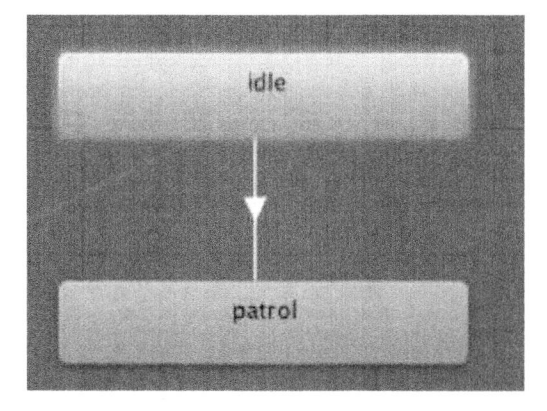

Once this is done, we just need to manage the transition that we have just created and specify when it should occur.

[284]

- Please select the transition (i.e., click once on it).

- In the **Inspector** window, scroll down to the section called **Conditions**, and click on the + button that is located to the right of the label "**List is Empty**".

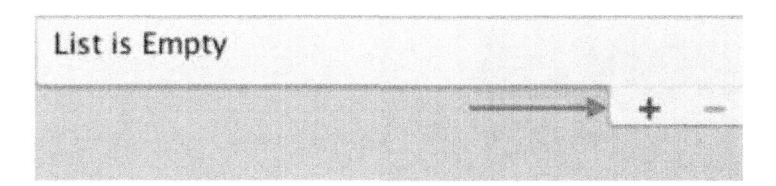

Figure 85: Creating a new condition

- By default, because **startPatrol** is the only parameter declared for our **Animator Controller**, it will be used as the default condition for the transition, as illustrated in the next figure.

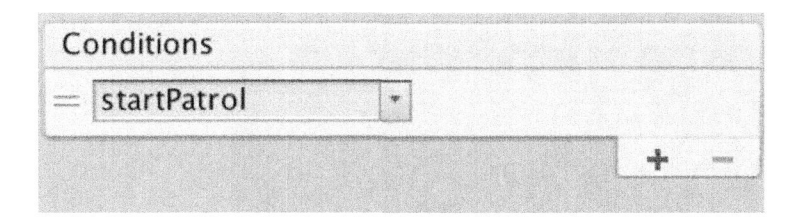

Figure 86: Setting a condition for the transition

- So this means that the transition from the state **idle** to the state **patrol** will occur if (and only if) the variable **startPatrol** is set to true.

Now that the **Animator Controller** is set-up, we can test it by doing the following:

- Play the scene.

- Press the escape key on your keyboard as the scene is playing; this will make it possible for you to click on any of the other windows in Unity while the game is playing.

- Select the **Scene** view.

- In the **Hierarchy**, double click on the object **NPC2**, so that the view is focused on this object. You should see that the NPC is idle.

Adding Vision and Hearing to NPCs

Figure 87: The NPC is idle

If you then look at the **Animator** window, you should see that the active state is the state called **idle**, based on the blue progression bar located below the state **idle**, that indicates that it is the active state, as illustrated in the next figure.

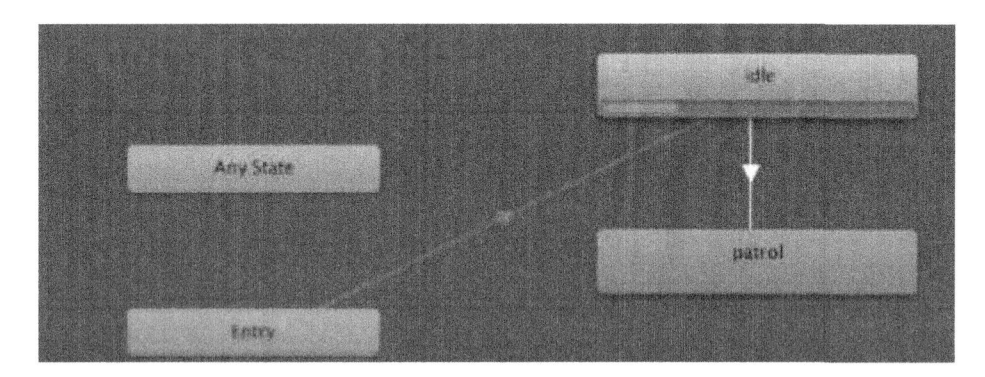

Figure 88: Checking the active state

- In the **Animator** window, in the tab called **Parameter**, click on the radio button called **startPatrol**, this should set the Trigger **startPatrol** to true.

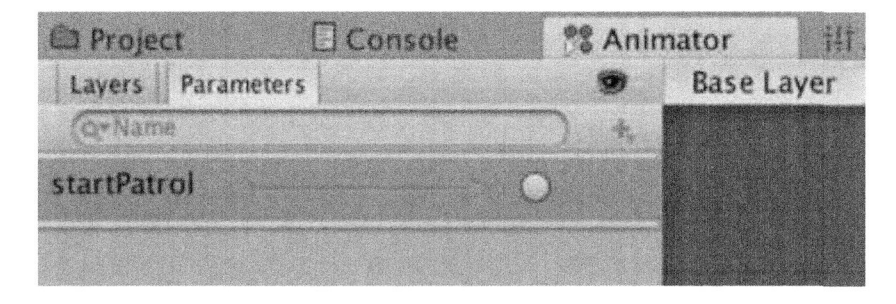

Figure 89: Activating the trigger called startPatrol

- As you do so, you should see that the **Animator Controller** has transitioned to the state called **patrol**.

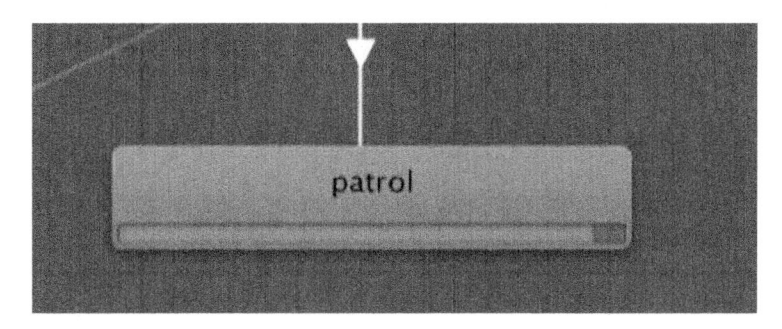

- You will also notice that the NPC is now walking, which is the default animation that we have defined for the state **patrol**.

Figure 90: The NPC is walking

ASSOCIATING A MOVEMENT TO A STATE FROM THE SCRIPT

As you have seen in the previous section, the NPC can now change its state, based on the trigger that we have defined. However, the NPC is walking on the spot, and is not yet patrolling; this is because, for now, we have only specified an animation for the state called **patrol**; this being said, what we would need now, would be for the NPC to follow a path when it is in this particular state. In addition, it would be great to trigger the change based on, let's say, a timer, so that the NPC goes patrolling after a few seconds or minutes.

First we will make sure that the NPC follows a path when in the state called **patrol**, and this will be done as follows:

- Modify the script **ControlNPC2**.
- Link the script to the **Animator Controller**.
- Check from the script whether the NPC is in the state called **patrol**.
- If this is the case, make sure that the NPC is following a path, as we have done in the previous chapter.

So, in the next section, we will make sure that the transition from the state **idle** to the state **patrol** is triggered at frequent intervals from the script, and this will be done as follows:

- Create a timer.
- When this timer reaches a specific time, trigger the transition between these two states by setting the trigger variable called **startPatrol**, from the **Animator Controller**, to true.
- Reset the timer.

So, with this in mind, let's start the first part, which consists in setting the NPC on a path when in the state called **patrol**.

- Please open the script **ControlNPC2**.
- Add the following code at the beginning of the script (i.e., just before the **Start** function)

```
Animator anim;
AnimatorStateInfo info;
```

In the previous code:

Adding Vision and Hearing to NPCs

- We declare two variables **anim** and **info**.

- The variable **anim** will be used to refer (or point) to the **Animator** component for the object **NPC2**.

- The variable **info** will be used to determine the current state for the object **NPC2**.

We can now use these variable to set-up the path.

- Please add the following code at the beginning of the function **Start**:

```
anim = GetComponent<Animator> ();
target = new GameObject ();
```

- Please add the following code at the start of the **Update** function.

```
info = anim.GetCurrentAnimatorStateInfo (0);
```

- In the previous code, we state that the variable **anim** will point to the current state for the **Animator Controller**; this is done through the built-in function **GetCurrentAnimatorStateInfo**; the parameter **0** means that we are referring to the first layer in the **Animator Controller**.

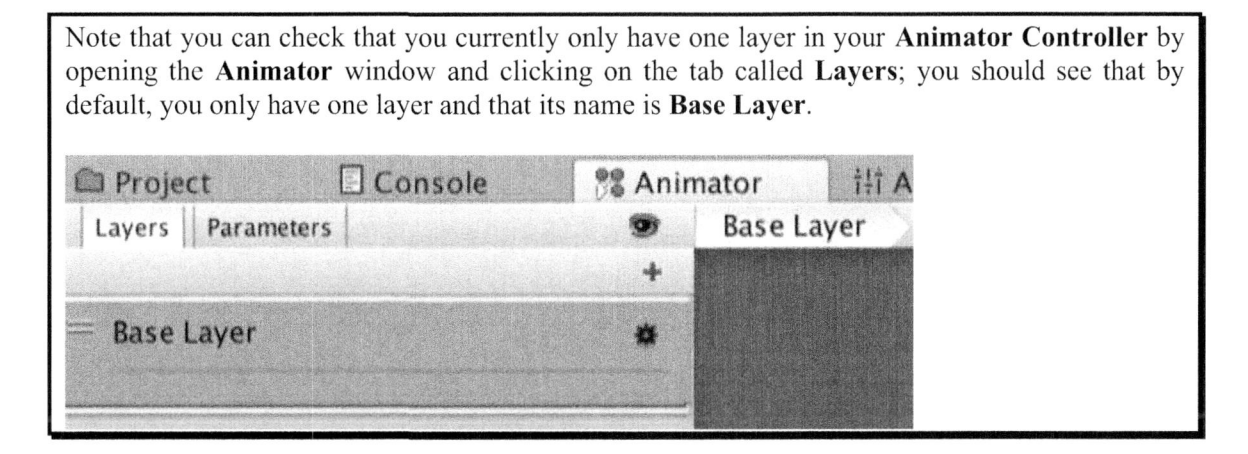

> Note that you can check that you currently only have one layer in your **Animator Controller** by opening the **Animator** window and clicking on the tab called **Layers**; you should see that by default, you only have one layer and that its name is **Base Layer**.
>
> [Screenshot showing Animator window with Layers tab and Base Layer]

Figure 91: Checking the layers for the Animator Controller

- In the **Update** function, replace this line:

```
//if (isFollowingWayPoints)
```

with this line:

```
if (info.IsName("patrol"))
```

In the previous code, we check that the current state for the NPC is **patrol**. If this is the case, we do as we have done previously (i.e., setting a new target).

Adding Vision and Hearing to NPCs

- Add the following code (new code in bold).

```
if(Vector3.Distance(transform.position,target.transform.position) < 1.0)
{
    //moveToNextWP ();
    moveToRandomWP ();
}
GetComponent<NavMeshAgent>().SetDestination (target.transform.position);
```

In the previous code, we just set the new destination for our NPC based on the target defined earlier.

> Note that, as it is, the function **moveToRandomWP** is used; however, you could also use the other function **moveToNextWP** instead, if you would prefer the NPC to follow the waypoints sequentially rather than randomly.

- Please save your code and check that it is error-free.

Once this is done, you can test your scene and trigger the transition by setting the parameter **startPatrol** to true in the **Animator** window; you should see that the NPC is now in the state called **patrol** and that it is following the waypoints.

> Note that, while the scene is playing, and if you'd like to see where the waypoints are located, you can temporarily select them all and enable their **Mesh Renderer** Component.

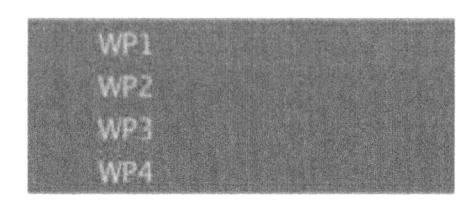

Figure 92: Selecting all the waypoints in the Hierarchy window

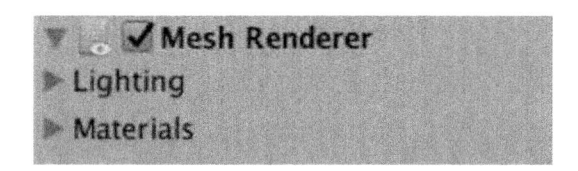

Figure 93: Activating the waypoints' mesh renderers

Adding Vision and Hearing to NPCs

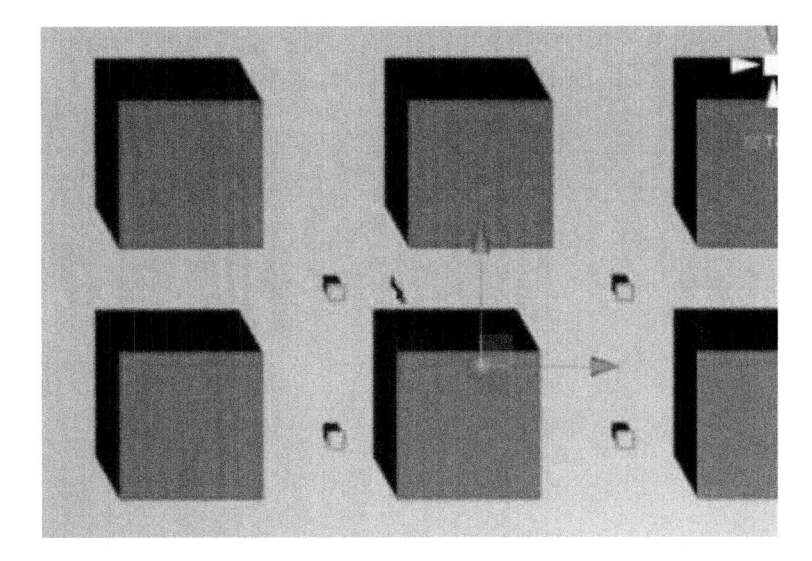

Figure 94: The NPC walking towards the waypoints

The next thing we need to do, is to be able to set the trigger between the two states at regular intervals; for this purpose, we will modify the script **ControlNPC2**.

- Please add the following code just before the function **Start**.

```
float patrolTimer;
```

- Add the following code at the beginning of the function **Start**.

```
patrolTimer = 0.0f;
```

- Add the following code at the end of the function **Update**.

```
if (info.IsName ("idle"))
{
        patrolTimer += Time.deltaTime;
        if (patrolTimer > 5) {
                patrolTimer = 0;
                anim.SetTrigger ("startPatrol");
        }
}
```

In the previous code:

- We check whether the **NPC** is in the state called **idle**.
- If this is the case, we increase the value of the variable **patrolTimer** by one every seconds.

Adding Vision and Hearing to NPCs

- When this value has reached 5 seconds, we then reset the timer and set the **Trigger** parameter of our **Animator Controller**, called **startPatrol,** to **true** using the built-in function **anim.SetTrigger**.

Please save your code, and play the scene; you should see that after 5 seconds the NPC will start to patrol.

So, when you have checked that the code works properly, we can now complete this behavior by setting the NPC to go back to its initial position after it has completed its path or gone through at least 4 waypoints. So we will proceed as follows:

- We will save the original position of the NPC as it is idle.

- When the NPC follows a path (randomly or sequentially), we will count the number of waypoints that it has reached.

- After reaching the 4th waypoint, the NPC will then go back to its original position.

For this, we will need to create additional states, as well as transitions. So let's get started!

- Please open the **Animator** window.

- Create an additional state called **backToStart**. This state will be used to identify when the NPC has completed its path and to define when it is walking back to its initial position.

- Associate the animation clip **walking** to this state, as we have done earlier.

- Create two new **Trigger** parameters: **startToGoBackToStart** and **hasReachedStart**.

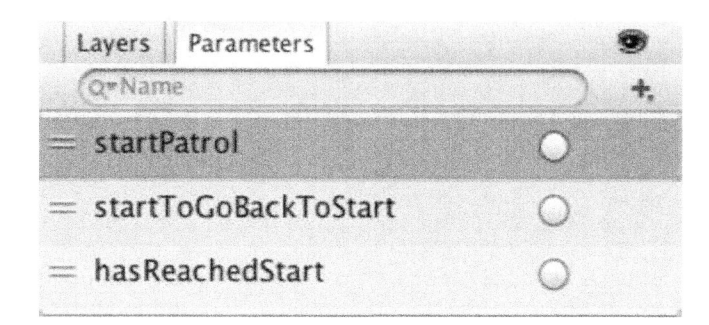

Figure 95: creating two new parameters

- Create a transition from the state **patrol** to the state **backToStart**, and use the parameter **startToGoBackToStart** as a condition for this transition to occur.

- Create a transition from the state **backToStart** to the state **idle**, and use the parameter **hasReachedStart** as a condition for this transition to occur.

Adding Vision and Hearing to NPCs

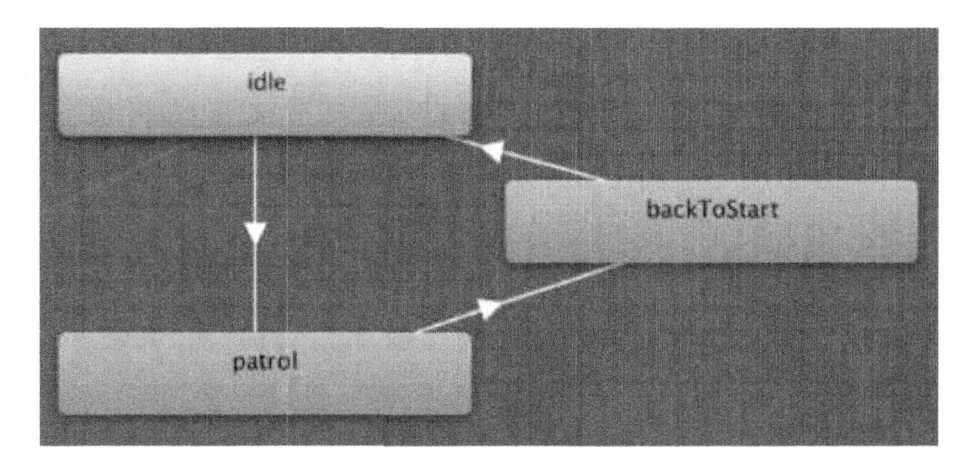

Figure 96: Creating a new state and associated transitions

Once this is done, we just need to modify our script **ControlNPC2**.

- Please open the script **ControlNPC2**.
- Add the following code just before the function **Start**.

```
int nbWPReached = 0;
Vector3 startingPosition;
```

- Add this code at the beginning of the function **Start**.

```
startingPosition = gameObject.transform.position;
```

- Modify the **Update** function as follows (new code in bold):

```
if(Vector3.Distance(transform.position,target.transform.position) < 1.0)
{
        moveToNextWP ();
        //moveToRandomWP ();
        nbWPReached++;
        if (nbWPReached >= 4)
        {
                nbWPReached = 0;
                anim.SetTrigger ("startToGoBackToStart");
        }
}
```

In the previous code, if we have reached 4 consecutive waypoints, then we reset the variable **nbWPReached**, and set the Trigger parameter **startToGoBackToStart** from the **Animator Controller** to **true**. We also set the patrol to be sequential between the waypoints.

Next we just need to ensure that the NPC goes back to the **idle** state once it has reached its initial position.

[293]

- Please, add the following code to the function **Update**.

```
if (info.IsName ("backToStart"))
{
        GetComponent<UnityEngine.AI.NavMeshAgent> ().SetDestination (startingPosition);
        if (Vector3.Distance(transform.position, startingPosition) < 1.0) anim.SetTrigger ("hasReachedStart");
}
```

In the previous code: if we are in the state called **backToStart**, we check whether we are near the initial position; if it is the case, we then set the Trigger parameter **hasReachedStart** from the **Animator Controller** to true.

You can now test your scene, and check that the NPC starts to patrol after a few seconds and that it also goes back to its initial position after completing the patrol (i.e., after the last waypoint).

ADDING HEARING

In the previous sections, the NPC was taking the decision to start patrolling or to go back to its original position, based on a timer; while this makes the NPC more believable, it would be great if this NPC could use simulated sense, such as smell, hearing, or sight, to detect the player or objects in the scene, and take action accordingly. So in his section we will add these senses to the NPC, as follows:

- We will create parameters, in the **Animator Controller**, related to sight, hearing, and smell.

- In the script, we will implement the code that simulates these senses.

- When the simulated senses have, through the script, detected something, the Animator Controller will be updated accordingly, and transitions may also occur.

So let's get started!

- Using the **Animator** window for the **Animator Controller** called **ControlNPC2**, please create a new state called **followPlayer** and associate the animation **walking** to this state, as we have done for the state called patrol.

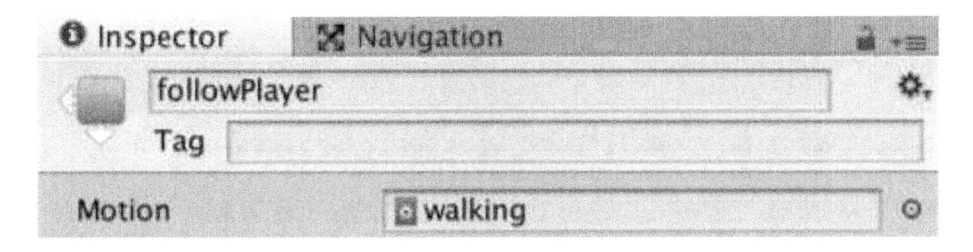

Figure 97: Associating the animation called walking

- Create a new **Boolean** parameter called **canHearPlayer**.

Figure 98: Creating a new Boolean parameter

- Create a transition between the state **Any State** and the state called **followPlayer**.

Adding Vision and Hearing to NPCs

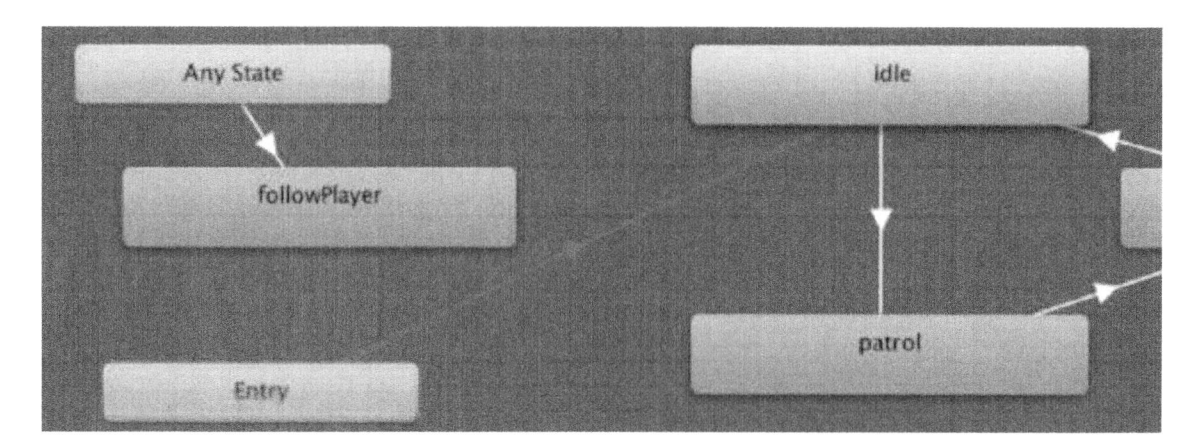

Figure 99: Creating a new state and a transition

- Set the variable **canHearPlayer** to be the condition for this transition.

Figure 100: Setting the condition for the transition

> The stated called **Any State** is a virtual state that correspond to any state that you have created in your **Animator Controller**. It can be used to create general transitions and associated rules, and to avoid repeating the same transition between states. In our case, we want to create a transition regardless of the original state to the state called **followPlayer**; in other word, this transition should occur regardless of the current state.

Once this is done, we can start to modify our script.

- Please open the script **ControlNPC2**.

- Create the following function at the end of the script (i.e., before the last closing curly bracket).

```
void listen()
{
        float    distance    =    Vector3.Distance    (gameObject.transform.position,    GameObject.Find
("FPSController").transform.position);
        if (distance < 3) {
                anim.SetBool ("canHearPlayer", true);
        }
}
```

In the previous code:

- We create a new function called **listen**.

- This function calculates the distance between the NPC and the player using the built-in function **Vector3.Distance**.

- If the player is within a radius of 3 meters, then we can assume that the NPC can hear the player and we set the parameter **canHearPlayer** to true accordingly.

Next we can modify the **Update** function:

- Please, add the following code to the **Update** function.

```
if (info.IsName ("followPlayer"))
{
        target = GameObject.Find ("FPSController");
        GetComponent<UnityEngine.AI.NavMeshAgent> ().SetDestination (target.transform.position);
}
```

- Please Save your script, check that it is error free, and play the scene.

As the scene is playing, you can open the **Animator** window (after pressing the ESC key), change the parameter **canHearPlayer** to true, and see how the NPC is now following the player.

Once you have checked that the transition is working, we will make it possible for the NPC to detect the player.

- Please modify the script to add the following code to the **Update** function (new code in bold).

```
info = anim.GetCurrentAnimatorStateInfo (0);
listen ();
```

Play the scene again, but this time, walk close to the NPC so that you are within a radius of about 3 meters. The NPC should start to follow you, as illustrated in the next figure.

Adding Vision and Hearing to NPCs

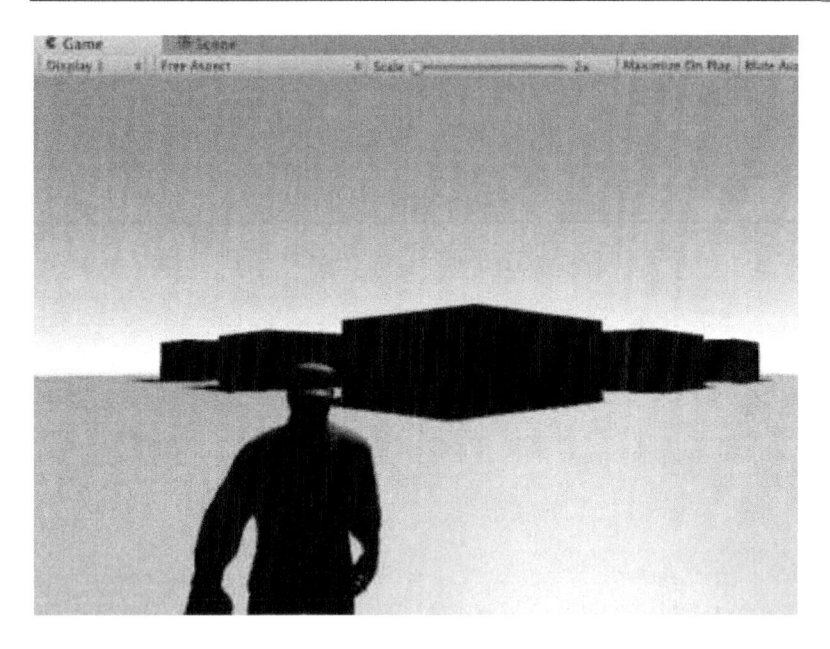

Figure 101: The NPC after detecting the player.

- You should also see that the **Animator Controller** has transitioned to the state called **followPlayer**. If you look at the **Animator Controller**, you may see that the NPC constantly transitions from **Any State** to **followPlayer** (the arrow is blue).

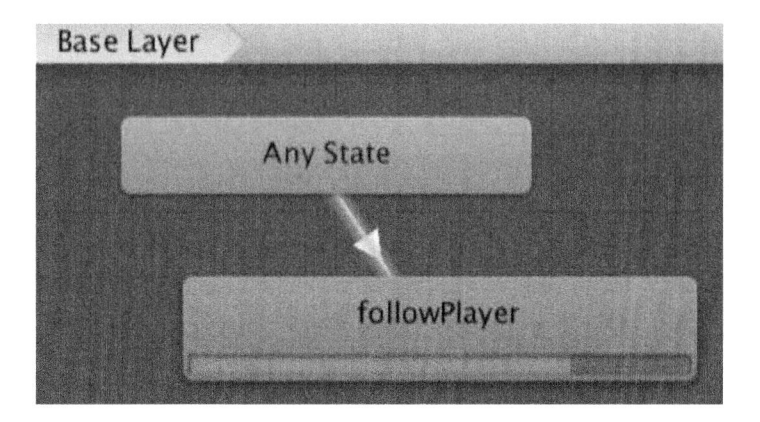

Figure 102: Constant transitions to the state followPlayer

To avoid this constant transition, we just need to let Unity know that the NPC should not transition to the state **followPlayer** if it is already in this state; in other words, it should not transition to its current state; this can be done as follows:

- Select the transition between the state **Any State** and the state **followPlayer** in the **Animator**.

Adding Vision and Hearing to NPCs

- Using the **Inspector** window, scroll down to the section called **Settings**, and untick the box called **Transition to Self**.

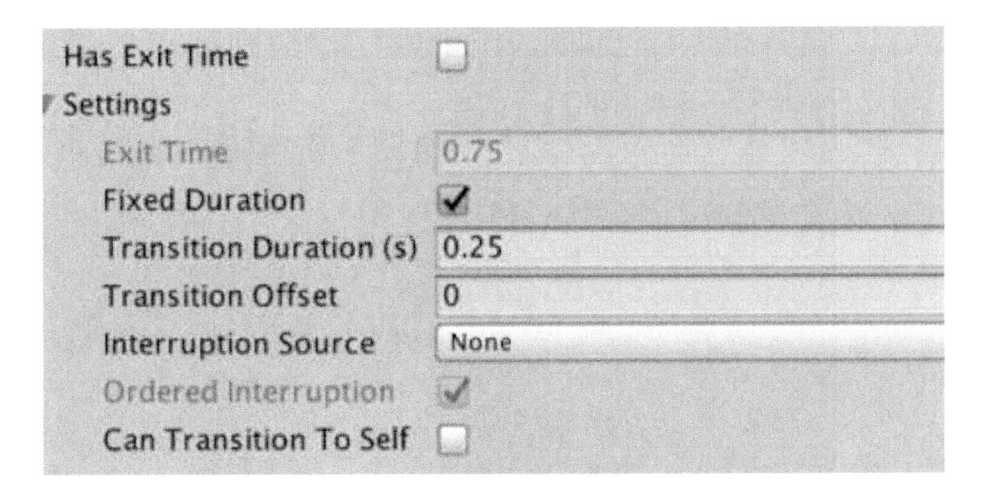

Figure 103: Disabling Transition to Self

- As you play the scene again and walk near the NPC, you should see, in the **Animator** window, that the NPC transitions only once to the state **followPlayer** (i.e., not constantly).

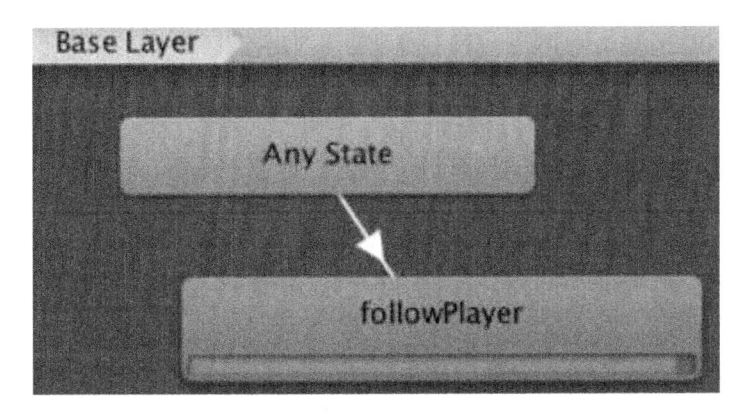

Figure 104: Correct transition to the state followPlayer

ADDING SIGHT

In this section we will add the ability for the NPC to detect the player, based on sight. We will also make sure that the NPC follows the player whether it sees or hears the player.

- Please create a new **Boolean** parameter called **canSeePlayer**.
- Create a new transition between the state **Any State** and the state **followPlayer**.
- You should see that it creates a link with three arrows. This means that the transition can occur based on multiple conditions.

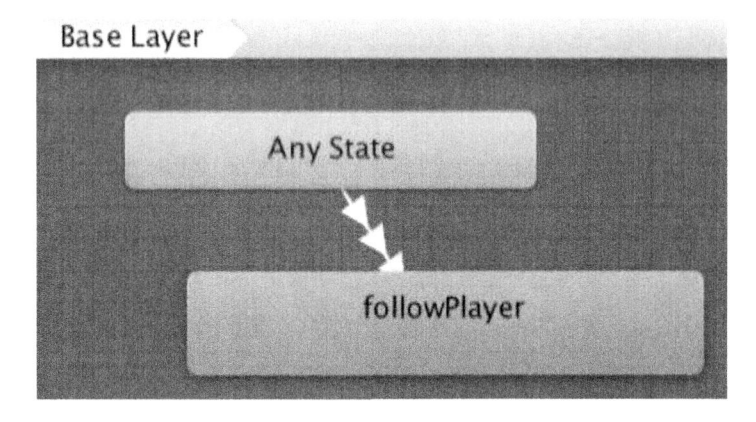

Figure 105: Creating multiple transitions

- If you click on this transition and look at the **Inspector**, you should see that the **Inspector** now displays two transitions.

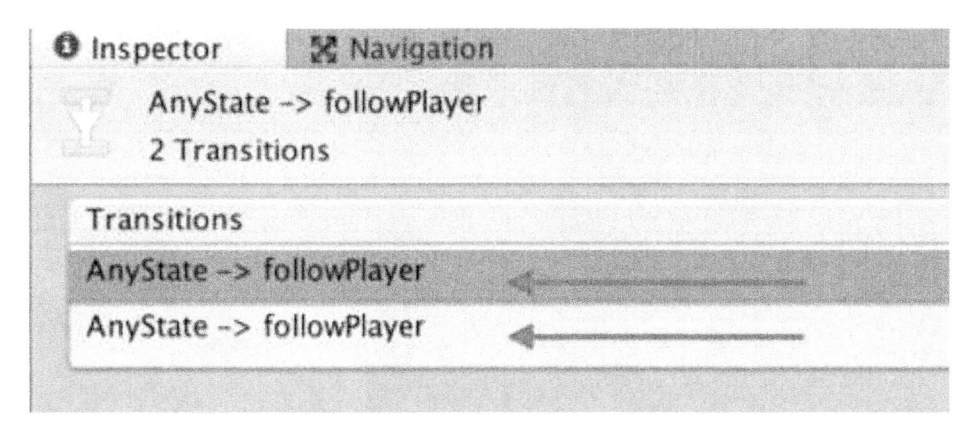

Figure 106: Displaying multiple transitions

[300]

Adding Vision and Hearing to NPCs

- If you click on the second transition, you will see that the corresponding condition in the section called **Transition** is based on the parameter **canHearPlayer**.

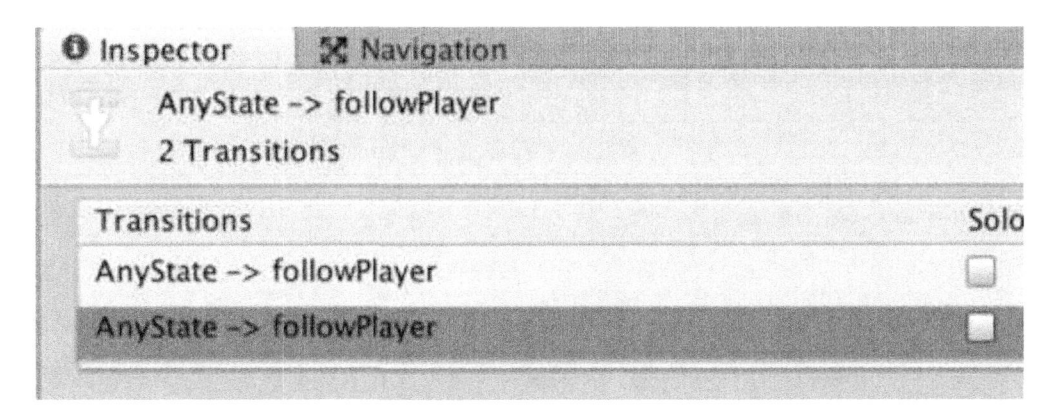

Figure 107: Displaying the details of each transition

Figure 108: Condition for the second transition

- Please click on the first transition (the last transition created will appear first in the list) you will see that no corresponding condition has been set yet.

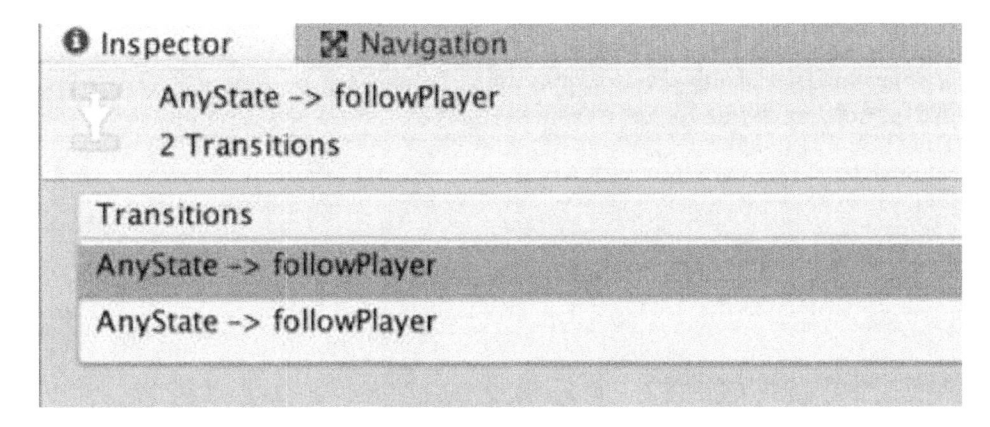

Figure 109: Condition for the first transition (part 1)

- Add the condition **canSeePlayer**.

[301]

Adding Vision and Hearing to NPCs

Figure 110: Condition for the second transition

- Also make sure that the state does not transition to itself, by setting the attribute called **Can Transition To Self** to **false**.

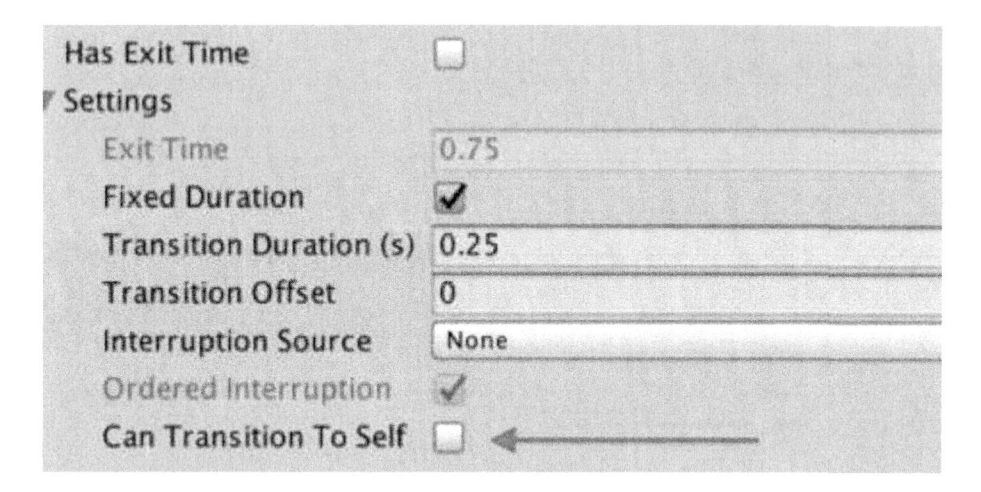

Figure 111: Setting the option "Can Transition to Self"

So effectively, we have specified that the transition will occur if **canSeePlayer** is true **OR** if **canHearPlayer** is true; this is a handy way to apply transitions based on a logical **OR**, which means either conditions need to be true for the transition to occur.

- Before you play the scene again, you can reset the parameter canHearPlayer to false.

Figure 112: resetting the parameter canHearPlayer

- You can now play the scene, set the parameter **canSeePlayer** to true from the **Animator** window, and check that the NPC start to walk **towards** the player.

Adding Vision and Hearing to NPCs

Once this is done, we can then modify the script **ControlNPC2** so that the sight is implemented for the NPC (rather than triggering it from the **Animator** window).

- Please, add the following function before the end of the class:

```
void look()
{
        Ray ray = new Ray();
        RaycastHit hit;
        ray.origin = transform.position + Vector3.up * 0.7f;
        string objectInSight = "" ;
        float castingDistance = 20;
        ray.direction = transform.forward * castingDistance;
        Debug.DrawRay (ray.origin, ray.direction*castingDistance, Color.red);
        if (Physics.Raycast (ray.origin, ray.direction, out hit, castingDistance))
        {
                objectInSight = hit.collider.gameObject.name;
                if (objectInSight == "FPSController") anim.SetBool ("canSeePlayer", true);

        }

}
```

In the previous code:

- We create a new function called **look**.

- We create a new ray that will originate from the NPC.

- If this ray collides with an object, we save the name of this particular object in the variable called **objectInSight**.

- If this object is the player, we then set the **Trigger** parameter **canSeePlayer** to true.

- We also cast a ray that can be seen in the **Scene** view using the built-in function **Debug.DrawRay**.

We can now modify the **Update** function as follows (new code in bold), so that the NPC looks ahead constantly (in order to detect the player).

Adding Vision and Hearing to NPCs

```
void Update () {
    info = anim.GetCurrentAnimatorStateInfo (0);
    //listen ();
    look ();
```

In the previous code: we comment the line starting with the call to the function **listen**, so that we can only test the sight (and not the hearing); however, we will remove the comments from this line as soon as we have tested the sight.

You can now save your script and play the scene. You should see that, as soon as you walk in front of the NPC, it will start to follow you.

Adding Vision and Hearing to NPCs

LOSING TRACK OF THE PLAYER

In this section, we will implement a feature by which, when the NPC loses track of the player (sight or hearing), it will go back to its patrolling state.

- Create a transition from the state **followPlayer** to the state **patrol**.
- For this transition, include two condition as illustrated below.
- To add a second condition, you can press the + button, to the right of the label **Conditions**.

Conditions

| = | canSeePlayer | ▼ | false | ⇅ |
| = | canHearPlayer | ▼ | false | ⇅ |

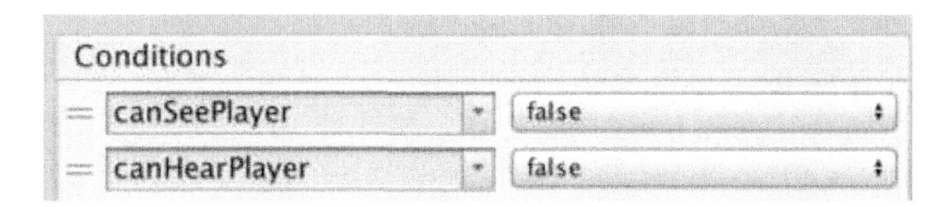

Figure 113: Combining two conditions

> When two conditions are added this way, it means that both conditions need to be true for the transition to occur; this is equivalent to a logical **AND**.

Once this done we can modify the script **ControlNPC2**:

- Please uncomment the following line:

```
listen();
```

- Modify the function called **look** as follows (new code in bold):

```
if (Physics.Raycast (ray.origin, ray.direction, out hit, castingDistance))
{
        objectInSight = hit.collider.gameObject.name;
        if (objectInSight == "FPSController") anim.SetBool ("canSeePlayer", true);
        else anim.SetBool ("canSeePlayer", false);
}
```

- Modify the function **listen** as follows (new code in bold):

Adding Vision and Hearing to NPCs

```
if (distance < 3) {
        anim.SetBool ("canHearPlayer", true);
}
else
{
        anim.SetBool ("canHearPlayer", false);
}
```

You can now test the scene, make sure that the NPC detects you through sight or hearing, and then navigate away from the NPC so that it can't hear you or see you anymore. You should then notice that the NPC goes back to patrolling.

ADDING THE SENSE OF SMELL

The sense of smell can be interesting to make the NPCs more believable; it can be simulated easily and this will be done in this section as follows:

- We will make it possible for the player to drop molecules (or what is commonly called breadcrumbs in AI terms) that can be compared to scent.

- These will be dropped at regular intervals.

- These molecules will disappear after a few seconds, leaving an invisible trail behind the player.

- Once the NPC senses (i.e., smells) any of these molecules, it will start to follow the player.

So the first thing we will do, is to make it possible for the player to drop breadcrumbs; these will be dropped every time the player moves one meter ahead;

> While we could set the code so that the NPC drops a breadcrumb every second, this would quickly overcrowd the scene with multiple crumbs created every seconds. Therefore, dropping crumbs only when the NPC has actually moved should be more efficient.

- Please create a new script called **BreadCrumbs**.
- Open this script.
- Add this code just before the **Start** function.

```
Vector3 previousPosition;
float counter = 0;
public GameObject BC;
```

- Add this code to the **Start** function (new code in bold).

```
void Start ()
{
        previousPosition = gameObject.transform.position;
}
```

- Modify the **Update** function as follows:

Adding Vision and Hearing to NPCs

```
void Update ()
{
        Vector3 currentLocation = gameObject.transform.position;
        float distance = Vector3.Distance (previousPosition, currentLocation);
        if (distance > 1.0f)
        {
                previousPosition = currentLocation;
                GameObject g = Instantiate (BC, currentLocation, Quaternion.identity);
                g.name = "BC" + counter;
                counter++;
        }
}
```

In the previous code:

- We store the current location in the variable **currentLocation**.

- We then calculate the distance between the current location and the previous location.

- If the player has moved further than one meter from the previous location, we instantiate a new breadcrumb.

- This breadcrumb is given a name that includes a number; this number could be useful later-on to determine the freshest breadcrumb.

- We then increase the counter by one.

- Please save your code, and drag and drop the script to the object called **FPSController**.

Next, we will be creating the breadcrumb that will be dropped by the player:

- Please create a new sphere (**GameObject | 3D Object | Sphere**).

- Rename it **BC**.

- Using the **Inspector** window, deactivate its **collider** component.

- Change its position to **(0, 0, 0)**.

- Change its scale to **(.2, .2, .2)**.

- Create a prefab from it.

- Delete (or deactivate) the object **BC** from the **Hierarchy**, as we don't need it anymore, now that the prefab has been created.

Adding Vision and Hearing to NPCs

- Select the prefab called **BC**.
- Create a new label called **BC** by clicking on the attribute called **Untagged** and by selecting the option **New Tag** from the drop-down menu.

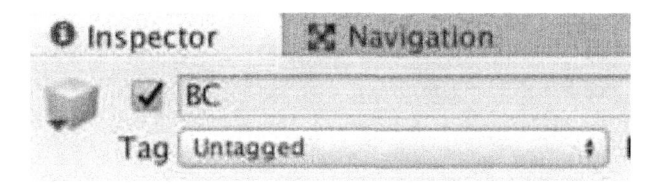

Figure 114: Creating a new tag (part 1)

Figure 115: Creating a new tag (part 2)

- Apply this tag to the prefab called **BC**.

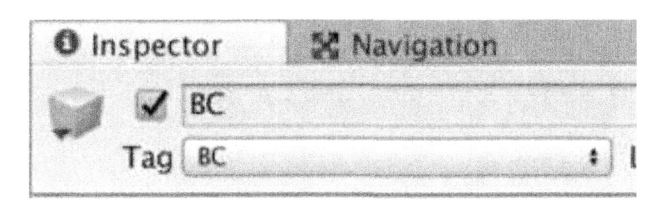

Figure 116: Applying the new tag

This tag will be used to detect all the breadcrumbs in the scene.

We will now create a small script that will be added to the prefab called **BC**:

- Please create a new C# script called **BC**.
- Open the script and modify the **Start** function as follows:

```
void Start ()
{
        Destroy (gameObject, 5);
}
```

- Save the script and drag and drop it on the prefab called **BC**.

[309]

Adding Vision and Hearing to NPCs

- Last but not least, select the object **FPSController** in the **Hierarchy**.

- In the **Inspector** window, if you scroll down to the component called **BreadCrumbs**, you should see an empty attribute called **BC**, as illustrated in the next figure.

Figure 117: Setting the breadcrumb to be instantiated (part 1)

- Please drag and drop the prefab called **BC** from the **Project** window to this attribute, as illustrated in the next figure.

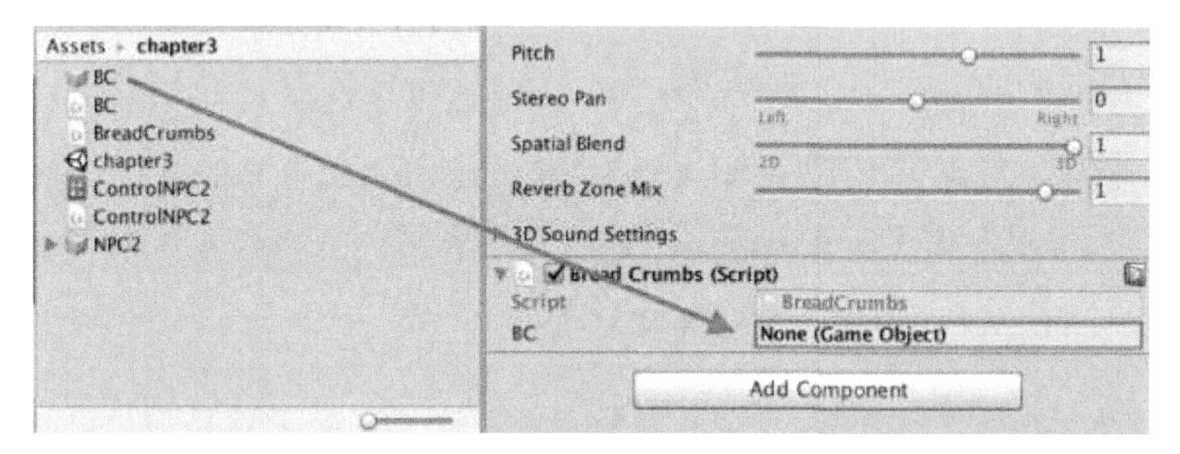

Figure 118: Setting the breadcrumb to be instantiated (part 2)

You can now play the scene; as you move your character forward, you can look behind you to see the breadcrumbs that have been created.

Adding Vision and Hearing to NPCs

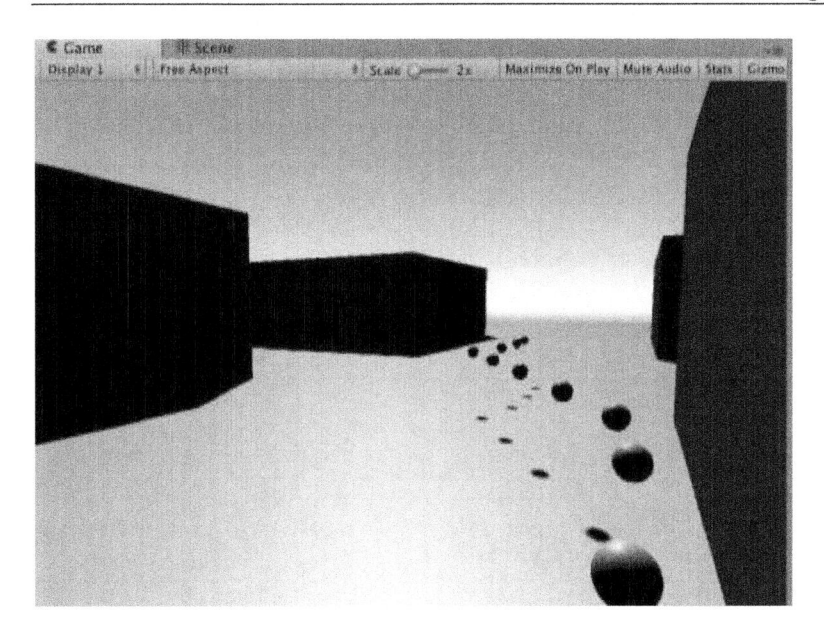

Figure 119: Instantiating breadcrumbs

If you stop moving, these breadcrumbs will start to disappear after 5 seconds, as illustrated in the next figure.

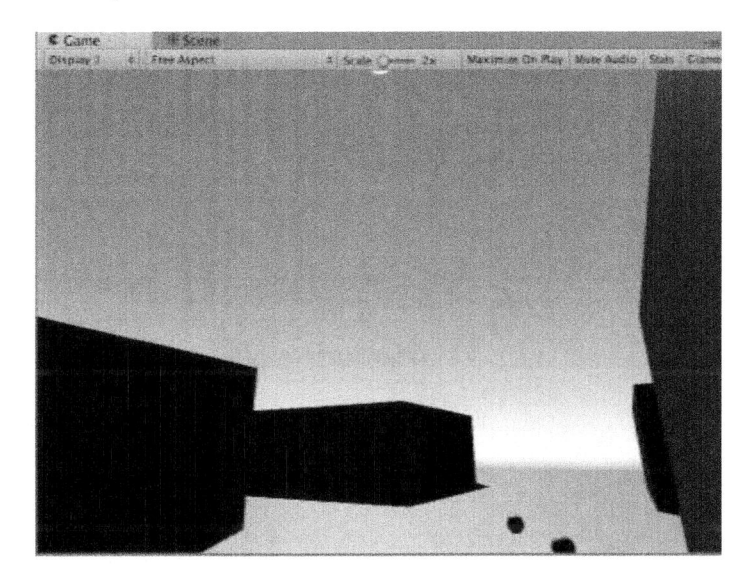

Figure 120: The remaining breadcrumbs

> Note that you can decide to hide the breadcrumbs by selecting the **BC** prefab and deactivating its Mesh renderer component.

[311]

Adding Vision and Hearing to NPCs

Now that we can drop breadcrumbs, we can make it possible for the NPC to detect these breadcrumbs, and we will need to modify the script for the NPC accordingly.

- Please open the **Animator Controller ControlNPC2** in the **Animator** window and create one additional Boolean parameter called **canSmellPlayer**.

- Select the transition from **followPlayer** to **patrol**.

- Add the condition **canSmellPlayer = false**.

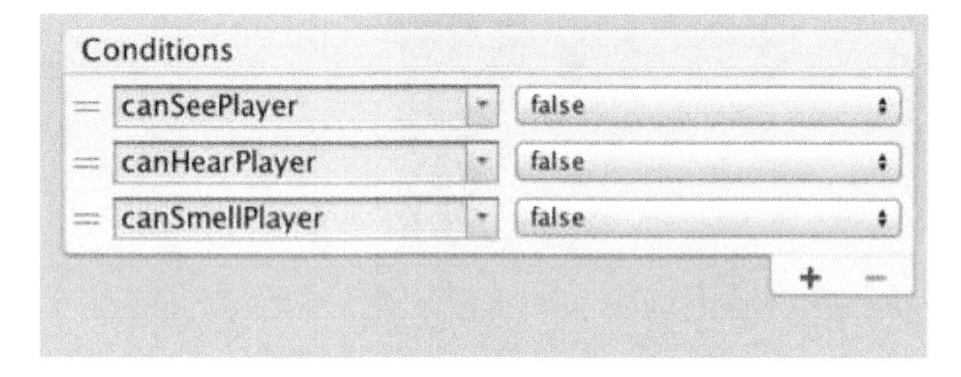

Figure 121: Adding conditions

- Create a new transition from **AnyState** to **followPlayer**.

- You should now see in the **Inspector** that there are three transitions between these two states now.

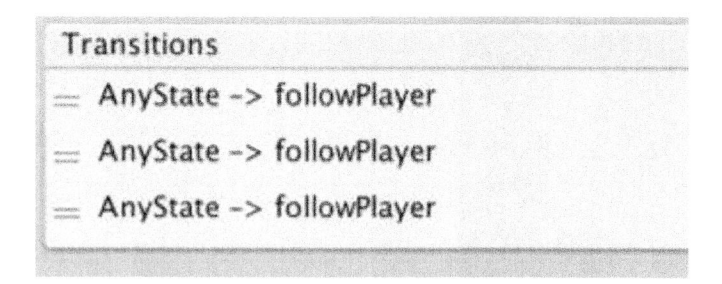

Figure 122: Configuring the transitions (part 1)

- Select the third transition.

[312]

Adding Vision and Hearing to NPCs

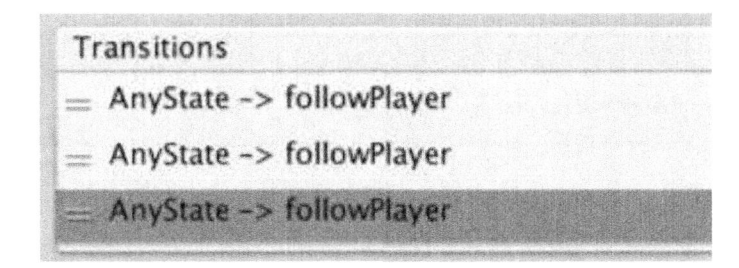

```
Transitions
= AnyState -> followPlayer
= AnyState -> followPlayer
= AnyState -> followPlayer
```

Figure 123: Configuring the transitions (part 2)

- Add the parameter **canSmellPlayer** as a condition for this transition.

```
Conditions
= canSmellPlayer    true
                         + -
```

Figure 124: Transition based on smell

- You may also check that the option **Can Transition To Self** is set to **false** (i.e., unchecked) in the **Inspector** window.

So, again here, this transition will occur if any of the variables **canSeePlayer**, **canHearPlayer** or **canSmellPlayer** is true.

Once this is done, we just need to modify our script **ControlNPC2**.

- Please add the following function to the script **ControlNPC2**.

Adding Vision and Hearing to NPCs

```
void smell()
{
        GameObject[] allBCs = GameObject.FindGameObjectsWithTag ("BC");
        float minDistance = 2;
        bool detectedBC = false;
        for (int i = 0; i < allBCs.Length; i ++)
        {
                if (Vector3.Distance(gameObject.transform.position, allBCs[i].transform.position) < minDistance)
                {
                        detectedBC = true; break;
                }
        }
        if (detectedBC)
                anim.SetBool ("canSmellPlayer", true);
        else
                anim.SetBool ("canSmellPlayer", false);
}
```

In the previous code:

We look for all the breadcrumbs and store them in the variable called **allBCs**.

- We define the variable **minDistance**, that can be used to define a radius within which breadcrumbs can be detected.
- We go through the array of breadcrumbs.
- If one of them is within the two-meter radius, then we consider that the player's scent has been detected.
- In this case, the parameter **canSmellPlayer** is set to **true**; otherwise, it is set to **false**.

We can now modify the **Update** function.

- Please, add the following code (new code in bold) to the **Update** function:

```
listen ();
look ();
smell ();
```

You can now save your code, and test the scene; you should see that the NPC, once near one of the breadcrumbs, will start to follow you.

Adding Vision and Hearing to NPCs

> Note that you can disable the Renderer for the breadcrumb prefab, if you wish, so that breadcrumbs don't appear in the game.

You may wonder where to use Triggers and Boolean parameters, since they are quite similar; well, as a general rule, if a parameter refers to an event (something that happens briefly) then a trigger makes sense; however, if you need a parameter for a state, something that lasts over time, then a Boolean may make more senses; for example, you can see that the variables **hasReachedStart** or **startPatrol** are triggers, because they are events that don't last long overtime; however, the variable **canSeePlayer** or **canHearPlayer** are Boolean because they can hold true or false for extended periods of time.

Adding Vision and Hearing to NPCs

LEVEL ROUNDUP

Summary

In this chapter, we have managed to create a challenging NPC character that has the ability to detect the player based on three different senses (smell, sight, and hearing) and to take simple decisions based on these (i.e., follow the player or go back to patrolling). Along the way, we have also learned to create states and transitions, and to combine transitions and parameters to create customized conditions for these transitions to occur. So well done! This is quite a significant leap from the last chapter.

Checklist

You can consider moving to the next stage if you can do the following:

- Understand how to implement sight detection using ray-casting.
- Understand how to create detection based on hearing using distance.
- Know how to create and detect breadcrumbs.

Quiz

Now, let's check your knowledge! Please answer the following questions (the answers are included in the resource pack) or specify whether they are correct or incorrect.

1. To remove a component from an object, you can select the option **Component | Remove** from the top menu.

2. An animation clip used to animate a 3D character cannot be modified.

3. A Trigger parameter is always reset to its original state (e.g., false) after the corresponding transition has occurred.

4. It is possible to access an **Animator Controller** from a script.

5. It is possible to access any of the parameters of an **Animator Controller** from a script.

6. An **Animator Controller** always has one layer.

7. The following code within the conditional statement will be executed if the current state is idle.

Adding Vision and Hearing to NPCs

```
AnimatorStateInfo info;
info = anim.GetCurrentAnimatorStateInfo (0);
if info.name("idle)
{

        //

}
```

8. It is possible to execute a transition between states, on the condition that several parameters are true.

9. If an Animator Controller keeps transitioning between two states, one of them being **Any State**, it could be that the variable "**Can Transition to Self**" was selected.

10. It is possible to create more than one transition between two states.

Quiz Solution

Now, let's check your knowledge!

1. False.
2. False.
3. True.
4. True.
5. True.
6. False.
7. False (it should read info.**isName**).
8. True.
9. True.
10. True.

Challenge 1

For this chapter, your challenge will be to modify the game as follows:

- Modify the radius used to detect the NPC based on its hearing.
- Modify the range used to detect the NPC based on its sight.

8
CREATING SMARTER NPCS WHO CAN FLEE OR AMBUSH

In this section, we will be implementing new types of behaviours for our NPC, some of these are found in many 3D games and can really add more challenge and playability to your game, including the ability for the NPC to:

- Look for some items based on senses and internal values (e.g., health)
- Flee from the player (for example, when health is low).
- Avail of and use weapons (e.g., gun or grenades).
- Ambush the player.

You will also learn to:

- Spawn NPCs.
- Spawn health packs at random locations.
- Improve the NPC's sight using dot products.

> The code solutions for this chapter are in the **resource pack** that you can download by following the instructions included in the section entitled "Support and Resources for this Book".

DECISIONS BASED ON INTERNAL VALUES (HEALTH, AMMOS, ETC.)

Ok. So, so far, we have managed to implement an NPC that navigates through the environment and that can also detect and follow the player accordingly, or go back to its patrol after losing sight of the player.

What would be even better, would be to make it possible for the NPC to make decisions (and to take action accordingly) based on specific parameters; for example, an NPC might need, now and then, to replenish its energy levels, or to collect ammunitions. In a game, this could correspond to several situations where an NPC may:

- be hit several time and may need to look for ammo packs when its health is running low.

- need to look for ammunitions after it has used-up its initial ammunitions.

- need to collect a specific weapon and the corresponding ammunitions to stand a chance to defeat the player.

In all these cases, the NPC will need to manage its current state (e.g., health) and levels of inventory (e.g., any object such as weapons or ammunitions) to be able to make a decision. These principles, of course, can be used for non-FPS games, to simulate an environment where NPCs make decisions based on their internal values.

Before we start we the new features, we will save some of the work we have done to date and also duplicate the current scene, so that the duplicate can be re-used for this chapter; this way, you will always be able to go back to the scene as it was when you completed Chapter 3.

- Please save the current scene.

- Create a new folder called **chapter4** in the **Project** window

- Duplicate the scene called **chapter3**, rename the duplicate **chapter4**, and save the duplicate in the folder called **chapter4** that you have just created.

Creating Smarter NPCs Who Can Flee or Ambush

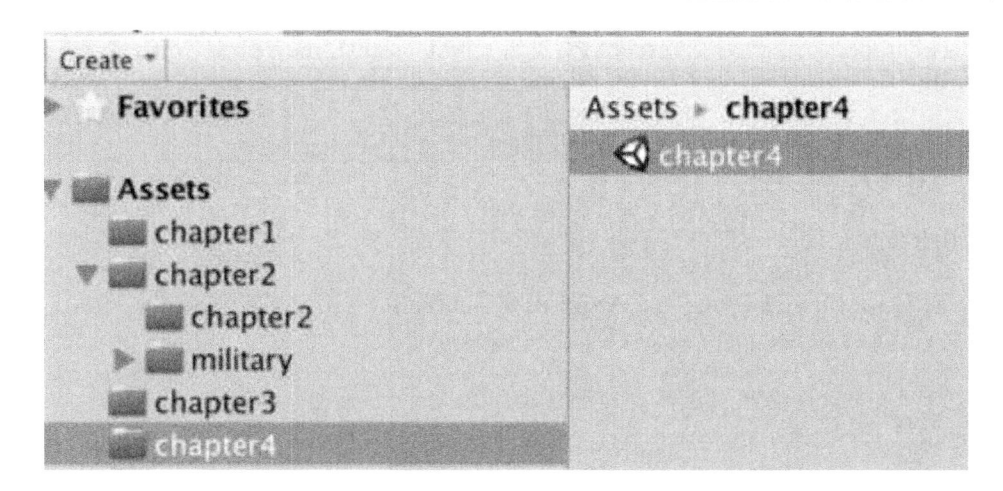

Figure 125: Creating the scene for chapter 4

Once this is done:

- Duplicate the script called **ControlNPC2**, rename the duplicate **ControlNPC3**, and open it to change the beginning of the class as follows (new code in bold):

```
public class ControlNPC3 : MonoBehaviour {
```

- Save the script and move it to the folder called **chapter4**.

- Duplicate the **Animator Controller** called **ControlNPC2**, rename the duplicate **ControlNPC3**, and move it to the folder called **chapter4**.

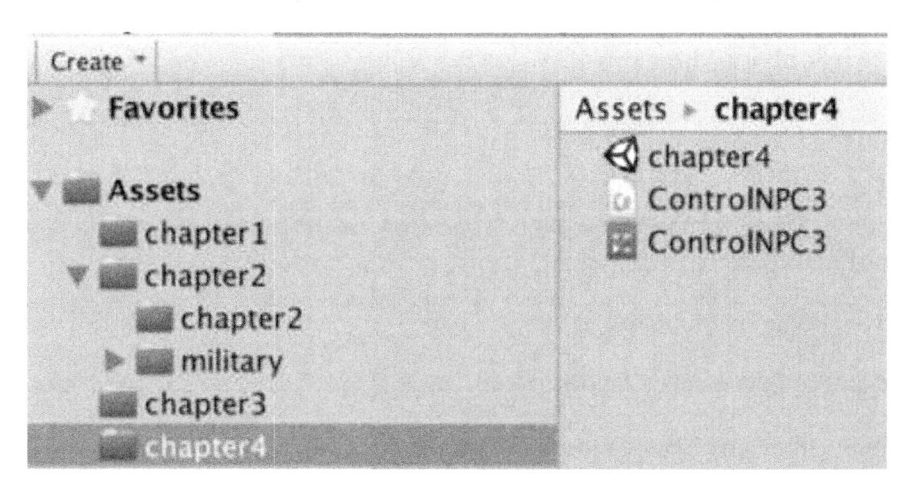

Figure 126: Duplicating the Animator Controller

- Click on the object called **NPC2** in the **Hierarchy**.

Creating Smarter NPCs Who Can Flee or Ambush

- Remove its component called **ControlNPC2**, and add, instead the script **ControlNPC3** to this object.

- Drag and drop the object **FirstPersonController** to its **target** attribute.

- Rename the object **NPC2** to **NPC3**, and drag and drop it to the **Project** view to create a prefab called **NPC3**.

- Last but not least, drag and drop the **Animator Controller** called **ControlNPC3** to the **controller** attribute of the component called **Animator**.

Figure 127: Changing the Animator Controller

That's it. We have managed to save the code and prefab used in the previous chapter so that you can always go back to it if needed.

So in the next sections, we create a mechanism by which the NPC can assess its current state and ammo levels, and decide to go to the corresponding resource accordingly (e.g., heal pack or ammunitions). For this purpose, we will create scripts that will account for these levels, and triggers that will be set when these levels run low; transitions will be created to states whereby the NPC is looking for the corresponding resource(s).

So let's get started:

- In the **Animator** window, for the **Controller** called **ControlNPC3**, please create a new state called **lookForHealth**.

- Link the animation called **walking** to this state.

- Create a new **float** parameter called **health**.

- Create a transitions from **Any State** to **lookForHealth**.

- Set the condition for this **transition** to **health < 20**.

- Create a transition from the state **lookForHealth** to the state **patrol**.

- Set the condition for this transition to **health > 90**.

Creating Smarter NPCs Who Can Flee or Ambush

- So effectively, the NPC should look for health when its health falls below **20** and it will then return to the **patrol** state when its health has reached **90**.

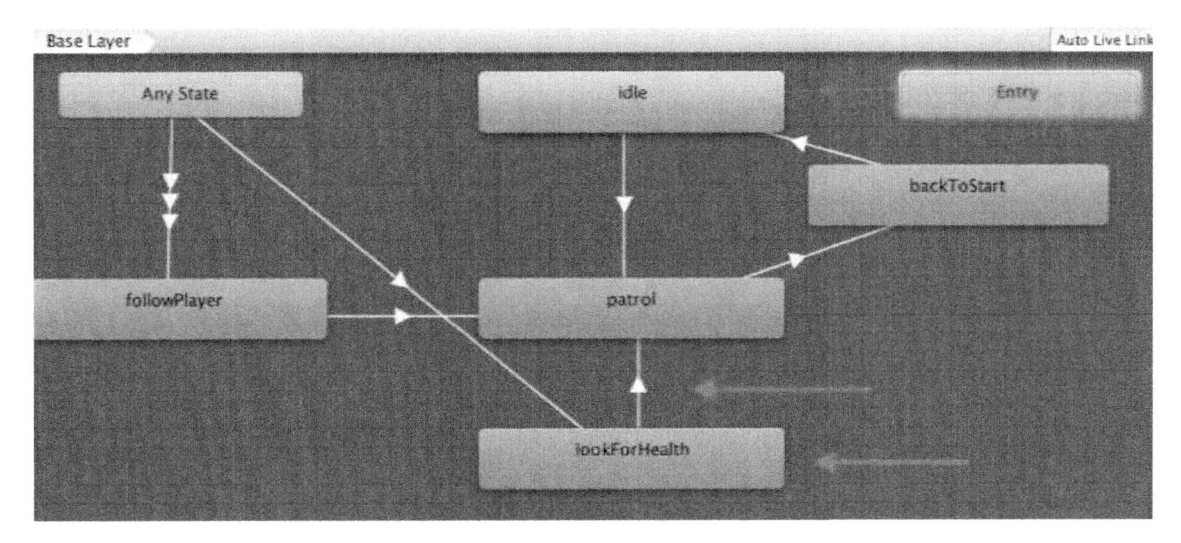

Figure 128: Creating a new state and associated transitions

- For the first transition (**Any State** to **lookForHealth**) please check that the option **Can Transition to Self** is set to **false** (i.e., unticked), as illustrated in the next figure.

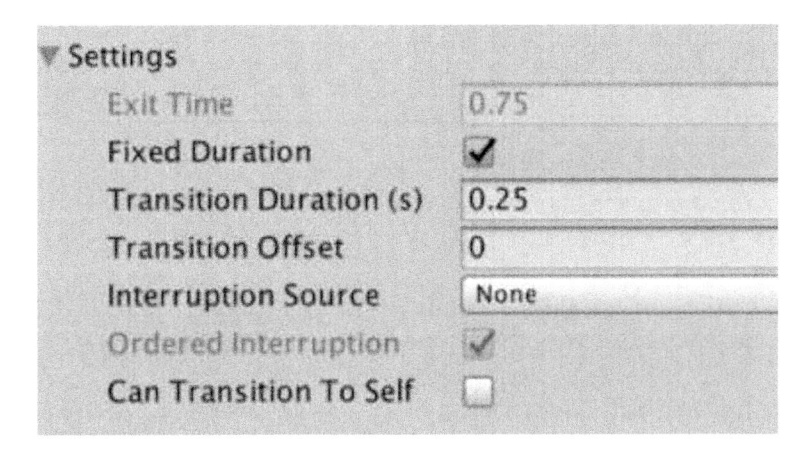

Figure 129: Disabling auto-transition

- Once this is done, please create a new **Cube**, rename it **healthPack**, and move it to a location of your choice, for example **(-20, 1, 26)**. You can, if you wish, apply one of the textures provided in the resource pack (e.g., **box_texture.jpg**).

Now that this is done, we will create a script that will manage the NPC's health and other assets.

Creating Smarter NPCs Who Can Flee or Ambush

- Please create a new script called **ManageNPC2**.
- Add the following code to it.

```
Animator anim;
float health = 100;
void Start () {anim = GetComponent<Animator> ();}

public float getHealth()
{
        return health;
}
public void setHealth(float newHealth)
{

        health = newHealth;
        anim.SetFloat ("health", health);
}
```

In the previous code:

- We declare a variable called **anim** that will refer to the Animator on the object linked to this script.

- We create a variable called **health**.

- We set its value to **100**.

- We create two functions **getHealth** and **setHealth**, that are public (and hence accessible from outside this class) and that respectively return the value of the variable **health** or set the variable called **health** to a specific value.

Now that this is done, we will modify the **Update** function so that the health of the NPC decreases overtime, forcing it to eventually look for health packs.

- Please modify the **Update** function as follows.

```
void Update ()
{
        setHealth (health -Time.deltaTime*10);
        if (health < 0) setHealth (0);
}
```

In the previous code, we update the variable called **health**, through the function called **setHealth**.

- Save your code, and drag and drop the script **ManageNPC2** to the object called **NPC3**.

Creating Smarter NPCs Who Can Flee or Ambush

- Open the script **ControlNPC3**, and add this code to the **Update** function (i.e., before the end of this function).

```
if (info.IsName ("lookForHealth"))
{
        target = GameObject.Find ("healthPack");
        GetComponent<UnityEngine.AI.NavMeshAgent> ().SetDestination (target.transform.position);
        if (Vector3.Distance (gameObject.transform.position, target.transform.position) < 2)
        {
                GetComponent<ManageNPC2> ().setHealth (100);
        }
}
```

In the previous code:

- We check if the current state is **lookForHealth**.
- If this is the case, the NPC will now head towards the **health pack**.
- When the NPC is close enough to the health pack, its health will be increased to 100.

> Note that this is for testing purposes; in many games, the health pack would usually be destroyed; however, in our case, the health pack will act as a zone where the NPC can replenish its health levels.

Please save your code, and test the scene, you should see that, after a few seconds, the NPC will start to transition to the state **lookForHealth**; once it has reached the health pack, its health will be replenished, and the NPC will then resume its patrol.

Note that we have not destroyed the health pack yet, but we could do so later on.

We could also add a state where the NPC dies as the health is 0; let's implement this feature:

- Using the **Animator** window, modify the transition between the state called **Any State** and the state called **lookForHealth** as follows (i.e., **health < 20** and **health > 1**):

Conditions
| = | health | Less | 20 |
| = | health | Greater | 1 |

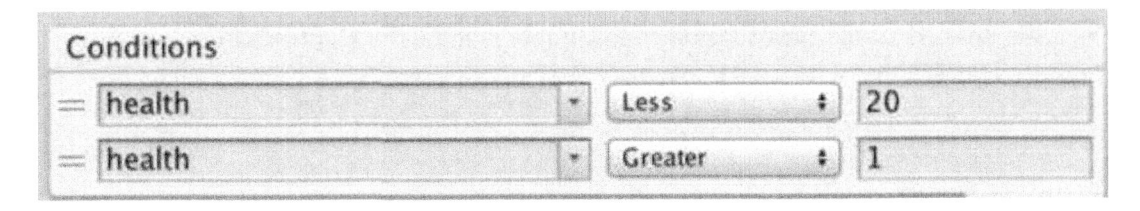

Figure 130: Modifying the transition

- Create a new state called **dies** and link it to the animation **dying**.

[325]

Creating Smarter NPCs Who Can Flee or Ambush

- Create a new transition from the state **Any State** to the state called **dies**, using the following condition.

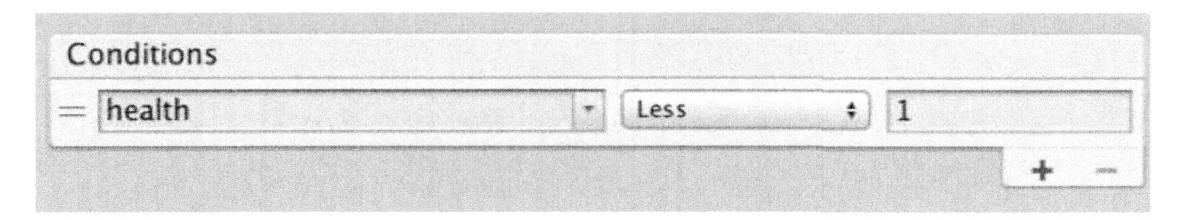

Figure 131: Adding a new condition

- Please also ensure that the option **Can Transition to Self** is set to **false** for this transition.

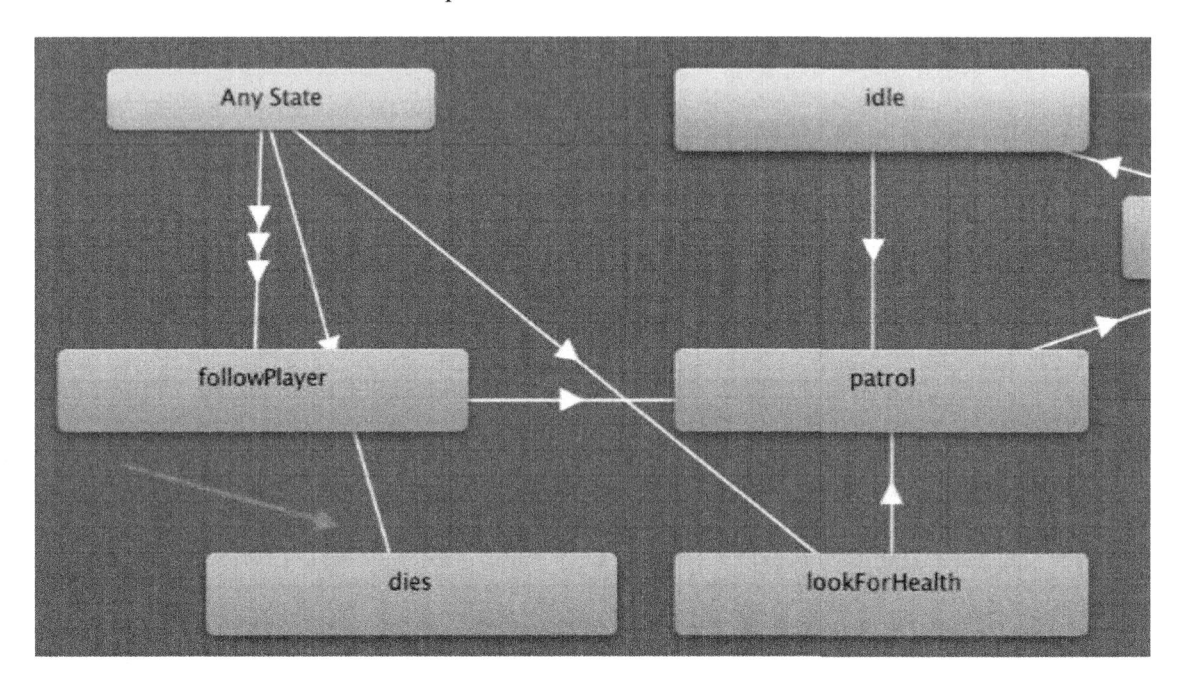

Figure 132: Adding the state called dies

- Add this code at the end of the function **Update** in the script **ControlNPC3**:

```
if (info.IsName ("dies"))
{
        GetComponent<UnityEngine.AI.NavMeshAgent> ().isStopped = true;
        Destroy (gameObject, 3);
}
```

In the previous code: if the NPC is in the state called **dies**, its navigation is stopped and the NPC is then destroyed after three seconds.

If you test the scene, you should see that he NPC, although it is going towards the health pack, will not reach it in time.

Figure 133: The NPC falls to the ground (part 1)

Figure 134: The NPC falls to the ground (part 2)

PROVIDING WEAPONS TO THE NPC

So far, the NPC could only look for health or follow the player; in this section, we will give the ability for the NPC to have a weapon, and ammunitions, and to chase the player when it detects him/her. As it is following the player, the NPC will shoot every 4 seconds and then resume following the player.

Let's implement this feature:

- Open the script **ManageNPC2**.

- Change **health** rate as follows.

```
//setHealth (health -Time.deltaTime*10);
setHealth (health -Time.deltaTime*2);
```

This change is so that the health decreases less quickly and hence allows for these features to be tested before the NPC dies.

- Using the **Animator** window, create a new state called **shoot**.

- Associate the animation called **shooting** to this state.

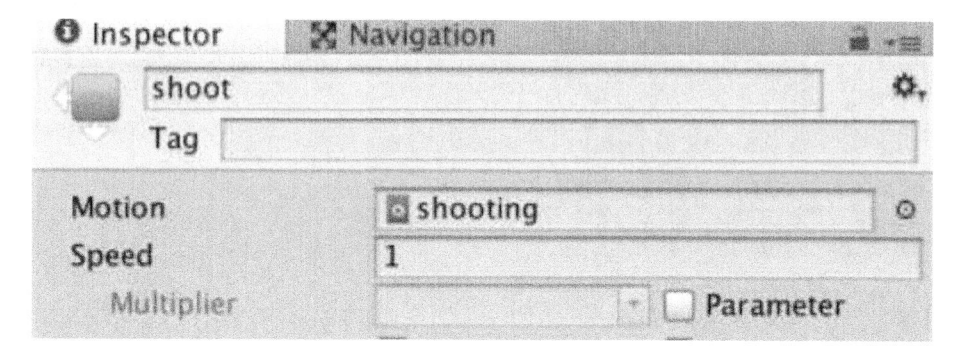

Figure 135: Associating the animation called shooting

- Create a new **Trigger** parameter called **startToShoot**.

- Create a transition from the state **followPlayer** to the state **shoot** using **startToShoot** as the condition.

- Create a transition from the state **shoot** to the state **followPlayer** with no condition so that the transitions to the state **followPlayer** state occurs directly after shooting.

Creating Smarter NPCs Who Can Flee or Ambush

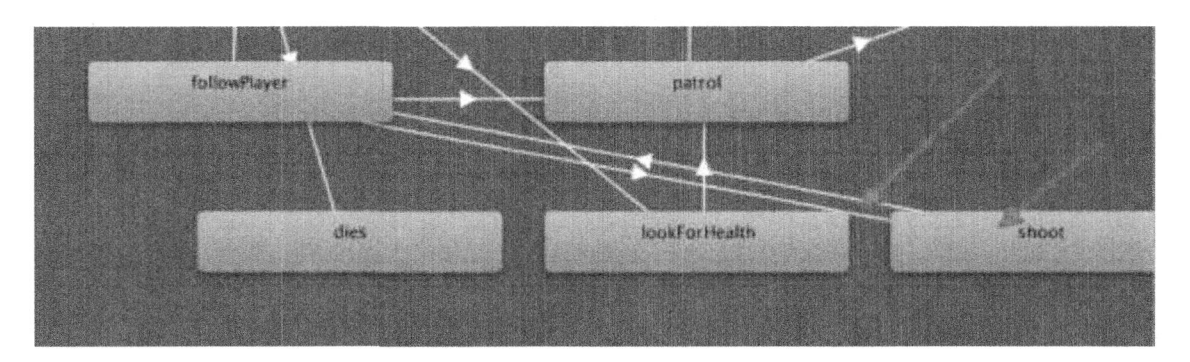

Figure 136: Adding a new state and corresponding transitions

Once this is done, we will modify our scripts:

- Please add the following code at the beginning of the script **ManageNPC2**.

```
int ammos = 100;
```

- Add the following functions to the script **ManageNPC2**.

```
public void decreaseAmmo()
{
        ammos--;
        if (ammos <= 0) ammos = 0;
}

public void setAmmos(int newAmmos)
{
        ammos = newAmmos;
}
public int getAmmos()
{
        return ammos;
}
```

In the previous code, we create three functions: **decreaseAmmo**, **setAmmos**, and **getAmmos**; they respectively decrease the ammunitions, set the ammunitions to a particular level, or return the amount of ammunitions available.

- Add the following code at the beginning of the script **ControlNPC3**.

```
float shootTimer = 0;
```

- Modify the **Update** function in the script called **ControlNPC3** (new code in bold).

Creating Smarter NPCs Who Can Flee or Ambush

```
if (info.IsName ("followPlayer"))
{
        shootTimer += Time.deltaTime;
        if (shootTimer >= 3)
        {
                if    (anim.GetBool("canSeePlayer")    &&    GetComponent<ManageNPC2>
().getAmmos() >0) anim.SetTrigger ("startToShoot");
                shootTimer = 0;
                GetComponent<ManageNPC2> ().decreaseAmmo ();
        }
```

In the previous code:

- The time is updated.

- Every three seconds, if the NPC can see the player and if it has enough ammunitions, it will fire its gun (that we yet have to add to the NPC).

- The ammunitions levels are decreased accordingly.

You can now test your scene; as the NPC is following you, it will be shooting every three seconds; note that the NPC doesn't have a gun yet, but we will add this feature later-on.

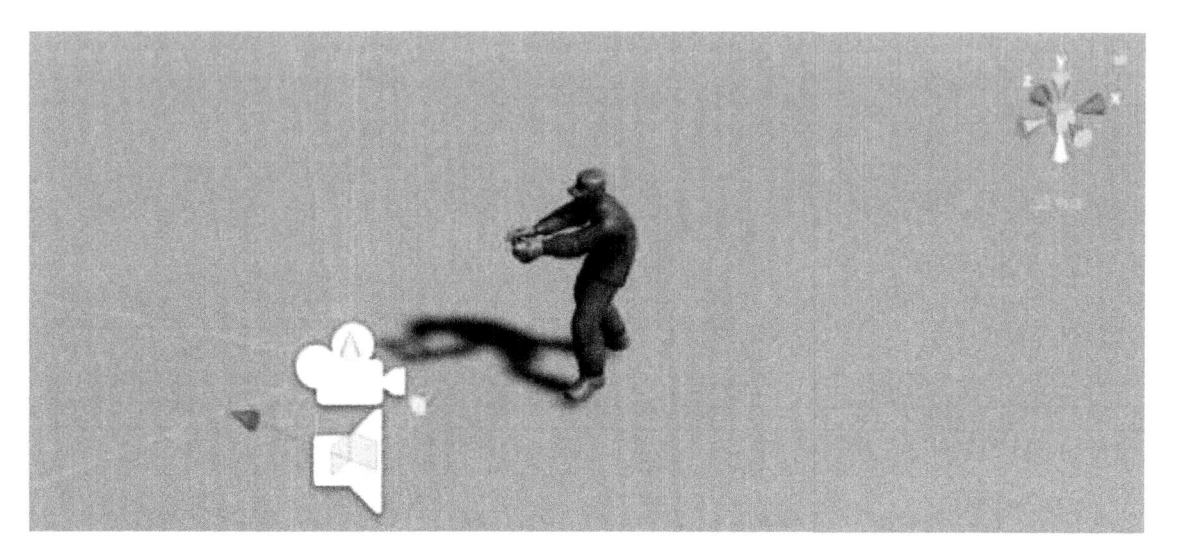

Figure 137: The NPC is shooting

Now that this behavior is working, we could add a feature by which the NPC needs to replenish its ammunition as they run low. For this, we will be using the same principle as we have for the NPC's health; this will consist in:

- Creating a new parameter for the ammunitions.
- Creating a new state called **lookForAmmos**.
- Triggering a transition to this state whenever the ammos are below a specific value.

So let's get started.

- In the **Animator** window, create a **float** parameter called **ammos**, and set its value to **100**.
- Create a new state called **lookForAmmos**, and associate the animation **walking** to this state.
- Create a transition from **Any State** to **lookForAmmos** with the condition **ammos < 5**, ensuring that the option **Can Transition To Self** is set to false for this transition.
- Create a transition from the state **lookForAmmos** to the state called **patrol** with the condition **ammos > 80**.
- In the script **ControlNPC3**, add the following code at the beginning of the function **Update**:

```
float ammos = GetComponent<ManageNPC2> ().getAmmos ();
anim.SetFloat ("ammos", ammos);
```

- Add this code to the **Update** function.

```
if (info.IsName ("lookForAmmos"))
{
        target = GameObject.Find ("ammoPack");
        GetComponent<UnityEngine.AI.NavMeshAgent> ().SetDestination (target.transform.position);
        if (Vector3.Distance (gameObject.transform.position, target.transform.position) < 2)
        {
                GetComponent<ManageNPC2> ().setAmmos (100);
        }
}
```

In the previous code, for the state called **lookForAmmos**, the NPC will go towards the ammo pack; once close enough its ammunition levels will be increased to 100. Note that, as for the health pack, the ammo pack will not be destroyed, and instead, it acts as an ammo-replenishing zone. If we were to remove the ammo now, we would also need to account for the possibility that they are no ammunitions left before transitioning to this state, and this can be done later-on.

- Last but not least, duplicate the object called **healthPack**, rename it **ammoPack**, and move it to a different location, for example **(-30, 1, 12)**.
- For testing purpose, modify the script **ManageNPC2** as follows:

Creating Smarter NPCs Who Can Flee or Ambush

```
//ammos--;
ammos-=40;
```

- Save your code and play the scene.

You should see that, after detecting you, the NPC will start to follow you and shoot every 3 seconds; once the ammunitions are below 20, the NPC should start to look for ammos.

This being said, if you make sure that the player is detected by the NPC, and don't move the player anymore, you will see that the NPC will shoot every seconds and eventually run-out of ammunitions; however, because it is close to the player, it will alternate between the two states.

So we need to specify that the NPC should follow the player only when its health and ammo levels are sufficiently high (e.g., greater than 20); for this purpose, we will modify each of the three transitions from **Any State** to **followPlayer**, to add the conditions **health greater than 0** and **ammos greater than 0**.

- Please identify the transitions from **Any State** to **followPlayer**.
- Select the first transition, as illustrated in the next figure.

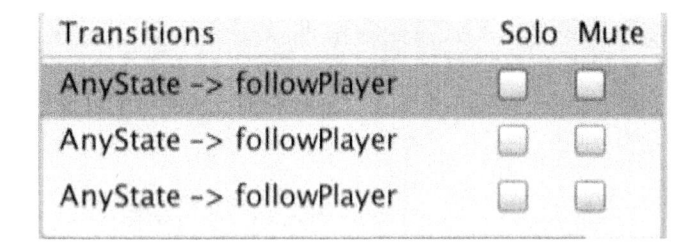

Figure 138: Selecting a transition

- Scroll down to the section called **Conditions**.
- Add the two conditions: **ammos greater than 20** and **health greater than 20**.

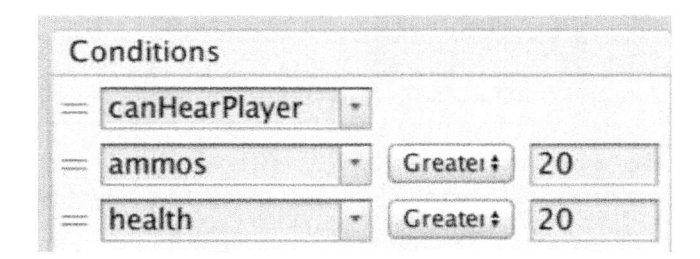

Figure 139: Including additional conditions

- Repeat the last steps with the two other transitions from **Any State** to **followPlayer**.

Once this is done, you can play the scene again and see that, when the NPC runs out of ammunitions, it will, even if it can detect the player, go to replenish its ammunitions levels.

AMBUSHING

In this section, we will implement a behavior whereby the NPC is ambushing the player as follows:

- There will be a zone, or area, that is ideal for an ambush, consisting of a long corridor where the movement of the player will be restricted, and where it can't escape any attack, as it is a cul-de-sac.

- Once this player enters this cul-de-sac, the NPC will be travelling to the ambush site.

- Once in place, it will launch a grenade in the direction of the player who won't be able to escape.

- Once this grenade is launched, the NPC will go back to its patrol.

For this purpose, we will be introducing the concept of **sub-state machines**; the idea of a sub-state machine is to group several actions of states; in our case, our sub-state machine will be including all the states necessary for the ambush, including: going to the ambush site and throwing a grenade towards the player.

So let's get started.

First, will create the corridor:

- Please duplicate one of the walls present in the scene three times.

- Rename these duplicates **corridorWall1**, **corridorWall2**, and **corridorWall3**.

- Change the position of **corridorWall1** to **(0, 2.5, -42)** and its scale to **(52, 4, 3.6)**.

- Change the position of **corridorWall2** to **(0, 2.5, -32)** and its scale to **(52, 4, 3.6)**.

- Change the position of **corridorWall3** to **(24, 2.5, -36.7)** and its scale to **(4, 4, 7)**.

- After your changes, the corridor may look like the one in the following figure.

Creating Smarter NPCs Who Can Flee or Ambush

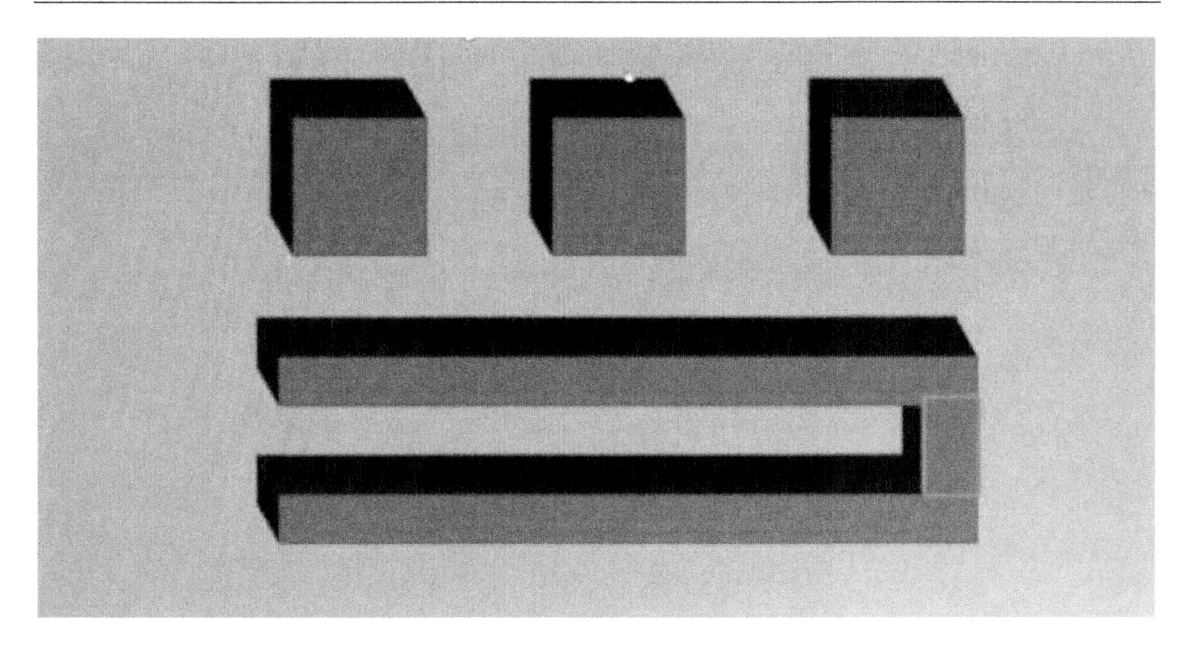

Figure 140: The corridor for the ambush

After creating these new walls, you may need to include them to the baking:

- Please select all the walls in the **Hierarchy**.

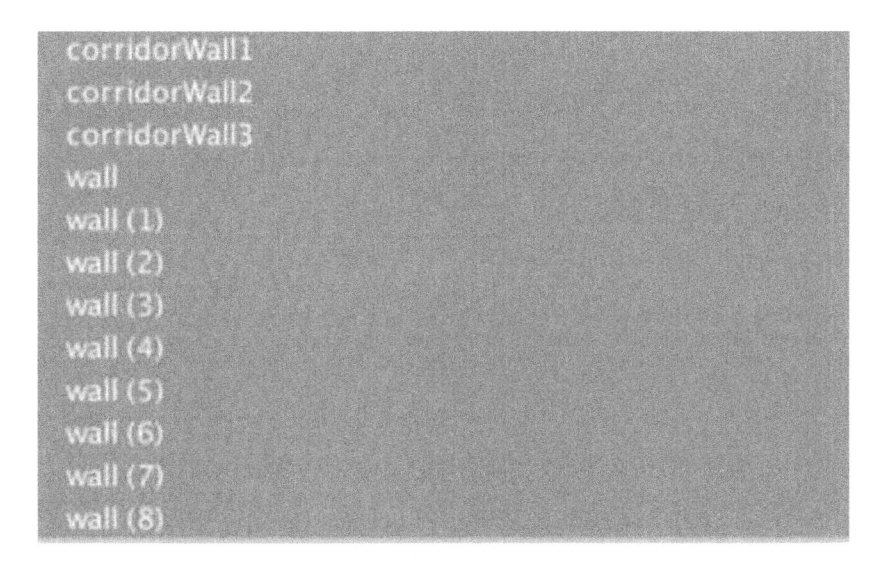

Figure 141: Selecting all the walls

- Open the **Navigation** window, and the tab called **Object**.

Creating Smarter NPCs Who Can Flee or Ambush

- Make sure that the options **Navigation Static** and **Not Walkable** are selected.
- Open the tab called **Bake** and click on the button called **Bake**.

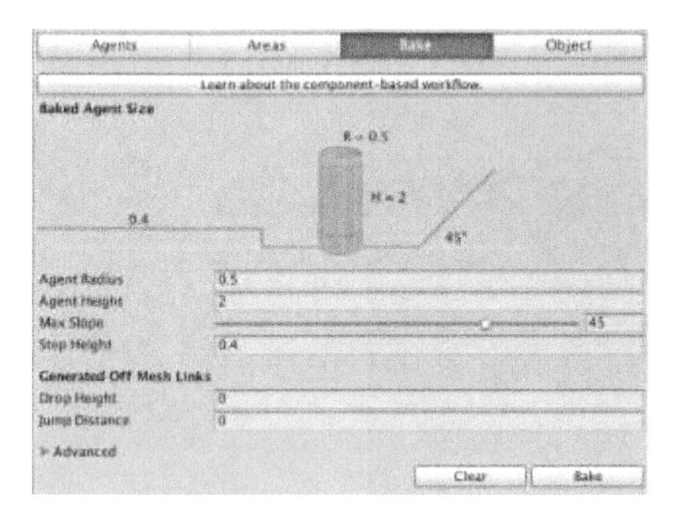

Figure 142: Baking the scene

Now that this is done, we can start to create the objects used to materialize the entrance and the end of the corridor.

- Create an empty object and call it **ambush_start**.
- Move this object to **(-24, 1, -37)**.
- This object will be used to locate the entrance of the cul-de-sac (i.e., where the NPC should go to when the player has been detected).

We can now create the area that will be used as a trigger:

- Duplicate one of the walls that you have already created.
- Rename the duplicate **ambush_area**.
- Select the object **ambush_area** and change its position to **(13, 3, -37)** and its scale to **(16, 4, 5)**.
- Deactivate the component **MeshRenderer** for this object.

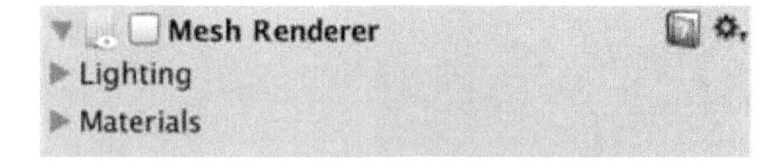

Figure 143: Deactivating the Mesh Renderer component

[336]

Creating Smarter NPCs Who Can Flee or Ambush

- The ambush area should look as illustrated in the next figure.

Figure 144: Deactivating the Mesh Renderer

Select the object **ambush_area**, and, for its **Box Collider** component, check the attribute **Is Trigger**.

> This means that the area defined by the cubical geometry will act as a trigger; no collision will be applied; however, Unity will be able to detect when this area was entered or exited. So this object will act as a zone that is motion-sensed, thanks to the trigger attribute set to true.

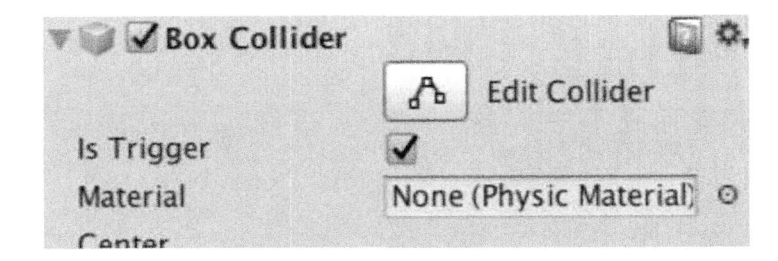

Figure 145: Setting the collider as a trigger

Now that the trigger has been defined, we will create our sub-state machine.

- In the **Animator** window, for the **Controller** called **ControlNPC3**, create two new Trigger parameters called **goToAmbush** and **reachedAmbush**.

- Right-click on the canvas, and select the option **Create sub-state machine**.

- Create a sub-state machine.

- Rename it **ambush**.

- Double click on it, this will open the sub-state machine, and a new tab called **ambush** will also appear at the top of the **Animator** window.

Figure 146: The new tab for the sub-state machine

- In this new window, create a new state called **goToAmbushSpot**; by default, Unity will link it to the **Entry** state; in other words, the state **goToAmbushSpot** will be the first one to be entered when we enter the sub-state machine **ambush**.

- Associate the animation **walking** to this state (i.e., the state **goToAmbushSpot**).

- Create another state called **throwGrenade** and associate the animation called **walking** to this state.

- Create a transition between the state **goToAmbushSpot** and the state **throwGrenade** and use the parameter **reachedAmbush** as a condition.

Finally, we will create a transition from the state **throwGrenade** to a state outside the sub-state machine and we will proceed as follows:

- Locate the state called **(Up) Base Layer** in the **Animator** window (you may need to scroll to the right by holding down the **ALT** key while dragging the mouse) within the sub-state **ambush**.

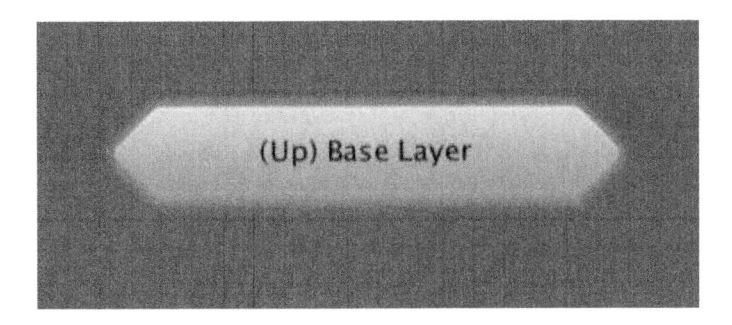

Figure 147: Locating the Up state

- You can then move this state closer to the other states that you have created in the sub-state machine (i.e., drag and drop).

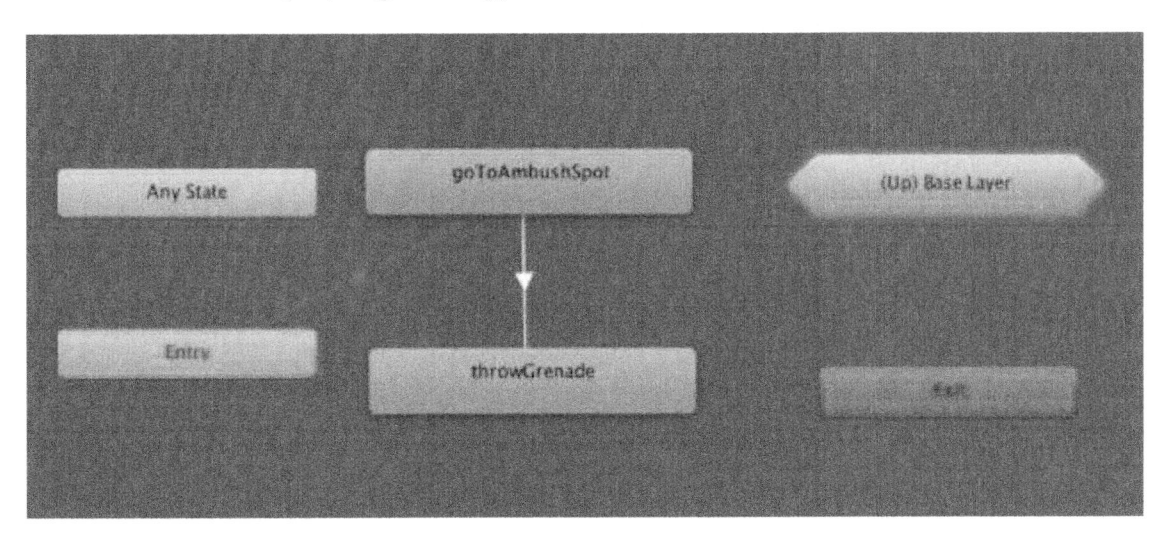

Figure 148: Visualizing all the states in the sub-state machine

- Right-click on the state **throwGrenade**, as you would usually do, to create a transition.

- Select the option **Make Transition** from the contextual menu, and click on the state called **(Up) Base Layer**.

- Once this is done, you can select the option **States | patrol**, as illustrated in the next figure.

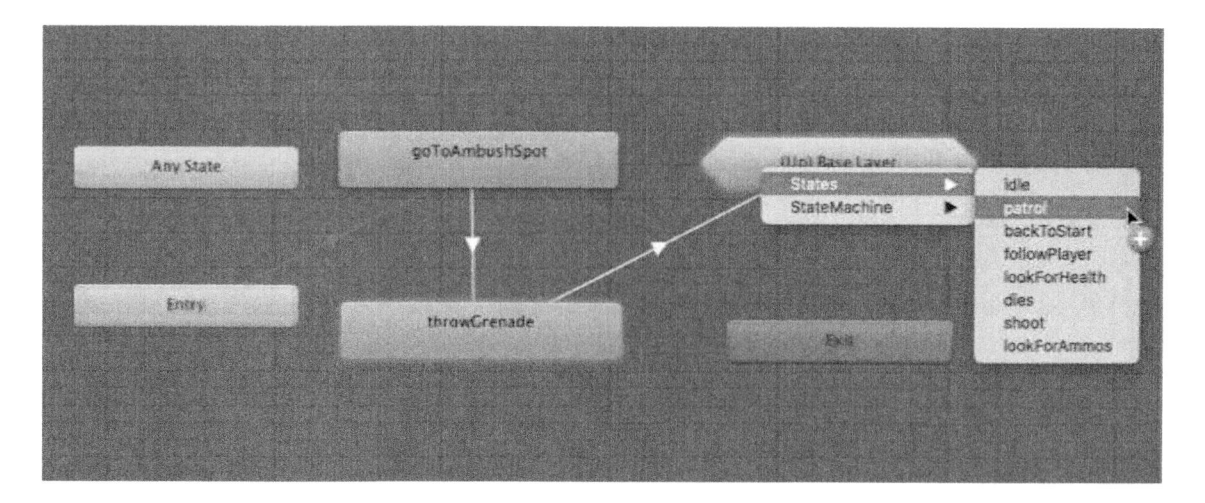

Figure 149: Linking the states

Last but not least:

- Create a transition from the state **Any State** to the state **goToAmbushSpot** with the variable **goToAmbush** as a condition. Please also check that the option "**Can Transition To Self**" is not selected.

So this means that, if the variable **goToAmbush** is set to **true**, then the NPC should transition to the sub-state machine called **ambush**, go to the ambush site (i.e., the cul-de-sac) and then throw a grenade towards the player.

So at this stage, there a few more things that we need to set-up, including:

- The movement of the NPC while in the state **goToAmbushSpot**.

- The action of throwing a grenade towards the player.

- Create the actual grenade that will be used by the NPC.

- Use the trigger area to set the NPC in the **ambush** mode.

So let's start with the first part, that is, setting the movement of the NPC while in the state **goToAmbushSpot**:

- Please open the script **ControlNPC3**.

- Add the following code to the **Update** function

```
if (info.IsName ("goToAmbushSpot"))
{
        target = GameObject.Find ("ambush_start");
        GetComponent<UnityEngine.AI.NavMeshAgent> ().SetDestination (target.transform.position);
        GetComponent<UnityEngine.AI.NavMeshAgent> ().speed = 5.5f;
        float distance = Vector3.Distance (gameObject.transform.position, target.transform.position);
        if (distance < 2.5f)
        {
                anim.SetTrigger ("reachedAmbush");
        }
}
else
{
        GetComponent<UnityEngine.AI.NavMeshAgent> ().speed = 3.5f;
}
```

In the previous code:

- We test whether we are in the state called **goToAmbushSpot**.

- If this is the case, the NPC will navigate towards the object called **ambush_start**.

- We increase its speed, so that it can get there quickly before the player exits the cul-de-sac.

- When the NPC has reached the area (i.e., when the distance to the object **ambush_start** is lesser than 2.5 meters) we set the parameter **reachedAmbush** to true; this means that the corresponding **Animator Controller** will transition to the state called **throwGrenade**.

- If we are not in this state, then the speed of the NPC is restored to **3.5**.

The next step is to get the NPC to throw grenades in the state called **throwGrenade**. For this particular feature, we will use a concept called **state events**; state events are triggered when events related to a state occur; for example, when the state is entered or exited; this is useful when an action needs to be performed **only once** during the state for example; in our case, we want the NPC to throw a grenade once, and then for the NPC to go back to its patrol; so for this purpose, we will use the event that corresponds to entering this state; when this occurs, we will get the NPC to throw a grenade. So let's proceed.

First, let's create a grenade:

- Please create a new sphere object.

- Rename it **grenade**.

- Change its **scale** attribute as follows **(0.2, 0.2, 0.2)**.

Creating Smarter NPCs Who Can Flee or Ambush

- Add a rigid body to this object (i.e., select **Component | Physics | Rigidbody**).
- Using the **Inspector**, select the option **Use Gravity** for this component.

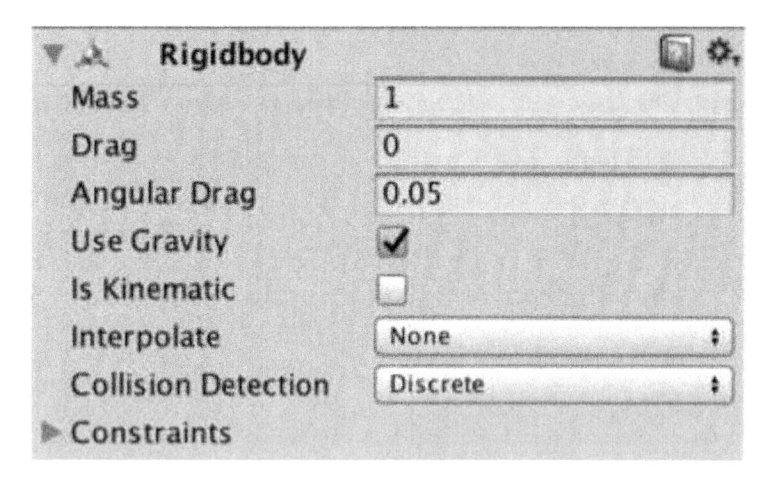

Figure 150: Adding a Rigidbody component

We can now create the script that will be used to detonate the grenade.

- Please create a new script called **Grenade**.
- Add the following code to this script (new code in bold).

```
public class Grenade : MonoBehaviour
{
        public GameObject explosion;
        float time;
        void Start () {
        }
        void Update () {
                time += Time.deltaTime;
                if (time >= 3) Instantiate (explosion, transform.position, Quaternion.identity);
                Destroy (gameObject, 3);
        }
}
```

In the previous code:

- We create a timer.
- We also declare an object called **explosion** that will be initialized with one of the explosion Assets.

- After 3 seconds, the explosion will be instantiated.
- The grenade is then destroyed 3 seconds after it has been created.

Once this is done, please do the following:

- Save your code, and check that it is error-free.
- Drag and drop the script **Grenade** to the object called **grenade**.

We can now associate an explosion to the grenade:

- Please import the **Particle** Asset bundle (i.e., select **Assets | Import Package | ParticleSystems**).
- This will create a folder called **ParticleSystems** within the folder called **Standard Assets**.

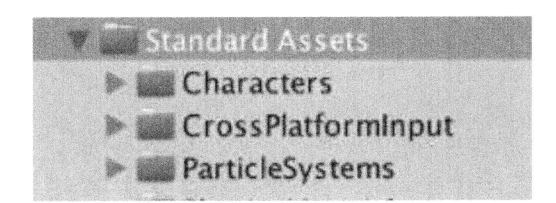

Figure 151: Importing the Particle System

- Using the **Inspector**, select the object called **grenade**.
- Then navigate to the folder **Standard Assets | ParticleSystems | prefab**.
- Drag and drop the prefab called **Explosion** to the field called **explosion**, as illustrated in the next figure.

Creating Smarter NPCs Who Can Flee or Ambush

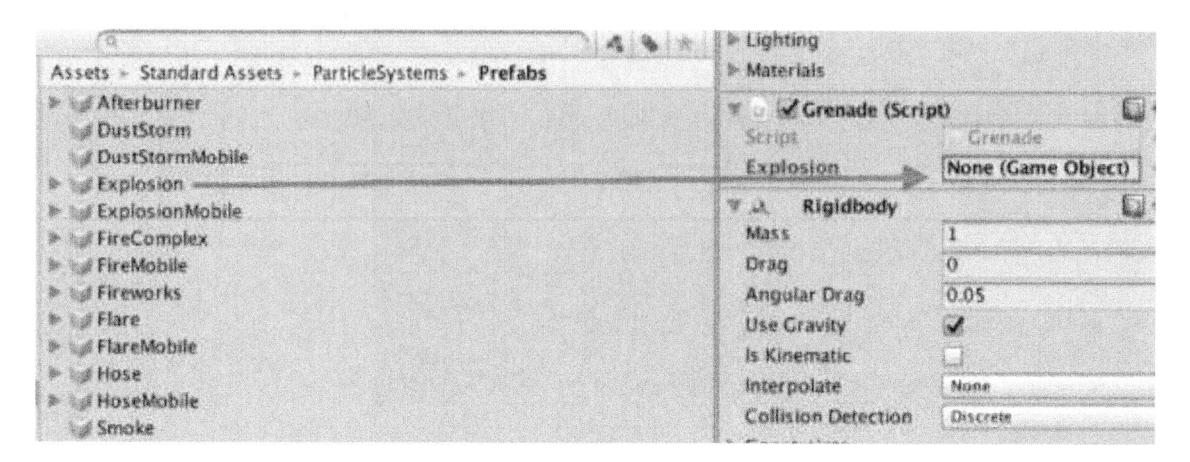

Figure 152: Setting the explosion

- Create a prefab called **grenade** with the object called **grenade** by dragging and dropping this object to the **Project** window.

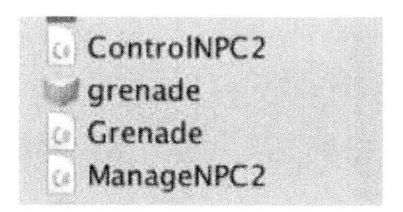

Figure 153: Creating the grenade prefab

- Remove or deactivate the object called **grenade** in the **Hierarchy** window.

Now that we have set-up our grenade, we can write code to instantiate a **grenade** when the NPC has reached the ambush site:

- In the **Animator** window, select the state called **throwGrenade** that is within the state called **ambush** (you may double click on the sub-state called **ambush** if it is not open yet).

- In the **Inspector** window, click on the button called **Add Behaviour**.

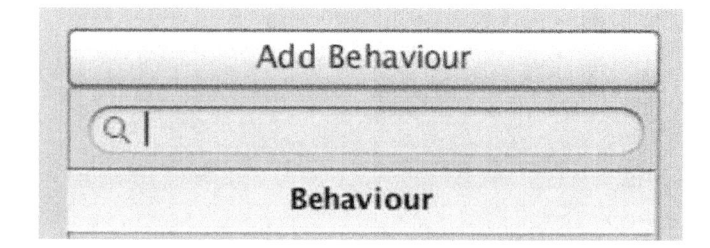

- and then select the option **New Script**.

Creating Smarter NPCs Who Can Flee or Ambush

Figure 154: Adding a new script (part 1)

- Name this script **ControlGrenade**.

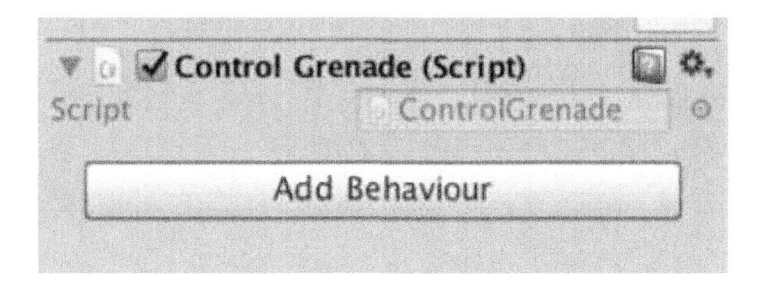

Figure 155: Adding a new script (part 2)

- Double click on the script **ControlGrenade** in this window to open it.
- As it opens, you may notice that the start of the script is different from the usual scripts, especially the next line.

```
public class ControlGrenade : StateMachineBehaviour {
```

This line specifies that this class extends the class **StateMachineBehaviour**; which means that, by default it will avail of its methods and attributes, including the method called **OnStateEnter**, that we will implement (i.e., override) in the next section.

- Please add the following code to the script (new code in bold).

Creating Smarter NPCs Who Can Flee or Ambush

```
public class ControlGrenade : StateMachineBehaviour {
public GameObject grenade;
void Start () {}
override public void OnStateEnter(Animator animator, AnimatorStateInfo stateInfo, int layerIndex)
{
        animator.gameObject.transform.LookAt(GameObject.Find ("FPSController").gameObject.transform.position);
        GameObject clone = Instantiate(grenade, animator.rootPosition, Quaternion.identity) as GameObject;
        Rigidbody rb = clone.GetComponent<Rigidbody>();
        rb.AddForce (animator.gameObject.transform.forward*1000);
}
```

In the previous code:

- We declare a public variable called **grenade**; it will be used to instantiate a new grenade.
- We use the built-in function **OnStateEnter** that is called whenever a state is entered.
- When this function is called, we ensure that the NPC is looking at the player.
- We then instantiate a grenade and throw it towards the player.

You may notice that to access the NPC's **gameObject** we use the syntax **animator.gameObject**.

You can now save your script.

If you look at the **Animator** window, you should see an empty placeholder called **grenade**.

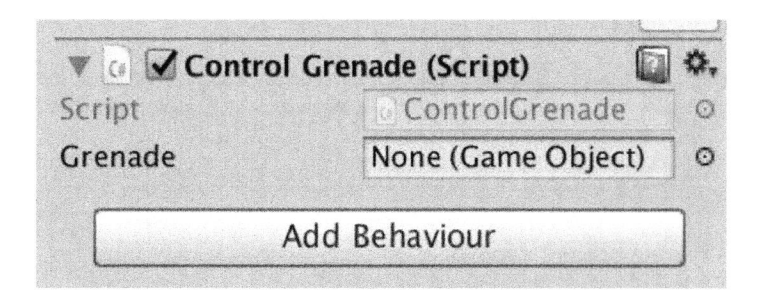

Figure 156: The empty placeholder for the grenade

- Please drag and drop the prefab called **grenade** from the **Project** window to this placeholder.

Last, but not least, we need to link the trigger in the ambush site to the NPC.

- Please create a new script called **Trigger** and drag and drop it to the object called **ambush_area**.

- Open the script called **Trigger**.

- Add the following code to it.

```
void OnTriggerEnter (Collider coll)
{
        if (coll.gameObject.name == "FPSController") GameObject.Find ("NPC3").GetComponent<ControlNPC3>().playerEnteredAmbushArea ();
}
```

In the previous code:

- The function **OnTriggerEnter** is called whenever a trigger is entered; this trigger can be linked to the object related to this script.

- In this case, we call the function **playerEnteredAmbushArea**, that we yet have to create, that will be part of the script **ControlNPC3**.

We can now create this function.

- Please save your script and open the script **ControlNPC3**.

- Add the following function to this script (i.e., **ControlNPC3**).

```
public void playerEnteredAmbushArea()
{
        anim.SetTrigger ("goToAmbush");
}
```

In the previous code, we declare the function **playerEnteredAmbushArea**; when this function is called, its sets the trigger parameter **goToAmbush** of the corresponding **Animator Controller** to **true**.

Et Voila!

Please save your code. At this stage all the mechanics should be in place for our NPC to go to the ambush site when the player enters the cul-de-sac. So you can test the game, move the player so that it enters the cul-de-sac, and the NPC should be going to the area, throw a grenade, and then return to patrolling.

Creating Smarter NPCs Who Can Flee or Ambush

Figure 157: The NPC throws a grenade

Figure 158: The grenade explodes

ADDING A GUN TO THE NPC

As you check the scene, you may notice that when the NPC is shooting, it has no gun yet in its hand; this is because the animation created did not include the weapon, so we need to add a gun object to this NPC when it is shooting.

So let's add this object:

- You can download a gun object from the following site and link (this model was created by Dennis Haupt):

http://tf3dm.com/3d-model/45-acp-smith-and-wesson-13999.html

- In case this link is not available anymore, it is also included in the resource pack, in the folder **3D models | handgun** (with the permission of the author of this object).

- Once this done, you can import the folder called **fbx** in Unity. This will include a folder with a prefab for the gun, as well as textures.

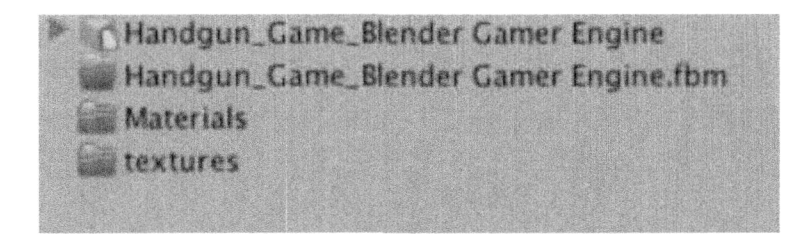

Figure 159: Importing a gun object

Once this is done, you can drag and drop the prefab (i.e., the blue box named **Handgun_Game_Blender Gamer Engine**) on the object **NPC3**, so that it becomes a child of the NPC.

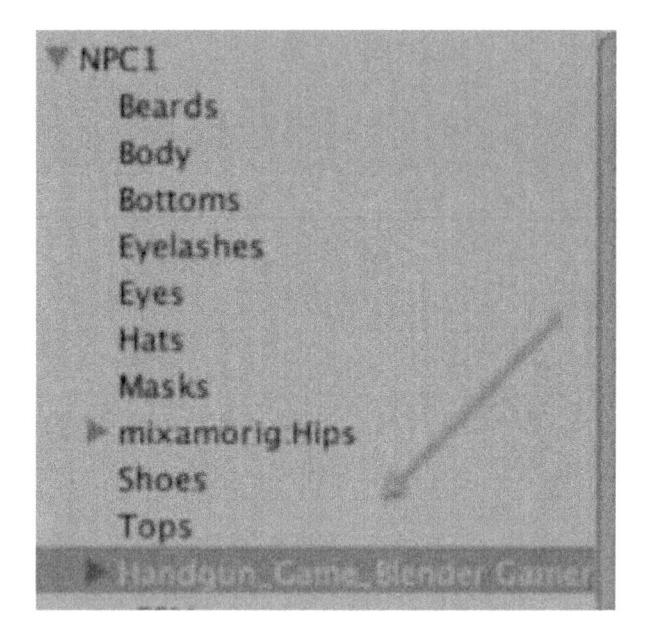

Figure 160: Adding the gun as a child of the NPC

We can then adjust its **Transform** settings as follows:

- Position **(0.115, 1.211, 0.759)**.
- Rotation **(0, 90, 0)**.
- Scale **(0.2, 0.2, 0.2)**.

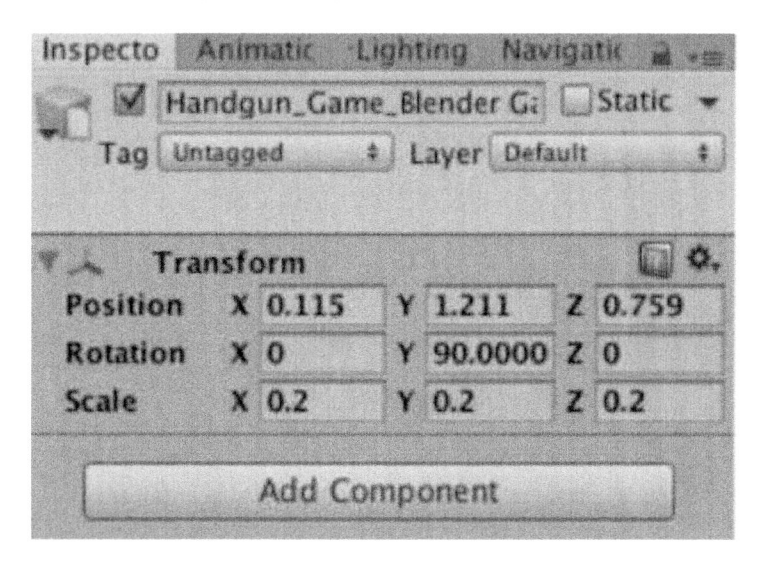

Figure 161: Adjusting the position and scale of the gun

Creating Smarter NPCs Who Can Flee or Ambush

- In the **Hierarchy** window, rename this object **hand_gun**.

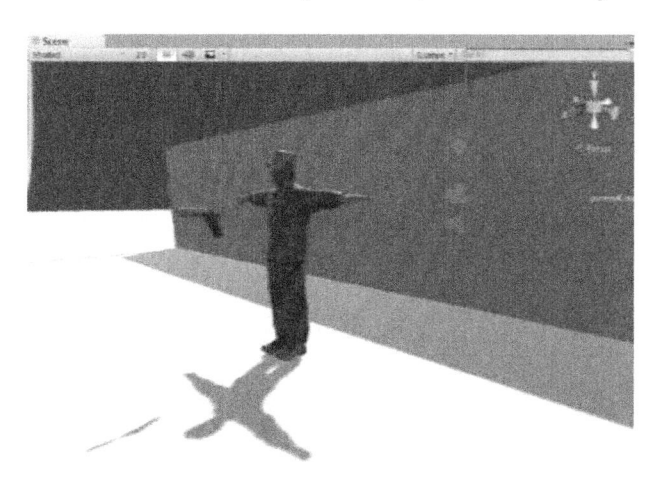

Figure 162: Adding the gun to the NPC

Next, we need to enable this object only when the NPC is shooting:

- Open the script **ControlNPC3**.
- Add the following code at the beginning of the class.

```
public GameObject gun;
```

- Then add the following code to the method **Start**.

```
gun = GameObject.Find("hand_gun");
gun.SetActive(false);
```

Finally:

- In the **Animator** window, select the state called **shoot**.
- In the **Inspector** window click on the button labelled **Add Behavior**.
- Create a new script called **ControlGun**.

Creating Smarter NPCs Who Can Flee or Ambush

Figure 163: Adding a new behaviour

- Open the script **ControlGun**.
- Add the following code to it.

```
override public void OnStateEnter(Animator animator, AnimatorStateInfo stateInfo, int layerIndex)
{
        animator.gameObject.GetComponent<ControlNPC3> ().gun.SetActive (true);
}
override public void OnStateExit(Animator animator, AnimatorStateInfo stateInfo, int layerIndex)
{
        animator.gameObject.GetComponent<ControlNPC3> ().gun.SetActive (false);
}
```

In the previous code: the gun is activated as we enter the state called **shoot** and deactivated when we exit this state.

You can now test the scene and check that the gun is displayed when the NPC is shooting.

Figure 164: The NPC shooting with apparent gun

USING DOT PRODUCTS FOR A MORE ACCURATE VISION

Now, as you play and test the scene, you should see that the NPC will follow you whenever you walk pass him. However, the sight detection, as it is, may not be as accurate as it could be. This is because, at present, the field of view of this NPC is extremely narrow, as we expect to detect only objects at a 0-degree angle from him; not only is this not accurate, but it can cause some undesirable effects and behaviors. However, we can correct this easily using a more realistic field of view. For this we will use a bit of algebra, that is, using the dot product. The **dot product** is a mathematical concept that basically tells us about the angle between two vectors; so to mimic the field of view of the NPC, we would like to know whether the player is in front of the NPC +/- several degrees, as illustrated on the next figure.

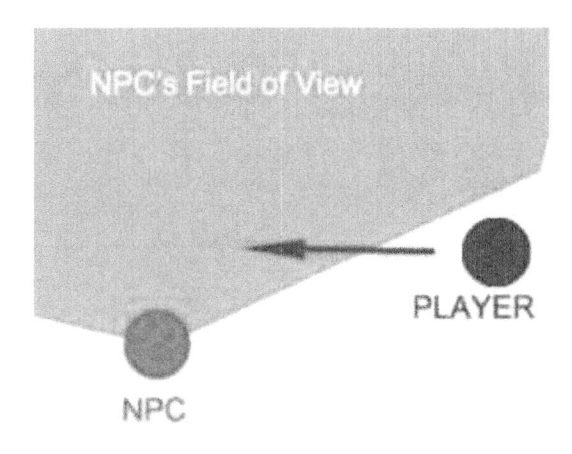

Figure 165: Illustrating the player's field of view

The definition of a dot product between two vectors is the product of their magnitude multiplied by the cosine of the angle between these vectors. In practical terms, we multiply the two vectors; however, to do so, we need to consider whether they are in the same direction. So the cosine will provide us with the projection of one of the vectors on the other one and multiply this projection then by the magnitude of the other vector.

> The dot product effectively tells us about the angle between these vectors and to what extent they are aligned; for example, a positive dot product indicates that the angle between the two vectors is between -90 and 90 degrees, a null dot product indicates that they are perpendicular to each other.

The formula is as follows:

D = |v1| x |v2| x Cos (alpha).

Where:

- D is the dot product between the two vectors.
- Alpha is the angle between the two vectors.

In Unity, the built-in classes make it easier to use the dot product, as demonstrated below:

```
Vector3 v1 = new Vector3 (1.0f,1.0f,1.0f);
Vector3 v2 = new Vector3 (-2.0f,-2.0f,-2.0f);
float productOfV1AndV2 = Vector3.Dot(v1,v2);
```

- Line 1: the vector v1 is created.
- Line 2: the vector v2 is created.
- Line 3: the dot product of these vectors is calculated.
- In this case, the dot product is -2; so we know that the angle between the vectors is between -90 and 90 degrees.

It would be great, however, to know more about the direction of these vectors, and more importantly if they are aligned or pointing in the same direction. For this purpose, we can normalize these vectors first (i.e., reduce their magnitude to 1). This way, if they are in the exact same direction, the dot product will be 1; and if they are in the opposite direction, the dot product will be -1. This is because when we calculate the dot product, if the magnitudes of both vectors are 1, the dot product will be equal to the cosine of the angle between these two. Because the cosine is equal to one if the angle is 0 and -1 if the angle is 180, it is now easier to check if these vectors are aligned. In Unity, we could do this as follows:

```
Vector3 v1 = new Vector3 (1.0f,1.0f,1.0f);
Vector3 v2 = new Vector3 (-2.0f,-2.0f,-2.0f);
float productOfV1AndV2 = Vector3.Dot(v1.normalized,v2. normalized);
```

- The first two lines are similar to the previous code.
- Line3: we calculate the dot product of these vectors, after they have been normalized; in this case, we will find that the dot product equals -1 (i.e., vectors are pointing to opposite directions).

If we call the field of view **alpha**, knowing whether the NPC is in the field of view is equivalent to know whether the angle determined by the direction of the NPC (V1 on the next diagram) and the vector that points at the player from the NPC (V2 in the next diagram) is comprised between -alpha/2 and alpha/2. So for a field of view of 90 degrees, the angle defined by V1 and V2 should be comprised between -45 degrees and +45 degrees. This is explained on the next diagram. As the player enters the NPCs' field of view, the vector V2 will rotate counterclockwise.

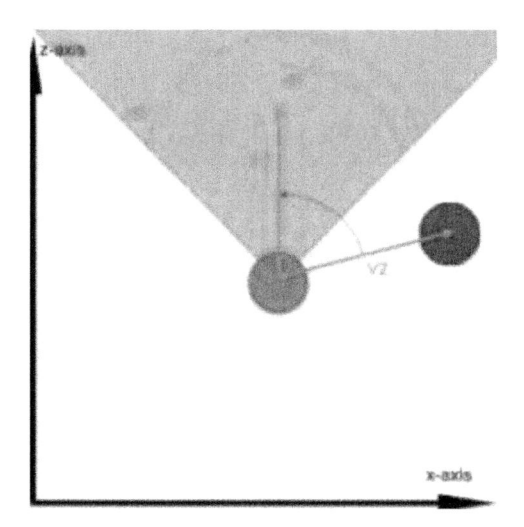

Figure 166: Illustrating the player entering the NPC's field of view

So, as described on the previous diagram, and knowing that cosine (45) is approximately 0.7 and that cosine (-45) is approximately also 0.7, we know that the player is in the field of view of the NPC if the angle between V1 and V2 is between -45 degrees and +45 degrees, or, in a similar way, if the cosine of the angle between the vectors V1 and V2 is comprised between 0.7 and 1. This is because when the player is on the right border of the field of view, the angle between V1 and V2 is -45° (i.e., cosine = 0.7).

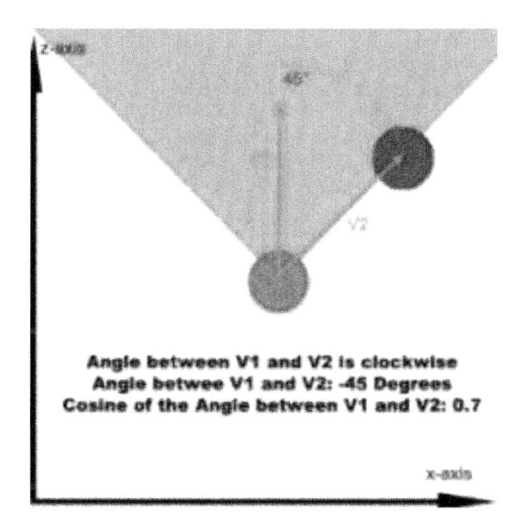

Figure 167: the player enters the right boundary of the field of view

- When the player is in front of the NPC, the angle between V1 and V2 is 0 (Cosine = 1).
- When the player is on the left border of the field of view, the angle between V1 and V2 is 45° (Cosine = 0.7). So effectively, when the NPC is in the field of view, the Cosine of the angle will vary between 0.7 and 1.

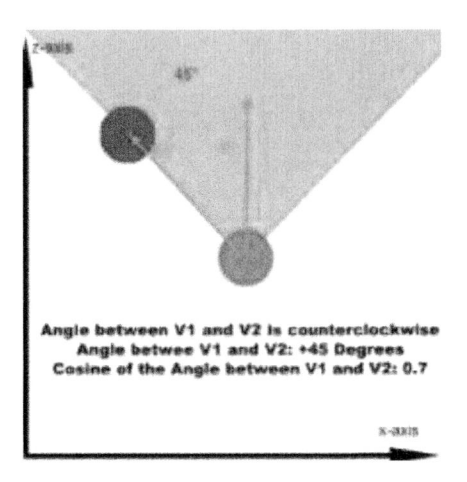

Figure 8-168: Exiting the NPC's field of view

- The field of view could be any number of your choice. We have arbitrarily chosen 90 degrees to simulate the horizontal field of view for some humans, but you could, if you wished, increase it to 100 degrees or more.

- Now that we have clarified the calculation of the **Cosine**, let's see how we can find the vectors V1 and V2.

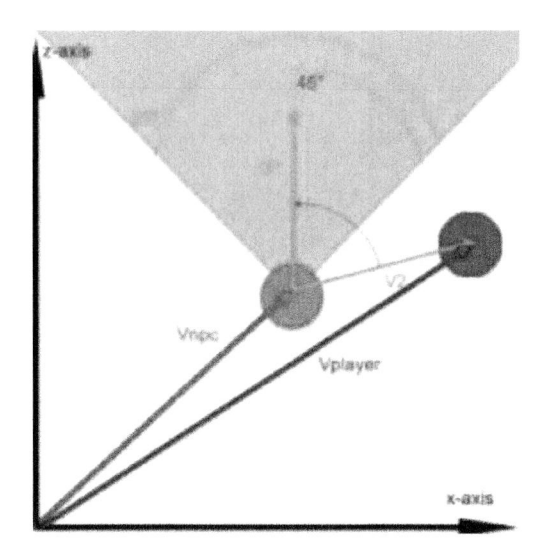

Figure 8-169: Calculating V2

- V1 is the direction of the NPC. This vector originates (on the previous diagram) from the NPC and is going in the direction of the positive z-axis. V2 is determined by the position of both the NPC and the Player. Let's see how. As you can see on the next diagram, V2, Vnpc and Vplayer form a triangle. Vnpc is the vector for the position of the NPC. It starts at the origin of the coordinate system. Vplayer is the vector for the position of the NPC and, as for the previous vector, it starts at the origin of the coordinate system. If we operate a loop from the origin of the coordinate system, we can go from the origin of the coordinate system to the NPC by following the vector Vnpc, we follow the vector V2 (in reverse: from the head to the tail), and then following the vector Vplayer (in reverse: from the head to the tail). So we could say that: **Vnpc + V2-Vplayer = 0**; in other words, by following Vnpc, then V2 in reverse and Vplayer in reverse, we end up at the same point. Following this, we can then say that: V2 = -Vnpc + Vplayer (we add -V2 to both sides of the previous equation). This is how we can calculate V2.

- Normalizing the vectors: so at this stage, we know V1 and V2 and we just need to calculate the dot product between these to have an idea of the cosine of the angle. However, if you remember the definition of a dot product, the cosine of this angle equals the dot product only if the magnitude of the vectors is 1, or in other words, if these vectors have been normalized. Normalizing can be done easily in Unity as each vector can access the function/method **normalized** which returns a normalized version accordingly.

- At this stage, we have two normalized vectors (magnitude equals 1) and we need to calculate the cosine of the angle defined by them. You will notice that so far, we have been using degrees for angles (FOV=90°). However, the function that calculates the Cosine in Unity only takes Radians (and not Degrees) as parameters. So we will need to convert our angle in radians first before the cosine can be calculated. This can be done using the function **Mathf.Deg2Rad** in Unity.

- Now we have an angle expressed in radians and we can calculate the dot product of the normalized versions of V1 and V2. That's great! Bearing in mind that when the player is on the right boundary of the field of view, the angle between V1 and V2 is -45° (Cosine = 0.7), when the player is in front of the NPC, the angle between V1 and V2 is 0 (Cosine = 1), and that when the player is on the left border of the field of view, the angle between V1 and V2 is 45° (Cosine = 0.7), we effectively know that for the NPC to detect the player (or the player to enter the Field of View of the NPC), the cosine of the angle between V1 and V2 should be comprised between 0.7 and 1.

- The last thing that we need to check for the vision detection is that there is nothing between the player and the NPC; this can be achieved using a simple raycast.

Now that the principle of dot products is clear, we could apply it to our own code, as follows:

- Please open the script **ControlNPC3**.

- Add the following code at the beginning of the script.

```
public Vector3 direction;
public bool isInTheFieldOfView;
public bool noObjectBetweenNPCAndPlayer = false;
```

- Add the following code at the beginning of the function called **look** (new code in bold).

Creating Smarter NPCs Who Can Flee or Ambush

```
direction = (GameObject.Find("FPSController").transform.position - transform.position).normalized;
isInTheFieldOfView = (Vector3.Dot(transform.forward.normalized, direction) > .7);
Debug.DrawRay(transform.position, direction * 100, Color.green);
Debug.DrawRay(transform.position, transform.forward * 100, Color.blue);


if (Physics.Raycast (ray.origin, ray.direction, out hit, castingDistance))
```

- Add the following code to the **look** function (new code in bold):

```
if (Physics.Raycast (ray.origin, direction, out hit, castingDistance))
{
        objectInSight = hit.collider.gameObject.name;
        if (objectInSight == "FPSController" && isInTheFieldOfView) anim.SetBool ("canSeePlayer",true);
        else anim.SetBool ("canSeePlayer", false);
}
```

In the previous code:

- We set the variable **direction** to be the direction between the player and the NPC.

- We then set the variable **isInTheFieldOfView** to true if the dot product between the direction of the NPC and the vector direction (i.e., direction if the NPC had to look at the player) is between .7 and 1. Note that we use normalized vectors, so the dot product can only be between -1 and 1.

- We also cast two rays that you will be able to see in the scene view: one in the NPC's direction (i.e., forward), and the other one from the NPC and toward the player.

- Once this is done, we cast a ray between the NPC and the player.

- So if this ray collides with the player, we know that there is nothing between the NPC and the player.

- Finally, if there are no objects between the NPC and the player and the player is in the field of view, we set the animation parameter to true, otherwise it is set to false.

Creating Smarter NPCs Who Can Flee or Ambush

You can now play the scene; you can look at the **Scene** view and the **Game** view simultaneously if you wish; as you move the player around, look at the two rays originating from the NPC and the angle between them, as illustrated on the next figure.

Figure 170: Detecting the player when it is in the field of view

- Once you reach the 45-degree angle within the NPC's field of view, the NPC will start to follow you.

So, as you can see, simple algebra can be very handy to solve some challenges paused by game design, and dot products are extremely useful in the case of fields of view.

SPAWNING NPCS

Ok. So at this stage we have an NPC that can detect the player and also complete an ambush; it would be great, to increase the challenge for the player, if we could spawn several versions of this NPC; so we will, in this section, manage to create an NPC spawner that will spawn NPCs at regular intervals.

So, let's go ahead:

- At this stage you should already have a prefab called **NPC3**; if this is the case, then please select the object **NPC3**, and click on the button called **Apply** located in the top-right corner of the Inspector window, to update the corresponding prefab.

- If you don't have a prefab for the object **NPC3**, then you can create one by dragging and dropping the object **NPC3** to the **Project** window.

- Please duplicate the prefab **NPC3** and rename the duplicate it **NPC_template**.

- Create an empty object called **spawner**.

- Change its position to **(36, 3, 11)**.

- Create a new script called **Spawner**.

- Add the following code at the beginning of the script.

```
public GameObject npc;
float timer;
public float spawningTime = 5.0f;
```

- Add the following to the **Update** function.

```
void Update ()
{
    timer += Time.deltaTime;
    if (timer >= spawningTime)
    {
        GameObject go = (GameObject)(Instantiate (npc, transform.position, Quaternion.identity));
        timer = 0.0f;
    }
}
```

In the previous code:

- We create a timer that will be used to spawn new NPCs.

Creating Smarter NPCs Who Can Flee or Ambush

- When we have reached a specific threshold (i.e., **spawningTime**), new NPCs are instantiated.

- The timer is then set to 0.

Once this is done, we can start to save our code and to apply it.

- Please save your code.

- Drag and drop the script **Spawner** to the object **spawner**.

- Select the object **spawner**.

- Drag and drop the prefab **NPC_template** from the **Project** window to the field called **npc**.

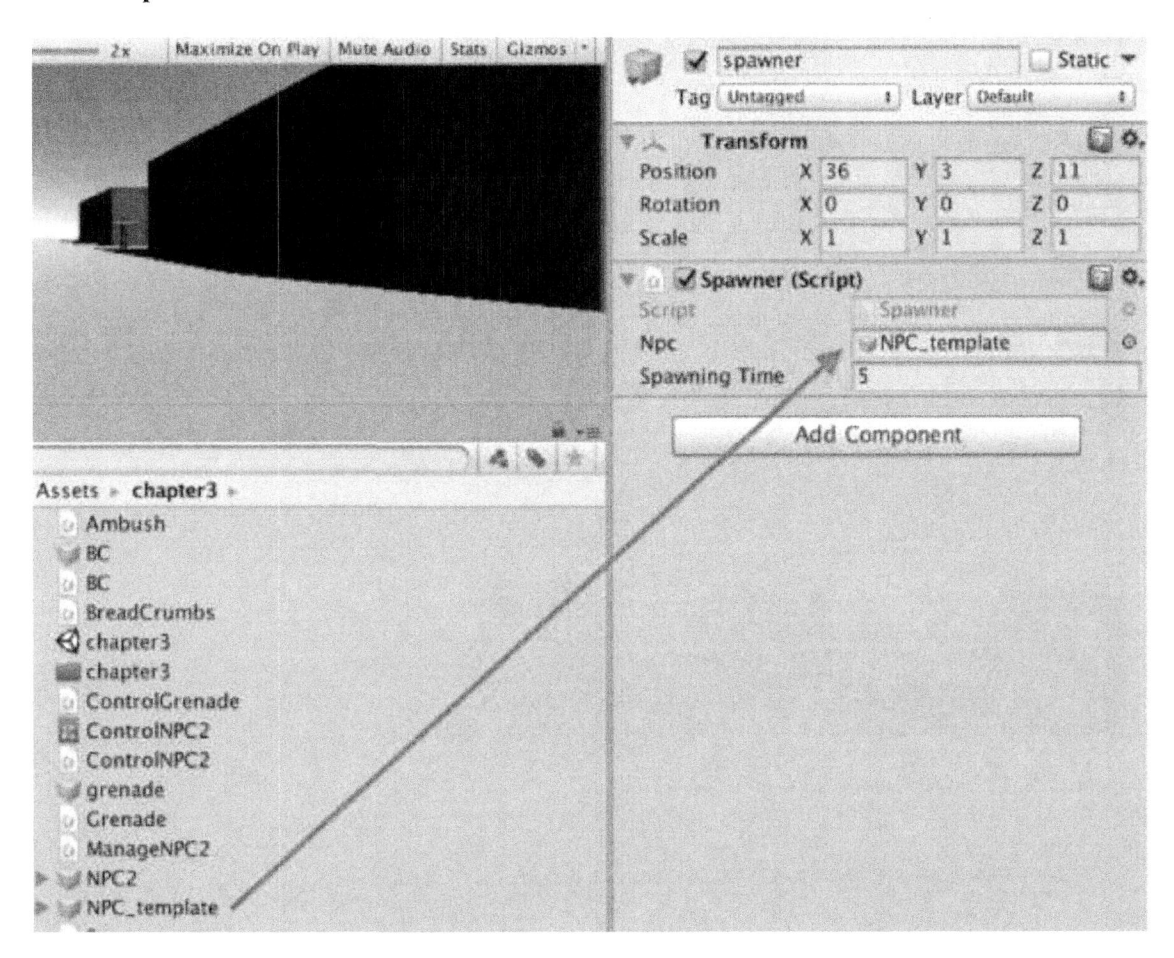

Figure 171: Instantiating new NPCs

Creating Smarter NPCs Who Can Flee or Ambush

Before we can start to test the scene, we just need to modify the **Animator Controller ControlNPC3** by setting its parameter **health** to **100** (otherwise the NPCs health will be zero just after being instantiated).

= health   100.0

Figure 172: Setting the health to a00%

Once this is done, you can start to test the scene and check that it is working properly (i.e., new NPCs spawn every 5 seconds). After a minute you should see that several NPCs have been instantiated.

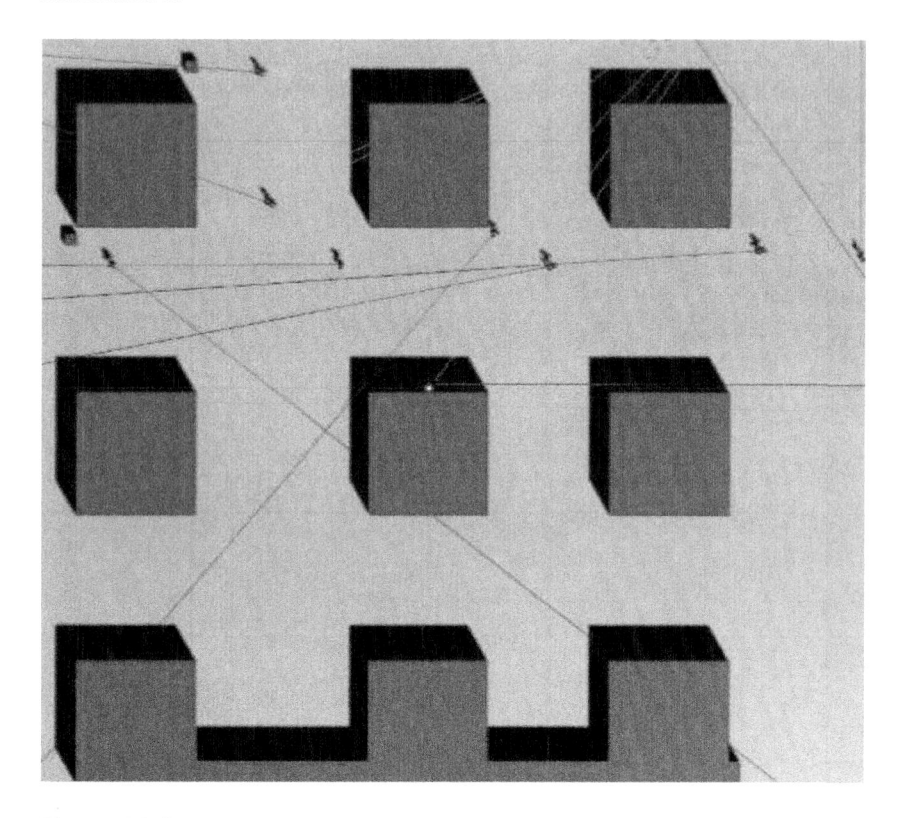

Figure 173: Several NPCs have been spawned

FLEEING

In this section, we will make it possible for the NPC to flee from the player; this will add more challenge and realism to your games; as the NPC is low on ammos, it may decide to flee until its ammunitions are replenished.

The concept of fleeing involves the NPC going away from and in the opposite direction of the player; so to be able to implement this state we need to do the following:

- Determine the position of the player.
- Determine the position of the NPC.
- Move to a point that is diametrically opposed to the player.

So let's get started:

- In the **Animator** window, for the **Controller** called **ControlNPC3**, create a new state called **flee** and associate the animation **walking** to it.
- Create a Trigger parameter called **startToFlee**.
- For testing purposes, create a transition between the state called **Any State** and the state called **flee** with **startToFlee** as a condition for the transition. Also make sure that the option **Can Transition to Self** is set to **false**.
- You can also disable the object called **spawner** for the time being and we will focus on the object **NPC3** that is already present in the scene (otherwise you can drag and drop a prefab based of this object in the scene).
- Open the script called **ControlNPC3**.
- Add the following code to it (in the **Update** function):

```
if (info.IsName ("flee") )
{
        float minumDistanceBetweenThem = 25;
        Vector3 playerPosition = GameObject.Find ("FPSController").transform.position;
        Vector3 towardsPlayer = (transform.position  + playerPosition)/2 ;
        towardsPlayer = towardsPlayer.normalized;
        target.transform.position = transform.position + - (towardsPlayer)*minumDistanceBetweenThem;
        GetComponent<NavMeshAgent> ().SetDestination (target.transform.position);
}
```

In the previous code

- We check if we are in the state called **flee**.

Creating Smarter NPCs Who Can Flee or Ambush

- If this is the case, we set the minimum distance between the player and the NPC.
- We then calculate the vector that points from the NPC to the player.
- Since we just want the direction of this vector, we then normalize the vector.
- We then set the target of the NPC to be in the opposite direction, and at a distance of 25 meters.

> Note that because, by default, the attribute **auto repath** is usually set to true, even if the NPC can't reach the target, a partial path is generated to the closest destination.

Before we test our scene, we will mute all the other transitions from the state **Any State**, so that we can isolate and only execute the transition from **Any State** to **flee**.

- In the **Animator** window, select the state called **Any State**.
- Tick the option called **Solo** for the transition from **Any State** to **flee**.

Transitions	Solo	Mute
AnyState -> followPlayer	☐	☐
AnyState -> followPlayer	☐	☐
AnyState -> followPlayer	☐	☐
AnyState -> lookForHealth	☐	☐
AnyState -> dies	☐	☐
AnyState -> lookForAmmos	☐	☐
AnyState -> goToAmbushSpot	☐	☐
AnyState -> flee	✓	☐

Figure 174: Soloing the transition

Creating Smarter NPCs Who Can Flee or Ambush

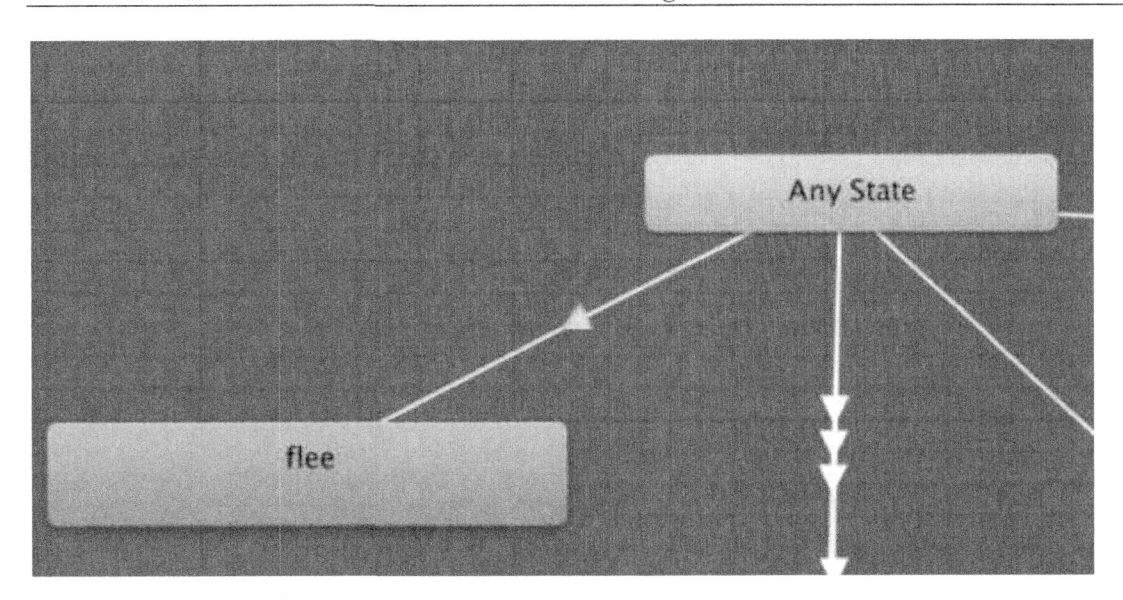

Figure 175: The transition is soloed

Because the transition from **Any State** to **flee** is soloed, the other transitions from **Any State** are muted by default.

You can now test your scene:

- Play the scene.
- Move the player around
- In the **Animator** window, set the parameter **startToFlee** to true.
- You should see that the NPC will start to move in the opposite direction of the player.

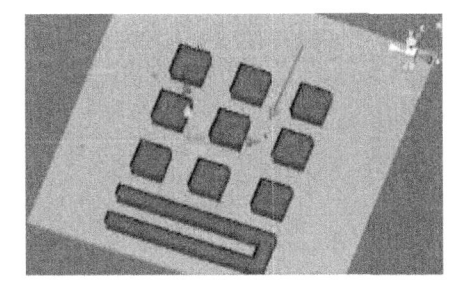

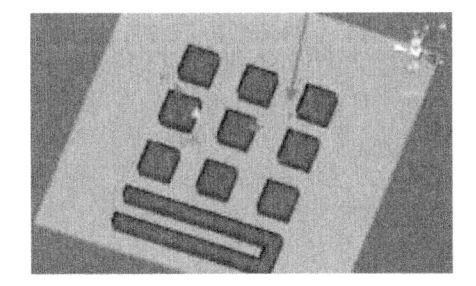

Figure 176: The NPC fleeing from the player (part 1)   **Figure 177: The NPC fleeing from the player (part 2)**

As you can see in the previous figures, the NPC is moving away from the player.

Creating Smarter NPCs Who Can Flee or Ambush

Now, we have just implemented this as an example, and you could implement this as part of the gameplay in various situations, for example, if the NPC is running out of ammos and health, or if it is looking for health but there are no health packs available.

Let's implement this feature:

- Please remove the transition between the states **Any State** and **flee**.

- Create a parameter called **healthPackAvailable** of type **Boolean**.

- Modify the transition from **AnyState** to **lookForHealth** as follows, so that the condition **healthPackAvailable** is also checked.

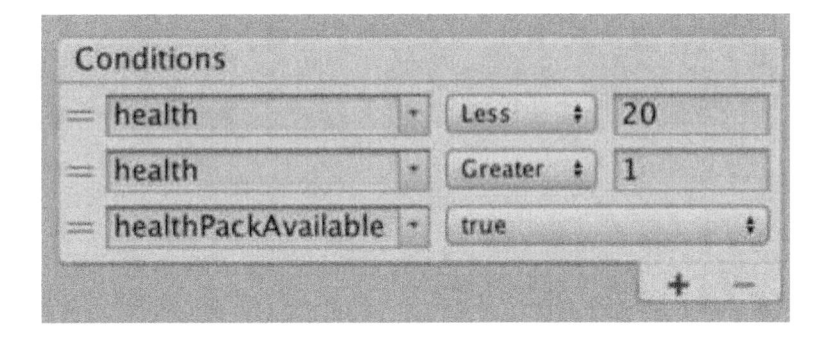

Figure 178: Modifying a transition

- Create a transition from **flee** to **lookForHealth** with **healPackAvailable is true** as a condition.

For testing purposes, you can modify the value of the variable **health** in the script **ManageNPC2** to **10**, and set the parameter **healthPackAvailable** to **true** in the **Animator** window.

As you play the game you should see that the NPC is transitioning immediately to the state **lookForHealth** and that it goes to the health pack.

This being said, to be more realistic, it might be better to have several health packs that disappear as the NPC collects them; so in the next section, we will make sure that health packs are collected and destroyed, but also that the NPC flees if its health is low and if no packs are available, until one becomes available. For this purpose, we will also create a health pack spawner.

So let's get started:

- Please create a **new** tag called **healthPack** and apply it to the object **healthPack** in the scene.

Creating Smarter NPCs Who Can Flee or Ambush

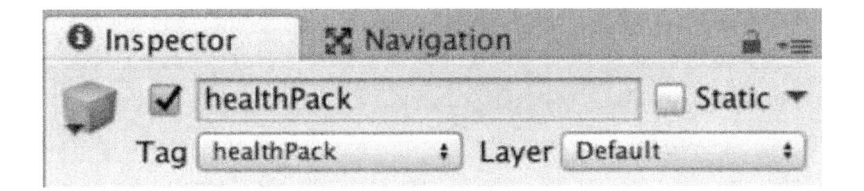

Figure 179: Adding a label to the health pack

- Create a new prefab called **healthPack** by dragging and dropping the **healthPack** object to the **Project** window.

Figure 180: Creating health pack prefabs

- Once this is done, drag and drop the prefab called **healthPack** in three different locations in the game; for example, **(1, 1, 5)**, **(20, 1, 5)**, and **(40, 1, 40)**.

- Modify the **Update** function in the script **ControlNPC3** as follows (new code in bold):

[367]

Creating Smarter NPCs Who Can Flee or Ambush

```
if (info.IsName ("lookForHealth"))
{
        //target = GameObject.Find ("healthPack");
        GameObject [] healthPacks;
        healthPacks = (GameObject[])GameObject.FindGameObjectsWithTag ("healthPack");
        if (healthPacks.Length == 0)
                //anim.SetTrigger ("startToFlee");
                anim.SetBool ("healthPackAvailable",false);
        else
        {
                anim.SetBool ("healthPackAvailable",true);
                float distanceToClosestPack = 1000;
                int rankOfClosestPack = 100;
                for (int i = 0; i < healthPacks.Length; i++)
                {
                        float distanceToCurrentPack = Vector3.Distance (gameObject.transform.position, healthPacks [i].transform.position);
                        if (distanceToCurrentPack < distanceToClosestPack)
                        {
                                distanceToClosestPack = distanceToCurrentPack;
                                rankOfClosestPack = i;
                        }
                }
                target = healthPacks [rankOfClosestPack];
        }
        GetComponent<UnityEngine.AI.NavMeshAgent> ().SetDestination (target.transform.position);
        if (Vector3.Distance (gameObject.transform.position, target.transform.position) < 2)
        {
                GetComponent<ManageNPC2> ().setHealth (100);
        }
}
```

In the previous code:

- We identify all the health packs present in the scene based on their tag.

- If no health packs are available, then the NPC will flee (until health packs become available).

- In case there are health packs available, we select (and go to) the closest one.

So that a health pack is destroyed after being collected, we can change the code just below the previous lines (new code in bold):

```
if (Vector3.Distance (gameObject.transform.position, target.transform.position) < 2)
{
        GetComponent<ManageNPC2> ().setHealth (100);
        Destroy (target);

}
```

- Please also create a transition from the state **Any State** to the state **flee** with the following conditions: **health > 1, health < 20, healthPackAvailable=false**.

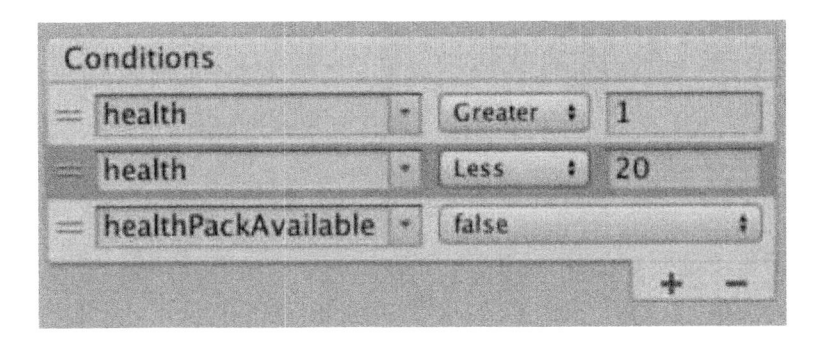

Figure 181: Modifying the transition

- Ensure that Can **Transition To Self** is set to **false** for this transition.

- Please save your script.

- For testing purposes, please check that the value of the variable **health** for the script **ManagePC2** is set to **20** initially, so that the NPC needs to find health packs immediately after the scene starts.

- Test the scene: you should see that the NPC goes to the health pack and the pack should then disappear.

You may notice an error in the **Console**, because the target is temporarily set to an object that does not exist; so you can change these lines within the code that deals with the state **lookForHealth** in the **Update** function.

Creating Smarter NPCs Who Can Flee or Ambush

```
if (target != null)
{
    GetComponent<UnityEngine.AI.NavMeshAgent> ().SetDestination (target.transform.position);
    if (Vector3.Distance (gameObject.transform.position, target.transform.position) < 2) {
        GetComponent<ManageNPC2> ().setHealth (100);
        Destroy (target);
    }
}
```

- Add the following code to the **Update** function in the section that deals with the **flee** state (new code in bold):

```
if (info.IsName ("flee") )
{
    GameObject [] healthPacks;
    healthPacks = (GameObject[])GameObject.FindGameObjectsWithTag ("healthPack");
    if (healthPacks.Length == 0)
        anim.SetBool ("healthPackAvailable",false);
    else anim.SetBool("healthPackAvailable",true);
```

To further the test, disable all the **healthPack** objects and replay the scene, and you should see that the NPC transitions to the state called **flee** immediately because there are no health packs available.

Last but not least, we will create a health pack spawner that will spawn health packs randomly in four different locations and ensure that there is at least one health pack available in the scene at all times.

First let's create the locations where the packs will be created:

- Please create an empty object and rename it **HPSpawn1**; duplicate it three times to create three other objects called **HPSpawn2**, **HPSpawn3** and **HPSpawn4**.

- Once this is done, change the position of the objects **HPSpawn1**, **HPSpawn2**, **HPSpawn3** and **HPSpawn4** respectively, to **(-39, 1, 35)**, **(-39, 1, -35)**, **(39, 1, 35)** and **(39, 1, -35)**, or other positions of your choice.

- Create an empty object called **healthPackSpawner**.

- Create a new C# script called **SpawnHealthPacks**.

- Add this code at the beginning of the script.

```csharp
float timer = 0;
GameObject [] healthPacks;
public GameObject healthPack;
```

- Modify the **Update** function as follows:

```csharp
void Update ()
{
        timer += Time.deltaTime;
        if (timer > 10)
        {
                checkPacks ();
                timer = 0;
        }
}
```

- Add the following function before the last curly bracket of the class.

```csharp
void checkPacks()
{

        healthPacks = (GameObject[]) GameObject.FindGameObjectsWithTag ("healthPack");
        if (healthPacks.Length == 0)
        {
                int randomPosition = Random.Range (1, 5);
                GameObject t = Instantiate (healthPack, GameObject.Find ("HPSpawn" + randomPosition).transform.position, Quaternion.identity);
                t.tag = "healthPack";
                t.name = "healthPack";

        }
}
```

In the previous code:

- We declare a function called **checkPacks**.
- We look for all the health packs in the scene.
- If no health packs are found, we generate a health pack.
- We also set its position randomly so that it is instantiated at the positions occupied by one of the objects **HPSpawn1**, **HPSpawn2**, **HPSpawn3** or **HPSpawn4**.

Once this is done, we can link this script to the object **healthPackSpawner**.

- Please drag and drop the script **SpawnHealthPacks** on the object **healthPackSpawner**.

- Select the object **healthPackSpawner**.

- Drag and drop the **healthPack** prefab from the **Project** window to the placeholder in the **Inspector** called **healthPack**.

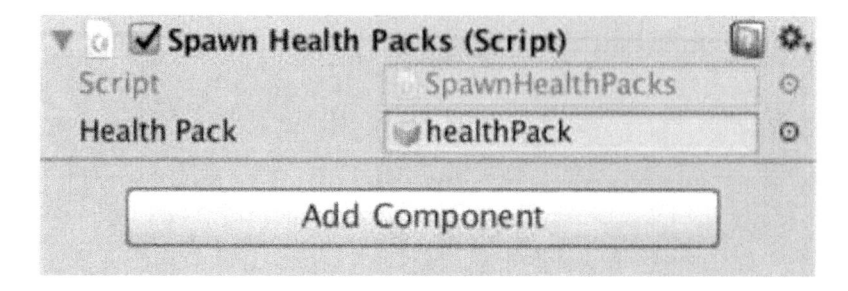

Figure 182: Setting the health pack to be instantiated.

- Deactivate all the health packs in the scene and test the scene.

- You can also modify the **Update** function in the script **manageNPC2** as follows, so that the health of the NPC decreases slowly (and so that it has the time to wait for new health packs).

```
//setHealth (health -Time.deltaTime*2);
setHealth (health -Time.deltaTime*0.5f);
```

- The NPC will flee first, and then, as a new pack is instantiated, the NPC will go towards it and collect it.

LEVEL ROUNDUP

Summary

In this chapter, we have managed to improve our NPC, providing some interesting features including making decisions based on internal values (e.g., ammos or health) or external values (e.g., player in the ambush area), and implementing related and common behaviors found in 3D games such as fleeing, ambushing, or attacking. Along the way, we have also managed to improve the vision of the NPC using dot products, and to also spawn health packs at random locations based on the number of health packs available in the scene.

Checklist

You can consider moving to the next stage if you can do the following:

- Understand how to create an Animator Controller.
- Understand how to create transitions.
- Know how to access Animator Controllers from a script.

Quiz

Now, let's check your knowledge! Please answer the following questions (the answers are included on the next page) or specify whether they are correct or incorrect.

1. By default, for a transition, the attribute **Can Transition To Self** is set to true.

2. The following code will set the new destination for an NPC.

```
GetComponent<UnityEngine.AI.NavMeshAgent> ().SetDestination (target.transform.position);
```

3. Transitions from the state called **Any State** can be created.

4. This code will stop the progression of an NPC linked to a navigation Agent.

```
GetComponent<UnityEngine.AI.NavMeshAgent> ().isStopped = true;
```

5. This code will access a float parameter called **health** set in the Animator Controller.

```
anim.SetFloatValue ("health", health);
```

6. For an object to act as a trigger, its **Collider** component must have the attribute **isTrigger** set to true.

7. It is possible to modify the speed of a **NavMeshAgent** from a script.

8. For any state in an Animator Controller, it is possible to associate a Script Behaviour.

9. A **Script Behaviour** extends the class **StateMachineBehaviour**.

10. A dot product can be used to determine the angle between two vectors.

Challenge 1

For this chapter, your challenge will be to modify the game as follows:

- Check that the NPC collects ammos when it is running out of ammos.
- Create an ammo spawner as we have done for the health packs.
- Make sure that the ammos disappear when they have been collected by the NPC.

Quiz Solutions

1. True.
2. True
3. True.
4. True.
5. False.
6. True
7. True.
8. True.
9. True.
10. True.

Challenge 1

For this chapter, your challenge will be to modify the game as follows:

- Check that the NPC collects ammos when its running out of ammos.
- Create an ammo spawner as we have done for the health packs.

- Make sure that the ammos disappear when they have been collected by the NPC.

9
ADDING AND CONTROLLING AN ARMY OF NPCS

In this section, we will be looking at group movements, whereby the actions of the members of a group are coordinated; after completing this chapter, you will be able to:

- Create groups of Non-Player Characters (i.e., armies).
- Coordinate the actions of NPCs who belong to the same group.
- Control the NPCs so that they follow the leader of the group.
- Coordinate one-to-one attacks as a group (i.e., each soldier will attack a predefined target or NPC).
- Control the NPCs so that they retreat and follow the leader when necessary.
- Generate melee combat.

> The code solutions for this chapter are in the **resource pack** that you can download by following the instructions included in the section entitled "Support and Resources for this Book".

WALKING BEHIND THE LEADER

In this new scene, we will create NPCs that follow a particular character that we will refer to as **the leader**; in this particular case, the leader will be the player, so the NPCs will follow the player, and stop whenever they are close to the player. For this purpose, we will complete the following tasks:

- Create the ground.
- Add the player (i.e., a First-Person Controller).
- Create NPCs, along with a finite state machine and its corresponding states.
- Coordinate the movement of the NPCs as a group.

So let's get started:

- Please save the current scene, and create a new scene and call it **chapter5**.
- Please create a new **cube** object; rename it **ground**, and change its scale settings to **(100, 1, 100)** and its position to **(0, 0, 0)**.
- Add a **First-Person Controller** to the scene from the folder **Standard Assets | Characters | FirstPersonCharacter | Prefabs** located in the **Project** window.
- Rename this object **player**.
- You can also change its position, for example, to **(11, 1, -9)**.
- From the folder called **military**, that you have imported in Unity in the previous chapters, select the prefab called **FuseModel** and drag and drop it to the scene; this will create a new object called **FuseModel**; rename this object **teamMember**.

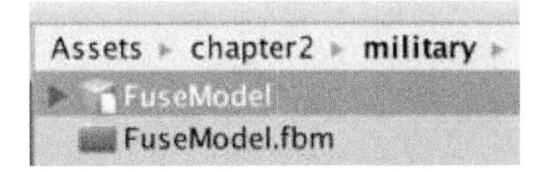

Figure 183: Adding a 3D model to the scene

- Change the position of this object to **(-8, 0.5, -11)**.

Adding and Controlling An Army of NPCs

- Select the object **teamMember** and add a **NavMesh Agent** component to it (i.e., select **Component | Navigation | NavMeshAgent**). This will be necessary so that the NPC can navigate in the scene.

Next, we will create an **Animator Controller** that will be used for the NPC.

- From the **Project** menu, select **Create | Animator Controller**. This will create an asset called **New Animator Controller**; please rename this asset **teamMember**.

- Open this **Animator Controller** by double-clicking on it.

- Create a new state called **idle** and associate the animation **idle** to this state.

- Then create another state called **moveTowardsLeader**, and associate the animation **walking** to this state.

- Create a new **Boolean** parameter called **closeToLeader**. This parameter will be used to determine when the NPC is close to its leader.

- Create a transition from the state **idle** to the state **moveTowardsLeader** and use the condition **closeToLeader=false** as a condition for the transition. So, the NPC will walk towards the leader until it is close enough.

- Create a transition from the state **moveTowardsLeader** to the state **idle** and use the condition **closeToLeader=true** as a condition for the transition, as illustrated in the next figure.

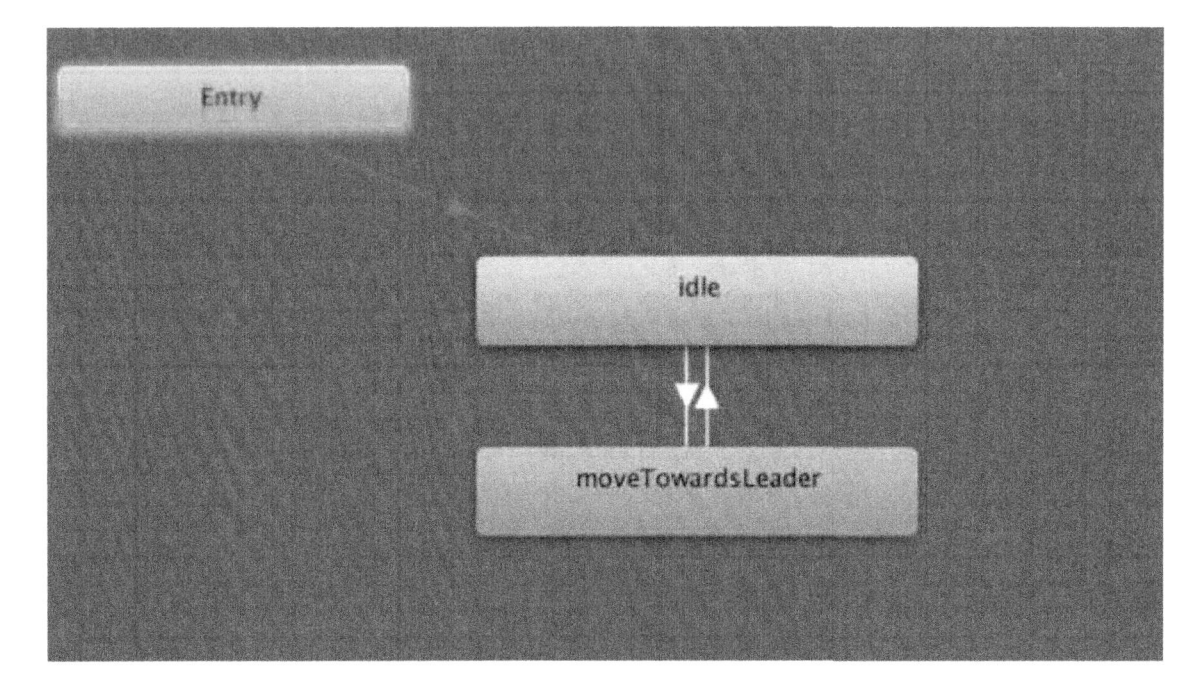

Figure 184: Setting-up the Animator Controller

Adding and Controlling An Army of NPCs

You can now drag and drop the Animator Controller called **teamMember** to the object called **teamMember**.

Now that we have set-up the **Animator Controller**, we create a script that will be employed to trigger transitions between the two states that we have defined earlier.

- Please create a new C# script and rename it **TeamMember**.
- Drag and drop this script on the object called **teamMember**.
- Open the script.
- Add this code at the beginning of the script:

```csharp
using UnityEngine.AI;
```

- Add the following code at the beginning of the class.

```csharp
GameObject leader;
Animator anim;
AnimatorStateInfo info;
float distanceToLeader;
```

- Modify the **Start** method as follows (new code in bold)

```csharp
void Start ()
{
    anim = gameObject.GetComponent<Animator>();
    leader = GameObject.Find ("player");
}
```

In the previous code, we create a reference to the **Animator Controller** linked to the NPC and we also define the object that will act as a leader for this NPC. In this particular case, the player will be the leader; so in other words, this NPC will be following the player.

- Please add the following code to the **Update** function (new code in bold).

```csharp
void Update ()
{
    info = anim.GetCurrentAnimatorStateInfo(0);
    distanceToLeader = Vector3.Distance (leader.transform.position, gameObject.transform.position);
    if (distanceToLeader < 5.0f)
        anim.SetBool ("closeToLeader", true);
    else anim.SetBool ("closeToLeader", false);
}
```

In the previous code:

- We update the variable called **info** so that we can detect the current (or active) state.

- We calculate the distance between the NPC and the leader (i.e., the **player**).

- If this distance is greater than **5 meters**, then we set the Boolean parameter **closeToLeader** (from the Animator Controller) to **true**; otherwise, this parameter is set to **false**.

We can now add the code that will be executed when we are in the states called **idle** or **moveTowardsPlayer**.

- Please add the following code just after the code that you have added in the **Update** function.

```
if (info.IsName ("idle"))
{
        GetComponent<UnityEngine.AI.NavMeshAgent> ().isStopped = true;
}
if (info.IsName ("moveTowardsLeader"))
{
        GetComponent<AI.NavMeshAgent> ().SetDestination (leader.transform.position);
        GetComponent<AI.NavMeshAgent> ().isStopped = false;
}
```

In the previous code:

- If we are in the state called **idle**, we ensure that the navigation is not active for the NPC; in other words, it will be stopped.

- If we are in the state called **moveTowardsLeader**, we set the destination (or the target) to be the leader (i.e., the player); we also ensure that the navigation resumes.

You can now save this script and drag and drop it to the object called **teamMember** (if not done yet).

So at this stage, we have implemented most of the features that will make it possible for the NPC to follow the player; the only thing that we will need to do is to bake our scene, so that navigation can be performed correctly.

We can now bake the scene:

- Please select the **ground** object and all the walls included in your scene (if any).

- Open the **Navigation** window.

- Select the **Object** tab, and then the options **Navigation Static** and **Walkable**.

Adding and Controlling An Army of NPCs

- Select the **Bake** tab and click on the button labelled **Bake**.

Finally, when this is done, we can create a prefab from our NPC and create duplicates to create a team of NPCs that share the same features.

- Please create a prefab from the object called **teamMember,** and rename this prefab **teamMember**.

- Drag the prefab **teamMember** three times to the scene; this will create three additional objects called **teamMember(1)**, **teamMember(2)**, and **teamMember(3)**.

You can now play the scene; you should see that the NPCs follow the player and stop once they are about 5 meters away from the player.

Figure 185: The NPCs are following the player

Adding and Controlling An Army of NPCs

Figure 186: The NPCs are idle once near the player

ATTACKING SEVERAL TARGETS AS A GROUP

In this section, we will start to coordinate group attacks as follows:

- We will create targets symbolized by cylinders.
- The leader will order the team members to launch an attack.
- Every team member will be attacking one particular target.

So let's go ahead!

- Please open the **Animator Controller** called **teamMember** (i.e., from the **Project** window).
- Create a sub-state machine called **attack-one-to-one** (i.e., right-click on the canvas and select **Create Sub-State Machine**).

Figure 187: Creating a sub-state machine

- Double-click on this sub-state machine (i.e., **attack-one-to-one**) to open it.
- Create two states within: a state called **goToTarget**, and then a state called **attackTarget**.
- Associate the animation **walking** to the state **goToTarget** and the animation called **punching** to the state called **attackTarget**.
- You will need to edit the **punching** animation to set the attribute **Loop Pose** and **Loop Time** to true, so that it loops indefinitely, as we have done earlier for the walking animation.
- Create a Boolean parameter called **closeToTarget**.
- Create a transition from the state **goToTarget** to the state **attackTarget** using the condition **closeToTarget=true**.
- Create a transition from the state **attackTarget** to the state **goToTarget** using the condition **closeToTarget=false**.

Adding and Controlling An Army of NPCs

- Once this is done, your **Animator Controller** should look as follows.

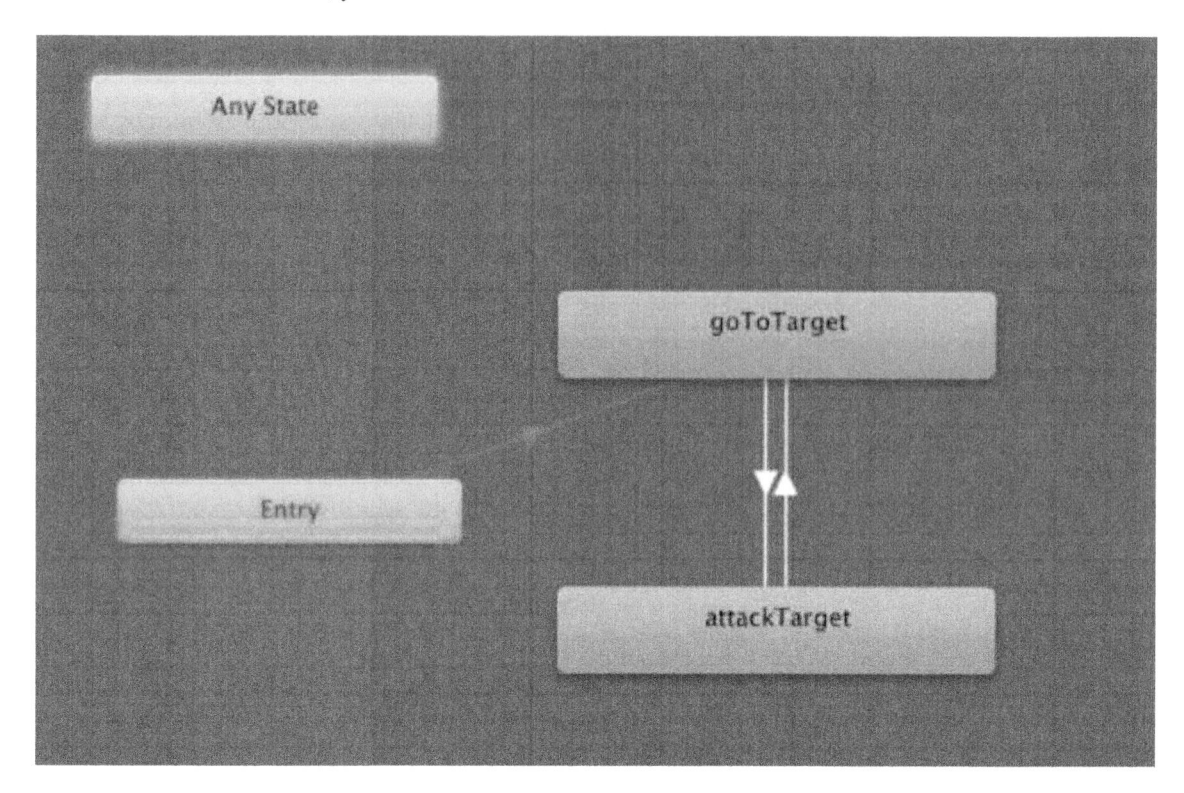

Figure 188: Creating transitions

- Create a new **Trigger** parameter called **attackOneToOne**.

- We will be using this parameter to create a transition between the **idle** state and the sub-state machine **attack-one-to-one**.

- In the **Animator** window, click on the tab called **Base Layer**.

- Create a transition from the state **idle** to the sub-state machine: right-click on the state **idle** and select the option **Make Transition** from the contextual menu.

- Then click on the sub-state machine called **attack-one-to-one** and select the option: **States | goToTarget**, as illustrated in the next figure. This means that the transition is made from the state **idle** to the state **goToTarget** that is within the sub-state machine called **attack-one-to-one**.

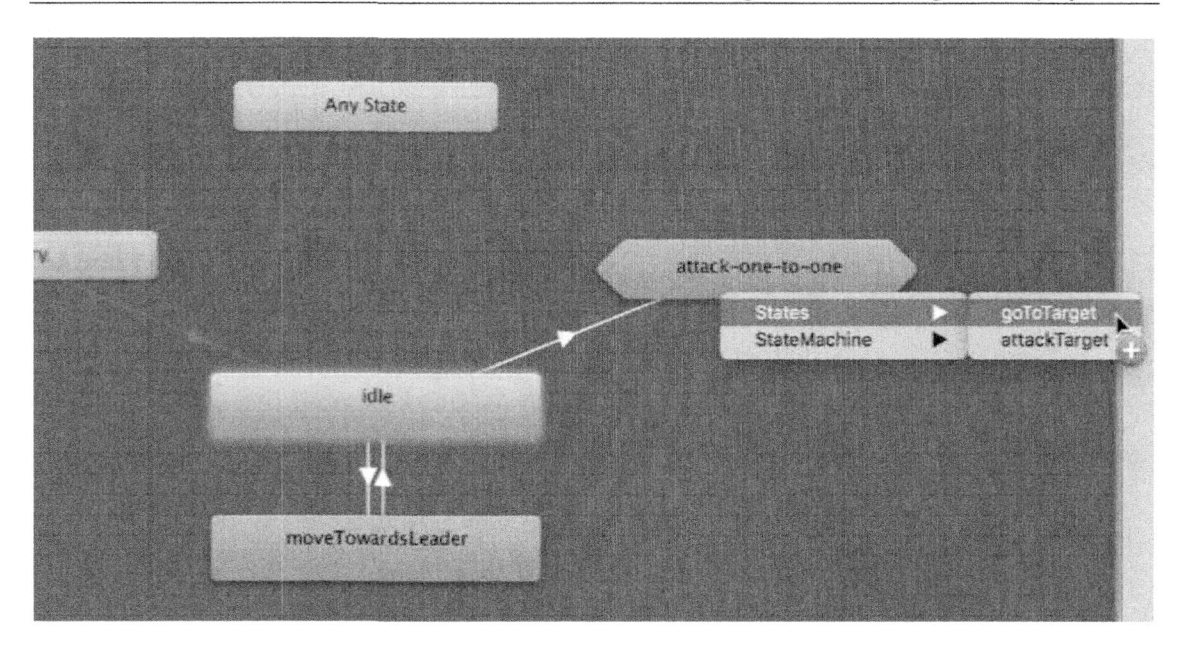

Figure 189: Creating a transition to the sub-state machine

As you open (i.e., double click on) the sub-state machine, you should see that the new transition is apparent within the sub-state machine, from a state called **(Up) Base Layer** as illustrated in the next figure.

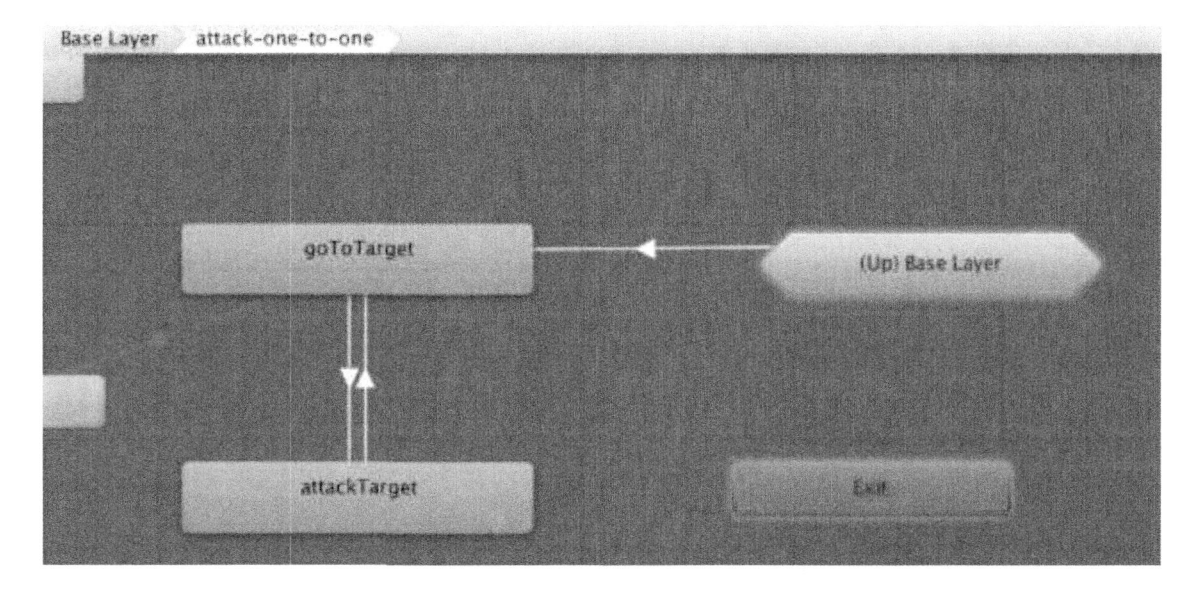

Figure 190: The transition from the Base layer

- Select the transition that you have just created and set the condition to **attack-one-to-one**.

Adding and Controlling An Army of NPCs

Now that our sub-state machine has been configured, we can start to modify the script for the NPC to specify what should be done in the different states that we have defined in the sub-states.

- Please open the script **TeamMember**.

- Add this code at the beginning of the class.

```
GameObject target;
float distanceToTarget;
```

In the previous code:

- We define two variables: **target** and **distanceToTarget**.

- The first variable will define the target that the NPC has to attack.

- The second variable will be used to determine whether the NPC is close enough to the target to start attacking; it will also be used to set the corresponding parameter in the **Animator Controller**.

Now that these variables have been defined, we can define a few methods that will be used to control the NPC.

- Please, add the following method to the script **TeamMember**.

```
public void attack (GameObject t)
{
        target = t;
        anim.SetTrigger ("attackOneToOne");
}
```

In the previous code:

- We define a method called **attack**.

- Note that this method is **public**; so it will be accessible from outside the class.

- This method will be accessed by the leader, when sending an order to attack a particular target to the NPC. Note that the target will be defined by the leader (not the NPC), so that a group attack can be coordinated easily.

- When the method is called, the target is defined and the trigger parameter **attackOneToOne** is also set.

We can now define the actions to be performed in the states present in the sub-state machine.

- Please add the following in the **Update** method within the script **TeamMember**:

```
if (info.IsName ("goToTarget"))
{
        GetComponent<UnityEngine.AI.NavMeshAgent> ().SetDestination (target.transform.position);
        GetComponent<UnityEngine.AI.NavMeshAgent> ().isStopped = false;
        distanceToTarget = Vector3.Distance (target.transform.position, gameObject.transform.position);

        if (distanceToTarget < 2.0f) {
                anim.SetBool ("closeToTarget", true);
                GetComponent<UnityEngine.AI.NavMeshAgent> ().isStopped = true;
        }
        else anim.SetBool ("closeToTarget", false);

}
```

In the previous code:

- We check that we are in the state called **goToTarget**.
- The destination is set for the NPC.
- The NPC moves towards the target until it is close enough.

Now, let's define the actions for the state **attackTarget**.

- Please add the following code to the **Update** method:

```
if (info.IsName ("attackTarget"))
{
        GetComponent<NavMeshAgent> ().isStopped = true;

}
```

In the previous code, the NPC will stop moving forward as soon as it is in the state called **attackTarget**.

You can now save your script. Now that we have defined how the NPCs should behave when receiving orders to attack, we just need to create a communication channel between the leader and the NPCs, so that the latter can receive orders from the former; this will consist in:

- Identifying all team members.
- Detecting when orders need to be sent to the team members.
- Allowing the player to send orders to these members.

Adding and Controlling An Army of NPCs

First, we will create a few targets that will be used for the attacks:

- Please create a new cylinder (i.e., select: **GameObject | 3D Object | Cylinder**).
- Set its position to **(7, 1.5, -7)** and leave the other options as default.

Figure 191: Creating a target

- Rename this object **target**.
- Create a new tag called **target**.
- Apply the tag **target** to the object **target**.
- Create a prefab from this object (i.e., **target**) and rename the prefab **target**.
- Drag and drop the **target** prefab three times to the **Scene** view. This should create three additional targets named **target (1)**, **target (2)**, and **target (3)**, all with a tag called **target**.

Once this is done, we will also create and apply tags to the NPCs; this is so that the leader can identify them and send them orders accordingly.

- Please create a tag called **teamMember** and apply it to the prefab called **teamMember**.

Once this is done, we can create a script that will be used to establish communication between the leader and the other team members.

- Please create a new C# script called **Leader**.
- Drag and drop this script on the object called **player**.

- Open the script.
- Add this code at the beginning of the class.

```
GameObject [] teamMembers;
int nbTeamMembers, nbTargets;
```

In the previous code:

- We define three variables: **teamMembers**, **nbTeamMembers**, and **nbTargets**.
- **teamMembers** is an array of all the team members that the leader will be able to control.
- **nbTeamMembers** is the number of NPCs (i.e., members) in a particular team.
- **nbTargets** is the number of targets in the current scene.

We can now add the code to identify the team members.

- Please modify the **Start** function, for the script **Leader**, as follows:

```
void Start ()
{
    teamMembers = GameObject.FindGameObjectsWithTag ("teamMember");
    nbTeamMembers = teamMembers.Length;
}
```

In the previous code: we look for all the NPCs that are part of the team, based on their tag, and add them to the array called **teamMembers**; we also store the number of NPCs in this team.

Now that we have identified the NPCs that are part of the team, we can add the code to control them.

- Please add the following method to the script **Leader**.

```
void attack()
{
    GameObject[] allTargets = GameObject.FindGameObjectsWithTag ("target");
    nbTargets = allTargets.Length;
    for (int i = 0; i < nbTargets; i++)
    {
        teamMembers [i].GetComponent<TeamMember> ().attack (allTargets [i]);
    }
}
```

In the previous code:

Adding and Controlling An Army of NPCs

- We define a function called **attack**.

- In this function, we look for all the targets in the scene, based on their tags, and add them to the array called **allTargets**.

- We then ask each NPC to attack a particular target, by accessing one of their public method called **attack**.

> We could customize this script to account for the fact that there could be more targets than NPCs or vice-versa; however, for the time being, we will assume (an set-up our environment accordingly) that there is one target for each NPC.

The only thing that we need to do now, is to trigger attacks; in our case, this will be done when the player presses the **P** key on the keyboard.

- Please add the following code to the **Update** function in the script called **Leader** (new code in bold):

```
void Update ()
{
        if (Input.GetKeyDown (KeyCode.P))
        {
                attack ();
        }
}
```

- Please save your script and play the scene (after checking that you have added the script called **Leader** to the object called **player**). The NPC will start to gather around the player. As you press the **P** key, the NPCs will start to go towards and attack a target.

Figure 192: The NPCs attacking their target

[390]

Adding and Controlling An Army of NPCs

Figure 193: Close-up on an NPC attacking its target

> Note that if you would like to look at the scene view while the game is playing, you can press the **ESC** key on your keyboard, and then select the scene view and focus on a particular object.

WITHDRAWING FROM A BATTLE

So at this stage, the NPCs are coordinated perfectly, and they will attack a target when asked by the leader; this being said, there may be cases when the group may need to retreat; it could be due to the need to attack other objectives, a much bigger number of soldiers in the opponent team, or too many casualties. For this reason, we will create a behavior by which all NPCs retreat from the battle and gather around the leader, when asked to do so by the leader.

So let's get started:

- Please open the **Animator Controller** called **teamMember**.

- Create a **Trigger** parameter called **retreat**.

- For the tab **Base Layer**, create a transition from the state **Any State** to the state **moveTowardsLeader**, and use the parameter **retreat** as a condition for this transition to occur.

So this means that whenever the parameter called **retreat** is set to **true**, the NPCs will go back to following the leader.

Next, we will modify the scripts **Leader** and **TeamMember** to be able to apply this behavior when needed.

- Please open the script called **TeamMember** and add the following method to it:

```
public void retreat ()
{
        anim.SetTrigger ("retreat");
}
```

- Open the script called **Leader** and add the following method to it:

```
void retreat()
{
        for (int i = 0; i < nbTeamMembers; i++)
        {
        teamMembers [i].GetComponent<TeamMember> ().retreat ();
        }
}
```

In the previous code, the leader identifies all its team members and sends them the order to retreat from the battle.

- Finally, add the following code to the **Update** function in the script **Leader**.

```
if (Input.GetKeyDown (KeyCode.O))
{
        retreat ();
}
```

So in the previous code: whenever the **O** key is pressed, the leader will contact all its team members and ask them to retreat. This means that the NPCs will go back to the state called **moveTowardsLeader**.

You can now save both scripts and test the scene. Press the **P** key so that the NPCs attack their respective targets; then press the **O** key; all NPCs should now retreat and follow the leader again.

MANAGING DAMAGE AND ATTACKS

So far, all NPCs can attack and retreat when asked by the leader. However, there are a few more aspects that could make this more realistic; for example, we could do the following:

- Apply damage to targets when they are being attacked.

- Apply damage to the NPCs during a battle if the target can inflict damage (we will use other NPCs as targets later-on).

- When a target has been eliminated or when the NPCs' health is low, the NPCs may return to the leader and await orders.

First, let's look after the targets and ensure that they are destroyed after they have been hit several times:

- Please create a new C# script called **NPC** and open it.

- Add the following code to it (new code in bold).

```
public class NPC : MonoBehaviour
{
        int health;
        void Start ()
        {
                health = 100;
        }
```

- Add the following functions to this script.

```
public int getHealth()
{
        return (health);
}
```

```
public void decreaseHealth(int amount)
{
        setHealth (health - amount);
}
public void setHealth (int amount)
{
        health = amount;
        if (health <= 0)
                destroyNPC ();
}
void destroyNPC()
{
        Destroy (gameObject);
}
```

In the previous code:

- We create four functions.

- The function **getHealth** will return the health of the NPC linked to this script.

- The function **decreaseHealth** will remove a specific amount from the current health; note that this function is public, and it will therefore be accessible from outside the class.

- The function **setHealth** sets the health to a specific value; it also calls the function **destroyNPC** if the health is lower than **0**.

- The function **destroyNPC** destroys the object attached to the **script**.

You can now save your script, and do the following:

- Check that the script called **NPC** is error-free.

- Drag and drop the script called **NPC** on the object called **target** in the **Hierarchy**.

- Select the object called **target** in the **Hierarchy**.

- Click on the button called **Apply** located in the top-right corner of the **Inspector**, as illustrated in the next figure; this will ensure that all objects based on the prefab called **target** are updated (and therefore that they include the script called **NPC**).

Adding and Controlling An Army of NPCs

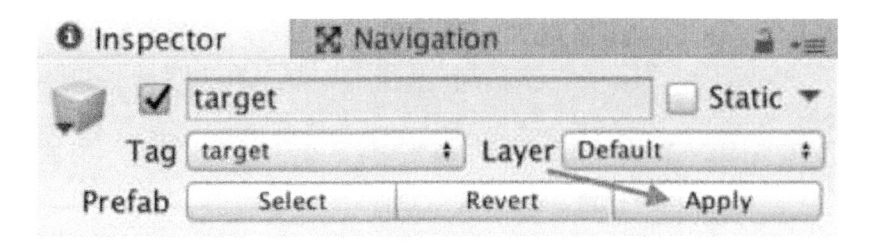

Figure 194: Applying changes to the other objects

Next, we will modify the **Animator Controller** used for each NPC, so that each NPC goes back to the leader after destroying its target.

- Please open the **Animator Controller** called **teamMember** in the **Animation** window (if it is not open yet).

- Create a new **Boolean** parameter called **targetDestroyed**.

- Create a transition from the state called **attackTarget**, that is within the sub-state machine called **attack-one-to-one**, to the state called **moveTowardsLeader**, using the parameter **targetDestroyed** as a condition for the transition to occur. To do so, you can right-click on the state **attackTarget**, chose the option **Make Transition**, then click on the state called **(Up) Base Layer**, and then select the option **States | moveTowardsLeader**.

- Create a transition from the state called **goToTarget**, that is within the sub-state machine called **attack-one-to-one**, to the state called **moveTowardsLeader**, using the parameter **targetDestroyed=true** as a condition for the transition to occur. To do so, you can right-click on the state **goToTarget**, chose the option **Make Transition**, then click on the state called **(Up) Base Layer**, and then select the option **States | moveTowardsLeader**.

- Once this is done, you should see that the transition is now visible from within and from outside the sub-state, as illustrated in the next figures.

Adding and Controlling An Army of NPCs

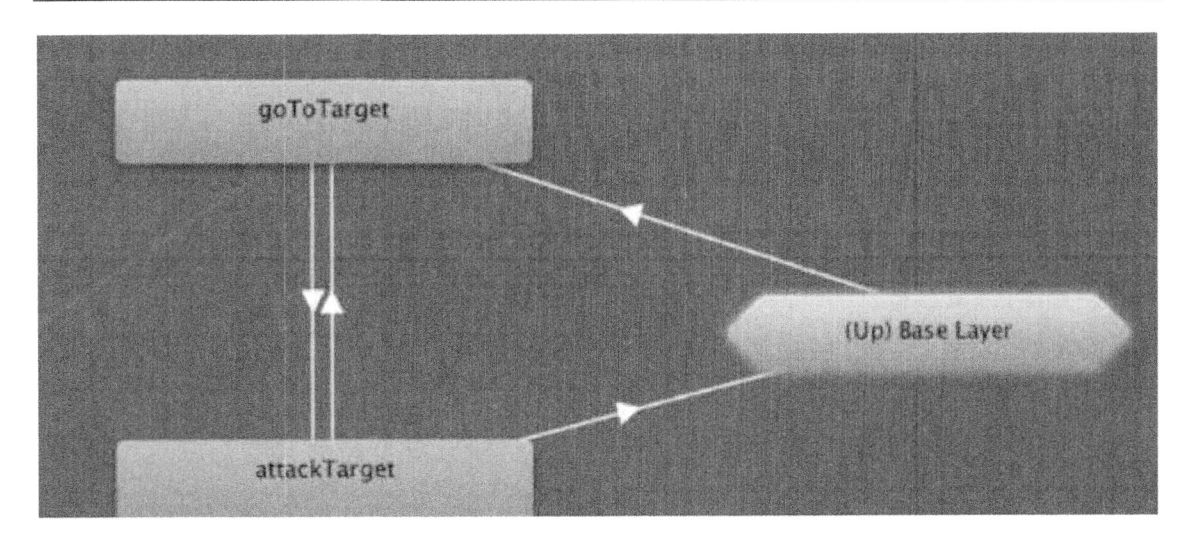

Figure 195: The transition seen from within the sub-state

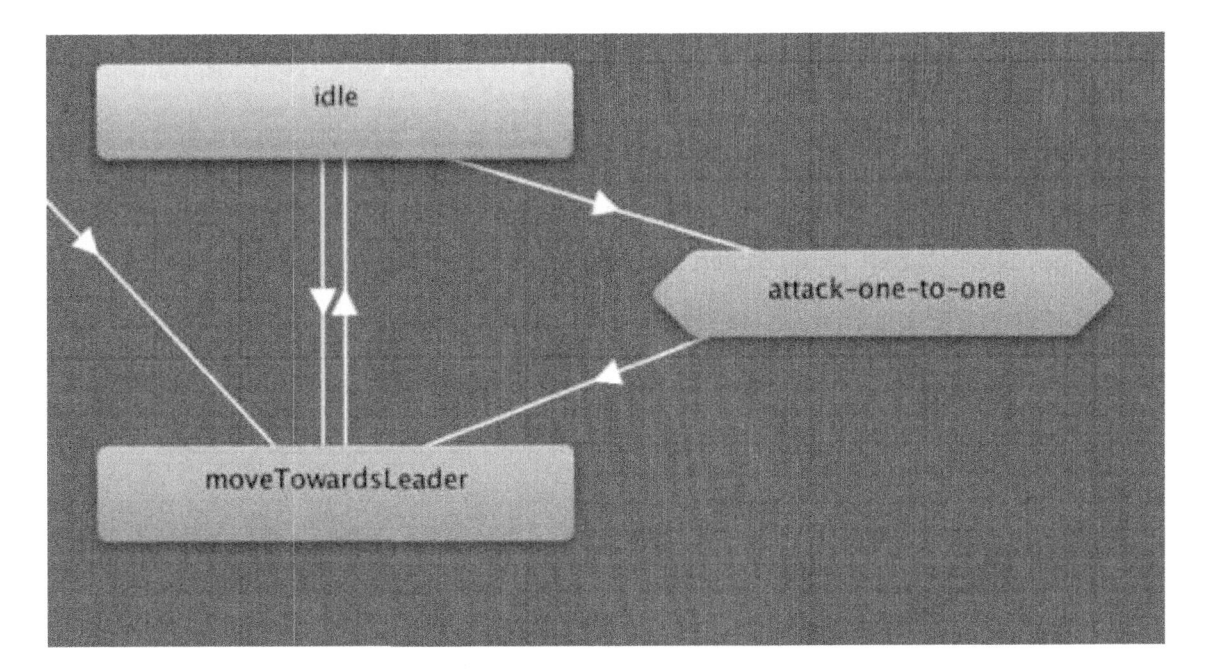

Figure 196: The transition seen from outside the sub-state

- Select this transition and set the condition to be **targetDestroyed=true**.
- Select the transition between the state **attackTarget** and **goToTarget** and add the condition **targetDestroyed = false**.

[397]

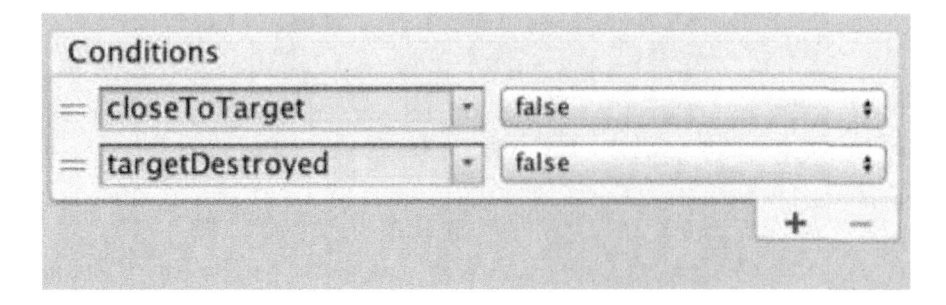

Figure 197: Modifying the transition

Next, we will need to modify our script called **TeamMember** so that some damage is applied to a target every time it is hit by an NPC.

- Please open the script called **TeamMember**.

- Add the following code to it (new code in bold)

```
if (info.IsName ("attackTarget"))
{
        GetComponent<NavMeshAgent> ().isStopped = true;
        if (info.normalizedTime % 1.0 >= .98)
        {
                if (target != null) target.GetComponent<NPC> ().decreaseHealth (20);
                else
                anim.SetBool ("targetDestroyed", true);
        }
}
```

In the previous code:

- The NPC is stopped (i.e., not moving forward) if it is in the state called **attackTarget**.

- We use the built-in function **info.normalizedTime** to check whether we have reached the end of the punching animation; if this is the case, we decrease the health of the target by 20; it is necessary to check for the completion of the current animation, otherwise the function **decreaseHealth** may be called constantly

- If we don't check that the animation is almost completed, we would decrease the player's health continuously while the animation is played; however, we just want to decrease the player's health after each round of attack (or punch); so we wait until the animation is 98% complete before we decrease the health.

> The variable **info.normalizedTime** returns a number that includes two types of information: an integer part tells us how many times the animation has looped, and a decimal value indicates the percentage of completion of the current loop. So since we are interested in the later (i.e., percentage of completion of the current loop), we use the operator modulo (%) to obtain this value.

Please modify the **Update** function, for the script **TeamMember**, as follows (new code in bold):

```
if (info.IsName ("goToTarget"))
{
    if (target != null)
    {
        GetComponent<UnityEngine.AI.NavMeshAgent> ().SetDestination (target.transform.position);
        GetComponent<UnityEngine.AI.NavMeshAgent> ().isStopped = false;
        distanceToTarget = Vector3.Distance (target.transform.position, gameObject.transform.position);

        if (distanceToTarget < 2.0f) {
            anim.SetBool ("closeToTarget", true);
            GetComponent<UnityEngine.AI.NavMeshAgent> ().isStopped = true;
        } else
            anim.SetBool ("closeToTarget", false);
    }
    else anim.SetBool ("targetDestroyed", true);
}
```

In the previous code, we ensure that the NPC goes towards the target only if the target exists.

That's it!

You can now save all your scrips, and test the scene. As you play the scene, let the NPC gather around you and press the key **P**. They should then go to their respective target, and hit the target five times (i.e., 5 x 20, resulting in 100% loss for each target); the targets should then disappear and the NPCs should then gather again around the leader.

SETTING-UP AN INTELLIGENT TEAM

As it is, we have a working group dynamic whereby we can associate NPCs to the player as a team and get them to either attack specific targets or to gather (e.g., retreat) around the player who acts as a leader. In this section, we will get to create an opposite team with a leader equipped with artificial intelligence that will control its own team and decide when they should engage in a battle or retreat.

This will involve the following steps:

- Creating an NPC and set it as the leader.
- Creating a new team of NPCs and set a corresponding tag for them.
- The leader and its team will initially patrol around the scene.
- Once the leader detects any member of the opposite team, it will launch an attack.

So let's go ahead:

- Please locate the **FuseModel** asset in the **Project** window and drag and drop it on the scene view.
- Rename it **teamLeader**.
- Create a new **AnimatorControler** and rename it **teamLeader**.
- Open this **Animator Controller** (i.e., **teamLeader**).
- Create a new state called **idle** and link it to the animation **idle**.
- Drag and drop the **Animator Controller teamLeader** on the object called **teamLeader**.
- Duplicate the object **teamMember** in the **Hierarchy** window; this should create a new object called **teamMember (4)**; rename this object **oppositeTeamMember**.
- Select the object **oppositeTeamMember**, create a new tag called **team2**, and apply it to this object.
- Create a new prefab from this object (i.e., **oppositeTeamMember**), called **oppositeTeamMember**.
- Drag and drop this prefab three times in the **Scene** view to create three other NPCs that will be part of the opposite team.

Now that we have created the NPCs for the opposite team (i.e., the team lead by an intelligent NPC), we can modify the associated script.

Adding and Controlling An Army of NPCs

- Modify the script **TeamMember** as follows (new code in bold).

```
void Start ()
{
    anim = gameObject.GetComponent<Animator>();
    //leader = GameObject.Find ("player");
    if (gameObject.tag == "teamMember") leader = GameObject.Find ("player");
    else leader = GameObject.Find ("teamLeader");
}
```

In the previous script, we define the leader for each NPC, depending on its tag.

- You can now save the script and play the scene, and you should see that four NPCs gather around the player, and that three other NPCs gather around the leader of the opposite team.

Figure 198: Gathering the troops

So, so far, we can see that each team member has recognized and followed its leader.

Next, we will get to define the movement and decisions of the leader of the opposite team; it will patrol the scene, and ask its team mates to attack a target whenever one of the targets is within 10 meters from the leader.

[401]

Adding and Controlling An Army of NPCs

> Note that for testing purposes, we test first an attack on targets; however, at a later stage, these NPCs will be attacking the members of your team.

- Please add a **NavMesh Agent** component to the object **teamLeader**.
- Open the **Animator Controller** called **teamLeader**.
- Create a **Trigger** variable called **startPatrolling**.
- Create a new state called **patrol** associated to the animation **walking**.
- Create a transition from the state **idle** to the state **patrol** using the parameter **startPatrolling** as a condition.

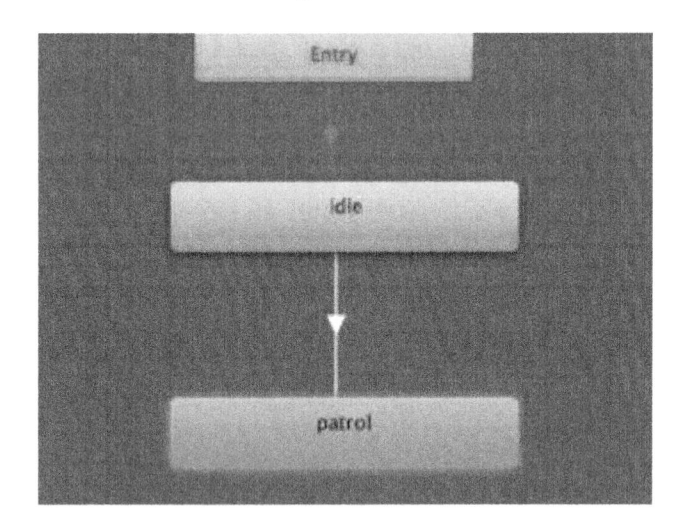

Figure 199: Creating a patrol state

So at this stage, we have set-up our **Animator Controller** and we just need to control the leader of the opposite team so that it starts patrolling and also so that it decides when its team should engage in a battle.

First, we will create the waypoints defining its path, and write the code related to the patrolling state.

- Please create four empty objects and rename them **WP0**, **WP1**, **WP2**, and **WP3**; these will be used as waypoints for the leader's patrol.
- Move these waypoints in the scene so that they form a path that the NPC will follow, for example **(11, 1, 2)**, **(-11, 1, -2)**, **(-4, 1. -20)** and **(11, 1, -20)**.
- Drag and drop the script **Leader** on the object **teamLeader**.
- Open the script **Leader**.

Adding and Controlling An Army of NPCs

- Add the following code at the beginning of the script.

```
Animator anim;
AnimatorStateInfo info;
float distanceToTarget;
float patrolTimer = 0.0f;
int WPIndex;
GameObject[] WPs;
```

- Modify the **Start** function as follows:

```
void Start ()
{
    //teamMembers = GameObject.FindGameObjectsWithTag ("teamMember");
    WPIndex = 0;
    WPs = new GameObject[] { GameObject.Find ("WP0"), GameObject.Find ("WP1"), GameObject.Find ("WP2"), GameObject.Find ("WP3") };
    anim = gameObject.GetComponent<Animator>();
    if (gameObject.name == "player") teamMembers = GameObject.FindGameObjectsWithTag ("teamMember");
    else teamMembers = GameObject.FindGameObjectsWithTag ("team2");
    nbTeamMembers = teamMembers.Length;
}
```

- Modify the **Update** function as follows (new code in bold):

```
void Update ()
{
    if (gameObject.name == "player")
    {
        if (Input.GetKeyDown (KeyCode.P)) {
            attack ();
        }

        if (Input.GetKeyDown (KeyCode.O)) {
            retreat ();
        }
    }
}
```

In the previous code we ensure that the keys **P** and **O** are processed only for the player; in other words, if you press them, orders will be sent to the player's team only, not the opposite team.

- Please add the following code just after the code you have just typed in the **Update** function.

```
else
{
        patrolTimer += Time.deltaTime;
        info = anim.GetCurrentAnimatorStateInfo(0);
        if (info.IsName("idle"))
        {
                if (patrolTimer >=5)
                {
                        patrolTimer = 0.0f;
                        anim.SetTrigger("startPatrolling");}
        }
        if (info.IsName("patrol"))
        {
                if (Vector3.Distance (gameObject.transform.position, WPs[WPIndex].transform.position) < 1.0f)
                        WPIndex++;
                if (WPIndex > 3) WPIndex = 0;
                GetComponent<UnityEngine.AI.NavMeshAgent> ().SetDestination (WPs[WPIndex].transform.position);
                GetComponent<UnityEngine.AI.NavMeshAgent> ().isStopped = false;
        }
}
```

In the previous code:

- We create a new timer.

- After 5 seconds, the leader will start to patrol.

- When in the patrolling state, the leader will successively navigate towards each of the waypoints

You can now save your script and test the scene. You should see that, after 5 seconds, the opposite team should start to patrol the scene, as illustrated in the next figure.

Figure 200: The opposite team is patrolling

Once this is working, we will implement the feature whereby the leader of the opposite team will order its troop to attack the targets whenever one of the targets is within 10 meters.

- Please create a new state called **attack** in the **Animator Controller** called **teamLeader**.

- Associate the animation called **idle** to this state.

- Create a **Trigger** parameter called **closeToEnnemy**.

- Create a transition from the state called **patrol** to the state called **attack** using the parameter **closeToEnnemy** as a condition for the transition.

Adding and Controlling An Army of NPCs

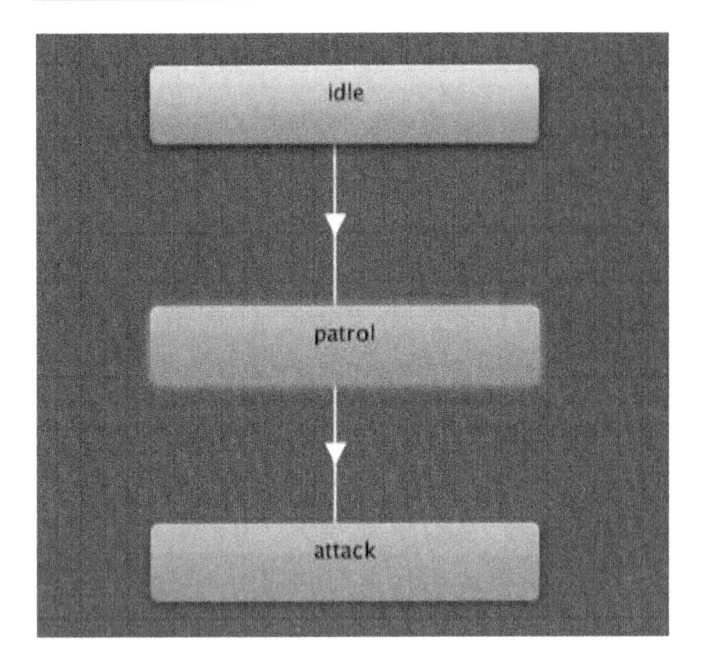

Figure 201: Creating the new state for the attack

Once this is done, we can modify the script called **Leader** to trigger the patrolling state.

- Please open the script called **Leader**.
- Please add this code to the script **Leader**.

```
if (info.IsName("patrol"))
{
        if (patrolTimer >= 4)
        {
                detectEnnemies ();
                patrolTimer = 0.0f;
        }
}
```

- Add this function.

```
void detectEnnemies ()
{
        if (Vector3.Distance(gameObject.transform.position, GameObject.Find("player").transform.position) < 10)
anim.SetTrigger ("closeToEnnemy");
}
```

- Make the function **attack** public, as follows (new code in bold).

[406]

| public void attack() |

In the previous code, we have just added the keyword **public** so that this function can be accessed from outside this class.

Now that it's done, we will be creating code that will be executed once the NPC has entered the state called **attack**; now, if we were to create code for a state the usual way (in the **Update** function checking for the current state), this code would be executed every frame. However, we just want this code to be executed once, for example, when the state called **attack** is entered. For this purpose, we will create a state **Behaviour**, as we have done previously; this means that we will be creating a script that will be used just for the state called **attack**. This script will include a method that will be called only when the state is entered (i.e., once). So let's go ahead:

- Please open the **Animator Controller** called **teamLeader**.
- Select the state called **attack**.
- Using the **Inspector** window, click on the button called **AddBehaviour**.

Figure 202: Adding a new Behaviour

- From the contextual menu, select the option **New Script**.
- Create a new behavior (i.e., script) by typing the text **LeaderAttack** in the text field.

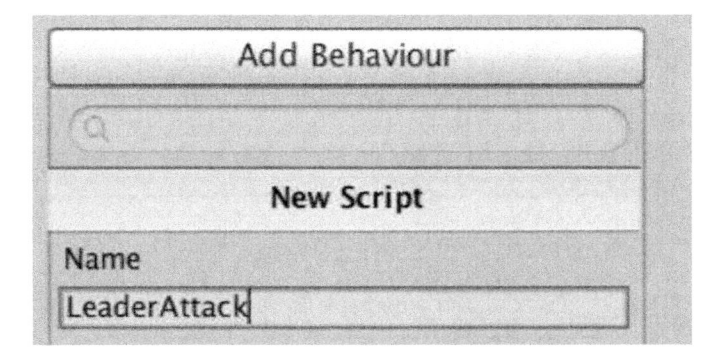

- This will create a new script (i.e., class) called **LeaderAttack**.

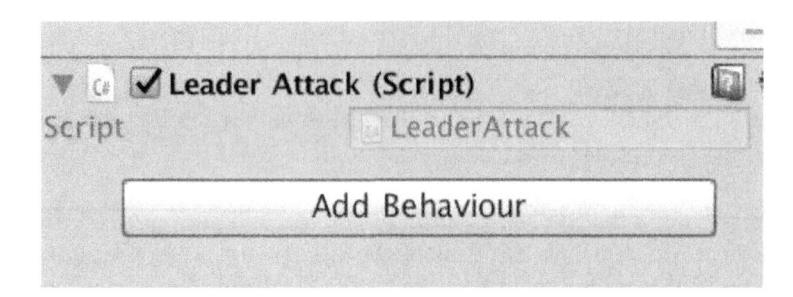

Adding and Controlling An Army of NPCs

- Open the script by double clicking on it and modify it as follows:

```
override public void OnStateEnter(Animator animator, AnimatorStateInfo stateInfo, int layerIndex)
{
        GameObject.Find("teamLeader").GetComponent<Leader> ().attack ();
}
```

In the previous code: whenever we enter the state linked to this script, the method **attack** (from the class called **Leader**) is called.

- You can now save your script and test the scene.

As you play the scene, the opposite team should start to gather around its leader. After 4 seconds the members of the team will attack each target and then go back to the leader, as illustrated in the next figures.

Figure 203: The other team attacking targets

Figure 204: The other team returning to the leader

So, at this stage, we have managed to create a group and its leader, and the leader can control its troops, including patrolling, launching an attack, and going back to the leader when the attacks have been completed.

APPLYING ATTACKS TO THE NPCS

So at this stage, all attacks were directed against targets; so now, what we need to do is to make it possible for both teams to launch attacks against each other.

This will involve the following:

- Each team member, during an attack, will be able to inflict damage to members of the other team.

- Once an NPC is attacked, it will fight back.

So let's go ahead:

- Please open the script called **Leader**.

- Modify the function **attack** as follows (new code in bold).

```
public void attack()
{
        //GameObject[] allTargets = GameObject.FindGameObjectsWithTag ("target");
        GameObject[] allTargets;
        if        (gameObject.name       ==       "teamLeader")        allTargets     =
GameObject.FindGameObjectsWithTag ("teamMember");
        else allTargets = GameObject.FindGameObjectsWithTag ("team2");
```

In the previous code, we define the targets based on the NPC's team.

- Drag and drop the **NPC** script to the objects **teamMember** and **oppositeTeamMember**.

- For both of these objects, make sure that you click on the button labelled **Apply** located at the top-right corner of the Inspector, so that these changes are applied to all the other team members based on this prefab.

- Open the script called **NPC** and add this function:

```
public void hitByOpponent(GameObject g, int amount)
{
        setHealth (health - amount);
        gameObject.GetComponent<TeamMember> ().attack (g);
}
```

In the previous code:

- We declare a function called **hitByOpponent**.

Adding and Controlling An Army of NPCs

- It takes two parameters: the amount of damage and the NPC who is currently attacking.

- This function will be called whenever an NPC attacks another NPC.

- In this case, the NPC that is being attacked will see its health decreasing

- However, it will fight back: this is done by calling the method called **attack**; the target of this attack is the NPC who launched an attack in the first place.

Now that this function is defined, we will need to modify the **Animator Controller** accordingly as well as the script that is executed when an attack is carried-out.

- Open the **Animator Controller** called **teamMember** in the **Animator** window.

- Create a new **Trigger** parameter called **respondToAttack**.

- Within the sub-state machine called **attack one-to-one**, create a transition from the state **Any State** to the state **goToTarget**, and use the parameter **respondToAttack** as a condition for this transition, and ensure that the option **Can Transition To Self** is set to false.

Now that the **Animator Controller** has been modified, we can modify the script **TeamMember**.

- Please open the script **TeamMember**.

- Modify the following code (new code in bold).

```
if (info.IsName ("attackTarget"))
{
        if (target != null)
        {
                GetComponent<UnityEngine.AI.NavMeshAgent> ().isStopped = true;
                gameObject.transform.LookAt (target.transform);

                if (info.normalizedTime % 1.0 >= .98)
                {
                        int damage;
                        if (gameObject.tag == "team2") damage = 10;
                        else damage = 20;
                        target.GetComponent<NPC> ().hitByOpponent (gameObject, damage);
                }
        }
        else anim.SetTBool ("targetDestroyed", true);
}
```

In the previous code:

Adding and Controlling An Army of NPCs

- For testing purposes, we adjust the damage depending on the target, so that the player's team inflict more damage than the other team.

- We also apply the attack only if the target exists.

At this stage, we need to specify that the NPC will attack when it is either ordered to do so by its leader, or as a response to an attack.

- Please modify the function attack in the script **TeamMember** as follows

```
//anim.SetTrigger ("attackOneToOne");
anim.SetTrigger ("respondToAttack");
```

In the previous code, since triggering the parameter **respondToAttack** will be used to trigger the NPC to fight back, we use this trigger in both situations, whether the NPC needs to attack in the first place or to respond to an attack; in both cases, the NPC will enter the state called **attack**.

Next, because the radius that we have used earlier was essentially for the static cylinders, we will modify it so that it is more suited to detect when an NPCs is close to its NPC target:

- Please modify the script **TeamMember** as follows (new code in bold), if you have not already done so:

```
if (info.IsName ("goToTarget"))
{
        if (target != null)
        {
                GetComponent<UnityEngine.AI.NavMeshAgent> ().SetDestination (target.transform.position);
                GetComponent<UnityEngine.AI.NavMeshAgent> ().isStopped = false;
                distanceToTarget = Vector3.Distance (target.transform.position, gameObject.transform.position);
                if (distanceToTarget < 1.5f) {
                        anim.SetBool ("closeToTarget", true);
                        GetComponent<UnityEngine.AI.NavMeshAgent> ().isStopped = true;
                } else
                        anim.SetBool ("closeToTarget", false);
        }
        else anim.SetBool ("targetDestroyed", true);
}
```

In the previous code:

- We check that the target exists.

- If it has been destroyed, then we set the Boolean parameter **targetDestroyed**.

- We also change the minimum distance to the target from **2** to **1.5**.

[412]

Adding and Controlling An Army of NPCs

Now, if we also need to make sure that the protagonists will face each other during a fight; this is necessary now, as some NPCs responding to an attack won't automatically face their opponent, so this can be done by using the built-in function called **LookAt**.

- Please modify the script **TeamMember** as follows (new code in bold), if you have not already done so:

```
if (info.IsName ("attackTarget"))
{

        GetComponent<UnityEngine.AI.NavMeshAgent> ().isStopped = true;
```
gameObject.transform.LookAt (target.transform);

Because we only want the NPC to rotate around the y-axis when it is looking at its opponent, we will also need to freeze its rotation around the x- and z-axes.

- Please select the prefabs **teamMember** and **oppositeTeamMember**.

- Add a **Rigidbody** component to these objects, and leave the options as default for this component.

- In the **Inspector**, modify the **Rigidbody** component of these objects as described in the next figure (i.e., **freeze rotation** for **x** and **z-axes**).

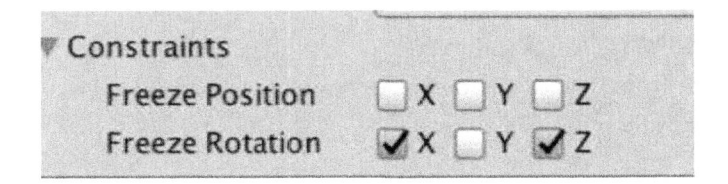

Figure 205: Freezing rotation around two axes

That's it!

Let's test the game now.

- Play the scene.

- Launch an attack using the **P** key.

- You should see that a battle starts between the two teams; each team member, after defeating its opponent will go back to its team leader.

- Because, the player's team inflicts more damage (as per the code that we have added), you should see that all the members of the opponent team will be eliminated, and that the player's team members then return to their leader.

[413]

Adding and Controlling An Army of NPCs

Figure 206: One-to-one fight between the two teams

That's it!

LEVEL ROUNDUP

Summary

In this chapter, we have managed to create more challenging NPCs that act as a group; we discovered how it is possible to create a group of NPCs that follow and receive orders from the player; we also managed to create another team of NPCs led by another NPC. Finally, we managed to simulate a battle between the two teams. You could, of course, add more features, based on the principles that we have learned so far; however, the principles that you have learned in this chapter can be used and further customized to implement some even more realistic group movements and battles.

Checklist

You can consider moving to the next stage if you can do the following:

- Understand how to coordinate a team.
- Understand how to send orders from a leader to the other members of the team.
- Know how to create transitions to sub-state machines.

Quiz

Now, let's check your knowledge! Please answer the following questions (the answers are on the next page) or specify whether they are correct or incorrect.

1. To create a sub-state machine you can right click in the Animator window and selected **Create | Sub-state Machine**.

2. To open a sub-state machine, you can just double click on it.

3. Only Boolean variables can be used to transition to a sub-state machine.

4. The following code will create an array of **GameObjects**.

```
GameObject [] objects;
```

5. If a function is **public**, it can be accessed from outside its class.

6. The following code will check whether a key has been pressed and released.

Adding and Controlling An Army of NPCs

```
if (Input.GetKeyDown(KeyCode.O)){...}
```

7. If several objects are based on the same prefab, clicking on the button called **Apply** located in the **Inspector** window, will update the properties of all these objects.

8. The built-in function **Vector3.Distance** can be used to calculate the distance between two objects.

9. The method **OnStateEnter** can be used to detect when a state is entered.

10. All script behaviors linked to a state inherit, by default, from the class **StateBehaviour**.

Quiz Answers

1. True.
2. True.
3. False.
4. True.
5. True.
6. True.
7. True.
8. True.
9. True.
10. False (it is the class **StateMachineBehaviour**).

Challenge 1

For this chapter, your challenge will be to modify the game as follows:

- Add more team members on both teams.
- Create a mechanism through which each leader can monitor the number of team members who have been destroyed

Ask the troops to retreat after losing half of the initial number of team members.

10 Creating a 2D Shooter (Part 1): Introduction

In this section, we will start by creating a simple level, including:

- A spaceship symbolized by a triangle that you will be able to move in four directions.
- The ability for the spaceship to fire missiles.
- The ability for the player to destroy targets with the missiles.
- A camera that displays the scene.
- Meteorites (or moving targets) generated randomly.

So, after completing this chapter, you will be able to:

- Detect keystrokes.
- Generate random events.
- Instantiate objects.
- Add velocity to objects (i.e., to the moving targets).
- Modify sprites' properties such as their color.
- Move objects from a script.

ADDING THE SPACESHIP

So, in this section, we will start to create the spaceship that will be used by the player; it will consist of a simple sprite (for the time-being) that we will be able to move in four directions using the arrow keys on the keyboard: left, right, up and down.

So, let's get started:

- Please launch Unity and create a new Project (**File | New Project**).

Figure 207: Creating a new project

- In the new window, you can specify the name of your project, its location, as well as the **2D** mode (as this game will be **2D**).

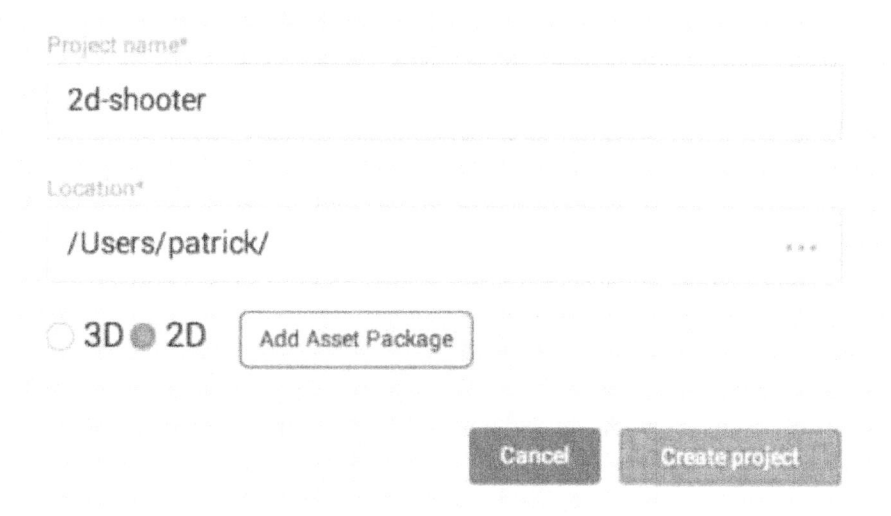

Figure 208: Specifying the name and location for your project

Creating a 2D Shooter (Part 1): Introduction

- Once this is done, you can click on the button called **Create project** (at the bottom of the window) and Unity should open.

- Once this is done, you can check that the 2D mode is activated, based on the 2D logo located in the top right-corner of the **Scene** view.

Figure 209: Activating the 2D mode

We will now create a new sprite for our spaceship; it will be made of a simple triangle.

- From the **Project** view, please select **Create | Sprites | Triangle**, as illustrated on the next figure.

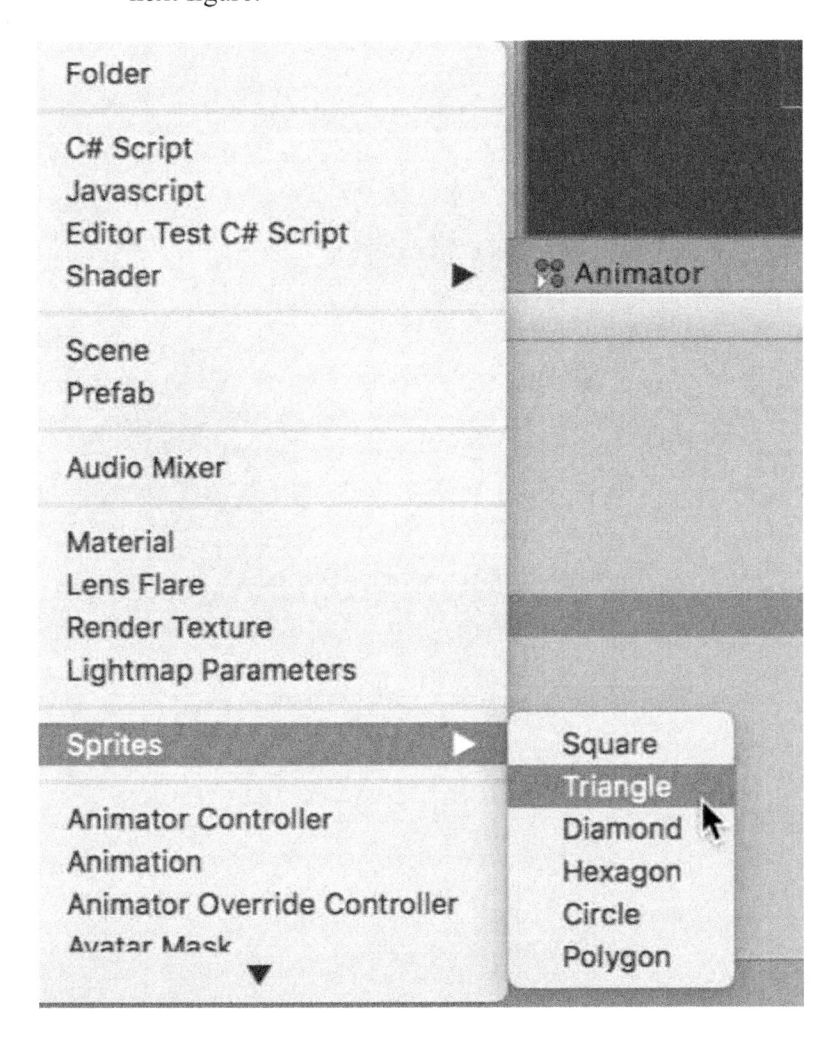

Figure 210: Creating a new sprite

[419]

Creating a 2D Shooter (Part 1): Introduction

- This will create a new asset called **Triangle** in the **Project** window.

Figure 211: Creating a new triangle asset

- Once this is done, you can drag and drop this sprite (i.e., the white object with the label **Triangle**) from the **Project** window to the **Scene** view; this will create a new object called **Triangle** in the **Hierarchy** view.

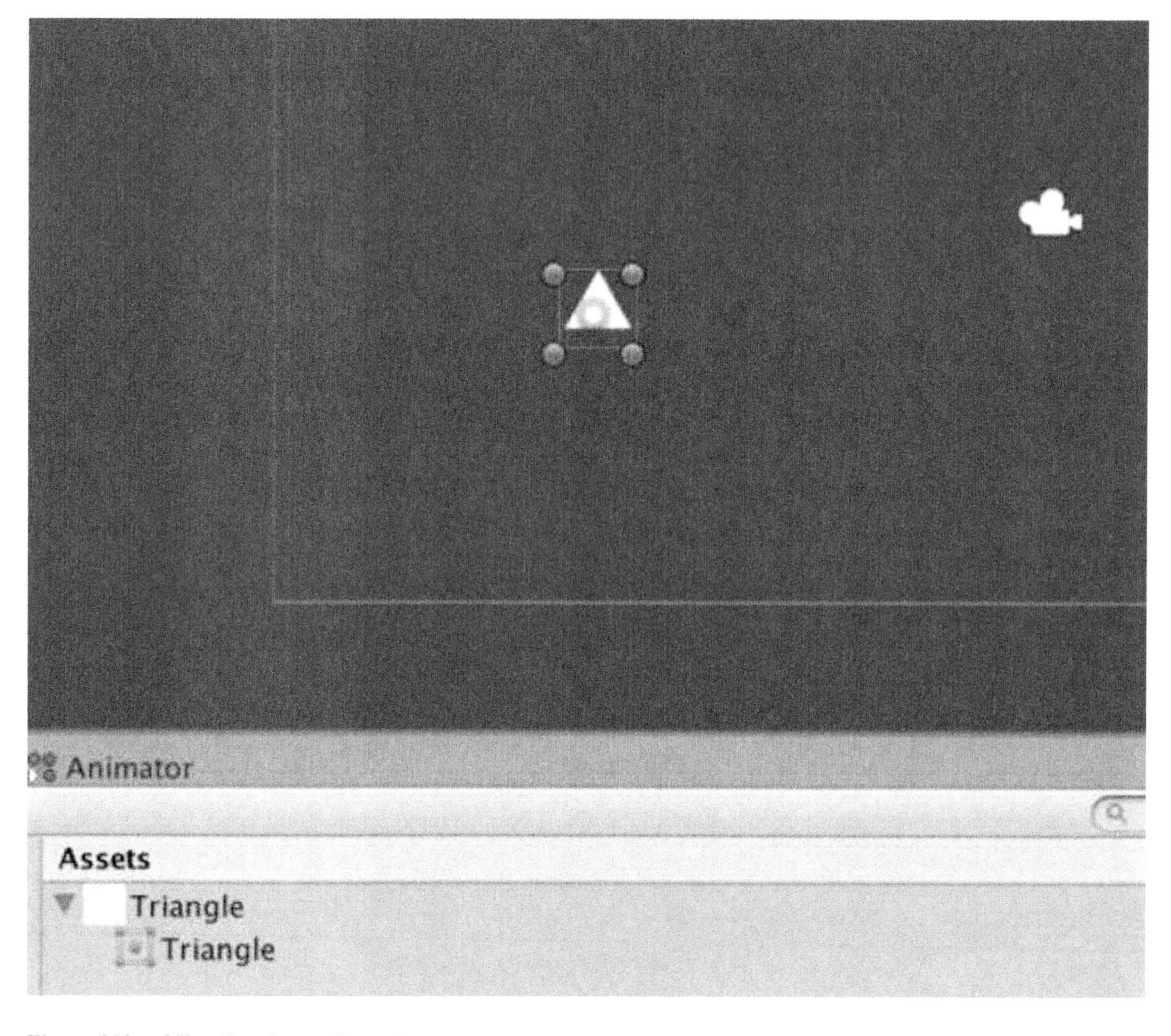

Figure 212: adding the player character

Creating a 2D Shooter (Part 1): Introduction

> In the previous window, you may notice the white lines at the bottom and to the left of the screen; these are the boundaries that define what will be visible onscreen; so by dropping your object within these lines, you ensure that the player will be seen (or captured) by the camera.

- Please rename this object **player** for now, using the **Hierarchy** window: to rename this object, you can right-click on it in the **Hierarchy** window, and then select the option **Rename** from the contextual menu.

So at this stage, we have a new player character (i.e., the spaceship) and we will need to move it according to the keys pressed on the keyboard; so let's do just this:

- Please create a new C# script (i.e., select **Create | C# Script** from the **Project** window) and rename this script **MovePlayer**.

- Once this is done, please open this script and add the following code to it (new code in bold):

```csharp
void Update ()
{
    if (Input.GetKey (KeyCode.LeftArrow))
    {
        gameObject.transform.Translate (Vector3.left * 0.1f);
    }
    if (Input.GetKey (KeyCode.RightArrow))
    {
        gameObject.transform.Translate (Vector3.right * 0.1f);
    }
    if (Input.GetKey (KeyCode.UpArrow))
    {
        gameObject.transform.Translate (Vector3.up * 0.1f);
    }
    if (Input.GetKey (KeyCode.DownArrow))
    {
        gameObject.transform.Translate (Vector3.down * 0.1f);
    }
}
```

In the previous code:

- We use the function **Update** to check for keyboard inputs.
- If the **left** arrow is pressed, we move the object linked to this script (i.e., the spaceship) to the **left** (i.e., 0.1 meter to the left).

- If the **right** arrow is pressed, we move the object linked to this script (i.e., the spaceship) to the **right** (i.e., 0.1 meter to the right).

> Note that we use the function **GetKey** that checks whether a key has been pressed; however, if you wanted to check whether a key has been released then you could use the function **GetKeyDown** instead.

You can now save the script, check for any error in the **Console** window, and link the script (i.e., drag and drop it) to the object called **player** that is in the **Hierarchy** view. Once this is done, you can play the scene and check that you can move the player left or right. After pressing the arrow keys on your keyboard, you should see that the spaceship moves in four directions.

> Note that to play and stop the scene, you can press the shortcut **CTRL + P**, or use the black triangle located at the top of the window.

SHOOTING MISSILES

In this section, we will get the player to shoot missiles whenever s/he presses the space bar; this will involve the following steps:

- Creating an object for the missile.
- Saving this object as a prefab (i.e., a template).
- Detecting when the space bar has been pressed (and then released) by the player.
- Instantiating the missile prefab and adding velocity to it so that it moves up when fired.

First, let's create a new object for the missile:

- You can now stop the scene (e.g., CTRL + P).
- Using the **Project** window, please create a new circular sprite (**Create | Sprites | Circle**), and rename it **bullet**.

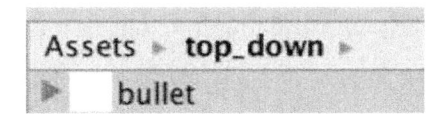

Figure 213: Creating a bullet

- Once this is done, please drag and drop this **bullet** asset from the **Project** window to the **Scene** (or **Hierarchy**) window, this will create a new object called **bullet**.
- Using the **Inspector**, rescale this object to **(0.1, 0.1, 0.1)**. The position of this object does not matter for now.

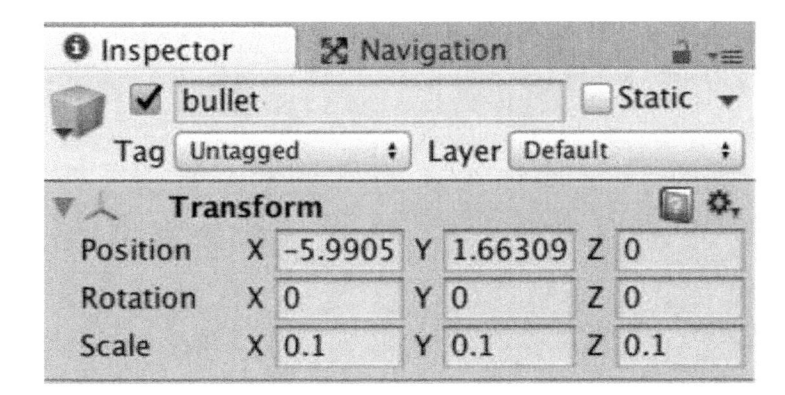

Figure 214: Scaling-down the bullet

[423]

Creating a 2D Shooter (Part 1): Introduction

- Add a **Rigidbody2D** component to this object (i.e., select **Components | Physics2D | Rigidbody2D** from the top menu) and set the **Gravity Scale** attribute of this component (i.e., **Rigidbody2D**) to **0**, as illustrated in the next figure.

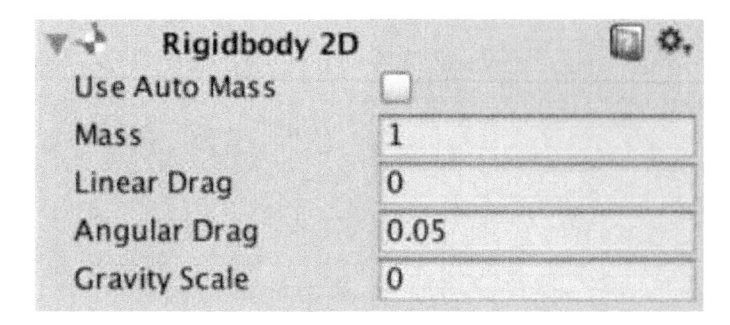

Figure 215: Setting the gravity scale

> By adding a **Rigidbody2D** component to this object, we ensure that we can apply forces to it, or modify its velocity; this being said, because we have a top-down view, we do not want this object to be influenced by gravity (otherwise it would fall down), and this is why we set the **Gravity Scale** attribute to **0** for this object.

- We can now convert this **bullet** to a prefab by dragging and dropping this object (i.e., **bullet**) to the **Project** view.

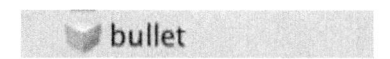

Figure 216: Creating a prefab for the bullet

- You can now delete the object called **bullet** from the **Hierarchy**.

Last but not least, we need to add some code that will be used to instantiate and propel this bullet if the player presses the space bar.

- Please open the script called **MovePlayer**.
- Add the following code at the beginning of the script (new code in bold).

```
public class MovePlayer : MonoBehaviour
{
    public GameObject bullet;
```

- Please add the following code to the **Update** function:

Creating a 2D Shooter (Part 1): Introduction

```
if (Input.GetKeyDown (KeyCode.Space))
{
        GameObject b = (GameObject)(Instantiate (bullet, transform.position + transform.up*1.5f, Quaternion.identity));
        b.GetComponent<Rigidbody2D> ().AddForce (transform.up * 1000);
}
```

In the previous code:

- We create a new **GameObject**.
- This **GameObject** will be based on the template called **bullet**.
- If the player hits the space bar, the new bullet is instantiated just above the spaceship.
- We then add an upward force to the bullet so that it starts to move.

You can now save your script, and check that it is error-free in the **Console** window.

- If you click on the object called **player** that is present in the **Hierarchy**, and if you look at the **Inspector**, you should see that a new field called **bullet** has appeared for the component **MovePlayer**.
- Please drag and drop the prefab called **bullet** to this field (as illustrated on the next figure).

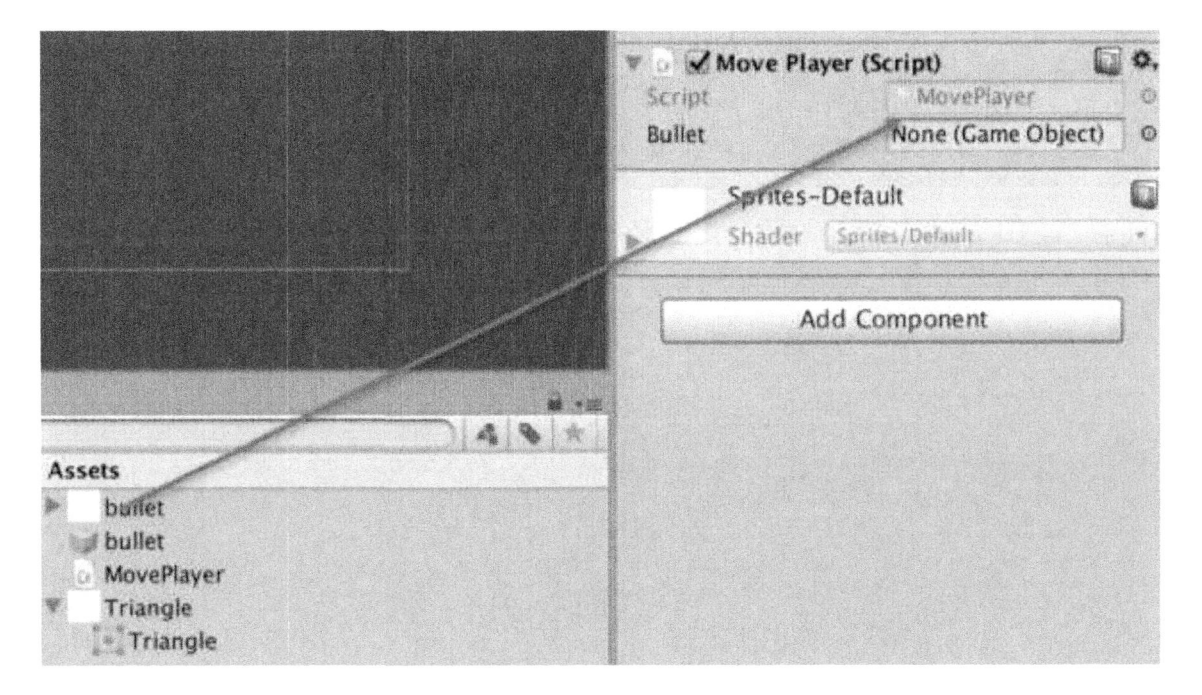

Figure 217: Adding the bullet prefab

[425]

Once this done, you can play the scene, and check that after pressing the space bar, you are able to fire a bullet.

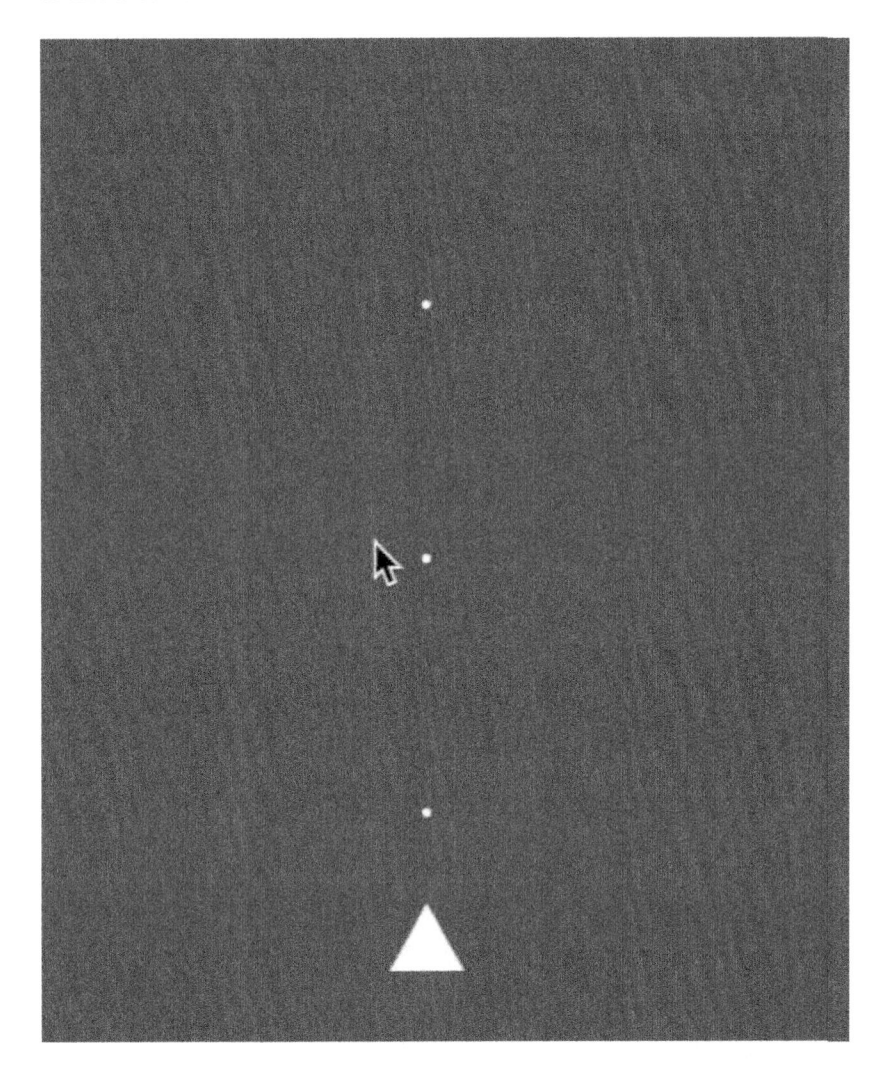

Figure 218: Shooting projectiles

DESTROYING THE TARGET

Now that we can shoot missiles (or bullets), we just need to be able to destroy the objects colliding with the missiles; so we will create new objects that will be used as targets for the time being.

- Please create a new **Square** sprite (from the **Project** window, select: **Create Sprites | Square**) or you can also duplicate the **player** sprite if you wish.

- Rename this new sprite **target**.

- Drag and drop this sprite to the **Scene** view.

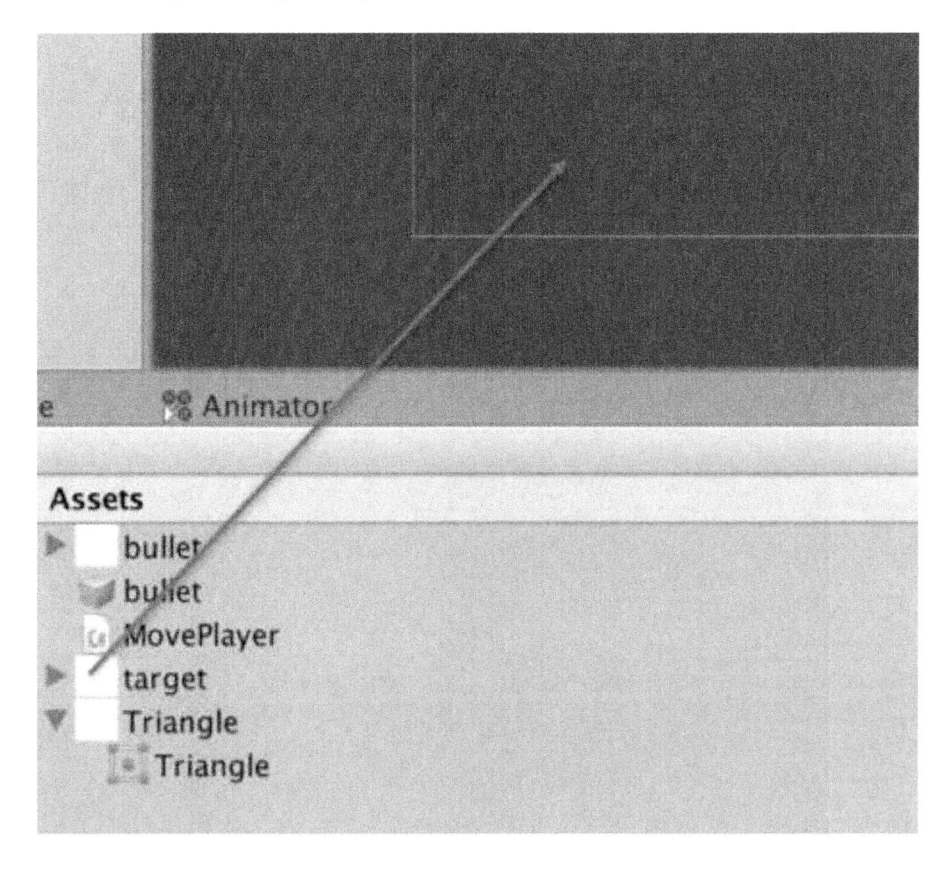

Figure 219: Adding a target to the scene

- This will create a new object; rename this new object **target**.

- Please select this object.

Add a **BoxCollider2D** to this object (i.e., select **Components | Physics2D | BoxCollider2D** from the top menu). This is so that collisions can be detected.

We will now create a new tag for this object. A **tag**; will help to identify each object in the scene, and to see the object that the bullets (or the player) are colliding with.

- Please select the object called **target** in the **Hierarchy**.

- In the **Inspector** window, click on the drop-down menu called **Untagged** (to the right of the attribute called tag), as described on the next figure.

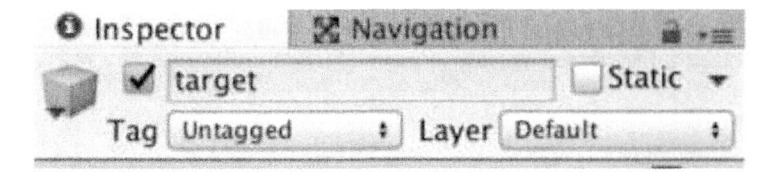

Figure 220: Creating a tag (part1)

- From the drop-down menu, please select the option **Add Tag...**

Figure 221: Creating a tag (part 2)

- In the new window, click on the + button that is located below the label "**Tags/List is Empty**".

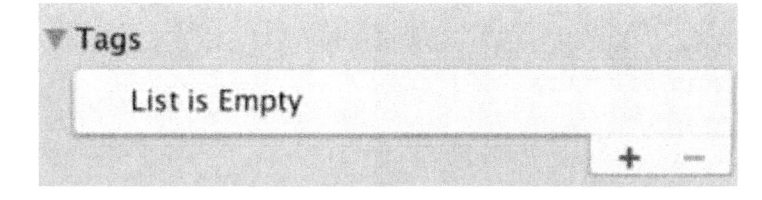

Figure 222: Creating a tag (part 3)

Creating a 2D Shooter (Part 1): Introduction

- Please specify a name for your tag (i.e., **target**), using the field to the right of the label **Tag 0**.

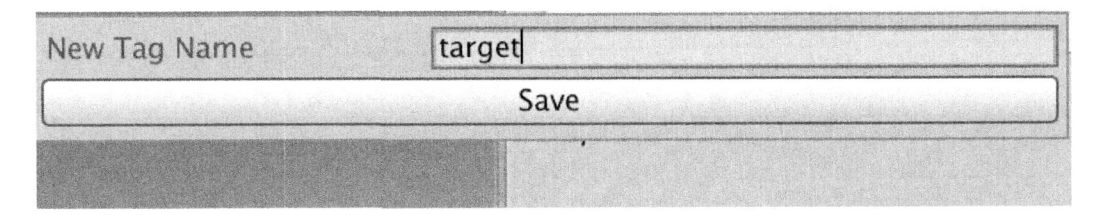

Figure 223: Adding a tag (part 2)

- Press the **Enter/Return** key on your keyboard to save your new tag.
- Select the object **target** in the **Hierarchy** again, and, using the **Inspector**, select the tag **target**, that you have just created.

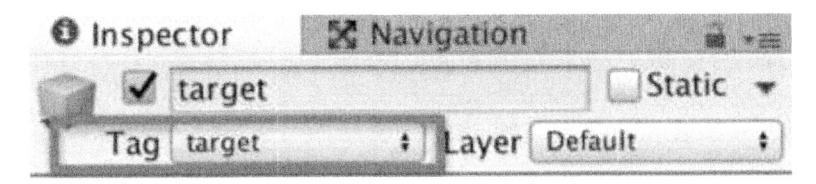

Figure 224: Adding a tag (part 3)

- Last but not least, we will create a prefab from this target by dragging and dropping the object **target** to the **Project** window.

Next, we will create a new script that will be linked to the bullet (or missile), so that, upon collision with a target, this target should be destroyed (based on its tag).

- Please create a new script called **Bullet**: from the **Project** window, select **Create | C# Script**.
- Open this script.
- Add the following code to it (just **after** the function **Update**).

[429]

```
void OnCollisionEnter2D(Collision2D coll)
{
        if (coll.gameObject.tag == "target")
        {
                Destroy (coll.gameObject);
                Destroy (gameObject);
        }
}
```

In the previous code:

- We detect the objects colliding with the bullet.

- When this occurs, we check if this object is a target; if this is the case, this target is then destroyed.

- The bullet is also destroyed in this case.

Once this is done, we can save our script and link it to the **bullet** prefab.

- Please save the script called **Bullet** and check that it is error-free.

- Once this is done, please drag and drop it on the prefab called **Bullet**, in the **Project** window.

- You can then click once on the prefab called **bullet**, and check, using the **Inspector** window, that it includes the script **Bullet**.

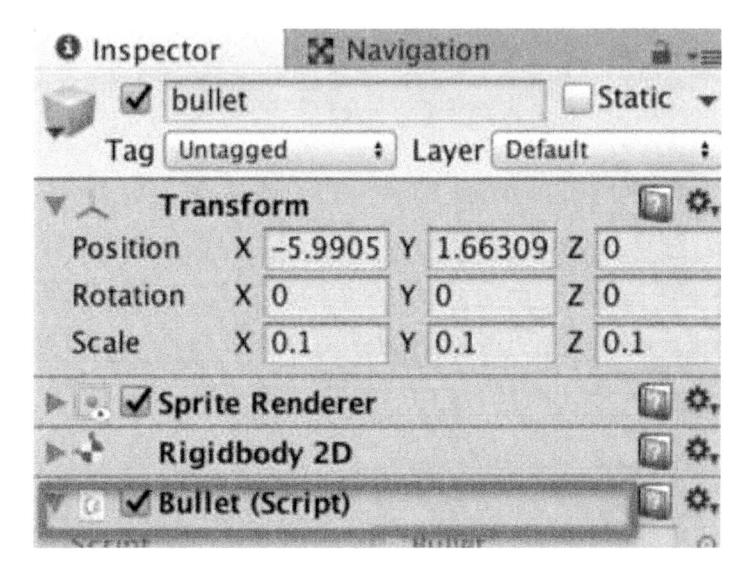

Figure 225: Checking the components of the Bullet prefab

Creating a 2D Shooter (Part 1): Introduction

Last but not least, we will need to add a collider to our **Bullet** prefab, so that it actually collides with other objects:

- Please select the prefab called **bullet**.
- From the top menu, select **Components | Physics2D | BoxCollider2D**.

You can now test your game:

- Move the target object just above the **player**, as illustrated in the next figure.

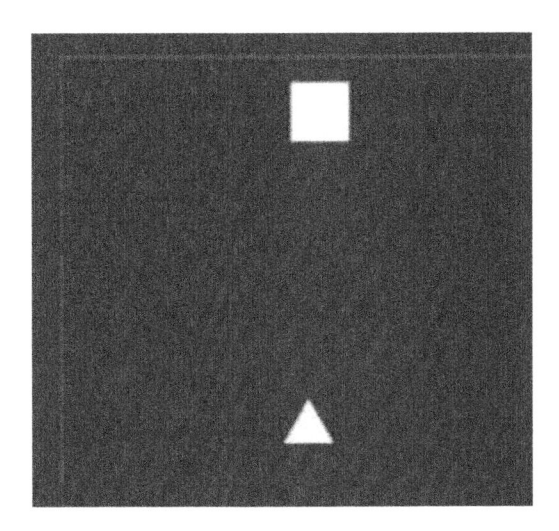

Figure 226: Checking the bullet prefab

- Please play the scene, fire a missile (i.e., press the space bar), and check that, upon collision between the bullet and the target, both objects are destroyed.

> Note that since you will be firing several bullets, we could choose to destroy a bullet after 10 seconds (by this time it should have hit a target), by modifying the script **Bullet** as follows (new code in bold):

```
void Start ()
{
        Destroy (gameObject, 10);
}
```

You can test your scene and see that after 10 seconds the bullet is destroyed.

Before we go ahead, it may be a good idea to save our scene:

[431]

- Please select **File | Save Scene As** from the top menu, and save your scene as **level1**.
- You can also save your project (**File | Save Project**).

Next, we will just create a slightly different type of target; that is: a moving target that will move downwards and that the player will have to avoid or to destroy; so let's implement this feature:

- Using the **Project** window, please duplicate the prefab called **target**, that we have just created (i.e., select the **target** prefab, and the press *CTRL + D*).
- Rename the duplicate **moving_target** (i.e., right-click + **Rename**).
- Select the prefab **moving_target** in the **Hierarchy** and add a RigidBody2D component to it (i.e., select **Component | Physics2D | RigidBody2D**).
- Using the Inspector window, set its attribute called **Gravity Scale** (for the component **Rigidbody2D**) to 0, as illustrated on the next figure. This is so that the object does not fall indefinitely (since it is a top-down view).

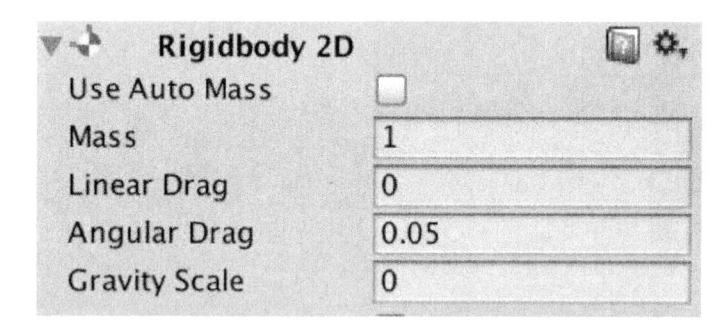

Rigidbody 2D	
Use Auto Mass	
Mass	1
Linear Drag	0
Angular Drag	0.05
Gravity Scale	0

Figure 227: Adjusting the gravity scale

Next, we will create a script that will be linked to this object and that will set its initial velocity downwards.

- Please create a new C# script called **MovingTarget**.
- Modify the **Start** function as follows (new code in bold).

```
void Start ()
{
        GetComponent<Rigidbody2D> ().velocity = Vector2.down * 10;
}
```

In the previous code, we access the **Rigidbody2D** component of the object linked to this script (this will be the moving target), and then set the velocity downwards.

- You can now save your script, check that it is error-free, and drag and drop it to the prefab called **moving_target**.

Creating a 2D Shooter (Part 1): Introduction

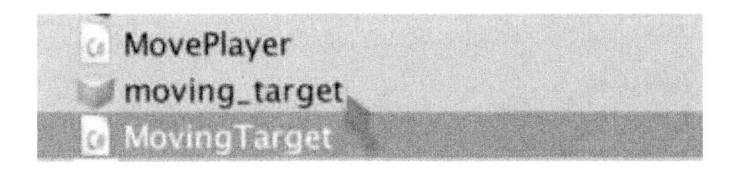

Figure 228: Linking the script to the target

- So that we can test the scene, please drag and drop the prefab **moving_target** to the **Scene** view and play the scene, you should see that this particular target moves downwards.

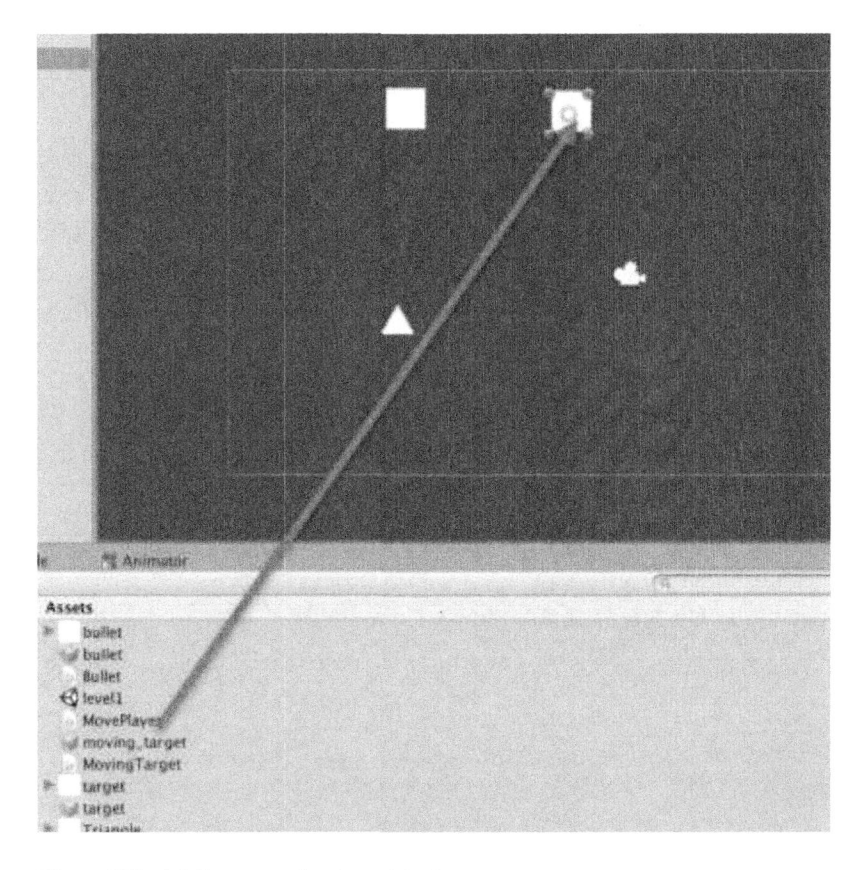

Figure 229: Adding a moving target to the scene

SPAWNING MOVING TARGETS RANDOMLY

Last but not least, we will create a mechanism through which the moving targets are created randomly, a bit like meteorites, so that flying "meteorites" appear randomly onscreen and move downwards. For this, we will be doing the following:

- We will create an empty object that will spawn these moving targets.
- These will be instantiated at regular intervals and at random positions.
- We will also ensure that the moving targets are spawned in the current view (i.e., relatively close to the player so that they can be captured and displayed by the camera).

So let's get to it:

- Please create a new empty object called **targetSpawner** in the **Hierarchy** window (i.e., select **GameObject | Create Empty**).
- Create a new C# script called **SpawnMovingTargets**.
- Open the script.
- Add the following code at the beginning of the class (new code in bold):

```
public class SpawnMovingTargets : MonoBehaviour {
float timer = 0;
public GameObject newObject;
```

- Add the following code to the **Update** function (new code in bold):

```
void Update ()
{
        timer += Time.deltaTime;
        float range = Random.Range (-10, 10);
        Vector3 newPosition = new Vector3 (GameObject.Find("player").transform.position.x + range, transform.position.y, 0);
        if (timer >= 1)
        {
                GameObject t = (GameObject)(Instantiate (newObject, newPosition, Quaternion.identity));
                timer = 0;
        }
}
```

In the previous code:

- We increase the value of our timer every seconds.

- We then define a variable called **range**; it will be a random number between **-10** and **10**; this variable will be used to define a random position that is to the left (i.e., **-10 to 0**) or to the right (i.e., **0 to +10**) of the player; this is so that the target instantiated is close enough to the player and within the field of the view of the camera.

- We then create a new vector called **newPosition** that uses the variable **range** defined earlier for the **x coordinate;** the **y-coordinate** of the object linked to this script (this will be the empty object **targetSpawner**) is then used for the **y-coordinate** of the object that is being instantiated.

- A new object is then instantiated every second: every time the value of the variable **timer** is greater than 1, **timer** is reset to 0 and a new prefab (i.e., moving target) is instantiated

There are of course many other ways to create this feature, but this version is relatively simple, to start with.

Next, we just need to set-up the **targetSpawner** object:

- Please check that the script that you have just created is error-free.

- Drag and drop this script (i.e., **SpawnMovingTargets**) to the object called **targetSpawner** in the **Hierarchy**. Alternatively, you can add the script to the object **targetSpawner** by selecting this object in the **Hierarhcy**, and by then dragging and dropping the script (i.e., **SpawnMovingTargets**) to the **Inspector** window, as illustrated on the next figure.

Creating a 2D Shooter (Part 1): Introduction

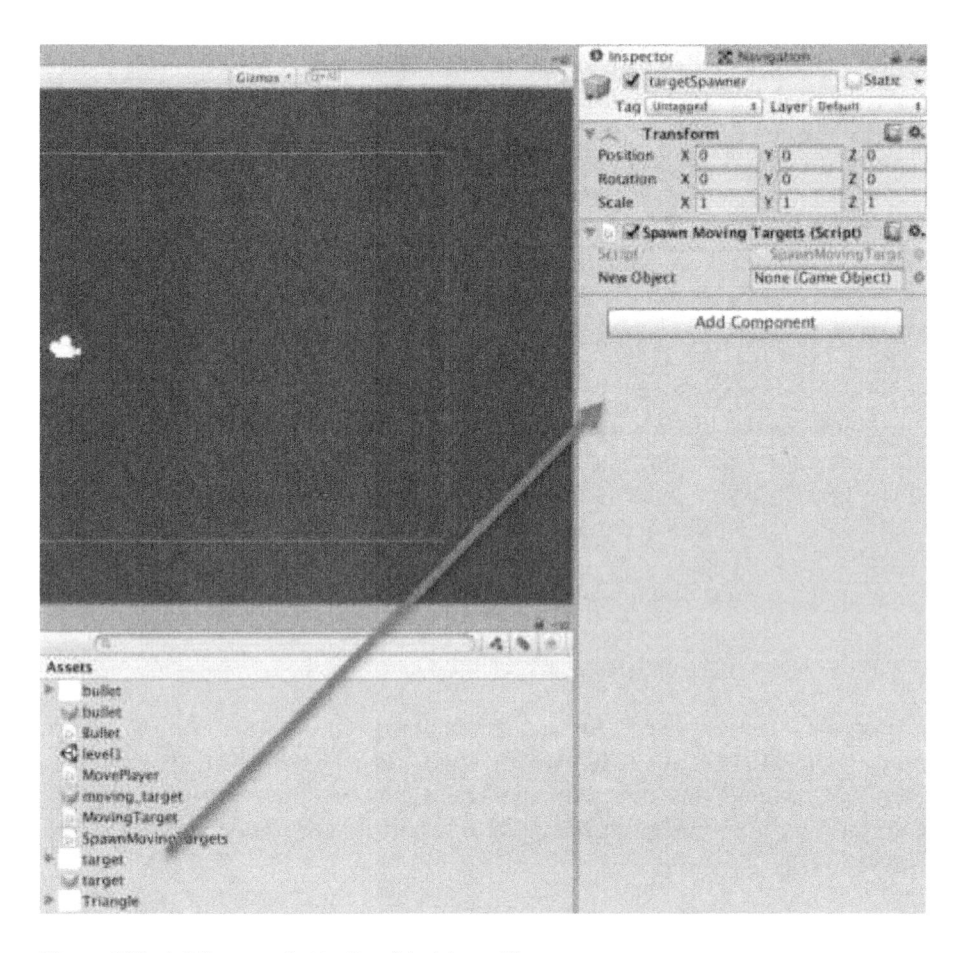

Figure 230: Adding a script to the object targetSpawner

- Please select the object **targetSpawner** in the **Hierarchy** window.

- Drag the prefab called **moving_target** from the **Project** window to the field called **newObject** in the **Inspector**, as described in the next figure.

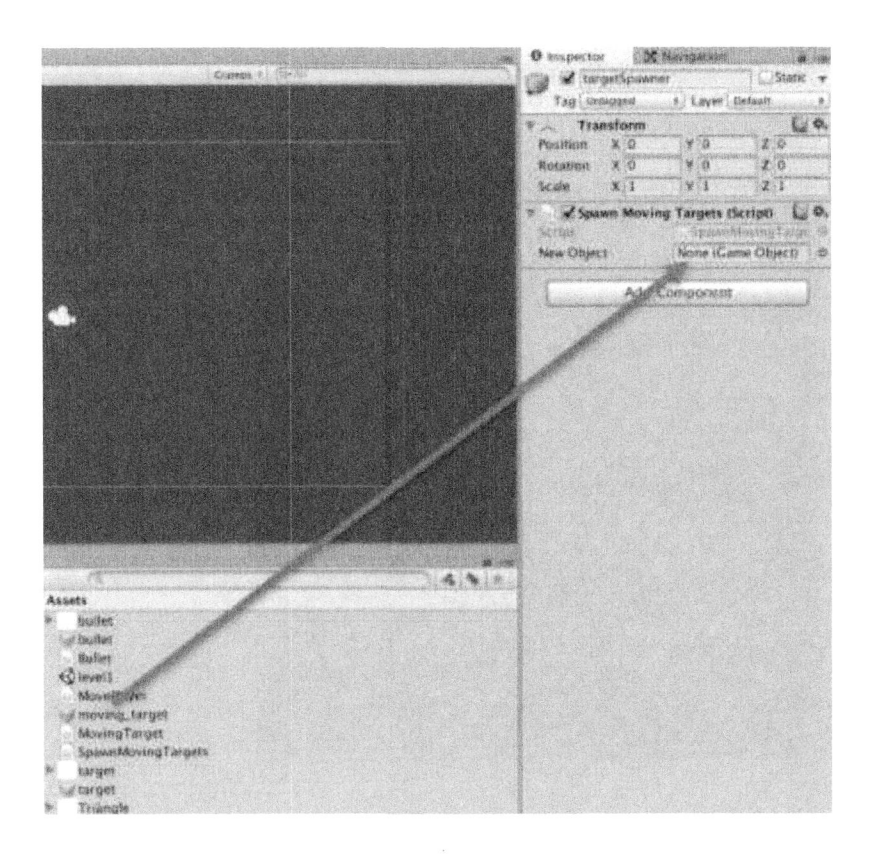

Figure 231: Setting the prefab to be spawn (part 1)

- The component **SawnMovingTarget** should then look as follows.

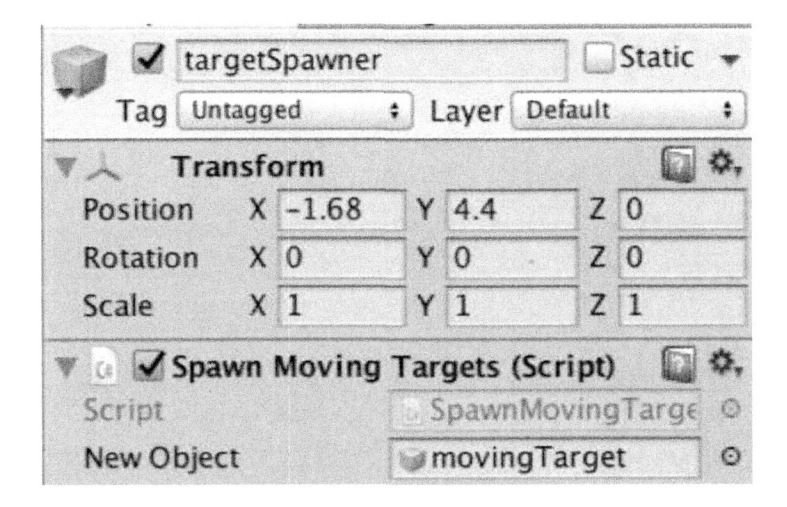

Figure 232: Setting the prefab to be spawn (part 2)

Creating a 2D Shooter (Part 1): Introduction

Last, using the **Scene** view, we just need to move the object called **targetSpawner** at the upper boundary of the screen; this is so that the moving targets are instantiated at the very top of the screen, just above the player.

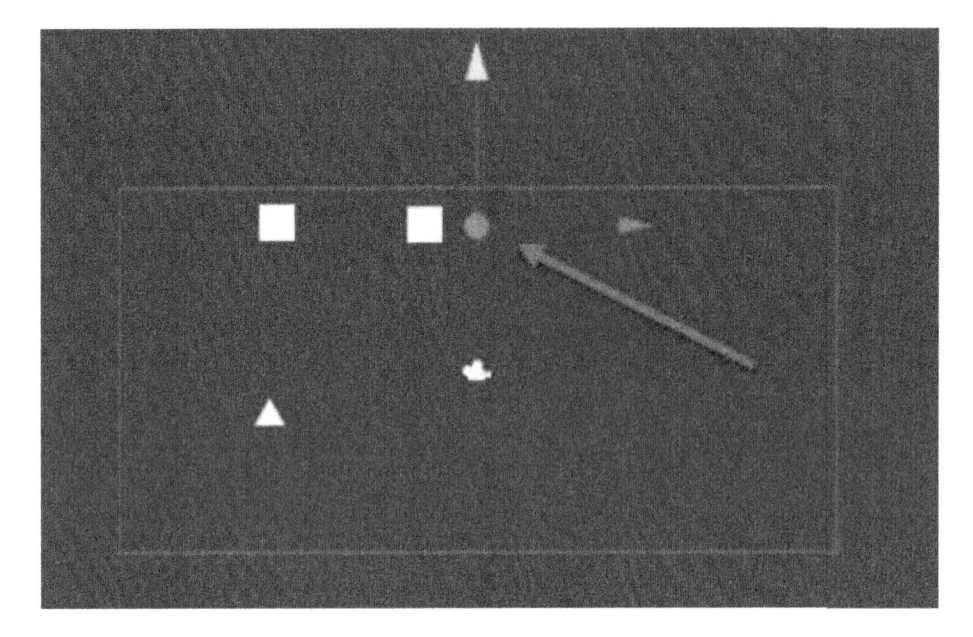

Figure 233: Moving the targetSpawner object

Once this is done, you can delete or deactivate the objects called **moving_target** and **target** that are already in the scene (i.e., the two squares that you could see in the previous figure), and test the scene. To deactivate these objects, you can select them and, using the **Inspector** window, uncheck the box to the left of their name.

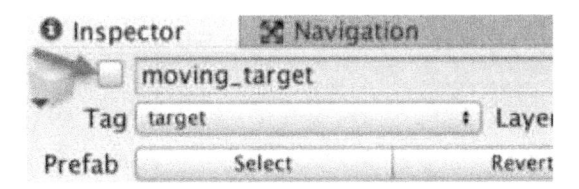

Figure 234: Deactivating the moving target

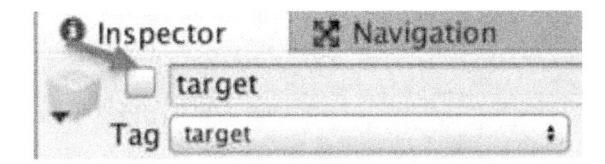

Figure 235: Deactivating the target

[438]

Creating a 2D Shooter (Part 1): Introduction

As you play the scene, you should see that a new moving target is instantiated every second at random, as described on the next figure.

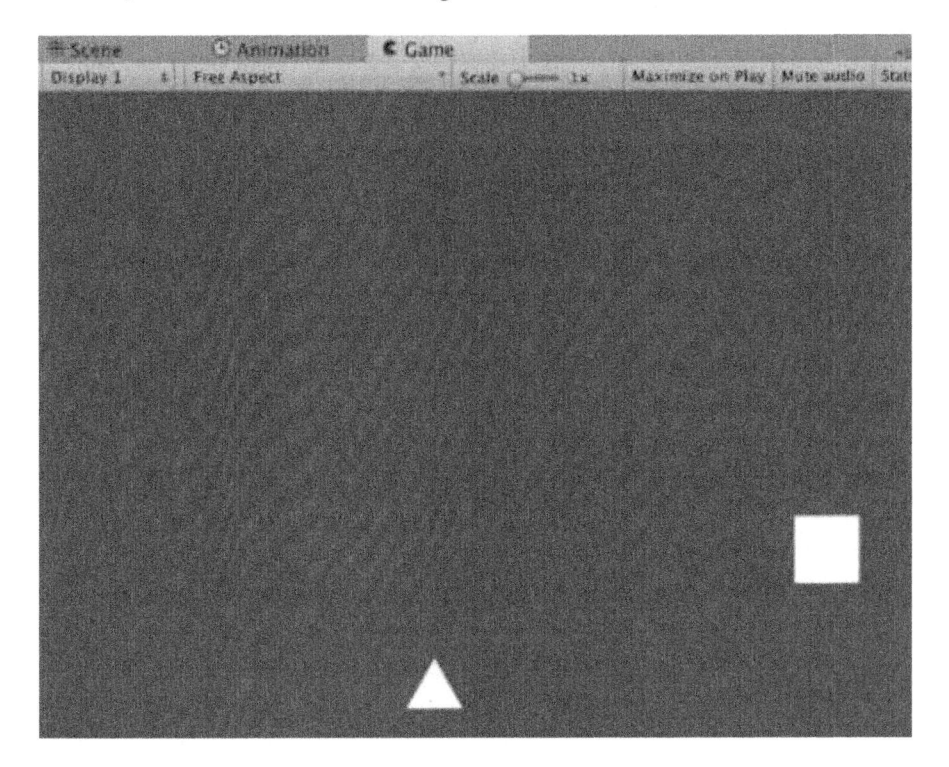

Figure 236: Spawning moving targets

MANAGING DAMAGE

Now that we have created a moving target that the player can shoot, we will create a script that manages the damage taken by the target so that it is destroyed only after being hit several times by the player's bullets.

- Please create a new script called **ManageTargetHealth** (i.e., select **Create | C# Script** from the **Project** window)

- Add the following code at the beginning of the class (new code in bold).

```
public class ManageTargetHealth : MonoBehaviour {
    public int health, type;
    public static int TARGET_BOULDER = 0;
```

- In the previous code, we create three variables: **health**, **type**, and **TARGET_BOULDER**.

- **health** will be used to determine the health (or strength) of each target so that we know how much damage it can sustain before being destroyed.

- **type** is used to set different types of targets; each of these will have different levels of health (or strength).

- **TARGET_BOULDER** will be used as a type for our moving targets (i.e., boulders). Note that this variable is both **static** and **public**; this means that it can be accessed from outside its class; also, because it is **static**, this variable can be accessed without the need to instantiate a new object of type **ManageTargetHealth**.

> We will come back to this principle later, but in a nutshell, static variables and functions can be used by other classes with no instantiation required; you can consider these static variables and functions as utility classes and variables that can be used without the need to be part of a particular class, a bit like a friend granting your access to his or her car without the need for you to be the owner. For example, the function **Debug.Log** can be used from anywhere in your game, although, you don't need to instantiate an object of type **Debug** for this purpose; the same holds true for the function **GameObject.Find**; again, you can use this function to find a particular object; however, you don't need to instantiate an object of class **GameOBject** to be able to use this function **Find**.

Now, we just need to specify the health (or strength) of the target, based on its type, in the **Start** function.

- Please add the following code to the **Start** function (new code in bold).

```
void Start ()
{
        if (type == TARGET_BOULDER) health = 20;
}
```

- Add a new function called **gotHit**, at the end of the class (i.e., before the last closing curly bracket) as follows:

```
public void gotHit(int damage)
{
        health -= damage;
        if (health <= 0)
        destroyTarget ();
}
```

In the previous code:

- We declare a function called **gotHit**; its return type is **void** because it does not return any value; it takes a parameter of type **int** that will be referred to as **damage** within this function.

- We then set the value of the variable **health** by subtracting the value of the variable **damage** from the previous value of the variable **health**; this is equivalent to the following code:

```
health = health – damage;
```

- If the **health** is **0** or less, we then call the function called **destroyTarget**.

We now just need to create the function called **destroyTarget**.

- Please add a new function called **destroyTarget** at the end of the class (i.e., before the last closing curly bracket) as follows:

```
public void destroyTarget()
{
        Destroy (gameObject);
}
```

In the previous code:

- We create a new function called **destroyTarget** of type **void** (since it does not return any value).

- This function destroys the object linked to this script (i.e., the target).

Once this is done, we can save and use this script:

Creating a 2D Shooter (Part 1): Introduction

- Please save your code and check that it is error-free.

- Using the **Project** view, drag and drop this script (i.e., **ManageTargetHealth**) on both the **target** and the **moving_target** prefabs.

Next, we just need to modify the script **SpawnMovingTarget** so that we specify the type of the target that is to be created.

- Please modify the spawning script (i.e., **SpawnMovingTargets**) as follows (new code in bold).

```
if (timer >= 1)
{
        GameObject t = (GameObject)(Instantiate (newObject, newPosition, Quaternion.identity));
        t.GetComponent<ManageTargetHealth> ().type = ManageTargetHealth.TARGET_BOULDER;
        timer = 0;
}
```

In the previous code: we specify that the value of the variable called **type**, for the script called **ManageTargetHealth**, that is a component of the object **t** is **TARGET_BOULDER**.

> Note that we have accessed the static variable **TARGET_BOULDER** from the class **ManageTargetHealth** without instantiating an object of type **ManageTargetHealth**; this is because the variable **TARGET_BOULDER** is static.

Last but not least, we can add the following code to the script **Bullet**.

```
if (coll.gameObject.tag == "target")
{
        //Destroy (coll.gameObject);
        coll.gameObject.GetComponent<ManageTargetHealth>().gotHit(10);
        Destroy (gameObject);
}
```

You can now play the scene and test that the moving targets disappear after being hit twice.

> For testing purposes, you can also drag and drop the script **ManageTargetHealth** on the prefab called **target**, reactivate the object **target** in the **Scene** view, and then fire bullets at this target. It should disappear after two bullets have been fired.

LEVEL ROUNDUP

In this chapter, we have learned how to create a simple level with a spaceship, for the player, that can fire missiles and destroy static or moving targets. We also managed to create moving targets spawn at regular intervals but at random locations. Finally, we also learned to create **Rigidbody2D** and **BoxCollider2D** components and detect collision between the player's bullets and the targets. So, we have covered considerable ground to get you started with the first level of your 2D shooter.

Checklist

You can consider moving to the next stage if you can do the following:

- Apply **Rigidbody2D** and **BoxCollider2D** components.
- Detect the keys pressed on the keyboard.
- Know the difference between **Input.GetKey** and **Input.GetKeyDown**.
- Apply a tag to an object.
- Understand how to generate random numbers.
- Detect collision from a script.
- Detect a tag from a script.

Creating a 2D Shooter (Part 1): Introduction

Quiz

Now, let's check your knowledge! Please answer the following questions (the answers are included in the resource pack) or specify if these statements are either correct or incorrect.

1. The method **Random.GenerateRandomNumber** is used to generate random numbers.

2. Sprites can be created using the menu **Create | Sprite**.

3. The function **Input.GetKeyDown** is called to detect when a key has been pressed and subsequently released.

4. The function **Input.GetKey** is called whenever a key is being pressed.

5. Static variables cannot be accessed outside their class.

6. The following code will add force to the **Rigidbody2D** component of the object linked to the script .

```
GetComponent<Rigidbody2D> ().AddForce (transform.up * 1000);
```

7. The following code will destroy 10 instances of the current object:

```
Destroy (gameObject, 10);
```

8. When a collision between two objects (each with a 2DCollider) occurs, the function **OnCollisionEnter2D** is called.

9. A function of type **void** does not return any value.

10. Only square sprites can be created in Unity.

Creating a 2D Shooter (Part 1): Introduction

Answers to the Quiz

1. The method **Random.GenerateRandomNumber** is used to generate random numbers. **FALSE**

2. Sprites can be created using the menu **Create | Sprite**. **FALSE**

3. The function **Input.GetKeyDown** is called to detect when a key has been pressed and subsequently released. **TRUE**

4. The function **Input.GetKey** is called whenever a key is being pressed. **TRUE**

5. Static variables cannot be accessed outside their class. **FALSE**

6. The following code will add force to the **Rigidbody2D** component of the object linked to the script . **TRUE**

```
GetComponent<Rigidbody2D> ().AddForce (transform.up * 1000);
```

7. The following code will destroy 10 instances of the current object: **FALSE**

```
Destroy (gameObject, 10);
```

8. When a collision between two objects (each with a 2DCollider) occurs, the function **OnCollisionEnter2D** is called. **TRUE**

9. A function of type **void** does not return any value. **TRUE**

10. Only square sprites can be created in Unity. **FALSE**

Challenge 1

Now that you have managed to complete this chapter and that you have created your first level, you could improve the level by doing the following:

- Modify the color of each target.

- Modify the speed (or frequency) at which the moving targets are created.

Challenge 2

Now that you have managed to complete this chapter and that you have created your first level, you could improve it by doing the following:

- In the script **ManageTargetHealth**, create different types of targets; for example:

```
public static int TARGET_BOULDER_2 = 1;
```

- In the same script, modify the **Start** function so that the health of this particular target is set accordingly (i.e., different strength for different targets). For example:

```
If (type == ) health =;
```

- Modify the script **SpawnMovingTarget**, so that the boulder created is created at random; for example, you could generate a number between 1 and 2; based on this number, you will generate a boulder of type 0, or a boulder of type 1.

11
CREATING A 2D SHOOTER (PART2): ADDING SPECIAL EFFECTS

In this section, we will learn how to create special effects for our initial game to provide more visual feedback to the player when targets have been hit, and to also provide the illusion of movement by adding a scrolling background.

After completing this chapter, you will be able to:

- Access and modify the color of objects at run-time to make them blink temporary.
- Create a simple scrolling background.
- Know how to use the **Sprite Editor**.
- Create animated images that will be used for explosions.
- Understand how to import and slice sprite sheets to create animations.

Creating a 2D Shooter (Part2): Adding Special Effects

INTRODUCTION

In this chapter, we will learn how to create visual effects when the target has been hit (a blinking color) and destroyed (i.e., explosion). We will also create a scrolling background from a texture to give the impression of continuous movement.

ADDING SPECIAL EFFECTS TO THE TARGETS

In this section we will add some special effects when the targets are being hit.

When they are hit, they should blink blue. For this we will proceed as follows:

- When the object is hit, we will change its color to red.
- We will then start a timer that will count for 0.2 seconds.
- Once the .2 seconds have elapsed, we will then switch this object back to its original color.

So let's proceed:

- Please open the script called **ManageTargethealth**.
- Add this code at the beginning of the class.

```
public bool isBlinking = false;
public float timer;
public Color previousColor;
```

In the previous code:

- We declare three variables.
- The variable **isBlinking** will be used to determine if the object is blinking (i.e., if it is being hit).
- The variable **timer** will be used so that a new color is applied to this object for a few milliseconds; this will create a blinking effect.
- The variable **previousColor** will be used to save the color of the target before it starts to blink, so that this color can be applied again after the color change.

Please add this code in the **gotHit** function (new code in bold).

```
public void gotHit(int damage)
{
    health-= damage;
    if (health <= 0) destroyTarget ();
    previousColor = GetComponent<SpriteRenderer> ().color;
    GetComponent<SpriteRenderer> ().color = Color.blue;
    isBlinking = true;
}
```

In the previous code:

Creating a 2D Shooter (Part2): Adding Special Effects

- The initial (i.e., the previous) color of the target is saved in the variable **previousColor**.

- The current color of the target is changed to **blue**.

- The variable **isBlinking** is set to **true**; it will be used to start a timer that will define when the blinking should stop (i.e., to determine how long the blue color should be applied for).

Finally, we just need to restore the previous color, after the delay has elapsed.

- Please add the following code to the **Update** function:

```
if (isBlinking)
{
    timer += Time.deltaTime;
    if (timer >= .2)
    {
        isBlinking = false;
        GetComponent<SpriteRenderer> ().color = previousColor;
        timer = 0;
    }
}
```

In the previous code:

- We check whether the sprite is in the blinking mode (i.e., if it is being hit).
- We then update the variable **timer** every frame.
- Once the time has reached .2 seconds, we then switch back to the original color for our sprite.

Please save the script, play the scene and check that upon firing at a target, its color turns to blue very briefly. For testing purposes, you can activate the object called target and fire at this target and see if it blinks upon being hit), as illustrated on the next figure.

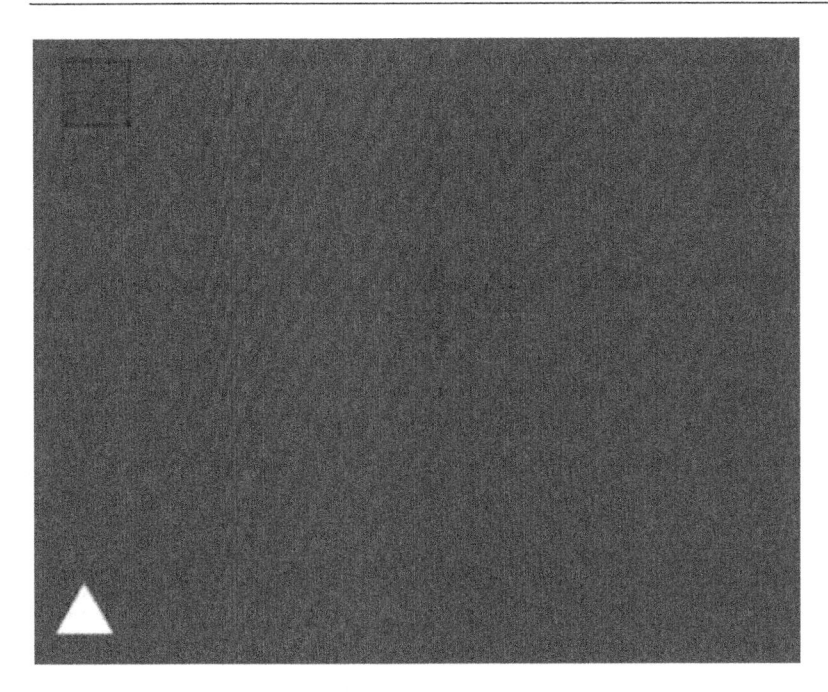

Creating a 2D Shooter (Part2): Adding Special Effects

Figure 237: The target blinks after being hit

Creating a 2D Shooter (Part2): Adding Special Effects

ADDING AN EXPLOSION

Now that the blinking effect is working, we will create an explosion when the target is destroyed; for this purpose, we will use existing sprites, and then sequence them to create an animation (or an animated sprite); when the target is destroyed, this animated sprite will be spawn at the target's position and subsequently removed once the explosion animation is complete.

- Please open the resource pack provided with this book.

- Import the texture called **explosion.png** from the resource pack folder to the **Project** window in Unity (e.g., drag and drop).

- After importing the texture, Unity will create a new asset called **explosion** in the **Project** window.

Figure 238: Importing the explosion sprite sheet

- Using the **Inspector**, change its **Sprite Mode** properties to **Multiple**, as illustrated on the next figure:

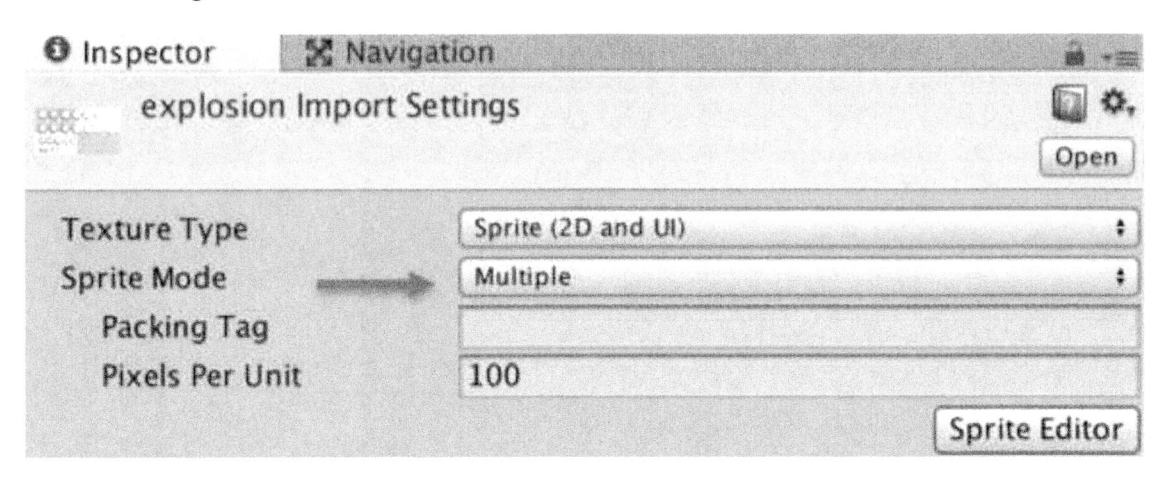

Figure 239: Importing the explosion sprite sheet

- By modifying this property, we indicate that this image includes possible sub-images to be generated for our animation.

- Please click on the button called **Apply** located in the bottom-right corner of the **Inspector** window, as described in the next figure.

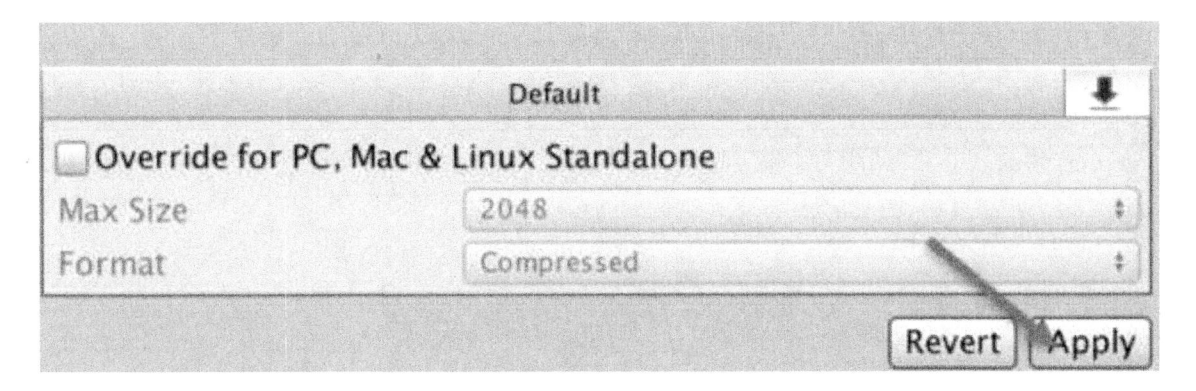

Creating a 2D Shooter (Part2): Adding Special Effects

Figure 240: Applying changes

- Then click on the button called **Sprite Editor** (as illustrated on the next figure).

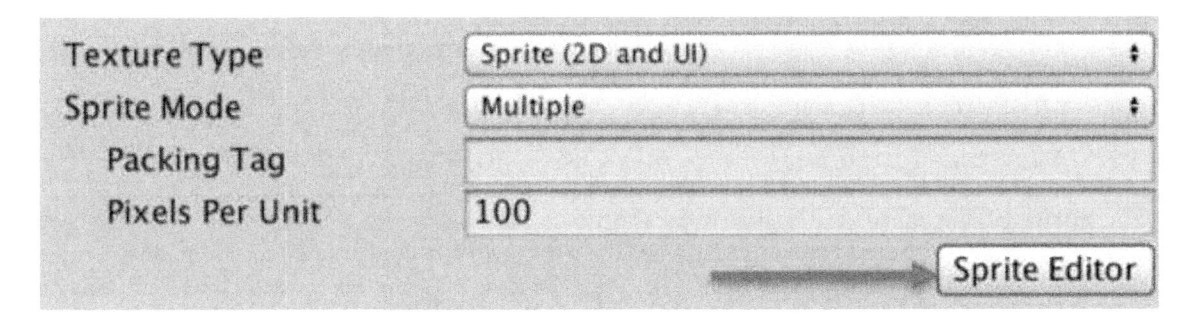

Figure 241: Opening the Sprite Editor (part 1)

- This should open the **Sprite Editor** window.

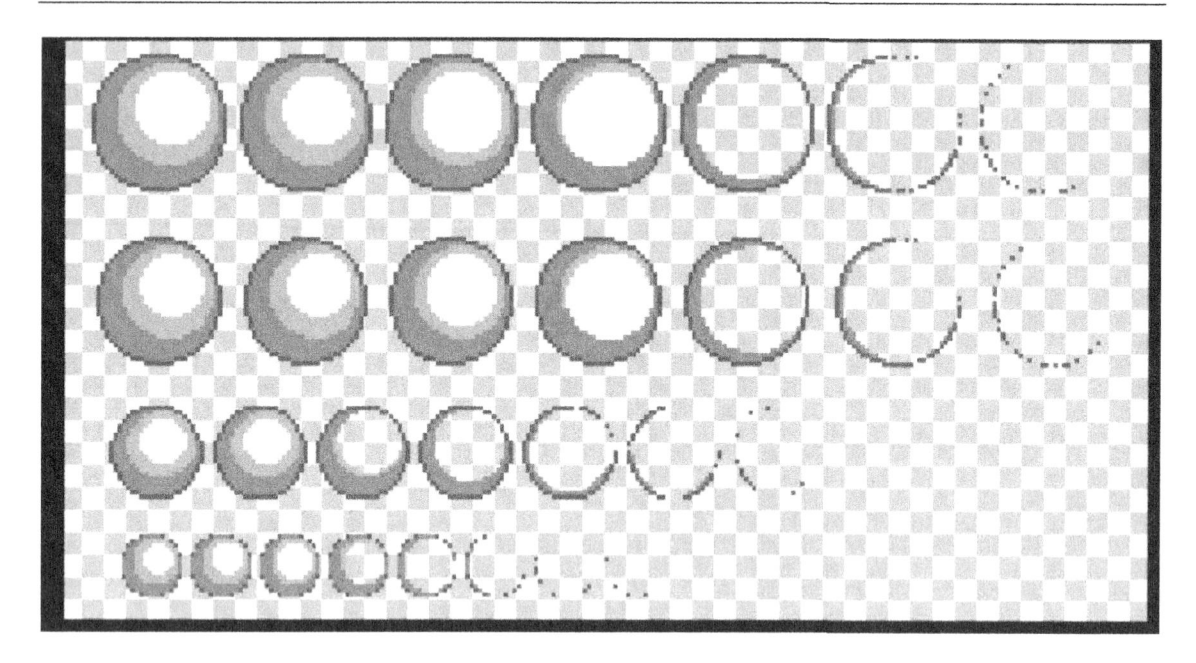

Creating a 2D Shooter (Part2): Adding Special Effects

Figure 242: Opening the Sprite Editor (part 2)

> The **Sprite Editor** makes it possible to edit sprites; in our case, we have imported a sprite sheet: an image made-up of other sub-images; what we want is to extract some of these images in order to create our animation. The idea is to "slice" this image (e.g., the sprite sheet) into sub-images and then to create an animation based on these "slices".

- When the **Sprite Editor** window opens, please click on the button called **Slice** located in the top-left corner of the **Sprite Editor** window.

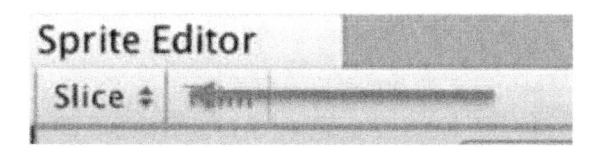

Figure 243: Clicking the Slice button

- A new window will appear.

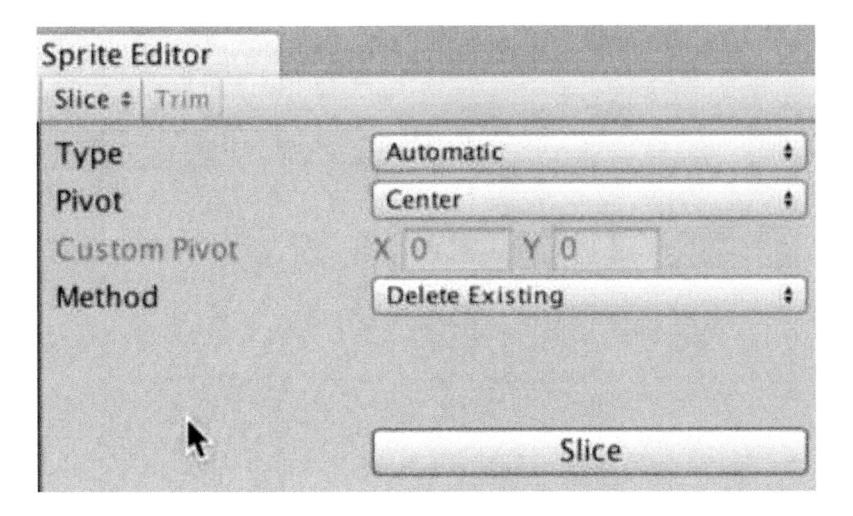

Creating a 2D Shooter (Part2): Adding Special Effects

Figure 244: Slicing the sprite sheet (part 1)

- Please modify its settings as per the next figure.

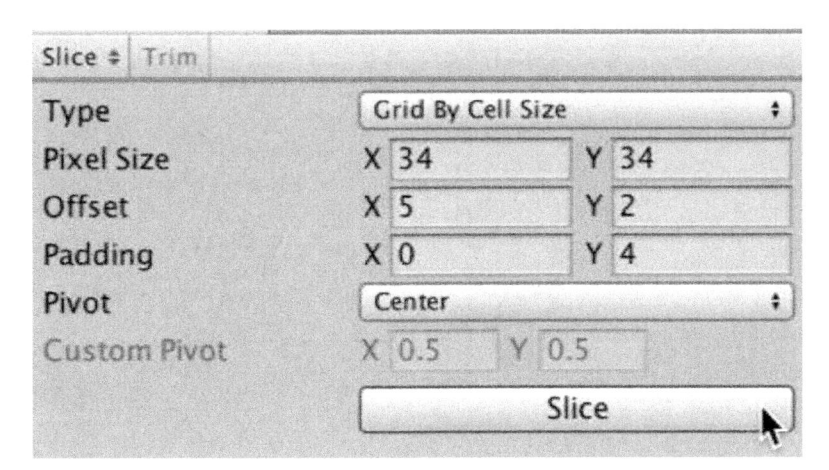

Figure 245: Slicing the sprite sheet (part 2)

The idea of this window is to specify how to capture the sub-images within.

- **Type**: By specifying "**Grid By Cell Size**" we mention that these are laid out as a grid.

- **Pixel Size**: Each sub-image (or sprite) is **34** by **34** pixels.

- **Offset**: For each row, there is a horizontal offset of 5 pixels and a vertical offset of 2 pixels from the start of the image (i.e., from the top-left corner).

- **Padding**: There is also padding between each cells, 0 horizontally and 4 pixels vertically.

- **Pivot**: If an image is rotated, the pivot used for this rotation will be its **center**, by default.

[455]

Creating a 2D Shooter (Part2): Adding Special Effects

Once this is done, you can press the button called **Slice**, to actually slice the image.

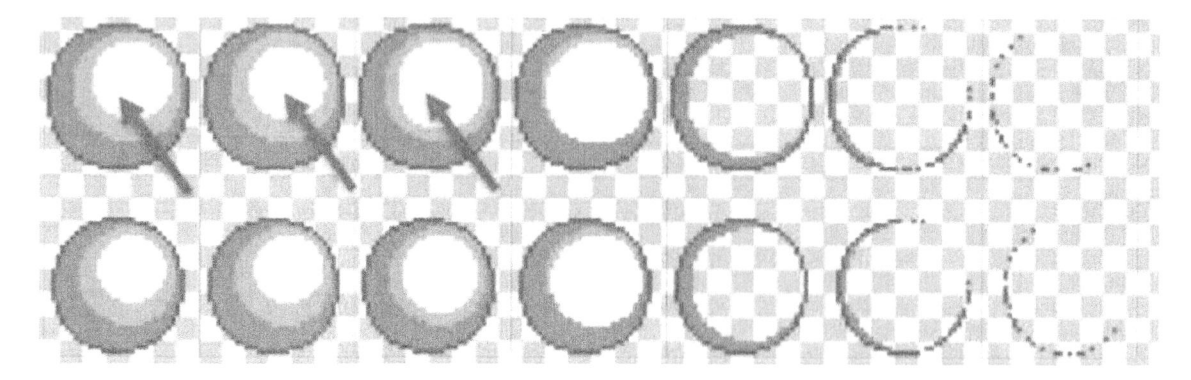

Figure 246: Slicing the sprite sheet (part 3)

- As you can see, we now have managed to define the sub-images from the original file. Each of these is defined by a grey square.

- Once this is done, you can, click on the button called **Apply** at the top of the **Sprite Editor** window.

Figure 247: Applying the slicing settings

- If you look in the **Project** window, you should now see that the original image for the explosion has now turned into a folder with several sprites.

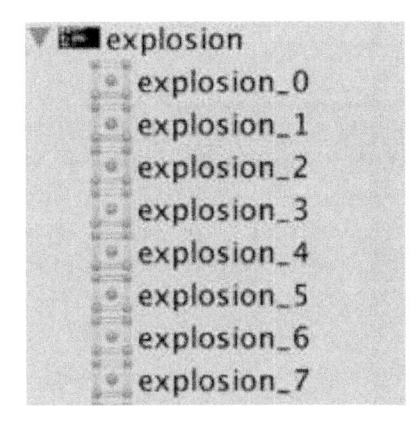

Creating a 2D Shooter (Part2): Adding Special Effects

Figure 248: The slices (sprites) from the original image

- If you click on the individual sprites in the list (e.g., **explosion_0**) and look at the **Inspector** window, you will be able to see what they look like; for example, **explosion_0**, may look like the next figure:

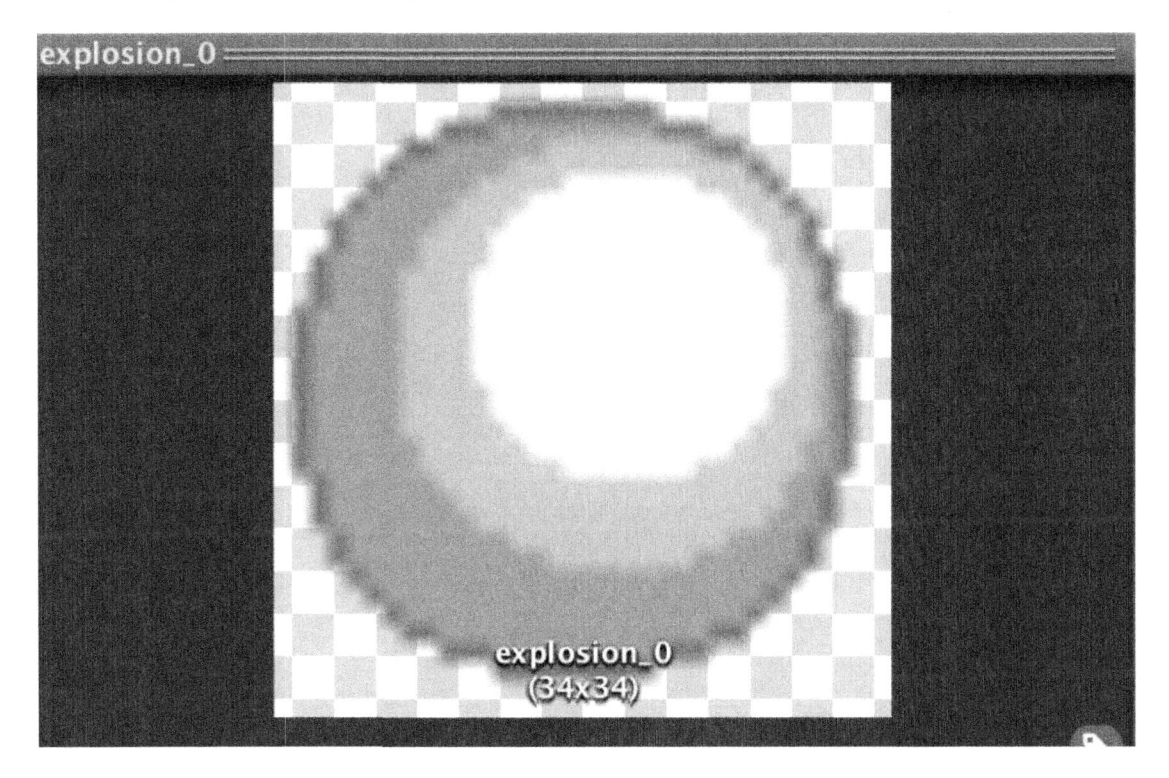

Figure 249: Visualizing the sprite explosion_0

Next, we will create an animation from the first seven sprites; if you remember well, the first row of the original image (i.e., the sprite sheet) included seven sprites that made up the animation that we needed; so now we will create an animation from these images.

[457]

Creating a 2D Shooter (Part2): Adding Special Effects

> Remember, an animation is a succession of sprites that, put together, give the illusion of movement.

- From the **Project** window, please select the seven first sprites (**explosion0, eplosion2, ..., explosion 6**) that we have created. To select all of these sprites, you can **left-click** on the first sprite (i.e., **explosion_0**), then press **CTRL** and then left-click on the six other sprites individually, as illustrated on the next figure. Alternatively, you can also **left-click** on the first sprite, and then press **SHIFT,** and left-click on the last sprite (i.e., **explosion_6**).

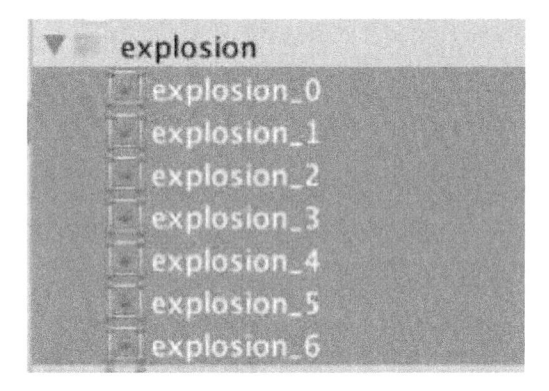

Figure 250: Selecting the seven sprites for the animation

- Once the seven sprites have been selected, please drag and drop these sprites to the **Scene** view, so that Unity can recognise this sequence of sprites (and save them) as an animation.

- As you drag these sprites to the **Scene** view, the mouse cursor will change to display the message <**Multiple**>, as illustrated on the next figure.

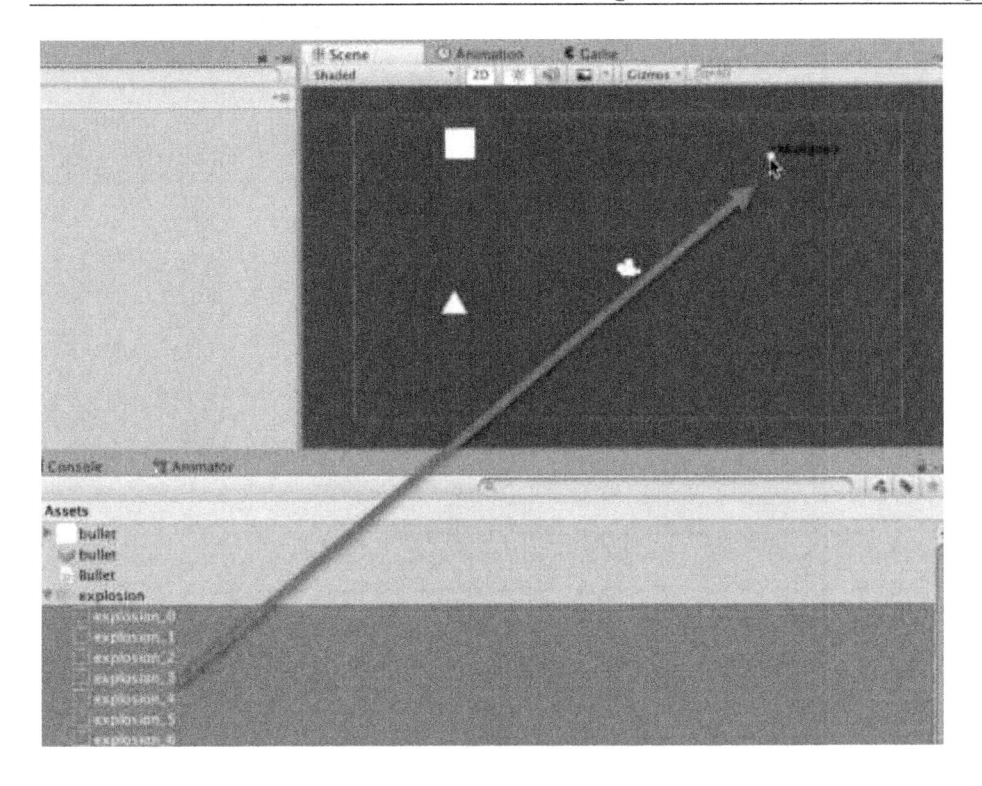

Creating a 2D Shooter (Part2): Adding Special Effects

- Once you have dropped the sprites in the **Scene** view, a new window will appear, asking you to save the resulting animation.

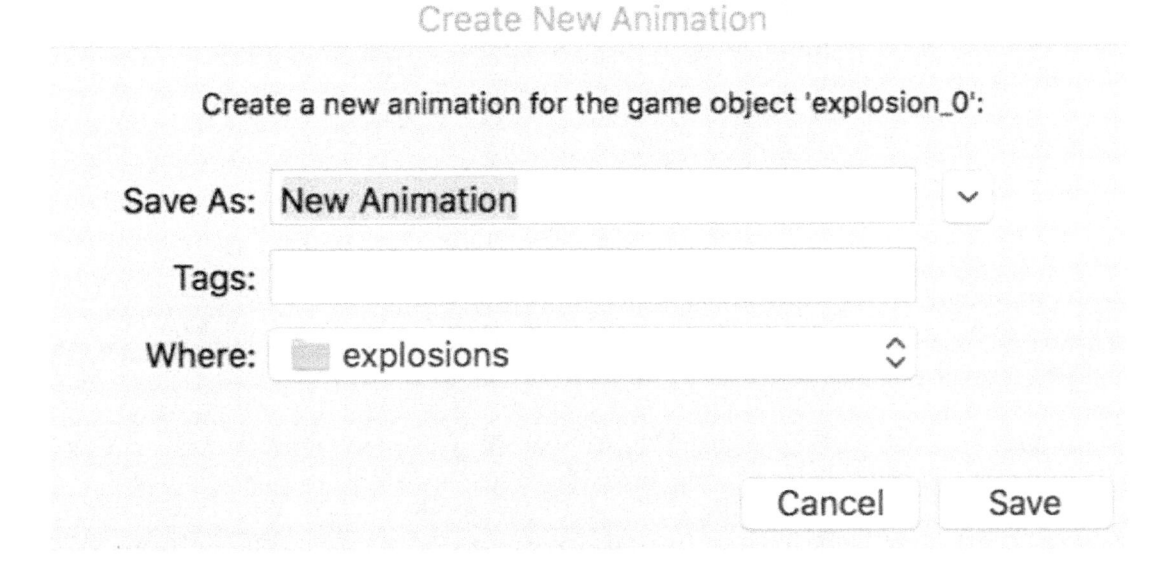

Figure 251: Saving the animation

- You can call this animation **explosion_animated_1** (or any other name of your choice) and then click on the button **Save**, in the same window.

[459]

Creating a 2D Shooter (Part2): Adding Special Effects

- This will create three different assets: (1) a new object called **explosion_0** in the **Hierarchy**, (2) an animation called **explosion_animated_1** in the **Project** window, and (3) an **Animator Controller** called **explosion_0** in the **Project** window.

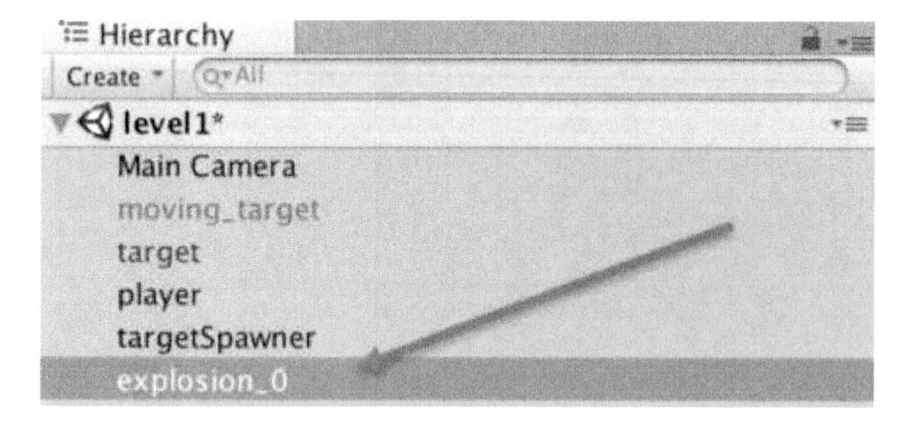

Figure 252: A new object created from the animation

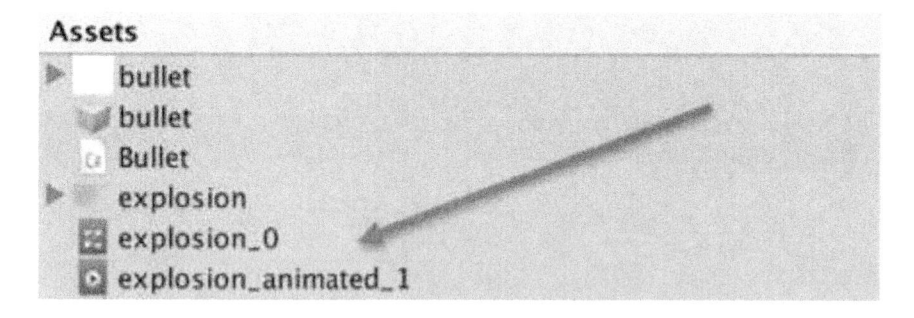

Figure 253: New assets created in the Project window

- In the **Hierarchy** window, please rename the object that you have just created (i.e., **explosion_0**) **explosion**.

If you play the scene, you should see the animated explosion, where you have dragged and dropped the animation in the scene.

You may also notice that the explosion is actually smaller than the target object; so we will rescale the explosion (so that it matches the size of the target) and also create a prefab from it.

- Please select the object called **explosion** in the **Hierarchy**, and, using the **Inspector**, change its scale to **(3.5, 3.5, 1)**;

You may also have noticed that this animation (i.e., the explosion) is looping continuously; however, for our game, we just want it to be played once; so we will modify the animation for the explosion.

Creating a 2D Shooter (Part2): Adding Special Effects

- Using the **Project** window, locate the file called **explosion_animated_1**.

> Note that you can use the search window located at the top of the **Project** to look for specific assets, and to find them quickly, as described in the next figure.

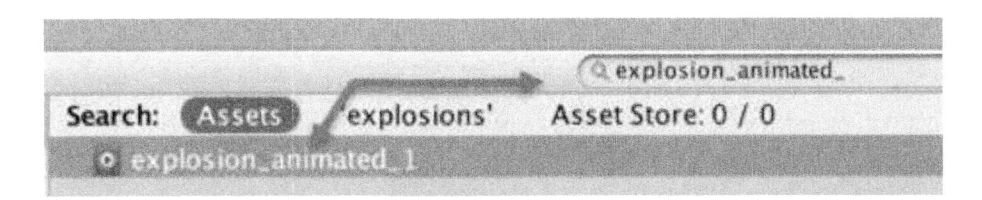

Figure 254: Looking for the explosion animation

- As you left-click on this asset in the **Project** window (i.e., **explosion_animated_1**), you can see its properties in the **Inspector** window.

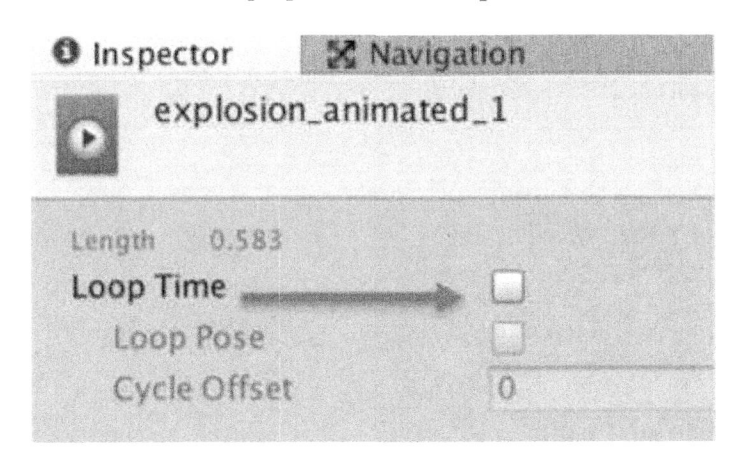

Figure 255: Modifying the explosion animation

- Please, set its attribute **Loop Time** to **false** (i.e., unticked); this means that the animation should not loop.

- Play the scene again, and you should see that the animation is played only once this time.

Once this is done, we just need to create a prefab from this explosion, as we will then instantiate this **explosion** prefab whenever a target is destroyed.

- Please clear the search field in the **Project** view, if you have used it earlier.

Creating a 2D Shooter (Part2): Adding Special Effects

Figure 256: Clearing the search field for the Project view

- Please drag and drop the object called **explosion** from the **Hierarchy** to the **Project** window. This will create a new prefab called **explosion**.

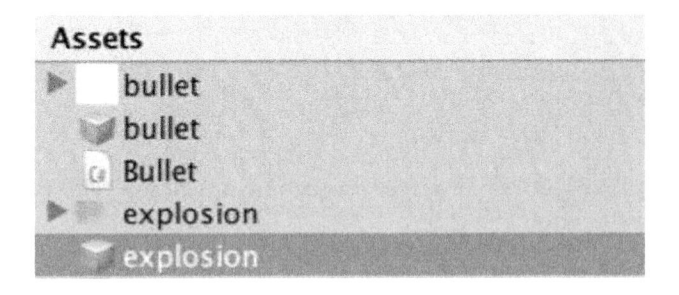

Figure 257: Creating the prefab called explosion

- You can then remove (i.e. delete or deactivate) the object called **explosion** form the **Hierarchy** now (since we have a corresponding prefab now). To do so, you can use the **SUP** or **DEL** keys on your keyboard.

We will then modify the script **ManageTargetHealth**, so that this prefab (i.e., **explosion**) is created at the point of impact between a bullet and a target.

- Please open the script **ManageTargetHealth**.
- Add the following code at the beginning of the script (new code in bold).

```
public float timer;
public Color previousColor;
public GameObject explosion;
```

- Add the following code to the function **destroyTarget** (new code in bold).

```
GameObject exp = (GameObject)(Instantiate (explosion, transform.position, Quaternion.identity));
Destroy (exp, .5f);
Destroy (gameObject);
```

In the previous code:

- We instantiate an explosion.
- This explosion is then destroyed after .5 seconds.

[462]

Once this is done:

- Please save your script.
- In the **Project** window, select the prefab called **target**.
- Using the **Inspector**, scroll down to the component **ManageTargetHealth**.
- Click to the right of the attribute **Explosion**, as illustrated in the next figure

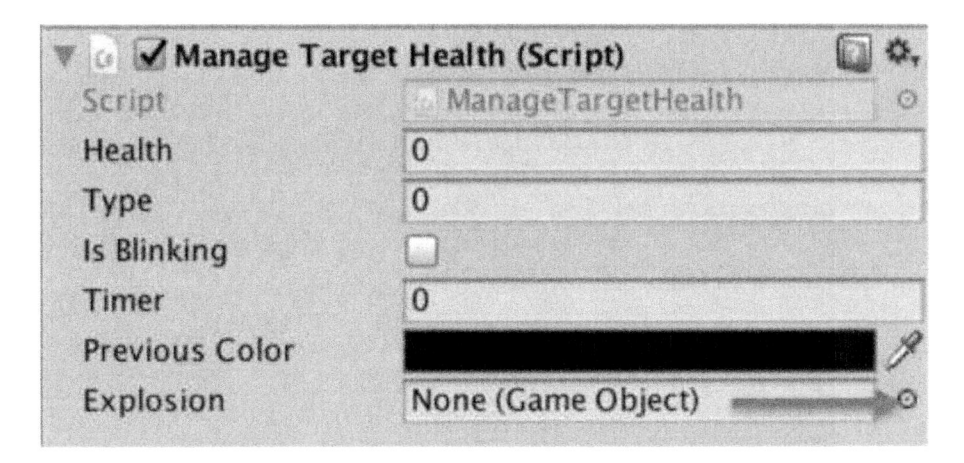

- Using the new window, search for and select the prefab called **explosion**.

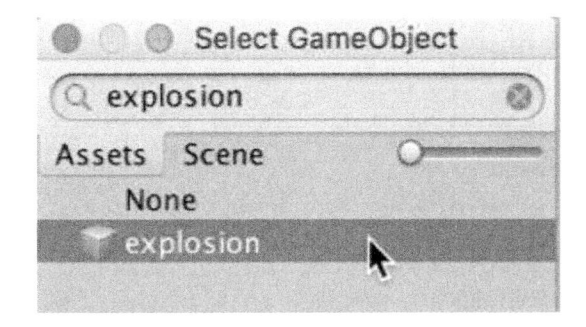

Figure 258: Selecting the explosion

Please repeat these steps for the prefab **moving_target**:

- In Unity, select the prefab **moving_target**.
- Using the **Inspector**, scroll down to the component **ManageTargetHealth**.
- Click to the right of the attribute **Explosion**.
- Using the new window, search and select the prefab called **explosion**.

Creating a 2D Shooter (Part2): Adding Special Effects

Before we can play our scene, we can delete (or deactivate) the explosion that is already present in the scene.

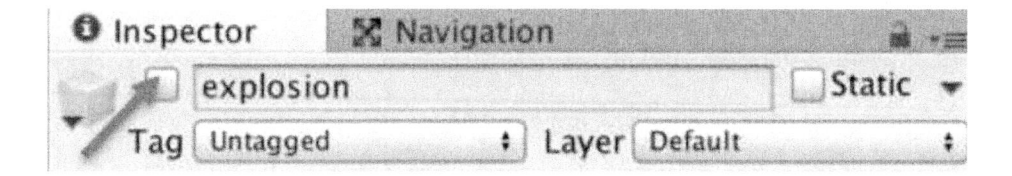

Figure 259: Deactivating the explosion present in the scene

Once this is done, you can play the scene. As you shoot at the static target, you should see an explosion after it has been hit twice; this explosion should then disappear after a few milliseconds.

CREATING A SCROLLING BACKGROUND

Ok, so now that we have created a moving object, we will start to create a moving background to give the illusion of movement; for this, we will do the following:

- Import a texture for our background.
- Modify its properties, so that it can be made scrollable.
- Apply this texture to a **Quad** object.
- Create a script that will make this texture scroll atop the **Quad** object.

So let's get started:

- Please locate the resource pack in your file system.
- Import the texture called **moving_bg_tile** to Unity's **Project** window.

Figure 260: Importing the scrolling background

Once this is done, please select this asset (i.e., **moving_bg_tile**) from the **Project** window and use the **Inspector** window to set its attributes as follows:

- **Texture Type: Texture** (we use a texture here, as textures can be made scrollable).
- **Wrap Mode: Repeat** (this is also so that the texture can be made scrollable).

Creating a 2D Shooter (Part2): Adding Special Effects

Figure 261: Setting the attributes of the scrolling background

- Once this is done, please click on the button **Apply** located at the bottom of the **Inspector** window, to apply these changes.

Next we will create a new object for our background and apply the texture to it:

- Please create a new **Quad** object (**GameObject | 3D Object | Quad**).

- Using the **Hierarchy**, rename this object **moving_background**.

- Drag and drop the texture **moving_bg_tile** from the **Project** window to this object in the **Hierarchy**.

- Rescale this object (i.e., **moving_background**) by changing its scale properties to **(40, 20, 1)**.

- Change its position to **(0, 0, 0)** so that its centre is close to the centre of the screen, as illustrated in the next figure.

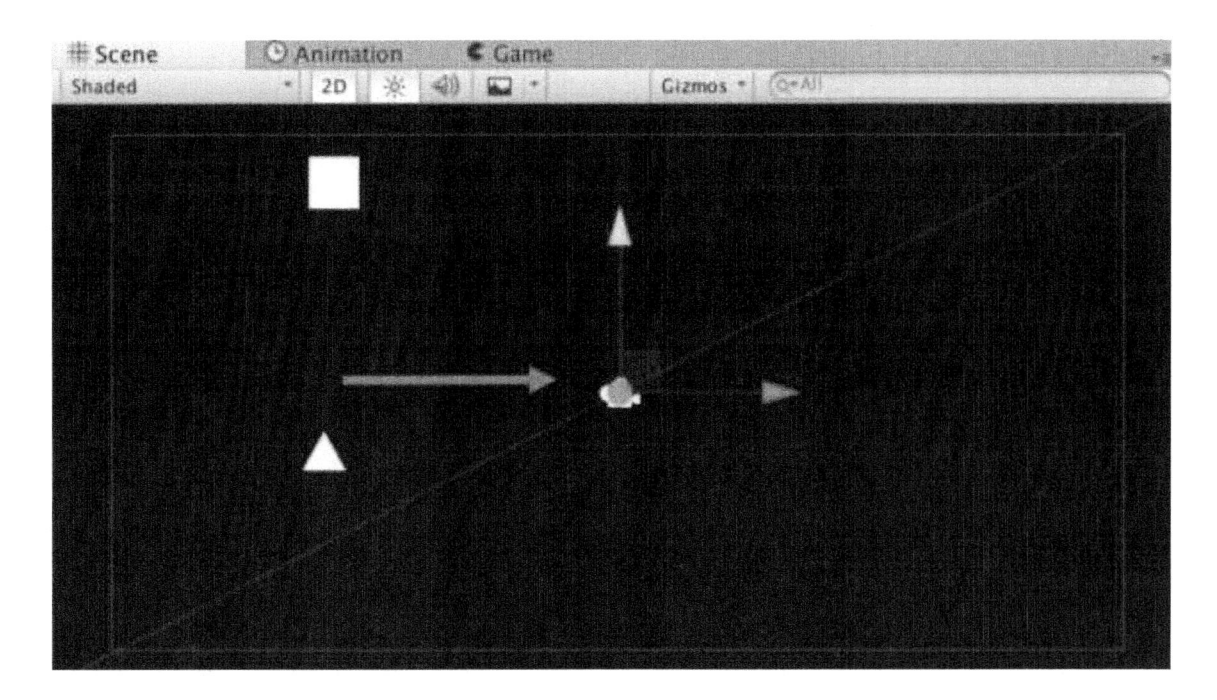

Creating a 2D Shooter (Part2): Adding Special Effects

Figure 262: Aligning the moving background with the spaceship

- To check that this is correct, you can look at the game view, and check that the background fills-up the screen (if not, you can scale-up the background a bit more).

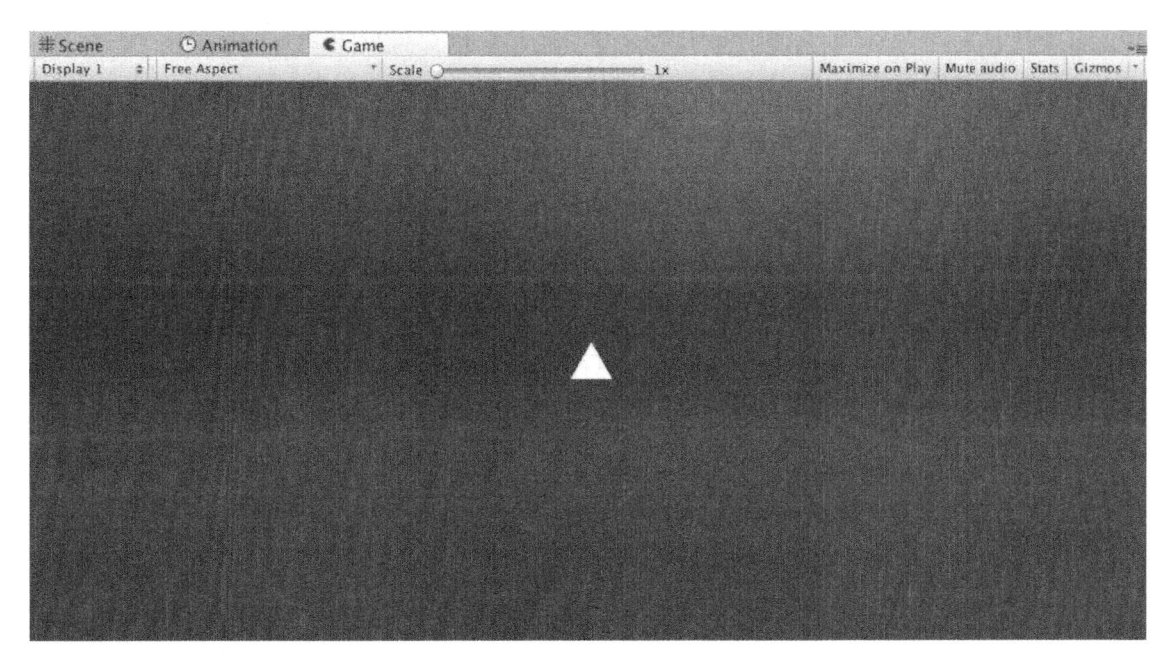

Figure 263: Checking the position of the moving background

[467]

Next, we will create a script that will perform the scrolling for us:

- Please create a new C# script and call it **ScrollingBackground**.
- Add the following code to it, in the function **Update** (new code in bold).

```
void Update ()
{
    GetComponent<Renderer>().material.mainTextureOffset = new Vector2 (0,0.5f*Time.time);
}
```

In the previous code,

- We access the **Renderer** component of the object linked to the script. This component can be used to modify the way a texture is displayed; in our case, we will manage its vertical offset.

- We then access the main texture (the texture that we have just added to the Quad).

- We finally modify the vertical offset for this texture; in other words, we move it along the y-axis at .5 units per seconds (this would be 50 pixels per seconds, since our import settings for the background specified 100 pixels per units).

Once this is done; please save your code, check that it is error-free, and drag and drop this scrip on the object called **moving_background**.

- If you select the object **moving_background** in the **Hierarchy** and then look at the **Inspector** window, you should see that it includes the component **ScrollingBackground**.

Please play the scene and you should see that the background is actually scrolling vertically. However, you may also notice that the scene is quite dark, preventing you from seeing the background clearly.

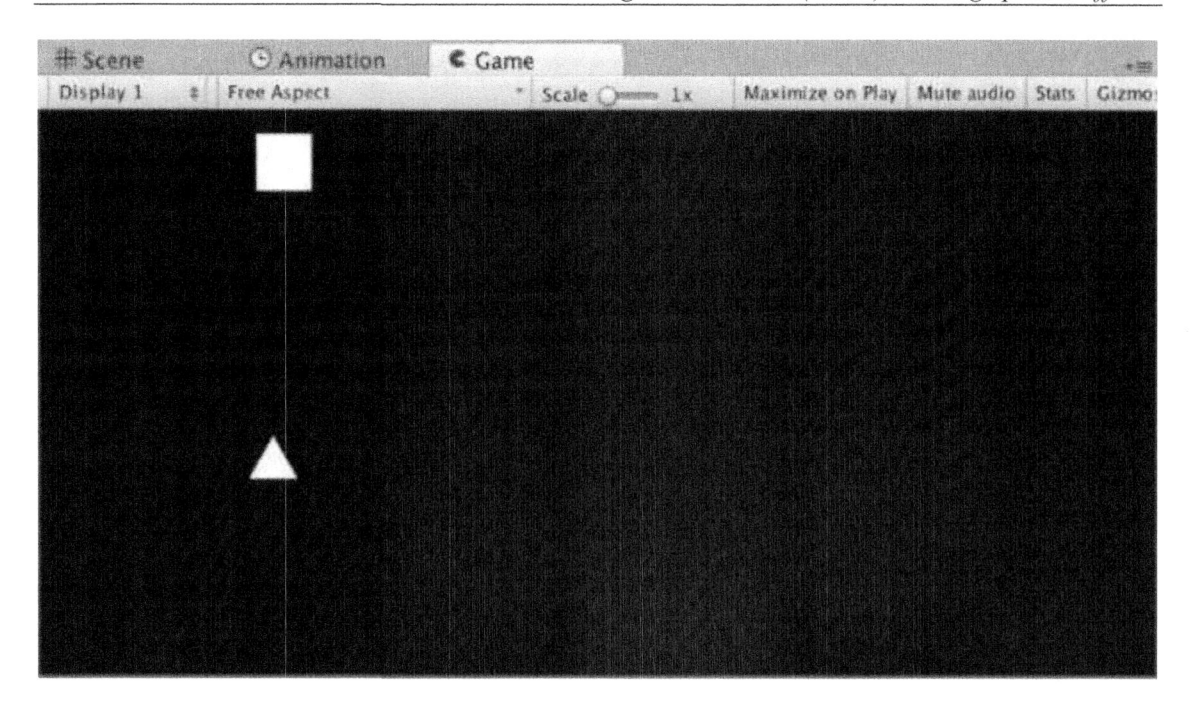

Creating a 2D Shooter (Part2): Adding Special Effects

Figure 264: The scene before adding light

So we could add some light to the scene to solve this issue, as follows:

- Please select **GameObject | Light | Directional Light** from the top menu.
- This will create a new object called **Directional Light**.
- Rename this object **light**.
- Then, select it, and, using the **Inspector** window, change its rotation to **(0,0,0)** and its position to **(0,0,0)**. You can also change its intensity if you wish.

You can test the scene again and the scene should be much brighter.

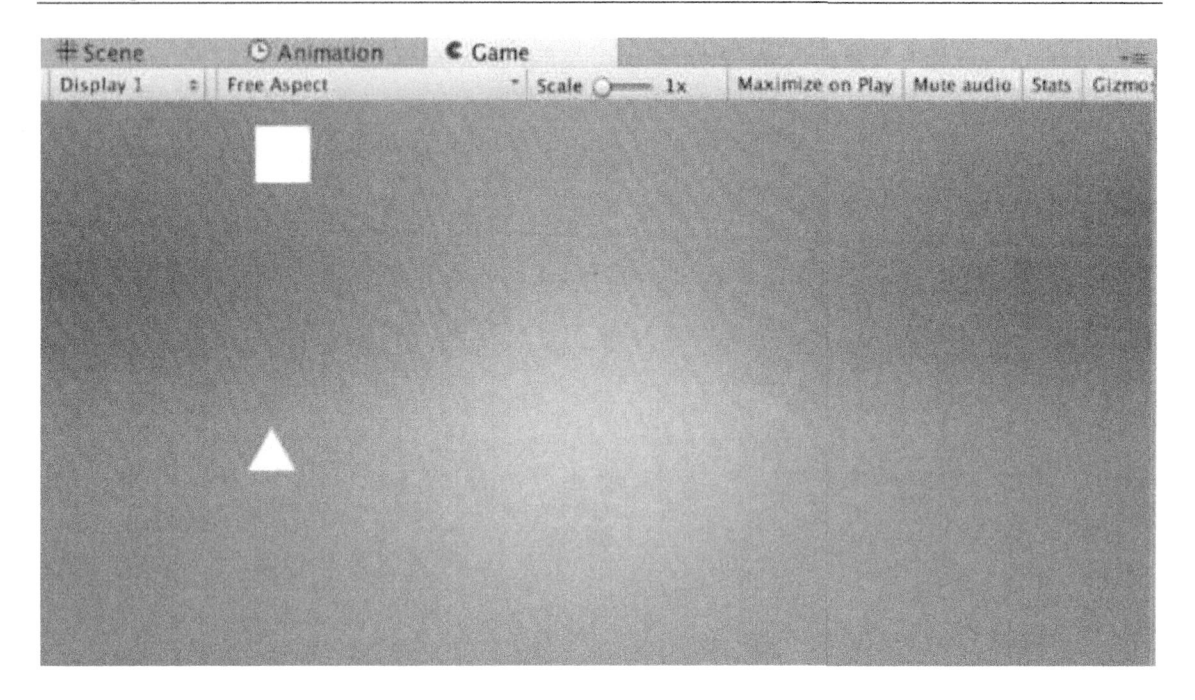

Creating a 2D Shooter (Part2): Adding Special Effects

Figure 265: The scene after adding light

LEVEL ROUNDUP

Well, this is it!

In this chapter, we have learned about creating simple but powerful visual effects, including a blinking object, explosions made from sprites, along with a scrolling. So, we have, by now, a very simple but almost complete 2D shooter game.

Checklist

> You can consider moving to the next chapter if you can do the following:
>
> - Slice a sprite sheet.
> - Create an animation from a sprite.
> - Create a scrolling background.

Quiz

It's now time to check your knowledge with a quiz. So please try to answer the following questions (or specify whether the statements are correct or incorrect). The solutions are included in your resource pack. Good luck!

1. You can select multiple assets by using CTRL + left-click.

2. You can select multiple assets by using SHIFT + left-click.

3. You can modify (i.e., change the color of pixels of) a sprite using the **Sprite Editor**.

4. For an image to be sliced, its **Sprite Mode** attribute should be set to **Single**.

5. You can create a new button, by selecting **GameObject | Text** from the top menu.

6. The following code will change the color of a sprite to red.

```
GetComponent<SpriteRenderer> ().color = Color.red;
```

7. The following code will scroll a texture vertically.

```
GetComponent<Renderer>().material.mainTextureOffset = new Vector2 (0.5f*Time.time,0);
```

8. The following code will scroll a texture horizontally.

```
GetComponent<Renderer>().material.mainTextureOffset = new Vector2 (0,0.5f*Time.time);
```

9. To create an animation from existing sprites, you need to select these sprites, and then select: **GameObject | New Animation**.

10. To create a directional light, you can select: **GameObject | Light | Directional Light**.

Creating a 2D Shooter (Part2): Adding Special Effects

Answers to the Quiz

1. You can select multiple assets by using CTRL + left-click. **TRUE**

2. You can select multiple assets by using SHIFT + left-click. **TRUE**

3. You can modify (i.e., change the color of pixels of) a sprite using the **Sprite Editor**. **FALSE**

4. For an image to be sliced, its **Sprite Mode** attribute should be set to **Single**. **FALSE**

5. You can create a new button, by selecting **GameObject | Text** from the top menu. **FALSE**

6. The following code will change the color of a sprite to red. **TRUE**

```
GetComponent<SpriteRenderer> ().color = Color.red;
```

7. The following code will scroll a texture vertically. **FALSE**

```
GetComponent<Renderer>().material.mainTextureOffset = new Vector2 (0.5f*Time.time,0);
```

8. The following code will scroll a texture horizontally. **FALSE**

```
GetComponent<Renderer>().material.mainTextureOffset = new Vector2 (0,0.5f*Time.time);
```

9. To create an animation from existing sprites, you need to select these sprites, and then select: **GameObject | New Animation**. **FALSE**

10. To create a directional light, you can select: **GameObject | Light | Directional Light**. **TRUE**

Challenge 1

Now that you have managed to complete this chapter and that you have improved your skills, let's do the following:

- Create your own background with the image editor of your choice, and use it as a scrolling background for the game.
- Modify the blinking color and the blinking speed used when a target has been hit.

12
CREATING A 2D SHOOTER (PART 3): ADDING AI AND WEAPONS

In this section, we will improve our game by including additional features that will help to keep the spaceship onscreen, to manage its health levels, and to also make the game more challenging with some AI-driven NPCs.

After completing this chapter, you will be able to:

- Check if the player is in the field of view of the camera.
- Apply damage to the spaceship and manage the player's health.
- Include some artificial intelligence to the NPCs.
- Trigger attacks from the NPCs when the player is detected.

INTRODUCTION

In this chapter we will improve the current game by including a few add-ons:

- We will detect if the player is outside the camera's field of view and ensure that it is always visible.

- We will create NPCs, each with artificial intelligence, that will be moving horizontally and shoot at the player.

- We will also manage the player's health and detect when the spaceship has been hit or when it has collided with targets.

KEEPING THE PLAYER IN THE FIELD OF VIEW

So, all works well so far; the only thing is that, as you may have noticed, the player might be going off-screen, at times, and become invisible; so we will build a mechanism that will solve this issue; we will proceed as follows:

- We will need to detect when the player is no longer in the camera's field of view.

- For this purpose, we will need to translate the **world position** of the player into its position in relation to the camera view.

- So, we will convert the position of the player to the actual camera view port.

- We will then ensure that this position, in the camera view, is within the field of view of the camera; the position of the player, if the player is outside the view, may be modified if need be, so that it is no less that 0, but no more than 1. This is because, the position of objects, in the camera view, is using x and y coordinates that range from 0 to 1; for example, along the x-axis, 0 means the left side of the screen, and 1, means the right side of the screen.

- Once we have made sure that the player is in the field of view, we can then convert this position from the referential defined by the camera view (between 0 and 1) to a world position (from 0 to infinity).

Ok, so let's get started:

- Please open the script called **MovePlayer**.

- Add the following code to the function **Update** (at the end of the function).

```
Vector3 viewPortPosition = Camera.main.WorldToViewportPoint(transform.position);
viewPortPosition.x = Mathf.Clamp01(viewPortPosition.x);
viewPortPosition.y = Mathf.Clamp01(viewPortPosition.y);
transform.position = Camera.main.ViewportToWorldPoint(viewPortPosition);
```

In the previous code:

- We define a new vector called **viewPortPosition**; this vector will be used to define the position of the object in relation to the camera view.

> Note that, in the camera view (or **viewport**), objects' positions are expressed using x and y coordinates that range between 0 and 1; for the x coordinate 0 means the left side of the screen and 1 means the right side of the screen. For the y coordinate 1 means the top of the screen and 0 means the bottom of the screen.

- We then clamp the value of both x and y coordinates; in other words, we ensure that their values are within 0 and 1 (i.e., onscreen); this is done using the built-in function **Clamp01**.

- We then translate this position from the camera view (or viewport) to world coordinates using the function **ViewportToWorldView**.

> In the previous code, what we have effectively done is a change of referential from the world view, to the camera view, and then back to the world view.

Please check your code and test the scene, you will notice that the player is now always onscreen; however, only half of the player is displayed when you try to move beyond the camera view, as illustrated in the next figure.

Figure 266: Improving position clamping

We could fix this as follows:

- Determine the size of our sprite on the x- and y–axis.

- Calculate how this size can be translated in the view port settings (i.e., what proportion of the screen the sprite would occupy).

- Clamp the player to the size of the screen (height or width) minus the size of the sprite.

Creating a 2D Shooter (Part 3): Adding AI and Weapons

- Translate this clamping to world view coordinates.

Please add (or comment) the following code to the script **MovePlayer**:

```
//Vector3 viewPortPosition = Camera.main.WorldToViewportPoint(transform.position);
//viewPortPosition.x = Mathf.Clamp01(viewPortPosition.x);
//viewPortPosition.y = Mathf.Clamp01(viewPortPosition.y);
//transform.position = Camera.main.ViewportToWorldPoint(viewPortPosition);

Vector3 viewPortPosition = Camera.main.WorldToViewportPoint(transform.position);
Vector3 viewPortXDelta = Camera.main.WorldToViewportPoint(transform.position + Vector3.left/2);
Vector3 viewPortYDelta = Camera.main.WorldToViewportPoint(transform.position + Vector3.up/2);
```

In the previous code:

- We comment the previous code.

- We create two new vectors: **viewPortXDelta** and **viewPortYDelta**.

- **viewPortXDelta** will be used to determine the relative size of the sprite along the x axis (i.e., its width). Note that we use **Vector3.left/2** because we want to know the distance between the center of the sprite and its edges (i.e., half its width).

- **viewPortYDelta** will be used to determine the relative size of the sprite along the y axis (i.e., its height). Note that we use **Vector3.up/2** because we want to know the distance between the center of the sprite to its edge (half its height).

> Note that our sprite, at present, has a scale of 1 on all axes; so the magnitude (length) of the vectors **Vector3.up** or **Vector3.left** will effectively describe the width or height of this sprite; however, if the scale had been **2** on the x axis, for example, we would then need to use **Vector3.left** instead of **Vector3.left/2 (i.e., Vector3.left/2** multiplied by 2).

- Please add the following code in the same **Update** function, just after the previous code:

```
float deltaX = viewPortPosition.x - viewPortXDelta.x;
float deltaY = -viewPortPosition.y + viewPortYDelta.y;

viewPortPosition.x = Mathf.Clamp(viewPortPosition.x, 0+deltaX, 1-deltaX);
viewPortPosition.y = Mathf.Clamp(viewPortPosition.y, 0+deltaY, 1-deltaY);
transform.position = Camera.main.ViewportToWorldPoint(viewPortPosition);
```

In the previous code:

- We declare two variables called **deltaX** and **deltaY**; these will be used to determine the actual distance, in the viewport, between the center of the sprite and its edges.

Creating a 2D Shooter (Part 3): Adding AI and Weapons

- We then clamp the position of the sprite using the values that we have calculated earlier; so the minimum x position will be the left side of the screen + half the width of the sprite; the same is done with the y position; all of these changes are done in the viewport referential (i.e., values ranging between 0 and 1)

- As we have done before, these new coordinates are then translated to world view coordinates.

Please save your code and check that it is error-free, and test your game; as you move towards the edges of the screen, you should now see that the player is properly "clamped" to each side of the screen, and that the full triangle is now displayed.

Figure 267: Clamping the player to the bottom-left corner

That's it!

Creating a 2D Shooter (Part 3): Adding AI and Weapons

APPLYING DAMAGE TO THE PLAYER

In this section, we will create code to implement a feature whereby, when the moving targets collide with the player, they destroy the player; in this case, the level should also be restarted automatically.

The process will be as follows:

- We will add collision capabilities to our player.
- We will then detect collision with moving targets.
- We will finally restart the level in case of a collision.

So let's get to it:

- Please add a **Polygon2DCollider** to the player: select the **player** in the **Hierarchy**, then select **Component | Physic2D| Polygon2DCollider** from the top menu. This will add a **Polygon2DCollider** to the object, as illustrated on the next figure.

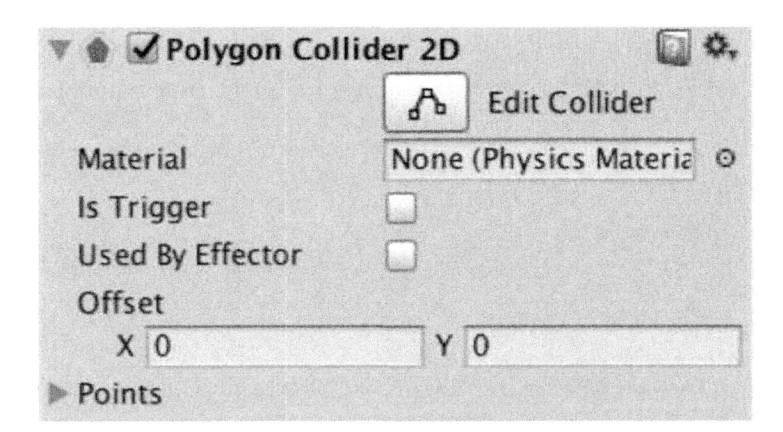

Figure 268: Adding a polygonal collider to the player

In the next sections, the player may be hit by other objects; so the mechanism involved in destroying the player and restarting the game may need to be performed several times (depending on the object that collided with the player); so to centralize this process and to make our code more efficient, we will create a function that manages this aspect of the game (i.e., player colliding with other objects), and add it to a script linked to the player. This way, upon collision with any object, this function will be called accordingly.

- Please create a new script called **ManagePlayerHealth**.
- Add the following code at the beginning of the class.

Creating a 2D Shooter (Part 3): Adding AI and Weapons

```
using UnityEngine.SceneManagement;
```

- Add the following functions at the end of the script (i.e., before the last closing curly bracket).

```
void OnCollisionEnter2D(Collision2D coll)
{
        if (coll.gameObject.tag == "target")
        {
                Destroy (coll.gameObject);
                DestroyPlayer ();
        }

}
void DestroyPlayer()
{
        SceneManager.LoadScene (SceneManager.GetActiveScene().name);
}
```

In the previous code:

- We detect collisions with targets.

- In case the player collides with a target, the target is destroyed, and the function called **DestroyPlayer** is called.

- The function **DestroyPlayer** reloads the current scene.

We can now apply this script:

- Please save your script and check that it is error-free.

- Drag and drop this new script (**ManagePlayerHealth**) on the object called **player** in the **Hierarchy**.

- Once this is done, you can test your scene and check that upon colliding with a moving target, that the scene is restarted.

ADDING ARTIFICIAL INTELLIGENCE

So at this stage, the game works relatively well, and we could also add a bit more challenge to it. So, to make this game more challenging to the player, we will add a few NPCs that will move and attack the player.

The NPC that we will add will be moving horizontally from left to right and it will shoot at the player whenever it is in front of the player (or close to it). It will consist of a simple triangle (the same as we have used for the player), that shoots projectiles towards the player, if the latter is detected.

- From the **Project** window, please drag and drop the asset called **Triangle** to the **Scene** view, as illustrated on the next figure.

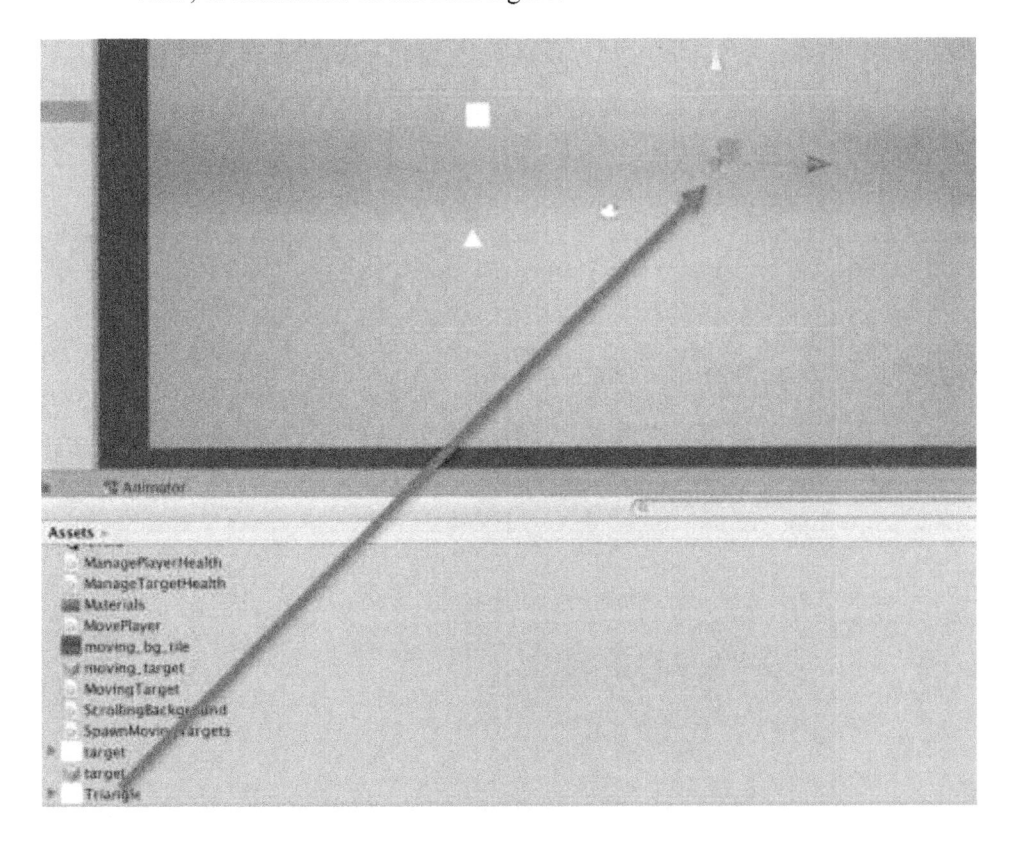

Figure 269: Recycling the triangle to create an NPC.

- This will create a new object called **Triangle** in the **Hierarchy** window.
- Please rename this object **npc1**.

[483]

Creating a 2D Shooter (Part 3): Adding AI and Weapons

- Using the **Inspector**, change the rotation of this object to **(0, 0, 180)**, so that it looks like the next figure.

Figure 270: Rotating the NPC

- Add a **Polygon Collider2D** to this object: select the object **npc1**, and then select the option **Components | Physics2D | PolygonCollider2D** from the top menu.

- Change its tag to **target**, as we have done previously using the **Inspector** window.

At this stage, we just need to make sure that this object, (i.e., **npc1**), can be destroyed in the same way as the targets that we have created earlier. So we will reuse the script called **ManageTargetHealth**, that was previously employed for the other targets.

- Please add the script **ManageTargetHealth** to the object **npc1** (i.e., drag and drop the script from the **Project** window to the object **npc1** in the **Hierarchy**).

- Select the object **npc1**, and then, using the **Hierarchy** window, click to the right of the attribute **Explosion** for the component **ManageTargetHealth**, as illustrated on the next figure.

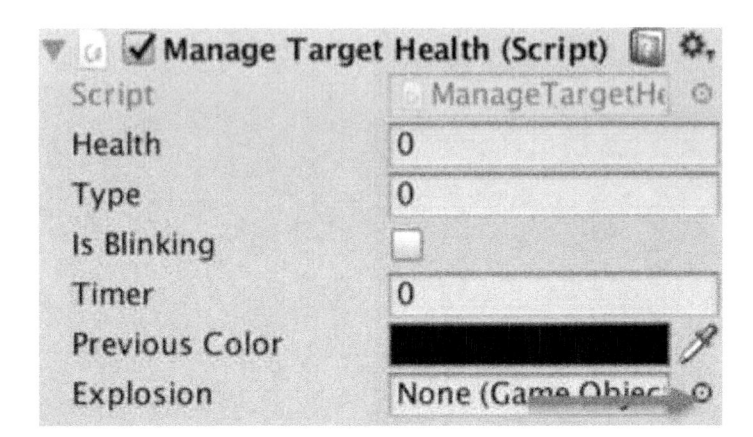

Figure 271: Adding an explosion

- Using the new window, search and select the prefab called **explosion**.

[484]

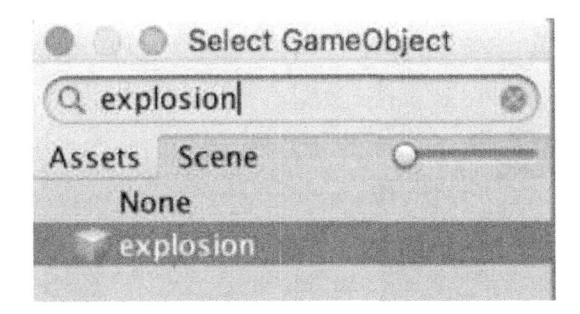

Creating a 2D Shooter (Part 3): Adding AI and Weapons

Figure 272: Choosing an explosion for the NPC

Next, we will create a new script that will be attached to the NPC; in this script, we will add some code that moves the NPC from right to left, and that also ensures that the NPC shoots at the player when it is in front of the player.

- Please create a new script called **MoveNPC**.
- Add the following code at the beginning of the class (new code in bold):

```
public class MoveNPC : MonoBehaviour {
public GameObject bullet;
public float direction = 1.0f;
public float timer;
```

In the previous code:

- We declare three variables.
- The variable **bullet** will be used as a placeholder for the bullet that we want to instantiate when the NPC shoots.
- The variable **direction** will be used to determine in what direction the NPC will be moving.
- The variable **timer** will be employed to determine when the NPC changes direction (e.g., from right to left or vice-versa).

- Please add the following code to the **Update** function.

```
timer += Time.deltaTime;
transform.Translate (Vector3.left *direction* Time.deltaTime * 2);
if (timer >= 2) {direction *= -1; timer = 0;}
```

In the previous code:

Creating a 2D Shooter (Part 3): Adding AI and Weapons

- We increase the variable **timer** by one, every seconds.

- Every second, we also move the NPC horizontally; it is moved to the left initially, as the value of the variable **direction** is **1** at the beginning.

- Then, after 2 seconds, the **direction** is reversed, and the **timer** is initialized back to **0**; so changes in the direction will occur every two seconds.

We can now save our script:

- Please save your code, and check that it is error-free.

- You can then drag and drop this script (i.e., **MoveNPC**) on the object **npc1**.

Once this done you can test the scene:

- Please deactivate the object **target** (i.e., f this is not already done).

- Move the object **npc1** to the upper boundary of the screen, as illustrated on the next figure.

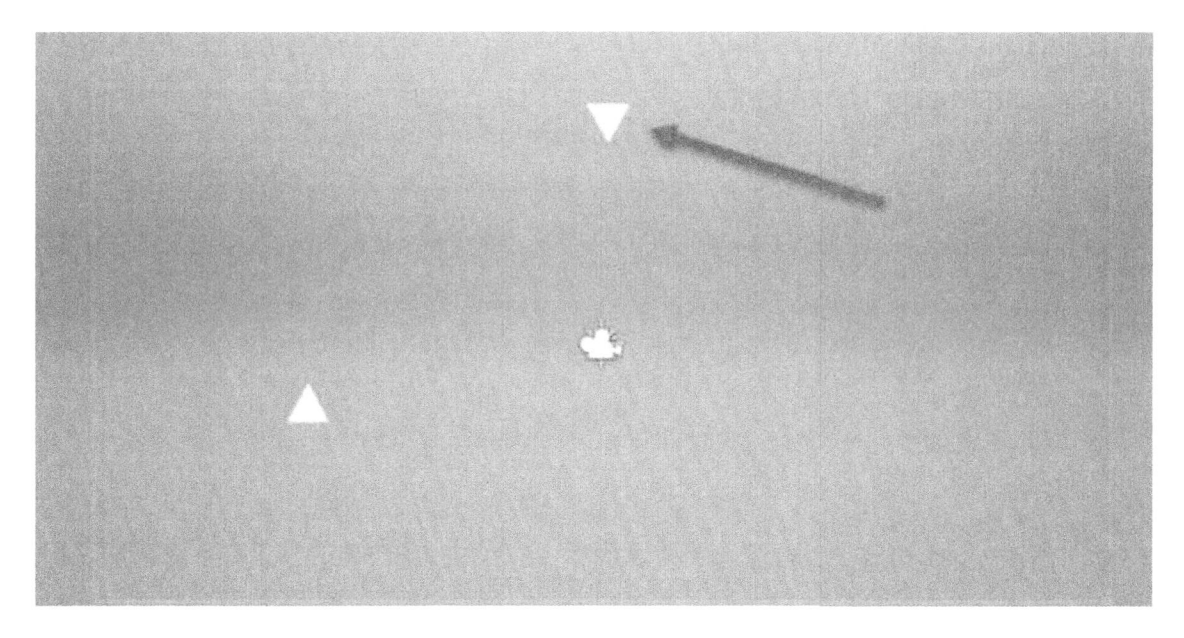

Figure 273: Moving the NPC

- As you play the scene, you should see that the NPC moves from left to right, as illustrated on the next figure.

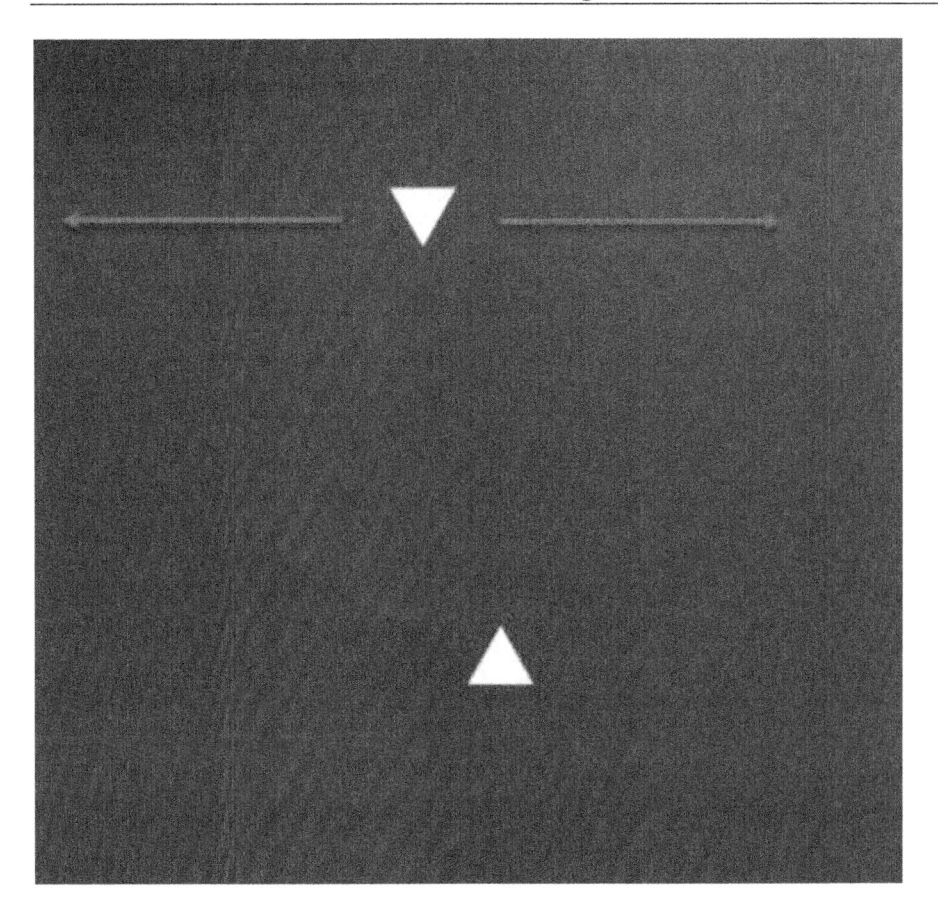

Creating a 2D Shooter (Part 3): Adding AI and Weapons

Figure 274: Testing the NPC's movement

Ok, so now that the NPC can move properly, we will add a feature whereby it shoots at the player when in front of the player. For this purpose, we will proceed as follows:

- Detect when the **NPC** is in front of the player.
- Shoot (i.e., instantiate a bullet prefab that moves towards the player).
- Ensure that the shooting stops after a few milliseconds, when the player is no longer in front of the NPC.

So let's start with this feature:

- Please open the script **MoveNPC**.
- Please add the following code to the function **Update** (new code in bold).

[487]

Creating a 2D Shooter (Part 3): Adding AI and Weapons

```
void Update ()
{
        timer += Time.deltaTime;
        transform.Translate (Vector3.left *direction* Time.deltaTime * 2);
        if (timer >= 2) {direction *= -1; timer = 0;}
        detectPlayer ();
```

This function (i.e., **detectPlayer**) will be called to check if the player is in front of the NPC.

Now let's declare this function by adding the following code to the class, just after the function **Update**.

```
void detectPlayer()
{
        float playerXPosition = GameObject.Find ("player").transform.position.x;
        if (transform.position.x < (playerXPosition + 1) && transform.position.x > (playerXPosition - 1)) Shoot();
}
```

In the previous code, we calculate the player's position on the **x-axis** and we then call the function called **shoot** if the player is in front of the NPC.

We just need to implement the function called **Shoot** now.

- Please add the following code at the end of the class, just after the previous function:

```
void Shoot()
{
        GameObject b = (GameObject)(Instantiate (bullet, transform.position + transform.up*1.5f, Quaternion.identity));
        b.GetComponent<Rigidbody2D> ().AddForce (Vector3.down * 1000);
}
```

In the previous code

- We define a new function called **Shoot**.

- We create a new object called **b** that is based on the variable **bullet** (the variable **bullet** will be initialized later using the **Inspector**).

- This projectile (i.e., the object called **b**) is then propelled downwards, by accessing its **Rigidbody2D** component and by then exerting a downwards force.

Please save your script and check that it is error-free.

Once this is done, we can now initialize the variable **bullet** defined in this script from the **Inspector**:

[488]

Creating a 2D Shooter (Part 3): Adding AI and Weapons

- Please, select the object **npc1** in the **Hierarchy**.

- Using the **Inspector**, click to the right of the attribute called **Bullet** for the script **MoveNPC**, as described on the next figure.

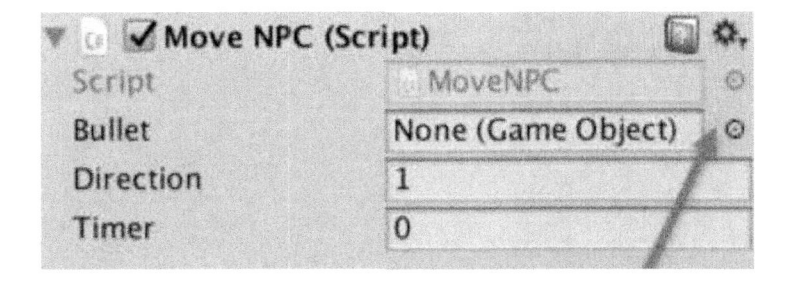

Figure 275: Selecting a bullet for the NPC (part 1)

- Using the new window, search and select the prefab called **bullet**.

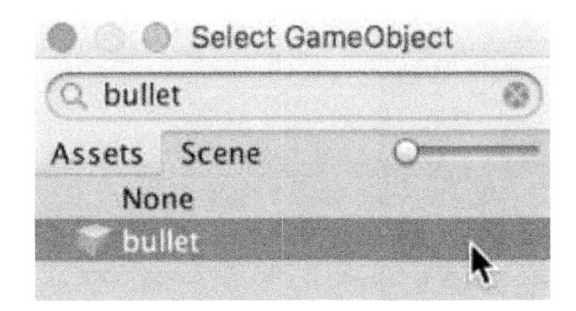

Figure 276: Selecting a bullet for the NPC (part 2)

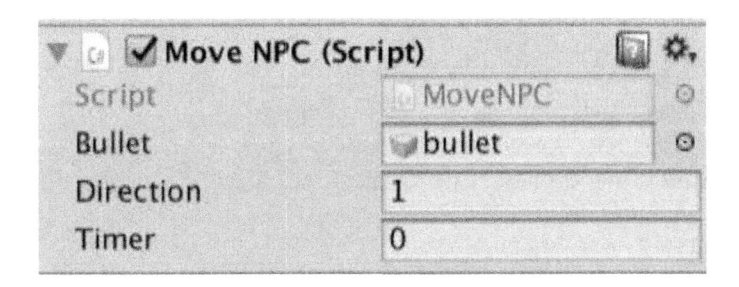

Figure 277: Selecting a bullet for the NPC (part 3)

Now that it is done, you can test the scene and check that the NPC fires bullets in the direction of the player when the player is in front of the NPC.

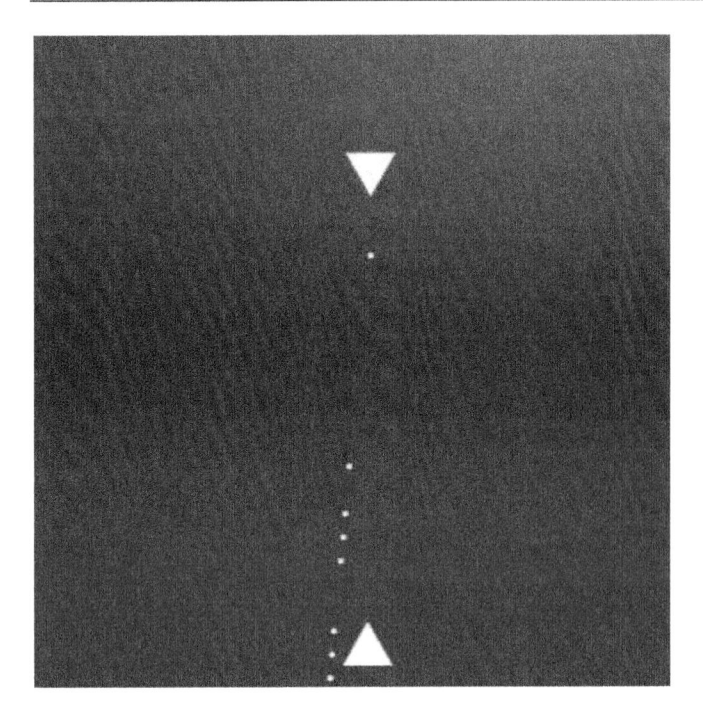

Figure 278: The NPC firing at the player

Now, this works well; however, there are a few things that we could improve, including:

- A slower firing rate for the NPC.

- Collision detection with the NPC's bullets.

- Restarting the level when the player has been shot.

Now, to start with, we will make sure that the game restarts if the player is hit by a bullet; to do so, we just need to add a tag to the bullets fired by the NPC, and then modify the script called **ManagePlayerHealth** to detect collision with these bullets. So, let's proceed:

- Please select the prefab called **Bullet** in the **Project** window.

- Create a new tag called **bullet**, as we have done earlier.

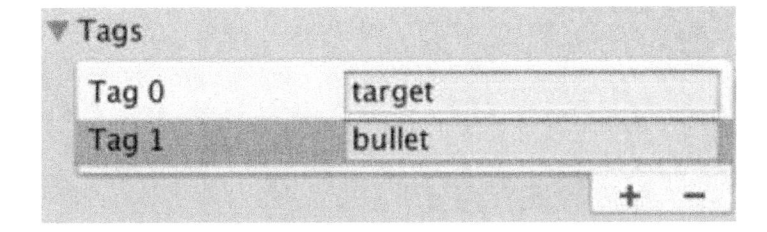

Figure 279: Creating a new tag for bullets

Creating a 2D Shooter (Part 3): Adding AI and Weapons

- Apply this tag to the prefab called **bullet**.

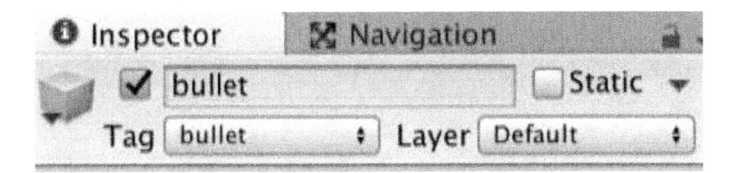

Figure 280: Applying the new tag to the bullet prefab

- Once this is done, please open the script **ManagePlayerHealth**.
- Modify the function **OnCollisionEnter2D** as follows (new code in bold):

```
void OnCollisionEnter2D(Collision2D coll)
{
        if (coll.gameObject.tag == "target" || coll.gameObject.tag == "bullet")
        //if (coll.gameObject.tag == "target")
        {
                Destroy (coll.gameObject);
                DestroyPlayer ();
        }
}
```

In the previous code, we check that the object colliding with the player is either a moving target or a bullet.

Please save your code, check that it is error-free, and then test the scene.

Now that this is working, we can look at the NPC's firing rate: as you test the scene, you may notice that the firing rate of the NPC is quite high; so you can either leave it as it is or modify it, by amending the script **MoveNPC** as follows:

- Please open the script **MoveNPC**.
- Add the following code at the beginning of the class.

```
public bool startShootingTimer = false;
public bool canShoot = true;
public float shootingTimer;
```

- In the previous code, we create three variables that will be used to determine when the NPC can shoot again.
- Please add this code at the beginning of the **Update** function:

[491]

```
if (startShootingTimer)
{
        shootingTimer += Time.deltaTime;
        if (shootingTimer >= .5)
        {
                startShootingTimer = false;
                canShoot = true;
                shootingTimer = 0;
        }
}
```

In the previous code:

- If the NPC has just fired a bullet (i.e., **startShootingTimer** is true), the timer is ticking and its value is increased every second by one.

- If the timer reaches 500 milliseconds, then the timer stops ticking (i.e., **startShootingTimer** is false), and the player can shoot again.

- The timer is also reset to 0.

Now, we just need to modify the function **Shoot**, so that the **timer** starts just after the NPC has fired a bullet and also so that the NPC cannot shoot another bullet for the next 500 milliseconds (i.e., as long as the timer has not reached 500 milliseconds).

- Please modify the function called **Shoot**, in the script **MoveNPC**, as follows (new code in bold):

```
void Shoot()
{
        if (canShoot)
        {
                GameObject b = (GameObject)(Instantiate (bullet, transform.position + transform.up * 1.5f, Quaternion.identity));
                b.GetComponent<Rigidbody2D> ().AddForce (Vector3.down * 1000);
                canShoot = false;
                startShootingTimer = true;
        }
}
```

As you save and complete the code, you may test the scene and check that the NPC fires at a lower rate.

There is one more thing that we could modify in our game: as it is, several of the moving targets may fall on the NPC; however, we could decide to ignore collisions between these boulders and the NPC, otherwise, these targets may accumulate at the top of the screen. To do so, we will

Creating a 2D Shooter (Part 3): Adding AI and Weapons

employ a built-in function called **IgnoreCollision** that will be used on every new moving target, so that collisions between NPCs and moving targets are ignored.

So let's proceed:

- Please create a new C# script called **IgnoreCollision**.

- Open this script.

- Add the following code to the function **Start** (new code in bold):

```
void Start ()
{
        Physics2D.IgnoreCollision        (GetComponent<BoxCollider2D>(),        GameObject.Find
("npc1").GetComponent<PolygonCollider2D> ());
}
```

In the previous code, we use the function **Physics2D.IgnoreCollision** to ignore collisions between the collider from the moving target (this object will be attached to this script) and the collider from the object with the name **npc1**. Although this function has some limitations when used with more than two objects (and we will see how this can be solved later), it is fine for the time being.

Please save your code, and check that the moving targets are not colliding anymore with the NPCs.

Once this is working, the next step will be to instantiate several NPCs at random positions; for example, we could instantiate one of these NPCs at the top of the screen, every 5 seconds; for this purpose, we will proceed as follows:

- We will create an empty object called **NPCSpawner**, that will be in charge of spawning NPCs.

- We will then set-up the **NPCSpawner** object so that NPCs are spawned at regular intervals.

So let's get started:

- Please create a prefab from the object called **npc1** (i.e., drag and drop the object **npc1** to the **Project** window); this will create a prefab called **npc1**.

Figure 281: The new prefab called npc1

- You can delete (or deactivate) the object called **npc1** from the **Hierarchy** window now.

[493]

Creating a 2D Shooter (Part 3): Adding AI and Weapons

- Please create a new empty object and rename it **NPCSpawner**.

- Create a new C# script called **SpawnNPCs** and drag and drop it to the object **NPCSpawner** in the **Hierarchy**.

We can now modify this script:

- Please open the script **NPCSpawner**.

- Add this code at the beginning of the class (new code in bold).

```
public class NPCSpawner : MonoBehaviour {
    public GameObject npc1;
    private float timer, respawnTime;
```

- In the previous code, we declare two variables that will be used to spawn NPCs at regular intervals.

- Please add this code to the **Update** function.

```
void Update ()
{
    timer += Time.deltaTime;
    if (timer >= 1)
    {
        timer = 0;
        SpawnNPC (npc1);

    }
}
```

- In the previous code, we create a timer that is used to spawn a new NPC every second.

- Please add this code at the end of the class (i.e., just before the last closing curly bracket):

```
void SpawnNPC(GameObject typeOfNPC)
{
        float range = Random.Range (-10, 10);//Screen.width);
        Vector3 newPosition = new Vector3 (GameObject.Find("player").transform.position.x + range, transform.position.y, 0);
        GameObject newNPC = (GameObject)(Instantiate (npc1, newPosition, Quaternion.identity));
        newNPC.transform.Rotate (new Vector3 (0, 0, 180));
        newNPC.name = "npc1";

}
```

In the previous code:

Creating a 2D Shooter (Part 3): Adding AI and Weapons

- We declare a variable called **range**, with a random value that will range between -10 and +10.

- This random value is then used to instantiated a new NPC for which the **x coordinate** is based on the x coordinate of the player +/- 10; this is similar to the code used to instantiate moving targets.

- The name of the new NPCs that has been instantiated is set to **npc1**.

You can now save your script and set-up the **NPCSpawner** object:

- Please, save your script.

- Using the **Hierarchy**, please select the object **NPCSpawner**.

- In the **Inspector**, you will see a field called **NPC1** for the component called **NPCSpawner**, as illustrated in the next figure.

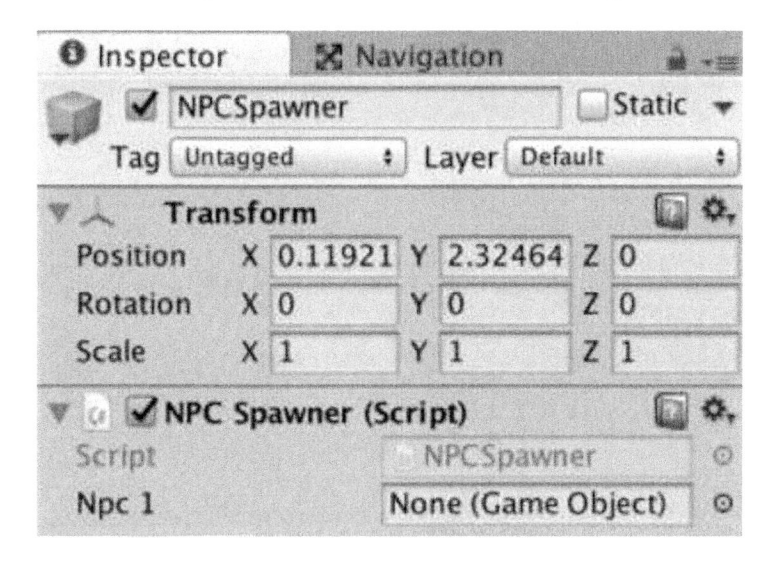

Figure 282: Setting-up the object Spawner (part 1)

- Please drag and drop the prefab **npc1** from the **Project** window, to the field **NPC1**, as illustrated in the next figure.

[495]

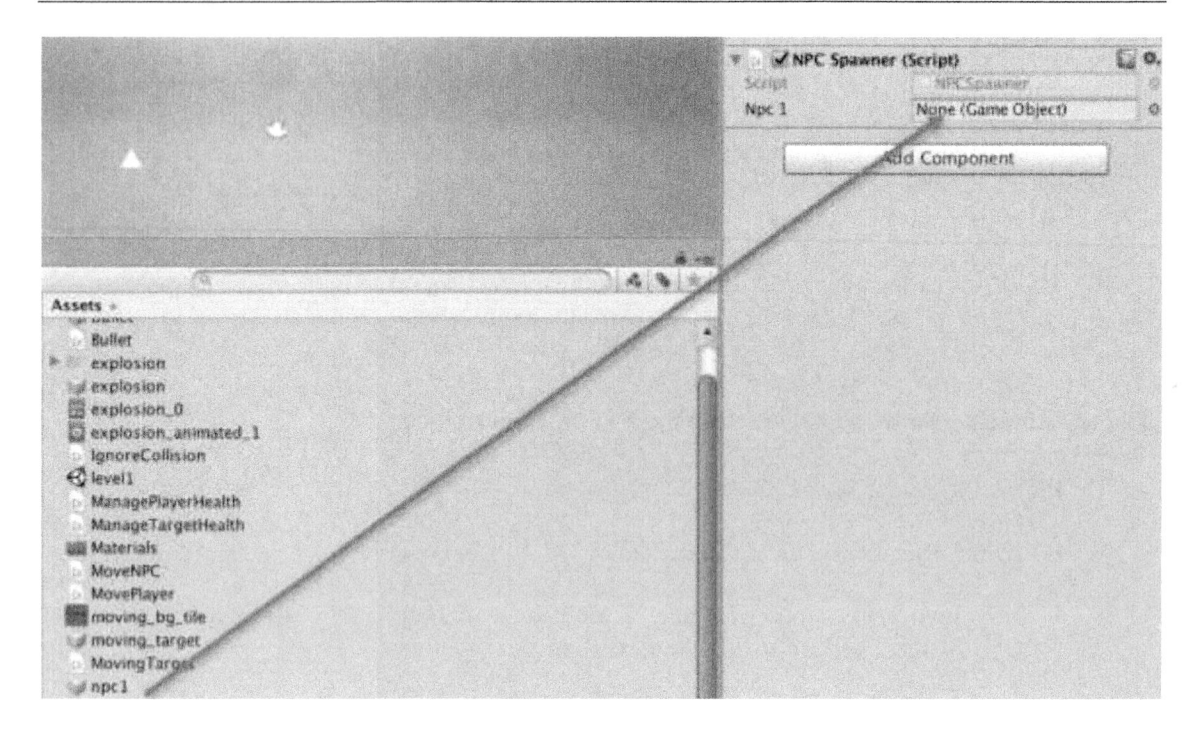

Creating a 2D Shooter (Part 3): Adding AI and Weapons

Figure 283: Setting-up the object Spawner (part 2)

- Finally, please move the object **NPCSpawner** close to the top part of the screen, as illustrated on the next figure.

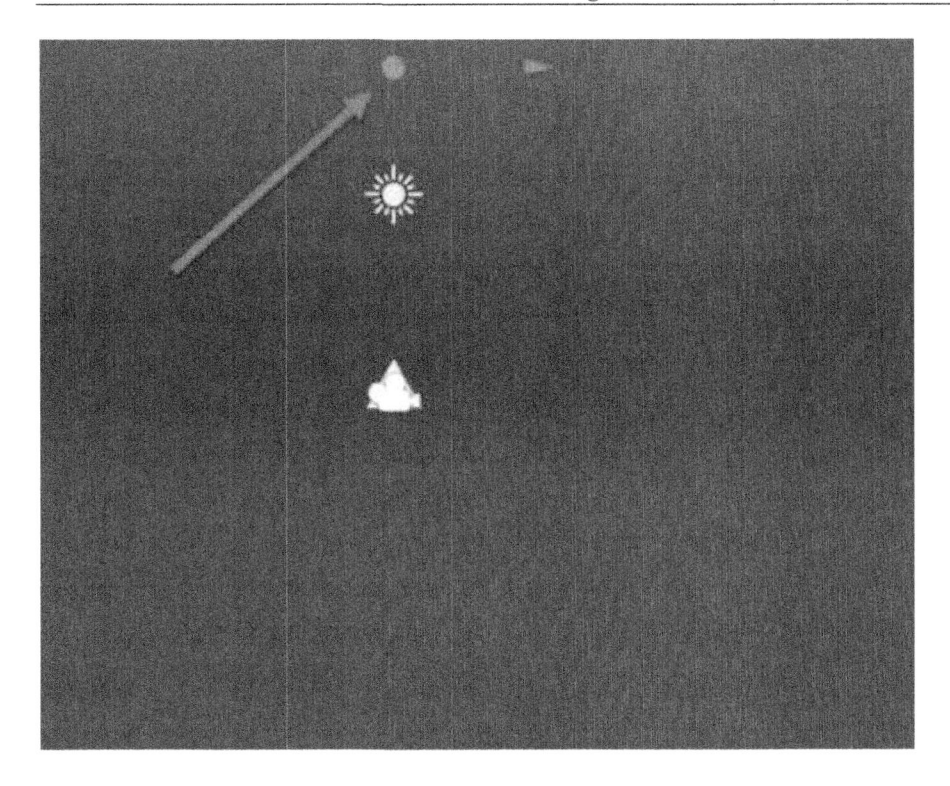

Creating a 2D Shooter (Part 3): Adding AI and Weapons

Figure 284: Moving the object NPCSpawner

As you play the scene, you will see that the NPCs are spawn at random positions.

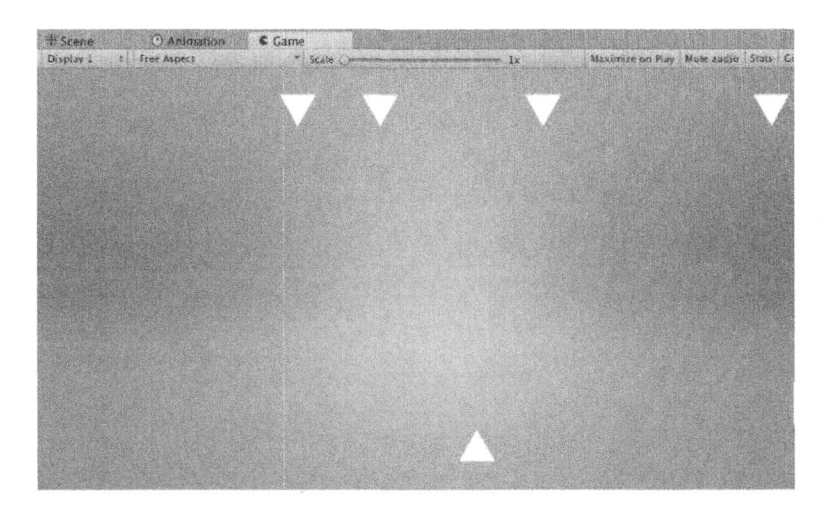

Figure 285: Spawning NPCs

You may notice that the moving targets collide with some of the NPCs; this is because we have previously used a function that ignores collision between two objects (i.e., the object **npc1** and a moving target); however, at this stage we would like to ignore collisions between more than two objects. This is because we now have not just one, but several objects called **npc1**.

[497]

Creating a 2D Shooter (Part 3): Adding AI and Weapons

So in the next section, we will be using a new technique to ignore collisions between more than two objects; this will involve **layers**. Layers are a way to group objects by adding them to a virtual group called a **layer**; we can then apply specific rules or features to all objects that are included in a specific layer; in our case we will specify that we should be ignoring collisions between objects belonging to two different layers; so, we will do as follows:

- Create a new layer, and add the falling (moving) targets to this layer.

- Create a second new layer, and add each NPC to this new layer.

- Make sure that collisions are ignored between the objects on the first layer and the objects on the second layer.

So let's start!

First we will create a layer for the NPCs and add any NPC based on the prefab **npc1** to this layer:

- Please select the prefab called **npc1** in the **Project** window.

- Then, open the **Inspector** window and locate the section called **Layer**, at the top of the **Inspector** window, as described on the next figure.

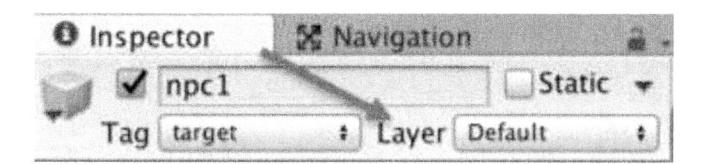

Figure 286: Adding a layer (part 1)

- Click on **Default** (to the right of the label **Layer**); this will display a list of existing layers.

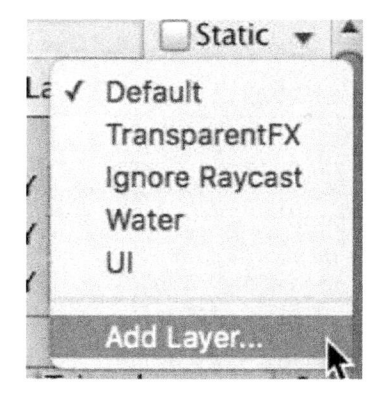

Figure 287: Adding a layer (part 2)

- You can then select the option **Add Layer** from the drop-down menu.

[498]

Creating a 2D Shooter (Part 3): Adding AI and Weapons

- In the new window, please type the name of the new layer called **NPC** to the right of the label **User Layer 8**.

Figure 288: Adding a layer (part 3)

- Once this is, done, select the prefab **npc1** in the **Project** window.
- Using the **Inspector** window, click on **Default** (to the right of the label **Layer)**; this will display a list of existing layers.
- This time, a list that includes your new layer (i.e., **NPC**) should appear; please select the layer called **NPC**.

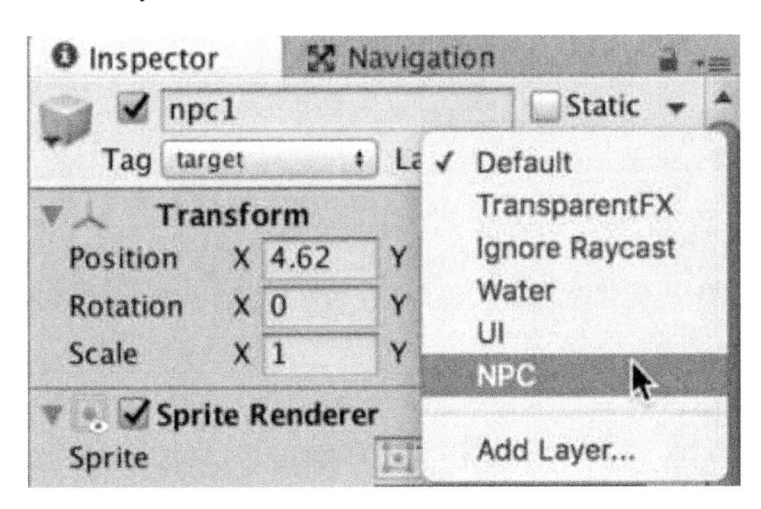

Figure 289: Applying a new layer

So by performing this action, we have specified that each object based on the prefab **npc1** will be on the layer called **NPC**.

Now we just need to specify a layer for the prefab called **moving_target**.

- Please select the prefab called **movingTarget** in the **Project** window.
- Then, open the **Inspector** window and locate the section called **Layer** (as we have done previously), at the top of the **Inspector** window, as described on the next figure.

[499]

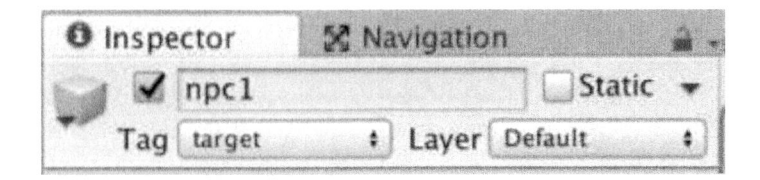

Creating a 2D Shooter (Part 3): Adding AI and Weapons

Figure 290: Creating a new layer for moving targets (part 1)

- Click on **Default** (to the right of the label **Layer**); this will display a list of existing layers.

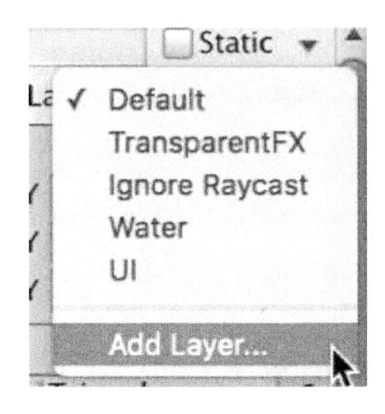

Figure 291: Creating a new layer for moving targets (part 2)

- Select **Add Layer**.

- In the new window, type the name of the new layer called **Target** to the right of the label **User Layer 9**.

Figure 292: Creating a new layer for moving targets (part 3)

- Once this is, done, please select the prefab **movingTarget** in the **Project** window.

- Using the **Inspector** window, click on the drop-down menu (to the right of the label **Layer**); this will display a list of existing layers.

- This time a list that includes your new layer should appear; please select the layer called **Target**, as illustrated in the next figure.

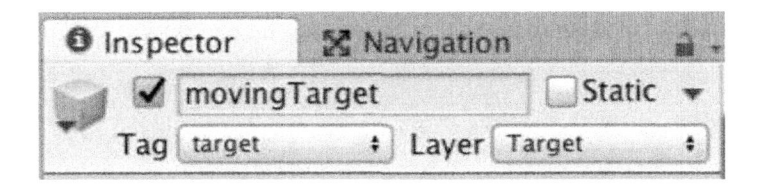

Creating a 2D Shooter (Part 3): Adding AI and Weapons

Figure 293: Applying a new layer to the moving targets

- So by performing this action, we have specified that each object based on the prefab **movingTarget** will be on the layer called **Target**.

Last but not least, we need to tell Unity that collisions should be ignored between objects belonging to these two new layers (i.e., objects that belong to the layers called **NPC** and **Target**); this will be done using scripting:

- Please open the script called **IgnoreCollisions**.

- Modify the **Start** function as follows:

```
void Start ()
{
        //if (GameObject.Find ("npc1") != null) Physics2D.IgnoreCollision (GetComponent<BoxCollider2D>(), GameObject.Find ("npc1").GetComponent<PolygonCollider2D> ());
        int layer1 = GameObject.Find ("npc1").layer;
        int layer2 = gameObject.layer;
        Physics2D.IgnoreLayerCollision(layer1, layer2, true);
}
```

In the previous code:

- We comment the first line that was originally used to ignore collisions between the object called **npc1** and the moving targets, since we will now use layers for this purpose.

- We then define the index of the two layers that we have created previously (i.e., **NPC** and **Target**). Note that to obtain the ids of these layers, we refer to objects that have been added to these layers. So to find the id of the layer **Target**, we refer to the layer on which the NPC called **npc1** has been added; the same is done for the moving targets (i.e., the object linked to this script).

- These layer indices are expressed as integers.

- **layer2** is the index of the layer (called **Target**) linked to the object (or prefab) that is attached to this script (i.e., **moving_target**)

- **layer1** is the index of the layer (called **NPC**) linked to the object (or prefab) named **npc1**.

Please save your code, and test the scene; you should see that the moving targets do not collide with the NPCs anymore.

Creating a 2D Shooter (Part 3): Adding AI and Weapons

LEVEL ROUNDUP

Summary

In this chapter, we have managed to add some interesting features, including artificial intelligence, applying damage to the player, and keeping the player in the field of view. Finally we also learned about layers and how to use them to ignore collisions between more than two objects.

Checklist

You can consider moving to the next stage if you can do the following:

- Understand how to create and apply layers.
- Understand how to ignore collision through scripting.
- Understand how to convert world coordinates to the camera viewport's coordinates.

Quiz

Now, let's check your knowledge! Please answer the following questions (the answers are included in the resource pack) or specify whether they are correct or incorrect.

11. Coordinates in the viewport range from 1 to 100.

12. The following code will convert world coordinates to viewport coordinates:

```
Camera.main.WorldToViewportPoint
```

13. Assuming that npc1 is on a layer called NPC, the following code will return the id of the layer called NPC.

```
int layer1 = GameObject.Find ("npc1").layer;
```

14. The following code will ignore collisions between objects belonging to the first layer and objects belonging to the second layer.

```
Physics2D.IgnoreLayerCollision(layer1, layer2, false);
```

15. By default, all new objects in Unity are allocated the layer called **Unity-Default**.

16. An object can be allocated to several layers.

17. The following code will create a variable that ranges from -10 to +10.

```
float range = Random.Range (-10, 10)
```

18. A polygon collider can be added to an object using the menu **Components | Polygon | PolygonCollider2D**.

19. For a particular script, the function **Start** is called when the script is loaded.

20. For a particular script, the function **Start** is called only when the game is loaded.

Answers to the Quiz

1. Coordinates in the viewport range from 1 to 100. **FALSE**

2. The following code will convert world coordinates to viewport coordinates: **TRUE**

```
Camera.main.WorldToViewportPoint
```

3. Assuming that npc1 is on a layer called NPC, the following code will return the id of the layer called NPC. **TRUE**

```
int layer1 = GameObject.Find ("npc1").layer;
```

4. The following code will ignore collisions between objects belonging to the first layer and objects belonging to the second layer. **FALSE**

```
Physics2D.IgnoreLayerCollision(layer1, layer2, false);
```

5. By default, all new objects in Unity are allocated the layer called **Unity-Default**. **TRUE**

6. An object can be allocated to several layers. **FALSE**

7. The following code will create a variable that ranges from -10 to +10. **TRUE**

```
float range = Random.Range (-10, 10)
```

8. A polygon collider can be added to an object using the menu **Components | Polygon | PolygonCollider2D**. **FALSE**

9. For a particular script, the function **Start** is called when the script is loaded. **TRUE**

10. For a particular script, the function **Start** is called only when the game is loaded. **TRUE**

Challenge 1

For this chapter, your challenge will be to modify the attributes of the game to make it more or less challenging:

- Modify the frequency at which the NPCs are spawn.
- Modify the speed at which the player moves.

13
CREATING A 2D SHOOTER (PART 4): ADDING AI AND SOUND

In this section, we will polish-up our game by adding a few features that will increase the game play, as well as the game flow; after completing this chapter, you will be able to:

- Improve AI by respawning NPCs given that specific conditions are fulfilled.
- Increase the difficulty of your game over time.
- Add a temporary shield to the player.
- Add sound effects.

IMPROVING AI

In this section, we will improve the AI in several ways:

- NPCs will be spawned after 5 seconds.
- The difficulty of the game will increase with time; as time elapses, the NPCs will be spawned more frequently and the falling targets will be generated more frequently also.

So let's get started:

- Please create a new empty object and call it **gameManager**.
- Create a new C# script and rename it **ManageShooterGame**.
- Open this script and modify it as follows.
- Add the following code at the beginning of the class (new code in bold).

```
public class ManageShooterGame : MonoBehaviour {
    public float timer;
    public float difficulty;
    public float timerThresold;
```

- In the previous code, we declare three variables that will be used to increase the difficulty of the game after a specific threshold has been reached by the timer.
- Add the following code in the **Start** function.

```
void Start ()
{
    timer = 0;
    difficulty = 1;
    timerThresold = 5;//difficulty increases after 5 seconds
}
```

- In the previous code: we initialize the time and set the initial **difficulty** level to **1**; the threshold is set to **5**, which means that the difficulty will increase every 5 seconds.
- Please add the following code in the **Update** function.

```
void Update ()
{
        timer += Time.deltaTime;
        if (timer >= timerThresold)
        {
                difficulty++;
                print ("Difficulty level: " + difficulty);
                timer = 0;
        }
}
```

- In the previous code, we update the variable **timer**, so that the difficulty level is increased every time the threshold (i.e., 5 seconds for now) has been reached. The difficulty level is also displayed in the **Console** window, for testing purposes.

- Please save this script (i.e., **manageShooterGame**), check that it is error-free, and then drag and drop it on the objet called **gameManager** in the **Hierarchy** window.

Now we just need to use this difficulty level for the scripts that spawn the moving targets or the NPCs. The idea is that the frequency at which these are spawn will be based on the difficulty level; the higher the difficult level, and the more frequently these objects will be spawn.

So let's modify these scripts:

- Please open the script called **SpawnMovingTarget**, and modify its **Update** function as follows (new code in bold).

```
timer += Time.deltaTime;
float range = Random.Range (-10, 10);//Screen.width);
Vector3 newPosition = new Vector3 (GameObject.Find("player").transform.position.x + range, transform.position.y, 0);
//if (timer >= 1 )
float respawnTime = 5/GameObject.Find("gameManager").GetComponent<ManageShooterGame>().difficulty;
if (timer >= respawnTime)
{
```

In the previous code:

- We create a variable **respawnTime** that is calculated based on the difficulty level; so at the start, **respawnTime** will be 5 and then 2.5, etc; so objects will be respawn twice as fast every time the level of difficulty increases by one; this will make the game extremely challenging over time.

- We then use this **respawnTime** variable to know when the prefab should be instantiated.

You can now save your script, and we can then perform similar modifications for the NPCs.

Creating a 2D Shooter (Part 4): Adding AI and Sound

- Please open the script **NPCSpawner**, and modify its **Update** function as follows (new code in bold).

```
//if (timer >= 1 )
float respawnTime = 5/GameObject.Find("gameManager").GetComponent<ManageShooterGame>().difficulty;
if (timer >= respawnTime)
{
```

- This code is identical to the one we have used to respawn the moving targets.
- You can now save your code.

Note that you can modify the variable **respawnTime** by multiplying it by a number of your choice. As it is, the game will quickly become very challenging as the spawning frequency is doubled every 5 seconds.

ADDING A TEMPORARY SHIELD TO THE PLAYER

While the player can shoot projectiles, given the frequency at which the NPCs are spawn, it would be great for the player to avail of a shield, even temporarily.

So, in this section, we will create a feature whereby:

- A bonus object will be instantiated randomly.

- After collecting this bonus, the player will avail of a shield and be invincible for 5 seconds.

- While it is invincible, a blue circle will be displayed around the player.

This will involve the following:

- Creating a tag for the bonus.

- Detecting collision with this bonus based on its tag.

- Creating a shield, based on a sprite.

- Initially deactivate the shield (i.e., make it invisible).

- Creating a timer to determine for how long the shield should be active.

- Activate the shield (i.e., make it visible) after the bonus has been collected, and ignore collisions with bullets or targets while the shield is active.

- Deactivate the shield when the timer has reached 5 seconds.

So let's implement this feature:

- Please create a new sprite: from the **Project** window, select **Create | Sprites | Circle**.

- Rename this asset **shield**.

Figure 294: Creating a new shield

- Drag and drop this asset (i.e., the shield) to the **Scene** view; this will create a new object called **shield**.

Creating a 2D Shooter (Part 4): Adding AI and Sound

- Using the **Hierarchy**, drag and drop this object (i.e., the shield) on top of the object called **player**, so that it becomes a child of the object **player**, as illustrated on the next figure.

▼ player
    shield

Figure 295: Adding the shield as a child of the object player

- Once this is done, you can click on the object called **shield** in the **Hierarchy**, and then look at the **Inspector** window.

- In the **Inspector** window, set the position of this object (i.e., the shield) to **(0, 0, 0)** and its scale attributes to **(1, 1, 1)**.

You can also change the color and transparency of the sprite for this object as follows:

- Using the **Inspector**, for the **Component** called **Sprite Renderer**, click on the white rectangle to the right of the attribute called **Color**.

▼ ✓ Sprite Renderer
Sprite   shield
Color

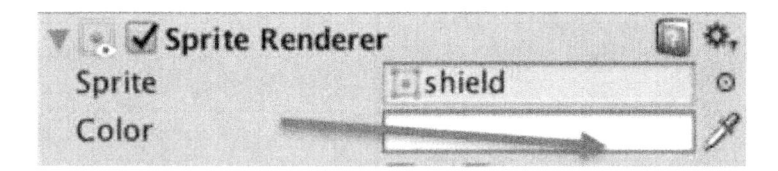

Figure 296: Changing the color of the shield

- This will open a new window; using this window you can pick a blue color of your choice, and also set the **opacity** to **70**, as illustrated on the next figures.

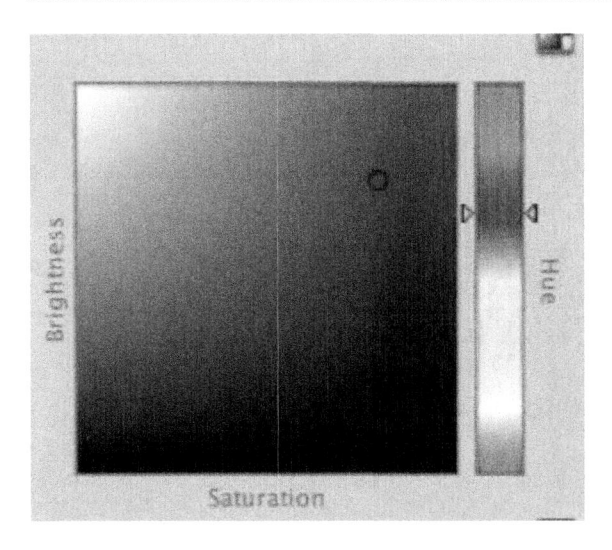

Figure 297: Painting the shield in blue

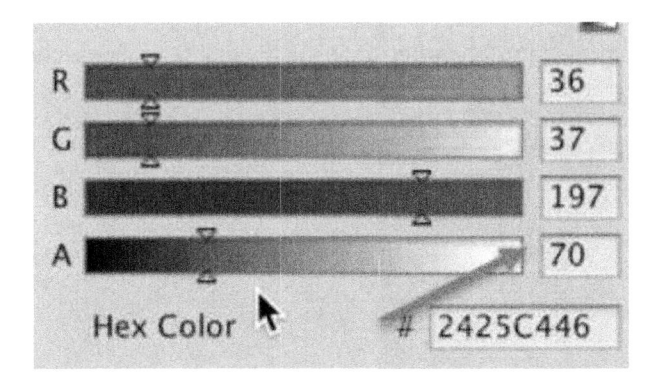

Figure 298: Setting the opacity to 70

- Once this is done, the player should look like the following figure:

[513]

Creating a 2D Shooter (Part 4): Adding AI and Sound

Figure 299: The player and its shield

Next, we will create a prefab that will be used as a bonus to be collected by the player to activate its shield.

- In the **Project** window, please duplicate the prefab called **movingTarget** (i.e., select the prefab and then press **CTRL + D**).

- Rename the duplicate **bonus**.

Figure 300: Creating a new prefab for the bonus

- Once this is done, please click on the prefab called **bonus** that you have just created in the **Project** window, so that we can modify some of its properties.

- Using the **Inspector** window, create a new tag called **bonus** and apply it to this object, as we have done previously for other objects.

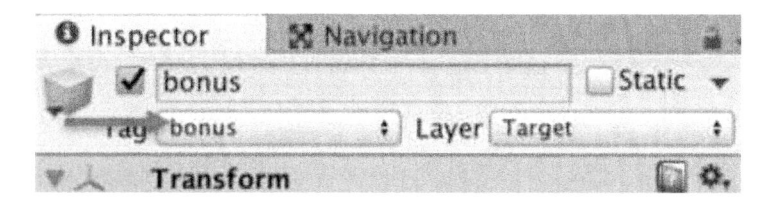

Figure 301: Adding a tag to the bonus prefab

- Please change the color of the sprite for this prefab to green using its **Sprite Renderer** component in the **Inspector**.

Creating a 2D Shooter (Part 4): Adding AI and Sound

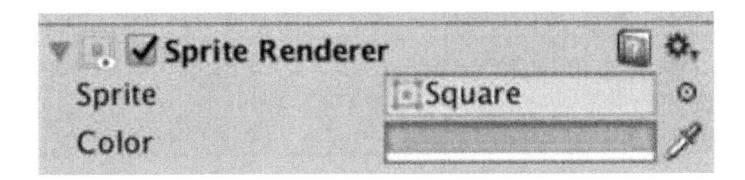

Figure 302: Changing the color of the bonus

So, this new prefab will behave the same way as the moving platforms, in the sense that, once spawned, it will move downwards; however, this **bonus** prefab has a different tag called **bonus**, so that he player can collect it; the **bonus** prefab also has a distinctive color (i.e., green) so that the player can tell it apart from the falling targets.

So now that we have created this prefab, we will need to spawn it and to ensure that when it is collected by the player, that the player's shield is activated accordingly.

So we will need to modify a few of the existing scripts: the script that spawns moving targets, and the other script that manages the player's health.

- Please open the script **SpawnMovingTargets**.
- Add the following code at the beginning of the class (new code in bold).

```
public GameObject newObject;
public GameObject bonus;
```

- Modify the function **Update** as follows (new code in bold).

```
if (timer >= respawnTime)
{
        float typeOfObjectSpwan = Random.Range(0,100);
        GameObject t;
        if (typeOfObjectSpwan >= 50)
        {
                t = (GameObject)(Instantiate (newObject, newPosition, Quaternion.identity));
                t.GetComponent<ManageTargetHealth> ().type = ManageTargetHealth.TARGET_BOULDER;
        }
        else t = (GameObject)(Instantiate (bonus, newPosition, Quaternion.identity));
        //GameObject t = (GameObject)(Instantiate (newObject, newPosition, Quaternion.identity));
        //t.GetComponent<ManageTargetHealth> ().type = ManageTargetHealth.TARGET_BOULDER;
        timer = 0;
}
```

In the previous code:

- We generate a random number between 0 and 100; this number will be used to determine what object should be spawn; here, we are effectively specifying a probability of 50% chance for bonuses to be spawn and a 50% chance for moving targets to be spawn. This is a very simple way to apply probabilities (and random behaviors) to your games.

- If the random number id **50 or more**, we instantiate a moving target. Otherwise, we instantiate a bonus.

> Note that **Random.Range** will generate numbers from a range that includes the boundaries of this range; in our case the number generated will range between 0 and 100 inclusive, which would include 101 possibilities; so to be more accurate, we could adjust the upper boundary of the range to 99, which would result in 100 possibilities.

- The previous code used to instantiate a moving target is commented.

That's it!

Please save your script and check that it is error-free.

Next, we can modify the script that manages the player's health.

- Please open the script **ManagePlayerHealth**.
- Modify the beginning of the class as follows:

```
public float timerForShield;
public bool startInvincibility;
void Start ()
{
        GameObject.Find ("shield").GetComponent<SpriteRenderer> ().enabled = false;

}
```

In the previous code:

- We declare two variables: **timerForShield** and **startInvincibility**.
- We also make sure that the shield is not displayed at the start of the game by **not** rendering the corresponding sprite.

We can now modify the collision detection to account for the shield (and the temporary invincibility).

- Please modify the function **OnCollisionEnter2D**, in the script **ManagePlayerHealth**, as follows (new code in bold):

```
if ((coll.gameObject.tag == "target" || coll.gameObject.tag == "bullet") && !startInvincibility)
{
        Destroy (coll.gameObject);

        DestroyPlayer ();
}

if (coll.gameObject.tag == "bonus")
{
        Destroy (coll.gameObject);
        startInvincibility = true;
        GameObject.Find ("shield").GetComponent<SpriteRenderer> ().enabled = true;
}
```

In the previous code:

- The player will sustain damage only when it is not invincible (i.e., when the shield is not active).

- We also check that the player has collided with a bonus.

- If this is the case, the bonus is destroyed, the player becomes invincible (for the time-being) and the shield is displayed. The variable **startInvincibility** is used to start a timer that will determine when this invincibility will stop.

Finally, we just need to modify the **Update** function to be able to implement the timer, and to check how long the shield should be active.

- Please modify the **Update** function in the script **ManagePlayerHealth** as follows (new code in bold):

```
void Update ()
{
        if (startInvincibility)
        {
                timerForShield += Time.deltaTime;
                if (timerForShield >= 20)
                {
                        timerForShield = 0;
                        startInvincibility = false;
                        GameObject.Find ("shield").GetComponent<SpriteRenderer> ().enabled = false;
                }
        }
}
```

In the previous code:

Creating a 2D Shooter (Part 4): Adding AI and Sound

- We check whether the player is invincible (i.e., if a bonus shield has been collected).

- If this is the case, the value of the timer is increased every second, until it reaches 20 seconds.

- In this case, the timer is reset to 0, the invincibility is set to **false**, and the shield is no longer displayed onscreen.

Last but not least, we need to add the bonus prefab to the object **targetSpawner**.

- Please select the object **targetSpawner** in the **Hierarchy**.

- Then drag and drop the prefab **bonus** from the **Project** window, to the field called **bonus** for the component called **SpawnMovingTargets**, as described on the next figure.

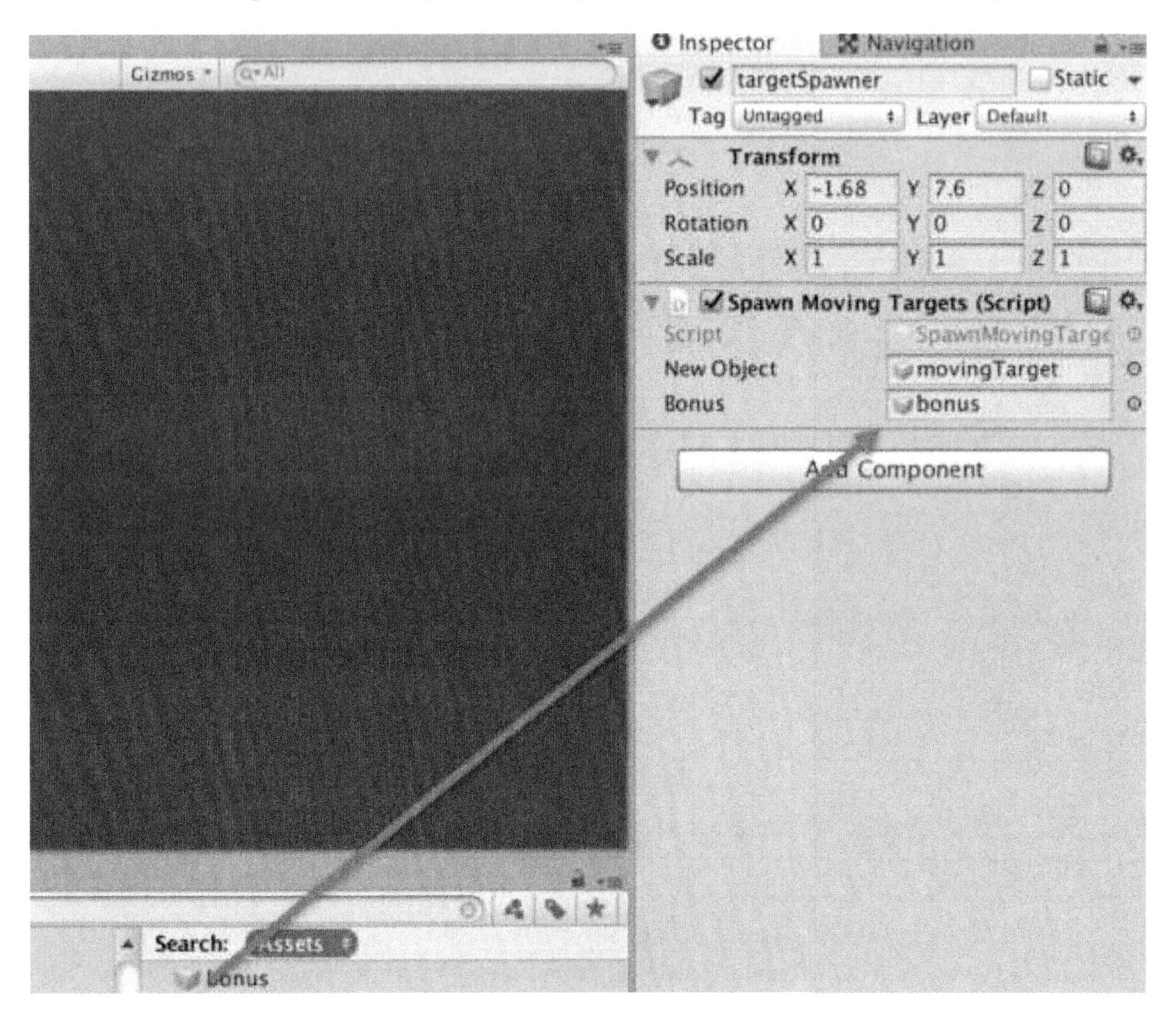

Figure 303: Adding the bonus to the targetSpawner object

Once this is done, you can now test your game: after collecting a bonus, the shield should appear for 20 seconds, allowing you to be invincible for that duration.

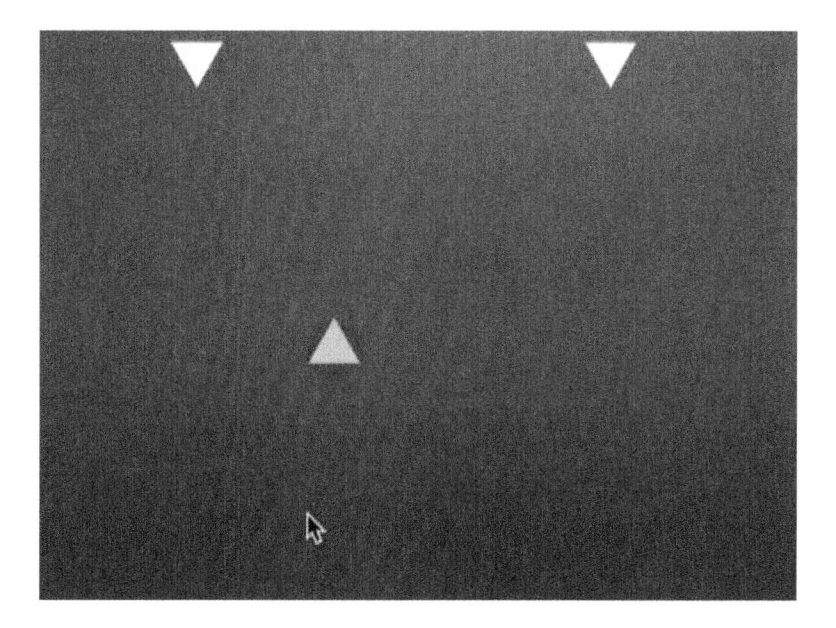

Figure 304: Using the shield

ADDING A SCORE

Now that our gameplay is improved thanks to randomly instantiated NPCs and an increasing difficulty, we could add and display a score. This will consist of a **UI Text** object that will be updated from a script every time the player manages to hit a target.

- Please create a new **UI Text** object; from the main menu, select: **GameObject | UI | Text**. This will create a new object called **Text**, along with a parent object called **Canvas**.

Figure 305: Adding a UI Text object

- To know where this object is in relation to the game screen, you can just double click on it in the **Hierarchy**.

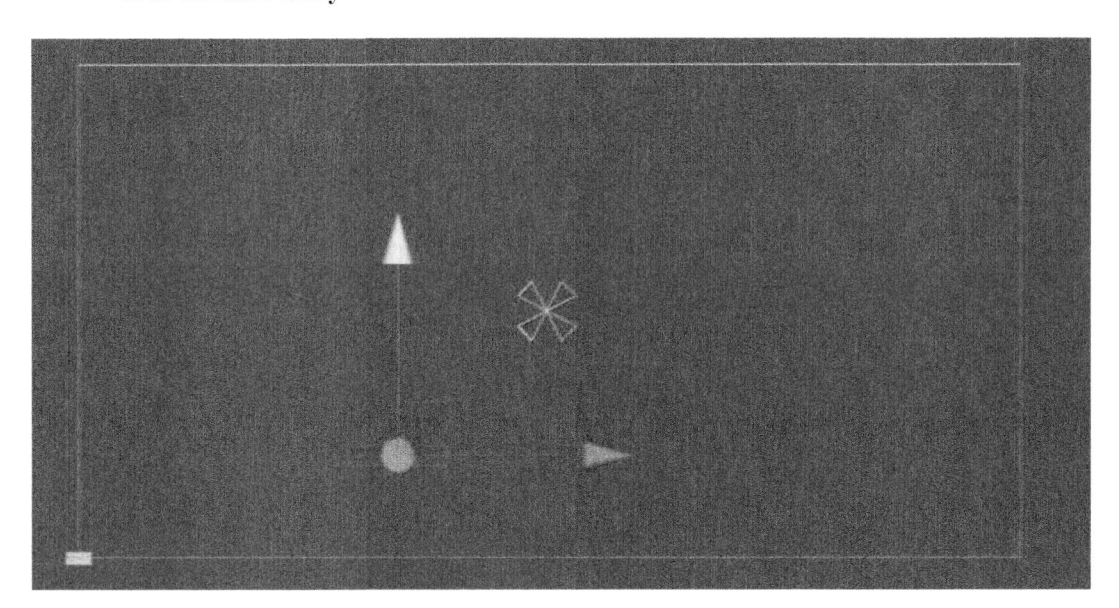

Figure 306: Locating the UI Text object

- Then, in the **Scene** view, move this object, to the top-left corner of the white rectangle that defines the game screen.

Creating a 2D Shooter (Part 4): Adding AI and Sound

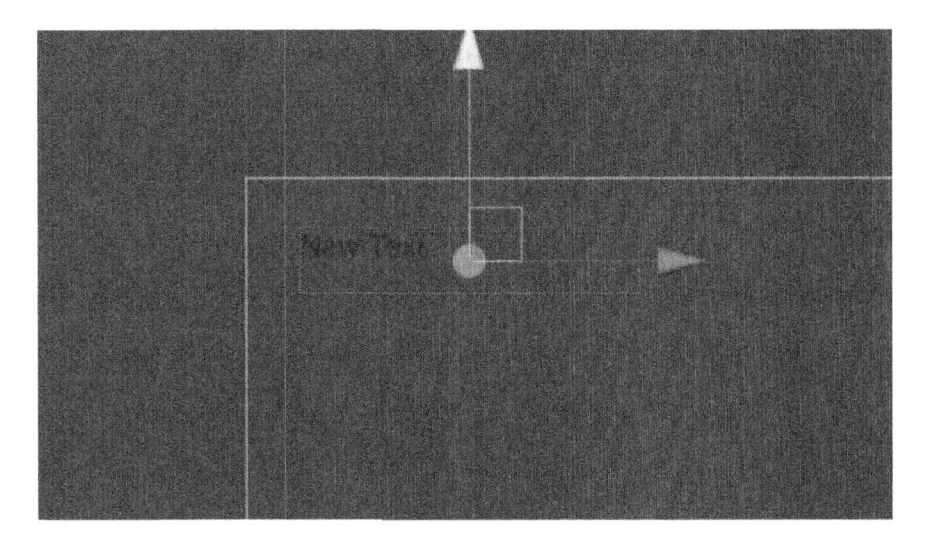

Figure 307: Moving the UI text object

We can now change some of the properties of this object (e.g., color and size):

- After selecting the object called **Text** in the **Hierarchy**, please use the **Inspector** window to change the color of its text to **white** (in the component called **Text**).

Figure 308: Changing the color of the text

- Please modify its alignment as described in the next figure:

Figure 309: Modifying the alignment of the Text object

- You can also rename this object **uiScrore**, using the **Hierarchy** window.

Once this is done, we just need to calculate the score and display it in the **UI Text** object.

- Please, open the script called **ManagePlayerHealth**.

[521]

Creating a 2D Shooter (Part 4): Adding AI and Sound

- Add the following code at the start of the script (new code in bold):

```
using UnityEngine;
using System.Collections;
using UnityEngine.SceneManagement;
using UnityEngine.UI;
```

- Add the following code at the beginning of the class (new code in bold).

```
public float timerForShield;
public bool startInvincibility;
public int score;
void Start ()
{
        score = 0;
        GameObject.Find ("shield").GetComponent<SpriteRenderer> ().enabled = false;
        GameObject.Find ("scoreUI").GetComponent<Text> ().text = "Score:" + score;

}
```

In the previous script:

- We declare a new variable called **score**.
- At the beginning of the scene, we set this variable (i.e., **score**) to **0**.
- We also initialize the text displayed by the **UI Text** component.

Please add the following code at the end of the class, just before the last closing curly bracket.

```
public void increaseScore()
{
        score++;
        GameObject.Find ("scoreUI").GetComponent<Text> ().text = "Score:" + score;
}
```

In the previous script:

- We create a new function called **increaseScore**.
- In this function, we increase the **score** by **1**.
- We also update the **UI Text** object to reflect the change in the **score**.

Please save this script, and check that it is error-free.

Creating a 2D Shooter (Part 4): Adding AI and Sound

The next thing we need to do is to call this function when the bullet fired by the player has hit a target; this will be managed in the script called **Bullet**.

> Note that the function **increaseScore** is public, which means that it will be accessible from outside its class, and as a result, from the script called **Bullet**.

So let's modify the script called **Bullet**:

- Please open the script called **Bullet**.
- Add the following code to the function **OnCollisionEnter2D** (new code in bold).

```
coll.gameObject.GetComponent<ManageTargetHealth>().gotHit(10);
GameObject.Find ("player").GetComponent<ManagePlayerHealth> ().increaseScore ();
Destroy (gameObject);
```

- Please save your code.

You can now check the game to see whether the score is displayed and updated accordingly as your bullets hit different targets.

Creating a 2D Shooter (Part 4): Adding AI and Sound

ADDING AUDIO

The last thing we will do is to add audio to our game whenever the player is hit, or s/he fires bullets. For this purpose, we will import two sound effects, and play them accordingly.

Please import the audio files **explosion.wav** and **bullet.wav** from the resource pack to Unity's **Project** window.

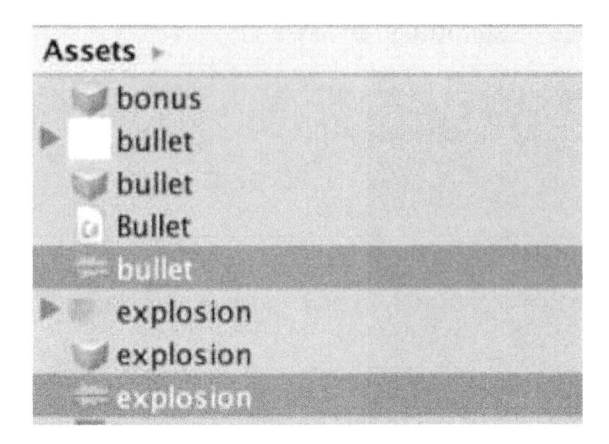

Figure 310: Importing audio

> The two audio files were created using the site http://www.bfxr.net/, which is a free tool to create your own sound effects.

Next, we will create the necessary components to be able to play these sounds, and we will start with the sound for the bullet.

- Please select the object called **player** in the **Hierarchy**.

- From the top menu, select **Component | Audio | Audio Source**; this will add an **Audio Source** component to your object.

> Whenever you need to play a sound, an **Audio Source** is needed, and it is comparable to an mp3 player in the sense that it plays audio clips that you need to select, the same way you would select a particular track on your mp3 player.

- Please, drag and drop the audio file called **bullet** from the **Project** window to the **Audio Clip** attribute of the **Audio Source.**

Creating a 2D Shooter (Part 4): Adding AI and Sound

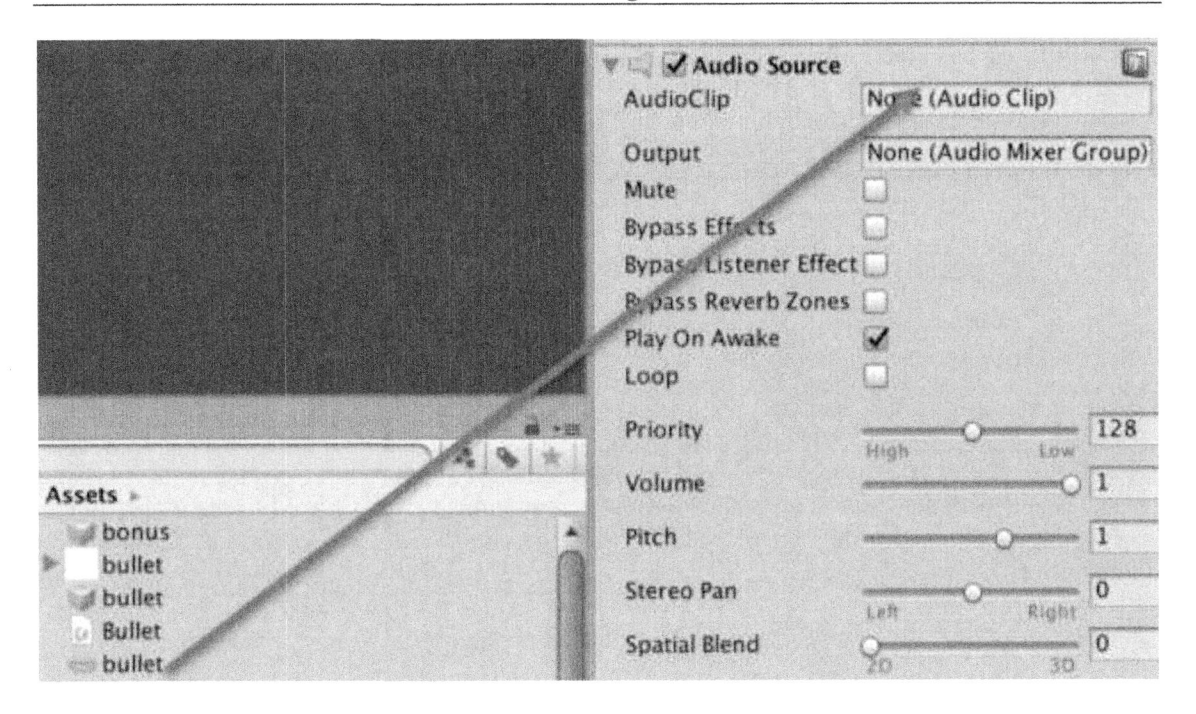

Figure 311: Adding an audio source

- You can then set the attribute **Play on Awake** to **false** (i.e., unchecked) so that this sound is not played automatically at the start of the scene, as illustrated on the next figure.

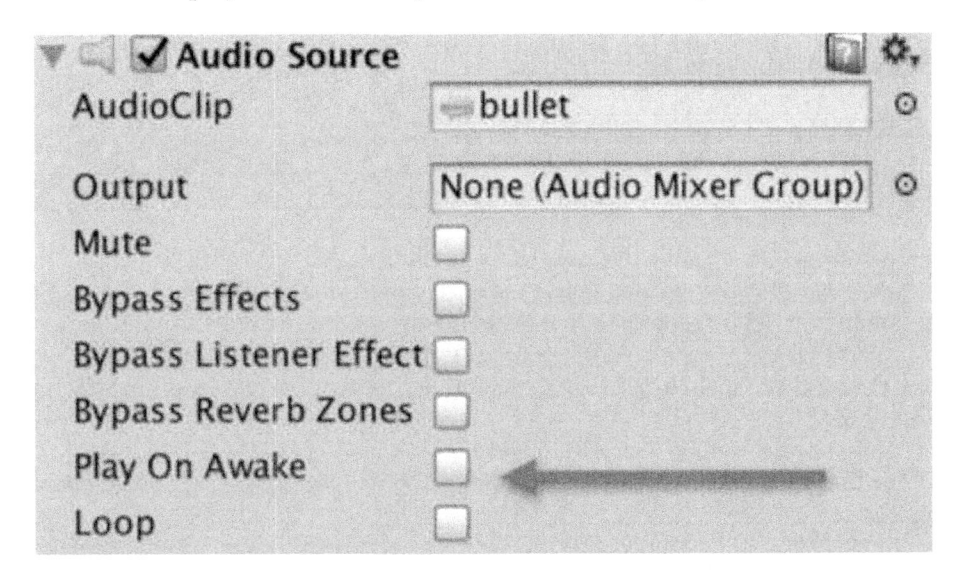

Figure 312: Setting the attributes of the sound effect

Next, we will write code that will access this **Audio Source** and play the clip, whenever the player fires a bullet.

[525]

Creating a 2D Shooter (Part 4): Adding AI and Sound

- Please open the script called **MovePlayer**.
- Add the following code to the function **Update** (new cold in bold).

```
if (Input.GetKeyDown (KeyCode.Space))
{
        GameObject b = (GameObject)(Instantiate (bullet, transform.position + transform.up*1.5f, Quaternion.identity));
        b.GetComponent<Rigidbody2D> ().AddForce (transform.up * 1000);
        GetComponent<AudioSource> ().Play ();
}
```

In the previous code, we access the **AudioSource** component that is linked to the object **player** (i.e., the object linked to this script), and we play the clip that is included in this **AudioSource** (i.e., **bullet**).

Please save your code, test the scene, and check that the audio clip is played whenever you press the space bar.

Next, using the same principle, we will generate the sound of an explosion when the player is hit.

Now, because the **Audio Source** will need to play several sounds (a different sound depending on whether the player fires a bullet or is hit), we will need to specify which track needs to be played, so we will modify our script accordingly.

- Please open the script **MovePlayer**.
- Add the following line at the beginning of the script:

```
public AudioClip fireSound;
```

- This code declares an audio clip; because it is public, it will be accessible from the **Inspector**, and as a result, we will be able to set (or initialize) this variable by dragging and dropping objects to its placeholders in the **Inspector** window.

- Please save your script, switch to Unity, select the **player** object and display the **Inspector** window.

- You should see that a variable called **fireSound**, that acts as placeholder, is now available in the component called **Move**.

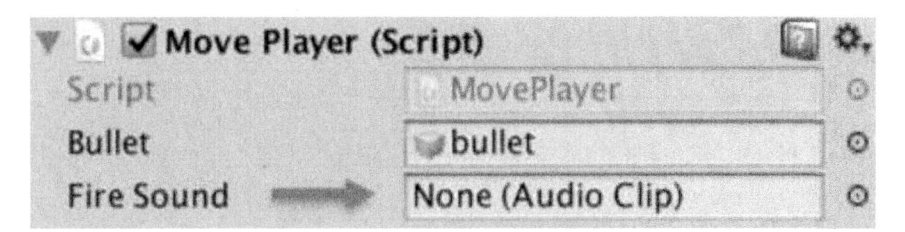

Move Player (Script)	
Script	MovePlayer
Bullet	bullet
Fire Sound	None (Audio Clip)

Creating a 2D Shooter (Part 4): Adding AI and Sound

Figure 313: Initializing the audio clips (part1)

- Please drag and drop the sound **bullet.wav** from the **Project** view, to the variable **fireSound** in the **Inspector**, as illustrated in the next figure.

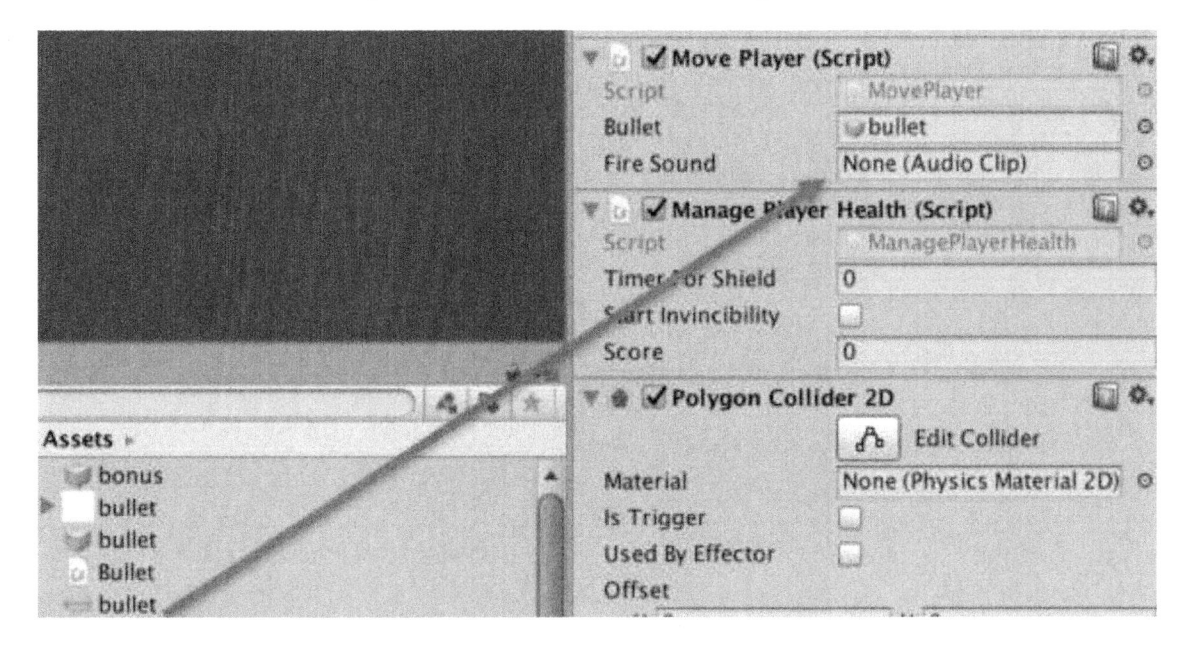

Figure 314: Initializing the audio clips (part 2)

Now, it's time to modify the script further to tell the system which audio clip to play and when.

- Please open the script **MovePlayer**.

- Add the following code to the **Update** function (new code in bold):

```
if (Input.GetKeyDown (KeyCode.Space))
{
        GameObject b = (GameObject)(Instantiate (bullet, transform.position + transform.up*1.5f, Quaternion.identity));
        b.GetComponent<Rigidbody2D> ().AddForce (transform.up * 1000);
        GetComponent<AudioSource> ().clip = fireSound;
        GetComponent<AudioSource> ().Play ();
}
```

In the previous code:

- We specify that we should play the clip called **fireSound** (which contains the audio **bullet.wav**); this track is now the default (or active) track for the **Audio Source**.

- We then play the track that we have selected.

[527]

Creating a 2D Shooter (Part 4): Adding AI and Sound

Next, we will use a similar technique to play a different sound when the player is hurt.

- Please open the script called **ManagePlayerHealth**.
- Add the following lines at the beginning of the script:

```
public AudioClip hitSound;
```

- This code declares an audio clip; because it is public, it will be accessible from the **Inspector**, and as a result, we will be able to set (or initialize) this variable by dragging and dropping objects to its placeholders in the **Inspector** window.
- Add the following code to the function **DestroyPlayer** (new code in bold).

```
void DestroyPlayer()
{
    GetComponent<AudioSource> ().clip = hitSound;
    GetComponent<AudioSource> ().Play ();
    SceneManager.LoadScene (SceneManager.GetActiveScene().name);
}
```

Once this is done, we just need to initialize the variable **hitSound** from the **Inspector** window.

- Please save your script, switch to Unity, select the **player** object and display the **Inspector** window.
- You should see that a variable called **hitSound**, for the component **ManagePlayerHealth**, that acts as placeholder, is now available.

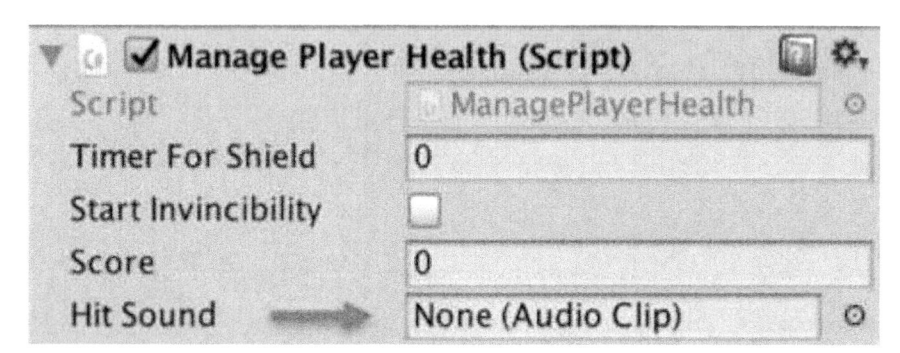

Figure 315: Initializing the audio clips (part1)

- Please drag and drop the sound **explosion.wav** from the **Project** view, to the variable **hitSound** in the **Inspector**, as illustrated in the next figure.

Creating a 2D Shooter (Part 4): Adding AI and Sound

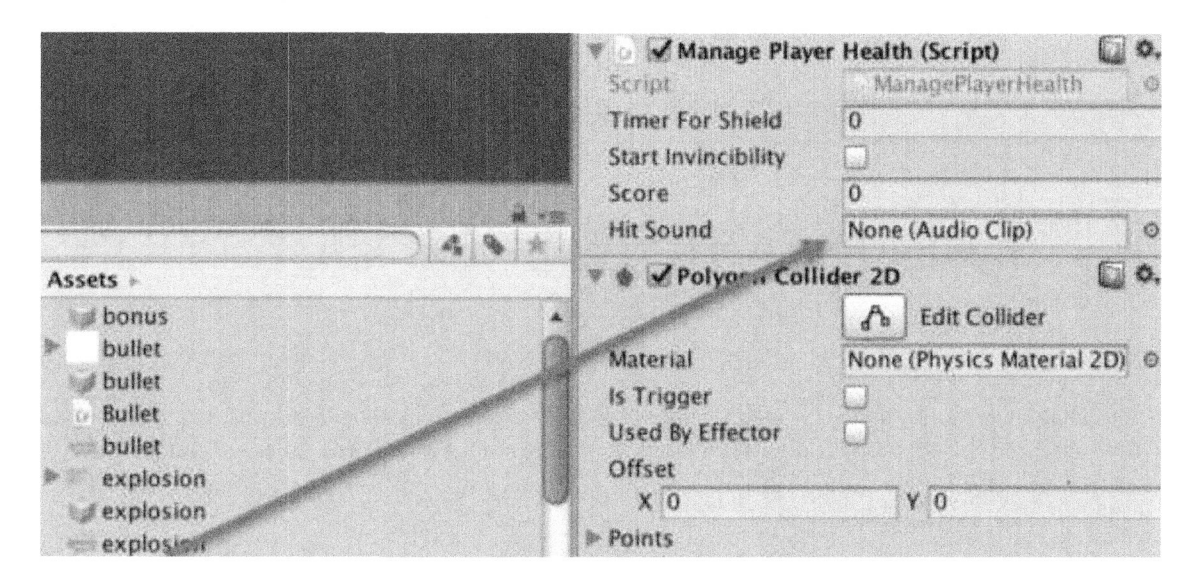

Figure 316: Initializing the audio clips (part 2)

You can now test your scene: when the player is hit, the explosion sound should be played.

14
FREQUENTLY ASKED QUESTIONS

This chapter provides answers to the most frequently asked questions about the features that we have covered in this book. Please also note that some **videos are also available on the companion site** to help you with some of the concepts covered in this topic, including AI, UI, collision, cameras, or paths.

RIGID BODIES

What are rigid bodies?

Rigid bodies are components that make it possible for an object to be subject to the laws of physics, including gravity.

How can I add a rigid body to an object?

This can be done in several ways, including by selecting the object and then the menu **Component** (from the top menu) or using **Add Component** in the **Inspector**.

How can I add force to an object that includes a rigid body?

When an object includes a rigid body, you can apply a force to it, from a script, using the method **AddForce**; for example:

```
gameObject.rigidbody.AddForce (New Vector3 (10,10,10));
```

USING PREFABS

What is a prefab?

A prefab can be compared to a template that can be reused (and updated) indefinitely.

How can I create a prefab?

Just drag and drop an object to the **Project** window or select **Create | Prefab** from the **Project** window.

How can I add a prefab to a scene?

You can either drag and drop the prefab from the **Project** window to the **Scene** view or instantiate this prefab from a script.

Can I use prefabs across scenes?

Yes, since the prefab is saved in your project, it can be accessed from any scene within this project.

FINITE STATE MACHINES

How can I create an FSM in Unity?

You will need to create an **Animator Controller**. This controller will include states, transitions and parameters.

How do I link my Animator Controller to an object?

You can add an **Animator** component to this object, and then add the **Animator Controller** to this **Animator** component (i.e., drag and drop the **Animator Controller** to the variable called **Controller** for the component called **Animator** for this object).

How do I control my Animator Controller from a script?

- Add the script to the object to which the **Animator Controller** is linked to; then you can create a reference to the **Animator Controller** from the script, as illustrated in the next code.

```
anim = GetComponent<Animator>();
```

- You can then access parameters using **SetBool** or **SetTrigger**.

```
anim.SetTrigger("gotHit");
```

How can I know the current state of an Animator Controller from a script?

- You will first need to gain access to information about the **Animator Controller** using the method **GetCurrentAnimatorStateInfo**.

```
info = anim.GetCurrentAnimatorStateInfo(0);
```

- Then you can use this information to access the state.

```
if (info.IsName("ATTACK_CLOSE_RANGE"))...
```

NAVMESH NAVIGATION

What is a NavmeshAgent?

It is a component that you can add to an object so that this object can navigate "intelligently" around the scene towards a target while avoiding some obstacles.

Why do I need to bake the Navmeshes before the NPC can move?

By baking the **Navmeshes**, Unity computes possible routes that can be used by a **Navmesh Agent** to reach its destination, accounting for the obstacles. This is done before the scene starts so it doesn't need to be done while the game runs, hence, keeping performance high for the game.

Is it possible to bake the scene at run-time?

Unfortunately, this is not possible at present; this being said, you can use **NavMesh Obstacles**, which means that they will be avoided without the need to bake the scene.

USER INTERACTION

How can I detect keystrokes?

You can detect keystroke by using the function **Input.GetKey**. For example, the following code detects when the key E is pressed; this code should be added to the **Update** function.

```
If (Input.GetKey(KeyCode.E)){}
```

How can I play sound?

To play a sound, you need to add an **Audio Source** component to an object; when this is done, you can either play its default audio clip, or select which audio clip should be played.

```
GetComponent<AudioSource>().Play();//plays the default sound
GetComponent<AudioSource>().clip = clip1;//selects the clip
GetComponent<AudioSource>().Play();//plays clip selected
```

How can I display text onscreen?

To display text onscreen you will need to create a **UI Text** object, and then access it through a script. For example:

```
GetComponent<Text>().text = "New Text";
```

FIRING OBJECTS

How can I ensure that a projectile will not be subject to gravity?

If a projectile includes a Rigidbody2D component, you can make sure that it is not subject to gravity by setting its **gravity scale** attribute to 0.

How can I set a projectile in movement?

To set a projectile in movement, you need to apply a force to it. For example, to move it up the screen, the following code could be used.

```
GetComponent<Rigidbody2D>().AddForce (transform.up * 1000);
```

15
THANK YOU

I would like to thank you for completing this book; I trust that you are now comfortable with scripting in C# and that you can create interactive 3D game environments. This book is the third in a series of four books on Unity, so it may be time to move on to the next book for the advanced level where you will learn more advanced features, including networking, database access, and much more. You can find a description of this book on the official page **http://www.learntocreategames.com/books**.

So that the book can be constantly improved, I would really appreciate your feedback. So, please leave me a helpful review on Amazon letting me know what you thought of the book and also send me an email (**learntocreategames@gmail.com**) with any suggestions you may have. I read and reply to every email.

Thanks so much!!